THE business. communication HANDBOOK

THE
business.
communication
HANDBOOK

6th edition   **Judith Dwyer**

Prentice
Hall

Pearson Education Australia
Unit 4, Level 2
14 Aquatic Drive
Frenchs Forest NSW 2086

www.pearsoned.com.au

Publisher: Julie Catalano
Senior Project Editor: Carolyn Robson
Copy Editor: Jo Rudd
Cover and internal design by DiZign
Cover photograph: Getty Images
Typeset by Midland Typesetters, Maryborough, Vic.

Printed in Malaysia, PA

7 8 9 10 08 07 06 05

National Library of Australia
Cataloguing-in-Publication data

Dwyer, Judith.
The business communication handbook.

6th ed.
Bibliography.
Includes index.
ISBN 1 74009 853 6.

1. Business communication. I. Title.

658.45

An imprint of Pearson Education Australia

Brief contents

Contents

How to use this book

The Business Communication Handbook, sixth edition, takes a 'hands on' approach. It is designed to help you understand communication theory and practise effective communication skills.

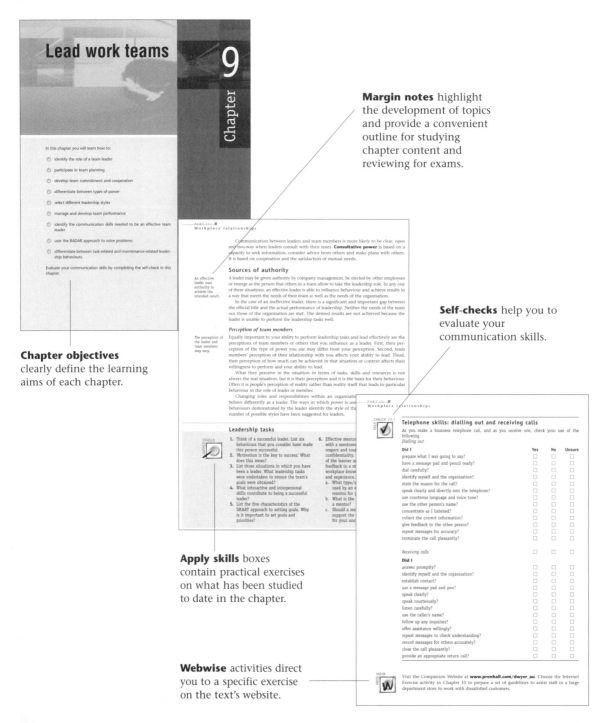

Margin notes highlight the development of topics and provide a convenient outline for studying chapter content and reviewing for exams.

Chapter objectives clearly define the learning aims of each chapter.

Self-checks help you to evaluate your communication skills.

Apply skills boxes contain practical exercises on what has been studied to date in the chapter.

Webwise activities direct you to a specific exercise on the text's website.

■ CHAPTER 10
DELIVER AND MONITOR A SERVICE TO CUSTOMERS

Chapter summary

Identify customers' requirements. Use a courteous approach and active listening to determine customers' requirements. For customer service, active listening is vital: be attentive, concentrate on the issue and not the person, target key points, investigate with questions, verify the customer's needs by restating them.

Develop customer service skills, particularly communication skills. Acknowledge the customer, listen with empathy, give feedback and use appropriate verbal and nonverbal communication so that you can offer the customer high-quality service.

Identify potential communication barriers. Some of these arise when there are not enough customer service staff, or when they do not know enough about the product and its features. Barriers may also be due to poor communication skills and lack of respect for or courtesy to the customer.

Provide product or service information and advice to promote the organisation. The person providing the service must know the product and explain it with courtesy. Listen carefully as you discuss the product so that you understand how much customers know about it and how much more they would like to know. Offer feedback that is appropriate to their needs and expectations.

Use problem-solving strategies to handle customer complaints and difficult situations. If customers express confusion or dissatisfaction, deal with the problem as promptly as possible. Two problem-solving strategies are the PAIR approval strategy and the five-step method. Use these to satisfy customer needs and expectations.

Deal with customers' special needs. Age, disability or cultural and language differences may cause problems and preclude a customer from accessing available services. To respond effectively to customers, you need to be aware of, and able to deal with, their special needs.

Use the telephone efficiently. When you use the telephone to answer inquiries and handle complaints, answer courteously and listen carefully. Once you understand what the customer wants, find the information or take action to satisfy them as quickly as you can. Courtesy and promptness are important.

Present the organisation in a positive way. Now, more that ever, customers expect high-quality service, short and reliable delivery times and innovative policies that respond quickly to their needs and expectations. Some positive features that successful customer service offers are a pleasant environment, friendly and well groomed staff, well informed staff with helpful supervisors, willing assistance and courtesy.

Deal with situations in a way that maintains and enhances goodwill. Establish and maintain a good relationship with your customers, to persuade them to keep using your product or service. The most direct way of doing this is to let customers know how they will benefit. Satisfy their needs and expectations by taking responsibility, using flexibility and showing initiative as you provide a high-quality service.

Chapter summaries parallel the learning objectives at the start of the chapter.

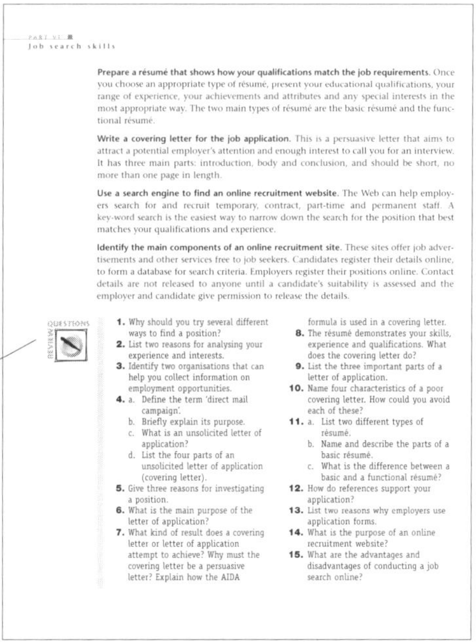

PART VI ■
Job search skills

Prepare a résumé that shows how your qualifications match the job requirements. Once you choose an appropriate type of résumé, present your educational qualifications, your range of experience, your achievements and attributes and any special interests in the most appropriate way. The two main types of résumé are the basic résumé and the functional résumé.

Write a covering letter for the job application. This is a persuasive letter that aims to attract a potential employer's attention and enough interest to call you for an interview. It has three main parts: introduction, body and conclusion, and should be short, no more than one page in length.

Use a search engine to find an online recruitment website. The Web can help employers search for and recruit temporary, contract, part-time and permanent staff. A key-word search is the easiest way to narrow down the search for the position that best matches your qualifications and experience.

Identify the main components of an online recruitment site. These sites offer job advertisements and other services free to job seekers. Candidates register their details online, to form a database for search criteria. Employers register their positions online. Contact details are not released to anyone until a candidate's suitability is assessed and the employer and candidate give permission to release the details.

REVIEW QUESTIONS

1. Why should you try several different ways to find a position?
2. List two reasons for analysing your experience and interests.
3. Identify two organisations that can help you collect information on employment opportunities.
4. a. Define the term 'direct mail campaign'.
   b. Briefly explain its purpose.
   c. What is an unsolicited letter of application?
   d. List the four parts of an unsolicited letter of application (covering letter).
5. Give three reasons for investigating a position.
6. What is the main purpose of the letter of application?
7. What kind of result does a covering letter or letter of application attempt to achieve? Why must the covering letter be a persuasive letter? Explain how the AIDA formula is used in a covering letter.
8. The résumé demonstrates your skills, experience and qualifications. What does the covering letter do?
9. List the three important parts of a letter of application.
10. Name four characteristics of a poor covering letter. How could you avoid each of these?
11. a. List two different types of résumé.
    b. Name and describe the parts of a basic résumé.
    c. What is the difference between a basic and a functional résumé?
12. How do references support your application?
13. List two reasons why employers use application forms.
14. What is the purpose of an online recruitment website?
15. What are the advantages and disadvantages of conducting a job search online?

Build skills activities incorporate skills and theory that give you practice in applying the whole competency.

Review questions provide opportunities for you to check your understanding of the theory contained in the chapter.

Case studies ask you to consider real workplace examples of communication issues.

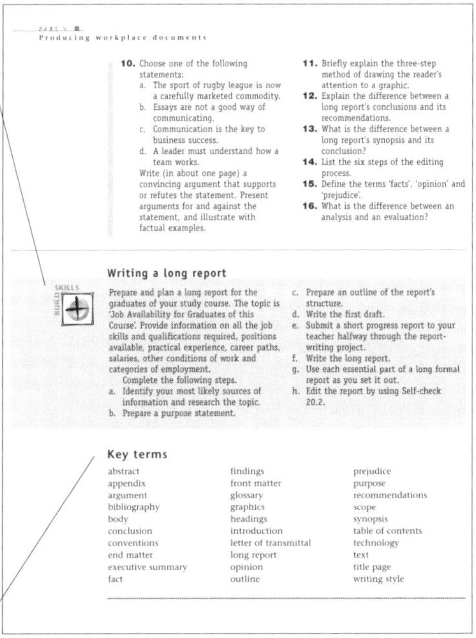

PART V ■
Producing workplace documents

10. Choose one of the following statements:
    a. The sport of rugby league is now a carefully marketed commodity.
    b. Essays are not a good way of communicating.
    c. Communication is the key to business success.
    d. A leader must understand how a team works.
    Write (in about one page) a convincing argument that supports or refutes the statement. Present arguments for and against the statement, and illustrate with factual examples.
11. Briefly explain the three-step method of drawing the reader's attention to a graphic.
12. Explain the difference between a long report's conclusions and its recommendations.
13. What is the difference between a long report's synopsis and its conclusion?
14. List the six steps of the editing process.
15. Define the terms 'facts', 'opinion' and 'prejudice'.
16. What is the difference between an analysis and an evaluation?

BUILD SKILLS

Writing a long report

Prepare and plan a long report for the graduates of your study course. The topic is 'Job Availability for Graduates of this Course'. Provide information on all the job skills and qualifications required, positions available, practical experience, career paths, salaries, other conditions of work and categories of employment.

Complete the following steps.

a. Identify your most likely sources of information and research the topic.
b. Prepare a purpose statement.
c. Prepare an outline of the report's structure.
d. Write the first draft.
e. Submit a short progress report to your teacher halfway through the report-writing project.
f. Write the long report.
g. Use each essential part of a long formal report as you set it out.
h. Edit the report by using Self-check 20.2.

Key terms

abstract	findings	prejudice
appendix	front matter	purpose
argument	glossary	recommendations
bibliography	graphics	scope
body	headings	synopsis
conclusion	introduction	table of contents
conventions	letter of transmittal	technology
end matter	long report	text
executive summary	opinion	title page
fact	outline	writing style

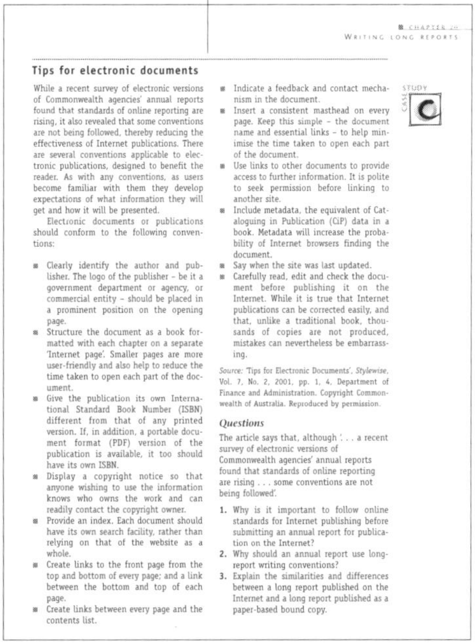

■ CHAPTER 20
WRITING LONG REPORTS

CASE STUDY

Tips for electronic documents

While a recent survey of electronic versions of Commonwealth agencies' annual reports found that standards of online reporting are rising, it also revealed that some conventions are not being followed, thereby reducing the effectiveness of Internet publications. There are several conventions applicable to electronic publications, designed to benefit the reader. As with any conventions, as users become familiar with them they develop expectations of what information they will get and how it will be presented.

Electronic documents or publications should conform to the following conventions:

- Clearly identify the author and publisher. The logo of the publisher – be it a government department or agency, or commercial entity – should be placed in a prominent position on the opening page.
- Structure the document as a book formatted with each chapter on a separate 'Internet page'. Smaller pages are more user-friendly and also help to reduce the time taken to open each part of the document.
- Give the publication its own International Standard Book Number (ISBN) different from that of any printed version. If, in addition, a portable document format (PDF) version of the publication is available, it too should have its own ISBN.
- Display a copyright notice so that anyone wishing to use the information knows who owns the work and can readily contact the copyright owner.
- Provide an index. Each document should have its own search facility, rather than relying on that of the website as a whole.
- Create links to the front page from the top and bottom of every page; and a link between the bottom and top of each page.
- Create links between every page and the contents list.
- Indicate a feedback and contact mechanism in the document.
- Insert a consistent masthead on every page. Keep this simple – the document name and essential links – to help minimise the time taken to open each part of the document.
- Use links to other documents to provide access to further information. It is polite to seek permission before linking to another site.
- Include metadata, the equivalent of Cataloguing in Publication (CiP) data in a book. Metadata will increase the probability of Internet browsers finding the document.
- Say when the site was last updated.
- Carefully read, edit and check the document before publishing it on the Internet. While it is true that Internet publications can be corrected easily, and that, unlike a traditional book, thousands of copies are not produced, mistakes can nevertheless be embarrassing.

Source: 'Tips for Electronic Documents', *Stylewise*, Vol. 7, No. 2, 2001, pp. 1, 4. Department of Finance and Administration. Copyright Commonwealth of Australia. Reproduced by permission.

Questions

The article says that, although '. . . a recent survey of electronic versions of Commonwealth agencies' annual reports found that standards of online reporting are rising . . . some conventions are not being followed'.

1. Why is it important to follow online standards for Internet publishing before submitting an annual report for publication on the Internet?
2. Why should an annual report use long-report writing conventions?
3. Explain the similarities and differences between a long report published on the Internet and a long report published as a paper-based bound copy.

Key terms are listed at end of each chapter and provide a quick review of important terms.

Preface

The Business Communication Handbook, sixth edition, is about understanding the knowledge underpinning communication, practising and acquiring communication skills and applying these in the workplace. Successful organisations have well established and efficient communication systems. Successful people have the ability to use and adjust their communication to the other person and the situation. They are able to communicate effectively in any context.

Effective communication within organisations and between people leads to increased understanding and more satisfying relationships. For those studying or working in our continuously changing social and economic environment effective communication skills are as important as ever.

The sixth edition is the ideal reference and support for the new Training Packages and in particular the BSB01 Business Services Training Package. How to communicate is built into all of the national Training Packages because effective communication is an essential part of a competent person's performance. Those who relate easily and positively to those around them appear to have good listening, speaking and nonverbal skills as well as good written communication skills. Good communication skills allow people to respond positively in their interactions. The BSB01 Business Services Training Package Volume 1 states '. . . communication skills . . . are central to and imperative to the performance of businesses' (2001: p. 30).

The sixth edition is organised into six parts. These are: *Interactive communication*; *Communicating in the workplace*; *Workplace relationships*; *Workplace writing and research skills*; *Producing workplace documents* and *Job search skills*. Chapter 7 'Organise personal work priorities and development', Chapter 9 'Lead work teams' and Chapter 24 'The job interview' are new chapters. Nonverbal communication and listening skills have been combined into one chapter (Chapter 2). A number of the chapters have been further developed to meet the ongoing changes in the vocational education and training sector.

Objectives at the beginning of each chapter establish the learning goals for the chapter. Margin notes highlight key terms and ideas and glossary terms are printed in bold the first time they appear. **Apply skills** activities in each chapter provide clear links to the business context and allow you to practise the communication theory and principles presented in the book. **Chapter summaries** contain the essential ideas presented in the chapter and the **review questions** provide a quick checkpoint for the main areas presented. **Build skills** activities at the end of the chapter allow you to practise, extend and self-assess your learning and skills development. **Self-checks** for each chapter let you evaluate your communication skills. **Case studies** demonstrate communication principles and practices in real workplace situations. The **webwise** activities provide further opportunities to practise and extend your skills.

I am grateful to the people at Pearson Education Australia for their continuing help and guidance. Special thanks are due to Jo Rudd for her careful editing of the text, Carolyn Robson, Senior Project Editor, and Julie Catalano, Senior Acquisitions Editor.

I thank Elizabeth Morrison for her constructive comments, enthusiastic support and ideas throughout the writing and editing of this edition. Special thanks are given to John and my family for their continuing support and encouragement.

Judith Dwyer
July 2002

About the Author

Judith Dwyer, M Mgt, BEc, Dip Ed, AIMM, has worked in education and training for many years. She is currently Managing Director of Austraining (NSW), a Registered Training Organisation (RTO) that offers a range of Certificate and Diploma qualifications. She has built the RTO into a leading edge provider of vocational education and training specialising in cross-industry management and communication studies.

In her early career she taught business students Communication Studies within Technical and Further Education for a period of twenty years. She has gained valuable experience in the learning needs of adult students. The book is based on proven educational and business principles. Through her involvement with industry she has observed the need for individuals, teams and organisations with the skills and knowledge to communicate effectively to achieve results. She promotes positive interactive communication as one of the essential components in any successful organisation.

In recent years she has become a leading vocational education and training author of textbooks and learning materials. The practical approach taken in her writing provides value to both students and trainers. People are able to put their learning into practice in their workplace.

Judith is a proactive member of the vocational education and training sector. She is a Director of the Australian Council of Independent Vocational Colleges (ACIVC) and has worked on a number of committees.

Judith earned her degree in Economics from the University of New England, Diploma of Education from the University of Newcastle and her Master in Management (Public) from the University of Technology Sydney.

Email: judith.dwyer@austrainingnsw.com.au

Interactive communication

Part I

How communication works

Chapter 1

In this chapter you will learn how to:

- define the term 'communication'

- list the different forms of communication

- identify each element of the communication process

- identify barriers to communication

- discuss the importance of good communication in the workplace

- apply ethics to your workplace communication

- identify the communication aspects of a multicultural society.

Evaluate your communication skills by completing the self-checks in the chapter.

Communication in the workplace occurs for a number of direct and indirect reasons. Primarily it is necessary for passing information between people working in the same organisation and between their organisation and others. In the workplace, your ability to communicate is reflected by the quality and range of your communication skills.

Communication – written, spoken or even nonverbal – is also used by leaders and managers for evaluating performance, directing or instructing staff and motivating others. People working as part of a team or department with a good communicator as its leader are generally more confident and competent because they understand what they are doing and what is required of them. They are able to work together in a purposeful, supportive and flexible manner.

Firms, businesses or agencies that provide a product or service to others must interact and operate with other people. This interaction with clients, customers, staff and members of other organisations requires communication and will succeed if the communication is effective. Observe people who are good in their relationships at work and with others. How do they interact with others? What skills do they use? These people have the means, the capacity and the will to communicate. Communication theory provides the means, their motivation provides the willingness and their communication skills provide the capacity. This book analyses the theory underpinning good communication, and its learning activities give you the opportunity to practise a range of skills that will help you communicate better.

Communication defined

People who are successful at work are often communication-oriented. They demonstrate empathy, awareness and concern for others; they use good listening skills and are aware of their own concerns and needs. These people are open, approachable and supportive of others.

Communication is any behaviour, verbal or nonverbal, that is perceived by another. Knowledge, feelings or thoughts are encoded and sent from at least one person and received and decoded by at least one other. Meaning is given to this message as the receiver interprets the message. A connection is made between the people communicating. Communication lets us learn more about ourselves and the world around us, share experiences with others, persuade and influence others, and relax and enjoy ourselves.

Communication is the transfer of meaning.

Forms of communication

Workplace communication is classified into three forms.

Each channel of communication requires skills suited to the **form of communication** that is used to send the message.

Communication is classified into three forms:

1. verbal communication, either spoken or written
2. nonverbal
3. graphic.

Communication skills in spoken, written, nonverbal and graphic communication are all essential in the workplace. These forms of communication send messages through various channels.

Verbal communication can take the form of spoken words between two or more people, or written words in written communication.

Nonverbal communication is sent by any means other than words or graphics. Nonverbal components occur in oral, written and graphic communication, and in oral communication these include facial expressions, body movement, posture and dress.

Format and layout are some of the nonverbal components of written and graphic communication.

Graphic communication represents ideas, relationships or connections visually with shapes, diagrams and lines. Graphic communication can have both verbal and nonverbal components – for example, some of the 'No Smoking' signs displayed in public places.

The ability to communicate is learned by gaining skills from others and from experience. As experience widens, new learning takes place. The communication style of individuals and organisations develops through using and adapting new techniques. Anyone who believes they can control the communication process is unaware that communication is an intricate, interactive process. The interactions of several elements affect the people communicating. You can do a great deal to influence the communication process but you cannot control someone else's perception, outlook, values and attitudes. Each of these affects the way communication is received.

The communication process

The process of communication is dynamic and interactive. Someone sends, someone receives and in between there is a message. As information flows, people place meaning and structure on the variety of messages received from others.

The **communication process** takes place in various situations for different reasons, with the potential for many interpretations. It has seven main elements.

Communication is an interactive process.

1. sender
2. message
3. receiver
4. feedback
5. channel
6. context or setting
7. interference or noise.

There are many models of the communication process. The diagrams presented in this chapter are representations of how communication works. It should be stressed that they cannot be a complete guide; they take the most significant elements of the process and place these in a useful sequence.

As communication occurs, the sender and receiver interact by sending (**encoding**) and receiving (**decoding**) messages.

Understanding communication

1. For an introduction activity, break into pairs.
   a. Person A takes three minutes to interview Person B and then the roles are exchanged.
   b. Person B interviews Person A for three minutes. When the interviews are complete, return to the large group.
   c. Person A introduces Person B to the large group.
   d. Person B introduces Person A to the large group.

2. This activity demonstrates the importance of nonverbal feedback. Work in groups of two. Stand back-to-back with one another and conduct a conversation for two minutes, then discuss how easy or difficult it was to speak in this way. Comment on the way in which nonverbal communication helps two people to talk to and understand one another.

APPLY SKILLS

The sender

Communication begins with the sender.

Figure 1.1 shows four elements of the communication process, which begins with the **sender**. Senders are individuals who react to situations from a unique vantage point, interpreting ideas and filtering experiences through their own perception (see Figure 1.2). Unique to individual senders, and integral to all the communication they engage in, is a background of accumulated attitudes, experiences, skills, cultural conditioning and individual differences that influences how they communicate. The sender encodes an idea or feeling in words or signs that the receiver will recognise and transmits this message to the receiver.

Figure 1.1 Four elements of the communication process

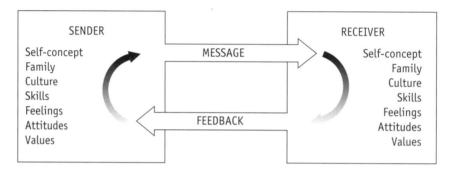

Message

The message connects the sender to the receiver.

The **message** is the idea or feeling transmitted from the sender to the receiver to achieve understanding. It makes a connection between sender and receiver.

The receiver

The **receiver** decodes or interprets the message to achieve understanding. In doing this, the receiver is also acting as an individual from a unique vantage point, interpreting the idea according to a particular personal perception of the message. This perception is the result of the receiver's unique background of experiences, beliefs, concerns and many other factors.

Perception

Since perception has a significant influence on communication, it is useful to look closely at it. The way a message is perceived by the sender may be quite different from the way the receiver perceives the message.

Perception influences communication.

Perception is the way people understand or give meaning to their environment. Perception and interpretation of the same message varies according to how each individual's perception is influenced by experience, attitudes and beliefs and a range of acquired skills or expectations. For example, one person may perceive the colour blue as cool, peaceful and comforting while another person may see blue as old-fashioned or formal. The particular or specific meaning is influenced by past experience. Even the context or setting of the communication affects perception. Blue may be calming and relaxing one day, too formal on another.

Perception can be compared with a pair of spectacles, through which we process all the signals received from others. The glasses place a particular focus on what we see, hear and understand, and influence the way we react to the message. The particular colour and focus of a message are affected by the pair of glasses worn. The glasses may distort the picture.

Figure 1.2 Perception

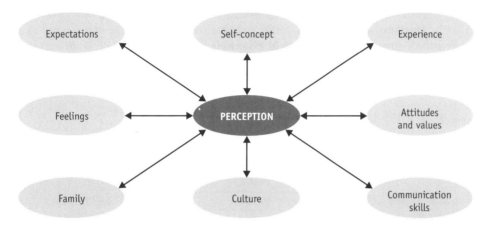

Feedback

There is a constant feeding back of information as people interact. As well as encouraging the speaker to continue, listeners respond in a way that shows their comprehension and acceptance or non-acceptance of the message. **Feedback** is an essential part of successful interpersonal communication. It is the receiver's response to the sender's message, and can be intentional or unintentional.

Feedback:

- gives the communication continuity
- indicates understanding or misunderstanding of the message
- stimulates further communication and discussion.

Both sender and receiver need feedback. As you communicate, check with your receivers to establish that their understanding of the message is correct. Ask the receiver to rephrase what has been said and acknowledge your agreement or disagreement. It is important to the speaker to determine how the message is being received and helps receivers understand how their behaviour affects others.

Feedback can help or hinder your communication and the climate you create. In the workplace most people communicate face-to-face with their leaders, supervisors and colleagues, so the ability to provide appropriate feedback can assist the development of good working relationships and the productivity of the business.

Feedback is an essential part of effective communication.

Communication channel

A **communication channel** is the means or technique used to signal or convey a message – for example, a conversation, letter, telephone call, radio or television program. Information technology provides a fast channel of communication that is becoming more widely available and easier to use than in the past. Information technology is used to store, send, receive and present information.

The channel is the vehicle for the message.

All organisations have internal channels of communication and external channels. Figure 1.3 shows three more elements in the communication process – the channel, interference and context.

Choose a channel that suits your communication purpose, your needs as the sender of the message, and the needs of the receiver.

The flow of communication moves through the organisation along different lines or channels. **Horizontal channels** operate between colleagues at the same level of the organisation's structure, while **vertical channels** move communication up and down between different levels.

Figure 1.3 The seven elements of the communication process

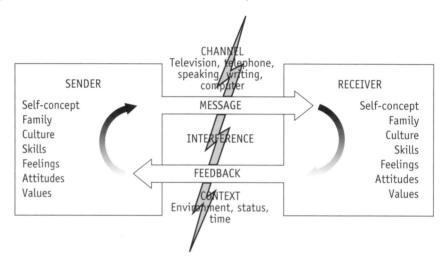

Context

Context affects
the message.

Context consists of the situation, circumstances or setting within which communication takes place. Context plays an important part in how a message is encoded and decoded. The same message can have a completely different meaning depending on the situation, since emotions and reactions to ideas and events vary in different situations. For example, communication at a conference, in the lunchroom, at a formal meeting or in the office is taking place in different settings. It may use different language, relationships and authority to achieve the different communication purpose in each situation.

Interference or noise

The message received is not necessarily the same as the message sent. Something other than the intended message is received because **noise**, or interference, interrupts the intended message.

Noise
interrupts the
communication.

Send a message by electronic mail to a person who is afraid of technology and unable to access the computer screen, and communication barriers will occur because the channel is inappropriate in this case. Write a memo or business letter to this person and the message is more likely to be easily understood and accepted.

Noise, or interference, that interrupts the message or communication flow between sender and receiver can lead to misunderstanding, or to confused or ambiguous communication. **Communication barriers** occur as a result of a misunderstanding or misinterpretation of the message. These barriers can be caused by the sender, the receiver, lack of feedback, a poor choice of channel, the wrong context or any other element in the communication model. Even when communication barriers occur, something is communicated but the noise, or interference, distorts the intended message.

Causes of communication barriers

Effective communication often passes unnoticed, while poor communication is obvious. The complete message and its meaning are distorted or interrupted.

Some of the factors that cause communication barriers are:

- inappropriate choice of words
- inappropriate channel
- inappropriate message
- receiver inattention
- lack of courtesy by the sender or the receiver
- nonverbal communication that does not support the words
- different cultural backgrounds
- poor layout and presentation
- inappropriate timing
- inadequate feedback.

Recognising these and other causes of poor communication is an important step towards avoiding them. Consider the possibilities shown in Table 1.1.

It is impossible for one person in the communication process to control the process, as one person cannot be responsible for someone else's communication style or for all the other factors that contribute to communication barriers.

Table 1.1 Communication barriers

Cause of barrier	Outcome	Strategies to avoid barrier
Differences in perception	People often see and interpret the same event or action in a different way.	Listen carefully. Speak clearly and directly to the other person. Ask questions. Give feedback.
Different attitudes and values	People often form different interpretations.	Listen carefully. Speak clearly and directly to the other person. Ask questions. Give feedback.
Inconsistency between spoken and nonverbal communication	Poor communication and confusion due to an ambiguous message.	Match the verbal and nonverbal parts of the total message.
Withholding information	Others operate with only part of the message so mistakes are more likely to occur.	Plan and structure the message to include all necessary information.
Passing judgment by telling people their reaction is stupid	The receiver can become angry and retaliate.	Listen actively. Ask questions. Give feedback.
Dismissing others' concerns or points of view	The receiver may withdraw.	Listen carefully. Show you are aware of the other's point of view. Ask questions.

Communication barriers

APPLY SKILLS

1. Michael works as a sales representative in the New South Wales showroom and warehouse of the Wood Panel Division of a large Australian company, Woodstone. Senior buyers for a large kitchen joinery firm based in Queensland and Victoria visit the New South Wales showroom and show a keen interest in the new products. Michael is able to make further contact with this client firm by letter, telephone or personal visit.
   a. Outline the advantages and disadvantages of the three possible channels of communication.
   b. Decide which of them Michael should use for the first follow-up contact with this potential client. Give reasons for your choice of channel.

2. a. 'One of the most important skills that any person in an organisation needs is the ability to communicate. Without communication your other skills are less useful.' Explain the meaning of this statement.
   b. Should an organisation train its staff in workplace communication? Give reasons for your answer.

3. Working in groups of three:
   a. List three statements that you have written or spoken (or observed) that were insensitive to the receiver's feelings.
   b. Discuss the sort of communication barriers caused by each of these statements.
   c. Restate, to the people you are working with, each of your three statements in a more sensitive way and ask them if they think the new version would be more effective.
   d. Discuss three ways in which communication barriers can affect interpersonal communication.

4. Two colleagues, Mary and David, meet in David's office to discuss the introduction of the new software package on the agenda at tomorrow's staff meeting. As they talk through the procedure to introduce this package to other staff:
   ■ David answers and deals with a telephone call and then continues the conversation with Mary;
   ■ Another person enters David's office and interrupts the conversation to ask Mary to solve a problem in the delivery times for stock;
   ■ When Mary has provided the solution, Mary and David resume their discussion;
   ■ Mary looks at her watch and exclaims that it is time for her next appointment;
   ■ As they rush to finish their plans they discuss who will present the new software procedures at the staff meeting. When that item comes up, Mary expects David to present the procedure; David believes Mary is to present it.
   a. Identify the communication barriers that occurred and explain briefly in two paragraphs how they contributed to the misunderstanding between Mary and David.
   b. List two sources of noise at the initial planning meeting.
   c. How could Mary and David have dealt with the noise or interference in their planning meeting? Self-check 1.1 can be used to evaluate your answers.

5. Checking what the other person said:
   a. Work in groups of three (A, B and C).
      ■ Persons A and B are to discuss a topic of interest by taking opposite sides. Person C is the observer.
      ■ Person A opens the discussion. Person B gives feedback to Person A by summarising what Person A has said before giving an opposing view. Person A summarises what Person B has said before Person A continues with their opposing view.
      ■ Continue this for 10 minutes. When Person C believes that either Person A or B has not summarised the other person's point of view accurately, Person C can give feedback to both A and B.
   b. After 10 minutes, discuss the advantages gained by checking what the other person said.

Communication barriers

In analysing the situation between Mary and David (see the previous Apply Skills) to identify noise or communication barriers, have I:

	Yes	No	Unsure
considered the responsibility of the sender?	☐	☐	☐
evaluated the appropriate channel?	☐	☐	☐
examined the message?	☐	☐	☐
considered the role of the receiver?	☐	☐	☐
identified the place of feedback?	☐	☐	☐
considered the impact of the context?	☐	☐	☐

Empathy

To reduce the chance of communication barriers and associated problems, communicate with **empathy** – a feeling for and awareness of your receivers and their point of view. Also, be willing to provide appropriate and sufficient feedback to achieve understanding.

Communication in the workplace

For business decisions to be sound and relevant, timely and appropriate information has to be conveyed throughout the organisation. The successful organisation is the one that communicates well both internally and with other companies and clients. In fact, information flow is crucial to any organisation and the better the flow the more successful it is.

Information flow is crucial to the success of any organisation.

Many factors apart from our individual communication skills affect communication in the workforce. The organisation's culture and values, the resources available to it and its power relationships all affect communication.

Being a good communicator means acknowledging and working with these factors as well as communicating skilfully. Good communicators are honest with themselves and others and have the ability to say what they want or feel, but not at the expense of others. They realise that communication is not all about getting their own way and winning every time. Nor is it a means to manipulate other people so that they achieve their aim while appearing to be considering others. A sincere communicator avoids quick-fix tricks or techniques.

As well as using listening, speaking, questioning and feedback skills when dealing with others about simple, routine matters, effective communicators also use their interpersonal skills to greet others, find out and satisfy their expectations and needs, and finish the interaction courteously.

Communication between colleagues

One of the routine tasks in any workplace is to gather, record and convey simple information. Another is to give and follow simple instructions. Good communicators use appropriate communication skills such as listening, speaking, questioning and offering feedback as they collect and organise information, and they give accurate, clear and comprehensive instructions. To complete these tasks successfully, they must also participate in discussions and interact in a supportive, efficient and effective way.

People who are able to communicate well in the workplace are generally happier in themselves and manage to handle difficult or tricky situations. They get the best from themselves and others at work. They are also much more likely to achieve outcomes that are satisfying for everyone. Stress in the workplace is reduced as people are more likely to cope with conflict early and in a competent manner.

Communication by leaders and managers

Leaders and managers who communicate well are able to work directly with people. Consequently, there are fewer hidden agendas and issues are resolved at an early stage before they become long-term problems. Good communication by leaders and managers leads to fewer direct controls and more understanding, commitment and motivation.

Leaders and managers communicate to control, motivate and balance needs and goals.

Control

Communication can be used by an organisation's management as a means to control procedures and to encourage employees to conform to company objectives, directives or work procedures. People in organisations participate in employee assessment schemes, read manuals of procedure for different work tasks and set targets for company plans. People are using their communication skills constantly.

The difficulty for leaders and managers is to communicate in a way that achieves a balance between control, motivation and efficiency. Too much control may reduce initiative and even productivity, with less response to what the client wants and more emphasis on what the workers think the managers want. Too little control may cause uncertainty and insecurity.

Motivation

An organisation's management, including leaders of small teams, can use communication to motivate employees. Each employee needs, in varying degrees, achievement, power and a sense of belonging to the organisation. When an organisation acknowledges the achievements of individuals and groups, job satisfaction and performance are improved. Acknowledgment (feedback) can involve verbal praise or written letters or circulars that reassure employees that they are an important part of the organisation and that what they are doing is appreciated.

Balancing needs and goals

Communication in the organisation has another important role. A firm's interests and expectations and its employees' goals and needs have to be balanced. To understand and achieve this balance, both employer and employee need to understand one another. Good communication is essential.

When this understanding is achieved and the needs and goals of both are compatible, the behaviour required at work to achieve the organisation's goals is satisfying to the employee. The possible differences between the needs of the organisation and the individual are highlighted in Table 1.2.

The organisation must convey its viewpoint to employees, and employees must persuade management to appreciate their viewpoint. Slow, inefficient lines of communication may mean dissatisfied customers and demoralised workers. For all these reasons, business organisations need skilled communicators and good communication channels to move information through the organisation efficiently.

Table 1.2 Organisational and individual goals

Organisational goals	Individual or team goals
Profit	Good pay
Return on investment	Job security
Employee efficiency	Fringe benefits
Production of quality goods and services	Scope for initiative and achievement
Competitiveness	Challenge
Low absenteeism and low turnover of employees	Satisfaction

Ethics in communication

We all have ideas about what is right and wrong, and we derive them from a variety of values and conventions throughout our lifetime. Personal **ethics**, professional ethics and corporate ethics are sets of moral principles by which we judge human actions and proposals as good or bad or right or wrong.

Why do we need ethics?

Ethical behaviour requires us to act with equity, fairness, impartiality and respect for the rights of others. Professional ethics are the conventions for the right professional conduct or practice. In the workplace we are expected to behave according to the established rules and standards. Ethical behaviour leads to professional behaviour. People working for an ethical company behave with integrity.

Ethical behaviour is equitable, fair and impartial.

Most organisations have a code of ethics, which is a statement of its primary values and the ethical rules it expects its employees to follow. In a company without a code of ethics people may be uncertain about how to deal with an issue or problem.

A code of ethics benefits the company and the individual by:

- reinforcing the organisation's standard of conduct
- reminding staff that management wants participants to consider ethical issues in their decisions
- identifying practices that are and are not permissible
- allowing leaders, managers and others to share experiences and ideas about what is and is not an ethical position
- developing a shared culture based on ethics and accountability.

What makes an ethical business communicator?

Business communication is an integral part of any company's activities. Professional business communicators behave ethically when they:

- follow the organisation's policies, procedures and guidelines
- communicate factual information objectively
- avoid using distortions of fact and misleading information
- respect the dignity of each person, irrespective of ethnic background, religion or gender
- follow their company's code of ethics.

Ethical dilemma checklist

Whenever you feel there is an ethical dilemma in your communication, use this checklist	Yes	No	Unsure
■ Is the intended action legal?	☐	☐	☐
■ Is my communication factual and objective?	☐	☐	☐
■ Who will gain from the communication or action? (Do I know?)	☐	☐	☐
■ Who will lose from the communication or action? (Do I know?)	☐	☐	☐
■ Would I be happy for my co-workers, family and friends to know about what I am communicating?	☐	☐	☐
■ Will I seek the opinion of other people who are knowledgeable about the subject?	☐	☐	☐
■ Am I willing to seek an objective second opinion?	☐	☐	☐
■ Does the language describing the issue talk about the real issue or something else?	☐	☐	☐
■ Am I willing to acknowledge the position and interests of those opposing my message or actions?	☐	☐	☐
■ Would I feel willing and confident to defend my message or actions at a meeting?	☐	☐	☐

Communication in a multicultural society

Never before has it been easier for people to move between countries. As a result, Australia has an expanding tourist industry, an increasing number of foreign students paying for education in this country, and greater opportunities to trade with other countries. Australia is a **multicultural society** with a population drawn from diverse cultural, racial, religious and ethnic backgrounds.

Intercultural communication

Intercultural communication is communication between people who live in the same country but come from different cultural backgrounds. Over time, a culture develops distinctive national patterns of communication and social behaviour. These patterns are the customs and conventions regarded as the characteristics of a particular culture. They affect the way people communicate and act as individuals or in groups.

Effective intercultural communicators acknowledge differences in perception.

What information we take in, which part of the message we choose to remember and which response we give are all a result of our perception. Effective communicators acknowledge differences in perception. They also use communication strategies that avoid the communication barriers caused by the ineffective intercultural communication strategies shown in Table 1.3.

Effect of perception

Although people may live in the same country, their various cultural backgrounds and rules may mean that they see the same event differently and place different interpretations on it. We are limited by the 'baggage' of background experience that we carry. Our perception is determined by a background consisting of:

Table 1.3 Communication strategies

Discriminatory communication techniques	Purpose	Inclusive communication techniques
Derogatory labelling	To put down people from another culture or group.	Refuse to use derogatory labels.
Stereotyping people belonging to a particular group	To isolate or exaggerate certain factors and apply them to all people in that group.	Recognise and avoid the use of language that stereotypes groups of people.
Invisibility	To subsume one group into another by label, name or term.	Use inclusive language and language preferred by the minority group.
Imposed labelling	To reinforce the majority group's view because the minority lacks the power to define themselves.	Avoid the use of one single generic name for a number of different groups of people.
Extra visibility	To emphasise a difference such as sex, race or ethnic background.	Avoid emphasis on differences such as sex, race and ethnic background.

- values
- attitudes
- life concerns
- cultural conditioning
- skills
- other factors.

If we can expand our view of events by being aware of our background and its impact on our perception, then we can choose more appropriate messages or responses. Consequently, we can perform better in the workplace and become more willing to learn new ways to communicate with people from different cultural backgrounds.

Intentional and unintentional messages

Both culture and individual experience shape each person's perception, style of communication and interpretation of others' **intentional** and **unintentional messages**. Some of the many aspects of nonverbal communication influenced by culture are tone of voice, inflection, rate of speech, facial expressions, touching and body movement. Intentional and unintentional messages may lead to misunderstanding because of a message that is poorly constructed by the sender, or due to the receiver's perception and cultural background.

Rules and patterns of behaviour

The common rules and patterns of behaviour of one country may be very different from those of another. **Cultural sensitivity** leads to effective **cross-cultural communication**. Whereas intercultural communication takes place between people living in the same country but from different cultural backgrounds, cross-cultural communication occurs between people living in different countries.

Cultural sensitivity leads to better communication.

Awareness of the different customs, rules and social behaviour in different cultures reduces the barriers caused by prejudice, stereotypes and discrimination. In Australia, people whose culture involves rigid rules on who speaks first or last in conversations, or the belief that to look down as someone speaks to you is courteous, would seem discourteous. This impression might lead to their exclusion from the conversation without them knowing why. What we assume and how we expect others to behave is affected by our cultural filter.

Different cultural groups have different rules for:

- humour and irony
- courtesies in speech, such as when to say 'please', 'thank you' or 'excuse me'
- the meaning of 'yes' and 'no'
- rules of politeness – who can speak to whom, and who can begin a conversation
- dress
- deference to others
- drinking alcohol
- use of time.

Discriminatory language

The language people employ as they communicate can be used as a vehicle of **discrimination** or a vehicle of **inclusion** (see Table 1.3).

The need to offer Australia's diverse population equality of access to opportunities in education, jobs and promotion makes communication strategies such as plain English and inclusive communication an essential part of workplace communication. These two strategies are presented more fully in Chapter 16.

Communication and perception

SKILLS
APPLY

1. Work in groups of three.
   a. 'Communication by leaders and managers can be used for three reasons.' Identify and discuss the three reasons and give a workplace example of each.
   b. List three organisational goals and three individual goals in the workplace.
   c. How can communication balance these needs and goals?
2. a. Define the terms 'values' and 'ethics'.
   b. Why should business communicators behave ethically?
   c. How can a company's code of ethics help staff in their workplace?
3. a. Define the terms 'multicultural society', 'intercultural communication' and 'cross-cultural communication'.

   b. What role does perception play in the communication process?
4. Identify two different communication 'rules' that people in different cultures recognise.
5. In an article in the *Harvard Business Review* entitled 'Barriers and Gateways to Communication', Rogers and Roethlisberger (1952) suggested: 'The major barrier to mutual interpersonal communication is our tendency to judge, to evaluate and to approve (or disapprove) the statements of the other person or the other group.'
   a. In small groups, discuss this idea, drawing from your own experiences.
   b. Report your findings to the large group.
6. *Quick Quiz*: Check your cross-cultural awareness.

Cross-cultural belief

Naming systems   T   F
 1. The Chinese naming system places the surname first.   ☐   ☐
 2. In China, descent is traced through the female line.   ☐   ☐
 3. The Vietnamese naming system places the surname first.   ☐   ☐
 4. The Arabic naming system places the surname last.   ☐   ☐

Etiquette
 5. In Australia, direct eye contact is a sign of discourtesy.   ☐   ☐
 6. In Asia, avoiding eye contact is a sign of respect.   ☐   ☐
 7. To touch South-East Asians on the head is an act of extreme
    discourtesy.   ☐   ☐
 8. In a Muslim culture, people do not pass things to each other with
    the left hand.   ☐   ☐
 9. In Asian cultures, people find it easy to say 'No'.   ☐   ☐
10. For Thai people, sharing the cost of an outing goes against
    accepted custom.   ☐   ☐

Visit the Companion Website at **www.prenhall.com/dwyer_au**. Choose the Good Practice/Bad Practice activity in Chapter 1 and complete the survey to analyse and evaluate how well you use the seven elements in the communication process.

Chapter summary

Define the term 'communication'. Communication is any behaviour, verbal or nonverbal, that is perceived by another.

List the different forms of communication. Successful communication sends or transmits ideas, values and attitudes to others through three different forms of communication: verbal, nonverbal and graphic. Meaning is derived from the message as the receiver perceives, structures and interprets it.

Identify each element of the communication process. The seven elements of the communication process are the sender, message, receiver, feedback, channel, context and noise (or interference).

Identify barriers to communication. Barriers to communication interrupt its flow and lead to confusion and misunderstandings. They can be caused by the sender, the receiver, lack of feedback, a poor choice of channel, the wrong context or any other factor that interferes with the message.

Discuss the importance of good communication in the workplace. Good communication establishes a connection and understanding between two or more people. It enhances individuals, work performance and relationships with others. It allows individuals to interact to satisfy their own needs and to develop their personal, social and work relationships. It also enables leaders and managers to control work procedures, motivate others and balance the needs and goals of individuals with those of the organisation. Successful people and organisations are usually those who communicate well, because they convey clearly to other people what they are doing and what they require. Successful communicators apply their interpersonal skills to listening, speaking, questioning, assertiveness, verbal and nonverbal communication.

Apply ethics to your workplace communication. Ethical communicators give honest and accurate information. They let others know about matters or information that affect them and maintain confidentiality of private information. They avoid spreading malicious gossip, putting others down or taking the credit for someone else's work. They communicate openly to achieve mutual understanding.

Identify communication aspects of a multicultural society. In a multicultural society, people in the same country have different cultural backgrounds. Intercultural communication occurs between these people. Culture conditions our perception of and reactions to signals and messages. It also determines the meanings we give to communication, events and situations. Aim to achieve successful intercultural communication by applying empathy and an open manner.

REVIEW QUESTIONS

1. 'Communication is an interactive process.' Briefly explain.
2. Define and give an example of verbal, nonverbal and graphic communication.
3. a. Define the terms 'sender' and 'receiver'.
   b. Define the term 'message'.
   c. Define the term 'feedback'.
4. a. Define the term 'perception'.
   b. List the four factors that may influence the perception of the sender or receiver of a message.
5. a. List four different types of communication.
   b. Define these and give an example of each.
6. a. 'Communication begins with the sender.' What are the remaining six variables at work in the communication process?
   b. As a sender, how do you obtain feedback from your receiver?
7. What are two factors that will influence your choice of channel? Give examples.
8. Define the term 'context' and give examples of how the context can affect the message.
9. Give five examples of possible 'noise' in the communication process.
10. What is wrong with this statement? 'The sender of the message has full control over how it is understood.'
11. a. Recall, and describe in writing, a situation in which you believe communication was successful.
    b. Give three reasons why the communication worked well.
12. a. List three possible differences between the needs of the organisation and the individual.
    b. Why is it important to balance the needs and goals of the individual with those of the organisation?
13. List four attributes displayed by an ethical business communicator.

Communication at work

BUILD SKILLS

Group discussion

Work in groups of three.
1. Each person is to think of someone who is good in their relationships with others at work and then discuss the following.
   a. How do these people interact with other people?
   b. What skills do they use?
2. Discuss and give examples of the ways we communicate:
   a. in words
   b. in pictures or symbols
   c. nonverbally.
3. Think of a situation when you tried to communicate with another person, or when somebody tried to communicate with you, and it failed. Think about the problems or barriers that interfered with the communication.
   a. Outline the situation to the members of your group and tell them why you think it failed.

b. List the reasons for failure identified by your group.

c. Come together as a large group to share the barriers identified by each group.

Role play: giving instructions

1. In your groups of three, nominate Person A to be Mitchell, Person B to be Carolyn and Person C, the observer.

2. Mitchell has been employed with the firm Arrow Ltd for five years. Carolyn has been working with Arrow for only one month.

   Mitchell has been asked by the Section Manager to show Carolyn how the communication process operates in the workplace. Mitchell must first identify each of the elements in the communication process, then describe their impact on personal interaction in the workplace.

   Persons A and B are to play the roles of Mitchell and Carolyn for ten minutes. Person C observes the role play and gives Mitchell feedback on how successfully he used his speaking, listening and questioning skills to instruct Carolyn.

3. All three people in the group should take a turn playing the roles of Persons A, B and C.

4. As a group, discuss the activity as follows. Did you find it easy to:
   a. organise information clearly and logically?
   b. speak confidently?
   c. ask questions clearly?
   d. listen to the other person?
   e. interact in a supportive way?

5. What did you learn from the activity about your capacity to communicate?

Key terms

communication
communication barrier
communication channel
communication process
context
cross-cultural
    communication
cultural sensitivity
decode
discrimination
empathy

encode
ethics
feedback
form of communication
graphic communication
horizontal channel
inclusion
intentional message
intercultural
    communication
message

multicultural society
noise
nonverbal communication
perception
receiver
sender
unintentional message
verbal communication
vertical channel

None the wiser

STUDY
CASE

by Louis Coutts

Recently, I had the privilege of taking a class of young executives from all over the world at the international extension to one of California's leading universities. There were people from Taiwan, Japan, South Korea, Denmark, Argentina and Brazil, aged from about 24 to 30 years.

After a couple of days of work, we broke up into groups of five or six. To facilitate the group discussion, I decided to give them some cases to work through. One of the cases was pretty simple.

'You have decided to leave your present job because you are frustrated at the working conditions and the lack of direction in the organisation. This means that you have formed an opinion of the working conditions that you don't like and you must have an idea of conditions you think you would enjoy. Describe why you want to leave your present job and describe the type of organisation in which you would like to work.'

The group that worked with this case was made up of people from Japan, Denmark, Germany and South Korea. The result was staggering. Most of those people had been working for a relatively short time, but they had worked long enough to develop a taste of what work was all about. The group documented first why they had left their previous job. The reasons were as follows:

- People were not talking with each other.
- There were no clear goals or direction.
- Communications were bad.
- There was no teamwork.
- Work was not fun.
- There was no feedback, positive or negative.
- There was no motivation, and this resulted in poor productivity.

They then turned to the question of the working conditions that they would look for in a new job:

- Open communication.
- Constructive feedback.
- Goals and the ability to verify them.
- Rewards for success.
- Opportunities to speak out.
- Work to be fun.

What was amazing about this was that, over the past 15 years in Australia, I have interviewed thousands of employees and they have expressed identical concerns to those expressed by this multinational group in California. This finding suggested to me that there must be something endemic in the manner in which we go about people management. It is significant that during this period of 15 years, there has been no variation in the stories that people tell me. Finally, when I sit down with a group of people from all over the world and they come up with the same concerns, I wonder whether we have really learnt anything about management during that time.

Before we began the group work, we had discussed the fact that so many people go into the workforce and are stifled by hierarchical institutions that prevent people from reaching their potential. One person mentioned that a previous lecturer in the program had made the point that this was no longer the case because of the liberation of youth and the fact that youth had become

used to having their say and were freer in how they went about their day-to-day activities. I had previously made the point that, in my experience, this freedom of youth only compounded the problem because, when they got into organisations that were focused on immediate financial performance, the organisation became dominated by financial factors, which resulted in a continuation of the stifling of youthful potential.

As the program progressed and the people in the class worked through the problems I set – taken from real life – it emerged that nothing had changed.

The disconcerting aspect of all this is that my expertise is in turning around companies that are in difficulty. And in every successful case I have dismantled the hierarchy and given much more responsibility to people in their areas of operation. I have to believe that, after the continual success of such a process, the correlation is not accidental.

Yet, the old hierarchical thing is alive and well and is making young people leave organisations in the hope that they will come across one that deserves their talent and energy.

I can only lament the loss that companies suffer when they lose such people or dissipate the energy that they can bring.

Source: Louis Coutts, 'None the wiser', *Management Today*, January–February 2002, p.37. Reproduced with permission of Louis Coutts, Management Consultant with Coutts & Connor, Melbourne.

Questions

1. The article highlights poor workplace communication as one of the main reasons why people are not happy in their workplace. Briefly describe the features of the poor workplace communication described in the case study.
2. What did the participant in the case study see as the key factors essential to good working conditions?
3. Describe the type of organisation in which you would like to work. In your answer, highlight the communication aspects of the organisation.

Answers to **Apply Skills**, question 6, on pages 16–17: 1T, 2F, 3T, 4T, 5F, 6T, 7T, 8T, 9F, 10T

Interactive skills: nonverbal communication and listening skills

Chapter 2

In this chapter you will learn how to:

- define the term 'nonverbal communication'
- identify its importance to the total message
- distinguish four types of nonverbal communication
- identify seven areas of nonverbal behaviour
- highlight the role of nonverbal behaviour in the communication process
- confirm with the sender of a message the meaning of their nonverbal communication
- interpret and use your own nonverbal communication appropriately
- identify the purpose of four different listening responses
- practise appropriate questioning responses
- provide feedback through reflective listening
- describe barriers to listening
- practise various listening skills
- use your nonverbal and listening skills appropriately.

Evaluate your communication skills by completing the self-checks in the chapter.

This chapter covers nonverbal communication and the listening skills and knowledge that enable people to interact effectively in their workplace. Effective interactions build positive workplace relationships.

In only a few situations do words alone send the message. Our impressions and images of others are affected by our perception of their verbal and nonverbal communication. Reactions to others' nonverbal communication influence our liking or dislike of them, our responsiveness and the way we respond and relate to one another.

There is a difference between hearing and listening. *Hearing* is a physical process. The ears receive sensations or stimuli and transmit them to the brain – for example, a loud, sudden or unfamiliar sound catches our attention. *Listening* refers to the interpretative process that takes place when we hear something. When we listen, we store, classify and label information, all of which involves attention, interpretation and understanding. Listening to another person takes time and effort.

The nonverbal communication accompanying the words reinforces and adds meaning to our message. Listening skills help us to understand and interpret the other person's message. Both these interactive skills assist us to send and receive the intended messages. Successful communication requires both sender and receiver to have interactive skills.

Nonverbal communication

The ability to focus on nonverbal communication allows us to plan and deal with situations in a purposeful, positive way and to communicate clearly. This in turn enables others to respond more easily because it lets them know what sort of person they are dealing with and how that person is likely to respond to various situations.

The nonverbal aspects of communication are so closely intermingled with the verbal that it is difficult to separate them. People receiving verbal and nonverbal messages combine them with the context in which the communication takes place and interpret the total message.

Actions speak louder than words.

Nonverbal communication consists of that part of a message that is not encoded in words. The nonverbal part of the message tends to be unconscious and often reveals the sender's feelings and preferences more spontaneously and honestly than the verbal part. If the verbal message does not match the nonverbal communication, people tend to believe the nonverbal message.

Nonverbal communication can be classified into four types.

In working towards better communication, particularly in interpreting the nonverbal part of the message, it is helpful to consider the four different types of nonverbal messages shown in Table 2.1.

Cultural nonverbal communication is shared by those in the culture.

Often we conform to the rules we learned as children about nonverbal messages. These rules create a level of cultural consensus and sense of belonging. However, cultural variations in the rules for nonverbal communication are great. While universal and random nonverbal communication are unlikely to cause communication barriers, personal and cultural nonverbal communication may raise barriers. For this reason, we need to be aware of the different ways individuals communicate nonverbally. We also need to be aware of variations caused by cultural differences.

Analysing nonverbal communication

Nonverbal behaviour should be interpreted in its context.

People communicate nonverbally with body movement and with personal relationship behaviours. This nonverbal communication changes or complements the verbal communication. Nonverbal communication always occurs in a **context**, or framework. The context often determines the meaning of the nonverbal behaviour. On different occasions the same nonverbal gesture may have completely different meanings. Without context and spoken words, nonverbal behaviour is almost impossible to interpret with any accuracy.

Table 2.1 Nonverbal messages

Type	Description	Example
1. Personal nonverbal communication	Involves various kinds of nonverbal behaviour that are unique to one person. The meaning is also unique to the person sending the message.	One person may work while talking, another may work in silence; someone may laugh due to nervousness or fear, while another may cry.
2. Cultural nonverbal communication	Characteristic of, or common to, a group of people. It is learned unconsciously by observing others in the society or group.	Women tend to feel free to touch each other, whereas men are generally more self-conscious about this. In Aboriginal culture, eye contact is less acceptable than it is in European culture.
3. Universal nonverbal communication	Behaviour that is common to humankind. It shows happiness, sadness or deep-seated feelings.	A smile, frown or tears
4. Random nonverbal communication	Unrelated to the verbal message; while it can distract from the verbal message it has little effect on the meaning.	A sneeze

Nonverbal cues and messages

1. Working in pairs, and without using words, use nonverbal cues to convey the following meanings.
   - No!
   - What do I do next?
   - Please help me finish.
   - Please stop badgering me.
   - What do you think?
   - I feel defeated.
   - I'm really happy.
   - I'm bored.
   - Let's get out of here.
2. Work with someone else in your group by standing together.
   a. Person A stays still, on exactly the same spot, while Person B takes up a position that feels comfortable in relation to Person A.
   b. Person B explains what made them choose that comfortable position.
   c. Person A talks about how they feel – that is, whether Person B is standing too close, the angle, the amount of contact, the impact of height difference, gender issues, body size and body space.
3. Explore the concept of eye contact by working in pairs. Each pair seats themselves comfortably and holds a two-way conversation for three minutes without making any eye contact at all. Once the conversation is finished, come together as a large group to discuss:
   - what it felt like to take part in the activity (the process)
   - what was talked about (the content)
   - what you liked most about the activity
   - what you liked least about the activity.

As a large group, close the activity by talking, with natural eye contact, about immediate activities such as the coming weekend, holidays or some other event.

APPLY SKILLS

Seven different aspects

Theoretical writings and research classify nonverbal communication into seven main areas.

1. body movement (kinesic behaviour)
2. physical characteristics
3. touching behaviour
4. vocal qualities (paralanguage)
5. space (proximity)
6. artefacts
7. environment.

Body movement

Body movement, or kinesic behaviour, includes movements of the hands, head, feet and legs, posture, eye movements and facial expressions – all these affect the message. Body posture – the way a person stands, leans forward or back, and moves the head – all affect the message. A person leaning forward, pointing and shaking a finger at someone is seen as trying to dominate the other person. The way this is received by others, and the type of feedback given, determines how the communication will flow. Ekman and Friesen's (1969) five main categories of body movement are listed in Table 2.2.

Table 2.2 The purpose of the five categories of body movement

Category	Definition	Purpose	Example
Emblems	Emblems are nonverbal acts learnt through imitation.	To reinforce or replace the words.	The nonverbal signal for 'okay' is a nod or a smile.
Illustrators	Illustrators are nonverbal acts that relate to, and illustrate, the spoken word.	To accentuate or emphasise a word or phrase.	A nod of the head and wave of the arm in a certain direction, accompanying the words 'Over there'.
Affective (or feeling) displays	Affective displays are changes in facial expression that display emotion.	Unconscious displays reflect feelings, whereas intentional expressions can disguise or hide feelings.	Facial muscles may 'drop' with surprise or shock; a smile may be used to deceive or disarm the listener.
Regulators	Nods and other head movements are nonverbal acts that regulate communication between people.	To maintain and control the flow of speaking and listening. Regulators indicate whether to continue, repeat, elaborate or change from speaker to listener.	A nod to encourage another person to continue speaking.
Adaptors	Nonverbal acts performed unconsciously in response to some inner desire.	To display instinctive responses.	Scratching an itchy ear; raising the arms in shock or horror

Figure 2.1 Six different facial expressions

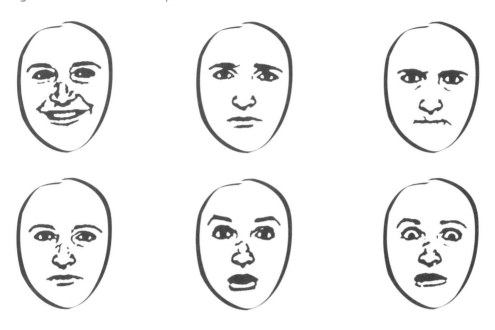

Physical characteristics

Physical characteristics such as body shape, general attractiveness, body and breath odours, weight, hair and skin colour are important parts of nonverbal communication. Because people react to these factors, they determine our responses in interpersonal encounters. First impressions and images of others can be associated unconsciously with past experiences of people with similar physical characteristics.

Physical characteristics can cause a reaction.

Touching behaviour

Stroking, hitting, holding or guiding the movements of another person are examples of touching behaviour that communicate nonverbally. Each adds a different meaning to a message. Touching can console or support the other person and show feelings such as affection, sexual interest or dominance. Hand gestures demonstrate feelings and convey thoughts and words through movement. A handshake, for example, can express dominance or equality. A pat on the arm can convey intimacy or control.

Touching adds meaning to the message.

Paralanguage (vocal qualities)

Paralanguage is that part of language associated with but not involving the word system. It consists of the voice qualities and vocalisations that affect *how* something is said rather than what is said. Voice qualities include:

Paralanguage is how something is said.

- pitch range
- pitch control
- rhythm control
- tempo
- articulation control
- resonance.

Vocalisations also give clues to the total message. Three of these are shown in Table 2.3. The tone of voice, rate of speaking and voice inflection are an important part of the total message. A tired person, for example, will speak more slowly than usual, a disappointed person may speak with a flat tone, while the tone of voice of someone excited about a coming holiday reflects this excitement.

Table 2.3 Vocalisations

Type	Examples
Vocal characterisers	Laughing, crying, sighing, yawning, clearing the throat, groaning, yelling, whispering
Vocal qualifiers	Intensity (loud/soft); pitch height (high/low)
Vocal segregates	Sounds such as 'uh-huh', 'um', 'uh', 'ah'; silent pauses

Proximity (use of space)

Proximity means nearness, in terms of physical space. How people use their personal space and that of others communicates a message. This response to spatial relationships in formal, informal and intimate settings indicates how that person perceives and feels in that space.

Space can be used to indicate status.

People also use their height and weight to convey a message. If you tower over other people in a way that intrudes on their personal space you may cause their discomfort and withdrawal.

Personal space varies according to:

■ gender
■ status
■ roles
■ culture.

Research has shown that Australians speaking to acquaintances or work colleagues leave about an arm's length of space between themselves and the other person. People speaking to friends and family leave about half an arm's length between themselves and others. People in intimate relationships allow direct and close contact when speaking to each other. The use of space reflects the way people feel about others.

Artefacts

Artefacts are objects used to convey nonverbal messages about self-concept, image, mood, feelings or style. For example, perfume, clothes, lipstick, glasses and hairpieces project the style or mood of the wearer. Many artefacts are common to the group but we also use artefacts, particularly clothing, as an individual form of communication.

Clothes are vehicles for conveying nonverbal messages.

Appearance and clothing are important and highly visible parts of nonverbal communication. Consider the difference between the clothes you wear to the beach and the clothes you wear to a job interview. The choice of clothes reflects your mood and your attitude to the occasion. Other people notice and place their own interpretation on your dress.

A police badge, a nurse's uniform, a university lecturer's gown and an Italian suit are all artefacts that can signal power or lack of power in a situation. If a plain-clothes police officer shows the police badge at an accident, others immediately perceive his or her authority. Even if you decide you will not bother about personal appearance or clothes, others will read this message as part of your nonverbal communication.

Environmental factors

The environment can influence the outcome of communication. For this reason, organisations give careful consideration to office space, factory layout, the sales area and conference venues. The environment should put people at ease and match their expectations; an unsuitable environment can produce 'noise' that causes communication barriers and interferes with the communication process.

Certain instincts, such as the desire for privacy, familiarity and security, need to be satisfied. Careful design of the workplace can meet these needs and in so doing improve communication, productivity and morale. Natural and artificial light, colour, temperature, tables, chairs, desks, lounges, plants, sound, artwork, magazines, and floor and wall coverings all have an impact on people's perception of an organisation.

In the workplace, attention to punctuality or a disregard for it can make a strong nonverbal impact. A disregard for punctuality may, like a sloppy appearance, merely reflect a casual attitude. However, a deliberate decision to keep a contact waiting may be a way of communicating a negative message.

While punctuality is a matter of courtesy, attitudes towards its importance vary between cultures. To be kept waiting for a business appointment on a tropical island will not have the same significance as a delay in some European countries where punctuality is highly regarded.

The above discussion of the seven aspects of nonverbal communication provides a theoretical analysis. However, to consider each aspect in isolation is artificial. In practice, what is sent as a total message is a cluster of nonverbal cues in association with the spoken words.

Environmental factors influence communication.

Communication without words

1. Visit a café and observe a customer and a waiter working.
   a. Compare the nonverbal behaviours of the waiter and the customer on each of the seven main areas of nonverbal communication. Use Table 2.4 on page 30.
   b. What were the major differences between the nonverbal behaviour of the waiter and the customer? Suggest reasons for the differences.
   c. Now observe the behaviour of two people sitting together in the café. Again, note each of the seven main areas of nonverbal communication.
   d. How did the interactions of the two people vary from the nonverbal behaviours of the waiter and customer? In your opinion, were the second pair enjoying themselves? Justify your answer.
   e. 'Nonverbal communication should be

interpreted in context.' What does this mean?

2. The purpose of this activity is to identify different aspects of nonverbal communication and to experience the effect of a stressful situation in a controlled environment.

   Work as a large group (15–20 people) to 'Walk the Circle':
   - Place as many chairs in a circle as there are people in the group, plus two extra chairs.
   - Each person in the group sits on a chair in the circle, with a chair on each side of the circle left empty. The rest of the activity is conducted in silence.
   - Each person takes a turn to stand up, walk across the circle to the first empty chair, sit down, then stand up and walk to the other empty chair and sit down, and then return to their own chair. The other

APPLY SKILLS

members of the group observe the person walking between chairs. Only one person should be moving at any time.

■ When each person has walked the circle, discuss as a large group:
a. their observations and impressions of the way people used nonverbal communication, such as eyes, pace, posture, facial expressions and other movements;
b. the messages conveyed by the nonverbal communication;
c. how people felt about walking the circle in silence in front of others.

3. Use Self-check 2.1 as you watch an interview or a political broadcast on television or video.

Table 2.4 Your response to behaviour

Nonverbal behaviour	Customer	Waiter
Body movements		
Physical characteristics		
Touching behaviour		
Vocal qualities		
Use of space		
Artefacts		
Environment		

SELF CHECK 2.1

Nonverbal communication

As you watch the program, identify nonverbal communication that interacts with the spoken message in a way that:	Yes	No	Unsure
repeats	☐	☐	☐
contradicts	☐	☐	☐
substitutes	☐	☐	☐
complements	☐	☐	☐
accents	☐	☐	☐
controls the message	☐	☐	☐

Matching the nonverbal and verbal parts of the total message

The **total message** combines spoken words with nonverbal communication. Nonverbal communication adds meaning, modifies or changes the spoken words in six ways.

1. *Repeating* – for example, pointing when giving directions.
2. *Contradicting* – for example, looking at your watch and backing away while telling someone, 'I'm very interested in what you're saying.'
3. *Substituting* – using facial expressions as a substitute for words, to show pleasure, disappointment and a range of feelings and experiences.

4. *Complementing* – modifying, emphasising or elaborating words in a way that conveys attitudes and intentions towards others; for example, standing in a casual way or using a careless tone of voice that conveys a lack of respect for the listener.
5. *Accenting* – moving the head and hands to emphasise parts of the verbal message; for example, shaking the head as you say 'No'.
6. *Controlling the flow of communication* – nodding your head or changing position can indicate that the speaker should continue or give you a turn.

Dealing with contradictions between the verbal and nonverbal message

The accurate interpretation of nonverbal messages comes from knowing people and their pattern of interpersonal communication, both verbal and nonverbal. The nonverbal communication is seldom consciously observed unless it confuses the receiver. On some occasions it is possible to ignore confusing nonverbal communication. At other times it must be acknowledged or even confronted. For example, when the verbal message conveys agreement while several nonverbal signals such as pitch of voice, facial expression or posture indicate lack of agreement or even ridicule, check the meaning of the nonverbal part of the message. It is useful to check the meaning when you:

Nonverbal messages may contradict or complement verbal messages.

- are in doubt
- are uncomfortable with the communication
- have to make a decision on the basis of the total message.

Consider the impact of culture

Because your cultural background influences the way you interpret the nonverbal messages of others, it is important to consider specific messages in context. If you discover inconsistencies between the verbal and nonverbal messages of someone from another culture, stand back and consider the message in the context of the situation. This allows you more scope for interpretation and a better chance of understanding the intended message rather than the one your cultural background suggests.

How to check the meaning of nonverbal behaviour

When you are in doubt about the meaning of nonverbal behaviour, confirm it with the sender and try not to make assumptions or pass judgment. Gestures and body movements are nonverbal behaviours that contribute to the total message. The total message is understood more easily when you follow the four-step process below.

The total message includes the words and the nonverbal behaviour.

1. Hear the words.
2. See the nonverbal behaviour.
3. Confirm their meaning with the sender when the verbal and nonverbal messages conflict or confuse you.
4. Consider the context or setting.

For example, suppose someone in a meeting sits back and folds their arms. If you say, 'I see you're in a closed posture', you are making an assumption about the nonverbal part of the message. It is more useful to confirm the meaning by replacing your interpretation with a simple description: 'You've just folded your arms'. This allows the person to reply: 'Yes, my shoulders are aching' or 'Yes, I feel uncomfortable, even threatened by the suggestion' or 'I'm cold' or 'I'm bored'.

Nonverbal communication can be misinterpreted.

Next time you are uncertain about the meaning of someone's nonverbal behaviour, simply check it out by completing these two steps.

1. Describe the behaviour.
2. Ask the sender what the response means.

In this way you avoid misinterpreting the communication. As a result, there are fewer communication barriers and misunderstandings. However, there are so many messages and so many variables it is impossible to check out everything.

Using nonverbal communication appropriately

SKILLS
APPLY

The object of this activity is to increase your nonverbal communication skills so that you give your message confidently and courteously—that is, so that you express *assertion*. You are asked to role-play aggressive and passive behaviours as well as assertive behaviour. Some of the nonverbal behaviour that indicates assertiveness, aggression and passivity is shown in the nonverbal behaviour checklist below.

Procedure

1. Divide into groups of three. Nominate Person A to be Jenny, the team leader; Person B is James, a team member; Person C is the observer. Jenny, the team leader, asks James to meet her at 4 pm. James responds with the question: 'What will we be discussing?'
2. The role of Jenny is to be played in three different ways:
   a. assertively
   b. aggressively
   c. passively.
      Person C, the observer, uses the nonverbal behaviour checklist (below) to give Person A feedback on how

successfully they used assertive, aggressive and passive nonverbal communication as they played the role of Jenny.

3. All three people in the group should take a turn playing the roles of Persons A, B and C.
4. Discuss the activity in the group as a whole by answering the following questions:
   a. Did you find it easy to use your nonverbal communication to show assertive, aggressive and passive behaviour in the role play?
   b. How well did each of you use behaviour that showed assertion, aggression and passivity nonverbally?
   c. Are there other ways to show assertion, aggression and passivity nonverbally?
   d. What effect did each of the three different ways of communicating nonverbally have on the person playing James?
   e. What were your reactions and feelings about the activity?

Nonverbal behaviour checklist

Nonverbal behaviour	Assertive	Y/N	Aggressive	Y/N	Passive	Y/N
Posture	Upright and relaxed	☐	Leaning forward	☐	Shrinking away	☐
Head	Firm and comfortable	☐	Chin pushed forward	☐	Head down	☐
Eyes	Direct and regular eye contact	☐	Staring, often piercing or glaring	☐	Glancing down with little eye contact	☐
Face	Appropriate, courteous and friendly expression	☐	Rigid and set	☐	Hesitant, smiling even when upset	☐

Cont'd

Nonverbal behaviour	Assertive	Y/N	Aggressive	Y/N	Passive	Y/N
Voice	Confident, with appropriate speed, pitch and volume	☐	Loud, fast and dramatic	☐	Soft, trailing off at ends of words or sentences	☐
Arms/hands	Relaxed, moving easily and reflecting the verbal message	☐	Controlled, sharp gestures with fingers pointing and jerky movements	☐	Still or slow, not reflecting the verbal message	☐
Movement/ walking	Confident and measured pace appropriate to the context	☐	Overly confident, heavy or fast, deliberate, hard	☐	Slow and without confidence, or fast and uncertain	☐

The process of listening

At work, people listen in order to understand instructions, receive new information, understand changes in procedure, and to interact with other people. Whatever the purpose, concentration and a deliberate effort to be interested in the speaker's message will increase listening effectiveness. If you listen well, you will understand the content, meaning and feelings of the message. If you are distracted, much of this will be lost.

Listening is an active process.

Listening serves two broad purposes in the process of talking to others:

1. As the sender of a message, listening to your receiver's answers tells you how the other person has interpreted your message.
2. As the receiver of a message, listening to the other person allows you to understand their meaning.

A variety of listening skills can be learned and developed with practice. Listening is so important that it is worth practising the different skills in each type of listening shown in Table 2.5. Sometimes you will use only one of these types of listening skills. On another occasion you might use all in combination. Each type of listening involves a set of behaviours or skills. They enable you to focus on the speaker, invite the speaker to continue, give feedback or show empathy with the speaker.

Each different type of listening skill involves a set of behaviours.

Table 2.5 Four listening skills

Type	Purpose
Attending listening	To focus on the speaker
Encouraging listening	To invite the speaker to continue
Reflecting listening	To mirror the feelings and content in the message
Active listening	To show empathy with the speaker

Focus on the speaker

In **attending listening**, you focus on the speaker by giving them your physical attention. You use your whole body and the environment you create to provide feedback that assures the speaker of your total attention. Some ways of offering this feedback are eye contact, posture and body movement.

The quality of your attending listening skills is also improved by:

- understanding the impact of moving into the personal space of others
- the impact of the environment
- the capacity to ignore distractions.

Listening is an active process. Show interest in the speaker by using the behaviours listed in Table 2.6.

Table 2.6 Attending listening

Factor	Behaviour
Eye contact	■ Use supportive eye contact.
	■ Focus your eyes on the speaker without being intimidating.
	■ Show sensitivity – avoid staring directly at the speaker for long periods as the speaker may feel uncomfortable.
Posture	■ Use your posture to show you are attending to the other person.
	■ Lean slightly forward towards the speaker in a relaxed way.
	■ Face the person squarely.
	■ Maintain an open position with arms and legs uncrossed.
Body movement	■ Avoid moving about a lot.
	■ Avoid fiddling with objects, crossing or uncrossing legs, signalling or speaking to passers-by.
Personal space	■ Position yourself at a distance that is comfortable for both you and the speaker. Comfort in the use of physical distance depends on culture and personal preference.
	■ Avoid moving into the speaker's personal space.
Environment	■ Create an environment without distractions or interruptions.
	■ Remove any physical barriers between you and the speaker.
	■ Establish an environment where you can both feel relaxed.
Avoid distractions	■ Face and maintain contact with the speaker.
	■ Ignore distractions rather than turning away from the speaker.
	■ Stop what you are doing and focus your attention on the other person.

Invite the speaker to continue

Encouraging listening indicates that the listener is willing to do more than listen. Encouraging listening provides feedback that invites speakers to say more and to disclose their thoughts and feelings. The following strategies will encourage the speaker to continue.

Invitation to disclose

Invite speakers to continue but without pressuring them to disclose their feelings or thoughts. It is their choice, so let them decide. They may be feeling ambivalent about whether to discuss their feelings or keep them private. Continue to give attention by using eye contact and an open posture and let them choose whether or not to disclose. For example, if the speaker seems upset or annoyed, you might say something like 'You seem to be upset about the discussion with that last client. Would you care to talk about it?'

Minimal and brief responses

Minimal and brief spoken responses let speakers know you are listening and encourage them to continue. Some of these responses are 'mm', 'hmmm', 'yes', 'I see', along with an attentive posture. Other nonverbal cues like nodding and facial expressions convey your interest without attempting to control or divert the conversation away from the area of interest.

Pause

A pause, or brief silence, allows the speaker time to consider, reflect and decide whether to continue the conversation. As a listener, use this time to watch the speaker's body movement. This can give you clues to the total message – its content and the speaker's feelings. Let the speaker have time to think. Allow silences.

Use encouraging questions

Asking open questions will encourage the other person to share more personal feelings and thoughts. An example of an **open question** is: 'How did you go about collecting the files?' An example of a **closed question** is: 'Did you collect the files?' Open questions encourage the speaker to answer at greater length and in more detail, whereas closed questions usually lead to a 'yes' or 'no' answer.

Use open questions.

Avoid 'why' questions because they can make the other person defensive. Rather than encouraging speakers to explore their actions, a 'why' question urges them to justify their actions. It can also sound disapproving.

By asking open questions about what, when, where, how and who, you can help the speaker to be more specific and revealing. Although encouraging questions show that you are interested in talking, they do not necessarily show that you understand. To show you understand, make reflective statements that clarify and summarise the other person's communication without interrupting the flow of words or thoughts.

Attending and encouraging listening

1. Work in pairs to practise attending and encouraging listening skills. Take turns to act as speaker and listener.

    As the speaker, choose a controversial topic on which you hold a very definite position, or a topic about which you feel strongly, and speak to your listener about this for three minutes.

    As the listener, use the following guidelines to focus your listening:

    a. Show your interest in the speaker by your body movement: face the speaker; make eye contact; lean forward, keeping an open posture.

    b. Notice the speaker's body movement. This may indicate the feelings underlying the spoken message.

    c. Use familiar, comfortable language that you both normally use and understand.

    d. Use feedback to invite the speaker to continue by using minimal responses.

APPLY SKILLS

e. Ask as few questions as possible. When you do ask questions, use attending and encouraging listening responses. (Some examples are shown in Table 2.7.)

2. At the end of the exercise, discuss with one another your effectiveness as listeners. Refer to points (a) to (e) in question 1.

Mirror the content and feelings in the message

Show the other person you understand.

Reflecting listening restates both the feeling and content of the speaker's message, to show that you understand. There are several techniques you can use to provide this kind of feedback.

Paraphrasing focuses on the content rather than the feelings. It rephrases the essential part of the message concisely in your own words. Listen for the main ideas and direction of the message and rephrase it for the speaker.

Paraphrasing helps to achieve a full understanding of the content. The speaker either agrees with your summary or disagrees and can then rephrase the message. For example, phrases such as 'You're saying that . . .' or 'I see, you would say that . . .' help you to paraphrase the message. Avoid repeating the other person's statements word for word.

Paraphrasing is useful at work to confirm instructions or information before you take action. Whether at work or in other situations, it is a very useful way of indicating to the speaker that you are concentrating on the message.

Reflective statements are made by expressing briefly the essential feelings you receive from the message. This helps the speaker to focus on them. For example, to reflect feelings from the message, 'I thought I would have got that last promotion. Seems like I miss out every time' the listener replies, 'It's really discouraging' or 'You feel discouraged' or 'You seem discouraged'. This lets the speaker know that you understand their feelings.

Clarifying establishes with the speaker that your understanding is correct. Make clarifying remarks in terms of your feelings rather than as criticisms of the speaker. For example, if you feel confused by what the speaker has said, you might say something like 'I feel a bit confused about that last remark. I think you are saying . . .' or 'Could you repeat that? I don't think I understood' or 'Could you give me an example of . . .? I'm not sure I followed what you said'.

If you have misunderstood, the speaker can then rephrase the message. Clarifying gives the speaker feedback and shows what the listener understands. It takes the guess-work out of communication.

Summarising is used to gather up and condense the most important points made in a long conversation, to conclude it and give it shape or direction. As you summarise, use statements such as 'So far we've covered . . .' or 'Your main concerns seem to be ...'. Summarising lets the other person know you understand what is most relevant, and their thoughts and feelings. Such feedback results in clear communication. Both sender and receiver understand the message.

Show empathy with the speaker

Understand the issue from the other person's point of view.

While reflective statements restate the feelings and content of the message, active listening goes one step further. It also communicates to other people that you understand the problem from their point of view. An active listener has **empathy** with the speaker.

This technique lets the speaker either confirm or correct the listener's feedback. Active listening also helps other people to reach their own decisions and form their own insights.

Active participation

The process of **active listening** involves actively participating in the conversation with the other person. It requires a conscious attempt to empathise with the speaker in terms of the content and feelings and to enable them to express and recognise those feelings. For example, a response by the listener such as 'You seem to be feeling down about this . . .' lets the speaker either agree or disagree with that response. Listening responses that help you to participate actively are shown in Table 2.7.

When you use active listening, you are giving the other person all your attention in order to understand their perspective, and to communicate your understanding. Active listening also lets speakers find their own understanding and insights.

Attending, encouraging and reflecting listening are separate listening skills that we combine as we interact with one another. As well as using these skills, an active listener understands the situation from the other person's point of view. It is a more intense form of listening. Speakers who are given the opportunity to talk with active listeners are more likely to find their own satisfactory resolution to the problem or issue of concern.

Table 2.7 Examples of listening responses

Type of response	Examples
Attending	■ 'I hear you . . .' ■ 'I see . . .' ■ 'Oh . . .' ■ 'Uh hmmm . . .'
Encouraging questions	■ 'I'd like to hear how you feel.' ■ 'Would you like to talk about it?' ■ 'You'd like to talk further?' ■ 'Perhaps you'd like to tell me?'
Reflective statements	■ 'You really dislike some . . .' ■ 'Sounds as if you're really . . .' ■ 'It's really exciting . . .' ■ 'You feel it is a good idea . . .' ■ 'You seem to be feeling discouraged . . .'
Clarifying questions	■ 'I think you're saying . . .' ■ 'Could you give an example . . .?' ■ 'I feel a bit confused. Could you repeat that?'
Active listening: empathy	■ 'I understand how you feel.' ■ 'You seem to be feeling upset about this.' ■ 'I see. It really means that . . .' ■ 'On another occasion you'd like . . .'

Feedback

What you choose to listen to, understand and interpret affects how you respond to the speaker. If you listen for both the words and the feelings and receive the message

Feedback is
the connecting,
continuing or
completing link.

accurately, it is possible to give feedback that helps the understanding of both speaker and listener. A good listener gives feedback in a way that is appropriate to the speaker's needs and to the situation. **Feedback** is the connecting or completing link between listener and speaker, and is discussed more fully in Chapter 4, Effective workplace communication.

By listening well, you can avoid directing or leading, blaming, judging or evaluating the other person. Rather than feeling the need to be responsible for others or to confront them, a good listener accepts and is accepted by others. Skill in listening lets you enjoy the company of others as you listen for pleasure, information, to help others or to interact in a work team.

Different types of questions are used for different reasons. Open questions such as 'Tell me about . . .' or 'Tell me how . . .' allow the person to give a lot of information. The listening funnel in Figure 2.2 shows how **probing questions** such as 'In what way were you able to . . .?' start to narrow the listener's range of responses. Closed questions such as 'When did you do that?' 'Where?' 'Who?' usually have only yes/no or specific answers. **Paraphrasing questions** are used to check that your understanding of the message matches the sender's meaning.

Figure 2.2 Listening funnel

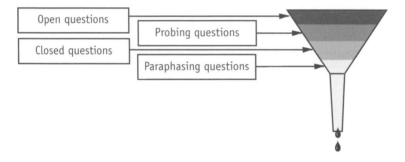

Reflecting and paraphrasing skills

SKILLS
APPLY

1. Work by yourself. Read the following statements and write a reflective response for each one. Reflect the feelings in the message.
   a. 'I know how to do it. Leave me alone.'
   b. 'I like to swim each morning. It makes me feel good all day.'
   c. 'I never know where I stand with you. Whenever I talk about the new project, I get the feeling you disapprove.'
   d. 'I never have enough time to get everything done.'
2. Work in groups of three to:
   a. Identify the content and feelings in each of the statements.
   b. Discuss the responses prepared in question 1.
   c. Discuss ways in which the responses could be improved.
3. Break into two groups. The first group is to create a 'top ten' list of reasons for listening well. The second group is to create a list of the 'top ten' excuses for not listening. Form one large group to compare and contrast the reasons for listening well and not listening.
4. *Quick Quiz:* Paraphrasing
   Tick true (T) or false (F) for the following statements.

Paraphrasing by the listener	T	F
1. focuses on the content rather than the feelings	☐	☐
2. allows the speaker to add new information	☐	☐
3. helps you listen carefully	☐	☐
4. shows speakers they are unimportant	☐	☐
5. mirrors to speakers what they have just said	☐	☐
6. lets the listener ignore the speaker	☐	☐
7. helps the listener to understand or confirm information	☐	☐
8. lets the speaker exaggerate	☐	☐
9. means that the listener always agrees with what the speaker said	☐	☐
10. helps to avoid mistakes	☐	☐
11. means the listener repeats word for word what the speaker said	☐	☐

Barriers to listening

Barriers may be due to the listeners themselves when some aspect of their own background interferes with their perception of the speaker or of the spoken message. Barriers may also be due to any one of the elements in the communication process – sender, receiver, message, channel, environment or ineffective feedback. An unclear message caused by static or interference on the telephone line is an obvious example of a communication barrier caused by the channel. Neither the listener nor the sender can prevent such a barrier. Listening is made easier when the speaker can send a clear, unambiguous message. It is also made easier when the listener avoids the following barriers.

Barriers interfere with the message.

Barriers in the listener

Often the most significant barriers to listening are present in the listener. Some examples of such barriers include:

- boredom or lack of interest
- the listener's dislike of the speaker's personality or physical appearance
- a desire to change rather than accept the speaker
- a tendency to make early conclusions or to listen only for a pause so the speaker can be interrupted
- the intrusion of the listener's own values or attitudes
- the listener's tendency to judge the speaker
- the listener's willingness to hear only that part of the message they agree with
- the listener's opinion that the speaker lacks credibility.

You will recognise some of these barriers, and perhaps be able to add to them from your own experience as a listener or as an observer of another listener. Table 2.8 gives examples of barriers to listening and their impact on the receiver. As a sender, no matter how skilled you are at speaking or communicating the message, communication will fail if the receiver does not listen.

Table 2.8 The impact of a listener's ineffective verbal response

Listener's ineffective response to the speaker	Example of barrier	Speaker's response to the barrier
Ordering, directing or commanding	'Stop it or else . . .' 'You must do this'	Resentment
Warning and threatening	'You'd better do this or else . . .'	Anger
Lecturing or preaching	'It's in your own best interest to do this'	Resistance
Judging, criticising	'I think you've gone too far this time'	Offence
Disagreeing	'I think you're totally wrong'	Put down
Blaming	'It's all your fault'	Defensiveness
Name calling	'You're stupid'	Distress
Probing, interrogating	'Why did you . . .?'	Defensiveness
Using ridicule or sarcasm	'Someone like you is not expected to know . . .'	Hurt

SELF CHECK 2.2

How good a listener are you?

How often have you noticed the following interfering with your ability to listen effectively?

	Often	Sometimes	Never
Your attention to the message	☐	☐	☐
The status or role of the speaker	☐	☐	☐
The rate at which the message is spoken	☐	☐	☐
The speaker's accent	☐	☐	☐
Familiarity with the subject	☐	☐	☐
A poorly organised message	☐	☐	☐
The speaker's resemblance to someone you dislike	☐	☐	☐
The importance of the subject	☐	☐	☐
Your lack of familiarity with the message	☐	☐	☐
The speaker's opposition to some of your opinions and beliefs	☐	☐	☐
The gestures made by the speaker	☐	☐	☐
Your tendency to think about something else	☐	☐	☐

WEB WISE

Visit the Companion Website at **www.prenhall.com/dwyer_au**. Choose the Multiple Choice activity in Chapter 2 and answer the questions. How would you describe your knowledge of nonverbal communication and listening?

Chapter summary

Define nonverbal communication. Nonverbal communication consists of all that part of a message that is not encoded in words – for example, tone of voice, facial expression or gestures and movement.

Identify the importance of nonverbal communication to the total message. Verbal and nonverbal messages communicate as a total message. They may be in agreement with each other, or contradictory. If the verbal and nonverbal messages are inconsistent, the nonverbal part of the message has the stronger effect and is the more credible part of the total message.

Distinguish four types of nonverbal communication. Nonverbal communication is either personal (unique to the individual), common to the group or culture, universal or random. The part of the nonverbal communication that is common to a range of people is a clue to what they consider to be acceptable behaviour. Personal nonverbal communication characteristics such as gestures and mannerisms create an impression of the sender's personality.

Identify seven areas of nonverbal behaviour. The seven aspects of nonverbal behaviour are body movement (kinesic behaviour), physical characteristics, touching behaviour, vocal qualities (paralanguage), use of space or proximity, artefacts and the environment. A combination of these aspects makes up the nonverbal part of the total message.

Highlight the role of nonverbal behaviour in the communication process. Nonverbal behaviour may be specific (e.g. pointing in the direction of the bus stop) or general (e.g. waving in the general direction of the next suburb). Body movement aims to communicate more than can be said with words alone. It is expressive (e.g. enthusiastic or weary) so it also conveys emotions or attitudes.

Confirm with the sender of the message the meaning of their nonverbal communication. When you observe other people's nonverbal communication, it is more useful to confirm with them the meaning of their nonverbal communication than to make your own interpretations or assumptions. Confirming the message reduces the chance of misinterpreting the nonverbal message.

Use nonverbal communication appropriately. Nonverbal communication is sent by at least one person and received by at least one other person. The accuracy with which it is interpreted and its value in clarifying the message depends on the sender's ability to communicate accurately and on the receiver's ability to interpret the message accurately. The appropriate use of nonverbal communication and the ability to interpret nonverbal communication accurately are two of the skills demonstrated by good communicators. These skills are used as each of us listens, speaks, questions and communicates with others. The seven main aspects of nonverbal communication have been presented in isolation in this chapter. In practice, they occur in clusters and must be read and used together.

Identify the purpose of four different listening responses. The four listening responses are attending, encouraging, reflecting and active listening. Attending listening focuses on the speaker. Encouraging listening invites the speaker to continue. Reflecting listening mirrors the content and feelings of the message. Active listening shows empathy with the speaker.

Practise appropriate questioning responses. Open questions encourage the other person to share their thoughts and feelings. Encouraging questions are open questions about what, when, where, how and who. Clarifying questions let you, as the listener, check your understanding of the message with the other person. Use closed questions only when a 'yes' or 'no' answer is required. Avoid 'why' questions because they may make other people feel defensive and justify their position rather than seek new ideas or further understanding.

Provide feedback through reflective listening. A good listener does this by paraphrasing, using reflective statements, clarifying and summarising. The result is a fuller understanding and clear communication.

Describe barriers to listening. These barriers can be caused by the sender, the receiver, the message, the channel, the environment or the way in which feedback is given. Barriers from the listener may be due to boredom, a difference in values, lack of interest or ineffective verbal responses.

Practise various listening skills. The learning activities in this chapter enable you to practise attending listening skills that focus your attention on the speaker, and encouraging listening skills that allow speakers to say more and to disclose their feelings and/or thoughts. You will also be able to practise reflective listening, a response that shows the other person you understand the content and feelings conveyed by the message. Active listening lets you restate the content and feeling, and also lets the other person know that you understand the situation from their point of view – that is, you demonstrate empathy.

Use your nonverbal and listening skills appropriately. Good listeners use all four listening responses, singly or in combination, to make their listening behaviour appropriate to the situation. Good nonverbal communicators identify the seven main areas of nonverbal communication and learn to blend them with the verbal and contextual information to convey or grasp the total message. Effective listening and nonverbal communication lead to positive interactions and mutual understanding.

REVIEW QUESTIONS

1. a. Define the term 'nonverbal communication'.
    b. It is often said that 'actions speak louder than words'. Explain.
2. List and define the four types of nonverbal communication.
3. Explain the difference between nonverbal messages that are personal to the individual and nonverbal messages common to a group of people.
4. List the main differences between the rule-governed behaviour for sitting and walking for men and women. In your answer, compare the socially acceptable ways in which arms, legs and the body are used when men sit and when women sit.
5. Define and give examples of cultural nonverbal communication and universal nonverbal communication.
6. Assume two people are standing side by side and will touch by one placing a hand on the other person's shoulder or arm. According to the etiquette rules of your culture, who would touch whom first in the following situations?
    ■ college principal and student
    ■ company director and new employee
    ■ interviewer and interviewee.
7. Researchers divide nonverbal communication into seven main areas. List these.
8. a. List and give an example of each of the five main categories of body movement.
    b. What is their purpose?
9. How does our use of space convey messages to others?

10. What part do artefacts play in nonverbal communication?

11. Identify two interpretations that a business executive might place on a colleague's lack of punctuality.

12. What are the two broad purposes served by listening?

13. a. Give a definition of listening.
   b. Think of a person you regard as a good listener, and one who is a poor listener. Identify three aspects of their listening techniques that make them either a good listener or a poor listener.

14. Identify three examples of nonverbal feedback you might use in attending listening.

15. a. Name four strategies that a listener can use to provide feedback when using encouraging listening skills.
   b. Explain the difference between open and closed questions.
   c. 'Avoid *why* questions because they can make the other person defensive.' Briefly explain this statement.

16. a. What is the main purpose of (i) encouraging listening, (ii) reflective statements?
   b. Define the term 'paraphrasing'

and explain its purpose as a listening response.
   c. Define the term 'empathy' and explain its purpose as a listening response.
   d. Define the term 'clarifying question' and explain its purpose as a listening response.
   e. Define the term 'summarising' and explain its purpose as a listening response.

17. a. 'Active listening goes one step further than mirroring content and feelings.' Explain this statement.

18. What is the role of feedback in the listening process?

19. 'Barriers interfere with the message.' Explain this statement.

20. Refer to Table 2.8
   a. List four inappropriate listening responses identified in this table.
   b. Give examples of a situation in which you have observed each of the inappropriate listening responses.
   c. Which of the four listening skills (attending, encouraging, reflecting or active listening) would have been more appropriate in each situation?

Good listening skills

Attending, encouraging and reflecting listening

Form into groups of three to practise listening skills. Allocate the roles of:

A Speaker
B Listener
C Observer

Take a turn at all three roles. A speaks, B listens and responds, C observes and assesses the listener's effectiveness according to the guidelines in the checklist.

Speaker's statements
The speaker makes the following statements, one at a time.

a. 'I keep getting all the worst

assignments in this section, and I just don't think it's fair!'

b. 'We have clients complaining every day about errors in delivery or late deliveries. If you can't meet the order you should let us know so that we can notify the client.'

c. 'It's not my job. Someone else can do it.'

d. 'What you expect from this job is unrealistic. The time needed to complete all the tasks varies and I can't control the number of tasks. How am I supposed to get my job done?'

The listener responds to statement (a) by paraphrasing; (b) by clarifying; (c) by reflecting feeling; and (d) by reflecting meaning.

BUILD SKILLS

Observer's guidelines

Observe the speaker and listener. Note when each listening skill has been used, decide whether the skill and the appropriate nonverbal behaviour – body language, facial expression and eye contact – was used successfully, fairly satisfactorily or poorly, and place a tick in the appropriate column of the checklist below.

Discuss your observations with the speaker and the listener.

Effective listening checklist

	Successfully	Fairly satisfactorily	Poorly
Paraphrased	☐	☐	☐
Clarified	☐	☐	☐
Reflected feelings	☐	☐	☐
Reflected meanings	☐	☐	☐
Used attentive body language	☐	☐	☐
Used facial expressions that encouraged the speaker	☐	☐	☐
Maintained eye contact	☐	☐	☐

Role play: active listening

Form into groups of five. Nominate one person to play the part of Susan and one to play the part of Jacob. The other three act as observers.

Susan

You have walked past the supervisor's office and witnessed your immediate superior presenting your report to the supervisor. You heard the supervisor say to him, 'You have done an excellent job.' You are angry because your superior has presented your work as his own. You go to his office and wait for him.

Jacob

You have taken Susan's report to the supervisor. The supervisor puts it aside and begins to discuss progress on the project you started last week. This project is now ahead of schedule. He says, as you are about to leave, 'You have done an excellent job. I will read Susan's report later.' You go back to your office to find Susan waiting for you.

Those playing the roles of Susan and Jacob are to act out the interaction between them. Susan is angry because she believes Jacob presented the report as his own work. Jacob is to use the cluster of listening skills – attending, encouraging, reflecting and active listening – to respond appropriately to Susan.

Observers

The observers are to complete three tasks.

a. Use the checklist below to assess the listening skills used by Jacob as he responds to Susan's anger.
b. List any barriers created by either Susan or Jacob.
c. Lead a discussion as a group of five and give feedback to the people playing the roles of Susan and Jacob. Suggest alternative responses they might have used.

Active listening checklist

	Yes	No	Unsure
1. Did the person playing the role of Jacob use			
a. body posture and position	☐	☐	☐
b. eye contact	☐	☐	☐
c. facial expression	☐	☐	☐
that conveyed the impression he was listening to Susan?			

2. Did Jacob use
   a. words ☐ ☐ ☐
   b. tone of voice ☐ ☐ ☐
   c. rate of speaking ☐ ☐ ☐
   that conveyed the impression he was listening to Susan?
3. Did Jacob provide enough encouragement for Susan to continue, either by
   a. minimal but positive responses, or ☐ ☐ ☐
   b. supportive body movement? ☐ ☐ ☐
4. Did Jacob use helpful questions? ☐ ☐ ☐
5. Circle the word that best describes Jacob's listening skills.
   Satisfactory Good Very good Excellent

Key terms

active listening
adaptors
affective displays
artefacts
attending listening
barriers
body movement
clarifying
closed question
context
cultural nonverbal
  communication

emblems
empathy
encouraging listening
feedback
illustrators
listening
nonverbal communication
open question
paralanguage
paraphrasing
paraphrasing question

personal nonverbal
  communication
probing question
proximity
reflecting listening
reflective statement
regulators
summarising
total message
universal nonverbal
  communication
vocalisations

Listening is the hardest of the easy tasks

CASE STUDY

by Harvey Mackay

Ask people if they are good listeners, and usually they'll say yes. And they'll say it's easy to be a good listener. Business publications are full of articles about the sorry state of communication in today's workplace. The chief culprit is always 'poor listening skills'. If being a good listener is so easy, what's the problem?

To answer that, we must identify the skills that make up good listening.

Many people think that communication means getting others to do what you want them to do. For them, good listening means, 'I talk, you listen.' Such an approach might work. These folks get their point across by shouting, 'Didn't you hear me?' Or by moralising, 'This is the only fair decision we can make.' Or by pulling rank: 'It's my way or the highway.'

Managers who use such tactics might get the staff to follow instructions. But these managers complain that their best staffers always seem to leave. 'I had no idea there was a problem until I got the resignation letter,' they whine. 'After all, we communicated so well!'

These people have forgotten the basic truth about being a good listener: Listening is a two-way process. Yes, you need to be heard. You also need to hear the other person's ideas, questions and objections. If you talk at people instead of with them, they're not buying in – they're caving in.

Believe it or not, being a good listener is more important in sales than being a good talker. Ben Feldman, the first insurance salesman to pass the sales goal of $25 million in one year, had a simple formula for his success. He was New York Life's leading

43

salesman for more than 20 years, operating out of East Liverpool, Ohio, a city of 20 000. His secret? Work hard. Think big. Listen very well.

Good listener's steer conversations toward other people's interests. This is what a good conversationalist is. And, remember, you can't learn anything when you are doing the talking.

More than a century ago, a young woman who had dined with both William Gladstone and Benjamin Disraeli explained why she preferred Disraeli: 'When I dined with Mr Gladstone I felt as though he was the smartest man in England. But when I dined with Mr Disraeli, I felt as though I was the smartest woman in England.'

Being a good listener also means paying attention to context as well as content. A listener who can paraphase what you've said without changing your meaning is a great listener. A listener who can merely repeat your words is a parrot.

It takes skill and determination to be a good listener, but the effort yields terrific results. Perhaps the biggest reward of being a good listener is that you also become a better talker. You learn the best way to get people to hear what you're saying, and you find that you don't need to force-feed your ideas and opinions to others. You'll know you've attained your goal when you can

utter two sentences in an hour-long conversation and the other speaker thanks you for your input and adds, quite earnestly, 'You always have so much to say!'

> Mackay's moral: Easy listening is a style of music, not communication.

Source: Harvey Mackay, 'Listening is the hardest of the easy tasks', *Minneapolis Star Tribune*, 24 May 2001. Also at <www.listen.org/pages/mackay.html>. Reprinted with permission from nationally syndicated columnist Harvey Mackay, author of *New York Times* bestsellers *Swim With the Sharks Without Being Eaten Alive* and *Pushing the Envelope*.

Questions

1. 'Listening is a two-way process.' What do you see as the key listening skills to use in the two-way process?
2. 'Being a good listener means paying attention to context as well as content.' Briefly discuss this statement.
3. The old saying 'There are none so deaf as those who won't hear' has implications for everyone in the workplace. Detail some of the barriers to effective listening.
4. 'Perhaps the biggest reward of being a good listener is that you also become a good talker.' What is meant by this statement?

Answers to **Apply Skills,** question 4, on pages 36–7: 1T, 2T, 3T, 4F, 5T, 6F, 7T, 8F, 9F,10T, 11F

Interactive skills: interpersonal communication

Chapter 3

In this chapter you will learn how to:

- use appropriate social skills in personal interactions

- interact in a supportive way

- use assertive communication

- construct 'I' statements

- use different types of feedback appropriately.

Evaluate your interpersonal communication skills by completing the self-check in the chapter.

Those who have effective workplace relationships and who seem successful in inter-personal communication appear to relate easily and confidently to those around them. They have good interactive skills – listening, speaking and nonverbal communica-tion – and can use assertion without alienating others. Overall, their perception of messages is accurate and their responsiveness allows others to use their own inter-personal skills to express their expectations and values. They develop good personal, social and work relationships and create a positive communication climate.

Creating a communication climate

Communication climate: the tone of a relationship, expressed by people's verbal and nonverbal messages.

The **communication climate** is created by the way people feel about each other. It is positive when people feel that they are valued, and when they interact confidently and courteously. Relationships can be built on openness, honesty and trust when people feel goodwill towards one another and are willing to speak with others, listen carefully, ask questions and offer feedback. Information and ideas are conveyed accurately this way.

A negative communication climate is created when someone's contribution is not appreciated. Such a climate makes it difficult for people to get and give information and to take action. If it is hard to communicate, people feel uncomfortable and unwilling to interact. They are less willing to ask questions, or offer ideas and feedback, and are more inclined to wait and see what happens. Communication is less accurate and inter-personal relationships are less effective in a negative communication climate.

Empathy

Empathy is the ability to understand and feel as the other person feels.

Those who respond appropriately and show **empathy** reassure others that their message has made contact. Empathetic people have the skill to:

■ attend to what is said
■ retain objectivity
■ recognise nonverbal cues about the feelings of others
■ understand the content of the message
■ understand others' feelings
■ communicate their understanding to others.

Empathy enhances the communication climate. The tone of the communication is pos-itive and the communication concentrates on the needs and interests of the people involved.

Win–win approach

The **win–win approach** concentrates on the needs and interests of the people commu-nicating. Rather than winning positions or gaining victories over the other person, the win–win approach lets you gather or give information in a way that creates a positive communication climate and transfers information accurately. The communication is more likely to get things done and to create and maintain goodwill because each person understands the needs and interests of the other. Figure 3.1 shows each person feeling positive about the message. The win–win approach is discussed more fully in Chapter 12, Negotiation Skills, and Chapter 13, Conflict Management.

Figure 3.1 Results of win–win approach

Self-disclosure

At work, people may learn a lot or very little about their colleagues. It depends on how much people are willing to disclose about themselves. **Self-disclosure** involves showing how you feel about a situation and revealing something about the past that affects your reaction; in this way, you allow others to know more about you. This openness comes from an acceptance and appreciation of yourself. Others come to understand you by observing how you react.

Self-disclosure does not mean you have to reveal intimate details about your past. It just means sharing ideas and feelings and giving feedback to others on how their behaviour is affecting you. The amount of self-disclosure is affected by the communication climate. In a positive climate people disclose more, in a negative climate they disclose less.

Both self-disclosure and feedback increase understanding and open communication. This allows you to establish more satisfying relationships at work and in your social and family life.

Self-disclosure involves your reaction to a situation.

Empathy and self-disclosure

1. Think of someone with whom you feel empathy. What helps you to feel it?
2. Think of someone with whom it is difficult to feel empathy. What makes this difficult?
3. Think of a person whom you consider has good interpersonal skills. How does this person show empathy for another? (Describe behaviour such as facial expressions, listening and nonverbal elements.)
4. List three of your strongest communi-

cation skills. How do these skills help you to communicate?
5. Think of your most recent pleasant interaction.
   a. Describe your communication skills in the interaction (facial expressions, type of listening and nonverbal elements).
   b. Describe the other person's communication skills.
   c. Briefly describe the amount of self-disclosure in the interaction.

APPLY SKILLS

How good is your interpersonal communication?

Technique	Very successful	Successful	Unsuccessful
I am able to:			
Express openness	☐	☐	☐
Show empathy	☐	☐	☐
Use supportiveness	☐	☐	☐
Be positive	☐	☐	☐
Demonstrate equality	☐	☐	☐
Use 'I' messages	☐	☐	☐
Listen	☐	☐	☐
Provide appropriate feedback	☐	☐	☐
Use appropriate self-disclosure	☐	☐	☐
Communicate assertively	☐	☐	☐

Effective interpersonal communication

Successful interaction requires confidence.

Interpersonal communication takes place in the workplace whenever two or more people interact with each other or in small groups. When the actions taken in response to your communication match your intentions, your interpersonal communication is effective: the message is received accurately, as you intend it to be received.

Workplace relationships built on good communication work well. Those built on poor communication do not work so well.

Some of the particular communication strategies that manage the interaction and achieve a balance that satisfies both parties are assertion, 'I' statements and feedback.

Assertive strategies

Assertive behaviour acknowledges your rights as an individual and the rights of other people. This is the ideal attitude to have at work and in our everyday lives. Assertive people tend to demonstrate open, expressive and relaxed behaviour. They are able to build honest, fulfilling relationships with others.

Assertiveness

An assertive person can negotiate and collaborate without feeling uncomfortable.

Assertive people acknowledge their rights and the rights of others.

Two assertive people can express different points of view. The assertive person wants to be heard and acknowledged. This does not necessarily mean winning. It means being accepted and treated as an equal – respecting the rights of others and being respected in turn. Two assertive people can accept that each has a different opinion or perspective.

Assertive leaders are able to manage others without feeling the need to manipulate or to be aggressive, because they recognise the rights of other workers. The assertive follower recognises the right of the manager or leader to make reasonable requests and to expect the job to be done. Such people feel comfortable with themselves and with others in the organisation. They get on with the job in a manner that satisfies their own needs and the needs of the organisation.

When the occasion demands, assertive people can disagree, stand up for their rights and present alternative points of view without being intimidated or putting anyone else down. Assertive people realise what type of behaviour is suited to a particular situation and recognise when their own behaviour is assertive, aggressive or non-assertive.

Aggressiveness

An aggressive person may have to win at all costs. This means dominating and, on occasion, humiliating others, even to the point of ignoring a suggestion that provides the best solution simply because it is someone else's solution. The rights of others to participate, enjoy a sense of satisfaction and receive acknowledgment for their work are ignored. An aggressive person is often in conflict with others.

An aggressive person may need to win.

Submissiveness

Submissive people are unable to assert or promote a point of view. They find it difficult to lead others because their style of relating means submitting to another's point of view, even to the extent of ignoring their own rights. When problems or unpleasant situations arise, a submissive person tends to avoid them, leaving them to someone else.

Submissive people are unable to promote a point of view.

The 'I' message

A useful technique to develop assertion and show openness with others is to use an **'I' message**. This is a way of sharing emotions and letting others know both how you perceive their behaviour and how it affects you. One of the best ways to begin assertive statements is to say, 'I feel . . . when . . .'. For example: 'I feel annoyed when I have not been notified that you will be late.'

We can all express our needs and wants with an 'I' message that shows our personal involvement and our willingness to share our feelings.

'I' messages can express our feelings about behaviour that is acceptable and pleasing, or unacceptable. Messages dealing with behaviour that is unacceptable to you are more difficult to express, so this section focuses on their construction.

An 'I' message can have two, three or four parts. The formulae for two-, three- and four-part 'I' messages are shown in Figure 3.2.

An 'I' message can have two, three or four parts.

In a two-part 'I' message, you:

1. 'own' the feeling
2. describe in concrete terms the behaviour that is causing the feeling.

Figure 3.2 Some formulae for 'I' statements

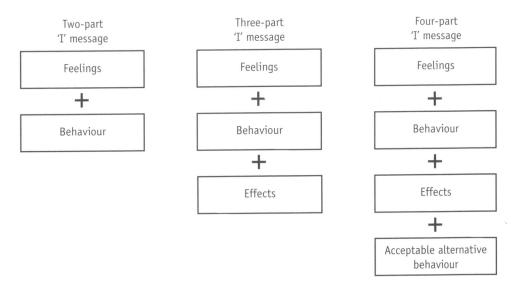

The formula in a two-part 'I' message is: feelings + behaviour. Following this formula, a two-part assertive message becomes: 'I feel angry when the dirty clothes are left in the bathroom'. In the second part, take care simply to describe the other person's behaviour rather than interpret, judge or evaluate it.

In a three-part 'I' message, you:

1. 'own' the feeling
2. describe precisely the behaviour that is causing the feeling
3. state what effects the behaviour has on you.

The formula in a three-part 'I' message is: feelings + behaviour + effects (the statements may occur in a different order). Following this formula, a three-part assertive statement becomes: 'I feel . . . when . . . because . . .'. For example, the message may be: 'I feel annoyed when I have not been notified that you will be late because I am unable to reschedule my time'.

In a four-part 'I' message, you:

1. 'own' the feeling
2. describe exactly what behaviour is causing the feeling
3. state the effect of the behaviour on you
4. offer an alternative, acceptable behaviour.

The formula in a four-part 'I' message is: feelings + behaviour + effects + acceptable alternative behaviour. Your assertive message would then say 'I feel . . . when . . . because . . . I would like . . .'. For example: 'I feel annoyed when I have not been notified that you will be late because I am unable to reschedule my time. I would like to be contacted if there is a reason to reschedule'.

You can use the fourth part of the message to suggest the alternative acceptable behaviour straightaway, or negotiate a behaviour that is acceptable to both people by using the problem-solving agenda described in Chapter 5.

Successful 'I' statements communicate how you feel in a non-threatening way that is acceptable to the other person. They produce a positive outcome. Though assertive, they do not blame or even interpret the other person's behaviour. On the other hand, aggressive statements often start with blame: 'You make me . . .'.

Once you become skilled at 'I' messages, you will frame them in your own words and may omit the words 'feel', 'when' and 'because'.

Communicating with others

SKILLS
APPLY

1. a. Stand up and move around the room. As you move around, greet everyone in the room nonverbally, with a smile, a handshake or any other nonverbal communication you like.

    b. Sit down with a person you do not know. Spend three minutes talking to each other about who you are and what you would like to gain from this course.

    c. Move to another person you do not know and spend three minutes repeating part (b) of this activity.

    d. Work with the same person for another three minutes, discussing how you see yourselves as similar to and different from each other.

2. Work by yourself to list the things you enjoyed when you were introducing yourself to others in the tasks above, and what you disliked. What, in your opinion, were your particular strengths and weaknesses in communicating with others? List these too.

3. Complete Self-check 3.1 to self-evaluate your interpersonal communication.

4. To explore eye contact, discuss in a small group any topic of interest for ten minutes. Throughout the discussion be aware of the eye contact you do or do not make. Think about when you:
   ■ began eye contact

   ■ stopped eye contact
   ■ avoided eye contact.

   Work in pairs to list the ways of using eye contact. Close by discussing as a large group what you liked most and what you liked least about the activity.

Feedback

Effective communication is based on giving and receiving **feedback**, the receiver's response to a sender's message. The message you send in words is sometimes received incorrectly or does not convey exactly what you meant to say. Feedback lets the sender understand how the message is received and helps the receiver confirm whether their perception of the message is correct or incorrect. In the communication process, feedback can be a continuing or completing link.

Effective feedback creates trust and an open relationship between sender and receiver. It is one of the main ways to assess how accurately your message has been received, how we affect others, and how others perceive us.

In an organisation, appropriate, constructive feedback creates a positive communication climate that, in turn, creates an open and encouraging organisational climate. In contrast, a rigid or competitive environment can make most people hesitant about communicating or offering ideas.

Several different types of feedback are used in organisations and businesses. They include negative feedback, positive feedback from leaders or managers, positive feedback from co-workers, and self-evaluation. People may evaluate their own work and their interactions with other people. Techniques for four different types of feedback are discussed below.

Immediate and specific feedback

Be specific about others' behaviour rather than general – for example, 'This file could do with a tidy up' is a more useful kind of feedback than 'Your files are always untidy'. Describe what needs to be done, and avoid judging or threatening the other person.

Give feedback only when the person is ready to accept it. Someone who is upset or defensive is less likely to accept suggestions or new material. Refer only to behaviour that the receiver is capable of changing, and include only what the receiver can handle at a particular time.

Immediate and specific feedback provides useful information.

It is destructive to bring up past behaviour and grievances. Deal with the current situation – for example, say 'We agreed to take turns answering the telephone. It's your turn' instead of 'You always expect me to answer the telephone'.

When you give immediate and specific feedback, respect the other person's right to respond. Take the time to listen. Acknowledge their response. In some cases their response and feedback may indicate that you need to change your behaviour.

Negative and positive feedback

Negative feedback is not necessarily detrimental to the receiver; the result depends on how it is provided. Positive feedback from superiors and peers encourages the repetition of that behaviour and acknowledges a worker's role in and contribution to the organisation. Chapter 4, Effective Workplace Communication, describes questioning skills you can apply to feedback.

Informative feedback

This type of feedback comes from listening to the words of a message and the feelings it conveys. Informative feedback is based on understanding and uses paraphrasing to help both the sender's and receiver's understanding. Effective listening focuses on the content of a message and identifies the speaker's purpose and main ideas. Good listeners rephrase or summarise the message. As you respond, consider why the speaker has expressed an idea. Try to withhold judgment. Try to work out what their unexpressed feelings are. Share your perceptions about the message instead of giving advice.

Perceptions are shared.

Appropriate and accurate feedback helps communication. Inappropriate and inaccurate feedback hinders it. The major barriers to good interpersonal communication and relationships are caused by approving or disapproving another person's statements, feelings or attitudes. In contrast, when you consider these from the other person's point of view, you stop making judgments and make an understanding connection. By acknowledging and expressing your own feelings as you give and receive feedback, you build a relationship based on trust and openness.

As well as achieving effective work relationships, feedback lets people know what needs to be done in the workplace. Tasks become easier to understand and complete accurately and efficiently.

Undercurrent message

The **undercurrent message** is something you sense that the sender wants to conceal or is unable to convey. If you can only sense it without understanding it, the undercurrent gets in the way of open and direct communication. By using feedback skilfully you come closer to understanding others' verbal, nonverbal and undercurrent messages. In addition, you gain a closer understanding of your own communication methods and how to improve them.

Interpersonal communication

APPLY SKILLS

1. Work in pairs.
   a. Stand back to back and talk to one another for two minutes about a topic of your choice. Do not turn towards one another until the two minutes are up.
   b. As a large group, discuss how it felt to speak in this way.
   c. Brainstorm to create a list of nonverbal behaviours that help you communicate.
2. Work in pairs.
   a. Each person (A and B) prepares two different distinctive shapes without letting the other person see them.
   b. Person A describes one of their shapes to B for one minute, while B sits with their back turned. As A describes the shape, B draws it without asking any questions, and without showing it to A until the minute is over.
   c. Change roles, following the procedure in step (b).
   d. Compare the shape described by each person with the shape drawn by the other person.
   e. Take turns to describe and draw the last two shapes. (Take one minute for each.) This time the listener can ask clarifying questions.
   f. Compare the shapes. Were the last shapes a better match than the first? Explain your answer.
3. Work in groups of three.
   a. Role-play the following situation: In front of another staff member, the supervisor of a computer store (Person A) requests an explanation why yesterday's sales dockets were not filed. The sales assistant (Person B) explains that he had left the last 15 minutes in the afternoon to do this job but a customer had come in

who was having difficulties with his computer software. Dealing with the customer had taken all the available time. The supervisor admonishes the sales assistant, stating that sales dockets are important and should take priority.

b. Change roles. In the second role play, Person A, after hearing the reason, praises the sales assistant for attending to the customer's needs, stating that customer service should always be the first priority. Person A then requests that the sales dockets be filed as soon as Person B has time this morning.

c. Identify how you felt as Person B in the two situations.

d. How could the supervisor have improved the way they handled this situation?

4. Identify the following examples of feedback as specific, negative or positive, and as peer or supervisor feedback.

a. Your supervisor tells you that you are doing a good job.

b. You have a regular staff appraisal.

c. Co-workers tease you about not working hard enough.

d. Co-workers tease you about working too hard.

e. The supervisor criticises your performance.

f. It is noted that you completed several jobs.

g. You find a new way of completing a task.

5. You are required to attend a weekly planning meeting scheduled to run from 9.15 am to 10.15 am. Jeremy, your colleague and the chairperson, invariably starts the meeting late and allows it to run over time. Develop an appropriate three-part 'I' message that will indicate your feelings about this behaviour and its effect on you.

6. Think about any situation where you have asserted yourself. Discuss with your group what you think was your greatest strength and weakness in that situation. Discuss how you could improve your ability to assert yourself.

Visit the Companion Website at **www.prenhall.com/dwyer_au**. Choose the Good Practice/Bad Practice activity in Chapter 3 to self-assess and practise using your interpersonal communication skills.

WISE
WEB

Chapter summary

Use appropriate social skills in personal interactions. Interpersonal skills enable you to communicate and to build personal, social and work relationships. These skills enable communicators to acknowledge and express their thoughts and feelings in words and actions that form a connection with the other person. At work, those who have effective workplace relationships and succeed in interpersonal communication relate easily and positively to those around them by using good interactive skills – by listening, speaking and using nonverbal communication well.

Interact in a supportive way. Supportive communication boosts confidence and self-esteem. People tend to perform better in their jobs when they are made to feel that they make a worthwhile contribution to the workplace interaction. The communication climate is positive.

Use assertive communication. Assertive people take responsibility for their actions and respect the rights of others. Their interpersonal skills give them direct contact with others. Overall, their perception of messages is accurate and their approach to people is positive and confident.

Construct 'I' statements. These statements are used to disclose how you feel about a situation and to show openness with others. They let you ask for what you want. An 'I' statement follows a two-, three- or four-part formula.

Use different types of feedback appropriately. Feedback is the continuing or completing link in the communication process. Feedback may be informative, specific, negative or positive. Appropriate and accurate feedback helps communication. Inappropriate and inaccurate feedback hinders it.

REVIEW QUESTIONS

1. Define the terms 'communication climate' and 'empathy'.
2. How does empathy affect the communication climate?
3. List the five skills demonstrated by an empathetic person.
4. Briefly explain the win–win approach.
5. Define the term 'self-disclosure'.
6. List the five qualities of a person who is good at interpersonal communication.
7. List the five specific interpersonal skills demonstrated by a person who is good at interpersonal relationships.
8. a. What are the main differences between assertive, aggressive and submissive behaviour? Describe two ways in which a person can be aggressive to another. What would be your typical response to this type of behaviour?
   b. If assertive behaviour is preferable to aggression or submission, define the basis of assertiveness.
   c. When is an assertive message effective?
9. What is the formula for a three-part 'I' message? What is the fourth part that can be added to make a four-part 'I' message?

Interpersonal skills

BUILD SKILLS

The object of this activity is to increase your capacity to use interpersonal tools as you interrelate with others.
1. Work on your own to list the things that increase and those that decrease the aspects of self listed in Table 3.1.

Think about who you are and what you value as you complete the table.
2. Work individually to indicate on a scale of 1 to 4 in Table 3.2 the importance of the items listed to your personal life.

Table 3.1 Increasing or decreasing self-esteem

	Things that increase	Things that decrease
Self-esteem	Being cared for	Being ignored
	Doing a job well	Handing an assignment in late
Self-awareness		
Self-confidence		
Self-image		

Table 3.2 My rating scale

	1 Little importance	2 Some importance	3 Important	4 Very important
Family				
Work				
Social life				
Social standing				
Relationships				

3. Work in small groups to:
   a. list the situations you have observed where someone with high self-esteem has created a positive communication climate
   b. decide why high self-esteem helps to create a positive communication climate
   c. discuss how the win–win approach helps to create a positive communication climate.
4. When someone describes something terrible that has happened, how often have you heard the reply 'Yes, I know'? If you were listening with a keen ear you would note that the 'Yes, I know' reply implies that they knew what had happened. In fact, the opposite is often the case. 'Yes, I know' is not an empathic response.

In small groups discuss the statements in Table 3.3 and tick the panel containing what you think is the most empathic response.

Table 3.3 Respond with empathy

Statement	Responses	Tick the empathic response
1. I can't believe it. I just drove my car into the back of another car.	What did the other person say?	
	I had that happen to me.	
	You feel upset.	
2. The loan company refused me a loan.	You feel at a loss as to what you can do now.	
	What made them do that?	
	I wouldn't go near them again if I were you.	
3. I just lost my job. What am I going to do?	Don't worry, there are lots of others.	
	You must be feeling devastated.	
	I was made redundant three years ago but it all worked out for the best.	

5. In small groups, discuss whether it is easy or difficult to talk about feelings, and focus on the following questions: What feelings are easy to express? Which ones are difficult to express? What feelings expressed by someone else are the hardest to deal with?
   a. Describe a context in which it is difficult to express feelings.
   b. Create a group list of the six best feelings from last weekend.
6. Work in pairs. Sit opposite one another. Each person is to describe themselves in the third person to their partner – for example: 'George Black is of average height and slim build. He has thick brown hair and looks fit. Today he is wearing . . .'. Each person describes themselves for three minutes and then the roles are reversed. Then discuss:
   a. what it felt like to describe yourself
   b. what you liked least about the activity
   c. what you liked most about the activity.

Key terms

communication climate	'I' message	self-disclosure
empathy	interpersonal	undercurrent message
feedback	communication	win–win approach

CASE STUDY

Think tank

To borrow a metaphor from modern psychology, an institution is like a tune; it is not constituted by individual sounds but by the relations between them.

Peter Drucker

Michelle Neasey
Executive officer, Camp Clayton, north-west coast of Tasmania

The best melodies often contain compelling phrases because the combination of notes seems to convey a significant message. Alone, the notes mean nothing; but their combination can evoke strong emotion.

When individuals in an organisation realise how their interaction and combination can produce varying results, the same depth of influence can shape their culture. Either all the notes can play at once, as loud and often as they like, or they can learn the sensitivity to know when and how to play with respect to others. Any organisation, regardless of its product or service, is a reflection of its internal relationships.

Although we all start out dependent, aspiring to become independent, the real challenge is to move on to interdependence, in which the spirit of sharing and the dynamics of a high-trust environment enable a team to thrive. Effective delegation, empowerment, mentoring and coaching are all tools to this end.

Often overlooked, interdependence comes from the basic principles of trust, respect, commitment and encouragement.

Clare Florence
Asian practice development director, Minter Ellison, Sydney

One of Peter Drucker's greatest strengths as management thinker is that while developing ground-breaking theories that pretty much define modern management, he has never lost sight of the fact that people make up an organisation. It is interpersonal relationships and team effort that make or break the largest and most powerful corporation. Any theory that loses sight of that simple fact is unlikely to be proved in the real world.

As businesses become globalised and the trend to closer international ties and interdependence grows, Drucker's 'tune' is fast becoming an entire, complex orchestral work, with many movements, in which not only the relationship between individual sounds defines the whole, but the relationship between different tunes, each with its own sounds, determines whether the result is a discordant mess or a thing of beauty.

Just as the work of a great conductor makes an orchestra's performance seem effortless to the point at which the listener wonders whether the piece could have been performed without someone in charge, so good management is an invisible conduit to harmony.

Matthew Foran
Government relations manager, AWB Ltd, Melbourne

A successful tune is one in which the whole is greater than the sum of the parts. No longer is it simply a collection of related sounds but a seamless integration from the development through to the execution. There is no one 'success' formula to guarantee a hit. The expectations of the audience, the instruments available and the skill and dedication of the musicians will all dictate the final outcome.

Building on Peter Drucker's analogy, it is the role of the manager, as the conductor of a company, to understand these variables and bring together the various elements to extract the greatest performance from the organisation and its resource base. Although the sum of the parts is critical, we should not underestimate the importance of the individual sounds. Having the right people with the right skills gives the organisation the best possible foundation on which to perform.

Finally, the organisation needs a clear vision and understanding of what has to be achieved. There is little point in creating Bach's Concerto No. 2 in F major if the market wants *No Sleep Till Brooklyn* by the Beastie Boys.

Source: Peter Drucker, Michelle Neasey, Clare Florence & Matthew Foran, 'Think Tank', *Management Today*, January–February 2002, p. 13. Reprinted by permission of the authors.

Questions

1. Michelle Neasey says, 'Any organisation, regardless of its product or service, is a reflection of its internal relationships.' Briefly describe the interpersonal skills that help you establish quality relationships.
2. Clare Florence says, 'Good management is an invisible conduit to harmony.' Discuss some communication strategies that managers can use to build trust, respect and harmony in an organisation.
3. Matthew Foran, continuing with the musical analogy of a successful tune, says, 'No longer is it simply a collection of related sounds but a seamless integration from the development to the execution.'
   a. Briefly describe the audience for the tune in a typical workplace.
   b. What are the instruments available to a manager to '. . . bring together the various elements to extract the greatest performance from the organisation and its resource base'?

Communicating in the workplace

II

Effective workplace communication

Chapter 4

In this chapter you will learn how to:

- give full, accurate and clear instructions

- prepare different types of questions

- follow a set of instructions

- develop a short oral report.

Evaluate your communication skills by completing the self-check in the chapter.

Every workplace includes a range of communication activities such as gathering, recording and conveying simple routine information; giving and following simple and routine instructions; and participating in small informal work groups. In each of these activities it is important to communicate well, by receiving and sending accurate messages. People who communicate well are likely to work cooperatively and more efficiently.

People who use spoken language well are in the best position to give and receive instructions about what happens in their workplace. They are able to inform, explain, make requests and consult in a way that improves understanding and encourages others. This chapter focuses on giving and receiving spoken instructions and making oral reports.

Giving instructions

Direct instructions are to the point and indicate who, what, when, where and how a task should be completed.

Successful instructions lead to the intended outcome.

Clear **workplace instructions** explain the objectives, provide background information and describe the intended outcome. Then it is up to the person receiving the instructions to decide how, when and where to reach this outcome.

Give clear instructions

When instructions are unclear, people cannot accomplish their workplace activities to the standard required. To do the job well, people need to understand how to do it and the reasons for doing it.

When giving instructions at work, follow these simple guidelines:

1. Determine what has to be accomplished – the intended outcome.
2. Give the reasons for doing the job.
3. Follow the steps of the task in the order given.
4. Use verbs (action words) rather than abstract words, and start with a verb.
5. Have the other person paraphrase the instructions back to you.
6. Use words appropriate to the receiver's level of understanding.
7. Use familiar and simple words.
8. Indicate clearly each step of the task, in sequence.
9. Demonstrate the skills required by the task if it involves machinery or equipment.
10. Encourage questions.
11. Ensure that your timing is appropriate.
12. Follow up the person's progress with the task.
13. Offer timely and specific feedback.

A systematic approach is helpful.

The instructor must explain precisely each step of the task, and the receiver must fully understand and follow the instructions, so a systematic approach to instructions is necessary. It follows the sequence shown in Figure 4.1.

A structured approach

Group your ideas into a logical structure that is easy to follow.

Once you have determined what needs to be accomplished, group the instructions into introduction, body and conclusion. The introduction gives the purpose of the job. Emphasise any dangers and highlight any safety measures that must be taken.

In the body of the instructions, outline the whole task and describe each step of the procedure slowly and clearly. Whenever it is possible for the other person to perform the step immediately, demonstrate how to do it first and then let them practise and ask

Figure 4.1 A systematic approach to workplace instructions

1	Explanation by the instructor.
2	Demonstrated by the instructor.
3	Review by the instructor.
4	Feedback: the receiver paraphrases the instructions.
5	Observe the receiver use the instructions in the workplace.
6	Feedback by instructor and receiver in the form of questions and answers.

questions. Check understanding by asking questions and observing how they complete the task. Lead the other person through each step of the process. Never assume that someone knows what workplace standard must be achieved: take time to explain it. Use videos, pictures and real objects to help people learn. They add meaning to verbal instructions.

In the conclusion, repeat the main points and state the standards again, particularly when safety is an issue. As you give feedback, be constructive. Correct any mistakes and let the other person know what they do well.

As you give the instructions, speak clearly and project your voice so that you are easily heard and understood. Use simple words.

Follow a set of instructions

1. How do you usually get your instructions for the tasks you have to do?
2. a. Think about an occasion when you received instructions that were easy to understand. How did the instructor make them clear to you?
   b. Think about an occasion when you received instructions that were hard to understand. What did the instructor do that made them so difficult?
3. Name some of the causes of unclear instructions on Figure 4.2.

APPLY SKILLS

Follow a sequence

Prepare the instructions in **sequence**, in one of the following three ways:

1. Move from the simple to the complex.
2. Move from the familiar to the unfamiliar.
3. Follow the required order of tasks.

Figure 4.2 Unclear instructions: some causes

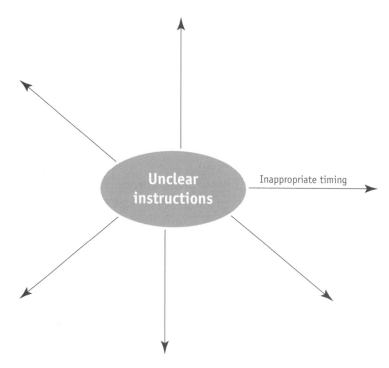

Good timing

Choose an
appropriate time.

When you give instructions, ensure that the timing is right and the communication climate is positive so that the people receiving the instructions have enough time to:

- listen and understand fully
- say what they think and feel
- ask questions
- show that they are willing and able to follow the instructions.

Instructions given in a thoughtful, appropriate and controlled manner at the appropriate time are more easily understood, and people are more likely to do the job well.

Questioning skills for giving instructions

Question to
confirm
understanding.

As you give instructions, you need to know how thoroughly they are being understood. Simple **routine instructions** usually only require questions to confirm that the person can:

- remember the facts
- rephrase the instructions in their own words
- apply the instructions to a new situation.

By asking these questions, you engage the other person in a two-way communication process. You are also offering them feedback.

Use a variety of methods

Workplace instructions that use a variety of communication methods are easier to remember. Some of the different methods are shown in Figure 4.3.

Sometimes you can simply give verbal instructions and demonstrate the task. On other occasions your spoken directions may need support from written instructions and graphics. Once people understand what to do, you want them to be able to carry out and complete the task. Written instructions and graphics are a handy reference.

Advantages of visual materials

The **visuals** (sometimes called 'graphics') used to support instructions should convey their message without words. Symbols do this very efficiently, and Figure 4.4 shows four symbols that mean the same thing anywhere in the world, regardless of what language is spoken.

Visuals create interest and add clarity to instructions. They also reinforce the main points and show the total picture. The visuals accompanying instructions must show an accurate picture of what has to be done. Their purpose is to explain, simplify and/or emphasise the main relationships.

Visual materials should be simple, clear and easy to see.

Receiving and following instructions

When you receive instructions in the workplace, be willing to ask questions and to share ideas and information. You want to be able to follow directions successfully because you are working with others towards a common goal. Strategies to help you follow instructions more easily are:

Listen well to avoid barriers and share ideas.

■ Listen carefully.
■ Concentrate on the instructions, and avoid thinking about anything else.

Figure 4.3 A range of communication methods

Figure 4.4 Four international symbols

■ Avoid jumping to conclusions.
■ Ask questions about what standards must be reached.
■ Paraphrase to check your understanding.
■ Double check any safety issues.
■ Ask for help if you cannot follow the instructions.
■ Ask general questions.

Prepare a set of instructions

SKILLS
APPLY

1. Work in small groups. Brainstorm to list different sorts of workplace instructions.
2. Prepare a set of instructions for one of the following tasks.
   a. install a door frame
   b. prepare a Brandy Alexander cocktail
   c. format a computer disk
   d. paint a wooden planter box
   e. change the tyre on a car
   f. put new strings on a guitar
   g. assemble a vacuum cleaner
   h. park a car on a steep slope
   i. any other familiar task.
   As you prepare the instructions, use an introduction, body and conclusion and check that each required step is described in clear, concise and specific terms.
3. What are the advantages of clear instructions?
4. What are the disadvantages of unclear instructions in the workplace?

Questioning skills

When receiving instructions, your questions should be:

■ brief and clear
■ focused on the work task
■ general, when you want an overview
■ specific, when you want to understand particular facts or ideas
■ rephrased, when the instructor does not understand your question
■ open, when you want more information and an idea of the instructor's understanding
■ closed, when you want a specific answer.

Questions like these help you think about and evaluate all the facts and tasks involved. As instructions are given and received, issues should be dealt with assertively and cooperatively. People who listen carefully and ask questions are able to achieve the intended outcomes.

Presenting oral reports

An **oral report** should always use the appropriate **workplace language** (the language used on the job). The sender uses oral communication skills to explain exactly what has happened and what the receiver has to do. Often a workplace hazard is reported orally to a team leader before a written report is prepared.

Certain factors that affect the impression we give when we report problems orally are:

■ sentence structure
■ order of information presented
■ knowledge of special terms
■ appropriate language
■ status of the person or people being addressed
■ cultural factors.

The report's purpose should be identified first and supported with accurate and objective information. Simple, direct language helps the receiver understand it.

Use 'first', 'second', 'third' and so on to indicate each stage of the report. Keep your sentences simple with one subject and one action rather than several complex ideas. This way the listener can follow your ideas easily.

Explain what has happened and what the receiver has to do.

An oral report should have a clear, logical structure and sequence.

Giving instructions

Did the instructor:	Yes	No	Unsure
1. Prepare people by putting them at ease?	☐	☐	☐
2. Use the introduction to give reasons for doing the task?	☐	☐	☐
3. Sequence the information in the body of the instructions appropriately?	☐	☐	☐
4. Begin each step with a verb (action word)?	☐	☐	☐
5. Give a clear overall picture of what was to be done?	☐	☐	☐
6. Use clear, simple language and explain any technical terms?	☐	☐	☐
7. Encourage questions to check that each step was understood?	☐	☐	☐
8. Demonstrate step by step?	☐	☐	☐
9. Give the instructions in different forms, such as verbal, written, diagram?	☐	☐	☐
10. Use the conclusion to repeat the main points and intended outcome?	☐	☐	☐

SELF CHECK 4.1

Plan your oral presentation by deciding what its purpose is, and sorting out your information. Discard anything irrelevant. Organise important material into the 'what, where, when, who and why' sections to give it a logical structure.

An oral report presents a subject by describing what, where, when, who and why it happened, as shown in Figure 4.5. Oral instructions that follow the order of tasks performed on the job make it easier for the listener to follow. One of the disadvantages of oral reports is their informality. An oral report can become distorted as the information is passed on. It is also easier to ignore than a written report.

Figure 4.5 Oral report sequence

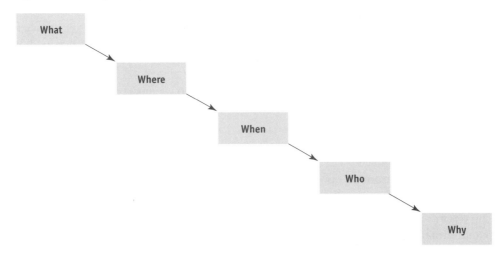

Oral reports

1. 'Oral communication is part of the job and cannot be separated from it.' Work in small groups to:
   a. Discuss this statement.
   b. List as many oral communication tasks performed at work as you can think of.
   c. Choose one job and decide approximately what proportion of work hours would be spent on oral communication.

2. a. Think about an oral report that you found difficult to understand. What caused the difficulty?
   b. What did you do to overcome the difficulty?

Visit the Companion Website at **www.prenhall.com/dwyer_au**. Choose the Internet Exercise activity in Chapter 4 to compare and contrast a set of instructions on the Web with a set of instructions in a trade journal.

Chapter summary

Give full, accurate and clear instructions. Instructions should develop ideas, knowledge and skills step by step. Determine what the intended outcome requires. Decide how to convey the details of who, what, when, where and how a task will be done. Plan the instructions first, and take a structured approach by using an introduction, body and conclusion. The language used for instructions should be appropriate for the tasks required. Present your instructions in a sequence (a) that moves from the simple to the complex; or (b) that moves from the familiar to the unfamiliar; or (c) that follows the order required by the job.

Prepare different types of questions. When you give instructions, ask questions to assess your receivers' understanding and encourage feedback. These questions should encourage them to remember facts, restate the information in their own words and apply the information to a new situation. When you are receiving instructions, ask questions to clarify your understanding. The questions should be brief, direct and relevant to the work task. Ask general questions when you want an overview, and specific questions when you want a particular idea or fact.

Follow a set of instructions. Listen carefully; ask questions to clarify any points that are unclear. By using your communication skills appropriately you will find out what you need to do and you will be able to work assertively and cooperatively with others as you follow the instructions.

Develop a short oral report. Oral reports describe what, where, when, who and why something happened. If you are clear about your objective, aware of your receiver's needs and able to use appropriate workplace language, your message will be easy to understand and likely to achieve the intended result.

REVIEW QUESTIONS

1. List three ways in which you can sequence the content of a set of instructions.
2. What is the purpose of organising the introduction, body and conclusion for a set of instructions?
3. Why should you choose an appropriate time to give instructions?
4. a. List three types of questions you can use as you give instructions.
   b. Why do you ask questions as you give instructions?
5. a. What sort of questions should you ask as you receive instructions?
   b. A good instructor asks for and gives feedback. Why?
6. Why should visual materials be used with instructions?
7. List the sequence used by the systematic approach to workplace instructions.
8. List three factors to consider as you make an oral report.

Receiving instructions

BUILD SKILLS

1. Work as a large group. The purpose of this activity is to listen to a set of instructions and respond appropriately. One person reads the instructions to the rest of the group.

Instructions

- Everyone seats themselves in a circle facing inwards.
- Everyone claps their hands once and then claps their hands on their knees.
- Then everyone points to the centre of the circle with their index finger.
- The instructor then says a word such as 'rain'.
- The person on the instructor's left responds with a word associated with the word 'rain' (e.g. 'wet' or a rhyming word such as 'plain') while everyone continues to clap their hands together, clap their knees, then point their index finger to the centre of the circle.
- Then the next person to the left says a word associated with the word 'wet' or 'plain', or a word rhyming with 'wet' or 'plain'. Maintain the momentum until you have been round the circle at least twice.
- Anyone who runs out of ideas may accept suggestions from others in the circle. It is a lot of fun and works better if everyone tries to maintain the flow.

Once the activity is complete, discuss the ease or difficulty of following the instructions.

a. Did you ask enough questions to clarify what you had to do before you began the task?
b. Would it be helpful if the activity was demonstrated first, then followed by a practice session?

c. What happened to the level of perform-ance as you moved through the activity?

d. How can you relate taking part in this activity to giving and receiving instruc-tions at work?

2. a. When you give instructions it is important to give feedback. Why?

b. What are the three links that feed-back makes in the communication process?

c. What are three features of good feedback?

d. Explain briefly why it is important to check your interpretation of your receivers' feedback.

3. Prepare two questions. The first question should encourage those receiving your instructions to remember the facts. The second question should ask them to restate the information in their own words.

4. Work in small groups. Each person in turn uses the instructions prepared in question 1 to tell the others how to complete the task. As you give the instructions, use the two questions pre-pared in question 3 (and any others you may need) to check the receivers' under-standing. Those receiving the instructions are to ask questions to clarify any points that are unclear.

Use Self-check 4.1 to evaluate the effectiveness of your instructions.

Key terms

direct instructions
oral report
routine instructions

sequence
visuals
workplace instructions

workplace language

STUDY
CASE

Developing the human resource

by Jack Collis

Communicating effectively is essential if we want to understand and be understood, as explained in the February issue of *Australian Business News*. Asking the right question at the right time as well as answering ques-tions concisely and effectively are the hallmarks of a first-class communicator.

So when asking questions the following techniques are very useful:

■ Ask the question to all of the group;
■ Allow time to think about the answer;
■ Nominate one participant to answer the question;
■ Listen to the answer. It is important to listen – that person is communicating with you. The more attention you give the answer, the more positive that person will feel about you;
■ Evaluate the answer. If it is correct let that person know it is. Let them also know that you are pleased with them getting it right. If it is not correct, thank the person for their effort; and

■ Redirect the question to the group by saying 'That's not quite right. Could you give us the right answer?'

If you have a problem getting the right answer it could be because your question was not clear enough. Rephrase the question and go through the procedure again.

Questions fall into two categories:

■ **Soft questions** deal with beliefs, feel-ings, attitudes, limits, directions. They are critical because you want to know how your people feel, what they believe, and their limits.
■ **Hard questions** are about facts, absolutes, where there is very little useful information.

For example, a hard question could be: What car do you drive? The information you get is limited. If you ask a soft question, this could be: How do you feel about your present car? In other words, you will get information that is meaningful.

When asking questions:

■ Be clear and to the point. If your audience know the subject you should get the right answer;

■ Avoid asking 50/50 questions which offer two alternative answers. You may get the right answer but it could be a guess;

■ Do not test your audience's power of expression. Questions that require long and involved answers waste time and can embarrass those trying to answer them. Ask concise questions to a number of your audience which will give better answers and cover the subject in detail;

■ Encourage participants to ask questions and give them positive answers. Their questions give you feedback on their progress and enable you to clear up any confusion. You can ask: Is any clarification needed on what has been done so far, or are there any disagreements?

■ Do not question a person's skill. Instead, have that person perform a skill rather than describe how it is done.

Source: Jack, Collis, 'Developing the human resource', *Australian Business News*, Vol. 32, March 2002, p. 27.

Questions

1. 'Communicating effectively is essential if we want to understand and be understood . . .'
   a. How does Jack Collis's opening statement impact on giving and receiving instructions in the workplace?
   b. Why do managers and supervisors need to find out if their instructions to an employee have been received and understood?
   c. Why is it important to engage in two-way communication as you give and receive instructions?

2. The article details some of the '. . . hallmarks of a first-class communicator'. What are the strategies used by communicators who can question effectively?

Effective meetings

Chapter 5

In this chapter you will learn how to:

○ determine the meeting's purpose

○ differentiate between formal and informal meetings

○ identify the roles of chairperson, secretary and member

○ draw up and distribute an agenda that covers all the business of the meeting

○ record clearly and concisely the decisions made at the meeting

○ use meeting conventions and processes to conduct a structured meeting

○ use communication skills and strategies to keep the meeting running smoothly

○ use problem-solving strategies

○ organise the venue and arrange the environment appropriately.

Evaluate your communication skills by completing the self-checks in the chapter.

Meetings, both formal and informal, are essential to ensure an organisation achieves its goals and objectives. Formal meetings are governed by rules, whereas informal meetings have very little structure.

Participating fully in a meeting allows you to express your viewpoint, discuss and debate relevant issues and reach an acceptable consensus. The opportunity to contribute makes you feel valued and increases your commitment to the work group.

Your willingness to be involved and to accept group responsibility for the team's decisions will make you an effective team member.

Determining the purpose

Meetings cover three main areas of responsibility. First, the organisation's responsibility is to provide the policy and procedures. Second, the meeting's executive is responsible for organising and running the meeting according to its standing orders and formalities. And, third, members are required to take part in decision making at the meeting and contribute to areas requiring their expertise. When the three areas of responsibility are dealt with efficiently, meetings give the executive and members the opportunity to create new ideas, solve problems and make democratic decisions.

Well run effective meetings achieve results and offer satisfaction to members.

Well run **meetings** enable everyone to contribute so that the maximum range of opinions and relevant information can be presented. This opportunity to contribute to decisions increases commitment by members of the work group and other co-workers. Meetings can:

■ provide information
■ clarify information
■ give and receive feedback
■ provide training
■ allow discussion
■ encourage problem solving.

Meetings vary to suit their purpose and the organisation's needs. Formal meetings suit a structured situation, informal meetings suit less structured situations. In both types of meeting, certain steps and procedures take place.

Formal meetings

Formal meetings have rules and regulations.

Formal meetings have rules and regulations, and sometimes follow the British Westminster system of government. Meeting rules and procedures provide a framework for the business or purpose of the meeting, and usually allow all members to participate. This chapter discusses only the formal procedures required for a structured meeting.

Even though interaction between members is generally limited by the formal procedures, and initiatives are taken by the leader who manages the meeting and the discussion, the meeting should be conducted in a democratic way. Table 5.1 lists some examples of formal meetings.

Informal meetings

Informal meetings are less structured than formal meetings.

Informal meetings at work are held to exchange information, solve problems, make decisions or set goals for a department or section. For example, a news reporter, camera operator and sound engineer are briefed by the news editor before going out to cover a story.

People can contribute their expertise in this give-and-take situation. Everyone

Table 5.1 Examples of formal meetings

Type	Purpose	Example
Annual general meeting	To inform interested parties of the year's progress and the plans for the next year.	CSR's Annual General Meeting
Extraordinary general meeting	To inform members of unusual circumstances and any potential advantages and disadvantages to shareholders, other interested parties and the company.	A company receives a takeover offer from another company
Board meeting	To provide a forum for management and the board of directors.	The board meeting of a student association
Departmental meeting	To discuss operations or to brief members.	Members of a university English department
Interdepartmental meeting	To discuss common policy with the most senior person from each section or division, and to exchange information.	Heads of department at an art college
Operational meeting	To discuss new equipment requirements or new safety procedures, for example.	Computer support committee
Briefing	To pass information along the organisation's channels; to save time.	Weekly briefing of public relations staff
Private meeting	To provide a forum for members and their invitees.	Clubs like APEX and professional associations
Public meeting	To allow the public to express opinions or give public support to an issue.	A proposal to close parkland to the general public

participates. Group discussion, participation, feedback and interaction lead to the final decision and action. This kind of procedure is ideal for the meeting held to make decisions and solve problems as it allows the group to define tasks, draw up plans of action and make decisions.

One of the main complaints about informal meetings is that they are often disorganised. The chairperson, usually the most senior person, not wanting to appear authoritarian, often allows discussion to become undirected. Without direction group members tend to debate an issue without achieving any consensus or worthwhile result. Alternatively, if the chairperson adopts an authoritarian role and controls the meeting, group members can become uninterested, bored and not committed to any decisions made.

Table 5.2 outlines an order to follow to achieve a meeting that is productive and reaches a consensus.

Table 5.2 Effective informal meetings

1. Familiarisation		Members familiarise themselves with the issues(s) to be discussed before the meeting. This can be achieved by the convenor distributing information on the topic either days before the meeting or allowing reading time of the information before the meeting commences.
2. Evaluation		During the meeting members discuss the issues, examine courses of action and make judgments on effectiveness.
3. Consensus		Members persuade, conciliate and compromise and move towards a group decision.
4. Action		Members make a commitment and agree on action to be taken.
5. Confirmation		Convenor sends a memo to group members confirming decisions made and actions to be taken.

Planning the seating arrangements

Seating arrangements influence the kind of interaction that takes place.

In formal meetings the chairperson and secretary plan the meeting and organise the order of business. In either of these roles, you should also consider the venue and seating arrangements. Round tables are ideal as people can see one another's actions and reactions. Rectangular tables give power to the people at either end. No table creates an informal atmosphere. If you sit above the rest, you have more power. If you sit below other people in a position where you have to look up, they have more power.

The ideal seating arrangement is the circular or oval shape illustrated in Figure 5.1. It allows everyone to see everyone else, which means better communication between members and better control and participation by the chairperson. This type of arrangement lessens the possibility of anyone dominating the meeting.

Figure 5.1 Circular or oval seating arrangement

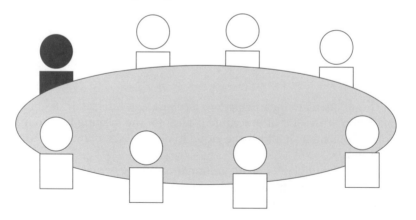

The long rectangular table illustrated in Figure 5.2 is less than ideal. It can lead to problems such as 'meetings within meetings'. The members farthest from the chairperson may talk among themselves. The chairperson may find it difficult to maintain control. It is not as democratic as the circle. Board meetings and international meetings often use this layout.

Figure 5.2 Long rectangular seating arrangement

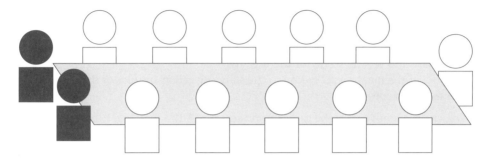

The U-shaped seating arrangement in Figure 5.3 presents problems similar to those of the long rectangular table. The person on the immediate left of the chairperson tends to have trouble asserting their presence. The person on the right is easily noticed, and so are the members closer to the chairperson.

Figure 5.3 U-shaped seating arrangement

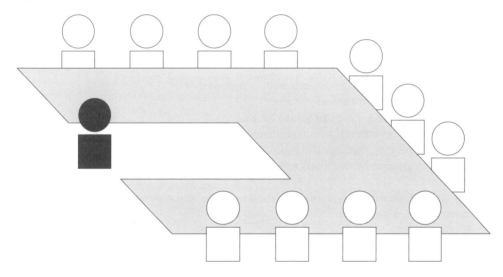

Conducting a structured meeting

People at a meeting may take an executive role or a membership role. Both roles involve two main responsibilities:

1. to prepare for the meeting
2. to participate in the meeting.

Members taking a leadership or membership role make the best contribution to any meeting if they realise that a group of people who meet to complete tasks should, in the process, also satisfy their need to belong to the group.

Duties of the chairperson

The **chairperson** should be able to achieve the goals of the meeting, maintain control, exercise impartiality and understand meeting procedures. The chairperson is either elected or appointed. Their responsibility is twofold:

1. to prepare and set the scene for the meeting
2. to conduct the meeting according to the standing orders or rules of the organisation, committee or meeting.

The chairperson's role is the most important role in the meeting. It covers the duties of a task leader and a maintenance leader. Therefore, a good chairperson needs a combination of technical skills and human relations skills. He or she must be able to prepare the agenda in consultation with the secretary, involve all participants in the meeting, keep the meeting focused on the order of business presented in the agenda, help everyone present to reach decisions and plan future action, and promote goodwill.

Other duties of the chairperson are discussed in more detail below.

Conducting the meeting

When acting as chairperson, conducting a meeting will involve you in the following duties.

- Check that a **quorum** (the minimum number needed to conduct the business of the meeting) is present.
- Declare the meeting open.
- Welcome people to the meeting and introduce any visitors.
- State the aims of the meeting.
- State that the order of the agenda will be followed.
- Indicate the time limit for each item.
- Give priority to the most important items.
- Sign the minutes when they are confirmed as correct.
- Guide the meeting through the business on the agenda.
- Allow each item to be discussed fully – this includes the presentation of information and plans.
- Control the moving and seconding of all motions and amendments.
- Delegate when necessary.
- Brief members.
- Give feedback.
- Encourage everyone's participation.
- Plan the action required by decisions reached.

Ruling on points of order

Formal meetings have a procedure. At any point in a meeting a member can draw the chairperson's attention to an irregularity such as a speaker speaking more than once or exceeding time.

The chairperson makes a decision on any **points of order** that are raised.

- Acknowledge that members can, at any time in a meeting, point out any improper proceeding or incorrect interpretation of the meeting's rules of conduct.
- Rule on the point as correct or incorrect after discussion or debate about it.
- Ask the meeting to vote for their ruling on a dissenting member's point of order – no seconder is needed.
- Accept the vote and take any necessary action required by the decision.

Following procedures

An important part of the chairperson's role is to ensure that correct procedures are followed, and to maintain control of the meeting.

- Allocate enough time for adequate discussion of each item on the agenda.
- Ensure that the meeting begins and ends on time.
- Follow procedures to keep the meeting democratic – but not a 'free for all', 'gossip' or 'gripe session'.
- Follow the meeting's procedure rules and keep order.
- Rule on difficult matters.
- Focus discussion on the meeting's objectives.
- Sum up the main points and ask for a decision or vote.
- Deal with any potential conflict before it becomes serious.
- Be objective and impartial.
- If business cannot be completed, put forward the motion or proposal to adjourn it to the next meeting.
- Determine the date and place of the next meeting.
- Close the meeting.

Moving and seconding proposals, motions and amendments

A **motion** is a specific proposal formally put by a member to the rest of the meeting; for example: 'I move that a pay increase of $30 per week be accepted'. Ideally, a motion should be put in writing and given to the chairperson before the meeting for inclusion in the agenda. At the meeting, the **proposal** is given in writing to the secretary for inclusion in the minutes.

A motion seeks action on a proposal.

Once the motion is put to the meeting, it must be seconded (supported) by another member before it can be discussed and voted on. The chairperson asks for a seconder. When the motion is seconded, the chairperson asks the mover of the motion to 'speak to it' (outline the motion). A time limit is imposed by the standing orders or by the chairperson. After the mover outlines the motion, the chairperson asks if anyone would like to speak against the motion. Then discussion on the motion is opened to all members present. Throughout the discussion, the chairperson aims to maintain a balance between those 'speaking to' the motion and those speaking against it by giving each side a turn.

Amendments

An **amendment** to the motion can be suggested by any member. It is an alteration that aims to clarify the motion (or improve it some other way) by rearranging, removing or adding words. The chairperson asks for a seconder to the amendment and then it is discussed and voted on. If it is accepted, the original motion is amended (changed) before the new version is put to the vote. An amendment is not permitted to negate or change the intention of the motion. Members who want to do this must wait until the motion is discussed and put to the vote, and then propose a separate motion to the meeting.

Right of reply

Once the general discussion on the motion is completed, the chairperson gives its mover the right of reply. This is the last discussion allowed and the mover's opportunity to reiterate and emphasise the main points.

Voting for the motion

The chairperson then asks members to **vote** for or against the motion. Occasionally, when members feel that the discussion is taking too long, they may pre-empt the chairperson and ask that 'the question be put' – that is, they request that the members vote for or against the motion at that point, without further discussion. However, it is more usual for the chairperson to ask for the vote. The simplest way to vote is by asking members to say 'aye' (yes) or 'nay' (no) and to judge the result by the volume of the voices.

A motion is won or lost by simple majority. When votes for the motion equal those against, the vote is tied. The chairperson then has the **casting vote** to break the tied vote. The chairperson abstains from voting unless the vote is tied. The chairperson also abstains from the discussion, but can join it if someone else agrees to take the chair.

Resolution

A motion put to the meeting and carried becomes a **resolution**; that is, the discussion about it has been resolved to everyone's satisfaction. All motions, whether successful or unsuccessful, should be recorded by the secretary in the minutes.

Table 5.3 explains some of the terms used in connection with meetings.

Duties of the secretary

The secretary assists the chairperson.

The duties of the **secretary** are numerous. The way in which they are carried out is important to the process of the meeting and the meeting's result.

Agenda

An agenda lists the order of business.

The secretary convenes all meetings and prepares the agenda in consultation with the chairperson. The **agenda** clearly states the time, date and place of the next meeting and the order in which items will be discussed. Agenda items can be separated into two groups:

1. items requiring decisions
2. items to be discussed.

By dividing the agenda in this way, the chairperson and secretary ensure that the most important items are dealt with first. Thus, the agenda lets members know:

- where and when the meeting will be held
- who is invited to the meeting
- what business will be covered
- when each item will be dealt with.

An example of an agenda is given in Figure 5.4.

A copy is sent to each member before the meeting, allowing them to think about and prepare for the business of the meeting. An agenda should be prepared and distributed in such a way that members can anticipate any problems and have time to consider solutions. The phrase 'other business' indicates that other items not on the agenda may also be discussed. The agenda may also indicate the time allotted to each item of business.

Documentation

The secretary deals with the paperwork that a meeting involves, including:

- preparing enough copies of documents for all members
- sending members the agenda for the next meeting and a copy of the minutes of the previous meeting, preferably 14 days after the last meeting
- answering inquiries from members.

Table 5.3 The terminology of meetings

Term	Meaning and purpose
Agenda	A list of the meeting's business items, prepared by the secretary in consultation with the Chair and distributed before the meeting. It gives participants at the meeting a brief to prepare information, form opinions and consider courses of action.
Amendment	A proposal to alter a motion by: 1. adding certain words 2. leaving out certain words 3. replacing certain words with others. An amendment must be debated and voted on before the original motion is dealt with. If there are two or more amendments, each is debated and voted on in turn. An amendment needs a mover and a seconder. The mover and the seconder of the original motion, plus anyone else who has spoken in debate on the original motion, may 'speak to' the amendment.
Casting vote	A vote from the Chair that will decide the issue in case of a tie. The Chair may choose not to use this casting vote.
Constitution	The constitution contains the organisation's name, aims and objectives, rules of administration, membership, office bearers and committee.
General business	The heading on the agenda under which 'new' business may be introduced. Notify the secretary, before the meeting, of any items you wish to raise under this heading.
Minutes	A record of what happens during the meeting: this includes who was present, motions and amendments passed, decisions taken, action decided on, people responsible for carrying out the decisions, and any matters that have been adjourned.
Motion	A proposal made by someone at the meeting. A motion becomes a resolution after it has been voted for by the majority. A motion can be classified as substantive (any motion of substance to do with the business of the meeting) or procedural (to do with the rules and regulations of the meeting).
Notice	A notice convening the meeting; sent to all members at a time specified by the organisation's rules.
Quorum	The minimum number of people who must attend a meeting for business to be conducted. The secretary should check that a quorum is present before voting proceeds. The size of the quorum is specified by the constitution.
Standing orders	Rules governing the way a meeting's business must be conducted.
Vote	At formal meetings members vote on issues by saying 'Aye' or 'Nay', by a show of hands, by a division or by a secret ballot.

Apologies

At the meeting, the secretary:

■ records the names of those present
■ reads **apologies** from absentees and asks the chairperson to call for any other apologies for absentees
■ records these apologies.

Figure 5.4 Example of a meeting agenda

Agenda: Sport and Recreation Social Club Meeting
Date: 4 October 2003
Time: 9–10 am
Location: Suite 11A, Level 2, Australian Institute
Purpose: To plan the annual Christmas function.

Order of business
  1. Opening of meeting.
  2. Apologies.
  3. Confirmation of minutes of previous meeting (copy attached).
  4. Business arising from minutes.
  5. Correspondence.
  6. Business arising from correspondence.
  7. Decision items:
      a.   Budget
      b.   Type of function
      c.   Date and venue
      d.   Collection and banking of money.
  8. Discussion items:
      a.   To invite partners or members only?
      b.   Will food and alcohol be provided?
  9. Other business.
 10. Closing of meeting.

Agenda distribution: Melissa Baxter   Peter Hill
                        Penny Baker   Willem Helvi
                        Colin Kees   Kay Wilson
                        Cheryl Kerr   Maria Pappas

Correspondence and minutes

The minutes are the official written record of the meeting.

The secretary also deals with all incoming and outgoing **correspondence**, and keeps clear and accurate **minutes**. When acting as secretary, you should:

- keep copies of any motions put without notice
- record in the minutes the names of those present, apologies, a list of correspondence, a brief summary of any discussion, and all conclusions and decisions reached
- check that the minutes clearly identify each motion and those who moved, seconded or amended it
- record in the minutes any action to be taken, and by whom
- check any doubtful points with the chairperson as soon as the meeting ends
- write up brief, clear and accurate minutes as soon as possible after the meeting, within 24 hours or sooner
- ensure that the chairperson initials any alterations to the minutes
- record the minutes in a minutes book
- ensure that the chairperson signs these at the next meeting to confirm that they are correct.

The secretary should be able to advise the chairperson on rules and procedures, and may also be required to handle details such as organising the seating in the meeting room. Figure 5.5 gives an example of the minutes of a meeting.

Figure 5.5 Example of minutes

Minutes of the Sport and Recreation Social Club Meeting held at Suite 11A, Level 2, Australian Institute on 4 October 2003

Present: Melissa Baxter (Chair)   Peter Hill (Secretary)
                Penny Baker   Willem Helvi
                Cheryl Kerr   Maria Pappas
Apologies: Colin Kees, Kay Wilson

1. Minutes of the previous meeting: Cheryl Kerr moved and Willem Helvi seconded that the minutes of the previous meeting be accepted. Carried.
2. Business arising from the minutes of the previous meeting: Nil
3. Business arising from correspondence: Nil
4. Purpose of meeting: Chairperson Melissa Baxter advised that the objective of today's Social Club meeting is to plan and organise the annual Christmas function and that the order of items on the agenda is to be followed.
5. Decision or action items
   Action
   The budget is to be $45 per person.
   Moved: W. Helvi   Seconded: M. Pappas   Carried
   Action
   The function is to be held on 11 December 2003.
   Moved: P. Baker   Seconded: C. Kerr   Carried
   Action
   The Christmas function is to be held at a local restaurant.
   Moved: P. Baker   Seconded: C. Kerr   Carried
   Action C. Kerr
   Determine the price and availability on 11 December 2003 of two different venues, Curlin House and the Satay Inn.
   Moved: M. Pappas   Seconded: P. Hill   Carried
   Action W. Helvi
   Money is to be collected from each member of the committee by S. Graham and held in a Credit Union account.
   Moved: M. Pappas   Seconded: P. Hill   Carried
6. Discussion items
   Action P. Hill
   To send a memo to all members asking for their preference on:
   a. inviting members and partners, or members only
   b. provide food only, or alcohol and food.
   Moved: C. Kerr   Seconded: W. Helvi   Carried
7. Other business
   General discussion on the format for next year's Little Athletics presentation night. Members decided to consider different formats and to present their views at the next meeting.
8. Date of next meeting: 5 November 2003
9. Meeting closed: 10.05 am

Chairperson's signature _____   Secretary's signature _____
Date: Date:

Duties of participants at a meeting

Productive meetings give results and satisfaction to those attending them. As a participant, you are able to make a meeting more productive by knowing how to prepare for it, how to conduct yourself there, and how to communicate with others.

Task-related roles

Before you attend a meeting, read the agenda and the minutes of the previous meeting. Prepare in writing any proposals or motions you wish to put to the meeting and forward these to the chairperson. Prepare your oral presentation so that you are ready to 'speak

A motion is presented to the meeting.

to' the proposal and exercise your right of reply. The following three steps help you keep to the main point.

1. State your main point to catch everyone's attention.
2. Explain your reason for the proposal.
3. Present concise, relevant background information.

Saying too much will distract members from your main point. Remember to reiterate the main point and its advantages or benefits in your right of reply.

Pay attention to task-related roles.

Task-related roles enable the meeting to move through each step in an organised way. As a member of a formal meeting, you must indicate to the chairperson your intention to speak, and wait for the chairperson's call to speak. Then you address your remarks to the chairperson before looking at the others present. Generally, you can speak only once when a motion or proposal is being discussed.

Maintenance-related roles

Attention to maintenance-related roles improves group cohesion.

The meeting's leader or chairperson, members of the executive and other members are all responsible for **maintenance-related roles**. Support and encourage others' contributions to create a positive atmosphere, reduce tensions and reconcile disagreements.

Be willing to negotiate, to modify your position or to admit an error. Open communication channels encourage discussion and contributions. Good maintenance skills enable task achievement in a cooperative environment. Maintenance-related roles use the human relations skills of support, encouragement and feedback. Delegating, guiding, influencing and motivating others are all part of the maintenance-related role.

Defensive and dysfunctional roles

Defensive and **dysfunctional roles** operate against task-related and maintenance-related roles, which help to achieve a group's goals. People take defensive roles – such as tension reliever or scapegoat – to protect others from the anxiety caused by a meeting that is not functioning well. People who play dysfunctional roles – such as show-off, blocker or rebel – to achieve their own hidden agendas prevent the meeting from achieving its goals. Both roles hinder the group's performance.

Task-related and maintenance-related roles are discussed more fully in Chapter 9. As you develop communication skills in speaking, questioning, listening and encouraging others, you become more productive and self-confident and better prepared to carry out task-related and maintenance-related roles in a meeting.

Behaviour at meetings

APPLY SKILLS

1. What makes a good meeting leader? What makes a good participant? Identify four characteristics that are common to both.
2. a. Briefly explain the difference between a motion and an amendment.
   b. List the steps involved in moving and voting on a motion (assuming that no amendment is made).
3. In pairs, recall and discuss a meeting one or both of you attended recently.

a. What were the seating arrangements? Why do you think participants were seated that way?
b. From your observations:
   i. Was the chairperson effective or not?
   ii. Identify two ways in which the chairperson or a participant helped others to communicate and participate.
   iii. How can a chairperson maintain control in a meeting?

    iv. What are two strategies a chairperson can use to create a pleasant environment?

c. Who was responsible for preparing and forwarding the agenda to members before the meeting?

d. Discuss two ways of collecting information and items for the agenda.

e. Why should the agenda reach members before the meeting?

f. Why does a meeting need minutes?

Communication skills that achieve results

People come together at a meeting to exchange views, ideas and knowledge. High-quality communication between them produces a meeting that enables decisions to be made and actions taken, with successful results. The communication skills you need in the preparation, participation and follow-up stages of a meeting are considered here.

Participate in a way that supports the meeting.

One of your responsibilities at a meeting is to be prepared for it. Before you arrive, read the agenda to become familiar with it. Research as much relevant background information as you can so that you are able to make a useful contribution. Consider why you are attending the meeting.

Participation means involvement in the meeting. Offer suggestions, and accept some of the responsibilities in a way that supports the group's efforts. As you become involved in the discussion, share your feelings and ideas. This way, new ideas and ways of doing things may emerge. Table 5.4 suggests strategies that will help you to perform well at a meeting.

Structured meetings

SELF CHECK 5.1 ✔

Did the chairperson and/or the secretary:	Often	Sometimes	Never
■ prepare and distribute the agenda?	☐	☐	☐
■ organise the venue and seating?	☐	☐	☐
■ state the meeting's purpose?	☐	☐	☐
■ guide the meeting through the business agenda?	☐	☐	☐
■ use strategies to complete the tasks?	☐	☐	☐
■ focus the discussion on the meeting's objectives?	☐	☐	☐
■ enable proposals or motions, discussion and resolution to take place effectively?	☐	☐	☐
■ help the meeting plan appropriate action?	☐	☐	☐
■ use strategies to maintain group cohesion?	☐	☐	☐
■ use problem-solving or decision-making strategies?	☐	☐	☐
■ encourage all members to participate?	☐	☐	☐
■ keep accurate minutes?	☐	☐	☐
■ use time efficiently?	☐	☐	☐

Did the members:			
■ follow structured meeting procedures?	☐	☐	☐
■ fulfil task roles?	☐	☐	☐
■ participate in group maintenance roles?	☐	☐	☐
■ give motions in writing to the secretary?	☐	☐	☐
■ speak logically, clearly and concisely to the motion from a prepared oral presentation?	☐	☐	☐
■ conform to the problem-solving or decision-making approach taken by the chairperson?	☐	☐	☐
■ show a willingness to comply with the meeting's decisions?	☐	☐	☐
■ participate constructively?	☐	☐	☐

Table 5.4 Strategies that aid participation at meetings

Practise courtesy and good meeting manners	■ Arrive prepared and on time. ■ Show your readiness to be involved in the meeting and in the decision making. ■ Express yourself clearly. ■ Listen to others and clarify points. ■ Accept and follow the agenda and the specified time limits. ■ Avoid causing unnecessary interruptions or distractions. ■ Cooperate to bring the meeting back to the agenda when others cause interruptions or distractions. ■ Apologise to the secretary if you must leave early. ■ Send an apology to the secretary or ask another member to do this if you cannot attend the meeting.
Express your ideas and give feedback	■ Participate fully in the meeting. ■ Direct your comments to all members and occasionally summarise your remarks. ■ Ask others for feedback on what you have said, to confirm that your ideas have been accurately received. ■ Give feedback that acknowledges and considers others' ideas.
Ask questions	■ Question others when you are unclear about something. ■ Avoid questioning in a way that causes unnecessary interruptions. ■ Aim to increase understanding and speed up the decision making. ■ Avoid interfering with the time limit or the order of the agenda.
Listen	■ Avoid making hasty judgments about other people's ideas. ■ Seek clarification by paraphrasing other people's comments. ■ Consider others' ideas carefully. ■ Give others the opportunity to expand or explain their ideas.
Match the nonverbal message to the spoken	■ Check that your nonverbal communication is assertive and treats others as equals. ■ Avoid using body movement that can be interpreted as aggressive or submissive. ■ Speak clearly and courteously, with open body language. ■ Attend the meeting with acceptable clothing and appearance. ■ Use your own and others' personal space appropriately – formal or informal.
Follow up	■ Check that everyone understands the decisions reached. ■ Before the meeting concludes, verify who will complete each agreed course of action. ■ Take part in the planning for the next meeting. ■ Offer any contributions you wish to add to the agenda for the next meeting. ■ Complete any required tasks before the next meeting.

Communication barriers

Communication barriers hinder productive results.

Communication barriers at meetings can result from poor leadership or poor membership skills or a combination of both. They interfere with and prevent productive results.

Poor verbal skills

Verbal communication barriers may be caused by the illogical organisation of words and by unclear or discourteous ways of speaking. Jargon, slang and negative language also interfere with the communication flow. Addressing a person by the wrong name or with the wrong level of formality may cause an immediate communication barrier.

Inappropriate nonverbal skills

Nonverbal behaviour such as your tone of voice, type or lack of eye contact, gestures, use of space, clothing and appearance all affect your communication with others. Use these in a manner appropriate to the meeting to match the needs of sender and receiver. Barriers occur when verbal or nonverbal behaviour is inappropriate to the type of meeting and its purpose.

Poor listening

Listening enables you to hear and comprehend the other person's message. Boredom, lack of interest, a clash of values, jumping to early conclusions, judging the speaker, dislike of the speaker and allowing the physical environment to distract you are all examples of poor listening. They cause communication barriers, and some of the message is lost.

Unwillingness to participate

The participants at a meeting usually have access to resources and power. However, unwilling, unsure participants are unable to make decisions or to organise the business of the meeting efficiently. Communication barriers develop. When people realise that the meeting is ineffective they tend to withdraw or behave in dysfunctional ways.

The success of any meeting is related to how well participants and the executive take part, solve problems, organise and manage the business in a way that achieves satisfactory results. Positive feedback, verbal and nonverbal, motivates the group, and gives it a sense of belonging and achievement. In fact, many of the potential barriers to communication at a meeting are avoided when participants use positive verbal and nonverbal feedback and follow up their decisions.

Decision making and problem solving in a meeting

When decisions are made at meetings, two important processes take place. First, members think and analyse to create ideas from the information presented. Second, decisions are made and a procedure or a plan of action is established to carry them out.

Two ways of creating new ideas are the *nominal group technique* and *brainstorming*. The nominal group technique lets you work independently and gives you time to consider the ideas. In the brainstorming process, you work with the group in a spontaneous way.

Nominal group technique

The main advantage of the **nominal group technique** is that it enables members of a group to work independently as individuals at the meeting, to think about and present new ideas. (The term 'nominal' means 'in name only'.) A disadvantage of this technique is that group members may feel their spontaneity is inhibited and that the situation is too controlled. Once the thinking process and presentation of ideas is finished, members work together again as a group to consider and evaluate the ideas.

Table 5.5 outlines the steps of the nominal group technique.

The nominal group technique encourages members to think independently.

Table 5.5 Nominal group technique

Step	Process
1. Discuss and clarify the situation or problem to be considered	The meeting's group of participants listen, ask questions, clarify the issue and decide how the nominal group process will work.
2. Work as individuals	Members are asked to think about the issue on their own and write down their ideas about possible solutions individually, without discussion. This usually takes 15–20 minutes.
3. Present and record the ideas	A 'round robin' contribution of ideas takes place. The leader records each member's contribution. No evaluation or discussion occurs at this time, but members may add further ideas to the list.
4. Clarify and evaluate	Once all the ideas are recorded, the group discusses, analyses and evaluates them.
5. Rate the ideas	Each member of the meeting independently rates the ideas. (If 20 ideas are presented, each person gives the best one a score of 20, the next best 19 and so on until the least favoured idea receives a score of 1.)
6. Choose the most preferred option	Each person's rating score for each idea is recorded alongside it. (If there are eight people at the meeting, each idea will be given eight different scores.) If you prefer anonymity, put your score rates on cards for the leader to collect and record. The scores are then totalled and divided by eight to give the average score. The idea with the highest average score is the preferred option.

Brainstorming

Brainstorming leads to new ideas.

When people in a meeting need to consider new ideas to reach a decision or solve a problem, brainstorming can quickly involve all members in the decision. **Brainstorming** is a process suited to stimulating innovative ideas and creative solutions. Table 5.6 explains it further.

Brainstorming lets each person contribute ideas and feel part of the process that produces the result. It is a quick and easy method to use at a meeting. It leads to new ideas and includes everyone. The meeting must then plan a course of action to ensure that the ideas are acted upon. Two ways to plan a course of action are the problem-solving process and the decision-making agenda.

Problem-solving process

Dewey's reflective thinking process offers a method of problem solving.

A very useful method of solving problems is Dewey's *reflective thinking process*, which suggests five stages in sequence for a meeting group to follow. It is creative, helps participants understand the reasons for the final decision, and encourages them to discuss the results with others. Problem solving is a useful way of creating new ideas on an issue that concerns everyone present. Table 5.7 outlines the process.

Schedule the action

In step 5 of Dewey's reflective thinking process you are able to plan a course of action. Then identify each step of the plan, create a schedule and give a copy to each group member. If, for example, the first step is to compile a set of computer printouts to give a database you could set a deadline of one week from the meeting date. The next step is

Table 5.6 Brainstorming

Step	Process
1. Define the main issue	Clarify for all participants the main purpose of the meeting. For example, a retail store employing 15 people may want to decide on ways to improve customer service. At a meeting of all staff, the group leader or chairperson states that the task is to 'identify ways to improve customer service'. Then the leader briefs the group on the brainstorming process.
2. Brief the meeting	Before the brainstorming begins, tell everyone that for two minutes the group is to suggest ways of tackling the task: improving customer relations. As the list of suggestions is created, no one must interrupt or comment on another person's contribution. It is important that no one speaks except to add new ideas.
3. Encourage all members to participate	Urge everyone to participate and feel part of the group. As people give their ideas they are written on a large sheet of paper or board that everyone can see. Simply throw ideas forward until a timekeeper calls 'time' at the end of two minutes.
4. Evaluate the ideas	Everyone at the meeting decides which ideas are a possibility and which should be discarded.
5. Choose the action	The possible ideas are considered further until one is chosen. At this point the brainstorming exercise is complete.

Table 5.7 Dewey's reflective thinking process

Step	Process
1. Define the problem	Define and clarify the meeting's understanding of its main purpose or task. Encourage each person to contribute ideas and opinions.
2. List all the possible alternatives	Brainstorming is a relatively easy way to list all the alternatives in the second stage of the process. Follow the brainstorming steps outlined in Table 5.6.
3. Discuss and analyse the alternatives	Work through the list with everyone until it is narrowed down to a few alternatives. Then use Self-check 5.2 to help you make the final decision. This process of group participation draws everyone into decision making and helps them to feel committed to the decision reached.
4. Choose a solution	Set your limits and identify the acceptable and unacceptable results. Agreeing to a solution that will bring undesirable results or one that is unrealistic simply wastes time. (You would not use this method for an issue that requires only a quick decision that can be dealt with by the executive or by a vote from all members.)
5. Plan the course of action	Ask all members to contribute ideas. State that planning is to be directed at the particular course of action decided by the group. Some members may ask to be involved in the plan. They may be willing to follow through until the task is finished.

to circulate the database printout for editing to remove out-of-date information or add new information. Set a date for return of, say, five working days. Work through each subsequent step of the plan. Make one person responsible for checking the plan's progress.

Follow-up stage

Add a follow-up stage to the problem-solving process, so that at the next meeting people report results to the group. If the results are acceptable, acknowledge one another's success. If the plan of action shows flaws, revise the plan.

SELF CHECK 5.2

Decision making

Next time you work with a group, use this checklist to decide if the group has:	Very successfully	Successfully	Unsuccessfully
defined the problem	☐	☐	☐
researched the issue	☐	☐	☐
considered accurate and factual information	☐	☐	☐
discussed the possible alternatives	☐	☐	☐
chosen a solution	☐	☐	☐
created an action plan	☐	☐	☐
delegated responsibility for taking action	☐	☐	☐
decided to monitor progress	☐	☐	☐
taken any necessary follow-up steps	☐	☐	☐
carried out the plan	☐	☐	☐

Strategies for meetings

APPLY SKILLS

1. When is the nominal group technique used?
2. Define the term 'brainstorming'. When is it useful in meetings?
3. List the five stages of Dewey's problem-solving process. Why is it important to have a follow-up stage?
4. a. Briefly describe three different seating arrangements suited to a meeting.
   b. How does each arrangement influence the interaction between the participants?
5. In groups of three or four, consider the following situation and complete the tasks below.
   As General Manager of a large manufacturing firm, you decide to call a meeting of the heads of customer relations sections: Accounts, Engineering, Human Resources and Public Relations. The purpose of the

meeting is to discuss how to improve customer relations.

a. Write a memo inviting section heads to the meeting and advising them of its purpose. Create an agenda for the meeting.
b. Prepare a written proposal offering one strategy that will improve customer relations. The proposal is to be put to the meeting as a motion.
c. Discuss one problem-solving technique you would use to ensure that the meeting solves any problems that are causing poor customer relations.
d. You decide to use brainstorming to encourage full input from all those present at the meeting. List and briefly describe the steps required for a brainstorming session.
e. List the physical resources you will need to create a suitable setting for the meeting.

Visit the Companion Website at **www.prenhall.com/dwyer_au**. Choose the Internet Exercise activity in Chapter 5 to create a list of handy hints to assist a meeting's chairperson.

Chapter summary

Determine the meeting's purpose. A meeting with a clearly defined purpose outlined in the agenda is more productive and satisfying than one that is held simply because 'We always meet on Fridays'.

Differentiate between formal and informal meetings. Formal meetings follow established structured proceedings. Informal meetings are less structured; the leader is usually chosen by the group and the roles worked out by the participants.

Identify the roles of chairperson, secretary and member. The chairperson's position is one of authority. He or she prepares for the meeting, conducts it, rules on points of order and initiates follow-up action. Some duties are completed before the meeting in consultation with the secretary. The secretary prepares the agenda, organises the documents for the meeting, accepts apologies and correspondence, and prepares the minutes. Members carry out task-related roles such as participating and passing motions and amendments. They also attend to maintenance-related roles to keep the group together.

Draw up and distribute an agenda that covers all the business of the meeting. Before the meeting the secretary prepares an agenda which tells members where and when the meeting will be held, what business will be covered and when each item will be dealt with. The agenda is distributed at least seven days before the meeting.

Record clearly and concisely decisions made at the meeting. The secretary prepares the minutes as the official written record of the meeting. The minutes must be confirmed by members at the next meeting as a true and accurate record.

Use meeting conventions and processes to conduct a structured meeting. When the chairperson, secretary and members work according to accepted conventions, the meeting is conducted with cooperation and efficiency. Proposals, motions, discussion of these, any amendments and the resolution of the motion are more easily achieved this way.

Use communication skills and strategies to keep the meeting running smoothly. The skills of speaking, listening, negotiation and conflict resolution are all used in meetings. The application of your own communication skills and knowledge will help or hinder the meeting.

Use problem-solving strategies. These strategies encourage members to extract new ideas from the information presented in a meeting and to create the plan of action required by the final decisions. Brainstorming draws new ideas from a group, while the nominal group technique has people working independently.

Organise the venue and arrange the environment appropriately. Consider the venue and seating arrangements for meetings carefully and choose the one that best suits your needs. Communication and interaction at meetings are affected by physical space and surroundings.

QUESTIONS

REVIEW

1. List six reasons for holding meetings.

2. a. What is the difference between a formal meeting and an informal meeting?
   b. Give an example of each.

3. a. Which system of rules and regulations do formal meetings often follow?
   b. What is the purpose of rules and regulations?

4. What is the purpose of an annual general meeting, an extraordinary general meeting and a board meeting?

5. List four duties of the chairperson, four of the secretary and four of the other participants.

6. a. Briefly explain the following: agenda, minutes, decision or action items, discussion items, other business, motion, quorum.
   b. Name and explain the main elements of an agenda.
   c. Name and briefly explain the main elements of the minutes.

7. a. Who prepares the agenda?
   b. How soon after a meeting should members receive the minutes of the meeting and the agenda for the next meeting?
   c. Who opens the meeting?
   d. Who gives the apologies?
   e. Who moves and seconds the minutes to confirm that they are correct?
   f. Who signs and confirms as correct the minutes from the previous meeting?
   g. Who keeps the minutes of the meeting?
   h. Who is involved in the resolution to confirm that the minutes of the previous meeting are correct?
   i. Who presents the correspondence in and out?
   j. Who moves and seconds motions?
   k. Who closes the meeting?

8. What is the difference between a task-related role and a maintenance-related role?

9. What are some of the factors that can cause communication barriers at meetings?

Plan and conduct a meeting

SKILLS

BUILD

Assume that the Society of Business Communicators is about to hold its annual conference, entitled 'Communication: Not Always Simple', at the Adelaide Hilton Hotel. You are the secretary of the committee planning the conference. In groups of six or seven, plan and conduct a committee meeting, following meeting procedures and the agenda. Work through the following tasks.

1. Prepare a memorandum and draft agenda for the initial conference planning meeting, and invent the details for the place, time and date of this meeting. Follow the agenda format for the Sport and Recreation Social Club's meeting shown in Figure 5.4. Include tasks 7 (b), (c) and (d) as items of business on your agenda.

2. At the meeting, brainstorm to create a range of ideas for each conference session. First, clearly define the purpose of the meeting. Use each of the five steps of the brainstorming process. Keep in mind that many participants at the conference will come from the public relations sections of large and small private business firms and of government departments. All consider themselves to be professional communicators.

3. Also at the meeting, decide how to publicise the conference. Use the nominal group technique to think independently about ways of doing this. Complete each of the six steps in the process. The group's goal is to create a list of publicity options ranked in order of preference.

4. Delegate someone to create a checklist that will help the committee make sure that the Adelaide Hilton Hotel meets its requirements for a highly professional venue.

Key terms

agenda	dysfunctional role	nominal group technique
amendment	formal meeting	point of order
apologies	general business	proposal
brainstorming	informal meeting	quorum
casting vote	maintenance-related role	resolution
chairperson	meeting	secretary
correspondence	minutes	task-related role
defensive role	motion	vote

Business protocol

Doing business in Asia can be very rewarding and enjoyable but cultural differences present pitfalls for the uninitiated. An understanding of Asian customs and business practices will smooth the way to fruitful negotiations.

First impressions

When conducting business in Asia, the first meeting is crucial to establishing relationships and credibility. Asian cultures emphasise dress, gesture and language more than Australian culture so it is useful to develop a basic knowledge of the culture you are dealing with. Business meetings in Asia are generally more conservative than in Australia, so formality in manner and dress will be appreciated.

In more westernised countries like Singapore and Hong Kong, it may be acceptable to use first names, but if in doubt always opt for the more formal mode of address, particularly in Japan.

Introductions

Because of the formality of business meetings in Asia, it may be useful to use a third person, or 'go-between', to arrange a meeting and introduce participants. This person should be regarded as a neutral party, but of significant rank and status. Observe protocol and decorum when arranging an appointment, and allow enough time for business counterparts to prepare for the meeting.

It is considered ill-mannered to list your own achievements at a meeting, so leave this job for a discreet 'go-between'. This person will also conduct the introductions in

a manner acceptable to the Asian participants. If a suitable 'go-between' cannot be arranged, observe strict formality in establishing business relationships in Asia. A meeting request should clearly state the reason for the meeting, who is to attend and a recommended date, time and venue.

Allow extra time to attend appointments in Asia as traffic congestion and other difficulties can play havoc with schedules.

Meeting people

If you are visiting another person's office in Asia, you will usually be seated facing the door. If an Asian colleague/s is visiting your office, the most senior person should be directed to sit facing the door.

When the people you are meeting enter the room, rise to your feet and move to greet them with a light handshake. Bowing is not always necessary and is better left to those who understand its value and intent.

After these initial introductions comes the important practice of exchanging business cards.

Business cards

Business cards are very important to Asians; they are seen by many cultures as an extension of yourself. The following tips will help minimise embarrassment.

■ Keep your cards in good condition by using a business card holder. Never use grubby or marked cards.
■ The visiting party is usually the first to hand over business cards. The correct way to do this is to present the card with two hands with the right hand forward.

CASE STUDY

- Hand over cards with your name facing upwards. If possible, have your cards translated into the local language and present this side of the card.
- Never produce a card from or return one to a back pocket.
- Never write on another's business card.
- Briefly study the card and, when seated, place the cards so you can see them clearly.

Small talk

Small talk is a common way of beginning business meetings. As in Australia, avoid discussing religion or politics and don't bring up family matters unless asked. Positive questions about your counterpart's business activities, natural or national events, sports and hobbies are safe. Small talk is useful in establishing business relationships in Asia, so don't dismiss it.

It is during this period of small talk that you should offer visitors some refreshment. Offer the most senior person a beverage first. If a guest, you may automatically be presented with a beverage. If this happens, you are not obliged to drink it.

Gift giving

Gift giving is common in Asian business; however, it is not necessary to present a gift at the initial meeting unless it has been preceded by considerable correspondence. Gifts should be presented at all subsequent meetings, however.

Hosts may present gifts at the conclusion of the first meeting – small promotional items are sufficient. The visiting party should not present a gift at this early stage as it could cause the host to 'lose face' if he/she is not ready to reciprocate immediately.

Using interpreters

Interpreters are useful in maintaining the flow of conversation if you do not speak the language. However, be aware that it is difficult to find a truly neutral interpreter, particularly if he/she is organised by the other party. Treat all information given to an interpreter cautiously.

Always look at your Asian contacts – not at the interpreter – during discussions. The

interpreter is considered to be a tool of the discussion, not a part of it.

Follow-up

It is important to follow up on the relationships established during the first meeting. If language is not a problem, telephone to thank your contacts before you leave their country.

Follow that up with a formal but friendly letter to the senior contact about a week later. This letter should outline your discussions and express hopes for an ongoing business relationship. Further correspondence should continue in a positive but undemanding manner.

Decision making

As in Australia, the people you meet may not be the decision-makers, particularly in large companies. It is useful to understand the decision-making process of the company you are dealing with. This will give you a better understanding of the timeframes of decisions and the likelihood of success.

Entertaining

Entertaining is a very important part of Asian business and is often used to establish and maintain relationships. When overseas, hosting dinner and/or drinks is one way to build business contacts. In Australia, dinners, drinks, golf, sightseeing and barbecues are also effective. Gifts should be presented at these occasions, with the senior member of the Asian delegation receiving the best gift.

While these occasions are important, don't expect to discuss much business. Social activities 'lubricate' relationships and help Asian contacts know you better so they are more comfortable doing business with you.

If personal favours are asked – e.g. to assist an Asian student to study in Australia – consider helping if you can, especially if the person seeking the favour ranks highly in the decision-making process.

When entertaining Asians in Australia, it is customary to insist on paying. It is also wise to pay if you have sought a lunch or dinner with a contact overseas. Entertaining overseas can be very expensive, especially in clubs, so select venues carefully.

Asians usually like to eat out but the

Japanese sometimes entertain at home. If you are invited to a Japanese home, it is a great honour and you should give your hosts an appropriate gift. Remember to remove your shoes before entering a Japanese home.

Source: This information was provided by Tourism Queensland, <www.qttc.com.au>.

Questions

1. The article details the manner in which business meetings are conducted in some Asian countries. Briefly compare the way business meetings are conducted in Australia with the way they are conducted in the countries described here.

2. Explain the role of the 'go-between' in Asian business meetings. Describe an Australian occasion on which a go-between might be used.

3. a. Why is it important to be sensitive to cultural differences at business meetings or conferences?

   b. In what ways might you offend your hosts if you are not familiar with their customs?

Speaking in public

Chapter 6

In this chapter you will learn how to:

- select relevant information

- organise material

- choose a speaking style appropriate to the situation

- use appropriate language

- express yourself clearly and audibly

- use appropriate nonverbal communication when speaking

- use audiovisiual aids to support the presentation

- deliver an effective presentation

Evaluate your communication skills by completing the self-checks in the chapter.

In the workplace you may sometimes have to speak on a work-related issue to a large group of people. The oral presentations you may be asked to make include introductions, instructions, team briefings, speeches of welcome or congratulation, brief oral reports and formal presentations. Usually such presentations aim to inform, persuade or entertain the audience. To achieve these aims, you need to plan well and present your material confidently.

Planning the presentation

At the planning stage you need to establish the context or setting in which the presentation will be given. Then you are able to design a presentation that is relevant to the specific task and audience. Design the speech to achieve one of three objectives, or a combination of them (Table 6.1).

A speech is designed to inform, entertain or persuade.

Table 6.1 The objectives of public speaking

Objective	Strategies
To inform	An informative speech delivers factual information, clear examples and supporting material. It may also aim to develop ideas, or show how something works or can be done. Balance the content and discussion to achieve an objective presentation.
To persuade	A persuasive speech aims to influence the audience, to change their attitude or convince them about a particular point.
To entertain	An entertaining speech uses a variety of techniques such as humour, anecdotes, examples and quotations, sometimes with a particular theme, so that the audience enjoys it. As a speaker, you may decide to combine informative or persuasive elements with entertainment.

No matter which style of speech you choose – informative, persuasive or entertaining – you must still prepare it so that it is relevant to your audience. In this preparation stage of your presentation, follow these six steps.

1. Define the purpose.
2. Analyse the audience.
3. Consider the context and setting.
4. Identify the main ideas.
5. Research supporting material.
6. Plan and organise the material.

Each step will help you achieve your goal: a confident, well paced delivery that engages and holds the audience's interest.

Define the purpose

Define the speech's purpose. Then develop the presentation to help the listener understand your message. Communicate directly to the audience to catch their attention and interest.

Analyse the audience

Analyse the audience in terms of their experience, age, interest and reason for attending the presentation. It is important to know these details so that you can pitch your

Consider your audience.

presentation to suit your audience's needs, interests and level of knowledge. If you do not prepare these details you may make the mistake of presenting material that is too difficult or too basic, or that entirely misses their needs and interests. It is, of course, easier to talk to a group of people with similar levels of skills or backgrounds than to a diverse group.

Consider the context and setting

Acknowledge the context or situation by preparing and delivering your presentation in a manner appropriate to that situation. The context may be an informal gathering of colleagues or a very formal public presentation. It is important to take it into account.

Take the context into account.

Identify your main purpose

As you plan and organise your material, focus on the main purpose of your speech. As your audience has only one chance to hear you, put your ideas into logical order in a way that is easy to understand. Check that they link together and that they cover everything your audience needs to know. Organise your speech into an outline that both highlights the main ideas and presents them clearly and logically for your audience.

Research

Research and investigation are necessary to find facts, and supporting evidence. Make sure that it presents an objective balance as you develop the ideas in the outline. Chapter 14, Analyse and Present Research Information, discusses this research stage more fully, identifying both primary and secondary sources available to you.

Research from a variety of sources.

Approaches to organising and arranging facts and ideas are discussed more fully in Chapter 15, Organise Workplace Information.

Organise main ideas into a clear and logical outline.

Approaches to public speaking

Several different approaches to speaking in public are possible. The appropriate one depends on the occasion and the purpose of the speech. This chapter discusses six different approaches to public speaking.

1. Prepared speeches
2. Impromptu speeches
3. Manuscript speeches
4. Memorised speeches
5. Briefings
6. Team briefings.

When using any of these approaches, you present your material orally for others to consider. Your intention is to encourage the group to respond in a certain way, so you need to prepare carefully and focus on the purpose of your speech.

The prepared speech

The **prepared speech** is planned and organised before presentation. You will need to prepare an outline and notes to prompt you. If you use the prompts well the delivery will appear spontaneous and relaxed even though you are fully prepared and know what you want to express.

Plan well ahead.

As you prepare your speech, put important ideas, phrases, quotations and statistics in note form. It is not essential to write down every word of the speech unless you are really nervous. To increase spontaneity, try to add some extra comments when you present your speech.

Try not to read the speech word for word – you may lose your place, and reading can bore the audience. If you can speak without reading all the time you can maintain eye contact with your audience, which holds their interest and allows you to note their response to your presentation.

Two of the most useful aids for people making a prepared speech for the first time in public are **overhead transparencies** and **palm** or (cue) **cards**. Outline your main points on the overhead transparencies. This will emphasise them for your audience, and act as a useful prompt for your delivery. Otherwise, you could prepare palm cards with the main points and notes and hold these in the palm of your hand as you deliver the speech. Cue cards and notes keep the outline and main points clearly before you and help you stay on the topic.

The impromptu speech

The **impromptu speech** is unexpected and thus delivered without preparation. Some impromptu speeches are special occasion or courtesy speeches such as welcomes, introductions and acknowledgments.

Think quickly to organise your information.

As this occasion for a speech usually takes you by surprise, it is important to think clearly, analyse the situation quickly and speak briefly and to the point. As you talk, use the following order of presentation.

- Clearly indicate the reason for the speech.
- Explain its relevance to the organisation or audience.
- Conclude with some of the characteristics of the individual or organisation receiving the recognition.

A successful formula used by many speakers for an impromptu speech is the PREP formula.

P stands for the main point
R stands for the reason for the speech
E stands for the example to illustrate the main point
P stands for restating the main point.

A speaker following this formula would start with explaining the main point – for example, their commitment to an environmental issue. Follow with an example to illustrate the main point, involve the audience and add interest. Draw examples from your own experience, a friend's experience or an experience the audience has shared. Alternatively, you may use statistics or a relevant quotation. Conclude by restating the main point in different words. This reinforces the main point and gives your speech strength and continuity. As you follow this formula, both speaker and audience reach the main point quickly.

The manuscript speech

The manuscript speech is read.

The **manuscript speech** is researched and structured, and usually read to the audience. It is suited to longer, more technical and difficult business presentations at meetings or conferences. It is also suitable for legal presentation, a parliamentary address, a press release or a speech that will be reported or quoted.

Even though you are reading the manuscript, look at your audience as often as possible to maintain eye contact. Devices like wide margins, large type and double spacing of the speech help you do this. Never read the entire speech word for word – you want to speak *to* the audience rather than *at* them, and this means using facial expressions and gestures. These are more interesting for your audience than looking at the top of your head as you read.

The memorised speech

The **memorised speech** is suited to short talks. Aim to memorise the ideas and concepts you want to get across without trying to recall every word. To sound relaxed and confident, try to memorise the introduction carefully – this applies to any speech. If you try to memorise a long talk, you may lose your place and panic.

A memorised speech is learned and recalled.

The briefing

A **briefing** is a short oral summary or report of a plan, event or operation. Its aim might be to inform, propose or justify solutions, or persuade your audience. An oral briefing that invites the audience to participate is usually more effective than a long speech. Very few people enjoy sitting for a half-hour or more just listening to one person. For this type of speech:

The briefing is an oral report.

- prepare the briefing, concentrating on its main purpose
- present background information
- discuss alternatives
- analyse their advantages and disadvantages
- outline their impact or outcome
- encourage audience participation, questions and suggestions
- show interest in audience response.

Team briefings

Team briefings are becoming more common. Together, all the team members consider the purpose of their presentation and the nature of the audience. Then the team designs the structure of the presentation and organises it into sections. A particular section is then allocated to each speaker. However, the team aims for a unified and coherent message rather than a series of individual presentations. So it is important to decide which team member will:

The team works together to plan and deliver the briefing.

- present the introduction
- develop the main body of the presentation and provide the supporting details
- reinforce the ideas outlined in the main body and present the conclusion.

Consider also the techniques you will use to tie the ideas together for a total presentation, and the audiovisual aids you will use to support the main ideas. Take care to speak to your audience rather than to the other members of the team. When appropriate, refer to the ideas presented by your team colleagues and link your content to theirs.

As you progress through an individual or team briefing define the main terms and restate the main ideas. Repetition emphasises the main points, helps understanding and reinforces the message.

Briefings and oral reports are most often used for staff meetings, customer contacts, and reports to supervisors and managers on progress, results or problems. Whatever the purpose of your briefing, it is often appropriate to give your audience a short memo or written summary. People are more likely to remember communication that combines both spoken and written forms.

Impromptu speeches and briefings

SKILLS
APPLY

1. Work in groups of six.
   a. Each person writes down two topics for a speech. Choose your favourite subject (e.g. a favourite leisure activity, a pet hate, the impact of newspapers on public opinion) or any other suitable subject.
   b. Shuffle the lists of topics and place them face down. Then each member of the group in turn selects one of the pieces of paper and gives an impromptu 2-minute speech on either of the two topics it contains. As you speak, follow the PREP formula. You might like to take turns by alphabetical order of family name, or by age from oldest to youngest.

2. Next time you attend a briefing at work, observe the person giving the briefing. Describe two ways in which that person could improve each of the following:
   a. content
   b. verbal presentation
   c. nonverbal presentation.

3. In groups of three, prepare and deliver a team briefing to the large group. Assume you are a team of salespeople for CARP, a wholesale distributor of electrical goods. The purpose of your presentation is to introduce the audience, a group of buyers from a retail store, to a new product you would like them to order and sell from their retail store. You may need to emphasise:
   - the product's features
   - the benefits the store gains by purchasing wholesale from your team
   - the benefits of selling the product
   - the advantages that this product has over other products.

   The team's intention is to instruct the audience and show them how to use, demonstrate and sell the electrical goods to the public.

   Evaluate the delivery by using Self-check 6.2, Delivering a Presentation, on page 108.

4. For each of the following occasions, decide whether you would use a prepared, impromptu, manuscript or memorised speech, or a briefing.
   a. instructions for operating a new machine
   b. a parliamentary address
   c. a thank-you for donations
   d. a talk to the National Press Club
   e. the opening address at a prize-giving function
   f. an appeal for aid for flood victims
   g. instructions on using a new forklift
   h. an unexpected toast to a guest at a function.

Preparing the presentation

Follow four steps.

After considering your audience and the context, clearly identifying your main purpose and topics, researching your material and organising it, you must write the speech. There are four steps to complete now.

1. Write the presentation.
2. Rewrite it for the ear.
3. Practise and revise it.
4. Organise the visual aids.

Your aim at this stage is to organise your presentation in a logical sequence and in clear, concise language. While it is important to suit the needs of your audience, you must also prepare the material in a way that suits your own particular needs as a speaker.

Write the presentation

Once you have made an outline of your main points, write the presentation. Each part of it should progress to and clearly connect with the next part. An oral presentation has three main parts.

1. The **introduction** states the topic and catches the audience's attention. It gives the audience a preview of the presentation, so it is important to stimulate their interest at this stage.
2. The **body** develops the theme and supports this with information. The body is the central part of the presentation in which you inform, persuade or entertain the audience.
3. The **conclusion** reinforces and summarises the main points. It is a brief overview that gives listeners a second chance to hear them.

Introduction

The introduction should be brief as it simply prepares the audience for what you are going to say. It leads them into the body of the talk by identifying your aim or main theme. Strategies to use in your introduction are to:

The introduction should stimulate interest.

- pose a question
- use humour appropriate to the audience and topic
- relate a short anecdote
- present an interesting fact.

Body

Acknowledge a typical listener's span of attention by presenting no more than three or four main points. Organise these under headings and subheadings. Emphasise the main points and expand them with supporting material such as:

The body develops the theme.

- personal experiences
- examples and illustrations
- facts
- statistics.

Make the presentation lively and interesting by including your own or other people's experiences. A relevant personal story or example can make all the difference between a dry presentation and a memorable one. Compile or collect examples from friends, business associates, newspapers, television and radio.

Table 6.2 gives examples of techniques you can use to enliven your speech. It indicates the purpose of each technique and the audience's likely response to it.

Be sure to choose appropriate language. When in doubt about the exact meanings of words, use a dictionary. A thesaurus can provide the best word and alternatives. Other reference books such as an encyclopaedia will give factual information, and a dictionary of quotations is useful for making introductions and conclusions more interesting.

Conclusion

To let the audience know you are about to end the talk, use signal phrases such as:

- 'in conclusion'
- 'to summarise'
- 'in closing'.

The conclusion reinforces the main points.

For a long presentation it may be easier to review or summarise each section separately.

Table 6.2 Techniques a speaker can use to enliven a presentation

Technique	Purpose	Audience response
Definition of a term	To sharpen understanding	Clearer understanding
Relating an experience	To arouse interest	Interest
Asking a question	To allow audience to reconsider the speaker's point	Thinking through the answer
Making an announcement	To catch audience's attention	Attending
Offering an explanation	To clarify a point for the audience	Clearer understanding
Presenting different views on the subject	To raise curiosity	Considering alternatives
Making a request	To receive cooperation or funding	Considering own response
Summarising	To reinforce points	Expecting end of talk
Using a visual aid	To illustrate, enhance or support	Better understanding, more interest

The conclusion rounds up the arguments or information you have presented in the main body of the speech. As a rule it contains no new material. It is sometimes the most memorable part of the presentation, and should always make an impact. Use:

- a relevant anecdote
- a quotation
- an example
- a recommendation.

You may also conclude by inviting your audience to take some action, or by challenging them, or by asking for their cooperation or support. Thank them for their interest.

Once you have written the first draft of the speech, practise the speech. You could record it on a tape recorder, then replay it and decide whether it needs rewriting for the ear.

Rewrite for the ear

Writing for the ear prepares the speech as a spoken rather than a written channel of communication. Read your speech aloud and listen for:

- a concise, simple structure that is easy to follow
- verbs in the active voice, with simple tenses
- words that are easy to hear and understand
- words that sound right together
- breathing spaces that give the message impact
- words that help the listener to connect the introduction, body and conclusion.

This technique enables you to refine the speech to suit the live audience who are listening to, not reading, your message.

Practise and revise

Practise and revise your speech by reading it several times to become familiar with your main points. Rewrite anything that sounds awkward. Allow for some audience participation, especially when preparing training sessions, seminars or instructions to staff. Be willing to answer questions from the audience – this creates an active exchange between audience and speaker. Before you begin to speak, indicate whether you will invite questions:

Be ready to answer questions.

■ throughout the talk
■ at certain breaks
■ at the end of the presentation.

An active audience responding to questions or becoming involved in discussions and small group exercises is more likely to remember your talk. This audience will also give you valuable feedback.

At your practice stage, organise visual aids to catch the interest of the audience and reinforce your points. Visual aids are discussed more fully in the next section.

Planning the presentation

SELF CHECK 6.1

Have I	Yes	No	Unsure
decided on the purpose?	☐	☐	☐
analysed the audience?	☐	☐	☐
chosen the most appropriate speaking approach?	☐	☐	☐
researched thoroughly?	☐	☐	☐
listed the main ideas in a logical order?	☐	☐	☐
prepared an introduction?	☐	☐	☐
prepared the main body?	☐	☐	☐
provided supporting ideas?	☐	☐	☐
prepared examples to illustrate the main points?	☐	☐	☐
prepared suitable audiovisual material?	☐	☐	☐
prepared a conclusion?	☐	☐	☐
practised the presentation?	☐	☐	☐

Delivering the speech

When you speak in public there is little opportunity for the two-way give and take of conversation and group discussions, so it is harder for you to establish and maintain a relationship with the audience, and to engage their attention. Therefore, an oral presentation must combine all explanations, information, visual aids, choice of words, vocal qualities, body movement and nonverbal communication in a way that catches the audience's attention and builds rapport. It must also, of course, be relevant.

Establish and maintain a relationship with the audience.

Audiovisual aids in presentations

Visual material is an important kind of signal, and improves any presentation. Since people receive messages in different ways, a delivery with a variety of communication channels makes a stronger impact than a delivery depending only on voice and gestures.

Each audiovisual item should be simple and present only one point, as too much detail can be distracting. Visual aids keep the listener and speaker active, and enhance the learning and understanding process with variety. A good visual aid:

Visual aids keep the listener alert.

■ gains attention
■ increases interest
■ supports your point

- emphasises connections
- clarifies
- aids the listeners' memory
- helps the presenter to arrange the content in a logical order
- keeps the focus on the topic, not the speaker.

Audiovisual aids should add to the message.

Consider carefully before deciding to use **audiovisual aids**. The budget available, the cost of equipment, the time you have to prepare and present, your preference for and ability to use different types of audiovisual equipment will all affect your decision. Any problems with using the equipment may distract the audience, and it is also worth considering how easy it is to carry or arrange.

Nonverbal communication in public speaking

Speaking well requires more than careful planning and preparing. It also involves choosing a verbal and nonverbal communication style that feels natural and appropriate to the presentation.

A confident speaker appears natural and comfortable.

The content of your talk and your physical and vocal behaviour all communicate something. Aim to establish and maintain a confident well paced delivery that sounds natural and looks comfortable. Be yourself and use nonverbal behaviour that matches your words. The first few times you give a business presentation or speech you may feel nervous or suffer stage fright. Experience and good preparation are the best strategies for overcoming this, and further advice is offered in the next section.

A range of **nonverbal behaviours** can modify or change your spoken presentation by repeating, contradicting, substituting, complementing or accenting certain words. Some examples are:

- posture
- facial expressions
- appearance and dress
- hand, arm, shoulder and head gestures
- voice quality
- volume
- articulation
- variation in the rate of speech.

When you speak in public your audience has only one opportunity to take in your message. You must therefore speak clearly and at a suitable pace, and use nonverbal behaviour in a way that helps to convey your message to the audience.

By practising the talk in front of a mirror, with someone listening, or with a video or tape recorder, you can hear what your voice sounds like and observe your nonverbal communication. As you practise you can decide how loudly or softly you want to speak, which parts of your speech to emphasise and where to pause. You can check how long the presentation will take. You can also pick up all the 'you knows', the 'ums' and 'ers', and another listener may help you pick up any errors in pronunciation. You will lose credibility if you use 'gonna' for 'going to' or 'youse' for 'you'.

Practise with your visual material, too, and decide where it is most appropriate in the presentation. Anticipate questions, prepare the answers and keep within the time limit.

Handling anxiety or stage fright

Careful preparation and a practised delivery reduce anxiety.

Anxiety is a normal response to any situation that involves risk. However, even nervousness can be useful if it provides the extra emotional or physical energy necessary to deliver the presentation successfully. If the fear of speaking becomes distressing, it has to be managed.

Deliver a presentation

APPLY SKILLS

1. Working in groups of three, choose one of the following topics. Each person is to prepare a three-minute speech on the topic you have all chosen, but one member must aim to inform the audience, another to persuade, and the third to entertain.
   ■ Why I work
   ■ Too much cricket is not enough
   ■ My favourite television shows
   ■ Sexual equality
   ■ Advertising is part of Western society
   ■ Competition is necessary
   ■ We have too much leisure time
   ■ My favourite music
   ■ Charities are necessary
   ■ The benefits of technology.

   a. As a group, choose the topic and decide who will prepare the informative/persuasive/entertaining speech.
   b. Write your speech outline, and clearly distinguish between its introduction, main body and conclusion. As you prepare, include at least one of the strategies suggested in this chapter for preparing the introduction, body and conclusion.
   c. Prepare a set of palm cards.
   d. Practise your speech in front of the other two members of your group. As observers, they should complete Self-check 6.1, Planning the Presentation, and discuss the checklist once the speaker has finished.
   e. After the discussion, list two ways to improve your nonverbal communication.
   f. Deliver the speeches to the large group. Ask them to identify which of the three speeches is designed to inform, persuade or entertain.

2. Watch a television speech by a politician or public figure.
   a. How did the speaker gain the audience's attention in the introduction?
   b. 'Both meaning and feeling are conveyed by your voice.' Briefly explain this statement and describe how the speaker you watched used their voice.
   c. Comment on the speaker's nonverbal communication.
   d. What strategy did the speaker use to conclude the speech?

3. Assume you work as a supervisor for a large organisation which has recruited 10 new people to start work in clerical positions in a fortnight. You have been asked to conduct the orientation session for the new employees. Your aim is to welcome them, introduce them to the organisation and raise their awareness of their role there. You must also instruct them about their hours of work, working conditions, pay periods and the company's expectations of performance. Invent the necessary details.

   Prepare and deliver a speech for this orientation session.

Thorough preparation and research reduce anxiety and **stage fright**, so make sure that you know the subject well. This will help you feel confident. Thorough preparation also helps you respond to any questions and challenges from the audience. Remind yourself that you have been asked to speak on the topic because of your knowledge and experience.

Check all equipment to make sure that the overhead projector, video player, the electrical outlets, seating arrangements, pens, paper and anything else you might need are available and in working order.

As an exercise to improve breath control, breathe deeply, concentrating on the diaphragm rather than the lungs. Erect posture allows deep breathing (and creates a good impression too). Movement before and during your presentation can ease muscle tension and assist breathing.

Relaxation can help anxiety, and it is worth finding a method you feel comfortable with. For example, some people focus on their positive and competent aspects.

Others choose to breathe deeply. Smile at your audience and someone is likely to smile back. This increases confidence and creates empathy between you and the audience.

Move around during the talk and remember that a visual aid gives you 'something to do' physically. This can help to take away some of the nervousness.

Most people are more critical of their performance than the audience is. An audience appreciates your preparation, knowledge and willingness to address them. The key to overcoming stage fright is to know your subject well, and to practise delivering it. The more opportunities you have to practise, to speak at meetings, to instruct staff or to address a group of clients, the more your confidence and skill will increase. Consider joining a public speaking group, a drama society or a professional association to gain experience, confidence and skills for public speaking.

SELF CHECK 6.2

Delivering a presentation

Did I	Very successfully	Successfully	Unsuccessfully
identify the presentation's purpose?	☐	☐	☐
use language suited to the audience?	☐	☐	☐
use suitable strategies in the introduction, body and conclusion?	☐	☐	☐
show progression and connections between each part of the presentation?	☐	☐	☐
use different forms of suitable support material?	☐	☐	☐
use my voice well?	☐	☐	☐
make eye contact with the audience?	☐	☐	☐
handle any stress or anxiety?	☐	☐	☐
demonstrate confidence?	☐	☐	☐
establish and maintain a relationship with the audience?	☐	☐	☐
finish within the time limit?	☐	☐	☐

WEB WISE

Visit the Companion Website at **www.prenhall.com/dwyer_au**. Choose the Good Practice/Bad Practice activity in Chapter 6 to decide how you would mentor a person who fears public speaking.

Chapter summary

Select relevant information. Your information should suit the context and audience. Decide on the main purpose of the talk, and analyse your audience and context.

Organise material. Careful planning allows you to present your main points clearly. Research your topic and arrange your main points in a logical structure. Prepare an interesting introduction, a body that develops the main points and a stimulating conclusion.

Choose a speaking style appropriate to the situation. The chapter suggests six different approaches to speaking in public. Successful speakers consider the advantages and disadvantages of each one.

Use appropriate language. Consider your audience, their age, interest and reason for being at the presentation. The language should be straightforward and neither too difficult nor too easy.

Express yourself clearly and audibly. A friendly voice and a smile also help to interest your audience. Enthusiasm, humour, gestures and facial expression attract the audience's attention. Vary your tone and speed to avoid a monotonous delivery.

Use appropriate nonverbal communication when speaking. Encourage participation, questions and suggestions, and listen to and acknowledge this feedback. Show your interest nonverbally with a smile, a nod, a hand gesture or by leaning forward.

Use audiovisual aids to support the presentation. Your aim is to reinforce your main points, so choose and illustrate them.

Deliver an effective presentation. As you gain experience and confidence in public speaking, you will need fewer notes and an outline that consists of key words and phrases. You will be able to speak directly to your audience and note their reactions. Your ideas will be relevant and accessible to the audience. By acquiring presentation skills you will improve your confidence and ability to communicate at work and in your personal life.

QUESTIONS

REVIEW

1. a. List six different approaches to public speaking.
   b. Define and briefly explain the difference between an impromptu and a prepared speech.
   c. What is the purpose of a team briefing?
2. What is the PREP formula? Use it to indicate the main points or structure you might use for an impromptu speech on the environment, education for adults, or Christmas holidays.
3. What six steps would you take when planning a presentation?
4. Why is it important to consider your audience? Justify your answer.
5. 'Select relevant information.' Apply this statement to public speaking.
6. 'A speech can be designed in three different ways.' Nominate these three options.
7. What is the role of the introduction? List two strategies you can use to improve it.
8. What is the role of the conclusion? Why do you think it is considered one of the most important sections of a speech?
9. Outline three strategies for reducing stage fright.
10. List two techniques that would provide a focus and maintain attention on the most important point of your speech.
11. List four types of supporting material and, in a few sentences, indicate how it can improve your presentation.
12. a. List three examples of visual or audiovisual aids.
    b. Describe how and why you might use two of these for a presentation.

Speaking in public

This activity will give you practice in planning and delivering an oral presentation. Your audience will be your fellow students. Read through the whole exercise before beginning.

Choose a workplace topic or issue. If you are not employed, choose a topic from one of these three general areas – food, social issues, fashion – or from the specific items listed in Table 6.3.

Table 6.3 Suggested topics or issues

Food	Social issues	Fashion
pasta	pollution	jeans
fast food	parks	designer haircuts
vegetarian food	sunbathing	fads
bread	road speed limits	ear-rings
seafood	pool safety	tweed jackets
takeaway food	tourism	sales

1. Write a memo report (see Chapter 19) on your chosen topic.
2. Research, plan, practise and deliver a 5–8 minute presentation on this topic.
   a. Use Self-check 6.1, Planning a Presentation, to evaluate the plan of your presentation.
   b. Use the audience analysis chart in Table 6.4 to help you decide whether you want to design a speech that:
      ■ informs
      ■ persuades
      ■ entertains
      ■ uses a combination of these.

Table 6.4 helps you analyse your audience so you can plan and prepare a speech that will catch their interest.
   c. Plan the speech. As you plan, consider your audience:
      ■ What do they already know?
      ■ What do they need to know?
      ■ What do they want to know?
   d. Practise the speech with a partner. As you speak, your partner completes Self-check 6.2, Delivering a Presentation. Use this feedback to refine your speech.
   e. Deliver the speech to the large group.

Table 6.4 Audience analysis chart

Name	Age group	Workplace	Interests	Plans for the future
1.				
2.				
3.				
4.				
5.				
6.				
7.				

Key terms

audiovisual aids

body

briefing

conclusion

impromptu speech

introduction

manuscript speech

memorised speech

nonverbal behaviour

overhead transparencies

palm card

prepared speech

stage fright

team briefing

Avoid presentation panic

STUDY
CASE

by Simon Tupman

A good presentation depends on making a good connection with your audience.

Do you get nervous when asked to get up on your feet and say a few words in front of an audience?

Don't worry, you are not alone. It is widely accepted that fear of public speaking comes second only to fear of death. However, your fear is easily overcome if you take the trouble to follow these sound steps.

First, ask yourself 'What am I frightened of?' I bet you are saying to yourself something like 'I want everything to be perfect'; 'I'm frightened I'll be lost for words'; 'I'm wondering if I'll look nervous'; 'What will they think of me?'

Certainly, these are the typical responses I get when teaching people in business how to connect with an audience. If you share similar anxieties, then you need to think differently about the whole concept of presenting. To help you overcome your anxieties, follow these tips and then put them into practice. You will notice a difference.

1. Focus on the audience, not on yourself

Presumably the principal reason for you being asked to present is because you have earned the right to present either through reputation, expertise or simply because it comes with the job. Stop worrying about having to convince an audience about your credibility. Every audience has a minimum threshold of expectation: you know what you are on about and that you will be informative and interesting. You do not have to be funny.

Every audience wants to see a presenter do a good job and can often be embarrassed for the presenter if he or she stumbles. The more you worry about your own performance, the less likely it is that you will have the desired impact. Instead, focus on the audience, not on yourself, and change your thought patterns so that you say to yourself: 'I'm thinking about the audience. I want them to enjoy and remember this presentation, and I know that they will because I'm prepared, I've got something interesting to say and I'm relaxed.'

2. Ask about your audience

When accepting an invitation to speak, find out as much as you can about the audience. For example, who will be in the audience, how many people will be attending, what is the male/female ratio? The more you can build up a mental picture of the audience in advance, the better.

Sometimes it can be a good idea to obtain the names and phone numbers of two or three people who are due to attend and to ring them up in advance and ask them some questions relevant to your speech. Brief yourself about any sensitivities and gauge their expectations about your presentation.

3. Ask about the event

It is important you have as much information about the event surrounding your presentation. Different events present different challenges for a presenter. Speaking to an audience of 500 can be quite different compared to speaking to an audience of just 50.

Find out who else, if anyone, is speaking at the event. If you find you are on the program just after a well known keynote speaker, ask to swap places so that you present first! Find out how much time you have got to give your presentation and make sure you stick absolutely to the time allocated. One of the biggest sins you can commit is to overrun on time.

4. Ask about the venue

This may sound obvious but I have heard of presenters who have dashed off to give a speech without having checked where the venue is and then arrived at the wrong place! Assuming you don't make this obvious mistake, you should try to visit the venue in advance of the day of your presentation. Check out the room, be clear about the layout, and find out what audiovisual requirements will be available on the day. Introduce yourself to the floor manager.

You need to be in total control of your presentation, so plan to set the platform up just as you require. Will you need a lectern or not? Will you require a lapel microphone or a hand-held microphone or none at all? Will you require a flipchart? Will you be using *Powerpoint*? If so, don't assume that the venue will have the necessary equipment.

5. Prepare your presentation

Do not leave it until the last minute to get ready for your speech in the hope that you can 'wing it' on the day. Chances are you will fall flat on your face, have a horribly embarrassing experience and be even more terrified of presenting next time! Do the research for your speech in advance.

Remember it's not just what to say but how to say it that's important.

Imagine you are with guests at the dinner table in your home and you are having to relate the information to them. Be natural, be interesting. If the topic is complex, by all means use notes to guide you, but try to avoid reading your speech. The ultimate insult to any audience is to read your speech if it is transcribed in any handout material. In such a case, why should they waste their time listening to you practise your reading skills?

6. Practise your presentation

Once your presentation is ready, practise it in the way that suits you. I like to prepare alone and mentally rehearse while walking along the beach near my home. Sometimes I rehearse aloud even though other beach walkers might be forgiven for thinking I just escaped from an asylum! However, it works for me and it's amazing how creative you can get when out in the open with nature. Other presenters like to rehearse their presentations in the company of friends or colleagues. Personally, I find this technique artificial, but if it works for you then do it!

7. Eat well in advance

Presenting will stimulate your adrenalin and soak up your energy, and so it is important to have given your body a dose of energy before you present. However, try to have eaten well in advance of your presentation to prevent you from any embarrassing moments! Believe me, it can happen! Try to have some water handy when you are presenting just in case you need it.

8. Introduce yourself to members of the audience before your presentation

One of the reasons presenters get nervous is that they are talking to strangers. It is much easier to present to people you know or have met. I was 21 when asked to give my first best man's speech at a wedding. I hardly knew anybody and I was nervous.

I recall walking from table to table at the reception and asking people if they were having a good time. This enabled me to meet several people on a one-to-one basis and, in so doing, enabled me to bridge the gap between audience and presenter. It is a technique I still use today. It helps me to make eye contact with those people when presenting and creates an impression of confidence. Try it; it will work for you too!

9. Be ready to make some mistakes

Yes that's right. Don't try to give a perfect presentation as I guarantee it will never go as planned. Except the unexpected. Just as TV audience like TV bloopers, presentation audiences can be amused when things go wrong or you make a mistake. But if that happens, don't be flustered. Your ability to take it in your stride will endear you to your audience. You will turn a potential cringe into a laugh.

Remember, you're only human, and your

audience will be forgiving because most of them would hate to be in your shoes anyway!

Source: Simon Tupman, 'Avoid presentation panic,' *Charter*, September 2000, pp. 56–7.

Questions

1. 'Connecting with the audience' is crucial to public speaking.
   a. What are the needs of a typical audience?
   b. Discuss some of the communication tools that will help to establish rapport with the audience.
2. a What are your fears in a public presentation?
   b. Choose some of the ideas from the article and describe how they would help you overcome your fear of speaking in public.
3. Thorough preparation for public presentations is the only guarantee for success. What do you see as the key factors essential to effective public speaking?

Workplace relationships

III

Part

Organise personal work priorities and development

In this chapter you will learn how to:

- prioritise activities

- set goals

- create an action plan

- use a time-management plan

- identify time wasters

- delegate effectively

- monitor use of discretionary and response time

- gather feedback on your work performance

- develop and maintain your competence level

- coordinate professional development.

Evaluate your interpersonal communication skills by completing the self-check in the chapter.

Constant changes in knowledge and technology mean that the skills, knowledge and capabilities that individuals need to perform competently in their workplace are also changing. As well as organising your own work schedule, and monitoring and obtaining feedback on performance, you also need to find the time to undertake career planning and development to maintain the required levels of competence. As you do all this you use time, a valuable but limited resource.

We all have the same amount of time each day, but how effectively we use that time is a matter of choice. We may allow time to control us so that we are pressured by it and achieve most of our workload in a haphazard way, dealing with tasks and people by reacting to them as they become urgent. Alternatively, we can choose to manage our time by establishing priorities, scheduling tasks and eliminating habits that slow down performance.

This latter approach will, of course, give you more control and less stress. Organising and completing your own work schedule will allow you to make time work for you. In organising and managing your own work performance it is useful to be aware of the various sorts of time, the different levels of priority and the strategies available for scheduling time and priorities effectively.

Organise and complete a work schedule

Effective prioritising and scheduling is about getting the most important things done. By giving you time to think and put things into perspective, setting **priorities** enables you to concentrate on important things and to keep trivial matters in perspective.

Decide what must be done by setting work priorities.

Prioritise activities

Prioritising helps you to distinguish between primary, secondary and urgent activities (see Figure 7.1) and to make choices that balance short-term and long-term goals. You are thus able to allocate time to activities in proportion to their real importance.

Figure 7.1 Activities

Type	Description
Primary activities	Primary activities are those that produce the most in results. They *should* be done. They have high priority and should have a considerable amount of effort given to them. Primary activities are the most important elements in your time management and personal planning.
Secondary activities	Secondary activities are the less important or secondary items that *could* be done. They receive lower priority than those that should be done, the primary activities. Some secondary activities may even be put aside until later.
Urgent activities	Remember: urgent matters are not part of your time-management plan. They are the interruptions that *must* be done. They cannot be avoided. When you bunch urgent tasks together and do them in one time slot, you save time.

Primary activities are the important activities in your work schedule. They have a high priority. They should be done but are not urgent, unless you plan badly or postpone them until the last minute. Think about your primary, secondary and urgent activities and distinguish clearly in your own mind those that *should* be done, *could* be done or *must* be done. Make the decision to do the primary activities according to the priorities on your work schedule.

While setting priorities is important, it is not the key to achieving work goals and objectives. The key is a time-management plan which allows you to schedule and complete tasks according to the priorities you set. Time-management plans are presented later in the chapter.

Set goals

A competent person understands work goals and objectives and is able to negotiate with others about the activities needed to achieve these goals. Once these activities are agreed, plans are made in accordance with the organisation's requirements.

Set goals to achieve the intended outcome.

A significant part of your work role is tied up in achieving the goals set by yourself or others. Long-term goals set jointly by managers and their staff are more likely to be accepted and implemented than those imposed on staff from the top down. When you are involved in the planning process, you can see the reason for the plan, its goals and sub-goals and recognise your contribution to it. However, it should be acknowledged that many of the plans that individuals, team leaders and supervisors work with are created by senior management and given to them to follow. In this case, you are told the objectives.

The BSB01 Business Services Training Package (p. 285) identifies the following workplace objectives and organisational requirements. The objectives may relate to:

- sales targets
- reporting deadlines
- production targets
- budgetary targets
- team participation
- team and individual learning goals.

Workplace goals support the organisation's strategic and business plans. An organisation's procedures, processes and requirements must be followed as goals are put into place. Organisational requirements are usually documented in:

- quality assurance or procedures manuals
- goals, objectives, plans, systems and processes
- legal and organisational policies, guidelines and requirements
- business and performance plans
- defined resource parameters
- access and equity principles and practice
- ethical standards
- occupational health and safety policies, procedures and programs
- quality and continuous improvement processes and standards.

As you set goals, keep in mind the workload and prioritise to ensure completion within the identified time frames and organisational requirements. Allow time for contingencies – that is, factors outside your control – that may affect the plan.

Develop SMART goals

Personal or team **goals** give a focus, purpose and direction to activities at work. In setting goals, whether personal or team, it is useful to keep in mind the **SMART formula.** SMART states that effective goals have five characteristics.

SMART goals are specific, measurable, achievable, relevant and time-referenced.

1. Specific
2. Measurable
3. Achievable

4. Relevant

5. Time-referenced.

Specific personal goals set by one person, or *specific team goals* set by co-workers or by management and staff are more likely to succeed. Since they are created in specific, concrete terms, it is possible to see what is to be done, when it is to be done, how and where it is to be done.

Measurable goals are those that can be checked and measured. They allow you to acknowledge achievement of your own personal goals. They also allow team members or management to acknowledge how well the team is progressing towards achievement of the goals. Measurable goals identify performance standards.

Achievable goals are those that can be attained. They can be accomplished effectively within the time you give to the project. Furthermore, they are neither too hard nor too easy. They are challenging and reasonable in that you can implement and complete them to the desired standard.

Relevant goals, whether personal, team or management and staff goals, support your planned long-term results. When achieved, they offer you the satisfaction and pleasure of knowing that the work is purposeful, relevant and necessary to the successful completion of the task.

Time-referencing the goals enables you to check progress against time deadlines. If the steps to accomplish the completed task fall behind schedule it may be necessary to plan again.

A realistic perception of the needs, capabilities and time needed to complete a task is easier to achieve when a time-management plan is created, using goals created and checked against the SMART formula. Further commitment to your personal goals or to the team's goals is encouraged by successful results and a feeling that the project is moving forward.

Complete your goals

With personal goals, the satisfaction comes from self-acknowledgment and recognition of your increasing abilities and skills in organising and completing your work schedules. Focus on one or two goals at a time and allocate enough time to achieve the goal. When you are working with a team, you are able to pool ideas, provide and receive support and develop one another's skills.

For effective results from goal setting, it is essential that management provide the necessary resources at the appropriate times to meet the planned deadlines. Another essential element is creating the action steps or action plans that must be carried out to achieve the goals. *Priorities* are the most important things. Check your goals to ensure they prioritise the most important things.

Goal setting based on the SMART formula helps to reduce or eliminate the digressions and diversions that can creep into a project. When you identify each goal, the standard to be reached and the time in which it is to be accomplished, you can reward yourself or your staff progressively as each goal is effectively reached.

Create an action plan

An action plan identifies the objectives, specific steps and key results.

An **action plan** is different from the time-management plan mentioned above. An action plan is a working document for a specific task or activity. It identifies the steps necessary to complete the activity.

The action plan can be limited to a specific task, such as the action plan to stock the stationery cabinet shown in Figure 7.2, or prepared for a wider task. A more extensive action plan could be a three-month working plan for a large division or department within an organisation.

The effort you put into preparing the plan is more than rewarded by the opportunity to complete clearly identified steps by focusing on the goals or objectives. Time is used well.

The third column in the action plan in Figure 7.2 could also be used as the basis of your progress or completion report. Each of the key results or indicators of performance is clearly identified and they become the headings in your report. In addition, the action plan is available for reflection, comment and variation, when necessary. There are four elements in an action plan:

1. what is to be achieved
2. the expected results, performance criteria and standards
3. the steps and resources to achieve the plan
4. the reporting mechanism to monitor, evaluate and report back on the plan.

Effective action plans are realistic and tangible and identify the deadlines. They enable you to focus on the actions to be taken and identify what is to happen, why and how it is to happen. An example of an action plan designed to stock stationery in a newly established firm is given in Figure 7.2.

A time-management plan and specific action plans provide a model for action or change, as well as motivation to achieve the change – that is, to bridge the gap between what is and what could be. Plans offer a structure within which the management of time

Figure 7.2 Action plan created 25 June: stationery stock

Goal To provide adequate stationery supplies before opening new firm on 19 July		
Objectives and anticipated time of completion	**Activity/step**	**Key result**
1. To stock the stationery cupboard by 19 July	1. Discuss with others their stationery needs. 2. Categorise the types of stationery by the name of available suppliers.	Compile the purchase orders by 28 June.
	3. Request quotes from three different suppliers 4. Telephone the suppliers who have not responded with a quote.	Receive the quotes by 9 July.
	5. Place the order with the most suitable supplier.	Place the order 10 July.
	6. Unpack stationery.	Receive and unpack the goods 18 July.
	7. Check invoices against order form. 8. Let people know their stationery is available.	
2. To create an order form for use by each section within the firm from August	9. Prepare the new order form.	
	10. Send form to printers.	Send form to printers 25 July.
	11. Distribute new form.	Distribute from 30 July.

can change. As a result, poor habits are broken and success in implementing the planned changes in time management takes place.

Use a time-management plan

To get the most important things done, you need to be able to manage time, to identify and organise different types of time, to prioritise and set goals. However, take care to build flexibility into the program so that opportunities can be used rather than ignored because you are overorganised. About 5–10 minutes a day is enough to give to time-management planning.

In addition, you need to use the four D's that take you from the planning stage of time management to the implementation stage:

1. **Discipline** to stay with the daily plan
2. **Dedication** and commitment to the plan
3. **Desire** to work through the time-management plan to accomplish the goals
4. **Delegation** to achieve more through trusting and training, and by communicating goals and task completion to others.

Once you have decided that it is worth changing the way you work and pinpointed what you would like to change to get the best use of your time, you are ready to create a time-management plan.

Create a time-management plan

You can change your management of time by preparing and staying within the guidelines of a **time-management plan**. Create the time-management plan as a personal management system aimed at using your time more effectively and saving time, perhaps up to two to three hours per day. Base the plan on facts and information to show how you use your time. However, as you prepare the plan, take care to avoid following Parkinson's Law, which says that 'Work expands to fill the time available'. If too much time is allocated to a task, people pace themselves to finish the task in that time.

A time-management plan is your personal tool.

A successful time-management plan identifies how time is used and managed. It also identifies what you can control or influence. Create your plan by completing the ten steps in Figure 7.3.

Implement the plan

Review your progress every two to three months. Check that you are keeping to your plan and give yourself the pleasure of acknowledging your success. An effective time-management plan lets you consider and choose between alternatives rather than rigidly defining your activities and type of experiences. Thinking about the alternatives enables you to create composite goals that best suit your needs and meet the requirements of your organisation.

Build definite and realistic goals into the time-management plan. An achievable plan is one that is within your mental and physical ability and acknowledges the opportunities and constraints placed on you or your team by the organisation. Effective time management allows you to work both efficiently and effectively. The subsequent successful achievement of goals is highly rewarding, motivating and satisfying.

Improve your use of time

Time management helps you to use the right strategies and develop the habits that improve the way you use your time. If your present ways of organising and planning are

Figure 7.3 Ten-step plan to effective time management

1. List your goals for the day first thing in the morning or on the afternoon of the previous day.
2. List the activities you will need to complete to achieve each of these goals.
3. Classify the list of activities into primary activities, secondary activities, those that can be delegated and things to do later. Focus on the primary (i.e. most important) activities.
4. Rank the primary activities from high to low priority; list the tasks necessary to achieve these; rank the list of tasks by order of importance and allocate time to each.
5. Create a set of priorities for the less important tasks (i.e. your secondary set of priorities) and list the activities necessary to achieve these tasks in order of importance.
6. Analyse the importance and urgency of the second set of priorities to identify what you must do, should do and will do later.
7. Allocate time on the basis of this analysis and delegate to others tasks that do not need your attention. Check priorities and time allocations against your deadlines.
8. Place your time-management plan on a desk or wall planner and display in a prominent position. This is your time log.
9. Mark off on your time log each completed step. This acknowledges your success in achieving your time-management goals.
10. Present your completed project on or before time.

frustrating your short-term or long-term goals, then make the effort to identify how you use your time and experiment with ways to improve it.

A number of strategies can be used to monitor your use of time. Developing practical strategies requires the skills listed in Figure 7.4. Choose from among these strategies to help you get more done and to complete important activities before you deal with less important tasks. The benefit to you is increased satisfaction and achievement.

Contingencies are unforeseen incidents. They may include technology or equipment breakdowns and occupational health and safety incidents. As you plan, acknowledge any workplace hazards that exist and ensure that your plans minimise the risks associated with them. In some workplaces environmental factors such as weather, noise and temperature can impact on the achievement of your goals and objectives.

Competent workers monitor and adjust their work performance to ensure the quality of their work. They take pride in the quality of their work and in the service they provide to others. They realise time is finite and irreplaceable and use it well to meet organisational requirements.

Identify time wasters

Many **time wasters** are common to most of the population but the causes and solutions lie with each individual. The most effective way to remove the causes of time wasting is

Figure 7.4 Practical strategies

■ Making lists	■ Preparing diaries
■ Sorting tasks into categories	■ Creating action plans
■ Ordering by degree of importance	■ Using response time well
■ Critically evaluating ways of doing things	■ Using discretionary time to think and plan
■ Questioning the reasons for doing things	■ Setting goals

Time wasters are distractions caused by human nature, environmental factors and poor management skills.

to create solutions that suit you. Identifying the cause and finding a solution is easier when you are able to recognise the three main categories of time wasters:

1. human nature
2. environmental factors
3. poor management skills.

Time wasters caused by human nature are personal. Some examples are disorganisation, an inability to say 'no' to requests, a tendency to procrastinate, and an inclination to socialise at the expense of work. Time is also wasted by environmental factors such as telephone interruptions, drop-in visitors, unnecessary mail and paperwork, inefficient meetings and poor workplace procedures.

Another time waster is poor management skills. An inability to establish priorities, set goals or delegate, a tendency to leave work unfinished and a failure to communicate all waste time.

As a consequence of these time wasters, too little time is left to complete tasks, and whatever time is available is filled by excessive amounts of work. Figure 7.5 gives examples of time savers and time wasters.

Time wasters reduce your efficiency and effectiveness.

Time wasters prevent you from achieving your specific goals. By removing the time wasters you will have more time to do the things you want to do.

Delegate effectively

Delegate authority and responsibility for carrying out a task.

Work that can be done by others should be delegated; otherwise, you will be overtaken by the routine details of administration. When you **delegate**, it is essential to do it in a way that effectively communicates your intention and plan to others, and to check progress so that the work is done on or before the deadline you set in your delegation. When both of these are achieved, there is an increased likelihood of a successful result.

Figure 7.5 Time savers and time wasters

Time savers	Time wasters
■ Time-saving technologies	■ Tyranny of the urgent
■ Time-saving products	■ Telephones
■ Having a clear desk	■ Poorly designed work space
■ Keeping a time log	■ Other people
■ Being able to reschedule	■ Going slow
■ Setting priorities	■ Too much pressure
■ Creating objectives	■ Lack of objectives
■ Being prepared to cancel	■ Conflicting demands
■ Completing everything on the list	■ Junk mail
■ Saying 'no'	■ Worrying
■ Combining tasks	■ Handling a piece of paper more than once
■ Having regular breaks	■ Doing instead of delegating
■ Doing it now	■ Doing something else
■ Doing the little tasks	■ Poor filing
■ Using action plans	■ Duplicated effort
■ Having clear lines of communication and authority	■ Lack of cooperation
■ Delegating	■ Confused lines of authority
	■ Indecision and procrastination

Some of the reasons for not delegating are:

- feeling inadequate because you cannot do everything yourself (when you believe you should)
- being afraid the job will take longer if someone else does it
- not knowing how to delegate.

Figure 7.6 offers guidelines for effective delegation.

Figure 7.6 Twelve steps to effective delegation

1. Determine your purpose. Identify the most suitable person.
2. Prepare a clear and coherent message.
3. Choose the most appropriate channel.
4. Select a suitable time and context.
5. Send the message clearly, confidently and courteously.
6. Allow the other person to give feedback and to clarify your instructions as you delegate the task.
7. Provide the necessary resources and training.
8. Establish at the beginning of the project suitable ways to report on progress and a realistic time for completion.
9. Give feedback.
10. Trust the delegate.
11. Follow up and follow through.
12. Acknowledge the completion of the task.

Eliminate unnecessary tasks and delegate to others the work that others can complete, while you get on with your primary tasks. Avoid saying 'yes' to requests or extra tasks when these will only add to an already overloaded work schedule.

Organise and prioritise work

1. Consider and make a list of your priorities for the coming week.
   a.
   b.
   c.
   d.
2. Write a sentence starting with 'I want to . . .' for each of the listed priorities.
3. Rewrite the list in order of importance – that is, rank your primary activites for the week.
   a.
   b.
   c.
   d.
4. Choose one of these primary activities and write a goal for it using the SMART formula. Do you think you can achieve this goal? Give reasons for your answer.

5. Create a list of the most common interruptions at work. Organise the interruptions into two columns: those caused by others and those caused by you.
6. Identify each interruption as an unexpected crisis (U) or a routine interruption (R). Break the routine interruptions into two groups: those that must be handled immediately (I) and those you can handle later (L).
7. Work in pairs to compare lists. In pairs, brainstorm for two minutes to suggest strategies that would control or minimise the number of routine interruptions on one person's list. Discuss the suggestions. Brainstorm again to suggest strategies for the other person's list.

Monitor your work performance

Efficiency is doing things in the right way.

Effectiveness is doing the right things.

The proportion of your time controlled by the boss, the system and you will influence your effectiveness and efficiency in getting the job done. **Effectiveness** is about results. At work, effectiveness is about doing well those things that are most important to you, while **efficiency** is about the *way* in which you get things done. Monitor the effectiveness and efficiency of your work performance.

Meet organisational requirements

Blanchard identified three types of organisational time.

In your workplace, **organisational time** is that time taken up with doing what the organisation expects you to do. An analysis of your **job description** shows where your organisation expects you to invest your time. When you allocate time to the tasks and responsibilities on your job description, you are on the way to meeting the organisation's expectations of you. The same analysis enables you to allocate quality or discretionary time to tasks that allow you to maximise your talents and achievements.

Types of organisational time

Once you identify the nature of tasks, aim to complete them in a way that matches the organisation's needs and objectives, and your needs and objectives. The tasks are completed within the organisation's time. There are three kinds of organisational time within any organisation:

1. boss-imposed time
2. system-imposed time
3. self-imposed time.

As you learn to recognise the three types of time shown in Figure 7.7, you are better able to think about your tasks and plan how you will use time to achieve them.

Figure 7.7 Types of time

Type	Description
Boss-imposed time	Boss-imposed time is hard to minimise or disregard. The boss (supervisor) makes the rules and accepts responsibility for the actions of others in the team, so they need to know what is happening. You must spend time with your boss and time completing the tasks your boss asks you to do. If you dislike what your boss wants, you may have to persuade your boss to accept an alternative.
System-imposed time	System-imposed time is time spent on tasks such as administrative paperwork, meetings and requests from others in the organisation. It involves working and interacting with others who are not your boss – for example, your peers or staff from other units. In some organisations, you may find that too much of your day is consumed by system-imposed time. A poorly organised system, for example, may not offer you sufficient staff to delegate, so your time is wasted on administrative tasks better completed by a clerical assistant. Alternatively, an inadequate Management Information System (MIS) can create too much paperwork with too little clear information and your time is wasted by searching through and filing far too much paper. As both these time wasters are caused by the system, it is difficult for you alone to solve the problem.
Self-imposed time	Self-imposed time is that part of time over which you have control. People who are unable to delegate because they do not know how, or because they are afraid co-workers will be unable to do the task, will use this time to carry out tasks that others might do. Unfortunately, they will find that the response time caused by self, the boss and the system will become too great, moving them from the stress stage to distress and sapping efficiency and effectiveness.

Some time wasters are caused by the boss, others by the system and others by yourself. While you are unable to control the time wasters caused by the boss or the system, you are able to control your own personal time wasters. These should be identified and dealt with. Before you proceed to the next section of the chapter, evaluate your own use of time by completing Self-check 7.1 (page 129). Those areas where you perform unsuccessfully will deserve special attention as you move through the chapter.

Monitor use of discretionary and response time

Discretionary time is the time available to you to think, plan and create ideas. You can use it to do those things that are an integral and rewarding part of your work. Using discretionary time leads to most of the effective results but, as it is only available for about 25% of the time, you must use it to complete your key tasks. As you organise and monitor your work performance, ensure you are using your discretionary time to do the important things.

Discretionary time is under your control.

Response time is when you are available to others for problems, inquiries or complaints. In some respects, it is that part of your time driven by others. A significant part of your personal and work time is response time – when interruptions such as telephone calls occur, co-workers call in for a chat or an unexpected crisis demands attention. Response time, then, is time spent responding to the demands of others. If most of your day and most days of your week are spent responding to these demands, you will have no time for the important activities and will start to feel the effects of stress.

Response time is when a person is available to others.

Your ability to reduce the number of disruptions or protect yourself from them is limited by your organisational skills and your boss's attitude to the need for discretionary time. Another limitation is your co-workers' acceptance of and respect for your use of time. They must be willing to accept your wishes. Aim to develop that respect. In addition, plan procedures for dealing with emergencies such as equipment breakdown. Look at problems that occur, and identify and treat the cause, rather than simply dealing with the symptoms. In this way, you save time in the future.

Solve the cause of the problem.

Create blocks of discretionary time

Monitoring the way you use discretionary time gives you factual information about how you use it. You are then able to plan to minimise the interruptions and disruptions that occur at work. Create a block of discretionary time at that time of day when you perform at your greatest efficiency. Aim to set aside that discretionary time period as private time in which you cannot be interrupted. It follows that you will achieve the high-priority, primary tasks in this block.

Let your co-workers know about your planned unavailability and that you are always unavailable in a certain time slot. The only exception is an emergency. Arrange for telephone calls to be diverted to another line and make appointments for times outside this block of discretionary time.

The level at which you operate in the organisation can help you to create the block of time. A new junior employee is unable to allocate time in this way. The more senior a person, the more power they have, including the opportunity to create a free block of time. This time can also be used to try out new methods and learn new skills.

The capacity to make good use of time and resources is critical.

By monitoring your own work performance well, you are able to maximise your discretionary time. Programming adequate discretionary time will allow you to achieve your primary activities, those of highest priority, first, and deal with the secondary activities later. This rationalisation of your time will reduce stress and enable you to respond to others in a way that is acceptable to you and to them. Personal work performance will reach a high standard and this will be reflected in quality customer service.

Gather feedback on your work performance

Feedback on performance is given in either formal or informal performance appraisals. Feedback may be gathered about your capacity to achieve goals and objectives in work plans. It may be about your capacity to comply with occupational health and safety policies, procedures and programs or to implement access and equity principles in your work practices.

At work we all use work space, the telephone and technology or equipment. We also prepare for meetings and deal with disruptions, interruptions and crises. Gathering feedback on how you do these activities enables you to improve your performance and gain greater satisfaction from your work.

Work from a clear desk

A desk is your work space, not a storage area. Some practical ways to improve the way you use this space are discussed here. Only those items that you use every day should be on your desk. Continually clearing a space on the desk where you can work is time-consuming and distracts you from your primary activities. If there is too much paper on your desk sort it into two piles: to keep and to throw out. File the 'to keep' pile and throw out the other pile.

Label each file and each drawer of the filing cabinet. Prepare a file index and keep it up to date. Working files are those you use frequently and should be the most accessible. Those files used less often are placed in less accessible places. Make it a rule to handle each piece of paper only once: by completing the action (e.g. responding to a memorandum), in the filing of it or throwing it out.

Control the telephone

The decision by another person to call you is outside your control. However, you can have calls screened or diverted for a set period of time or have an answering machine installed. Once you answer the telephone, you can be ready to take down the details of the call and shorten any lengthy calls to the amount of time that suits you. Reflective answers such as 'So you want to meet next week?' move the caller on to the main point. Try to avoid socialising on the telephone in work time.

When you talk on the telephone, adopt a positive attitude. Be willing to answer questions, say 'thank you', be courteous and helpful, and follow through. Before you make a telephone call, have an agenda – that is, decide what you want to say and the action you would like completed. In this way you, as the caller, and your receiver are able to move courteously and easily through to the completion of a call that has every chance of achieving its purpose.

Prepare for meetings

Read the agenda and minutes before you attend a meeting. Before you speak or ask a question, determine your purpose instead of wasting time with irrelevant questions and diversions. If you have an executive role, ensure you are prepared and are able to conduct an effective meeting. Most importantly, if there is no need for the meeting cancel it, rather than waste time on poorly run meetings with no business to complete. Chapter 5, Effective Meetings, discusses meetings more fully.

Avoid procrastination

Procrastination is 'putting things off'. By putting off the important activities because they are too difficult, or because you feel like doing something else, you waste time on unimportant tasks. Break the important tasks into smaller, easier tasks. Create a deadline for the important activities and give yourself a reward when you finish the activity. With unimportant tasks, do only those that must be done.

As you use these strategies monitor your performance and gather feedback from your team leader, mentor, coach or peers. Ask them open questions. The answers provide you with their perception of your work performance.

Positive feedback encourages you to repeat effective work practices. Informative feedback about ineffective work practices gives you the opportunity to make changes and improve your work performance.

Monitor own work performance

Work in small groups.
1. a. Discuss three types of organisational time and name two ways in which employees can improve their use of each type of time.
   b. Which of the three types of organisational time is the most difficult to control?
2. a. Identify six time wasters and six time savers.
   b. What is your greatest time waster?
   c. Discuss ways in which you can eliminate this time waster.
3. Consider your desk or work space. Briefly discuss three different ways in which you could improve this space to save you time.
4. a. Think of a time when a task was delegated to you.
   b. What worked well in the way the task was delegated and what worked badly?
   c. Consider the 12 steps to effective delegation and identify those that would have helped you complete the delegated task.
   d. Why is it important to delegate effectively?
5. Use Self-check 7.1 to evaluate how well you use time.

APPLY SKILLS

How well do you manage your time?

CHECK 7.1

SELF

I am able to:	Very successfully	Successfully	Unsuccessfully
■ achieve my goals.	☐	☐	☐
■ share time between work, leisure and other activities.	☐	☐	☐
■ control the telephone.	☐	☐	☐
■ work from a tidy desk or work space.	☐	☐	☐
■ prepare for meetings.	☐	☐	☐
■ handle disruptions and interruptions.	☐	☐	☐
■ delegate to others.	☐	☐	☐
■ have some uninterrupted time every day.	☐	☐	☐
■ say 'no'.	☐	☐	☐
■ combine tasks.	☐	☐	☐
■ use a diary.	☐	☐	☐
■ set priorities.	☐	☐	☐
■ use a daily work plan.	☐	☐	☐
■ audit my own use of time.	☐	☐	☐
■ avoid feeling stressed.	☐	☐	☐
■ review my goals and plans?	☐	☐	☐

Score

V___   S___   U___

How to score: Very successfully   (V) = 3
                   Successfully   (S) = 2
                   Unsuccessfully   (U) = 1

Total score of V + S + U = _____

Check how you rate as a time manager:

10 Unsatisfactory   30 Very Good
20 Satisfactory   40 Outstanding

Develop and maintain your competence level

To build your own performance and professionalism at work you need to know how to fill any gaps in your work skills. You also need to know how to work well with others. Assess your performance by answering the eight questions in Figure 7.8. (Bold face indicates key competencies.)

Figure 7.8 Eight questions on work skills

> 1. What is expected of me in my job role?
> 2. How do I use the **technology**, equipment and processes?
> 3. How do I **communicate ideas and information**, both formally and informally?
> 4. How do I **collect, analyse and organise information**?
> 5. How do I **plan and organise activities**?
> 6. How do I **solve problems**?
> 7. How do I use **mathematical ideas and techniques**?
> 8. How do I **work with others and in teams**?

Identify your competence against your job description

First, identify what is expected of you by referring to your job description. Cole states:

> The job description specifies the duties, tasks and activities to be performed – that is, what is to be done and, often, the standard to which it is to be done. It should also list the internal and external relationships, responsibilities and accountabilities and any other information that is relevant to the job. (p. 453).

The key duties, tasks and activities to be performed in your job are the primary activities in your job because they produce the most in results and must be done. These are your **technical competencies**. Identifying these clearly will enable you to focus on them and develop and maintain your own level of competence to perform them well.

Technical competencies are the knowledge, skills and attitudes required to perform the duties, tasks and activities in your job.

Access learning and development opportunities

Given the rapid change in knowledge and technology in the 21st century you may have to update your skills to meet the changing requirements of your position. On occasions, you may decide to do this by yourself. At other times, you may take opportunities provided by your workplace in the form of action learning, mentoring or coaching in the workplace. These are discussed in Chapter 8, Develop Teams and Individuals.

You may choose to attend formal courses in Technical and Further Education (TAFE), with private Registered Training Organisations (RTOs), at universities or in-house courses run by your organisation. By participating in professional development activities organised by your workplace you are able to access support from the human resources or training people. The exchange of information with other participants is a useful way to learn and network.

Key competencies

Questions 2–8 in Figure 7.8 are the key competencies (identified in bold). **Key competencies** are generic competencies that apply in all workplaces – communicating, organising, collecting, analysing, planning, problem solving, using mathematical ideas and working with others and in teams. Key competencies describe '. . . capabilities which are commonly used as key selection criteria by employers and which underpin the ability of employees to adapt to technological, organisational, societal and functional change.' (Business Services Australia, p. 137). We all need to develop our capabilities in each of the key competencies to be able to respond and adapt to current and future changes in the workplace.

As you progress from new staff member to experienced staff member and then on to promotion, the standard at which you are expected to perform the key competencies moves through three performance levels. The first level is the level required to manage yourself and undertake activities efficiently and effectively. The second level of performance is that required to undertake and manage tasks and processes. The third level is the level required to make changes, reshape processes and decide how to evaluate the quality of both processes and outcomes in the workplace. So, when you enter the workforce, you are expected to work at level 1. As you progress to more complex and higher-level positions, you are expected to use the competencies identified in questions 2–8 in Figure 7.8 at higher levels. As you progress, you need to access learning opportunities to extend not only your technical competencies but also your key competencies.

Key competencies are required in all workplaces.

Carry out a skills audit

An effective way to identify your development needs is to conduct a skills audit. A **skills audit** identifies what you can do. The audit should focus on measuring your skills against what you are required to do in your position. It shows you where you are in your current position. Performing a skills audit also lets you think about where you might like to be in the future.

A skills audit identifies what you can do.

Identify your development needs

The first step in the audit is to identify the skills that you need. The second is to identify the standard of performance (performance criteria) required in your position. The third is to measure your current level of skill and performance against the standard of performance required in your position. You might also decide to conduct a fourth step – measure your current skills against future requirements. This fourth step gives you an idea of how you might plan your professional development.

A skills audit takes a systematic approach to identifying your skills or competencies. The results of the audit should be recorded and used to create a professional development plan. A simple format for a professional development plan is shown in Figure 7.13 on page 137.

Coordinate professional development

Part of your work role may be to determine the professional development needs of individuals or teams and facilitate their **professional development**. Competency standards identify the level of performance required in the workplace so they are a useful starting point for determining the specific knowledge and skills that are needed. Individual and team development is aligned to workplace needs when learning program goals and outcomes match the performance criteria in a competency standard. The term **professional development** describes the activities we undertake to improve our personal and technical knowledge.

Principals of adult Learning

Collaborate to prepare professional development plans

A professional learning and development plan identifies what the individual/team needs to learn.

Professional development plans identify what the individual or team needs to learn, the intended outcomes and the methods by which the learning will take place. Learning methods should be appropriate to the:

- learning goals
- learning style of participants
- availability of equipment and resources.

Learning methods include off-the-job training, on-the-job training, action learning, coaching, mentoring, problem solving and attendance at seminars and conferences. Some learners prefer distance learning and self-directed study. Others prefer performance appraisals of their work to help in career development and planning.

A professional development plan should be prepared in consultation between individual and supervisor, or team and team leader. The plan will identify the learning goal and outcomes, the learning methods, resources, time frames, how the learning will be assessed and how feedback will be given. Its processes and activities should be non-discriminatory, include activities that provide success and encouragement and be fair and ethical in its approach. Consultation ensures that the ideas of the individual and the team are included and respected. Individuals are acknowledged for their achievements.

Balance individual needs and organisational needs

Match individual professional development plans with the organisation's goals and future directions.

As you take opportunities for improvement and access sources of learning, you need to balance and match your individual needs and the organisation's needs as closely as possible. Examples of organisational and individual needs are shown in Figure 7.9.

Teamwork, learning opportunities and career paths exist within an organisation that supports professional development and learning. Lack of information and teamwork makes it difficult for individuals to develop and maintain their level of competence. Poor management and inadequate preparation for new technology and work practices are barriers that prevent individuals from pursuing career planning and development.

Professional development enables you to acquire the '. . . personal and technical knowledge, skills and attitudes required to effectively and efficiently undertake the day to day tasks and duties of the practitioner's work function' (Business Services Australia, p. 365). By accessing opportunities for improvement and sources of learning you are able to facilitate continuous learning, improve your knowledge and skills and enhance your career development. The initial purpose of professional development may be to bring your expertise to a satisfactory level for effective job performance. As you continue in the job, additional training in the workplace provides opportunities to acquire more skills and knowledge and places you in a better position to qualify for advancement.

Figure 7.9 Individual and organisational needs

Organisational need	Individual needs
New directions	Clear organisational plans and objectives Knowledge of intended outcomes Opportunities to contribute Resources and support from management to pursue new directions
Current goals	Clear organisational goals and objectives Links between the team and other teams Opportunity to contribute to goals Resources and support to achieve goals Power delegated to achieve goals
Empowered teams	Clear team purpose Clear responsibilities and accountabilities Participation in team planning Commitment and cooperation across the team Open communication
Increased productivity	Clear organisational plans Training in new techniques Shared knowledge and skills Flexible working arrangements Teamwork
Quality assurance	Learning and development in quality assurance processes Participation in development of quality assurance systems and internal audits Opportunity to participate in corrective actions Positive communication and feedback about quality assurance processes
New technologies	Skills and knowledge to operate technology in the workplace efficiently and safely Assurances that the technology will not replace them Knowledge of occupational health and safety (OH&S) Safe work practices

Professional development for anyone in the workplace depends on support from management. Management does have responsibility to provide a career path for its employees. Before undertaking professional development you should have a thorough understanding of the organisation's goals and future directions. An awareness of where your organisation is headed and how it will get there enables you to make informed choices. Organisations with equitable policies and procedures market professional development opportunities to all staff. Professional development is managed by the Human Resources Division, manager or training coordinator. Emails to all staff, newsletters, direct mailing and organisation publications are some of the communication methods used to publicise professional development opportunities.

Management has responsibility to support individuals in their professional development.

Coordinate and develop competence

1. Use Figure 7.10 to:
   - establish the overall purpose of your job
   - identify at least four primary activities in the job
   - rank the primary activities in order of importance
   - establish the percentage (%) of time spent on each primary activity.

Figure 7.10 Primary activities performance work sheet

The overall purpose of my job is . . .

In order to . . .

So that I can. . .

Primary activity	Importance	% time currently spent	% time that I should spend

2. Reflect on your prioritising. How much time do you spend on key activities? Could you manage your time more effectively? If so, how?

3. Choose one of the primary activities you identified in Figure 7.10 and write it in column 1 in Figure 7.11. In column 2, identify two or three specific tasks you carry out as you do the primary activity. In column 3, identify the skills you need to perform each task.

4. How would you fill any gaps in your skills and knowledge for this primary activity? (You have just conducted a mini skills audit.)

Figure 7.11 Performance of primary activities

Primary activity	Tasks	Skills

Visit the Companion Website at **www.prenhall.com/dwyer_au**. Choose the Multiple Choice activity in Chapter 7 and answer the questions. How would you describe your capacity to prioritise, set goals and manage time?

Chapter summary

Prioritise activities. Distinguish between primary, secondary and urgent activities as you prioritise activities. Primary activities have high priority. Secondary activities are less important and urgent activities are the interruptions that must be done.

Set goals. Set SMART goals that are specific, measurable, achievable, realistic and time-referenced. Goals provide focus and direction. They may be short term, medium or long term.

Create an action plan. Identify the objectives, specific steps and key results for any task or activity in an action plan. An effective action plan is realistic and describes what has to happen in concrete terms. It should also identify deadlines.

Use a time-management plan. Identify how time is used and managed in a time-management plan. A time-management plan helps you break old habits and control your use of time to get more done. An effective plan identifies what you can control and influence.

Identify time wasters. Differentiate between three causes of time wasters – human nature, environmental factors and poor management skills. Take the time to identify and avoid time wasters and you are able to accomplish your primary activities.

Delegate effectively. Give someone else the authority and responsibility for carrying out a task by delegating. To delegate effectively you must let the other person know what is to be done, why it is to be done, why they have been asked to do it, how to do it and how they will know the task has been completed successfully.

Monitor use of discretionary and response time. Break organisational time into discretionary and response time so you can use each sort of time to accomplish more. Discretionary time is the time available to you to think, plan and create ideas. It gives the most effective results. Response time is when you respond to problems, inquiries or complaints from others. It is time driven by others.

Gather feedback on your performance. Analyse and improve your performance by gathering feedback and taking action on the basis of the feedback. Your job description specifies the duties, tasks and activities to be performed. Focus on these to ensure you are able to do them well.

Develop and maintain your competence level. Conduct a skills audit to identify any of your development needs. Then fill any gaps you identify in your technical and key competencies by undertaking professional development. Continual changes in modern workplaces require competent workers who are able to adapt to new ways of doing things, be multiskilled and work effectively with others. Ensure you are one of these people by accessing formal and informal learning and development opportunities.

Coordinate professional development. Determine the professional development needs of individuals or teams by identifying the specific knowledge and skills and level of performance required in the workplace. Align individual and team development to the competencies required in the workplace. Changing knowledge and technology requires professional development that enables people to stay up to date or ahead of these changes. By coordinating professional development you are able to support people as they access opportunities for improvement, facilitate continuous learning in your organisation and enhance their career development.

REVIEW QUESTIONS

1. a. Define the terms 'primary activities', 'secondary activities' and 'urgent activities'.
   b. Why should you set priorities?
2. What are the five characteristics of SMART goals?
3. a. How is an action plan different from a time-management plan?
   b. What are the four elements of an action plan?
4. a. List the ten steps of a time-management plan.
   b. What are the four D's that help you implement the time-management plan?
5. a. List the three main categories of time wasters.
   b. Name four strategies to deal with time wasters.
6. Why is it important to delegate both authority and responsibility for a task?

7. What are the three kinds of organisational time?
8. What is the difference between discretionary and response time?
9. a. Define the term 'technical competence'.
   b. What are the key competencies?
10. a. How can a skills audit help you develop and maintain your own competence level?
    b. What is the difference between a skills audit and a professional development plan?
11. List three different learning methods appropriate to learning and development in the workplace.
12. Why is it important to balance individual and organisational needs as you take opportunities to improve your competence?

Skills audit and professional development plan

BUILD SKILLS

1. Conduct a skills audit of your current skills. The learning objectives for the first section of this chapter are the skills listed in Figure 7.12, column 1.
2. In column 2, write down the evidence you have to verify your skill to complete the task.
3. In column 3, tick those areas you need to develop further. These are your areas of identified weakness and can be improved by training, mentoring, coaching, practice or other technique.
4. Auditing your skills is the first step in

planning to improve your performance. You have identified some areas you need to develop further. A professional development plan maps out how you will achieve your goal of improved performance in your identified areas. A format for a simple professional development plan is shown in Figure 7.13. Use this plan to show how you will improve the skills you identified as needing further improvement by writing a goal statement and then filling in columns 1, 2, 3 and 4.

Figure 7.12 Skills audit

Skill required	What evidence do I have that I can do that?	Needs further development
Prioritise activities		
Set goals		
Create an action plan		
Use a time-management plan		
Identify time wasters		
Delegate effectively		
Use business technology well		

Figure 7.13 Professional development plan

Goal statement:			
Skills that need further development	**How I will improve the skill**	**By when**	**How I will measure performance against the standard required**

Key terms

action plan
delegate
discretionary time
effectiveness
efficiency
feedback
goals

job description
key competencies
organisational time
primary activities
priorities
professional development
response time

secondary activities
skills audit
SMART formula
technical competencies
time-management plan
time wasters
urgent activities

Wake up to yourself

by Jeremy Bass

What drives you at work? What is it that gets you through the office doors each morning?

Maybe it's the thought of a fat pay packet at the end of the week. Maybe it's a heartfelt sense of useful contribution to the world's wellbeing. Maybe it's a sense of having nowhere better to go, nothing better to do. Probably it's a bit of everything.

Whatever it is, for your employer what counts is that you're getting the work done. And your level of motivation is the crucial factor in making sure that happens.

However you define motivation, it is about more than the instant thrill of hearing some visiting rock-star super-salesman at the Entertainment Centre. And it certainly needs more than a control-freak boss angrily demanding a little more 'positive thinking around here'.

According to Michael Rennie, of the management consultancy McKinsey & Company, motivation is largely concerned with the amorphous notion of 'meaning'.

'A job has to fulfil other needs as well – things like physical safety, intellectual and emotional stimulation,' he says. 'But in maintaining motivation, meaning is arguably the most important.

'To do our job well, we have to be able to answer that critical question, "Why am I doing this?" with something beyond money, intellectual challenge and emotional satisfaction. Meaning encompasses those things, but it extends beyond them.'

Countless people have discovered that money and prestige can get in the way here. Great money, a suitably important title and perks such as travel can make a job look great and feel great for a while.

But there's no shutting up that little voice that keeps saying 'Yeah, but so what' when you're in a job that means nothing beyond those things. Eventually, it will catch up. And when it does, woe betide those who keep trying to ignore it.

'A lot of our clients come to us full of blame and looking for external sources of their dissatisfaction – boss, colleagues, the work, etc,' says Hugh Christie, NSW director with careers consultancy Executive & Professional Register.

'People tend to get in a rut and complain rather than look at themselves or take risks.

'Part of our charter is to tap them on the shoulder and get them to think about their part in their predicament.'

Christie says lack of recognition is one of the major causes of dissatisfaction, much more so than money issues.

'But to many people who complain of it, I'd say "what do you expect?" People's natural modesty about their achievements can hinder their progress. So if you feel people treat you as part of the furniture, maybe it's because you're acting like part of the furniture.

'If you're feeling undervalued, how much are you valuing yourself by staying where you are and grumbling?'

A major demotivator is the notion that the perfect job is out there, says Christie.

'That's illusory, like the search for the perfect partner. In the right frame of mind, people can derive some satisfaction from virtually any job.'

People sometimes need to reassess their skills and adjust their aspirations, he says. 'Under guidance, most find they're aiming too low. But there is the odd one who's getting resentful because he's aiming too high and not getting anywhere.'

Motivation and demotivation can be contagious. Chances are that a control-freak boss demanding more positive thinking is feeling his own motivation threatened by the negativity of others. That's why in some European countries and companies they factor 'fed-up days' into workers' annual leave entitlements. These are days where you can legitimately hit the snooze button, roll over and say, 'Sod off the lot of you.'

And you don't even have to waste energy inventing stomach bug excuses.

'You simply can't stay energetic and excited all the time,' says Alison Rich, psychology services manager with Industrial Psychology Consultants (IPC). 'Life gets in the way.'

In showing people how to psych themselves through the low times, she says, the first step is to find out their driving forces.

'Do they crave credit and recognition from above? Do they fear anger and bad feedback? Do they need a sense of control? Do they want clear evidence of personal or professional development? Do they like variety? How much of their sense of worth do they derive from their work? And so on.

'Then we progress to finding out their working modus operandi. Are they a team player or a sole operator?

'Ultimately, it's about empowering people by getting them to know themselves, understand their needs and expressing those things without fear. People often need to be taught how to play an active role in their own lives.'

Rich says this is where managers need to be creative, especially with those jobs that give little intrinsic fulfilment.

'The idea is to infuse the menial with meaning – for example, by clearly expressing recognition without being patronising, and setting up clear career and development paths and inspiring people down them.'

At senior executive level, people are faced with the problem of keeping external market forces satisfied alongside their own people, says McKinsey's Rennie.

'Workers expect more than ever in the way of entitlements, safety, challenge, job satisfaction and meaning. Employers have translated that into a war for talent.'

The dilemma for executives, he says, has become to keep everyone satisfied on both sides of that divide. 'Plus, they're so often driven by fear of disappointing the market. They simply can't afford to – that's been what's behind the executive obsession with inflating shareholder value at all costs, often to the detriment of internal relations.'

Rennie says this is the big challenge many companies haven't yet begun to address. 'People need to learn that part of running a company rationally is accommodating the irrational, the emotional. It's not hard-nosed versus touchy-feely – it's a matter of integrating the two.'

The use of fear is a double-edged sword. 'A little fear can be used very effectively as a motivator, for example by setting deadlines,' he says. 'But if there's an atmosphere where work is stripped of all meaning, it's one where people dread going in to work each day.'

Source: Jeremy Bass, 'Wake up to yourself', My Career, *Sydney Morning Herald*, 2–3 February 2002, p. 1.

Questions

1. 'People sometimes need to reassess their skills and adjust their aspirations.'
   a. Comment on this statement from the case study.
   b. What role do you take in your professional development?
   c. Describe how setting goals and creating action plans can impact positively on your professional development.
2. The article refers to 'lack of recognition . . . as one of the major causes of job dissatisfaction'.
   a. Comment on this statement and describe how you would like your work performance monitored in the workplace.
   b. What do you see as the main motivators for you in the workplace?
3. a. Why is it important to gather feedback on your performance?
   b. Suggest some strategies you can use to develop your competence as you respond to feedback on your performance.

Develop teams and individuals

Chapter 8

In this chapter you will learn how to:

- establish an appropriate team communication climate

- work effectively with diversity

- analyse five work-team enablers

- identify the stages of work-team development

- distinguish a team's task, maintenance and liaison roles

- distinguish between mentoring and coaching roles

- outline the advantages and disadvantages of team decisions.

Evaluate your communication skills by completing the self-check in the chapter.

Teams are useful in the workplace as they give people an opportunity to work together, and to focus on the team's purpose and the tasks that achieve this purpose. Each individual can make a contribution. The level of contribution depends on a complex interaction between several factors – supportive team communication, members' personal skills, recognition of individual and team efforts, the recognition of diversity and a sense of belonging. The leadership and membership skills of those in a team also significantly affect members' opportunities to make a contribution.

A work team's results are evaluated by considering two aspects. One involves what it does, in terms of production, service or costs. The other involves how it achieves those results, in terms of teamwork, cooperation and initiative. This chapter explains how a team operates to complete its tasks. Communication, involvement and commitment to the team's goals are important parts of that process.

The communication climate

Openness and empathy help members to interact.

At all stages in the development of a team, the communication **climate** reflects the quality of the team's communication. An open supportive team encourages people to offer suggestions and solutions and to be part of the team process. Supportive communication considers both the needs of the receiver and how to solve the problem or complete the task. Supportive communication is genuine, spontaneous and empathetic. It creates a positive communication climate and positive personal relationships in the team.

Interactive communication skills

Working in a team is an interactive process. Consequently, the quality of its members' skills in speaking, offering support and empathy, and responding openly to others is important to the team's performance.

Speaking skills

Team decision making works well when all members actively take part. By sharing ideas people share their knowledge. The exchange of ideas can occur in a spontaneous, brief conversation or in a lengthy, planned and formal speech. People are more likely to make frequent team contributions informally. No single person should monopolise the discussion or control the team interaction as this impedes the exchange of knowledge and ideas.

Two-way communication and an understanding of interactive communication skills help the team adapt to one another's needs as the task is completed. If you fail to consider factors such as feedback and context, the team may misunderstand your intentions and ideas.

Supportive communication

Maintain or enhance self-esteem.

Supportive communication creates a climate of openness, trust, respect and team cohesion. Alternative ways of doing things, criticisms and conflict are accepted and handled in a positive way. Members speak out on issues and test ideas in a way that evaluates the ideas, not the speaker, so that self-esteem is not damaged. Members should be allowed to express their opinions without interruption.

Responding to others

Before you respond to another person, check that you fully understand their point of view. Listen carefully, ask for clarification, and check that others understand your ideas.

Watch for the reactions of others. A willingness to be flexible and to restate your ideas to improve understanding makes it easier for everyone to cope with problems and issues. Another advantage is sharing the success gained by cooperation and flexibility in communicating and making decisions. Be as specific and concise as you can when answering others' questions or comments.

Use listening, attending, reflecting and encouraging skills to increase others' understanding and willingness to contribute. These listening skills are discussed in Chapter 2.

Listen and respond with empathy.

Commitment to the team is one of the outcomes of a positive communication climate. If you do not feel committed or valuable to your team, or you feel unable to change the team, you may be working in a negative communication climate or perhaps creating one yourself. In that case it may be better to leave the team.

Workplace diversity

Work teams should take advantage of the diversity within the team. Diversity is the overall consequence of the individual differences present in the workplace. People may differ in their nationality, gender, intellectual and physical ability, language, experience, race, religion, sexual orientation and work style.

Workplace diversity results in many individual differences.

Work-team leaders should recognise that individual differences exist in the workplace and that these differences can be utilised to benefit both the workplace and the individual. Each person comes to the workplace with their own cultural differences, ideas, attitudes, expectations, educational level, biases and prejudices.

A clear understanding of individual differences helps in the recognition of the benefits of a diverse workforce. Working effectively with diversity can stimulate innovative and creative approaches to using the positive contributions that diverse skills, talents and perspectives can make.

Benefits of workplace diversity

In the workplace, utilising employee diversity can result in such benefits as:

- greater breadth of skill, knowledge, experience and creativity available to provide superior levels of service to internal and external clients
- greater utilisation of staff talents
- greater encouragement of staff to contribute to their full potential
- different approaches to problem solving
- increased productivity and innovation
- diminished conflict and grievance issues
- improved job satisfaction
- improved reputation in the local community

Demonstrating sensitivity

In a diverse workforce the challenge is for everyone to show respect for others. Demonstrating respect for others is achieved by:

Show respect for others.

- treating people with dignity and sensitivity
- considering the needs of others
- accepting individual differences
- respecting cultural differences
- valuing diversity.

Non-discriminatory behaviour

Non-discriminatory behaviour treats all individuals equally.

Non-discriminatory behaviour means that in words and actions all individuals are treated equally. Policies, practices and procedures in the workplace should incorporate systems that promote equity and diversity and eliminate any discriminatory practices.

Equal Opportunity Legislation (EEO) not only requires organisations to promote equity and diversity but also requires individuals, teams and business units to behave in a non-discriminatory manner. Discriminatory practices and harassment can result in distress, distrust, disharmony, inequities, absenteeism, low morale and complaints. Workplaces are legally liable if discriminatory behaviour is proven.

Anti-discrimination legislation, its schedules and regulations, help an organisation to develop guidelines and procedures that enable staff to give standard interpretations and consistent application of services. The diversity of the Australian population provides many challenges to those working in human resource management and industrial relations. People in these positions must work within the legislative framework.

The Australian Commonwealth Government has passed legislation to ensure that there is no discrimination in employment and occupation on the grounds shown in Table 8.1. An organisation that implements EEO, equity and diversity principles encourages better performance and better relationships.

Table 8.1 Illegal grounds for discrimination

Race and colour	Age	National extraction
Parental status	Criminal record	Political opinion
Sex	Sexual preferences	Social origin
Religion	Trade union activities	Physical disability
Medical record	Marital status	Intellectual disability

Culturally aware communication

Cultural diversity impacts on communication.

Choice of words, voice intonation and expressions differ between cultures. There are variations in the approach to time, environment, comfort, personal feelings and motivations. The use of body language and its interpretation can vary between cultures.

Acknowledgment of **cultural diversity** allows oral and written communication to be used effectively. Internal communications such as memoranda, short reports and emails can be used to explain team goals, strategies and progress. Team meetings, coaching and mentoring are examples of internal communication that rely on verbal communication to involve groups and individuals in discussion, problem solving and clarifying issues.

Good communicators use strategies in their oral and written communication to include the individual differences in the workplace. By being culturally aware and behaving with sensitivity, they are able to communicate openly in the workplace.

Workplace diversity

Work in small groups.

1. List some of the differences that exist between individuals.
2. Discuss cultural diversity and describe how it can benefit the workplace.
3. List at least three ways in which respect for cultural diversity is demonstrated.
4. Briefly explain the principles of Equal Employment Opportunity (EEO) legislation.
5. List ten illegal grounds for discrimination.
6. Brainstorm to create a list of reasons for complying with anti-discrimination legislation.
7. What is culturally aware communication?

Work-team development

The terms 'team' and 'group' are frequently used interchangeably, since on many occasions they share almost identical characteristics. However, though a team can always be loosely classified as a group, a group may not conform to the more specific criteria for a **team**, which are as follows.

■ Members operate according to a mandate.
■ They are assigned specific roles.
■ They consider the team is responsible for achieving specified organisation goals.

A work team may form in various ways. The most common kind of team is set up by management. A team may, however, gradually evolve with its own particular structure and behaviours.

Work-team enablers

The organisation, the team and each team member must all communicate with one another to learn what tasks are to be completed at each organisation level by each different team. Cooperative relationships help work teams to develop efficient workplace practices. The five **work-team enablers** are:

Work-team enablers are vital to communication and collaboration.

1. power
2. accountability
3. capability
4. direction
5. transparency.

Each work team must:

■ establish the enablers
■ agree on ways to develop
■ create positive relationships
■ maintain relationships with other teams.

The five work-team enablers shown in Figure 8.1 are the key to developing positive and efficient communication and cooperation within and between teams.

Power

For a team to develop and work well it must have *power*. That power is given by its mandate (reason for being). The team leader and each member must all be clear about

Figure 8.1 Work-team enablers

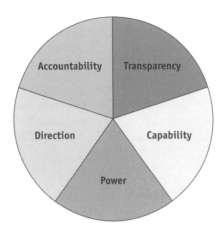

the team's role and their own role. They must also understand the authority held by their team.

The three sources of team power are:

1. *Personal power* held by each team member.
2. *Positional power* delegated by the organisation to the team leader or any other team member.
3. *Situational power* determined by environmental factors and by team interactions.

Any one of these three sources of power can influence the way the work team develops.

Accountability

The term accountability describes the team's responsibilities.

Each work team has a *mandate* – that is, an authorisation, order or contract to perform its particular duties. A mandate, or clear definition of the work team's role and each team member's role, is vital for everyone involved to perform their work tasks, singly and cooperatively.

A team's effectiveness in meeting its accountabilities depends on the quality of the team leader. The more the team respects the leader, and the less a leader has to rely on formal status in the organisation, the better it is for the team. The more organised and well informed the team leader, the better the team will work together. Finally, if the leader has good human relations and communication skills, there is less chance of conflict.

Not only is the team, as a whole unit, accountable: each member is individually accountable. The qualifications, skills and attitudes of each member are central to how well the team performs. If members are underqualified, uninterested or overconcerned with their own objectives, then team discussion and actions will be less productive.

Capability

A team's potential depends greatly on the *capability* of its members – that is, their qualifications, knowledge, skills and attitudes. It also depends on the team's **operating structure**. This is the framework in which individual team members' capabilities are used. The operating structure enables the organisation, its teams and individuals to meet legislative, industry, market, customer, operational and personal requirements. A team needs an operating structure for its collective achievement.

The team's operating structure also affects its functioning and how people feel about belonging to it. Team members who know what is happening and feel confident can contribute to, and influence, the team's outcomes. They are able to work productively through the combination of individual and team capabilities.

Direction

Direction is the line the team works along to reach its goals. Sometimes these goals are simply to complete the team's day-to-day activities. Other goals may be longer-term: for example, changing to new team systems and ways of doing things. If the direction and goals are clear it is easier for the team to complete its activities.

A team with clear direction is more likely to achieve its intended outcomes. A common purpose and direction, and commitment to the team from its members lead to team **cohesion**. In a cohesive team, members obtain a high level of job satisfaction. They feel needed, and will not let other team members down. Communication flows freely between members of such a team and decisions are rapidly acted on.

Transparency

Transparency means that it is easy for all members of a team to understand fully what is happening in the team. Each member can participate and trust the capacity of others to get the job done. With transparency, team members collaborate to achieve the team's goals. Every member has needs – for example, status, friendship or achievement – which they expect the team to meet. Transparency helps individuals to contribute information and ideas clearly, to work towards establishing harmony, and to minimise power struggles and conflict in the team.

Transparency enhances a team's performance.

A team that understands its mandate and has a joint commitment to the task usually has a positive attitude and communication climate. If, on the other hand, there is dissatisfaction, lack of unity and low morale, the climate is negative and the team will inevitably be less efficient.

While the organisation provides the setting, the work team provides the forum where people interact, develop relationships, and take a common approach to tasks and goals. Each team in an organisation is constantly changing, and has a clearly defined life cycle.

Stages in a team's development

As the team forms and gets on with its mandate it moves through several stages of its life cycle and develops its own team structure. This may evolve slowly or quickly. The following discussion deals with the four stages of development identified by Tuckman (1965), and a fifth stage, the adjourning stage. The five stages occur in the following sequence.

1. Forming
2. Storming
3. Norming
4. Performing
5. Adjourning.

While most teams move through all five stages, some may overlap stages or even miss out one or two completely.

The forming stage

The *forming stage* occurs when a team is established and its members begin to interact. At this stage they may be uncertain about the team's membership, leadership and goals.

Interaction
begins.

Great importance may therefore be attached to the team's leaders as members look to them for support, guidance and direction.

Except in the most highly structured team, with clear rules laid down for it, members spend this early stage of team development finding out about each other and determining their status. They also try to establish the real purpose of the team.

When people interact for the first time in a team, differences in operating methods emerge. Some seek information, some give opinions, others like to encourage everyone to participate.

The storming stage

Conflict emerges.

When conflict arises, the team has reached the *storming stage* – the stage where there is conflict and upheaval. This may arise over leadership, goals, the way goals are being achieved, or how individuals perform or feel in the team. Issues of inclusion or exclusion and the individuality of some members can cause conflict. Personal agendas or a lack of commitment to the team's goals also arise in the storming stage.

Hidden conflict may take the form of disagreement or lack of involvement. It jeopardises the team's efficiency. However, conflict that clarifies ideas and is then resolved is a positive force, and allows the team to become more cohesive and reach the next stage.

The norming stage

Team norms or
rules of
behaviour are
established.

As team members interact, similarities and differences emerge. Patterns of behaviour and relationships develop. This is the *norming stage*, when each member starts to feel part of the team: team structure, a common approach and shared goals have emerged. Perhaps a 'pecking order' is established.

Besides relationships, the team must also develop a common approach to tasks. In this stage, goals and the actions and activities necessary to achieve the goals are identified. Team norms – acceptable behaviour, attitudes, work patterns and related behaviour – emerge at this stage. The team becomes cohesive and members learn to tolerate each other's differences. The accomplishment of work goals begins.

The performing stage

Tasks are
accomplished.

Once the team has established its goals, its decision-making methods and its expectations of each member, it can proceed with the task. The *performing stage* has been reached. By this stage, the team's structure and identity are fully formed. The team gets on with the job but strikes a balance by maintaining interpersonal relationships.

The adjourning stage

The team breaks
up.

The *adjourning stage* occurs when the team is restructured, the committee is wound up or the task force dissolved after realising its objectives. Members check the achievement of goals, plan for the future, finalise any outstanding task or relationship matters, and leave the team. Even a team established by a company's management does not last forever.

These five stages form the general pattern of team development. It is not essential for every team to pass through every one of them. Some may bypass certain stages, or pass through two or more (e.g. the norming and performing stages) at the same time. As a team develops, the behaviour of each member changes in response to the activities required at each stage. Team members also need to build the skills these activities require. Table 8.2 describes some of their behaviour at each stage of the team's development.

Table 8.2 Typical behaviour at each stage of a team's development

Stage	Behaviour of members
Forming	• Clarification of goals • Commitment to the team's purpose • Establishment of relationships • Tentative contributions • Communication between members
Storming	• Criticism of team's performance • Presentation of various points of view • Emergence of conflict over power or leadership • Provision of negative and positive feedback • Discussion of problems or concerns • Resolution of conflict
Norming	• Support for other members • Problem solving • Decision making • Improvement of plans • Verification of goals • Development or extension of skills
Performing	• Improvement in ways of doing things • Development of interpersonal relationships • Acceptance of delegated tasks • Involvement in decision making • Achievement of goals
Adjourning	• Movement away from group • Commitment no longer needed • Fading of relationships • Finalisation of tasks as the team disbands

Team members' roles

A **role** is the behaviour that is expected of someone who holds a particular position. Work teams operate with set expectations about how each team member should behave. For example, a leader's roles differ from the roles played by other members. A leader is expected to behave differently from other members (refer to Chapter 9, on leadership).

There are three general roles that help a team achieve its goals.

An individual can take several different roles.

1. Task-related roles
2. Maintenance-related roles
3. Liaison-related roles.

An understanding of these different roles helps to explain some of a team's interactions. Some of the roles are constructive, others are destructive.

Task-related roles involve team members in briefing others, reporting, evaluating their own performance and assessing the performance of others. One of the task-related roles – that of the initiator, for example – starts procedures or finds new ways of tackling a problem.

Task-related roles involve the activities required by the team's specific goals.

Table 8.3 gives seven examples of task-related roles. Team members may assume any of these roles, but an efficient leader will keep control of proceedings and ensure that roles are properly performed.

Table 8.3 Team behaviour: task-related roles

Role	Example
1. The *initiator* starts a procedure, defines problems and organises solutions.	'Why don't we define the problem and then move on from there?'
2. The *information seeker* draws out facts by asking questions.	'As the Safety Officer, Jill, could you tell us about the problem?'
3. The *information giver* (preferably an expert) provides facts.	'The annual report shows that output has decreased by 2%.'
4. The *opinion seeker* asks questions to discover the team's views on a particular topic.	'I'm not sure about that proposal. What do you think about it?'
5. The *opinion giver* offers useful opinions based on personal experience.	'One way to overcome the problem might be . . .'
6. The *clarifier* paraphrases, asks for feedback on a member's comment, and integrates ideas.	'Are you proposing we complete the manuals ourselves rather than ask consultants?'
7. The *summariser* restates the main points and the team's ideas and plans for action.	'So far we have heard from Data Processing, Accounts and Sales. The proposals seem to be . . .'

Maintenance-related roles are concerned with people and their relationships. These roles help to keep the team together so that its tasks can be completed efficiently. Maintenance-related roles include advising and counselling others. Another, the harmoniser role, helps to maintain team relationships by working to avoid conflict and reduce tension. Examples of team-maintenance roles are given in Table 8.4. A team member may assume any of these.

A work team's emotional climate is continually changing, and so the maintenance roles change too. The tasks a team is asked to complete also change. External environmental changes also affect the team. A decision by management – for example, to diversify the company's activities – means that the team will have to complete new tasks.

Liaison-related roles involve team-to-team relationships and collaboration. They are responsible for identifying needs and setting ground rules to meet those needs. Then teams can work together for mutual benefit. Without successful team-to-team relationships, work is much more difficult.

Mentoring

Mentoring is the deliberate pairing of a skilled and experienced person with a less skilled and experienced colleague. The mentor is an encouraging and supportive counsellor who spends time with a less experienced employee, guiding, listening and advising on workplace problems, training needs and ways of working.

Mentoring is wise and supportive counsel.

Mentoring in an organisation is useful in ensuring that teams and individuals achieve competence and work effectively. Mentoring can increase productivity and assist an organisation to achieve its goals and objectives in a cost-effective manner. Mentoring has become an integral part of an organisation's ongoing employee support program since the 1980s when enforced restructuring caused organisations to consider their training options.

The mentoring program can be either formally or informally structured. A formal

Table 8.4 Team behaviour: maintenance roles

Role	Example
1. The *harmoniser* seeks to avoid conflict, reduce tensions and mediate between members.	'Both suggestions are useful, Sue and Carlos. I think we can combine both in our plan.'
2. The *encourager* ensures that each team member participates and gives appropriate recognition to all contributions.	'That's a terrific suggestion. You obviously put a lot of work into it.'
3. The *communication facilitator* ensures that team members communicate well with each other, and that no single member dominates the discussions or activities.	'That's interesting. What do other people think?'
4. The *interpersonal problem solver* ensures that any conflicts that emerge in the team are quickly identified and resolved.	'There appears to be a problem about this. Let's talk about it.'
5. The *standard setter* suggests norms and standards of behaviour.	'I've noticed the team prefers to keep management structure issues out of these meetings. Is this a subject to be avoided?'

mentoring program defines its goals and creates an action plan. It identifies how the results and benefits of the program will be measured and the resources required. An informal mentoring program leaves individuals and their leaders or managers to self-select the areas to include in the mentoring program. It is often impromptu and unplanned. Measuring the results of the informal mentoring program will depend on the mentor and mentoree taking the time to plan and decide on the intended results.

Mentoring skills

To be successful, both mentor and mentoree should be goal-oriented and committed to the mentoring process. Mentors should be willing to pass on their skills and glad to acknowledge a mentoree's work. Mentors need strong interpersonal skills and an interest in working with other people. Effective listening and use of positive nonverbal communication by the mentor build the mentoree's trust in the mentor and confidence in their own ability to learn. Mentorees should be willing and able to learn from their mistakes.

Often it is the leader who mentors a team member and is responsible for their development. The leader acts as a role model. Communication is a critical success factor in the mentoring process. Leaders who can use their interactive communication skills well are able to mentor well and inspire support.

Coaching

Coaching differs from mentoring in that it takes place on the job and assumes that people can learn from everything they do. It is more than simply issuing instructions and telling people what to do. Coaching is being aware of what people need to be able to do, guiding them in how to do it and encouraging them to do it well.

Effective coaches establish rapport and help the other person learn. They ensure there is sufficient time and opportunity for team members to practise and reflect on the skills and knowledge passed on in the coaching process. Table 8.5 lists the different roles of a workplace coach.

Coaches transfer their skills to a less experienced person.

Table 8.5 Roles of a workplace coach

Type of role	Purpose
Guiding role	Assist members gain knowledge about the organisation. Help the member work within the organisation's culture. Identify and support career development opportunities.
Tutoring role	Gain agreement on intended outcomes. Help the member think through a process. Provide intensive one-on-one training. Encourage and supervise as member practises new task.
Training role	Model how to do the activity in the workplace. Demonstrate the task skills. Transfer the underpinning knowledge. Encourage two-way discussion.
Empowering role	Involve members in what needs to be done and how it will be done. Motivate members to deliver enhanced performance. Help members solve their own problems rather than provide all the answers. Show interest in the needs, work and concerns of work-group members.
Counselling role	Build on strengths. Share insights. Work through conflict.
Managing performance role	Consult and set direction. Clarify goals. Support action plans. Acknowledge strengths. Provide support and opportunities to improve performance. Agree to what will be done, how it will be done and by when.
Communicating role	Create a positive communication climate. Offer suggestions. Use empathy. Listen actively. Gain feedback to check learning. Give constructive feedback.

Team groupthink

Groupthink is a term for the situation where no team or group member challenges the rest of the team or wishes to seem out of step with the others. It impairs the team's performance: the team fails to study objectives or research adequately, does not consider alternatives and may take unnecessary risks. Groupthink leads to the selective evaluation of information. Members may tend to look after their own interests rather than those of their organisation.

Teams suffering from groupthink display the following characteristics:

Janis first described the concept of groupthink.

- the illusion of invulnerability
- a tendency to stereotype outsiders
- a readiness to ridicule members if they criticise or put forward new ideas
- a failure to express doubt because of 'self-censorship' and social pressure by other members
- an illusion of internal harmony, maintained by avoiding disagreements.

Groupthink can be avoided if you are aware of it as a potential problem and if you, as either a leader or member, attempt to increase your critical evaluation of alternatives. A team that is able to express opinions, different points of view and new ideas usually has a more encouraging climate than one that suffers groupthink.

Team decision making

The purpose of any team at work is to achieve a **goal** or perhaps several goals. These may be short term and specific, such as planning an advertising campaign for the company, or they may be open-ended and broad, such as the continuing distribution of a company's products by its transport section. How the team's decisions are made and communicated determines the extent to which the team achieves its goals.

Communication affects the quality of decision making.

Ways of making decisions

Work-team members are part of a work unit and also a social unit. They depend on one another to reach objectives and to derive satisfaction from being part of the team. The way in which decisions are made affects the completion of tasks and the relationships between members. Four different ways of making team decisions, and the processes involved, are shown in Table 8.6.

Table 8.6 Ways of making decisions

Method	Process	Outcome
Decision by authority	The decision is made outside the team, or by one member and then communicated to the others. Decision by authority after team discussion is one of the most common ways of making team decisions. The team discusses the issue, then either the leader or even an outside supervisor makes the decision.	This may be the quickest way of reaching a decision, but over the long term it can produce resentment and low morale, and reduce the team's sense of purpose.
Decision by consensus	The decision is made by all team members. Sometimes this approach can be a disguised way of authoritarian decision making or decision by the loudest. Its disadvantages are that this method takes time and well developed communication skills.	Members feel they have contributed to the decision and, therefore, will work towards acting on it, but it is very difficult to get real team consensus.
Decision by majority	Agreement is reached by the majority of team members. This may be the best option if there is insufficient time to reach consensus, or if it is clear that members will not all agree.	A majority decision leaves a minority who may be hostile about it.
Decision by compromise	Made when several members of the team clearly will not agree on anything. The team leader can either make the decision or offer a compromise.	A compromise might appeal to both sides without really satisfying either.

Team interactions

SKILLS
APPLY

1. Assume your organisation wants to create a new office layout that will give each member of staff their own workstation. Ten members of staff will be affected by the changes.

   A task team has been called together to prepare a floor plan and to determine which new furniture and equipment should be purchased. The team's leader, Bryce, is the Assistant Accountant. The members are the Accounts Clerk, Marion, the Marketing Manager, Jenny, and the Human Resource Officer, Tom.

   Jenny does not want to be part of the team because she has a large project to complete within the next two weeks. Bryce is anxious to have the task completed and the purchases made before the end of the month. Marion realises she will have to collect quotes and prepare the orders. Tom wants the workstations to improve staff working conditions.

   a. List five possible stages in the development of the team.
   b. Briefly describe what aspects of the forming and norming stages will affect the team's success. Describe the roles of the team leader and the team members.
   c. Identify any differences between the team members that may cause conflict.
   d. Suggest three different ways in which the task team could communicate with, and present the proposed changes to, the ten people who will be affected by the changes.

2. Briefly explain two differences between task-related roles and team-maintenance roles.

3. The following statements by a team leader are either task-related to help members to focus on the task, or maintenance-related to encourage participation and team unity. Identify each one.
   a. 'That's a good idea, Jenny.'
   b. 'Tom, I think Marion would like to make a point.'
   c. 'Are we agreed on the proposal?'
   d. 'Should we discuss the production issue first?'
   e. 'You sound disappointed with the suggestion.'

Decision-making agenda

Encourage all members to participate in planning.

A useful planning strategy that encourages all members of a team to participate in planning the actions required to complete the tasks is the **decision-making agenda**. This agenda moves through nine stages.

1. *Clarify and establish an agenda.* Clarify the task, problem or issue and encourage members to ask questions to define it.
2. *Establish clear objectives on which to base decisions.* Brainstorm and list as many objectives as possible.
3. *Rank the objectives.* Determine which objectives must be met, which are desirable but not essential, and which need not be met.
4. *Identify the obstacles.* Consider what could prevent the team from reaching the objectives.
5. *Consider all the alternatives.* Brainstorm again at this stage to determine which alternatives will allow the team to reach its essential objectives, and perhaps some of the desirable objectives.
6. *Check the alternatives.* Analyse each alternative again in terms of the musts and wants, so that you are sure which objectives must be met, which are not essential and which need not be met.
7. *Make a tentative decision.* Choose from the alternatives identified.

8. *Test the tentative decision.* Evaluate the chances of success and failure by testing the tentative decision.
9. *Choose the best alternative.*

Efficient decision making

By asking all members to contribute their ideas, a greater range of creative decisions is made possible. Strategies that include all the team will prevent the discussion from being dominated by some members and overcome others' fears that their ideas will be rejected.

Two useful techniques for stimulating ideas are *brainstorming* and the *nominal group technique*. (Both are discussed in Chapter 5, Effective Meetings.) **Brainstorming** allows everyone to participate. It channels their energy into creating new ideas without fear of criticism.

The **nominal group technique** involves team members working alone. It often produces more ideas than brainstorming does, because anonymity can be maintained and the pressure to conform is not as great. There are, however, disadvantages. Members may feel, for example, that their spontaneity is inhibited and that the steps of the technique exert too much control.

Incomplete participation leads to a false consensus.

Team development plan

A team development plan is useful once the team makes a decision. The plan shown in Figure 8.2 organises the task of identifying who will do what, when it will be done and the intended outcome or result.

Advantages and disadvantages of teams

It seems that in many workplaces the inevitable answer to overcoming a problem or completing a new task is to set up a new team or reform an old one. In determining whether a team decision is more appropriate than an individual decision for a particular situation, you need to consider a range of issues.

The advantages a team has over a person working alone will depend on team members' competencies and efficiency. A team can provide and work on more information than one person can. On the other hand, teamwork has some disadvantages (see Table 8.8). However, the disadvantages of teamwork can be minimised and the benefits

Teams offer a wider range of alternatives and opinions.

Figure 8.2 Example of a team development plan

Decision: To _____			
Who	**What**	**When**	**Result**

increased if members (particularly those who lead them) are aware of the methods for improving performance and making decisions.

Table 8.8 Working in teams

Advantages	Disadvantages
■ The quality of the decision making is better.	■ More time may be needed to reach a decision and take action.
■ A wider range of alternatives and opinions is considered.	■ There may be pressure to conform to team norms and attitudes.
■ More attitudes and experiences are shared.	■ There may be resistance to change if the team's culture is negative.
■ A team has a greater capacity to evaluate ambiguous situations and promote unique ideas.	■ A dominant person may influence the team's decision making.
■ Several people are involved, so new ideas are more easily accepted.	■ There is more opportunity for conflict to emerge and continue.
■ A greater sense of involvement produces better morale and motivation.	■ It may be difficult to work out who is responsible for action.

SELF CHECK 8.1

Team communication

As I work in a team, do I:

	Very successfully	Successfully	Unsuccessfully
listen?	☐	☐	☐
give feedback?	☐	☐	☐
ask questions?	☐	☐	☐
present ideas?	☐	☐	☐
influence others?	☐	☐	☐
handle conflict?	☐	☐	☐
recognise the stage of development?	☐	☐	☐
contribute to decisions?	☐	☐	☐

Working with a team

APPLY SKILLS

In teams of five discuss, for about 15 minutes, a topic where a lot of differences of opinion might arise. Choose your own topic or discuss 'Sport is an Essential Part of Society'. As a team try to reach a decision about the topic – you may, perhaps, support or reject it, or reach some other kind of decision.

1. Each person is to perform a task-related role from Table 8.3 and a maintenance-related role from Table 8.4.
2. As you work with the team, observe:

a. how decisions are made (authority, consensus, majority or compromise)
b. how often each person speaks and for how long
c. how differences of opinion are settled
d. how often people listen
e. how task-related roles and maintenance-related roles help or hinder the team.

3. When the teamwork is finished, evaluate your contribution by using Self-check 8.1.

4. Discuss, as a large team, how the use of good communication techniques, such as supportive communication and responding to others, can improve the way a team performs.

5. Define the term 'team performance'.
6. Brainstorm, as a large team, for two minutes to list the communication skills that help team performance.

Visit the Companion Website at **www.prenhall.com/dwyer_au**. Choose the Internet Exercise activity in Chapter 8 to prepare a checklist of the factors that allow supportive relationships to develop within a team.

Chapter summary

Establish an appropriate team communication climate. The organisation provides the setting in which a work team develops. By creating an open and encouraging climate, an organisation promotes the willingness of co-workers to communicate, participate and be involved in achieving its overall targets and objectives. A closed and rigid climate makes this more difficult.

Work effectively with diversity. Leaders should recognise the individual differences that exist in the workplace and make use of them. Sensitivity to and respect for individual differences should be practised. EEO legislation requires all individuals to be treated equally and prohibits discriminatory practices and harassment at the workplace. Acknowledgment of cultural diversity in the workplace allows oral and written communication to be used effectively.

Analyse five work-team enablers. Teams operate with a mandate, have a specified role and are accountable for achieving specified workplace goals. A good work team uses five enablers: power, accountability, capability, direction and transparency.

Identify the stages of work-team development. A team usually moves through five stages of development: forming, storming, norming, performing and adjourning. Sometimes one stage overlaps another, or is missed out.

Distinguish a team's task, maintenance and liaison roles. When people work together, task and maintenance roles emerge. Task roles focus on achieving goals, while maintenance roles encourage the relationships between team members to develop. Each team member's role can vary according to their tasks. Liaison-related roles focus on team-to-team relationships.

Distinguish between mentoring and coaching roles. Mentoring is the deliberate pairing of a skilled and experienced person with a less experienced employee, to guide and advise. A mentoring program can be either formally or informally structured. Coaching occurs on the job and can involve guiding, tutoring, training, empowering and counselling. Communication is a critical success factor in both mentoring and coaching.

Outline the advantages and disadvantages of team decisions. The advantages a team has over people working alone depends on its members' competence. Some of the advantages of the involvement of several people are the consideration of a wider range of options, a greater sense of involvement and more ideas. On the other hand, a team may take longer to make decisions and take action. Team decision making may increase the opportunity for conflict and the difficulty of allocating responsibilities.

REVIEW QUESTIONS

1. a. Define the term 'communication climate'.
   b. List three interpersonal communication skills that affect the communication climate.
   c. What role does supportive communication play in a team?

2. a. Define the term 'workplace diversity'.
   b. How can respect for others be demonstrated?
   c. What measures does Equal Employment Opportunity (EEO) legislation require organisations to implement?
   d. How does cultural diversity impact on communication?

3. What are the three identifiers of a team?

4. a. Define the term 'work-team enabler'.
   b. Describe five work-team enablers.

5. List three sources of power in a team.

6. a. Define the terms 'task-related role' and 'maintenance-related role'.
   b. Give an example of each role.

7. a. List the five stages in the development of a team.
   b. List three things that happen in the forming stage of team development.
   c. List four things that happen in the norming stage.
   d. List four things that happen in the performing stage.
   e. Why do people behave in different ways during different stages of a team's development?

8. In what ways do mentoring and coaching differ?

9. a. What is groupthink?
   b. How does it affect team performance?

10. How can liaison-related roles make a work team's job easier?

11. a. Define the term 'role'.
   b. Name two different types of roles that can develop in a team.

12. List three interpersonal concerns that affect a team.

13. a. Briefly outline four factors that affect team performance.
   b. Name two communication skills that improve team performance.

14. What are three advantages and three disadvantages of teamwork?

15. a. List four different ways to make team decisions.
   b. Which of these do you prefer to use? Why?

16. Briefly explain the difference between brainstorming and the nominal group technique.

17. In teams of three:
   a. Recall either a social or work team you belong to, or have belonged to, and discuss whether individual contributions were valued or not.
   b. How would you describe the team's cohesion and climate?
   c. Which of the four decision-making methods – authority, consensus, majority and compromise – were demonstrated by the team? Give one example.
   d. Discuss how you feel (or felt) working in this team.

18. How would you define a good work team?

Team problem solving and decision making

BUILD SKILLS

The goals of this activity are to:
■ work together as a team
■ consider how the members of your team interact
■ identify your contribution to the team's final product.

Materials required

Two packets of pipe cleaners for each team. Pen and paper for each participant.

Procedure

1. Form teams of six.
2. Choose one person from each team to act as an observer. Follow the instructions in the 'Observer's role' section below.
3. Select a leader for each team.
4. *Task*: Each team is to build a structure from the pipe cleaners. Time allowed: 20 minutes. Then evaluate each structure by four criteria: height, strength, shape and beauty.
5. When the task is finished, each participant rates their work-team experience according to three criteria: satisfaction with the leader, satisfaction with their own participation, and satisfaction with the final product. Record your scores by circling a number on the rating scale below.
6. As a team, calculate the average score of your members for each of the satisfaction criteria on the rating scale.
7. Each team should bring its structure to a display area.
8. Record the average ratings for each team on a chart.
9. Vote, as a large group, for each structure in terms of its height, strength, shape and beauty.
10. In your teams of six, complete the debrief sheet.
11. Discuss how you worked as a team on this task. Consider team-member roles, the factors affecting participation, and how decisions were made.

Observer's role

Your task is to observe the team's behaviour. You do not participate. Position yourself where you can observe every team member.

1. Who was the team's leader?
2. Did anyone else emerge as a natural leader?
3. Describe each team climate.
4. Describe each team member's participation in this task.
5. Describe some team members' behaviour. How did they communicate and participate? Record their names. Then take 10 minutes to discuss your observations with the team. (Remember constructive feedback.)

Rating scale

Satisfaction with the leader

Low	1	2	3	4	5	6	High

Satisfaction with your participation

Low	1	2	3	4	5	6	High

Satisfaction with your team's product

Low	1	2	3	4	5	6	High

Use the scores you record here to calculate the average score of the team members for each of the three satisfaction criteria (step 6).

Debrief sheet

How well did the team plan the structure?

Low	1	2	3	4	5	6	High

To what extent did the team achieve its goals?

Low	1	2	3	4	5	6	High

How well did the team cooperate to achieve the task?

Low	1	2	3	4	5	6	High

How did the team form into members and a leader?
Low   1   2   3   4   5   6   High

How well did the team work together?
Low   1   2   3   4   5   6   High

What did you like most about the activity? _____

_____

_____

What did you like least about the activity? _____

_____

_____

Key terms

brainstorming	groupthink	operating structure
coaching	liaision-related role	role
climate	maintenance-related role	supportive
cohesion	mentoring	communication
cultural diversity	nominal group technique	task-related role
decision-making agenda	non-discriminatory	team
goal	behaviour	work-team enablers

Finding a fresh perspective

CASE STUDY

by Mark Borkowski and Sherif Alaily

Coaching in the business context is not about bringing solutions to the person being coached – that is what consulting entails. Coaching is about accelerating that person's learning. When determining which type of service would help you or your team the most in achieving your goals, being clear about the difference between consultants and coaches is a good place to start.

To help understand the differences between the two, there are questions you must ask yourself. Suppose you have something important to do. The first question is 'Can I delegate or outsource this task to someone else?' If the answer is 'yes', then a consultant (internal or external), an employee or a subcontractor could execute the task.

If the answer is 'no', meaning that *you* have to execute the task, and you are running into obstacles that prevent you

from performing effectively or you want to improve your performance significantly, then you need a coach, not a consultant.

Coaching is about facilitating self-improvement, not in the sense of 'knowing' but in the sense of 'doing', by systematically acquiring the skills and tools to uncover the barriers that stand in your way of performing and achieving your desired results.

Coaching or mentoring?

Successful coaching is determined by whether there is movement towards a desired goal. We undertake coaching because we are 'stuck'. We can be stuck for a number of reasons. For example, we might not take any action because we are frozen by fear, or we could be stuck in a pattern, doing the same thing over and over again but not getting the results we want. Coaching, then, can be defined as setting up structured conversations and learning activities that result in clients performing new actions toward desired goals.

In deciding whether a person needs coaching or mentoring, two questions must be considered:

1. Is the person *executing* a function or process, but not achieving the desired results; or
2. Is the person new to a function or process?

Situations falling under number one need a coach. When the goal is change – that is, the need to do something differently – it is coaching territory. Coaching is real-time; directly concerned with immediate improvement of performance and development of skills. Coaching focuses on how to execute.

Situations falling under number two need a mentor. Mentoring deals with filling a knowledge gap. Chip R. Bell, author of the book *Managers as Mentors*, describes a mentor as 'simply someone who helps someone else learn something the learner would otherwise have learned less well, more slowly, or not all'. He goes on to say that, 'From the junior's point of view, a mentor is someone outside one's usual chain of command who helps me understand the informal system, and offers guidance on how to be successful.'

Why do we need coaches?

We are all creatures of habit and without an outside perspective it is very difficult for us to see our habits and to change them. Thus, there are several reasons for using an outside agent, all of which point to the fact that we can't do it alone – the eye cannot see itself.

We must first become consciously aware of our habits, which by definition are things we do automatically and unconsciously. We then have to confront our habits and find ways to 'unlearn' and let go of them before we replace them with more appropriate ones. This is difficult to do because we have become comfortable with our old habits, and because our brain doesn't have a delete function.

In order to change, we have to learn to perform something new and different, we have to practise, and we need to apply discipline and have the fortitude to stick with it. This discipline is seldom achieved alone, especially in doing things we don't like or

---

How a coach works

A coach can help a person change without telling him or her what to do. An effective coach uses one or more of the following processes:

- **Reflecting:** A coach can help us step back, think through different perspectives, and discover new connections.
- **Giving feedback:** By acting as a mirror, a coach allows us to see that which resides in our blind spot. We all have blind spots and we need others to help us see them.
- **Confronting:** A coach helps us face up to those things we dislike or what we secretly fear. These are the issues that keep us mired in our problem situations.
- **Re-framing:** A coach can help us connect what was previously unconnected. Metaphors, analogies and new definitions are powerful tools used in this activity.
- **Questioning, probing or prompting:** These are the primary tools a coach uses to scan our thoughts and feelings, and focus on the critical variables and contexts. The outcome here is the increased non-judgemental awareness of what *is* – as verified by others – as opposed to what we think something is, or what we would like it to be.

---

that we don't have the natural talent for. Because we can't see our own 'blind spots' we need outside mechanisms – like the rear- and side-view mirrors on a car – to overcome the problem.

It is also difficult to step back and gain perspective in a fast-moving operational environment by standing outside our assumptions, that is, thinking 'outside the box'. The value of coaching lies precisely in the fact that the coach is not you and can see things differently.

In the work environment, we need someone who is not part of the operational team, and therefore does not have a position or agenda to advocate, to help us reflect. Through critical reflection, the learner comes to see the world through a different set of lenses; to re-frame the problem from alternative points of view.

Source: Mark Borkowski & Sherif Alaily, 'Finding a fresh perspective', *CMA Management*, December/January 2002, pp. 12–13. Reprinted with permission of Certified Management Accountants of Canada.

Questions

1. 'Coaching in the business context . . . is about accelerating that person's learning.'

   Discuss this statement and comment on any coaching you have received in the workplace (or elsewhere) and describe the positive outcomes achieved as a result of the coaching.

2. What benefits does a company gain by providing coaches and mentors in the workplace?

3. 'The value of coaching (in the workplace) lies precisely in the fact the coach is not you and can see things differently.'

   a. Describe the main reasons for using a coach.

   b. Comment on the value of a workplace coach to someone who is new to a task.

Lead work teams

In this chapter you will learn how to:

- identify the role of a team leader

- participate in team planning

- develop team commitment and cooperation

- differentiate between types of power

- select different leadership styles

- manage and develop team performance

- identify the communication skills needed to be an effective team leader

- user the RADAR approach to solve problems

- differentiate between task-related and maintenance-related leadership behaviours.

Evaluate your communication skills by completing the self-check in this chapter.

At some stage in your working life you may be called upon to act as a leader, and in that role to exercise leadership. Leadership is the ability to guide, direct and influence others. A leader or manager has the capacity to use interpersonal influence in a way that communicates a need and encourages the actions necessary to fulfil that need.

Leaders and group or team members interact or work together to achieve a team's goals, plans and objectives. It is the leader's task to assist the team to establish its purpose, role, responsibilities and accountabilities. This role demands skills and flexibility.

A readiness to use communication strategies that promote discussion and encourage effective listening and quality feedback will help you to become an effective leader. Using open communication processes to obtain and share information will develop commitment and cooperation within your work group or team. Effective leaders and team members are able to maintain harmony and cohesiveness as they work together to realise the team's objectives.

As a leader you will need to manage and develop the team's performance, using individual team members' knowledge and skills. It is important also to monitor the team's competencies as well as encouraging innovation and initiative to ensure that the team's goals are achieved.

Your leadership style will need to adapt to any changes within the team, the task or the organisational environment. Your needs, the needs of the team and the demands of the situation will vary. They require a leader who is capable of adapting and of communicating effectively.

An effective leader is able to develop plans, provide leadership and supervise the performance of the team. The focus throughout this chapter is on the way a leader can influence team members to achieve the team's goals.

The role of the leader

A leader
influences
others.

A **leader** is defined as a person who has the ability to influence followers in a work group or team in order to achieve predetermined goals. A team is defined here as a group with a charter or specific reason for being.

The role of a leader can be very complex. Its complexity will vary with the size of the team, the tasks facing the team, the length of time the team is together and the expectations of both the organisation or company and the team itself.

A person elected by a committee to be its chair for a meeting will have a different role from a long-term supervisor of a team. The leader of a large public sector organisation will have different problems from an employer leading a workforce of six people.

Whatever the size or complexity of the team, every leader influences the behaviour of team members at work in a positive or negative way, or somewhere in between. As you complete your leadership tasks, the challenge is to try new leadership skills and strategies and to apply those that improve the effectiveness of your team.

Participate in and facilitate the work team

The fact that the leader has influence means that a leader does something to affect the performance of others and to produce **results**. A leader's capacity to influence others – that is, to affect performance and achieve results – is a factor of the leader's aptitude for leadership and their willingness to fulfil and complete a range of activities. A leader participates in and facilitates a work team by:

■ motivating the team
■ organising it

- directing its activities
- coping with unexpected developments
- developing team cohesiveness and the right climate for work
- consulting with others
- counselling members
- ensuring the team achieves the right objectives
- ensuring effective communication within the team and between the team and the rest of the company.

Many of these activities involve workplace interaction and interpersonal communication between the leader and team members. The leader encourages team members to take individual and joint responsibility for their actions. Both leader and team members participate actively in team activities and communication processes. Leadership activities can be grouped into eight different tasks:

A leader completes a range of tasks.

1. developing a vision and setting goals
2. making jobs meaningful
3. giving feedback
4. developing teamwork
5. motivating team members
6. representing and supporting members
7. counselling members
8. providing mentoring and coaching.

Each task requires the leader to develop open communication, effective listening skills and the ability to give and receive feedback. A leader without these abilities finds it difficult to direct, change or influence others because team members are unable to understand where the team is going and what it hopes to achieve.

Developing a vision and setting goals

As a leader you have an impact on the climate and culture in your work team because you have both influence and the scope to achieve results. To be an effective leader you must know how you want things to be. You need a **vision** of what the team is doing and will do in the future. It is not enough, however, to have the vision in your head. You must be able to communicate that vision in a way that is understood and accepted by team members.

A vision must be understood and accepted.

Team members need to see how the vision for their team fits in with the organisation's vision or mission statement. They also need to understand how it relates to them and how their efforts will complement the organisation's vision and contribute to the organisation itself. If you and your team members understand and accept the vision, it is much easier to set goals that will lead to successful team outcomes.

One strategy to achieve a common understanding of the team's purpose is to set **goals** and priorities. When the goals and priorities are clearly established and clarified, each person in the team is able to commit to those goals or at least to accept that the tasks being completed are consistent with the goals.

Set clear goals.

An effective way to set goals is to follow the **SMART approach**. It states that goals should meet the following five characteristics:

1. Specific
2. Measurable
3. Achievable

4. Relevant
5. Timely or time-limited.

SMART goals are discussed more fully in Chapter 7, Organise Personal Work Priorities and Development. As a leader you may prefer to set the goals by yourself or in consultation with members of your team. Before you make the decision, however, it is worth noting that the most effective teams are those where leader's and members' views and priorities are in agreement. A team needs to establish its purpose, roles, responsibilities and accountabilities in accordance with the organisation's goals, plans and objectives.

In setting goals, remember also that both leader and team members need not only to set the goal, but to achieve that goal. Members and leaders need to feel they are noticed and are part of the team. Involvement in goal setting is one way of providing a sense of purpose and a feeling of belonging.

Making jobs meaningful

Achievement and acceptance make tasks more meaningful.

As a leader, you must develop clear lines of communication and ways for people to contribute. Ensure that team members understand their responsibilities and tasks, and acknowledge their contribution to the team's efforts.

Whenever possible, provide variety and challenge for team members. Be willing to adapt jobs to the individual styles of the members, their abilities and willingness to perform. If members demonstrate a lack of knowledge or ability, provide the opportunity for training and development. Empower individuals and the team to take individual and joint responsibility for their actions.

A team is able to achieve its intended results when all members know what they are doing and are able to complete the tasks in a purposeful way. The team can work well together with an integrated and cohesive approach to the task.

Giving feedback

If, as a leader, you acknowledge and give attention to the members of your team – that is, provide **feedback** on their performance – you will develop a team of people who have a sense of belonging to the team.

Sometimes you will provide feedback on successful performance; at other times, you will have to comment on unsuccessful performance. In both cases, useful feedback can be provided by:

■ focusing on behaviour
■ using factual information rather than hearsay or gossip
■ making it timely, that is, close to the event
■ delivering it in an open and appropriate way.

Give relevant and timely feedback.

As your feedback can affect the willingness and ability of the person to work within the team, always make it a rule to give feedback that is relevant and of value to the receiver. Open feedback is given for the right reasons to the right person at the right time in the right way. Recognising accomplishments reinforces behaviour that will lead to satisfactory performance – for example: 'Alison, your immediate contact and follow-up by telephone of the complaint from Ellnet Pty Ltd on late deliveries has led to an increase of 5% in next month's order from Ellnet. Well done'.

An example of feedback on unsatisfactory performance could be: 'A telephone call came through from Ellnet Pty Ltd saying that you did not respond to their telephone complaint about late deliveries. As they are afraid of late deliveries again, next month's order has been cancelled. Alison, this is a sign of poor performance on your part. Is something wrong?' Negative feedback is best given in private.

As you give feedback, avoid focusing on characteristics in the person or behaviours long past that have irritated you. Your immediate task is to reward or discourage the specific behaviour that is causing success or failure right now, rather than 'dumping' onto a team member your past frustrations or more than they can handle at one time. It is also important to avoid hidden agendas such as 'pay-backs'. Effective feedback provides support and motivates team members to participate actively in the team.

Developing teamwork

Teamwork is necessary whenever a leader and team members contribute towards achieving a goal. Both leader and team members have a need for attention and a sense of belonging. Promoting teamwork is a process that involves the leader, the team members and the work environment.

Teamwork depends on trust and cooperation.

As a leader you can ask for help and encourage team members to be involved. You can consider the ideas of others and work with them to implement the ideas. By using open communication processes you are able to assist the team to obtain and share information.

Teamwork develops in a situation where trust, cooperation and compatibility exist between leader and members. As a leader you work with the team to develop mutual concern and camaraderie. Team members must help in this process. So too must the organisation's culture. Where problems exist with the leader, the team members or the work environment, teamwork and efficiency will decrease.

Motivating team members

The capacity to **motivate** is an essential skill for leaders. Most successful team leaders have the ability to motivate people to work towards achieving the team's goals and objectives. Many team leaders rely on formal directions and control to motivate. Others seem to be able to get the most from team members without directly ordering or threatening them.

An organisation's strategic and business plans identify continuous improvement as a key goal. Team leaders are expected to develop and encourage team members to adopt the attitude that things can be done better. Effective team leaders encourage team members to look for improvements. Everyone in the team strives for excellence and works towards achieving the goals in the organisation's business plan. Team members are motivated.

Motivation directs behaviour or actions towards a goal.

Highly motivated team members are usually energetic, enthusiastic, determined and cooperative. They are willing to accept responsibility, continuously improve processes and achieve a high performance. They will also take the initiative to exploit innovative ideas and actions. Team members with poor motivation are apathetic, indifferent, resistant to change and uncooperative. Absenteeism is usually a consequence of poor motivation.

Rewards are another way to develop teamwork. People tend to do things for which they are rewarded and not to do things for which they are not rewarded. It follows then that a leader can use rewards constructively to encourage the desired performance from team members and to increase satisfaction and productivity.

It is important for leaders to reward the desired behaviour with rewards that the team values or desires. This may be formal recognition of the team's efforts in achieving the organisation's goals – for example, a letter of appreciation from management, an article in the organisation's newsletter or a thank-you at the team leaders' meeting. Informal recognition could be 'Well done', 'Great job', a bottle of champagne or a box of chocolates.

For a reward to be effective – that is, to produce the desired behaviour again – the people receiving the reward need to see the connection between their efforts and the reward. Feedback and rewards provide encouragement and recognition for the activities and involvement of both leaders and members.

The approach to workforce motivation often changes as the pressures on leaders cause them to respond to particular situations. Thus, when things are going well, the leader may be relaxed and fairly democratic but, if problems arise, the leader may suddenly become authoritarian and panicky. Inconsistency and unpredictability in a leader can create major problems.

Your ability to motivate well will depend on the way you interact with others, your leadership style and your interpersonal and communication skills.

Representing and supporting team members

A leader is a source of help and guidance.

The leader is the link between the work team and higher management. The leader represents and, at the same time, supports team members. The effective leader must remove potential communication blocks, define tasks and motivate employees to achieve the team's goals. Therefore, part of the leader's task is to be a source of help and guidance. As a leader you should praise, support and be involved with the members. This gives recognition to, and acceptance of, their efforts.

At work both leaders and team members have practical and personal **needs** to satisfy. Practical needs include receiving advice, hearing new ideas, increasing abilities in an area of weakness and getting help when a problem occurs. There are occasions when members need the support of the leader. Members should understand what actions to take and how to proceed in order to have their personal needs heard. Personal needs include feeling valued and respected, being heard and being able to participate.

A leader can support team members by making it possible for them to be involved in problem solving and decision making. Team members should be encouraged to be innovative and take the initiative in implementing new strategies. The ideas and opinions of team members should be sought and action taken on the basis of their ideas once the ideas have been listened to, discussed and agreed to as workable solutions that fit in with the goals and objectives of the team.

To represent and support team members you require a clear understanding of their needs, an ability to let members know what you require from them and a capacity to match the team's activities to the organisation's priorities. Leaders must not only be able to communicate clearly the organisation's needs and expectations – they must also be aware of, and receptive to, employees' needs and be able, on occasion, to present these needs to higher management. By seeing both sides, the leader is able to provide information relevant to organisational and team priorities, to ensure they match, and to provide direction and guidance as the work team moves towards the completion of its goals.

Counselling members

Counsel by listening actively.

Counselling is another important function of the leader. It involves discussing an emotional problem in order to eliminate or reduce the problem, whether caused by frustrations, conflict, stress or other personal matters. One of the most powerful tools when discussing an emotional problem is active listening. The active listening process is discussed in Chapter 2, Interactive Skills: Nonverbal Communication and Listening Skills.

Sometimes, you may wish to help a member of the team understand a personal problem. Rather than acting as counsellor, you may decide to listen and then help the person to link into an agency or other resource that has the skills to help in a purposeful and effective way.

When completing the counselling task the leader provides advice, reassurance, a release for emotional tension, guidance for retraining or refocusing of goals and a link to other agencies or resources.

Providing mentoring and coaching

At times the leader may recommend that a team member be matched with a mentor, or suggest coaching that will further develop the team member's skills and competence. Mentors have workplace skills, knowledge and experience. Mentors look for ways to improve work and encourage continuous improvement and learning. They are willing to adapt to change and are motivated to do the job well. They are good at developing networks and supporting their mentorees.

Mentoring pairs a team member with a more experienced person. Sometimes the leader undertakes this mentoring role. Alternatively, a coach may work with the team member to provide encouragement, guidance and training. The roles of mentoring and coaching are discussed in Chapter 8, Develop Teams and Individuals.

> Mentors are people with knowledge, skills and experience.

Leadership and power

Power is defined as the capacity to influence, the possession of delegated authority or an ability to act. Power thus involves more than personal power; it also involves positional power delegated by the organisation to leaders to get the job done. At least five different types of power can be used by a leader:

> A leader has the power to influence others.

1. legitimate power
2. expertise power
3. reward power
4. coercive power
5. consultative power.

Each type of power or a combination of them is used by leaders. **Legitimate power** is held because the organisation has given power and authority to the position held by the leader. **Expertise power** is held because of the leader's knowledge, aptitude and ability. Others are willing to defer to expertise power.

Reward power is held because the leader has the opportunity, through the control of resources, either to give or withhold things wanted by others. A leader can use reward power well to reinforce effective behaviour or can use it badly to manipulate the behaviour of others. **Coercive power** is held when a leader compels others to behave in certain ways.

A leader who uses reward power or coercive power in a way that deprives members of something they need is likely to lose the ability to influence the team. Members become resentful, do only the minimum to get by, and tell the leader only what the leader wants to hear. Facts are withheld from the leader.

By flattering the leader, particular members may ingratiate themselves. Others may submit and conform to the leader's will, while some may become rebellious and defiant or withdraw in an attempt to escape the leader's abuse of power. Team members may compete with each other for the leader's attention or blame one another when problems arise rather than working towards solutions. Communication barriers develop.

Communication between leaders and team members is more likely to be clear, open and two-way when leaders consult with their team. **Consultative power** is based on a capacity to seek information, consider advice from others and make plans with others. It is based on cooperation and the satisfaction of mutual needs.

Sources of authority

An effective leader uses authority to achieve the intended result.

A leader may be given authority by company management, be elected by other employees or emerge as the person that others in a team allow to take the leadership role. In any one of these situations, an effective leader is able to influence behaviour and achieve results in a way that meets the needs of their team as well as the needs of the organisation.

In the case of an ineffective leader, there is a significant and important gap between the official title and the actual performance of leadership. Neither the needs of the team nor those of the organisation are met. The desired results are not achieved because the leader is unable to perform the leadership tasks well.

Perception of team members

The perception of the leader and team members may vary.

Equally important to your ability to perform leadership tasks and lead effectively are the perceptions of team members or others that you influence as a leader. First, their perception of the type of power you use may differ from your perception. Second, team members' perception of their relationship with you affects your ability to lead. Third, their perception of how much can be achieved in that situation or context affects their willingness to perform and your ability to lead.

What they perceive in the situation in terms of tasks, skills and resources is not always the real situation, but it is their perception and it is the basis for their behaviour. Often it is people's perception of reality rather than reality itself that leads to particular behaviour in the role of leader or member.

Changing roles and responsibilities within an organisation may require you to behave differently as a leader. The ways in which power is used by the leader and the behaviours demonstrated by the leader identify the style of that person's leadership. A number of possible styles have been suggested for leaders.

Leadership tasks

SKILLS
APPLY

1. Think of a successful leader. List six behaviours that you consider have made this person successful.
2. 'Motivation is the key to success.' What does this mean?
3. List three situations in which you have been a leader. What leadership tasks were undertaken to ensure the team's goals were obtained?
4. What interactive and interpersonal skills contribute to being a successful leader?
5. List the five characteristics of the SMART approach to setting goals. Why is it important to set goals and priorities?

6. Effective mentors develop relationships with a mentoree based on honesty, respect and trust. They maintain confidentiality. They focus on the needs of the learner and provide support and feedback in a manner that passes on workplace knowledge, skills, wisdom and experience.
   a. What type/s of power is/are best used by an effective mentor? Give reasons for your answer.
   b. What is the source of authority for a mentor?
   c. Should a mentor represent and support the mentoree? Give reasons for your answer.

Leadership styles

Leadership style is the consistent pattern of behaviour adopted by a leader. Most leaders have a preferred leadership style by which they influence the performance of members of a team. It is not easy to change your leadership style, but leaders who can adapt their style can be effective in a range of situations.

A leader's style can be directive, supportive or in between.

Leadership styles have been the subject of study for many years. On the basis of the findings from these studies, researchers have divided leadership styles into two distinctive sets of behaviour (or a combination of them):

1. directive behaviour
2. supportive behaviour.

In a leadership situation you have the choice of using either one of these or a combination.

Leadership styles can be further divided into three general categories:

1. authoritarian
2. participative
3. laissez-faire.

No one style of leadership is the most effective. Each style has advantages and disadvantages. But if you have the capacity and willingness to use a range of leadership styles, you will be able to adapt your style to respond to different situations.

Authoritarian leaders

Authoritarian leaders determine the policies and work of the team with little discussion or input from team members. They direct others from above. The authoritarian leader assumes all the power, holds key information and maintains overall control of what goes on in the team. Team members are informed, and report back to the leader. An authoritarian leader makes and announces the decisions and accepts total responsibility for implementing and enforcing policy and rules.

Authoritarian leaders direct others.

Communication in a team that is dominated by an authoritarian leader is usually one-way between leader and team. Two-way communication, from the leader to members and from members to the leader, is limited to immediate tasks. An authoritarian leader usually makes decisions that are task-oriented and in the interests of the organisation ahead of the interests of the leader or the team.

While authoritarian leaders may save time and avoid some of the problems of democratically run teams, they may also find poor team motivation, few ideas and team members who only work to the rules. Authoritarian leaders may find that the lack of communication means that team members live in a world of crisis, and the leaders do not know what is happening in the section, committee or company they run.

Participative leaders

Participative leaders encourage members of the team to take an active role in decision making within the organisation. These leaders delegate authority, encourage feedback, discuss objectives and provide the chance for members to satisfy their esteem and self-actualisation needs. The team is part of the decision-making process. A two-way exchange of information flows from leader to members and from members to the leader, and between members themselves. A number of communication channels are used and

Participative leaders share decision making.

greater emphasis is placed by the participative leader on regular meetings and one-to-one discussion with team members.

The participative leader manages others but asks for ideas and suggestions. An effective participative leader delegates tasks and decision making because members have the skills and are willing to become involved in organising their own work. As team members become more involved, the leader moves from concentrating on management and decision making to promoting teamwork, supporting members and cooperating with them. The participative leader often directs from the centre and delegates some of the leadership tasks to team members.

Figure 9.1 Leadership styles

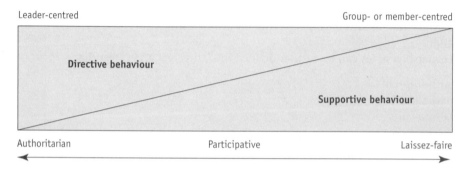

Leader-centred   Group- or member-centred

Directive behaviour

Supportive behaviour

Authoritarian   Participative   Laissez-faire

Laissez-faire leaders

Laissez-faire leaders let others direct their own activities.

The **laissez-faire** or permissive leadership style is at the other end of the leadership spectrum from the authoritarian leader. The laissez-faire leader has a policy of non-interference. This leadership style allows the team to run itself.

While there may be some specialised and highly motivated teams that operate well with laissez-faire leadership, generally the lack of unity and direction in a permissively led team will soon be obvious. Other people in the team will emerge as leaders and all the problems that occur in a work environment where there is no clear leadership will appear – unless the team has the skill to operate as a self-managed team.

Communication between leader and members in a laissez-faire team can be either unclear, limited and lacking direction, or clear, effective and purposeful. When it is unclear and limited, it causes frustration and poor performance as people are unsure where they fit in the team and, consequently, their input may be limited. When a laissez-faire leader is effective, communication flows well between leader and members, and between members themselves. It is clear and purposeful. Members have a sense of belonging to the team and a clear direction.

An effective laissez-faire leader may coach and support the members. The members are expected to make decisions while the leader coordinates and supports their activities. As a result, members are more involved and are able to see the reasons for what happens at work and the way in which things happen. In contrast, laissez-faire leaders who simply delegate and remove themselves from any responsibility for coaching, supporting or taking part in decision making are ineffective. Members may feel resentful that they are expected to take so much responsibility.

Choose from a number of leadership styles.

Figure 9.2 shows the flow of communication between the leader and team members for authoritarian, participative and laissez-faire leadership styles. There is no one best way to lead – a leader with any of these styles can be an effective leader. However, the ability to communicate with others is the common factor demonstrated by any effective leader in any style of leadership.

When effective interpersonal communication and an appropriate leadership style is used, there is every chance of achieving the intended result. At times, leaders will need to modify their behaviour to suit the tasks, situation or people they are working with. In

Figure 9.2 Leadership styles and the flow of communication

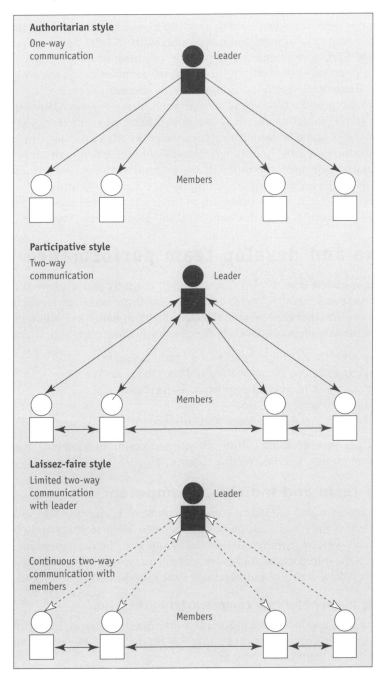

other words, leaders may choose to use any of the above leadership styles rather than just their preferred leadership style. As a leader, if you can use a variety of styles suited to the needs of team members and different situations, you have a variety of ways in which to tackle the complex task of leadership.

By either directing or consulting others, a leader establishes a course of action, commits to that course of action and allocates the necessary resources. In addition, leaders use their skills in interpersonal communication to motivate and guide team members to implement the plan.

A leader who is comfortable letting others take responsibility for part or all of the project can empower team members by creating a sense of ownership in the project or task. Effective leaders also need communication skills to offer help without removing responsibility from team members, to provide coaching when necessary and to help clarify ideas, directions and expectations. In return, members need to be willing and able to take part if the sharing of responsibility is to be successful.

It is unusual to find a completely authoritarian leader or laissez-faire leader. Leadership styles tend to fall somewhere between these two extremes. Many leaders deliberately use a range of leadership styles suited to the particular situation. Others have a style which is probably not even thought out and which varies according to the situation and perhaps even the mood of the leader. Figure 9.1 presents a summary of the emphasis placed on different leadership styles in the 21st century.

Whichever style of leadership is used, as the result of either a conscious or unconscious choice, it affects team performance and the motivation of members.

Manage and develop team performance

Effective team leaders have a team that can achieve results that support and contribute to the organisation's business plans. They monitor team and individual competencies regularly to confirm that the team has the capability and hence the willingness and confidence to achieve team goals. Modern organisations expect their team leaders to:

- contribute positively to the organisation's business plans
- encourage the team to be innovative and take the initiative
- monitor team and individual competencies regularly
- ensure the team achieves its goals
- encourage team members to share and enhance their knowledge and skills.

Teams with a positive learning culture are more successful in achieving goals and individual or team targets. They are willing to learn.

Monitor team and individual competencies

A skills gap exists when there is a difference between what an individual/team can do and what they are required to do.

By monitoring team and individual competencies team leaders are able to identify any skills gaps. When there is a skills gap, team members need to share and enhance their knowledge and skills by training, coaching or mentoring. The need may arise from a performance gap, the introduction of a new procedure, the need to comply with new statutory requirements such as a change in legislation or the introduction of new technology.

Identifying the need for new competencies in the team

Identifying a skills gap involves a process of asking questions, receiving answers and verifying that training, coaching or mentoring will fill the gap. Some of the methods used by team leaders to identify the need are:

- observation of performance
- skills audits
- surveys and questionnaires
- performance reports
- interviews.

Individuals in the team may identify their own level of competence and their training, coaching or mentoring needs by self-assessing their knowledge and skills against a performance checklist such as Self-check 9.1 in this chapter.

Facilitate task and maintenance behaviours

Effective leaders are skilled in the tasks that need to be achieved, and in the interpersonal skills needed to convey the requisite messages to complete the tasks and maintain the team. They lead the team towards the attainment of goals and help in the process that leads to completion of these goals. An effective leader participates in and facilitates the work team.

Leaders who are aware of the communication process recognise the seven elements involved and are able to understand where, in the process, communication is going well and where communication barriers occur (see Chapter 1, How Communication Works). They recognise the different forms of communication (verbal, nonverbal and graphic) and know how to use them appropriately. For example, if you wanted to increase customer service, would you discuss the issues with staff, write a newsletter, use the noticeboard or email, or a combination of all of these?

Effective interpersonal skills help convey the message.

Differentiate between task and maintenance functions

As a leader, your role is to manage the team, communicate ideas, facilitate work and show how the task completed by the team contributes to the organisation. The leader also encourages individuals and the team to take responsibility for their actions. Hence, when leaders and members are working together in a team to complete a particular task, they perform two basic functions (see Figure 9.3):

1. task-related functions
2. maintenance-related functions.

Task-related functions or behaviours focus on the task to be achieved, the problem to be solved or the purpose of the meeting. Designing a new product, planning an advertising campaign or hiring new staff are all task-related functions that aim to get the task done.

Task-related functions focus on the output.

Maintenance-related functions focus on what is happening in the team, the way members listen and relate to each other and the behaviour developments within the team. Many of the task and maintenance functions should be performed by the team leader, although other members in the team can also perform them. Thus, leaders of teams should be able to distinguish between task-related and maintenance-related

Maintenance-related functions focus on relationships.

Figure 9.3 Examples of task-related and maintenance-related behaviour by a leader

Task-related behaviour	Maintenance-related behaviour
Setting goals	Communicating
Planning and organising	Providing feedback
Controlling	Supporting
Directing	Interacting
Meeting deadlines	Listening

functions and be able to use them. These functions are discussed in Chapter 8, Develop Teams and Individuals, pages 149–150.

The most effective leader of team discussions and activities is one who ensures that there is good use of task-related functions and also confirms that maintenance-related functions are carried out in the team. The problem is to ensure that they are used at the right time and in the right way. Thus, the leader has to balance the task-related functions (which include questioning and seeking opinions) with maintaining harmony and good morale in the team.

The key to good team leadership is good communication. This is not just the ability to let the team know what the leader wants, but includes listening skills and the ability to ensure the goals of the team are met with the maximum contribution from everyone in the team.

Communicate to solve problems

A leader who facilitates the work team is able to work with the team to solve problems by devolving responsibility and accountability for problem solving to the team and gaining their commitment. The leader will ensure specific goals to solve the problem are set and monitor and assess the team's performance. This process not only solves the problem. It also facilitates team development and improvement.

RADAR five-step approach

When, as leader, you need to discuss practical problems and turn ideas into actions, try using the **RADAR** five-step approach to effective two-way communication:

1. Request that the other person identifies the what and why of the problem or situation.
2. Ask for the details.
3. Develop ideas.
4. Agree on the actions to be taken.
5. Review the main points and decide how to follow up.

In a continuing team, leaders and members become used to one another's communication styles. A leader's predominant or preferred style may be either task- or people-oriented. The leadership style you prefer will determine the amount of effort you put into task-related and maintenance-related functions.

Leadership styles

APPLY SKILLS

1. Name two differences between an authoritarian and a laissez-faire leader.
2. In small teams, select a leader and role-play the following situation:

   Your organisation has recently joined forces with another technology company. The new company needs to change its name and logo and advertise these changes to the public. The Managing Director has asked the team to produce a marketable name, logo design and advertising campaign.

   After the role play, briefly discuss the leadership style adopted to achieve the team's goal. Use Self-check 9.1 to evaluate the team leader's skills.
3. What role does communication play in the different leadership styles?
4. List six characteristics that assist you when you are in the role of leader.
5. a. Identify one area in which you feel you need to develop your leadership-related competencies.
   b. Prepare an action plan that will assist you to obtain these competencies.

Teams

Think of a team you are currently involved in. You might choose a team at work or the team you are currently studying with.

Has the team	Yes	No	Unsure
a clear team leader?	☐	☐	☐
an effective leader?	☐	☐	☐
an authoritarian leader?	☐	☐	☐
a participative leader?	☐	☐	☐
a laissez-faire leader?	☐	☐	☐
participation from team members?	☐	☐	☐
a member who is an initiator?	☐	☐	☐
a dominant member?	☐	☐	☐
motivation to complete the task?	☐	☐	☐
a sense of belonging?	☐	☐	☐
a readiness to make a decision and take action on the decision?	☐	☐	☐

As a team member do I			
take the initiative and contribute ideas and information?	☐	☐	☐
give and ask for information and ideas?	☐	☐	☐
state my feelings and opinions?	☐	☐	☐
clarify?	☐	☐	☐
encourage and support the contributions of others?	☐	☐	☐
help others by attending, encouraging and listening?	☐	☐	☐
structure and organise the thoughts of the team?	☐	☐	☐
use conflict constructively by disagreeing or asking for supporting examples?	☐	☐	☐

Visit the Companion Website at **www.prenhall.com/dwyer_au**. Choose the Multiple Choice activity in Chapter 9 and answer the questions. How would you describe your knowledge of leadership styles?

Chapter summary

Identify the role of a team leader. A leader is a person who can influence team or team members to produce results. As a leader you must be willing to be involved with the team, using your skills and strategies to improve the team's effectiveness. You need to be able to organise, motivate, direct the team's activities, consult, give feedback and develop team cohesiveness.

Participate in team planning. Effective leaders assist the team to establish its purpose, roles, responsibilities and accountabilities in accordance with the organisation's plans, goals and objectives. As the team interacts, its role is to complete the tasks that enable the organisation to achieve its goals.

Develop team commitment and cooperation. Team leaders assist the team to use open communication processes and share information. This develops mutual concern, trust and confidence within the team. A team with open communication is able to make decisions in accordance with its agreed roles and responsibilities.

Differentiate between types of power. A leader may use five different types of power: legitimate power, expertise power, reward power, coercive power or consultative power.

Select different leadership styles. Leaders can adopt different styles. No one style is the most effective and sometimes you may adapt your leadership style in response to different situations. Leadership styles can be authoritarian, participative or laissez-faire.

Manage and develop team performance. Effective team leaders encourage the team to use the competencies of each member for team and individual benefit. Team members are encouraged to share and enhance their knowledge. The team leader monitors competencies regularly to confirm that the team is able to achieve its goals.

Identify the communication skills needed to be an effective team leader. To be an effective leader you need to use your interpersonal, listening and nonverbal skills appropriately as you interact with team members to achieve the team's goals.

Use the RADAR approach to solve problems. This approach involves: asking the other person to identify the what and why of the problem; asking for details; developing ideas; agreeing on the actions to be taken; and reviewing the main points and deciding how to follow up.

Differentiate between task-related and maintenance-related leadership behaviours. As an effective leader, you should be able to use both task-related and maintenance-related functions to achieve the team's goals and at the same time maintain the team's cohesiveness. Task-related functions focus on the task to be achieved or the problem to be solved. Maintenance-related functions focus on what is happening in the team, and the way in which members relate to each other. The needs of members for acceptance, respect and involvement are recognised.

REVIEW QUESTIONS

1. List four tasks completed by a leader.
2. Describe two different leadership skills.
3. List at least five types of power used by leaders.
4. What is the difference between a directive leadership style and a supportive leadership style?
5. List three characteristics of:
   a. an authoritarian leader
   b. a participative leader
   c. a laissez-faire leader.
6. What differences are evident between highly motivated and poorly motivated team members?
7. List the five steps in the RADAR approach to practical problems.
8. Briefly outline the differences between task-related and maintenance-related leadership functions.
9. List three competencies demonstrated by an effective leader.
10. List three ways in which a leader can monitor an individual's or team's competencies.

Leadership

1. a. List three situations in which you act or have acted as a leader.
   b. Name three people who have in your opinion been successful leaders.
   c. List six behaviours that made these people successful leaders.
   d. 'Our values affect the way we react.' What does this mean?

2. Compare the difference between the leader's role and the role of members in a team. How is the role of a leader and the role of members similar?

3. a. Identify three leadership styles.
   b. Briefly describe the most important aspect of each style.
   c. Differentiate between personal power and position power.
   d. Who should control a team, the leader or the members? Justify your answer.

4. In groups of three, discuss the following questions.
   a. How does the style of leadership affect the flow of communication between the leader and the team?
   b. 'People skills are more important to a manager's progress than intelligence, decisiveness or job skills.' What does this statement mean?
   c. Prepare a list of six communication skills that help leaders use their 'people skills'.

   d. Compare effective and ineffective nonverbal communication you have observed in leaders.
   e. As a team leader, you notice that two members seem to withdraw from the team. To maintain team cohesion you wish to draw these people back into the team. In your group of three, decide on a strategy that would help you to do this.

5. Think of a team you are involved in at work or in your studies.
   a. Identify the team leader.
   b. Briefly explain this person's approach to leadership.
   c. Name three ways in which team members participate in the team.

6. a. Differentiate between supportive and directive behaviour by a leader by nominating three supportive behaviours and three directive behaviours.
   b. Give examples of two situations suited to supportive behaviour and two situations suited to directive behaviour by the leader.

7. a. What communication skills does a leader need to be able to participate in and facilitate a work team?
   b. Briefly describe at least two other skills required to lead a work team.

Key terms

authoritarian leader
coercive power
consultative power
expertise power
feedback
goals
laissez-faire leader
leader

legitimate power
maintenance-related functions
motivation
needs
participative leader
RADAR
results

reward power
rewards
SMART approach
task-related functions
teamwork
vision

Think tank

Leadership, like swimming, cannot be learned by reading about it. Leadership skills are so closely related to innate personality, however, that it may be difficult to effect really significant behavioral change in the classroom.

Henry Mintzberg

James Pirie
Assistant director, Basslink Development Board, Hobart

Leadership is not something that you can define, or place in a box and say 'there's leadership'. From my experience, I equate leadership with politics. The simplest rule of politics is that it is all in the eye of the beholder. If we accept that leadership is about other people's perceptions, then we need to think about what we want from our leaders.

I want our leaders to be people who are able to cope with, or indeed excel in, a rapidly changing and complex society. The command-and-control structures are rapidly losing relevance. This is, in part, because progress has led us to expect greater involvement in the institutions and concepts that govern our lives. If we accept that our society is becoming more complex, then we must accept that our future leaders must not just be able to cope with this complexity but actually enjoy it.

So, if this is what we want and expect, how do we equip future leaders to meet this high benchmark?

Although, as Mintzberg says, leadership cannot be learnt from a book, the concept of 'university' (which has withstood the test of time), with its intellectual rigour and quest for learning, must play a role in shaping future leaders. The test will be: Will the classroom environment be true to the university ideal?

Michael Haddy
Managing director, Innovation Science, defence software engineering, Adelaide

Leadership draws heavily on practical life skills and experiences. I agree it is not something that can be learnt by rote. Good leaders should have an appetite for the lessons learnt by others who have succeeded (or failed) before them. Blindly reproducing documented disasters only confirms one's ignorance.

Possibly the classroom's greatest contribution is to gather and instil some of the basic tools necessary for leadership. Like any artistic endeavour: teach the principles for applying the tools, and let each personality craft their own solution.

Leadership is an art. Perhaps the biggest behavioural change we can achieve is to persuade our prospective leaders to yearn for critical riposte, absorb their surroundings, and analyse their actions and apply innovation. And why not pick up a book or two along the way?

Swimmers may not be able to learn their art through rhetoric alone, but they may learn a few neat tricks.

Peta Woodard
2001 National president of Australian Junior Chamber, group accountant/company secretary for The International Learning Foundation Group, Roleystone, Western Australia

Given the right circumstances at the right time, many more people possess the qualities that make a leader than we may realise. It is such circumstances that are far more likely to affect behaviour than anything that can be taught in a formal sense. Some may never realise that potential, never find themselves in the situation where they can put their leadership ability to the test.

Pursuit of leadership through attending courses and adding to your skills base will make little change to that reality. Placing yourself in positions of leadership is more likely to make the difference.

When you consider true leaders, they just seem to 'have it', which makes you wonder, where did they learn that? How did they get that passion? Where did they learn that vision? It is such qualities that cannot be taught – only brought out in someone under the right circumstances.

There is no doubt that practical skill development can and does help people to perform at a superior level.

But when it comes to the qualities that make a person a leader, courses on leadership can offer no more than the icing on the cake.

Source: Henry Mintzberg, James Pirie, Michael Haddy & Peta Woodard, 'Think tank', *Management Today*, November/December 2001, p. 13. Reprinted by permission of the authors.

Questions

1. Outline the qualities that make a person an effective team leader.

2. Michael Haddy suggests: 'Leadership draws heavily on practical life skills and experiences.' How can life skills and experiences help team leaders to perform their leadership role well?

3. Michael Haddy suggests: 'Possibly the classroom's greatest contribution is to gather and instil some of the basic tools necessary for leadership.' Identify and briefly describe some of the tools (or skills) necessary for leadership.

Deliver and monitor a service to customers

10

In this chapter you will learn how to:

- ○ identify customers' requirements

- ○ develop customer service skills, particularly communication skills

- ○ identify potential communication barriers

- ○ provide product/service information and advice to promote the organisation

- ○ use problem-solving strategies to handle customer complaints and difficult situations

- ○ deal with customers' special needs

- ○ use the telephone efficiently

- ○ present the organisation in a positive way

- ○ deal with situations in a way that maintains and enhances goodwill.

Evaluate your communication skills by completing the self-checks in the chapter.

Customer service means assisting customers. Service organisations cater for their customers' needs by making them feel comfortable and respected and by anticipating and meeting their information and action requirements efficiently and courteously. The role of the organisation, and your role as a staff member providing that service, is to focus on customer needs and expectations.

To deliver high-quality customer service, you must be able to communicate well with the customer.

Your role in customer relations

A customer's first impression is lasting.

A **customer** is any person who purchases or seeks goods or services from another person or organisation. The first impression that your customer receives is lasting; therefore, greet the customer by using a range of communication skills that shows your interest and your ability to provide the service. Your workplace challenge is to provide service of a consistently high quality in as short a time as possible. In doing this, it is important to use the following communication skills appropriately.

1. Greet the customer and show empathy.
2. Listen and provide feedback.
3. Use appropriate verbal and nonverbal behaviour.
4. Problem-solve and consult customers.

Establish a positive communication climate to give customers a positive impression and create **goodwill** between them and the organisation. At the first contact the customer gets an impression of the quality of your service. A satisfying interaction between the customer and you as the service provider is the basis of quality customer service.

Greeting the customer

Prompt and courteous service is appreciated.

As customers have expressed a need or interest simply by approaching your business, make them feel welcome. Greet them with a smile. Say 'Good morning' or 'Good afternoon' and address them by name if you can. Always acknowledge their presence. As you talk to customers, aim to create:

- empathy
- a recognition of their needs
- a feeling of comfort and the impression that they are special.

Communicate with positive statements that focus on the customers and their needs. Some examples of positive statements and an opportunity to rephrase negative statements are presented in the Apply Skills activity, 'Communicate with Customers Positively', on page 190.

Communicate in a way that shows you respect customers' opinions, values and experience. If they have to wait, let them know how long it will be before you can attend to them. A customer's seeking of information (usually by questioning) is defined as a **cusomer inquiry**. A positive and considerate attitude towards a customer as you respond to their inquiry goes a long way towards meeting a customer's needs and expectations.

Identifying customer requirements

Once you have established empathy with customers, use your listening and questioning skills to find out how your product or service can best fill their needs.

Repeat in your own words what you think the customer has said, beginning with something like: 'What I hear you saying is ...'. The customer then has the opportunity to agree or disagree and to give you further information if necessary. This is *paraphrasing*, explained in earlier chapters. When you understand each other, you can proceed with the conversation. Energise your response by looking at the other person, leaning forward and showing interest in what they are saying. Active listening and how to use it in customer service is shown in Figure 10.1.

However, use the technique carefully. If you keep saying: 'What I hear you saying is . . .' the customer is likely to become irritated. Ask for clarification: 'Could you tell me a little more about what went wrong?' Follow the customer's response by asking a probing question – for example, when a customer says 'I really liked what you did last time', you could respond with: 'What exactly was it that you liked last time?' Be open and honest in the interchange and be aware of the customer's feelings as well as the content of their spoken words.

Customers have **expectations** that should be met. Before you go to a restaurant, consider your expectations. Are they the same at a very expensive restaurant as the expectations you have at McDonald's? The answer is probably 'no'.

Effective listening and questioning allow you to identify and take action to meet customer expectations, and to solve any existing problems or prevent problems happening. Listening techniques that are useful in customer relations are discussed in Chapter 2, Interactive Skills.

Using appropriate verbal and nonverbal behaviour

Be willing to deal with a justified complaint to the customer's satisfaction. Nonverbal behaviour is very important here. If you say positive things but frown, cross your arms or move away from the customer, they are likely to believe that you are feeling defensive or uncomfortable and withdrawing from them. Look at the customer as you speak and listen. It is most frustrating for a customer to feel that their point of view and comments are not being heard.

Demonstrate confidence and professionalism by showing respect for both the

Nonverbal behaviour should complement your verbal message.

Figure 10.1 Active listening

Attentive to the customer

Concentrate on the issue, not the person

Target key points

Investigate with questions

Verify cutomer's needs

Energise your response

customer and yourself. Confidence in your own skills and abilities is demonstrated by assertive behaviour – the way you speak and your nonverbal behaviour.

SELF CHECK 10.1

Nonverbal communication in customer service

Have I dealt with the customer in a way that included	Yes	No	Unsure
appropriate speed, pitch and volume of voice?	☐	☐	☐
assertion?	☐	☐	☐
direct eye contact?	☐	☐	☐
appropriate posture?	☐	☐	☐
courteous facial expressions?	☐	☐	☐
smiling?	☐	☐	☐
confidence?	☐	☐	☐
nonverbal behaviour that complemented the verbal message?	☐	☐	☐

Communication barriers in customer relations

Remove any communication barriers.

Even with the best of intentions, **communication barriers** can occur. Strive to avoid them, and concentrate on the customer's needs and expectations. The following techniques are useful.

- Keep staff and clients informed.
- Employ sufficient staff to handle customers' needs.
- Train staff well.
- Avoid gossip.
- Treat customers with respect and sincerity.
- Be clear and concise and aim to solve the customer's problems.
- Provide the service when the customer needs it, or as soon as possible.
- Make sure messages are passed on from customers to staff.
- Recognise and be sensitive to cultural differences.
- Avoid inappropriate levels of formality or informality.
- Use appropriate nonverbal behaviour.

SELF CHECK 10.2

Avoid communication barriers

Choose an organisation and observe a staff member providing service to a customer. How does the organisation rate on the following characteristics? Tick *Very Good* to indicate a high level of service, *Fair* for a mediocre level, and *Poor* for a low level of service.

	Very good	Fair	Poor
1. Acknowledge the customer by:			
a. greeting the customer immediately	☐	☐	☐
b. smiling and using the customer's name	☐	☐	☐
c. escorting the customer to the point of service	☐	☐	☐
d. being courteous.	☐	☐	☐
2. Establish the customer's needs by:			
a. asking the customer to state their needs	☐	☐	☐
b. questioning them to clarify their meaning	☐	☐	☐

c. repeating the customer's order or request ☐ ☐ ☐
d. reassuring them that their expectations can be satisfied. ☐ ☐ ☐

3. Deliver the service by:
   a. acting in a prompt, courteous and helpful manner ☐ ☐ ☐
   b. satisfying the customer's expectations of service ☐ ☐ ☐
   c. speaking clearly ☐ ☐ ☐
   d. using appropriate body language. ☐ ☐ ☐

4. Conclude the service by:
   a. inviting the customer to return ☐ ☐ ☐
   b. smiling and using a closing phrase ☐ ☐ ☐
   c. waiting until the customer departs before moving to the next one. ☐ ☐ ☐

Customer service

1. a. Working in groups of three, recall the worst experience of service that you have received as a customer. List four features that made it so bad.
   b. Take it in turns to discuss the experience with the rest of your group. Rate each experience on the scale in Table 10.1, and then decide which one is 'the worst example' of customer service.
   c. List the three features that make it the worst experience. List as many reasons as you can why customers become upset over poor service.
2. In groups of three, consider a business or government department that you regard as successful.
   a. List five factors that contribute to its professional image.
   b. Identify one of its services and decide whether the organisation provides average, good or superior service.
3. As a group, develop a definition of customer service.
4. As a group, discuss and compare the impact of positive and negative customer service on:
   a. the image of an organisation
   b. the staff of an organisation.

Table 10.1 Different levels of service

Service	Poor	Very poor	Worst
Experience of Person 1	☐	☐	☐
Experience of Person 2	☐	☐	☐
Experience of Person 3	☐	☐	☐

Dealing with difficult situations

Aim to give a high level of service to both pleasant and difficult customers. Irrespective of the quality of service, some customers can be very hard to please and difficult situations can arise. If a high level of service is not provided, the result will not only be loss of business, but often an increase in the number of difficult and even abusive customers. Abusive customers are difficult to cope with, but they are still customers. They have not yet been lost. Deal with them professionally.

Customer types

It is sometimes useful to classify difficult customers into three categories.

1. Impatient, frustrated customers
2. Rude customers who are never satisfied
3. Boring customers

Impatient customers

Impatient customers demand immediate service. They may express frustration. However difficult it is, respond to impatient customers with courtesy. Treat them in the following way.

- Be professional.
- Try not to get personally involved.
- Calm them down as quickly as possible.
- Sort out any problems in private as a public airing may be embarrassing.
- Apologise for any problem.
- Solve the problem.
- Use assertive skills.

Professionalism ensures that your behaviour is appropriate for the issue. Distance your feelings and yourself to avoid personal involvement.

Rude customers

When you are the first point of contact between the rude customer and the organisation, the responsibility to cope rests solely with you. Apologising is not sufficient – you must also take action to solve the problem. Some suitable strategies have already been mentioned. You can also add the following.

- Always stay cool and ignore rudeness; it is not necessarily personal – these customers may be like this with everyone.
- Speak clearly.
- Offer helpful suggestions and keep to the point so you are not sidetracked into an argument.

The rude, never satisfied customer is more difficult to work with than other types.

Boring customers

Handling over-fussy or talkative customers is also a demanding task. There will always be customers who talk too much and are boring. The following techniques help customer relations in this situation.

- Try not to show your boredom.
- Use directive or closed questions to bring customers to the point.
- Wait patiently for them to come to the point.

No matter how good your service or products, sometimes you will have to deal with this kind of customer. As you handle difficult customers, use your communication skills.

Problem solving

Sometimes you have to deal with customer complaints. A **customer complaint** happens when a customer is dissatisfied with the product or service. Some complaints are justified, others unjustified. Each type of complaint must be addressed and resolved in a way that allows you to maintain the customer's goodwill. Your intention is to turn customer complaints into goodwill and future business.

Justified customer complaints

Deal with a **justified complaint** by using negotiation and conflict-resolution skills. Acknowledge that the complaint is justified, and do your best to solve the problem. Since the customers' needs or expectations have not been met, there is no point in hedging or asking them to take further action on their own behalf. Your role is to solve the problem and avoid further ill-feeling. Two strategies available for resolving complaints and problems are shown in Figures 10.2 and 10.3.

Justified customer complaints should be acknowledged and resolved promptly.

Figure 10.2 The PAIR approval strategy

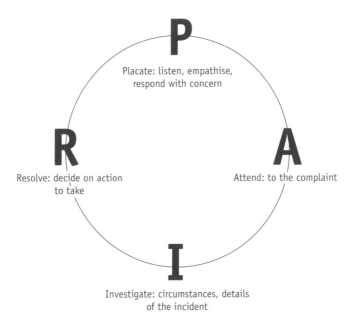

Figure 10.3 A five-step method of resolving complaints

1 Listen: Be open-minded; remember, this is not a personal complaint against you.

2 Repond: Show concern and empathy and apologise for any inconvenience. Remember, the customer may be embarrassed about complaining – put yourself in their position.

3 Decide on action: What factors will influence you here – the justice of the complaint, company policy? When uncertain, seek advice from your supervisor.

4 Take action: Act promptly.

5 Follow up: Confirm that the problem has been solved and the customer is happy.

Communicate with customers positively

1. Consider the negative statements in Table 10.2 and rewrite them in a more positive way.

2. In pairs, consider the following conversations and play the customer and staff roles. Read the statements with different tones of voice. Write a new response for the staff member in each example in a way that centres on the customer's need rather than irritating them.

   a. *Customer:* I would like to open an account with you.
      Staff member: We only open accounts for major customers.

   b. *Customer:* I need a summary of my account.
      Staff member: We're too busy to do it now.

   c. *Customer:* Where is the hotel's gymnasium?
      Staff member: Can't you read the board over there?

   d. *Customer:* I was promised a refund last week. Why hasn't it come?
      Staff member: You gave us inadequate information.

   e. *Customer:* I want to complain to the manager.
      Staff member: The manager's too busy to see you now.

   f. *Customer:* Can you hold that in stock for me?
      Staff member: No, I can't.

3. Think of the worst experience you have had as a customer. List the communication barriers that arose. Compare your answer with the rest of the group.

Table 10.2 Negative and positive statements

Negative	Positive
You have to . . .	Would it be all right with you if . . .?
I can't do that.	I haven't the authority to do that but I will get someone who can help you.
You don't understand . . .	
Wait a minute . . .	
What's wrong?	
It's not my job . . .	

If the customer is already angry, use the conflict-resolution skills described in Chapter 12, Negotiation Skills. Note both the content and emotions expressed by the customer, but avoid reacting emotionally to the complaint yourself. You want to resolve the complaint, not escalate the situation into an argument. Obtain the facts by using listening and questioning skills. Acknowledge the customer's position and indicate that you understand how they feel.

Always check that the course of action to solve the problem suits the customer. Clearly explain each step. As you do this, ask questions to encourage feedback and make sure that the customer understands what is happening, agrees to the solution and will be happy with the results. When you take the time to consult the customer in this way you are able to take a course of action that meets their needs and expectations.

A course of action that enables you or your staff to deal with the problem immediately gives the most positive results. If solving it is going to take a little longer, explain the steps clearly to the customer and make sure that they are completed.

Follow up by making a courtesy telephone call or posting a card to the customer. Dealing efficiently with the justified complaint gives you a chance of maintaining the customer's goodwill.

Unjustified customer complaints

Complaints are not always justified. When dealing with an **unjustified complaint**, use a conflict-resolution or negotiation strategy, and try active listening. Other chapters in this book discuss these techniques. **Active listening** allows customers to air their feelings and know that you have understood them. This helps to defuse the emotional content. Acknowledge the complaint, ask the customer to explain it, and ask how it can be solved. Quite often this is enough to make them realise the complaint is unjustified. If they cannot think of an answer, then perhaps there are no grounds for complaint.

As you ask the customer to explain the facts, they might come round to your point of view. If not, you may finally have to explain that the complaint is unjustified.

Unjustified customer complaints call for active listening and courteous negotiation.

Dealing with customers' special needs

Many customers have special needs. They may be unable to access an organisation's premises because of disability or age. They may be unable to understand what services an organisation offers due to language or cultural difficulties. Literacy deficiencies may lead to an inability to complete an organisation's forms or understand instructions.

These difficulties may preclude some customers from accessing the available services. Being aware of these special needs allows you to respond effectively.

Respond effectively to customers with special needs.

Cultural differences

Accommodating **cultural differences** is of particular importance. Cultural misunderstanding often leads to customer dissatisfaction. Different cultural groups respond to situations in different ways. Their perceptions and interpretations may differ considerably from your own. Their social values, roles and status, concepts of time and personal space, body language and the way in which they make decisions may be markedly different. Dwyer (2002) points out that it is important to learn the value systems of different cultures to avoid costly misunderstandings. You should realise that what is considered right and valid in one culture might be frowned upon in another.

Bovée & Thill (2000) comment that in China and Japan decisions are made by a negotiating team that requires complete consensus. All Chinese and Japanese business managers are expected to continue this time-consuming practice in all countries with which they do business. Latin Americans also prefer to spend a considerable amount of time discussing a business transaction before coming to a decision.

Cultures differ in their use of personal space. Gamble & Gamble (1996) point out that Latin, Arab and African people carrying out business transactions are comfortable with only half a metre of personal distance, whereas Oriental, Nordic, Anglo-Saxon and Germanic peoples require just over a metre. Similarly, there is a difference in eye contact preferences. Westerners prefer eye-to-eye communication in contrast to Japanese, who believe that continued use of eye contact is disrespectful.

Nonverbal communication can also differ markedly. The Japanese find it offensive if you use an index finger to summon someone. Cultures may differ in the way they signal 'no'. Some cultures indicate 'no' by nodding up and down, the opposite to Western cultures. These variations in body language can cause problems.

Being culturally aware will help you to communicate and deal effectively with

Awareness of cultural differences helps you to improve customer service.

customers culturally different from you. Communication in a multicultural society is discussed more fully in Chapter 1.

Communicating on the telephone

Good voice skills are essential for telephone users.

People meet each other, talk and sometimes form long-lasting business contacts over the telephone. Good voice skills are essential for telephone duties as the voice alone has to make the impression. Overcome the visual handicap by developing a clear and pleasant vocal presence and courteous telephone techniques.

Answer the telephone courteously

Answer the phone promptly, preferably by the third ring. Greet the customer by saying 'Good morning', 'Good afternoon' or 'Good evening'. Immediately after this greeting, give the name of the organisation and your name. This enables the person on the other end to speak to an identity rather than an anonymous voice.

Listen carefully

Listen carefully to the speaker. If you assume what is going to be said before it is said you may miss something else. Wait until the person finishes speaking before you reply. Don't interrupt.

The skills of attending, reflecting and encouraging listening all help speakers to explain themselves fully. These skills are discussed in Chapter 2, Interactive Skills: Non-verbal Communication and Listening Skills. Feedback helps the listener to receive and fully understand all the information, particularly when complex material is being presented on the telephone. Provide accurate information promptly and give clear feedback with a well modulated speaking voice, at a steady rate. Sound interested in the customer's needs and request for service.

Find the information

If you do not have the information ready, explain to the caller that you are moving away from the telephone to get it; or that you have to make further inquiries and will contact them later; or that you have to transfer their call to another person. Never say, 'Hang on a minute' and then disappear. The other person can obtain information only from your voice, so let them know you are leaving the telephone rather than just leaving them to wait. State clearly that you have to find the information from another source or room.

Courtesy and efficiency on the telephone demonstrate an organisation's professionalism.

If you have to ask someone else for information the caller has requested, let the caller know this and suggest that it might take some time. Ask if they would prefer to wait or have you ring back. Some people dislike being kept waiting on a silent telephone. The question is a courtesy as it lets customers make the choice in terms of their own needs. Once you make a commitment to return the call, always ring back promptly.

Before you transfer a caller, give them the name of the person who should answer and the number of the direct line to that person. Then, if the call gets lost in the transfer, the caller can ring the appropriate person easily, without the frustration of delays.

Throughout the call, show interest in the customer, use courtesy and satisfy their request. It is worth checking your style of telephone communication occasionally to ensure that you offer assistance readily. Conclude pleasantly and with courtesy.

Answering customer inquiries

The telephone links your organisation with your customers.

The telephone is a direct communication link between your organisation and customers. Telephone calls come in – as a customer inquiry or a customer complaint – or they go out to others. For a customer inquiry, use the following strategies.

- Open the call with a greeting, the organisation's name and your name.
- Listen to the inquiry.
- Provide the relevant information.
- Sound interested in the customer's needs.
- Explain how the organisation can help to satisfy them.
- Suggest what actions customers can take to satisfy their needs.
- Conclude courteously.

It helps you to identify the main points if you make notes as you talk to the customer. Always record relevant details such as name, address and telephone number for future transactions. Repeat information, particularly specific details, back to the caller to ensure accuracy.

Whenever you take a message for someone else, record the caller's name and phone number, the date and time, the name of the person to receive the message, and the important elements of the message. Ensure that the message is passed on to that person. Conclude the call with courtesy.

Handling complaints

If the complaint is justified, acknowledge this and try to solve the problem. This may mean replacing a faulty product or apologising for previous poor service. When the call is a complaint:

Deal with a complaint promptly.

- acknowledge it
- ask questions that encourage the customer to explain in detail
- paraphrase the complaint back to the customer
- deal with the complaint.

If the complaint is unjustified, be politely assertive: for example, explain that the problem was not caused by your organisation. Restate the customer's answer to confirm your understanding of their problem. Make any reasonable offer to the customer that is possible and let the customer know that the organisation is interested in their needs and expectations. Each time you deal with a complaint, make sure that the problem is solved to the customer's satisfaction and follow up with any necessary action.

Telephone instructions and listening skills

1. From your knowledge of telephone skills and from Self-check 10.3 create a set of instructions entitled 'Receiving a Telephone Customer Inquiry'. Make them appropriate to your workplace. If you are not working, create instructions for the reception desk of a small exclusive hotel. Ensure that the instructions include telephone courtesy and useful hints, and that they reflect the image of your firm. Give them a one-paragraph introduction describing the importance of vocal presence and correct diction.

2. List three listening skills that could be used to deal satisfactorily with a customer's telephone call stating that the service in the hotel has not met their expectations.

3. Write a reflecting question, an open question, an attending question and a closed question that you could use as the person receiving and attempting to resolve the complaint. Read Chapter 2 for further advice on listening. Check that your questions do not sound emotional or sarcastic: you want to maintain the hotel's goodwill.

APPLY SKILLS

Telephone skills: dialling out and receiving calls

As you make a business telephone call, and as you receive one, check your use of the following.

Dialling out

Did I	Yes	No	Unsure
prepare what I was going to say?	☐	☐	☐
have a message pad and pencil ready?	☐	☐	☐
dial carefully?	☐	☐	☐
identify myself and the organisation?	☐	☐	☐
state the reason for the call?	☐	☐	☐
speak clearly and directly into the telephone?	☐	☐	☐
use courteous language and voice tone?	☐	☐	☐
use the other person's name?	☐	☐	☐
concentrate as I listened?	☐	☐	☐
collect the correct information?	☐	☐	☐
give feedback to the other person?	☐	☐	☐
repeat messages for accuracy?	☐	☐	☐
terminate the call pleasantly?	☐	☐	☐

Receiving calls

Did I			
answer promptly?	☐	☐	☐
identify myself and the organisation?	☐	☐	☐
establish contact?	☐	☐	☐
use a message pad and pen?	☐	☐	☐
speak clearly?	☐	☐	☐
speak courteously?	☐	☐	☐
listen carefully?	☐	☐	☐
use the caller's name?	☐	☐	☐
follow up any inquiries?	☐	☐	☐
offer assistance willingly?	☐	☐	☐
repeat messages to check understanding?	☐	☐	☐
record messages for others accurately?	☐	☐	☐
close the call pleasantly?	☐	☐	☐
provide an appropriate return call?	☐	☐	☐

WISE
WEB

Visit the Companion Website at **www.prenhall.com/dwyer_au**. Choose the Internet Exercise activity in Chapter 10 to prepare a set of guidelines to assist staff in a large department store to work with dissatisfied customers.

Chapter summary

Identify customers' requirements. Use a courteous approach and active listening to determine customers' requirements. For customer service, active listening is vital: be attentive, concentrate on the issue and not the person, target key points, investigate with questions, verify the customer's needs by restating them.

Develop customer service skills, particularly communication skills. Acknowledge the customer, listen with empathy, give feedback and use appropriate verbal and nonverbal communication so that you can offer the customer high-quality service.

Identify potential communication barriers. Some of these arise when there are not enough customer service staff, or when they do not know enough about the product and its features. Barriers may also be due to poor communication skills and lack of respect for or courtesy to the customer.

Provide product or service information and advice to promote the organisation. The person providing the service must know the product and explain it with courtesy. Listen carefully as you discuss the product so that you understand how much customers know about it and how much more they would like to know. Offer feedback that is appropriate to their needs and expectations.

Use problem-solving strategies to handle customer complaints and difficult situations. If customers express confusion or dissatisfaction, deal with the problem as promptly as possible. Two problem-solving strategies are the PAIR approval strategy and the five-step method. Use these to satisfy customer needs and expectations.

Deal with customers' special needs. Age, disability or cultural and language differences may cause problems and preclude a customer from accessing available services. To respond effectively to customers, you need to be aware of, and able to deal with, their special needs.

Use the telephone efficiently. When you use the telephone to answer inquiries and handle complaints, answer courteously and listen carefully. Once you understand what the customer wants, find the information or take action to satisfy them as quickly as you can. Courtesy and promptness are important.

Present the organisation in a positive way. Now, more that ever, customers expect high-quality service, short and reliable delivery times and innovative policies that respond quickly to their needs and expectations. Some positive features that successful customer service offers are a pleasant environment, friendly and well groomed staff, well informed staff with helpful supervisors, willing assistance and courtesy.

Deal with situations in a way that maintains and enhances goodwill. Establish and maintain a good relationship with your customers, to persuade them to keep using your product or service. The most direct way of doing this is to let customers know how they will benefit. Satisfy their needs and expectations by taking responsibility, using flexibility and showing initiative as you provide a high-quality service.

QUESTIONS
REVIEW

1. Nominate three factors that contribute to good customer relations.
2. Explain two listening skills and two questioning skills that help to resolve customer complaints.
3. Explain four aspects of nonverbal communication that could help you establish a customer's needs.
4. List seven communication skills that add to the quality of customer service.
5. Name two communication barriers that prevent efficient customer service.
6. List the steps required for handling a customer complaint. Compare a justified and an unjustified customer complaint.
7. What is the PAIR approval strategy? When is it used?
8. What is the five-step method of handling customer complaints?

9. Why is it important to be aware of customers' special needs?
10. Identify three ways in which cultural differences may cause difficulties in customer service.
11. Why is it important to give a positive first impression when you answer the telephone?
12. Identify the strategies you might use when answering a customer inquiry.
13. List four steps you might take when handling a complaint on the telephone.
14. How would you deal with a telephone caller who has asked for information you do not have?
15. Why is it important to prepare what you are going to say before you make a call?
16. Why is it important to return a call promptly?

Customer service situation

SKILLS
BUILD

1. Kim enters a large department store to buy an electric razor as a twenty-first birthday present. As she cannot find any electric razors, she asks Leanne, a salesperson, where they are. Leanne, who is talking on the telephone, shrugs and points to another section of the electrical department. Kim moves in that direction and looks for about five minutes (which seems much longer) while Leanne continues to talk on the phone. Finally, Kim leaves the store without purchasing anything. She is very angry at having been kept waiting by a large department store that prides itself on customer service. Kim then decides to return to the store and complain to the department supervisor.

Task

1. In groups of three or four, consider the supervisor's role.
   a. Develop a four-point plan, following

the PAIR approval strategy, for handling this complaint.
   b. Highlight the action you will take immediately to satisfy Kim's needs.
   c. Discuss how staff should respond to customers in the future.
2. Describe two communication barriers that could occur in a telephone conversation between a person inquiring about an advertised special and a member of staff. Determine whether the barriers are caused by the sender or receiver of the call.
3. Several complaints from angry customers have been made to your firm. Write a memorandum to sales staff advising them how to handle telephone calls from angry customers. (This question assesses your knowledge of customer relations and telephone skills, and your ability to write a memorandum.)

Key terms

active listening

communication barriers

cultural differences

customer

customer complaint

customer inquiry

expectations

goodwill

justified complaint

professionalism

unjustified complaint

Superior service costs nothing

by Joanna Tovia

The one advantage small business has over big business is personalised service. If you fail to treat good service as the most important aspect of your business, you are only harming your prospects.

Some businesses assume their service is up to scratch but either fail to have high enough standards themselves, or don't take enough care to make sure their staff are upholding those standards.

Good service is not to be underestimated. The customer who has a bad service experience will tell an average of 10 people. Word of mouth can ruin your reputation and your business.

Satisfied customers usually tell an average of five people of their good experiences. Author of *Good Service is Good Business*, Catherine DeVrye, reminds us service comes from people, not companies.

'If employees feel good about themselves and who they work for, some of that positive outlook transfers to the customer,' Ms DeVrye says.

Ms DeVrye says taking time to hire positive people in the first place is worth the effort.

'It is easier to change people than it is to change people,' she quips.

It takes time to devise the right advertisement that outlines your expectations for serving customers, and it takes time to sort through the applications and to interview the applicants.

Ms DeVrye says it's better to invest time to get the best person than to settle for just anyone.

'If you're not sure that the person will fit in and have the same high standards that you do, don't hire them, even if it means you have to readvertise.'

The NSW Department of State and Regional Development suggests avoiding hypothetical questions when interviewing potential employees. Rather than asking them how they would deal with a situation if it arose, ask how they have dealt with such a situation in the past.

'A real example of an action is a far greater indicator of performance than an imagined guess.'

Leading by example is one way of letting your staff know how you expect them to treat customers.

The NSW DSRD advises going to any amount of trouble for all of your customers. Don't treat big or small customers any differently. Customer referrals are powerful and a customer who feels complimented that you've gone out of your way to help them with a small matter is very likely to know someone who'd fit into your 'big and best' customer category.

Follow these tips to service your customers better:

- Your whole company has a responsibility to become involved in understanding customers.
- Ask your customers how well you're currently serving them. Give them a chance to tell you what they want, where you're failing and where you're succeeding. Question customers regularly.
- Listen to what customers tell you, watch how they use your product, allow your customers to complain and then use these complaints to address the causes behind dissatisfaction.
- Visit your customers regularly; arrange for your staff to visit customers too so that they have a better understanding of your customers' operation.
- Train your frontline people to listen to customers and communicate back to you what they have heard from the customers.
- Call your company occasionally and

check how long it takes for the phone to be answered. How well is the phone being answered – did you feel welcome?

- Find ways that you and your staff can look at your product from the customers' point of view.
- Emphasise to your staff the importance of providing a quality service, not just the minimum required to get by.
- Make sure you convey courtesy and a knowledge of your product. Customers must have confidence in you and your word.
- Make sure you attend to the little details. Show that you care and that you are prepared to provide individual attention to every customer.
- Take a look at your shop front or office from the point of view of a new customer. Is it tidy? Is it easy to find? Are the staff clean, tidy and appropriately dressed?
- One of the most important things your customer expects from you is accuracy. Make sure your employees are well aware that any information given or sent to clients must be accurate.

Source: Joanna Tovia, Journalist, 'Superior service costs nothing', *Daily Telegraph*, 29 January 2002, p. 32.

Questions

1. The following statement from the article identifies the need for small business to hire the right staff: 'If you're not sure that the person will fit in and have the same high standards that you do, don't hire them, even it if means you have to readvertise'.
   a. What are some of the characteristics of a person who can provide quality customer service?
   b. Outline some communication strategies that enable them to deliver quality service.
2. a. Brainstorm to create a list of communication barriers you have experienced as a customer.
   b. Discuss the tips in the article for giving better customer service, and explain how following these tips could have prevented the barriers from arising.

Coordinate and implement customer service strategies

In this chapter you will learn how to:

- identify customer needs and expectations and the organisation's role in providing the service or product to fill these needs

- identify four types of customer values

- develop a plan for establishing a working relationship with customers

- prepare a customer value package

- maintain a working relationship with customers

- implement corrective actions

- make customers feel valued

- take account of customer needs

Evaluate your communication skills by completing the self-check in the chapter.

An organisation that focuses on the customer's point of view rather than its own point of view is well on the way to providing high-quality customer service. It achieves this by clearly defining its customers' needs and expectations, and by communicating regularly with them. An organisation's customer service is designed around the things customers value, and is continually improved to meet their needs and expectations.

When the product and price of one organisation are similar to those of another organisation, it is the quality of the service that makes the difference. The organisation with the better service maintains and builds goodwill because it can meet the needs and expectations of its regular customers, who enjoy the service package and like the environment. As regular customers are the base of the business, they should never be taken for granted. Have you ever heard someone say: 'Oh, they'll be back. They've been coming here for years'? Upset a regular customer and you have a dissatisfied one who may complain or seek service elsewhere.

The needs and expectations of regular customers determine the quality of the service. Ensure that the first impression regular and potential customers have of your organisation and of the service you provide as a staff member is positive and welcoming.

Establishing working relationships with customers

A customer value package meets customers' needs and expectations.

Putting customers' **needs** and **expectations** first is the best way to establish a relationship with them. However, a good relationship cannot be established in this way unless the organisation's most senior management (and managers at other levels) support the rest of the staff in their efforts to provide **high-quality service**. The organisation as a whole must have a clearly identified customer service vision or goal.

Albrecht's service triangle model

A total service package meets customers' needs and expectations.

A **total quality management (TQM)** approach to customer service has been adopted by several organisations. TQM involves everyone in the organisation. As a result, its culture ('the way things are done around here') focuses on the delivery of high-quality service.

Albrecht's model (1992), shown in Figure 11.1, focuses on three essential ingredients of a **service culture**:

1. A strategy for the product or service
2. Customer-oriented staff
3. Customer-friendly systems.

In this model, the **service strategy**, system and people (the organisation's staff) all focus on the customer. The flow of ideas and actions moves between the elements to support those staff who work directly with customers. The organisation responds to the needs and expectations of its customers.

Know your customers' needs and expectations

Before a customer service plan can be designed to satisfy customers' needs and expectations, the organisation must:

- have full knowledge of the product and market demand
- understand customers' needs and expectations
- be committed to its goals and strategies

Figure 11.1 Albrecht's model of essential ingredients in a customer service culture

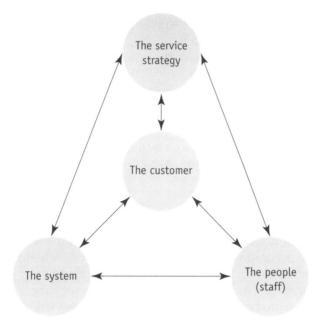

Source: Adapted from Karl Albrecht, *Customer Service: The Only Thing that Matters*, Harper & Row, 1992.

- adopt workable practices to establish a high-quality customer service culture
- access the funds and necessary resources to maintain the customer service culture
- be willing to do things differently
- review and improve customer service
- inform customers about the improved customer service and products.

It is necessary to understand your customer base and their service expectations, and to fulfil these. Customers want high-quality service with short, reliable delivery times and innovative policies that respond quickly to their needs. Some features of successful service are:

Understand your customer base and their expectations; provide at least the expected level of service.

- pleasant environment
- friendly and well groomed staff
- informed staff with helpful supervisors
- willing assistance
- a fast service
- politeness.

Customer service involves assisting customers by making them feel comfortable and respected, and by anticipating and meeting their needs efficiently and courteously.

Prepare a customer value package

The **customer value package** is a range of strategies designed to give customer service based on the things that customers value. By basing this package on the customer's needs and expectations, the organisation creates more opportunities to provide service. The following steps will help to create a customer value package.

Organisations that give good service have a high chance of success.

- Ask your customers what they value by using surveys, listening to their comments and asking questions.
- Set customer service goals.
- Decide what strategies will achieve the goals.
- Decide what service is needed to give the customer value.
- Decide what you will do differently.
- Decide how you will inform your customers about any improvements to the customer value package.

A customer value package brings together product quality and customer service. It is necessary not only to offer the customer a quality product but also to give them high-quality service. By bringing together the product and service into a quality package, you can give customers the service they value.

Customer values

Albrecht identifies four types of customer value.

Albrecht (1992) identifies four types of **customer value** (see Figure 11.2). Table 11.1 explains the different types of customer value from the lowest level (basic value) to the highest level (unanticipated value). Classifying customer values in this way enables you to focus on customers' needs and identify what gives them value.

The concept illustrated in Figure 11.2 helps you to identify the standards your customers expect and to incorporate these into your customer service package. This enables you to provide the expected level of service consistently and the desired and unanticipated levels of service when required.

Continuous research helps you and the organisation to stay in touch with your customers' needs and expectations. Ask questions, send out surveys and listen to your customers. Try to use the win–win approach, to meet the needs and interests of both parties. This way you are building customer loyalty. Customers will return to an organisation that offers them a high-quality product and high-quality service that concentrates on their needs.

Figure 11.2 Customer values

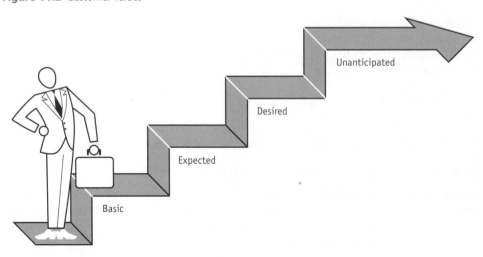

Table 11.1 Customer values

Type	Description
Basic service	The very basic services or products offered to your customers – they are the organisation's reason for existence; for example, to supply newspapers.
Expected service	Customers' expectations about how the service will be given – the service level that the customer expects as a right.
Desired service	Value-added service – that is, superior or excellent levels of service; the organisation's preparedness and capacity to offer customers more than they expect. Providing desired service increases satisfaction but, in the long run, customers may become used to it and expect it.
Unanticipated service	Anything that can be added to the desired service in the future. Once customers become used to superior levels of service, they may expect something more or different. Thus it is necessary to find ways of giving the customer a different and better service that gives unanticipated value.

Strategies to maintain a working relationship with customers

Organisations communicate with their customers through different channels. Personal contact, counter skills, telephone skills, and print and screen media can all be used in customer relations. Staff provide the most important and most effective way of communicating. Chapter 10, Deliver and Monitor a Service to Customers, discusses the communication strategies used for customer service.

Staff are the main channel for customer relations.

Internal and external customers

A **customer** is a person who buys a service or product from another person or organisation. They do business because the organisation or person has a product or service the customer requires. It is how this product or service is perceived by the customer that defines the level of service. Providing what the customer values is quality customer service from the customer's point of view.

Providing what the customer values is the key to customer satisfaction and loyalty.

Though customer service is integral to customer satisfaction it goes beyond mere service. A satisfied customer is one whose needs have been met to a predetermined standard. Customer satisfaction is interpreted by the customer rather than the person providing the service.

A customer may be internal or external to the organisation. **Internal customers** are the people you work with. The **external customer** is a person or organisation who purchases goods or services from your organisation. The issue of quality customer service is just as important to internal customers as it is to external customers.

A major problem with internal customer service is lack of cooperation between people. Cooperative partnerships between internal customers give more rapport and better quality service at each stage of the product or service line. Customer service is well managed when staff supply their internal customers with service that allows them to provide high-level service to external customers. Internal customers should be able to tell others in the organisation what will satisfy their needs as they supply service to others. Internal customers value services that give them satisfaction and enable them to do their work well as they provide service to their internal and external customers.

To understand your internal and external customers you must get to know what their needs and expectations are. Offer service in a way that lets them know you are interested and willing to be of service.

Deal with customer needs and expectations

One of the best ways to avoid problems is to make sure your product or service delivers the results promised by the organisation and expected by the customer. By asking customers for feedback, you can check that the results meet their expectations. Strategies that will help you deal with their needs and expectations are as follows.

1. Survey to find out what customers need and expect.
2. Inform customers about the organisation's activities.
3. Develop a good customer service 'climate' (or culture) in the organisation through communication, staff training and development.
4. Plan ahead to meet customers' needs and expectations.
5. Create a set of customer service performance standards.
6. Review the customer service outcomes and be willing to improve the service.

For an organisation to develop a service culture, and to operate efficiently with a focus on customer relations and service, communication skills such as speaking, questioning and listening are essential. The verbal and nonverbal aspects of these skills must complement one another. Monitor the interaction between customers and your organisation to check that these communication skills are used fully. They are the most important part of your customer service.

Solve problems

Apologise for misunderstandings with customers, or for communication barriers that give rise to other problems. Aim to resolve problems quickly and make no promises you cannot keep. If you avoid the problem, it will develop further and the customer may leave with ill will. Customers who express their dissatisfaction to family and friends create poor publicity for your business. Refer to Chapter 10 for problem-solving approaches to customer complaints.

Advertise

Advertise to influence customers' perception of your organisation. Tell your customers or potential customers what you can do for them and how your product or service is of value to them. Demonstrate why your organisation is ahead of others. Remember that potential customers are also your long-term prospects.

Show commitment to your customers.

Let your customers know about your commitment to meet their needs and expectations with the things they value. Advertise your high-quality customer service and support this with startling statements or statistics about your organisation's service and your customers' satisfaction.

Advertising is a proactive way to attract new customers. Remember, in your advertising or promotion of specials, to include your long established customers. Their loyalty and commitment should be acknowledged and on occasions rewarded.

Maintain customer records

In service industries such as dentistry or hairdressing, it is essential to keep a record of relevant personal details. Keep these **customer records** up to date and be systematic so that staff can record details easily and efficiently.

To gather information for customer records, staff need to speak to customers, either face-to-face or on the telephone. As you speak, remember to listen and ask questions so that you can provide feedback and record responses accurately. Let customers know why you keep their record and the benefits for them personally. Stress that records are confidential and ensure that the record is put into the appropriate index or file immediately. Do all this in a courteous, interested way.

Maintain the confidentiality of records.

Organisations are accountable for their actions. Records are a key component of accountability, as they provide evidence of what has happened. An organisation expects its individuals and teams to maintain high standards in their record-keeping practices. The record system documents actions and outcomes.

An effective and efficient record-keeping system:

■ reflects compliance with appropriate legislative and regulatory requirements
■ ensures record management and monitoring procedures are in place
■ has secure storage, including backup of electronic records
■ is well organised and readily accessible by appropriate personnel.

Records provide evidence to support any request for additional resources to fulfil customer service objectives. Records can be used to identify changes to customer service standards that will enhance the services and meet the customer's expectations. They also show that the team is working within the organisation's business plans and procedures to fulfil the organisation's requirements.

Inform customers

Keep your customers informed to build good relationships. Before, or as you provide service, explain the purpose and outcomes of the procedure, the principal steps and the order in which they take place. This contact with customers helps to prevent anxiety and stress. Obtain feedback from customers in terms of their comfort, feelings and perception of expected outcomes.

Customers are entitled to accurate information.

Give precise instructions to staff and accurate information to customers. Acknowledge customers' expectations but state what you can and cannot deliver. Deal with unrealistic or inadvisable customer requests confidently and without aggression. It is better to state clearly and courteously that it is not possible to fulfil the request than to make a commitment or promise you cannot keep.

On occasion, you will need to give advice and make recommendations that benefit the customer. Always consider your service from the customer's point of view. Does your service meet their needs or does it create barriers that encourage them to go elsewhere? Take into account age, disability, literacy skills and cultural differences when assessing customer needs. (Chapters 1 and 10 discuss communicating in a multicultural society.)

Skill in communicating and a preparedness and capacity to deliver the kind of service the customer expects and needs are essential for successful customer relations.

Where appropriate, explain your booking or service conditions to your customers. This way you can match their needs and expectations with yours and avoid any future awkwardness or communication barriers.

Figure 11.3 gives examples taken from newspapers of **service conditions** presented to customers before a transaction, to avoid false expectations.

Figure 11.3 Transaction conditions

> **RETAIL COMPLEX**
> No delivery on specials ■ Limit of 6 per customer ■ Retail sales only ■ No lay-bys at these prices ■ Available only while stocks last
>
> **THEATRE RESTAURANT**
> Dress rules apply ■ No entry after the dinner show starts ■ Cover charge on Saturdays, Sundays and public holidays
>
> **PROMOTION PRIZES**
> All the winners will go into the draw ■ Prizes not redeemable for cash ■ Prizes not transferable ■ Employees of the company or their families may not enter

What is a customer value package?

APPLY SKILLS

Work in small groups.
1. Consider the customers of a large department store. Identify the type of value they would want at the *expected* level of service in the customer value package. Be specific about their needs for, and expectations of, products and service.
2. Suggest one way in which a department store could reach the *desired* level of service.
3. Give an example of a department store offering *unanticipated* levels of service.
4. What do you value most when you are a customer in a large department store?
5. As a group, compare your answers.
6. Use Self-check 11.1 to decide whether an organisation is providing the expected level of service.
7. Scott (1991) states 'Customer service is defined by the organisation. Customer satisfaction is customer defined'. Explain why it is important to go beyond service and aim for customer satisfaction.

SELF CHECK 11.1

Achieving the expected level of service

Does the organisation	Yes	No	Unsure
■ offer all that each customer needs and expects?	☐	☐	☐
■ give all customers equal access to the service?	☐	☐	☐
■ use a service delivery style that recognises customers as central to the organisation?	☐	☐	☐
■ provide the service when it is needed?	☐	☐	☐

Customer complaints policy

Respond to feedback from customers.

Improving customer service and resolving customer complaints is a continual process. Each modification to a customer complaint policy needs factual information to plan the proposed change. Data should be collected from satisfied and dissatisfied customers. Collecting data from these sources involves three key tasks:

1. Analyse raw data such as customer complaints in order to turn it into useful information.

2. Identify and cluster customer complaints into categories.

3. Identify the organisation's customer service policies, procedures and goals in order to produce outcomes and overall trends that match these service goals.

As you respond to customer feedback aim to:

■ develop customer trust and confidence in your ability to provide the service

■ reduce customer complaints and increase their satisfaction

■ improve the effectiveness of the service by finding out what the customer expects and desires and plan to deliver at these two levels – the *expected* and the *desired* levels described by Albrecht

■ increase staff motivation and job satisfaction by achieving improvement goals.

Some simple rules for managing customer feedback will make the process both effective and efficient. These rules should:

■ concentrate on customer satisfaction

■ focus on a limited number of indicators

■ be ongoing and specific

■ be available to all staff on a timely basis

■ be written and have a visual impact.

Monitoring and improving customer service allows organisations to gather feedback and improve customer service on the basis of what customers say they want rather than on what the organisation believes its customers want. Its goal is to gather information about customer satisfaction.

Propose changes based on customer feedback

The key to implementing corrective actions regarding complaints is careful planning based on factual and objective data. Any proposed changes to customer service delivery should be based on customer feedback and documented.

Seek customer feedback

Seeking feedback from customers will help you to focus on their service priorities and match them with the organisation's requirements. An organisation's key priorities should include:

■ *effectiveness* – is the service providing the targeted outcomes?

■ *efficiency* – how well is the service being provided?

■ *equity* – does the service ensure equal access and provision to all targeted customers?

Requesting regular feedback earns respect from customers and allows you to capture the positive comments as well as the problems. Regularity of feedback enables trends to be identified, problems solved by improvements to the service design and conformance to standards. It also lets you know service standards are being maintained.

> Find out what the customer likes and dislikes.

Gathering customer feedback is about asking questions. If the right questions are posed then the answers will provide useful data to enable the service to be measured for customer satisfaction and your organisation's key priorities and requirements.

Prepare a proposal

On those occasions when modifications to customer service are major, you may have to submit a formal proposal that recommends and seeks approval for the changes. As a formal proposal is prepared for a decision-maker to approve the recommendations it should be a well organised and persuasive document.

Aim to make your customer service proposals effective to gain maximum benefit from the time, energy and costs involved in preparing it. A proposal seeks approval from those who have the responsibility and power to authorise the actions in the recommendations. To be successful you should:

- identify the objectives clearly
- identify the organisation's need to modify customer service
- present strategies for meeting that need
- outline the direct benefits of these strategies
- offer ways to evaluate the results.

Refer to Chapter 22, Writing Technical Documents, for more information on technical proposals.

Authorise, take action or refer

Implementation of corrective policy to avoid customer complaints often involves all levels of the organisation. Customer service delivered by managers, supervisors, team leaders and staff must focus on the needs of the customer and take place within the guidelines in the organisation's policies and procedures. An effective customer service organisation empowers its staff to take action or refer the complaint to the person with responsibility to authorise changes to procedures.

Involve team members in the customer service improvement process and you are likely to gain their cooperation. One practical way to involve team members is to encourage them to bring any research and feedback data they have collected to meetings. The data they have gathered is used to modify customer service processes on the basis of facts rather than opinions. Another way is to assign responsibility for customer service improvements to team members on the basis of their competencies. Figure 11.4 is a checklist that can be used to assess the customer service competencies in your team.

Action procedures to resolve customer difficulties and complaints.

Figure 11.4 Checklist of competencies for resolving customer complaints

Competency	Tick
■ Communication skills	
– speaking	
– listening	
– questioning	
■ Product knowledge	
■ Problem identification	
■ Data and fact gathering	
■ Problem solving	
■ Customer research	
■ Collecting and collating feedback	
■ Process redesign	

Encourage staff to become familiar with customer complaints procedures and ensure they know how to work within the guidelines in the procedures. Mentor or coach colleagues through the steps in the customer complaints procedure. Customer complaint procedures usually follow these four steps.

1. Identify the key features, tasks and processes of your customer service and prioritise them.

2. Make a list of all the processes customers go through each time they use your service. Remember to consider your internal customers as well as your external customers. Analyse each process according to:
   - factors that lead to customer frustration
   - barriers that prevent customers getting what they need

3. Review each process to ensure it is efficient, effective and equitable.

4. Implement improvements, solve problems and reset goals.

Develop a customer service action plan

1. Work in small groups.
   Step 1. Brainstorm to create a list on a flipchart of the forces that are likely to oppose any changes to customer service delivery.
   Step 2. Brainstorm to create a list on a flipchart of the forces that are likely to support any changes to customer service delivery.
   Step 3. Discuss how a proposal for changes to the customer service delivery process can minimise the likelihood of opposition to the recommended changes and maximise the likelihood of success.

2. It is well known that the service attributes outlined in Figure 11.5 are what customers use to judge the quality of service delivery. In column 3 tick the attributes that exist in the customer service you provide in your role at work.

Figure 11.5 Customer service attributes

Attribute	Definition	Tick
Reliability	The ability to provide the service that was promised and communicated dependably and accurately.	
Tangibles	The appearance of the physical attributes of facilities, equipment, personnel and communications material.	
Responsiveness	The willingness of servers to help customers and provide a prompt service.	
Assurance	The knowledge and courtesy of servers and the ability to convey trust and confidence.	
Empathy	The provision to customers of caring, individualised attention.	

3. Prepare an action plan in Figure 11.6 that could guide your implementation of an improved level of service to one of your organisation's customer groups. The action plan should:
   - identify your overall goal
   - identify each of the steps to be taken to achieve this goal
   - state the resources required
   - include a time frame for both the goal itself and each of the steps
   - state the measure that will determine the success of the service provided.

Figure 11.6 Customer service action plan

Goal statement			
Action plan			
Step	**Resources**	**Dates**	**Indicator of success**

Implement proposed changes

Modifications to the customer service delivery process should improve service and resolve any recurring customer complaints. Any change in policy leads to changes in the workplace. So any action plans for implementation of the modifications should identify steps, resources, dates and indicators of success clearly.

Implement changes to service standards consistently and equitably.

At the beginning of the implementation process double-check your plan to ensure the goal, steps and time lines are realistic and that you have allocated sufficient and competent personnel and resources to finalise the work. Also check the responsibilities are defined clearly. By double-checking process and resource issues before implementing changes to the customer service process, any problems that arise should relate only to details in the project rather than the processes.

Modifications to the customer service process could take place for the following reasons:

- To improve its effectiveness in achieving targeted outcomes
- To improve efficiency in the use of resources
- To ensure equity of access and provision to targeted customers
- To increase customer satisfaction
- To reduce customer complaints
- To improve staff motivation and job satisfaction
- To support changes in the organisation's objectives
- To comply with legal and regulatory requirements.

The Plan-Do-Check-Act cycle

The PDCA cycle (Plan-Do-Check-Act) shown in Figure 11.7 is an effective tool for implementing proposed changes. It was developed by Walter Shewhart (cited in Cole 2000), a

Figure 11.7 PDCA cycle

proponent of the Total Quality Management movement. Its purpose is to ensure that improvements are consistent and retained.

The implementation of customer service changes will benefit from team involvement in each of the four steps in the cycle. Empowering staff to take responsibility for planning and implementing recommended improvements motivates them to introduce the improvements successfully. The matrix in Figure 11.8 is a useful tool for an organisation or team to use as it analyses its customer service processes. The maxtrix was used to record the problems experienced by staff and customers in using the loan application form. Figure 11.9 gives the proposed solutions in the form of recommendations.

Involve team members and empower them to take responsibility for changes to customer service.

Figure 11.8 Problem analysis matrix

| Source of problem | Effects from problems | | | | |
	Incomplete details	Incorrect details	Late submission	Late processing of claims	Total
Form for collecting information is confusing and lengthy	36	56	92	105	289
Too many interruptions – staff are too busy	50	24	48	126	248
Staff unclear about the procedure			65	73	138
Customers do not understand the process	29	76	32	94	231
	115	156	237	398	906

Figure 11.9 Proposed solutions

| Recommendation 1 | That the form be reviewed and written in plain English to reduce staff time in checking and contacting customers who make mistakes. |
| Recommendation 2 | That communication such as customer briefings be used to increase the number of forms submitted on time. |

Any modifications to customer service must be carried out within your area of responsibility and the limits imposed by your organisation. Before implementing any modifications that are outside your area of responsibility you must propose the changes to your team leader or designated person and receive written approval for the changes.

Resolve a customer service problem

SKILLS
APPLY

1. Case Study: *Beverley's Complaint*

   A customer, Beverley, complains to Nathan about his company's credit policy. In her view the company is overbearing and has demanded payment for a service that needed to be done because Nathan's company had changed the name of her account without her consent. Beverley is irate. She explains she is visually impaired. Nathan's company wrote to her to ask if she would like the account name changed. In the letter the company stated they would make the change if she did not respond in seven days. As Beverley's reading camera was at the technicians being repaired at the time the letter arrived she was unable to read it until the reading camera was returned. The reading camera was returned 10 days after Beverley received the letter. She tells Nathan she has been treated badly and she will complain to the Consumer Affairs Bureau.

   Nathan does not know what to do. He realises he will have to work within his company's code of conduct as well as the guidelines in consumer legislation such as the Consumer Credit Code and the *Privacy Act* as he resolves the problem.

   What should Nathan do? In your answer discuss what Nathan can do immediately. What can he do later?

2. Use Self-check 11.2 to evaluate your skill in resolving customer complaints.

3. Choose any two of the skills for which you ticked the 'No' or 'Unsure' box. Describe how you could improve your performance for that skill.

   _____

   _____

   _____

   _____

SELF CHECK 11.2

Resolving customer complaints

Check whether you can:

Identify customer complaint/dispute	Yes	No	Unsure
■ establish the nature of complaint by listening, questioning and confirming needs of customer	☐	☐	☐
■ establish rapport with customer by displaying empathy towards customer's needs	☐	☐	☐

Record complaint/dispute			
■ describe and record complaint and documentation accurately and in simple language	☐	☐	☐
■ prepare any further documentation required to support complaint	☐	☐	☐

■ verify complaint with customer to ensure it has been recorded accurately   ☐ ☐ ☐

Refer complaint/dispute

■ identify complaints that need to be referred to other personnel or external body   ☐ ☐ ☐

■ forward documentation and the investigation report promptly   ☐ ☐ ☐

■ follow up with appropriate personnel to gain a prompt decision   ☐ ☐ ☐

Implement corrective action policy regarding customer complaints

■ authorise, action or refer procedures to resolve customer complaints to appropriate personnel, according to organisation's policies and procedures   ☐ ☐ ☐

■ satisfy customers' special needs in accordance with organisation's policies and procedures   ☐ ☐ ☐

■ provide operational information to appropriate personnel in order to facilitate customer service planning   ☐ ☐ ☐

■ monitor service standards to ensure corrective action policy in regard to customer complaints is implemented   ☐ ☐ ☐

■ refer current practices and policies regarding customer service issues that may affect the operation of the organisational unit to management   ☐ ☐ ☐

Process complaint/dispute

■ process complaint/dispute in accordance with dispute resolution procedures established under company policy, legislation or codes of practice   ☐ ☐ ☐

■ obtain necessary reports relating to the complaint   ☐ ☐ ☐

■ take into account applicable law, company policy, codes and any relevant considerations as decisions are made   ☐ ☐ ☐

■ maintain a register of complaints/disputes   ☐ ☐ ☐

■ inform customer of outcome of investigation   ☐ ☐ ☐

Follow up

■ inform customer of the outcome of the referral   ☐ ☐ ☐

■ discuss any further action with appropriate personnel and customer to ensure satisfaction   ☐ ☐ ☐

This checklist is based on the unit of competence FNBFSO6A Resolve Customer Complaints from the Finance Industry Training Package FNB99 ANTA.

Visit the Companion Website at **www.prenhall.com/dwyer_au**. Choose the Good Practice/Bad Practice activity in Chapter 11 to prepare a customer service plan designed to reduce customer complaints and improve customer service.

WEB WISE

Chapter summary

Identify customer needs and expectations and the organisation's role in providing the service or product to fill these needs. Customers choose your organisation because it satisfies their needs by providing them with a service or product. Customers also have expectations about the style and type of service. An organisation with a customer service focus identifies customer needs and expectations and offers service that satisfies them.

Identify four types of customer value. Customer value is classified as basic, expected, desired or unanticipated. Basic value means simply the standard product and service; expected value is the quality of service that meets the customer's needs and expectations; desired and unanticipated value go beyond the value expected by the customer – a superior level of service.

Develop a plan to establish a working relationship with customers. Plan a pleasant environment with friendly and well informed staff. Provide the service courteously and efficiently. The working relationship flows from the interaction of the three ingredients in the service package: the service strategy, the staff and the organisation's systems, all focused on customers' needs and expectations.

Prepare a customer value package. To achieve the expected level of service, or a higher level of service at the desired or unanticipated levels, ask your customers what they value most. Set customer service goals and decide what strategies will achieve them. Decide how you will improve the customer value package, and tell customers about it.

Maintain a working relationship with customers. Communicate skilfully with customers, deal with their problems efficiently, advertise, and maintain accurate customer records. Staff should be able to advise on and carry out service strategies to the standard required in their organisation and expected by the customer. Customer service should meet customers' needs and expectations.

Implement corrective actions. Procedures to resolve customer complaints should be authorised, actioned or referred to appropriate personnel according to your organisation's policies and procedures. Plan and implement corrective actions in consultation with others. Follow up to ensure the changes satisfy customers.

Make customers feel valued. By putting customers' needs first, you let them know that the organisation values their custom. The service should meet their expectations and, on occasions, exceed their expectations. Consult with customers, listen to their comments and aim to improve the customer value package.

Take account of customer needs. Whenever an organisation provides a service to someone, that customer has a certain idea of what the organisation should be offering. That idea is based on the customer's needs. An organisation and those who represent it must identify those needs, and use flexibility and initiative when striving to satisfy them.

REVIEW QUESTIONS

1. What is the best way to establish a relationship with a customer?
2. Define the terms 'customer needs' and 'customer expectations'.
3. Why should an organisation identify its customers' needs and expectations?
4. Briefly explain the three essential factors in Albrecht's service triangle.
5. List four features of successful service.
6. Define the term 'customer value package'.
7. Explain the four types of customer value.
8. List four ways in which an organisation can meet customers' needs and expectations.
9. Why is it important to solve problems quickly?
10. What is the purpose of advertising?
11. What is the purpose of customer records?
12. What is the purpose of consultation?
13. Why should customers be informed about conditions?
14. Why is it important to meet the customer's needs and expectations?
15. What benefits does an organisation gain by having a customer complaints policy?

1. Modify customer service delivery

There may be systems and procedures in existence in your organisation or team that you can use or adapt to help you modify customer service delivery processes. In Figure 11.10, describe the ways in which the procedures or systems in column 1

might help you implement a change to customer service delivery. An example is given in the first row of Figure 11.10.

Add another specific procedure or system that exists in your organisation in the last row of Figure 11.10.

Figure 11.10 Procedures and systems

Complaints log	Helps to spot common problems that need to be removed when the changes in customer service are implemented
Customer service feedback forms	
Departmental or team meetings	
Informal observation	
Formal reviews	
Your example	

2. Customer value package

The environment is a combination of surrounding things, conditions and influences. Elements in the environment such as furniture, architectural style, smells, music and colour all communicate something. Consider the following two situations in terms of this statement and observe how the staff of each office followed customer service principles.

Scene A

Michael Daniels, a newcomer to the city, had purchased a second-hand car with a registration due to expire. He had arranged his transfer of insurance and approached the local Motor Registry Office to register the car in his name. As he entered the office, he

was struck by its freshness and friendliness. The decor was smart, the office businesslike and the staff looked professional and well groomed. They appeared relaxed, but alert to the presence of customers and prompt in attending to newcomers.

Nicole, the person who dealt with his inquiry, was friendly and efficient. She listened attentively when he questioned the cost, and explained that the transfer attracted a stamp duty fee of $100. She issued an interim registration sticker and advised him that new papers and sticker would be posted to him within the next two days. As he left, he noted that he had spent only five minutes negotiating the transfer. He was very pleased.

Scene B

Six months later Michael Daniels approached another Motor Registry Office in response to a request that he apply in person for a photo licence. This time he noticed the general untidiness of the office, with cardboard boxes under the counters. He was aware of the tired air of staff member Marilyn, who explained that he would have to wait until the photographer was available. Michael waited for 20 minutes before deciding to cut his losses and make another visit when he was less busy.

The experience of Michael Daniels reflects the expectations of contemporary Australians. Customers have become used to a certain customer service approach: a pleasant smile, attractive surroundings, fast and efficient service and a consistent standard of product and service, whatever the outlet.

1. List the ways in which the needs of the customer, Michael Daniels, were satisfied in Scene A.
2. Consider Scene B and list the factors that caused customer dissatisfaction.
3. At which level of the customer value package did each office offer service?
4. Identify two communication skills that Marilyn would need to improve her quality of service to Michael.
5. In small groups, prepare a customer service action plan for Scene B. First, explain how the Motor Registry Office staff could provide the expected level of service. List each objective and the steps needed to achieve it. Put your answer on an overhead transparency or flipchart and report back to the large group.

Key terms

advertise
customer
customer records
customer value
customer value package

expectations
external customers
high-quality service
internal customers
needs

service conditions
service culture
service strategy
total quality management (TQM)

CASE STUDY

Great service is a learned skill

by Jack Fraenkel

One of the saddest things in business is to watch the gap between competitors narrow to the point where the only differential is price. There's an Alaskan saying: 'If you're not the lead dog, the view never changes'.

In other words, what are you doing and what can you do to stand out from the rest?

The courtesy of service

While product quality, reliability, price and performance will continue to serve as part of the buying decision process, service is rapidly becoming the ultimate determinant of value in the mind of your consumers/clients. Decisions are based on both emotion and logic. Unfortunately, logic only contributes 5 per cent to the process. Great service can save an average meal, but poor or even ordinary service will destroy a great meal.

No matter what business you're in, it is 50 per cent process/production and the other half is sales/marketing. It is vital to the future of your business that you train every member of your team in how to deliver outstanding service to your clients and prospects.

Step 1: you need to explain to the team that without customers there won't be any teeth to drill, lawns to mow, accounts to prepare, widgets to sell, hair to cut, legal cases to argue or bricks to lay. No matter how well you generate leads, it will all be a waste of time if your conversion rate from lead to sale isn't working.

Step 2: you need to set service standards. For example, in a retail store that might mean acknowledging customers within 30 seconds, in a professional practice it must be seeing your client within 5 minutes of the appointed time, on the telephone it could be answering all calls within 3 rings. Having set the standard, you must measure and monitor it continuously and reward or retrain accordingly.

Step 3: you need to train your team in how to build rapport and communicate effectively with your customers and prospects. This starts with the simple concept of introducing themselves and learning the client's name. 'Hi, I'm Jack' works really well and most people will respond with their name.

This step is probably the least understood and yet it is vital to providing great service. The human brain is commonly divided into left and right but there is also the prehistoric brain in the middle, just on the end of the stem. This is the *fight or flight* response mechanism. It has no powers of deductive reasoning. It simply decides emotionally whether or not to stay and listen to whatever message you have to deliver.

Effective communication wins

So you have to train yourself and your team in the modalities of effective communication. The ability to mirror and match communication styles is amazingly helpful in breaking down the barriers created by the adversarial nature of customer/salesperson relationships. Once you have gained your customer's trust, you can take the relationship to a much higher level and turn your clients into a part of your marketing strategy – through referrals, for example.

Providing great customer service will translate into an improved bottom line. Your clients will keep coming back and will refer your business to their friends and acquaintances so you won't have to spend so many marketing dollars.

You will also attract clients who want to do business with you because they believe that you can fulfil their needs better than any of your competitors. This of course means that they, your competitors, will get all the price shoppers while your business grows through the endless referrals generated by your great service.

What is great service?

Great service means acknowledging customers quickly and introducing yourself by name. It means building your clients' esteem by learning their names and using them, asking questions about their needs and wants and listening attentively to their answers. Great service involves offering solutions to their needs, ensuring that your solution meets their wants, making it easy for them to buy from you. It means thanking and warmly congratulating them for the great decision they made (this will reinforce their self-esteem) and, finally, farewelling them with an invitation to return to your business.

The three most important words in providing great customer service

- *Integrity:* never compromise yourself or company by being less than 100 per cent honest with everyone you come into contact with
- *Wisdom:* continually build your knowledge so that you always deliver the best solutions to match your customers' needs
- *Customers:* always treat customers as you want to be treated and ensure that they benefit in some way from every contact they have with you

Source: Jack Fraenkel, 'Great service is a learned skill', *Australian Business News*, Vol. 31, February 2002, pp. 25–6.

Questions

1. The article identifies the three most important words in providing great customer service as 'integrity', 'wisdom' and 'customers'. Briefly explain the place of these three concepts in the customer service context.
2. The article says 'effective communication wins'. Outline the communication strategies that lead to positive interactions between customers and the organisation's staff.
3. Why must a team leader or manager integrate an organisation's service strategy with its staff and systems if they want their customer service to stand out from their competitors' service?

Negotiation skills

In this chapter you will learn how to:

- distinguish several negotiation strategies

- analyse personal styles and the way they affect negotiation

- identify five power bases

- plan a negotiation

- use principled bargaining

- use persuasive interviews

- use negotiation to solve problems

- analyse various negotiating options

- use appropriate interpersonal skills.

Evaluate your communication skills by completing the self-check in the chapter.

Negotiation is a process in which two or more parties try to resolve differences, solve problems and reach agreement. Good negotiation meets as many interests as possible with an agreement that is durable.

Successful negotiators are able to collaborate with another party (or parties) to reach a mutually beneficial agreement. They use empathy appropriately because they can see the situation from other points of view. To be a successful negotiator you must put yourself in the other person's position to show them that you fully understand their needs and concerns.

People who are genuine about negotiation usually respond with honesty. A positive regard for yourself and the others involved will communicate your warmth and acceptance of them. Negotiators who have respect for themselves are also more likely to show respect for others. Good negotiators' verbal and nonverbal communication is open, confident and oriented to the needs and concerns of both parties.

Negotiation strategies

Good negotiation results in agreement.

Although negotiation has a specific purpose – to reach agreement – it does not always achieve this aim. Before attempting to negotiate, consider the differences between the following four strategies.

1. Win–win strategy
2. Win–lose strategy
3. Lose–win strategy
4. Lose–lose strategy.

Each strategy has a different result. The first strategy lets both parties win; the second and third makes one party win and one lose; the fourth strategy has both parties lose.

Win–win strategies meet the needs of both parties.

Win–win strategies produce the situation shown in Figure 12.1: both parties are satisfied with the settlement negotiated. This strategy aims to meet the needs of both parties, not to win positions or gain victories at one party's expense.

The win–win result is hard to achieve. Assertive communication, 'I' messages, good verbal and nonverbal communication and careful listening all help to achieve it. These skills are discussed in Chapter 3, Interpersonal Communication.

The win–win strategy succeeds only if both parties concentrate on problem-solving strategies and on communicating well. They must negotiate the situation on its merits

Figure 12.1 Win–win outcome: both parties satisfied

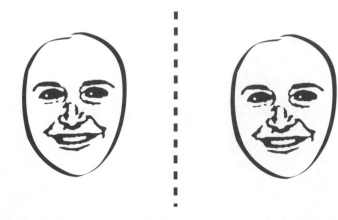

and base all bargaining on the interests of both parties. Each party is then more likely to be committed to the outcome.

Even as you reach a win–win conclusion that suits both parties, circumstances can change. After successfully negotiating a difficult or important issue, take the time to follow up to check that the other party also considers that the result is win–win.

Win–lose strategies result in the party who initiates the conflict being satisfied and the other dissatisfied. This strategy focuses on the initiator's problem to the exclusion of the other's. The initiator wins. Many people who adopt this strategy use a confusing presentation or a dominating style of speech and body movement. This invites the other side to be just as difficult, or to withdraw from conflict.

Lose–win strategies give a situation in which the initiator is dissatisfied and the other is satisfied. The losing party usually makes too many concessions. In an extreme case, the win–lose and the lose–win styles of negotiation can lead to a deadlock followed by the lose–lose result. Deadlocks can occur when neither party is satisfied by the negotiations. Figure 12.2 shows the outcome when the negotiators use the win–lose or lose–win strategy.

Figure 12.2 Win–lose or lose–win strategies: one party feels satisfied, the other feels dissatisfied

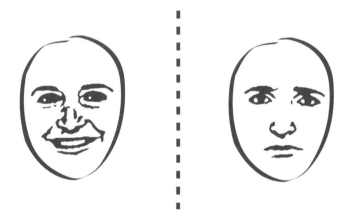

Lose–lose strategies result from a situation in which the objectives of both parties are too rigid, or when both parties are unable to collaborate, or are unaware of the opportunity to do so. The result is that both parties walk away from the negotiation dissatisfied. When agreement cannot be reached, a third party may mediate to help them reach a solution, or arbitrate and make the decision on behalf of both parties. Both sides may lose.

In any negotiation, be aware of your own and the other person's objectives and expectations. Keep your objectives reasonable and try to avoid the lose–lose outcome shown in Figure 12.3.

Personal styles in negotiation

Whenever people come together to negotiate, they bring their own personal styles, and these affect the way they communicate and handle the conflict. Table 12.1 presents Hellreigel's (1988) classification of five different ways of handling negotiation and conflict.

This classification also shows how personal style can help or hinder the negotiation

Personal styles can help or hinder conflict resolution.

Figure 12.3 Lose–lose strategy: both parties feel dissatisfied

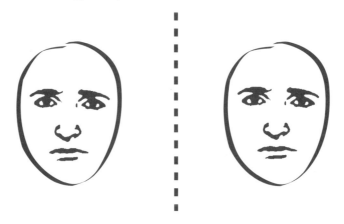

and how it can cause, prevent or resolve conflict. If you can recognise what style someone is using in the negotiation process you will become more capable of distinguishing the *real* message from *how it is delivered*. This skill will also help you to respond clearly.

Table 12.1 Personal negotiation styles

Type	Description
Self-denying	*Self-denying* people may be difficult to negotiate with as they are introverted and reticent with information, especially feedback. They hide their feelings and ideas from others.
Self-protecting	*Self-protecting* people use diversionary tactics such as discussing other people or side-tracking to other issues. They use these tactics to hide their true feelings and their ideas.
Self-exposing	*Self-exposing* people wish to be the centre of attention. They may demand this attention by speaking loudly, speaking over others, using attention-seeking body movements, or ignoring feedback and others' views.
Self-bargaining	*Self-bargaining* people will show you their feelings and ideas if you show yours first. These people wait until you lead them into negotiation. They may open up and negotiate when others initiate the process.
Self-actualising	*Self-actualising* people are the ideal negotiators as they want information and feedback from others. They present this information and feedback constructively to aid the negotiation process and to achieve goals and results without any conflict.

Psychological barriers

When you are negotiating, psychological barriers may arise. They may be produced by you or the other party. Be on the alert for signs of these barriers. 'Listen' for their effects and use your communication skills to ease or lower them. Psychological barriers to negotiation may include:

■ fear of being taken for a ride
■ wanting to be liked

- guilt about wanting to be assertive
- wanting to be 'nice'
- feeling intimidated by so-called powerful people
- fear of conflict or confrontation
- fear of losing face with the boss or colleagues
- lack of self-confidence.

Power in negotiation

When an organisation delegates work to its people to get the job done, it gives them power to act. **Power** may be used to influence and, in some cases, to control people. It can also be used to bring about change. Power can be exerted over one person or a group by another person or group. Power used well achieves good communication and results. Power can be used to manipulate others.

Power is the capacity to influence.

Each person has and can enjoy power. Observe how you use power. If you use it properly you will make an impact on workplace decisions and actions. Abuse or misuse it and people will mistrust you. Power is a useful tool in the negotiation process; however, if you misuse it or refuse to use it correctly, the likely result is tension and conflict.

Five types of workplace power are shown in Table 12.2. They operate in any workplace, either singly or in combination. Perception of what power is and how it should be used varies between people and organisations. Acknowledgment of, and deference to, power depends on peoples' perception of power and its use.

Table 12.2 Power at work

Type	Base of power	Example
Legitimate power	*Legitimate power* is based on a person's position or role in an organisation. Their authority and control over resources give them power that is acknowledged by others.	Chief Executive Officer (CEO) of a large organisation
Expertise power	People who have more skills and strengths than others have *expertise power*; their colleagues defer to them.	Graphic designer or computer expert
Reward power	*Reward power* is exerted by someone who has control over resources desired by others. Such a person can influence and manipulate others.	Employer who distributes a bonus annually
Coercive power	*Coercive power* is exerted by those who use their authority or any force, emotional or physical, against the interests of the other party.	Team leader who allocates duties, hours of work, overtime, holidays
Consultative power	*Consultative power* is exerted by someone who seeks information, considers others' advice and makes plans with others.	Union official who negotiates hours and wages in consultation with management and staff

Use of power

A person who has power, particularly over the allocation and use of resources, must be willing and able to use that power to make decisions and take action. If they refuse, or are unable to do this, conflict will arise because processes that are essential to the running of the workplace do not take place.

Rather than depending solely on your workplace power source or your personal power, develop strategies that achieve results. Use your communication skills to present your ideas without producing conflict.

Negotiation strategies

SKILLS
APPLY

Work in small groups.
1. Create a list of recent negotiations in which you have been involved.
2. For each situation, discuss your reasons for negotiating.
3. Were the needs and concerns of each party taken into account?
4. Choose one of the negotiations from your list and decide which strategies were used for it.
5. Which personal negotiation style did you use?
6. Briefly discuss how two different psychological barriers affect negotiation.

A five-step approach to negotiation

Follow five steps to negotiate an agreement.

Negotiation is a process in which two or more people (or parties) with common or conflicting interests decide on a specific issue or business transaction. This may at times produce win–win, win–lose, lose–win or lose–lose outcomes. The five-step approach is suited to a situation where the issue is more important than the relationship: for example, it is appropriate for purchasing a car or house but not for resolving a crisis with your partner. Fisher and Ury (1991) refer to this five-step approach as *positional bargaining* – that is, when a position is taken by each side, argued for and concessions are made to reach a compromise. The five stages of the negotiation process are shown in Figure 12.4.

Figure 12.4 The five-step approach to negotiation

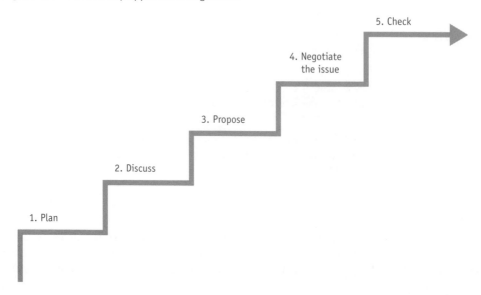

Plan for negotiation

Careful and thoughtful planning is essential before you negotiate. First, create a set of clear objectives to steer you towards the results you want. Prepared objectives allow you to progress through the five stages of negotiation. Think about how your objective can be achieved.

Gather data that helps you to:

■ give the other party relevant information
■ make sure this information is accurate and objective
■ develop and maintain good relationships with the other party
■ consider the other party's point of view.

Organise all the relevant information as this provides the ideal starting-point for your discussion. Plan your approach and the sequence of issues you wish to raise.

Assess the other party's objectives. Identify links and common ground. Anticipate the party's likely response to each of your issues, and prepare answers.

Here's an example of a negotiation.

> You have decided to buy a new four-wheel-drive vehicle. You want this type of vehicle as you will be driving on beaches and are concerned about safety. Your price range is $40 000–$45 000. Your preferred colour is blue. The vehicle must have air-conditioning and power steering. You have a 1994 Commodore sedan you want to trade in and expect the trade-in figure to be $6000–$8000. The car dealer has advertised a special deal for this weekend only of a Pegasus four-wheel-drive with power steering for $44 000 and free registration. You have previously test-driven this vehicle and decided this was the make you wanted to purchase.

Discuss

Set the communication climate by exchanging greetings; aim to establish trust and confidence. By being sociable you are able to establish a tension-free atmosphere.

Review proceedings leading up to the meeting. Iron out any differences in 'facts' before you start to negotiate. Confirm both parties' broad objectives and feelings. Listen carefully. Identify areas of agreement and try to establish some rapport with the other party. Your intention is to establish common ground before moving into areas of difference.

Create a positive communication climate.

> You were unable to visit the car showroom at the weekend. You approach the car dealer the following Monday with the advertisement offering the Pegasus for $44 000. After introductions, you refer to the advertisement and say that this is close to the price range you want to pay but you need to trade in your existing car. Also, you want air-conditioning. You ask whether the vehicle is available in blue duco. The car dealer confirms that they do have a vehicle available in the colour you want and with air-conditioning. He points out, however, that the deal in the newspaper was only on offer for that weekend and was for a vehicle without air-conditioning. They would be prepared to trade in your Commodore.

Propose

Define the issues and specify in detail what you wish to resolve. Where appropriate, link issues to the other party's objectives and focus on interests rather than positions.

Deal with one issue at a time. Try to keep to the point and avoid generalising, passing judgment on the other person, or confusing the other party's personality with the issue that must be negotiated.

Focus on interests rather than positions.

If the other party presents more than you can comprehend, or sounds confused, paraphrase their message to check that you understand it correctly. It is also useful for both parties to summarise the content, ideas and feelings being communicated.

The car dealer says he can sell you the Pegasus for $46 000 with air-conditioning but without free registration. You say that the maximum you can pay is the $44 000 offered in the weekend deal. The car dealer suggests that they examine the Commodore and gives you a trade-in price of $5500. You say that you want $8000 for the Commodore.

Negotiate the issue

Start by asking for what you want, but accept that your goals may have to be modified or compromised. Your intention is to collaborate with the other party to produce a solution that is satisfactory to both. Remember the phrase: 'If . . . then . . .'. Separate the people from the issue. Try to generate as many options as possible – this gives both parties room to negotiate a solution.

Throughout the discussion, keep summarising the points to confirm understanding, particularly when complex issues are involved. Take the time to confirm what you have negotiated so far. Unless agreement is fully understood by both parties, the settlement may not last.

The dealer suggests that they could offer you $6500 for the Commodore but are unable to reduce the price of $46 000 for the Pegasus. If you are prepared to accept the Pegasus without air-conditioning then he could lower the price to $44 000. Your counter-offer is that you would pay $45 000 for the Pegasus with air-conditioning but only if the trade-in price for the Commodore is raised to $7000. The car dealer considers your offer and, after consulting head office, agrees to sell you the Pegasus on those conditions.

Confirm

Once the agreement is concluded, check that each party is committed to it. This confirmation is the final stage in the negotiation process.

The contract is signed and you take delivery of the blue Pegasus with power steering and air-conditioning.

The five-step approach to negotiation will help you negotiate more effectively. Good negotiation strategies enable you to solve the problem in such a way that both parties win. Clearly state your needs and goals as you negotiate and listen to those expressed by the other party. This allows each party to evaluate the other's needs and goals and the areas of common interest. People who negotiate honestly treat one another as equals. Another approach to negotiating is *principled bargaining*.

Principled bargaining

Negotiate to satisfy the interests of both parties.

In contrast to positional bargaining, as illustrated in the negotiation steps above, Fisher and Ury (1991) developed a concept known as **principled bargaining**. This works well when a group of stakeholders have a common interest. An acknowledgment to work together for mutual outcomes is the essence of the principled bargaining approach: it acknowledges the Australian ethic of a 'fair go'. Everyone is treated equitably. In Fisher and Ury's view, each negotiated agreement should satisfy the following three criteria.

1. It should be a wise agreement, if possible.
2. It should be efficient.
3. It should improve, or at least not damage, relationships.

The principled negotiation method takes time, energy and commitment. Its four elements in the Fisher and Ury method are shown in Table 12.3.

Table 12.3 The principled negotiation method

Element	Purpose
People	To separate the people from the problem
Interests	To focus on interests rather than positions
Options	To generate a range of possibilities before choosing one
Criteria	To ensure that results are based on some objective standard

To implement the principled negotiation method you need to:

- state your case clearly and persuasively
- organise your facts well
- be aware of the timing and speed of the talks
- assess the others' needs properly
- be sensitive to those needs
- have patience
- not be unduly worried by conflict
- be committed to a win–win philosophy.

The purpose of the negotiation is to satisfy the interests of the parties involved. Sometimes these interests are not met; for example, a goal that is too rigid or a position from which you will not move. A negotiation based on satisfying both party's interests means that each must consider the view of the other. On some occasions you may have to settle for something less than your original goal.

BATNA stands for the 'best alternative to a negotiated agreement'. When you are not able to negotiate an agreement that meets your goal, it is useful to have a BATNA ready. Remember, the reason why both parties negotiate is to achieve something better than what they would achieve otherwise.

WATNA stands for the 'worst alternative to a negotiated agreement'. If the person you are negotiating with is your manager or supervisor you may have to think about a WATNA. If the other person has the legitimate power, or if you want the relationship to continue as it is, you may have to settle for less than your preferred outcome. You might have to modify your goal to maintain the relationship, especially if the other person is your boss. Sometimes your goal may be unrealistic and you have to modify it to make it more realistic. You may even decide not to negotiate if you feel that it will not achieve something better.

By identifying the BATNA and WATNA, you are exploring the alternatives available if negotiation is not possible. Rather than accept an unsatisfactory outcome you can say 'no' to negotiation.

Interviews and negotiation

Interviews are used in many negotiation situations to gain acceptance of a particular course of action or a new idea or change. As you structure this kind of interview, refer to the principles of persuasion outlined in Chapter 18, Writing Business Letters. Decide on an approach that will catch your target audience's attention, interest and willingness to take action. The persuasive interview is a useful selling as well as negotiation technique. It can also be used to negotiate and gain acceptance of policy changes.

Objectives of persuasive interviews

Consider and answer the following four questions to achieve your objectives as you negotiate in a persuasive interview.

1. What results do you expect?
2. When do you require the results?
3. Whose action do you want?
4. What is your plan to achieve what you want?

Plan the persuasive interview by knowing exactly what you want to change or accomplish: your objectives. Determine what you know already and ask questions to find out more. Anticipate objections, prepare responses and evidence.

A persuasive interview aims to persuade the interviewee to change their attitude, or accept something new. Conduct it by establishing rapport, using your negotiation skills well, identifying or creating a need, and obtaining agreement. Involve the interviewee in generating goals and solutions and move them towards their commitment to these solutions.

Problem solving by negotiation

Problem solving by negotiation is dealt with by a team or group of people who already have a working relationship and want to solve a work-related problem. The six-step approach to problem solving by negotiation will succeed only if the relationship is important to both parties and if they have a genuine desire to solve the problem rather than to win (see Table 12.4).

Negotiating methods

In the negotiating process, the parties involved may choose one of five different negotiation methods. Each has a different possible outcome. A skilful negotiator is able to identify them and recognise which one is being used by the other person.

1. Compromise
2. Collaboration
3. Competition
4. Accommodation
5. Withdrawal or avoidance.

Compromise means to settle differences through concessions made by one or both parties. A compromise usually produces a win–win or win–lose result. When the settlement meets the needs and goals of both parties (win–win), both are satisfied with the outcome. When the solution meets the needs and goals of only one party (win–lose), the other party is dissatisfied with the outcome (see Figure 12.5).

Table 12.4 Problem solving by negotiating: the six-step approach

Step	Strategy
1. Select best time	Choose a time when both or all members involved with the problem are relatively calm. If one party has strong or uncomfortable feelings, it will be difficult to communicate.
2. Define needs	Needs are defined by listening and sharing with each other. It is important to discover the basic needs of each party at the start, and not jump in too early with solutions.
3. Brainstorm solutions	It is important to list every solution suggested and not evaluate or judge any of them at this stage.
4. Evaluate solutions	Everyone must do more listening and talking ('I' statements) here so that all ideas and feelings about each proposed solution are heard and valued.
5. Choose solutions	Pick solutions that everyone can agree on, then plan when and how to carry them out.
6. Carry out solutions	Check to see how the solutions are working. Listening and sharing at this point are important to resolve any further problems.

Collaboration involves people cooperating to produce a solution satisfactory to both parties (win–win). It improves personal relationships and allows the exploration of new ideas. Permanent solutions and commitment to them can be achieved this way. On the other hand, it is time-consuming and demands good negotiating skills on each side.

Competition often leads to one party gaining advantage over the other, if it can negotiate at the expense of the other's needs. Since the competitive approach usually

Figure 12.5 The probable impact of negotiation styles and conflict resolution strategies on relationships and goal achievement

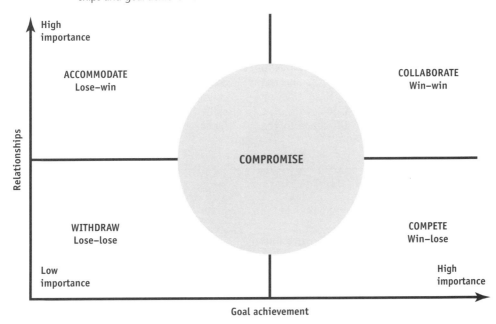

produces a win–lose result, it is bad for personal relationships. The solution is likely to be temporary as there is no commitment from the losing party, so the problem will occur again. It also leaves the losing side in a difficult situation.

Accommodation means that only one party is willing to oblige or adapt to meet the needs of the other. It produces a win–lose outcome. However, this method is useful for negotiating on minor matters. The result can go one way or the other. It is suitable if the accommodating party does not really care about the loss. However, the negotiating parties may not bother to look for creative solutions. With this negotiation method, points of view are easily swayed.

Withdrawal (avoidance) is a negotiation method that makes both parties lose, because one party retracts their point of view or backs away from the situation. This means that negotiation is broken off before either party can find an acceptable solution. Such dissatisfaction may lead to conflict in the future.

The negotiation context

Consider the context.

The choice of negotiating method will be influenced by the context in which you negotiate and by your range of personal communication and negotiation skills (see Table 12.5). This context is the situation within which the negotiation takes place or the circumstances surrounding the particular negotiation.

Applying negotiation skills to solve a problem

APPLY SKILLS

Joe is the human resource officer of a firm that is going through a period of cost-cutting. Joe sees the need to create a new position and appoint a highly qualified and skilled person for it.

The new position will require a person who can travel throughout the state, liaise with staff and establish close links with the firm's clients to achieve a more client-directed service.

Joe realises the cost of this appointment is not acceptable to the firm, but believes it is vital for the firm's growth. Joe prepares to negotiate with his manager, Beth. She has been told by her Divisional Head that no more staff can be employed unless the new position will make a real difference to the

firm's performance. In their last meeting, her Divisional Head said: 'Remember, don't be soft when your staff ask you to make a new position. Unless it is essential we can't afford it.'

1. Define Joe's problem.
2. What are the sources of potential conflict in this situation?
3. Role-play the situation in groups of three, using the six-step approach to problem solving. One person plays Joe, another plays Beth, and the third observes. The observer is to use Self-check 12.1 to note what communication skills are used and to give Beth and Joe feedback after the negotiation.

SELF CHECK 12.1

Negotiation

In this negotiation have I:	Yes	No	Unsure
Identified my needs?	☐	☐	☐
Been willing to identify the other party's needs?	☐	☐	☐
Used accepting and cooperative body movement?	☐	☐	☐
Used demanding or threatening body movement?	☐	☐	☐
Used positive and constructive language?	☐	☐	☐

Used negative or destructive language?	☐	☐	☐
Acknowledged the needs of the other party?	☐	☐	☐
Established realistic goals?	☐	☐	☐
Generated a range of options?	☐	☐	☐
Found common ground between me and the other party?	☐	☐	☐
Identified any points I am willing to trade?	☐	☐	☐
Become aware of any points the other party is willing to trade?	☐	☐	☐
Negotiated the issue, not the people?	☐	☐	☐
Chosen an appropriate environment?	☐	☐	☐
Used a negotiation method appropriate to this context?	☐	☐	☐

Table 12.5 Negotiating methods

Method	In practice
Compromise	The manager of a small organisation requests ideas for a sales promotion. Two employees each make presentations to the manager. He suggests they negotiate and make a decision on which is the better proposal. During negotiations, the two employees compromise and agree to present a proposal that includes ideas from both submissions.
Collaboration	Two training companies are involved in information technology training. Both are competing for limited federal funding. The training companies arrange a meeting and, after much deliberation and negotiation, decide to join forces and collaborate in tendering and allocating resources to meet the demand.
Competition	Two divisional managers have arranged staff meetings on the same day. Secretarial assistance is required to prepare agendas and record minutes of the meetings. It will not be possible for the secretarial staff to accommodate both and one of the meetings will have to be moved to another day. The two divisional managers confer and the competition over available resources results in one divisional manager having to postpone his staff meeting to later in the week. He resolves that, should this situation happen again, he will make certain he is not the one to postpone his meeting.
Accommodation	Two teachers have been given programs that result in one teacher having all senior classes and the other only junior classes. The teacher who has been given the junior classes feels there should be a more equitable distribution of classes as the senior students are more interesting to teach. After discussion, and in consultation with the head teacher, the teacher who has been given the senior classes agrees to change her program and both teachers are given a mixture of senior and junior classes.
Withdrawal or avoidance	Two partners have agreed they need more space and more exposure to passing customers. One partner wants to rent a large office in an up-market area at a rent considerably more than they are paying at present. The other wants to rent larger premises in the area they are presently in, stating they are known there and the small increase would be affordable. After three meetings to negotiate the move into larger premises one partner decides it is not worth the effort and refuses to discuss the matter. This is withdrawal from the negotiations. Negotiations break down and they remain in the smaller premises. Neither is satisfied.

Negotiation methods used to resolve conflict

SKILLS
APPLY

In groups of three, complete the following tasks.

1. a. List five types of power and give examples of how each could be used in the workplace.
   b. Discuss the similarities between coercive and reward power and list two differences between them.
   c. Discuss the similarities between legitimate power and expertise and list two differences between them.

2. The negotiation method and the conflict resolution strategy you choose influences the result of the negotiation, both in terms of your relationship with others and the achievement of your goals.

a. In Table 12.6, column 2, rank the importance that each negotiation method places on relationships. Use high (H), low (L) or a combination of both (C).

b. In Table 12.6, column 3, rank the importance that each negotiation method places on the achievement of goals or tasks. Use high (H), low (L) or a combination of both (C).

c. In Table 12.6, column 4, identify the conflict resolution strategy most likely to be used with each negotiation method. Refer to Figure 12.5.

Table 12.6 Likely strategies

Negotiation style	Relationship	Goal achievement	Likely strategy
Those who collaborate			
Those who compete			
Those who accommodate			
Those who withdraw			
Those who compromise			

Skills in conflict resolution and negotiation

In your organisation several negotiating styles and strategies are likely to be observed. Some achieve acceptable responses, others hinder negotiation and conflict resolution. Some solutions may be simple and practical. Others may be complex and difficult and may even require attitude changes and commitment from each party.

Negotiation involves a range of positions by both parties. You might change the other party's position, change your own position or arrive at a compromise. Clearly define your own objectives as well as the other party's. This places you in a better position to understand what is happening.

Negotiation methods affect relationships and the achievement of goals.

Figure 12.5 shows how each negotiation method affects relationships and the achievement of goals. It also matches each method with the most likely conflict resolution strategy. Once you understand them all you are in a position to decide which one is suited to a situation and your intended result.

Negotiation based on empathy for the other party establishes a climate where both parties can communicate easily. By contrast, **confrontation** leads to disputes and extreme positions. Check to see that both parties are working from the same agenda. Ensure that this agenda is clear and covers the full list of items to be negotiated.

Focus on the problem, not individual personalities. Ask questions to check that you understand the other side's expectations and position. Avoid aggression. Use your assertive communication skills. Listen carefully to the other party.

Establish the criteria that will make a realistic solution acceptable to both parties. This may involve several options. Successful negotiation develops these options into a plan of action.

Personal qualities of a good negotiator

Each negotiation method and the personal qualities of each negotiator affect the relationships between the people involved and their chances of achieving their goals. Their personal qualities affect the way they state their case, organise information, make proposals, discuss the issues and acknowledge the interests of the other party. Personal qualities also affect the choice of negotiation strategy. Good negotiators have good communication skills, create a positive communication climate and have some of the personal qualities listed in Table 12.7.

Stress is also a factor that should be taken into account. Lengthy negotiations can increase the level of stress experienced and result in a less desirable outcome.

Personal qualities affect the communication climate.

Table 12.7 Personal qualities of a good negotiator

Quality	Strategy
Ability to plan	Plan before negotiating; identify your own position and that of the other party.
Capacity to think clearly under stress	Be aware of your stress level and know how to deal with it.
Ability to be practical	Be flexible and solution-oriented; focus on the 'big picture' and all interests.
Capacity to communicate well	Listen, question, give feedback and speak clearly in the negotiating process.
Ability to act assertively and with integrity	Approach the issue assertively and negotiate with empathy.
Ability to identify the interests of each party	Separate the people from the problem; focus on the interests of both parties to work things out.
Capacity to identify standards	Ensure that the result is based on objective standards.
Willingness to follow up	Check agreement and take follow-up actions.

Visit the Companion Website at **www.prenhall.com/dwyer_au**. Choose the Good Practice/Bad Practice activity in Chapter 12 to apply the five-step negotiation process.

Chapter summary

Distinguish several negotiation strategies. Each negotiation strategy is named after the outcome it is likely to produce: win–win, win–lose, lose–win or lose–lose.

Analyse personal styles and the way they affect negotiation. Personal styles can help or hinder a negotiation. Self-denying, self-protecting and self-exposing styles make it difficult for one party to evaluate the other party's interests and issues. On the other hand, people who use self-bargaining and self-actualising styles communicate well with the other party. Once both parties understand one another, it is easier to negotiate their mutual interests.

Identify five power bases. These are legitimate power, expertise power, reward power, coercive power and consultative power.

Plan a negotiation. The five-step approach to negotiation (*positional bargaining*) is built on the first stage, the planning stage. Once you have planned, you can complete the discussing, proposing, negotiating and checking stages more successfully.

Use principled bargaining. This negotiation method has four elements: people, interests, options and criteria. It aims for a wise agreement, if possible, and one that is efficient, and designed to improve or at least not damage relationships. After an agreement is reached, record together mutually acceptable follow-up actions to minimise any potential communication barriers. This will help to keep the relationship constructive and positive.

Use persuasive interviews. To gain acceptance of a particular course of action, the persuasive interview is a useful technique. The interview should be planned to achieve your objectives. Consider the results you expect, when they are required, whose action you want and your plan to achieve what you want.

Use negotiation to solve problems. First, make sure that the relationship is important to you both and that neither party intends to compete and win. Aim to base a solution on the interests of both parties. Complete six steps: choose an appropriate time, define the needs, brainstorm solutions, evaluate solutions, choose solutions and carry them out. As you negotiate the issue, check that both parties understand it the same way. Once an agreement is reached, check the areas of agreement to avoid any misunderstanding or problems in the future.

Analyse various negotiating options. The five negotiating methods are compromise, collaboration, competition, accommodation and withdrawal. Those who withdraw have little chance of achieving their goals or of building relationships. Those who compete may achieve their goals at the expense of the relationship with the other party. Those who compromise are less likely to achieve their goals but more likely to maintain a good relationship with the other party. Those who accommodate adapt their needs to meet the needs of the other party. Those who collaborate are most likely to achieve mutually acceptable goals and maintain a good relationship with the other negotiators.

Use appropriate interpersonal communication skills. To achieve the best outcome from negotiation each party has to be able to exchange information in a way that establishes trust and confidence. A range of important listening, questioning, speaking and non-verbal communication skills is required for each stage of negotiation.

1. Define the term 'negotiation'. Why do people negotiate?
2. Define and briefly explain the terms 'win–win strategy' and 'win–lose strategy'.
3. List and define five different personal negotiation styles.
4. List five types of power. How is power used in negotiation?
5. Briefly explain two psychological barriers to negotiation.
6. How does the win–win approach make people partners, not opponents?
7. List and explain the purpose of each step in the five-step approach to negotiation.
8. a. Why is it important to base negotiation on the merits of a situation?
   b. Why is it important to distinguish between the issue and the people?

9. a. What are the three criteria of the principled bargaining approach?
   b. List the four elements of the principled negotiation method.
   c. What is the purpose of each element?
10. Define the terms 'BATNA', 'WATNA' and 'agreement chart'.
11. List the six steps to use when solving problems by negotiating.
    a. Briefly describe the five different negotiating methods.
    b. What is the likely outcome of each?
12. Choose two personal qualities a good negotiator has and explain how they affect the communication climate for negotiation.
13. a. What does a persuasive interview aim to achieve?
    b. Name two strategies that help the interviewer achieve this objective.

Workplace negotiation

During negotiations each party's position must be distinguished from the interests at stake. *Positions* are the possible solutions that individuals see as their answer to the issue being negotiated. *Interests* consist of the needs and concerns each party wants to satisfy, and the basis for bringing the parties together to negotiate. These must be made clear to reach a durable agreement based on cooperative solutions.

Work in groups of three to role-play the following situation.

Situation: Lisa is one of five employees in a fashion design business in the central business district of the city. She is responsible for reception duties, word processing and clerical work. Lisa attends a desktop publishing course at college two nights a week from 6 pm to 9 pm. Two months ago she injured her back in a car accident and now requires physiotherapy at least twice a week.

Marion is Lisa's employer. She wants Lisa to start and finish work at regular times and to be at work on time.

To make it possible for Lisa to visit the physiotherapist twice a week and attend college, Marion has agreed to allow Lisa to start work at 9.30 am two days per week. However, for the past two weeks Lisa has been arriving at work late on the two mornings she visits the physiotherapist. Marion decides it is time to talk to Lisa about the situation.

When Marion raises the issue of late arrival at work, Lisa says: 'Because I go to physiotherapy from 8.30 to 9 am it's harder to find a park in the city and this makes me late.'

Task: One person plays the part of Marion, another plays Lisa and the third person takes the role of observer. Those playing Marion and Lisa are to:

- use the principled bargaining method to focus on people, interests, options and criteria (rather than positions)
- outline clearly as many interests as possible

■ collaborate to reconcile any conflicting interests

■ reach a durable agreement.

The purpose of the negotiation is to meet Lisa's and Marion's needs and concerns by reaching a collaborative, durable agreement.

The observer should use Self-check 12.1 to observe (without speaking) the role play and then to offer feedback on how well the participants completed each of the tasks above.

Key terms

accommodation
BATNA
coercive power
collaboration
competition
compromise
confrontation
consultative power
expertise power

legitimate power
lose–lose strategy
lose–win strategy
negotiation
power
principled bargaining
reward power
self-actualising
self-bargaining

self-denying
self-exposing
self-protecting
WATNA
win–lose strategy
win–win strategy
withdrawal

CASE STUDY

Everything is negotiable

by Linda Jenkins

It's all negotiable. Every new job – every performance review, in fact – is an opportunity to negotiate base salary, various kinds of bonuses, benefits, stock options, and other incentives that add to job satisfaction and provide financial security. Taking control of your job search and conducting a smart search that takes into account more than just financial considerations can also lead to that elusive condition called happiness. Are you prepared to negotiate for happiness?

The negotiation process is an opportunity to define, communicate, and achieve what you want. But to get the right job that pays what you deserve, you'll need to do your homework. The first step in the negotiation clinic is to understand the negotiation basics.

Negotiation requires gathering information, planning your approach, considering different alternatives and viewpoints, communicating clearly and specifically, and making decisions to reach your goal. In her book, *Job Offer! A How-to Negotiation Guide*, author Maryanne L. Wegerbauer describes how each party in a negotiation can fulfil specific needs and wants of the other party, a concept called 'relative power'. According to Wegerbauer, understanding your strengths and resources, being able to respond to the needs of the other party and knowing your competition enable you to assess your bargaining position more accurately.

Learn the power factors

What is your power over the other side of the table? Relative power, Wegerbauer says, is a function of the following.

Business climate factors

■ Overall state of the economy and the industry in which you compete

■ Overall unemployment rate and the general employment picture

■ Demand for industry – and profession-specific knowledge and skills

Company factors

■ Profitability

■ Position in the business cycle (startup, growing, stable, turnaround)

Hiring manager factors

■ Urgency of the company's need to fill the position

■ Decision-making authority

■ Staffing budget

Applicant factors

- Other opportunities
- Technical expertise, unique knowledge/skill set
- Resources (financial depth, networks, etc.)
- Level of competition/availability of other candidates
- Career risk

Plan and communicate

A negotiation is composed of two major steps: planning (research and strategy) and communication (information exchange and agreement). In the planning step, get as much information as you can up front and, using both the company's written and unwritten signals, map your skills against what the company values.

Give it time

Timing is also important. Remember that the best time to negotiate is after a serious job offer has been made and before you have accepted it. Once you are clear about the initial offer, you can express interest and even enthusiasm, but ask for more time to consider the job offer. Wegerbauer suggests that this request is made 'in light of the importance of the decision'. Sometimes you can split up the negotiating session into two meetings: one to firm up the job design and responsibilities and the second to go over compensation and benefits. The key message here is not to make an impulsive decision. If they really want you, there's time.

Consider the alternatives

You should be prepared with a rationale for everything to strengthen your position.

Counteroffers are an expected part of many negotiations, so be sure to remain flexible. Keep in mind that different companies can give negotiations more or less latitude. Smaller companies may be more flexible than large, bureaucratic companies. Unionised companies usually have very little room for individual negotiations.

Negotiate for a win–win

Remember that the negotiation is not about strong-arm tactics or win/lose. It is a two-way process where you and your prospective employer are each trying to get something you need. In a negotiation, you're both designing the terms of a transaction so that each of you will receive the maximum benefit from the final agreement.

Source: Linda Jenkins, 'Part 1: Everything is negotiable', reprinted with permission from <www.salary.com> accessed 31 December 2001.

Questions

1. The article suggests that, in a negotiation about salary levels, you should 'remember that the negotiation is not about strong-arm tactics or win/lose'. Explain how planning, communicating, giving it time and considering the alternatives can help you negotiate for a win–win salary agreement.
2. The principled bargaining negotiation method works well when people have a common interest and will work together for mutual outcomes. Discuss the elements in the principled negotiation method and describe how it can be used in salary negotiations.

Conflict management

In this chapter you will learn how to:

- describe the five levels of conflict

- identify signs of conflict

- prepare a map to identify issues, key needs and concerns

- use active listening for conflict resolution

- give feedback assertively

- use communication skills that encourage constructive responses to conflict in the workplace

- identify the purpose of different types of interviews.

Evaluate your communication skills by completing the self-check in the chapter.

A capacity to manage conflict is one of the most important skills you can possess in your personal and work life. Conflict is caused by a clash of opinions, values or needs. It can be positive and constructive or negative and destructive, depending on the way people deal with it.

Conflict is a part of life. It arises when people's needs are not met. These needs can be physical, financial, social, educational, intellectual, recreational, spiritual, tangible or intangible. However, even when conflict arises it is possible, by finding areas of common ground, to remove some of the differences and emphasise the similarities between people.

People who acknowledge a source of conflict and negotiate to remove it tend to learn more about the situation, each other, and each other's needs.

What is conflict?

Conflict can be positive or negative.

Everyone experiences **conflict** at some time. It occurs whenever two people, teams or groups have different wants or goals and one party interferes with the other's attempts to satisfy these. Differences in the way people interpret facts, differences in values, and the various ways people take action to satisfy their wants and **needs** can all cause conflict.

Before dealing with any conflict, make sure you understand what is happening: identify what is causing the conflict. Is the problem a difference in facts, goals, methods or values? By understanding the real cause of the conflict, you will be better equipped to choose from the range of constructive responses suited to conflict resolution.

Levels of conflict

Conflict moves through several levels before it reaches the crisis level. At the first level, people experience discomfort, a feeling that things are not quite right. At the next level, an incident occurs. Emotions are not running high yet, but something has come between the people concerned.

Stay alert for signs of discomfort and incidents.

People who are aware of discomfort or an incident can use their communication skills to clarify the problem at this point, before the situation escalates to the next level: misunderstanding. A misunderstanding between individuals or groups can interfere with their relationship. It can arise over facts, or it may be about the goals or intentions of the parties involved.

Once **tension** arises over the misunderstanding, the situation is very close to a crisis. When people feel anxious about talking, working or coming into contact with each other, emotions run high. Negative attitudes and any negative response – an outburst of anger, or avoidance of the other party – will lead to a crisis, the fifth level of conflict. By staying alert for signs of discomfort and incidents (the first and second levels of conflict), you will be able to use the most appropriate resolution strategy before the conflict moves to higher levels.

The five levels of conflict are illustrated in Figure 13.1.

Mapping the conflict

A conflict map enables you to see the total picture.

A **map** is a useful way of finding the cause of the conflict. The cause may be a difference in facts, goals or values, or in methods of taking action. A map allows you to see the whole picture – your perception of the conflict, the other person's perception and the issues involved. Figure 13.2 shows some of the points identified on a conflict map. An example of a conflict map is shown in Figure 13.3.

Figure 13.1 Levels of conflict

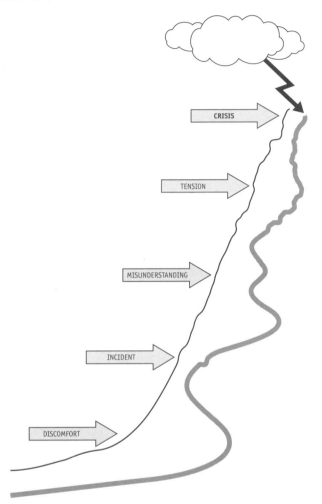

Prepare the map

There are four steps to mapping a conflict, each with a specific purpose.

1. Define the issue – to gain a clear idea of the issue/s to be mapped.
2. Identify who is involved – to identify and group together people with shared needs and concerns.
3. List each party's main needs and concerns – to work out the win–win approach and generate appropriate solutions.
4. Read the map – to draw together common threads and highlight points of special concern or importance.

By preparing and reading the map together each party in the conflict can see common threads and points of **concern**. Then the parties design the **options** and select the most appropriate one.

Figure 13.2 Points to look for on the map

Area where more
information
is needed

Common ground,
similar needs
and concerns

Leads worth
following through

MAP
SHOWS

New perspectives
and insights

Special concerns,
areas of difficulty

Hidden agendas,
(hidden fears/payoffs)

Mapping the conflict

SKILLS
APPLY

1. Think of a conflict that was difficult to resolve.
2. What was the main issue?
3. What made it difficult to resolve?
4. How were people's key needs and

concerns – including interests, values and hopes – identified?
5. Map this conflict, using the layout shown in Figure 13.3.

Fgure 13.3 Mapping a conflict

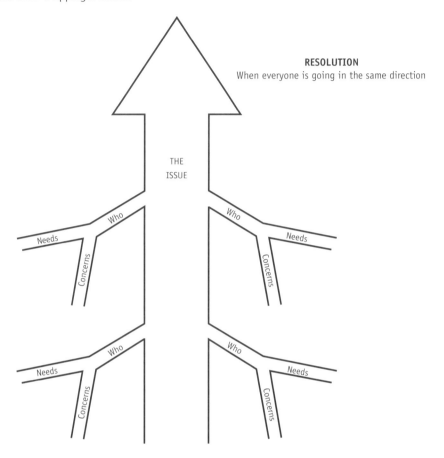

Understanding conflict

1. Work in pairs to discuss conflict. What does the term mean to you?
2. a. Think of a conflict that has been handled in a destructive way. Discuss the likely outcome of such an approach.
   b. Think of a conflict that has been handled in a constructive way. Discuss the likely outcome of such an approach.
   c. Complete Table 13.1 to identify the outcomes produced by handling conflict in a destructive way and in a constructive way.
3. a. Discuss a conflict you have recently experienced.
   b. What level did the conflict reach?
   c. Identify each level through which the conflict moved.
   d. What was the final outcome?
4. How can conflict be positive?
5. What are some of the sources of conflict at work?

Table 13.1 Likely outcomes

Handling conflict in a destructive way	Handling conflict in a constructive way
1.	1.
2.	2.
3.	3.
4.	4.

Design the options

Various strategies can be used to design the options before taking action.

- Brainstorm to list the options available.
- Use Dewey's reflective thinking process.
- Use the decision-making agenda.
- Divide, or chunk, the problem into small parts.
- Use a trial and error approach.

For more information on brainstorming, refer to Chapter 5.

Select the most appropriate option

Before you can select the most appropriate option it is important to link any similar or complementary options developed in the brainstorming session. The simplest way to do this on the map is to join similar options with a line. Then remove any options that are inappropriate. Analyse those that are left in terms of how well they will meet the main need or concern. Then list the options in the order in which they will be acted on.

Act on the chosen options

Set out *what* will be done, *how* it will be done, *who* will do it, *when* it will be completed and the expected *results* in an **action plan**. This is the working document for carrying out the chosen options. Keep the plan realistic and identify the time by which the options must be carried out. Unless you act on the options, the conflict will continue.

Constructive responses to conflict

Responses to conflict are learned early in our childhood. These responses become habits and reactions which we tend to use without thought in our adult life. By recognising early behaviour patterns and by learning new ways to handle conflict we can sometimes avoid repeating the conflicts of the past and respond more appropriately.

Communication is essential in conflict resolution.

Some of the techniques used to resolve conflict are shown in Table 13.2. However, no matter what the source of conflict is, or what level of conflict is involved, the key to conflict resolution is the capacity to communicate well.

Assertion

People who are able to say what they mean and acknowledge other people's rights to express opinions and feelings are assertive communicators. They are better able to use a variety of communication strategies to resolve conflict.

Table 13.2 Responses to conflict

Type	Purpose	Behaviour	Intended outcome
Fight	To be in control and defend a position	Aggressive	I win – you lose
Flight	To escape the situation and its outcome	Submissive	I lose – you win
Flow	To acknowledge the situation and respond appropriately	Assertive	I win – you win

Source: Adapted from materials of *The Conflict Resolution Network*, PO Box 1016, Chatswood, NSW 2067, Australia. Phone: 02 9419 8500; email: crn@crnhq.org; website: <www.crnhq.org>.

Assertive behaviour

Assertive behaviour shows in your way of speaking and questioning, and in your listening and other nonverbal behaviour. This kind of behaviour is constructive and helpful when conflict arises because the needs of both parties are acknowledged and dealt with. Both parties are also more likely to understand one another and the situation.

Acting assertively in a conflict means standing up for your rights and expressing what you believe, feel and want in direct, honest and appropriate ways that respect others' rights.

Assertive behaviour increases our self-esteem, develops respect for each other and helps us achieve our goals. It allows us to express our feelings in a way that is unlikely to make others feel defensive or aggressive.

Assertive behaviour builds mutual respect.

Non-assertive behaviour

Non-assertive behaviour is another term for **aggressive** or **submissive behaviour**. By behaving in this way we fail to express honest feelings, thoughts and beliefs. Aggressive people usually try to win at all costs by dominating and humiliating others. Such behaviour shows little respect for others. Submissive people, by contrast, are unable to promote their point of view and even ignore their own needs. They lack self-respect.

Non-assertive behaviour is best illustrated by the **drama triangle** (Figure 13.4). People who play the role of **victim** behave in a helpless manner. They speak and act as

Non-assertive behaviour is another term for aggressive or submissive behaviour.

Figure 13.4 Drama triangle

Source: Steiner, C.M. *Scripts People Live*, Grove Press, New York, 1974.

if everyone is against them and as if they cannot do anything for themselves. In a conflict situation they are unable to act, and give up. They are not real victims, but behave like helpless victims just to have someone else rescue or persecute them.

People who play the role of **persecutor** offer rewards or punishment to those who play the helpless victim role. Persecutors put the other person down and bully them. In contrast, people who play the role of **rescuer** offer help and support, sometimes denying their own needs. They may try to protect the victim from the persecutor.

The submissive behaviour shown in the **flight response** (see Table 13.2) can increase the conflict that the submissive person is trying to avoid. The aggressive behaviour shown in the **fight response** widens the differences between the two parties and increases the conflict. Contrast this with the assertive behaviour in the **flow response** shown in the **success triangle** (Figure 13.5).

Assertion lets you express your needs and concerns in a conflict. When it is used with the win–win approach, and with others who also use the win–win approach, each party can consider the needs of the other and move towards a solution that satisfies as many needs as possible. Those who keep alert for the discomfort and incident levels of conflict are able to prevent the escalation of conflict to higher levels.

Figure 13.5 Success triangle

Source: Steiner, C.M. *Scripts People Live*, Grove Press, New York, 1974.

Assertive statements

Assertive statements make people aware of your rights.

Assertive statements are used to make people aware of your rights while you respect theirs. If their behaviour is aggressive (not respecting your rights), or dangerous to themselves or others, send clear assertive messages and listen to the message from the other party. Assertion and 'I' messages are discussed more fully in Chapter 4, Effective Workplace Communication.

Three-part assertive messages

A basic assertive message has three parts.

The goal of assertiveness is to be caring, honest and accepting in our relationships with others. The basic message has three parts:

1. This is what I think . . .
2. this is what I feel . . . and
3. this is how I see the situation.

For example:

1. I know we're really busy,
2. but I feel stressed when everything is given equal importance
3. and I would like some way of grading the work from most important to least important.

'I' messages are assertive statements that help to send a clear message, particularly in a conflict, about what you want or how you feel. It increases other people's understanding of your situation and your point of view.

In a conflict situation, the 'I' message has three parts. It states the other person's action or behaviour, your response to the action and your preferred outcome.

action + your response + your preferred outcome

The 'I' message clearly states how the negotiation and the suggested result affect you. The other person receives an impartial message about this effect. The 'I' statement does not judge or put the other person down. Communication is continued on the basis of this statement and understanding. As you identify your needs and deal with the issues, discuss one specific issue at a time. The likely impact of an assertive 'I' message response to an aggressive message is shown in Figure 13.6.

Nonverbal messages

In a conflict, speak in a pleasant way, send appropriate verbal messages to the other person and match your nonverbal behaviour to the spoken message. Check your style of relating, to see whether your spoken and nonverbal messages say the same thing. Many of the messages we receive from others are affected by their nonverbal messages.

Match the verbal and nonverbal parts of the message.

Pay attention to the other person's nonverbal behaviour and identify what is aggressive, assertive or submissive. Self-check 13.1 gives some examples of nonverbal body and facial behaviour. Practise using assertive nonverbal behaviour and avoid aggressive and submissive nonverbal behaviour.

Figure 13.6 Possible outcomes of an assertive 'I' message response to an aggressive message

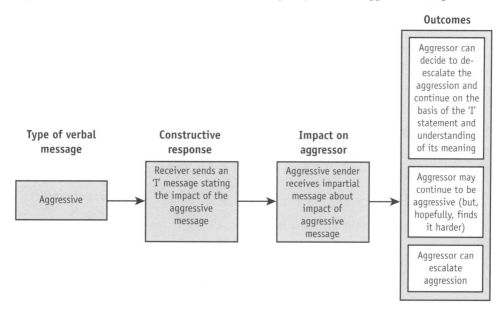

If you can interpret someone else's nonverbal behaviour as well as their verbal messages, you have two ways of checking the content. This feedback is very important as you negotiate to remove conflict. Ask the other person questions to check that your interpretation of their information is correct.

Responding to conflict

SKILLS
APPLY

Work in small groups.
1. Discuss the three types of response to conflict – fight, flight and flow.
2. List some examples of fight, flight and flow behaviour.
3. What is the likely outcome from each of the three types of response to conflict?
4. Describe the win–win approach to conflict resolution. In your opinion, what are its main benefits?
5. a. Read each of the following statements aloud with what you think is the appropriate tone and inflection. Distinguish between the 'I' messages and the non-'I' messages.
    i. 'I feel angry when my conversation is cut off.'
    ii. 'I find it hard to work when you stand and look over my shoulder.'
    iii. 'I'm unable to work with you constantly leaning over my shoulder and upsetting me.'
    iv. 'I feel angry when you interrupt because you're more interested in other things.'
    v. 'You always look after yourself. What about my needs?'
    vi. 'You're always late and that makes it so hard for us.'
    vii. 'I missed you when you were late this morning.'

viii. 'You keep me waiting because you don't care about me.'
  b. Reframe the non-'I' messages as 'I' messages.
6. One of your colleagues frequently remarks on how carefully and slowly you think before making a contribution to staff meetings. Even though these comments seem humorous, you feel that others who hear them are starting to label you as 'slow'. You've had enough of the comments.
  a. Write a two-part 'I' message, using the two-part formula, to:
    i. state the action
    ii. state your response.
  b. Change your two-part 'I' message into a three-part 'I' message using the three-part formula.
7. Imagine that it is 3 pm and you feel tense because you have two telephone calls to make and a major piece of work to finish in the next two hours. A colleague asks you to help him immediately with the agenda for next week's committee meeting. It has to be in the internal mail this afternoon.
   Write a three-part assertive message saying that you are unable to help with the agenda. Follow the three-part 'I' message formula.

CHECK 13.1
SELF

Levels of conflict

Next time you feel you are in a conflict use this checklist to identify its level.
(D = Discomfort, I = Incident, M = Misunderstanding, T = Tension, C = Crisis)

Type of behaviour	Level of conflict				
	D	I	M	T	C
What level of conflict do the following statements indicate?					
I feel discomfort.	☐	☐	☐	☐	☐
I have difficulty identifying the problem.	☐	☐	☐	☐	☐
I feel criticised.	☐	☐	☐	☐	☐

I feel accused of something.	☐	☐	☐	☐	☐
I feel irritation.	☐	☐	☐	☐	☐
I am left with a result I did not want.	☐	☐	☐	☐	☐
I feel like using sarcasm.	☐	☐	☐	☐	☐
My ideas seem misunderstood.	☐	☐	☐	☐	☐
I can't stop thinking about the problem.	☐	☐	☐	☐	☐
I avoid eye contact.	☐	☐	☐	☐	☐
My arms are folded across my chest.	☐	☐	☐	☐	☐
I feel that negative attitudes are affecting the relationship.	☐	☐	☐	☐	☐
There are tears in my eyes.	☐	☐	☐	☐	☐
I keep my hands on my hips.	☐	☐	☐	☐	☐
I feel like pointing an accusing finger.	☐	☐	☐	☐	☐
I have fixed opinions.	☐	☐	☐	☐	☐
I constantly worry about the relationship.	☐	☐	☐	☐	☐
I disapprove of the other person.	☐	☐	☐	☐	☐
I feel like using extreme gestures.	☐	☐	☐	☐	☐

The active listening process

Listening is vital to good communication and to conflict resolution. Good listening skills can be learned and developed. Listening with empathy helps you to identify both the content of the other person's message, and their feelings. One way to create empathy is to check that you have understood the speaker's message by restating or summarising: 'What you're saying is . . .'.

Listen with empathy.

By listening well you are better able to resolve conflict before it reaches a higher level. Applying the active listening process to a conflict is illustrated by Figure 13.7.

1. Pay close attention to the other person:
   ■ use eye contact
   ■ face them
   ■ be aware of personal space
   ■ adopt an open position
   ■ keep still
   ■ let them speak
   ■ be enthusiastic and/or encouraging
   ■ use an appropriate tone of voice.

2. Encourage the other by:
   ■ using conversation openers
   ■ inviting them to speak
   ■ making brief minimal responses without asking too many questions
   ■ pausing.

3. Reflect or mirror the message by:
   ■ paraphrasing
   ■ clarifying or exploring
   ■ reflecting feelings
   ■ reflecting meanings
   ■ summarising.

Figure 13.7 The active listening process

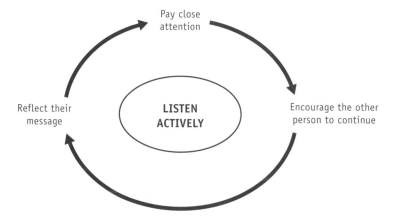

4. Listen actively to the whole message. This will allow you to relay the total message (content and feelings) back to the speaker. The speaker can then confirm or correct your feedback.

Empathy blockers

Empathy blockers increase the level of conflict.

Empathy blockers tend to have a negative impact on communication. Barriers arise and increase the difficulties of conflict resolution. Empathy blockers include:

■ listening ineffectively
■ passing judgment
■ changing the topic
■ giving unwanted advice
■ looking away from the speaker.

Empathy blockers cause defensiveness and lower people's self-esteem. When either party uses them, conflict is increased rather than resolved. In contrast, the opportunity to resolve conflict and find new opportunities for cooperation is enhanced when strategies such as active listening, 'I' statements and assertive behaviour are used to increase understanding and show empathy.

Using constructive responses

SKILLS

APPLY

1. 'An "I" message is non-evaluative.' Explain the meaning of this statement. Why are 'I' messages used?
2. How can conflict be positive?
3. How can negotiation and conflict overlap?
4. Consider this statement: 'Conflict is caused by a clash of opinions, values or needs.' Briefly explain the statement and give an example of a workplace situation in which each of the following could occur:

a. a clash of opinions
b. a difference of values
c. a failure to meet people's needs.

5. What do you find most difficult about disagreeing with another person in front of others?
6. 'Make partners not opponents.' Explain how you can do this in a conflict situation.
7. Complete the questionnaire in Figure 13.8 to determine your preferred style for handling conflicts.

Figure 13.8 What is your preferred style for handling conflict?

Indicate how often you use the following behaviours in conflict situations by scoring your response in column 2.	Score: 1 = seldom or 3 = sometimes or 5 = usually

Section A

1 I explore our differences, without imposing my view.
2 I tell the other person that I disagree and then talk about the reasons for our differences.
3 I seek a solution that will satisfy both parties.
4 I like to make sure that both parties have a chance to give their point of view.

Section A subtotal (add up your scores for statements 1 to 4) _____

Section B

5 I look for a solution that will be agreeable to both parties, even though it may not satisfy anyone completely.
6 I meet the other person halfway even if we don't understand why we don't agree fully.
7 Most people would agree that I prefer to meet halfway.
8 I don't fully expect to say everything that I want to say during the discussion.

Section B subtotal (add up your scores for statements 5 to 8) _____

Section C

9 If I can't change the other party's mind, I will concede.
10 I don't discuss aspects of the issue that might be controversial.
11 I avoid argument by agreeing about a point.
12 If the other party becomes too emotional, I will concede.

Section C subtotal (add up your scores for statements 9 to 12) _____

Section D

13 I attempt to convince the other person of my point of view.
14 I try to win at any cost.
15 I throw myself into the argument with gusto.
16 I prefer to win rather than meet halfway.

Section D subtotal (add up your scores for statements 13 to 16) _____

Refer to the end of chapter for an indication of your preferred style.

Workplace interviews

Interviews are regularly conducted at work and some of them will involve a level of conflict. You may, for example, conduct an interview to assist an employee in career planning and goal setting, or to correct a problem. While their purposes vary, all such interviews are conducted either to meet the organisation's objectives and needs or to support staff and help them to meet their own workplace needs and objectives. As a supervisor or interviewer, you need to be aware of communication and interview skills, and the planning necessary to match the organisation's goals with those of the employee.

While some workplace interviews are conducted regularly and involve hours of preparation, others arise from unexpected opportunities for gathering information and involve little preparation. Some of the more important interviews at work are discussed below.

Workplace interviews can involve a level of conflict.

Performance interviews

Performance interviews seek to evaluate the employee's performance and provide feedback on the organisation's perception of it. Aim to establish a supportive climate by greeting the interviewee and explaining the process clearly. The **performance appraisal** thus becomes motivational (encouraging) and part of the organisation's regular feedback.

An effective performance interview is motivational.

Both interviewer and interviewee can set goals together and check their perceptions of one another. Written evaluations by the interviewer and the employee's self-appraisal help this discussion along, and clarify each other's perceptions. The performance interview is often used for a promotion assessment. Conflict can enter a performance interview, for example, when the manager gives a performance grade lower than the person being interviewed expects. The interviewee may respond aggressively with a statement such as: 'You failed to take into account all my extra effects. What's the matter with you?'

Remember, for those being appraised it is a personal experience that involves their ego, feelings and self-image in relation to work. Always keep the discussion relevant to the job to avoid side-tracking and to minimise the employee's defensiveness.

Goals in a performance interview

Always aim to make an objective and factual assessment of the employee's job performance. Your goals in a performance interview are to:

■ support decisions on promotion, salary increases and transfers
■ control feedback about performance
■ establish mutual work goals
■ identify training needs and career counselling requirements.

In the performance interview, give employees helpful feedback about their performance. Do this by describing what the employee does in specific terms. For example, tell them where they need to improve: 'You don't look at customers or greet them with a smile when you are on the Help Desk'. Balance this by commenting on areas where they perform well. Questions should be open or probing. Closed questions help to establish facts. Avoid 'Why did you . . .' questions as they make the interviewee defensive and can lead to conflict.

Feedback and questioning skills are discussed more fully in Chapter 3, Interactive Skills: Interpersonal Communication.

Discipline or reprimand interviews

An effective discipline interview corrects undesirable behaviour.

Discipline or **reprimand interviews** aim to identify unacceptable or undesirable behaviour and to discuss how to change the behaviour. Plan the interview carefully and choose a place free from interruptions. Listen to the employee to determine reasons for their behaviour. Dealing with the facts rather than the employee's personal characteristics helps to reduce emotional reaction and defensiveness. Plan the course of action and solutions together. Acknowledge any positive aspects of the employee's behaviour.

Before you reach the stage of a discipline interview, try other communication techniques such as instructions, training, corrections and counselling. If these fail, then use the discipline interview.

Goals of the discipline interview

The **discipline interview** is a formal organisational procedure used by management to correct unacceptable behaviour. It seeks to:

- describe the unacceptable behaviour
- relate this behaviour to the organisation's rules and practices
- examine the causes and who is responsible
- obtain the employee's view of the situation
- work out what corrective action is necessary to solve the problem or eliminate the unacceptable behaviour.

At the beginning of the discipline interview, state its purpose. Begin with open-ended questions to encourage employees to discuss their perceptions of the situation. Use your listening and questioning skills to collect information and identify specific points. Follow up later with feedback on the interview's effect on the employee's behaviour. Be aware that conflict may arise and be willing to deal with it at the discomfort or incident levels. Ignoring conflict at the lower levels may allow it to escalate to a crisis level.

Counselling interviews

Counselling interviews aim to help employees to deal with issues and solve problems. They may also deal with issues that affect work performance. In a counselling interview it is important to remain non-evaluative, to use a range of questions and to develop active and reflective listening skills.

An effective counselling interview supports the employee.

Most supervisors have the empathy and skills to perform adequately, or better than adequately, in a counselling interview on work performance. This kind of interview is not meant to be a deep psychological probing of the employee's problems. If you feel that this is what they want, it is better to refer them to a qualified psychologist or therapist. Keep a list of professional and other referral services handy in case they are required.

Goals of the counselling interview

A counselling interview should be conducted privately, and confidentiality should be respected. As a counselling interviewer you will aim to:

- help the employee clarify the problem
- use active listening skills to help the employee define the problem
- offer feedback and alternative solutions
- assist the employee to select the solution that most suits their needs
- provide a supportive environment
- help the employee find professional help if required.

Conducting workplace interviews

1. In groups of three:
   a. Discuss and list three objectives of a performance interview and three objectives of a discipline interview.
   b. Briefly discuss the differences between a performance and a discipline interview.
   c. Why can different perceptions of performance cause conflict in a performance interview?
   d. Why does a performance interviewer prepare a written evaluation of the interview, and why does the interviewee prepare a self-evaluation sheet?
2. Work in pairs.
   Assume you are Leisa and Janet. Leisa is Janet's supervisor. Janet has been absent from work without a doctor's certificate on nine separate occasions over the last four months. Staff are allowed seven days' absence without having to produce a medical certificate. Leisa feels that Janet is

APPLY SKILLS

suffering from stress. Janet feels that she is being asked to do others' work as well as her own. The only way she can cope with her stress is by taking a day off sick. Leisa decides to speak to Janet and explain that this is unacceptable.

a. List Leisa's reasons for conducting the discipline interview.

b. How can Janet lessen the stress from work? Brainstorm to list strategies such as ways to communicate, delegate or negotiate.

Visit the Companion Website at **www.prenhall.com/dwyer_au**. Choose the Good Practice/Bad Practice activity in Chapter 13 to identify and record signs of conflict. Reflect on your records to identify both 'good practice' and 'bad practice' in dealing with conflict.

Chapter summary

Describe the five levels of conflict. These are discomfort, incidents, misunderstandings, tension and crisis.

Identify signs of conflict. People who keep alert for discomfort and incidents can use their communication skills to deal with lower levels of conflict before it progresses to the misunderstanding, tension or crisis level.

Prepare a map to identify issues, key needs and concerns. A map is useful when you need to determine the cause of a conflict. It highlights who is involved, their needs and concerns, and the issues. Using the map, the parties in the conflict can work together to design appropriate options and act on them to solve the conflict.

Use active listening for conflict resolution. Active listening enables you to attend closely to the other party, to encourage them and reflect their message, showing your empathy for their interests. Active listening lets you hear the whole message.

Give feedback assertively. Send clear, assertive 'I' messages and listen carefully. Check your nonverbal messages and their appropriateness to the situation. Feedback should focus on the issue rather than the person.

Use communication skills that encourage constructive responses to conflict in the workplace. The challenge is to develop confidence in deciding what communication skills are suited to the situation. Develop skills in dealing with conflict so that it is positive and constructive, not negative or destructive.

Identify the objectives of different types of interviews. The interview is essentially an exchange of information for a particular purpose. Interviews at work usually aim to inform, instruct, obtain ideas, counsel or solve a problem. Specific purposes for interviews include performance appraisal, discipline and counselling. Some of these interviews may involve a level of conflict.

1. Define the term 'conflict'.
2. What are the four components of a conflict map?
3. List five strategies that can be used to determine the options before taking action in a conflict situation.
4. a. List three responses to conflict.
   b. Which is the most constructive response and why?
5. a. What three roles are played in the drama triangle?
   b. What three roles are played in the success triangle?
   c. Briefly explain the difference between the drama triangle and the success triangle.
6. List and briefly explain three empathy blockers.
7. a. List three goals of a counselling interview.
   b. Briefly explain the differences between a discipline and a counselling interview.

Dealing with potential conflict

1. Suppose that you are Kieran, the Senior Purchasing Officer in a large organisation. You feel that Therese, a section supervisor, is ordering excessive amounts of stationery and duplicating some orders. How would you approach Therese with your concerns? Your aim is to reach a mutually acceptable solution in an assertive way. You know that Therese can be defensive and, on some occasions, quite aggressive.
2. Your opening statement to Therese at a meeting in her office is: 'Therese, I need to speak to you about the latest purchase requisition.'

   Work in pairs to create the script and act out the two roles. Identify assertive ways for Kieran to:

   a. present his point of view
   b. disagree
   c. give feedback
   d. negotiate a win–win situation.

   Refer to Chapter 3, Interactive Skills: Interpersonal Communication, particularly the assertive strategies section.
3. a. Use a map to give you an overall picture of the conflict.
   b. Identify ways for Kieran to:
      i. separate the person from the problem, and
      ii. focus on interests, not positions.
4. Outline the benefits Kieran is likely to gain by behaving assertively.

Key terms

action plan	drama triangle	options
aggressive behaviour	empathy blocker	performance appraisal
assertive behaviour	fight response	persecutor
assertive statement	flight response	rescuer
concerns	flow response	submissive behaviour
conflict	'I' message	success triangle
counselling interview	map	tension
discipline/reprimand interview	needs	victim
	non-assertive behaviour	

A nasty piece of work

by Guy Allenby

> People who cop a lot of flak often enjoy defusing hostile situations.

For most people there is no surer way to have their day ruined than to have to cope with an irate client, colleague or member of the public.

For others, however, copping snide remarks, dirty looks or outright aggression is just business as usual.

Those in the line of fire include parking inspectors, telephone operators taking calls on complaints lines and community case workers.

It takes a special type of person with an uncommon facility for listening to and deflecting an enormous amount of aggression to do the 'tough jobs'. What quality do you need most? Stoicism or masochism?

'People with extroverted personalities are more attracted to job roles where there is more people interaction,' says a University of Melbourne psychologist and spokesperson for the Australian Psychological Society, Dr Peter Cotton. 'Other people are a bit more emotionally sensitive and these people tend to avoid roles where they have to deal with people in an adversarial context.'

Cotton says an important attribute is the ability to be something of a sponge. 'If you emotionally absorb what the person is throwing at you, that helps defuse things. And that takes a lot of skill.'

But that's not to say anyone should take the abuse to heart. 'You have to be emotionally detached, as it were,' he says. 'Otherwise, you can become defensive and that can be like a red rag to a bull. Some people take things personally and it gets them down. You should never take anything personally.'

Easily said but far more difficult to do. Until recently, Steve Yatman, who works on the metropolitan south-west foster care team with the Department of Community Services, was responsible for visiting the homes of sexually and physically abused children.

He had to talk to the children and their parents and, in some cases, remove the youngsters and place them in a foster home. These days he works with the foster carers 'making sure we have enough people to meet the demand of children that come into care'.

Yatman says some people can cope with such 'highly contentious and difficult issues'.

'There are people who see their jobs of protecting kids as being fundamentally important. Often they are highly committed and they have support around them to assist them through [the difficult times].

'I've gone into houses where we've had to remove young kids,' he says.

'It's extremely difficult to cope with at times but that's where we have systems in place to help. Otherwise you end up getting out [of the job] and finding something completely different to do.'

Cotton agrees, saying that it is when a worker feels trapped in a difficult job that the daily stresses can have adverse consequences. 'The unfortunate thing in these tough times,' he says, 'is that people sometimes stay in jobs because they don't see there are any alternatives. This can be problematic because they feel stuck.'

When people feel trapped, problems and anxieties can easily compound.

'If you are not very robust you can start to feel down, become despondent and that can lead to depression,' he adds. 'It really depends on the level of support that is available. The bottom line is that it's crucial to be able to debrief with work peers or a supervisor so you can cope.'

However, if someone is in a tough job out of choice, the chances are he/she will be able to deal with the accompanying stress, Cotton says.

Yatman says the Department of Community Services recognises this need for support. 'The department has quite a strong philosophy of supervision to make sure people are supported through difficult times,' he says.

Not that it's all grind and grim reality. In tough jobs the potential for emotional lows is very real, but so are the potential rewards.

'When I interview people in these [demanding] roles,' Cotton says, 'they tell me that they get a lot of satisfaction out of the challenge of calming down and defusing someone who is aggressive and angry, having a rational engagement with them and then ending up with a positive outcome.'

Source: Guy Allenby, 'A nasty piece of work', *Sydney Morning Herald*, 13 March 2002, My Career, p. 4. Guy Allenby is a journalist at the *Sydney Morning Herald*.

Questions

1. The article suggests: 'If you emotionally absorb what the person is throwing at you, that helps defuse things. And that takes a lot of skill'.
   a. Describe two skills that help defuse conflict.
   b. What advantages flow to people who can defuse conflict?
2. Compare and contrast the outcomes from defensive behaviour and assertive behaviour in a conflict situation.
3. Choose a constructive response to conflict and explain how it helps to deflect aggression.

Preferred style for handling conflict

The subtotal scores in each section of the questionnaire indicate the strength of your preference. Figure 13.9 shows the strength of your preference. Figure 13.10 shows likely outcomes from each of the conflict styles – collaboration, compromise, accommodation and forcing.

Figure 13.9 Scores, preferences

Section score	Strength of your preference
17 and above	High
12 to 16	Moderately high
8 to 11	Moderately low
7 and below	Low

Figure 13.10 Likely outcomes from each conflict style

Section	Style
A	Collaboration – *I win, you win.*
B	Compromise – *Both win some, lose some.*
C	Accommodation – *I lose, you win.*
D	Forcing or domination – *I win, you lose.*

Workplace writing and research skills

IV

Part

Analyse and present research information

In this chapter you will learn how to:

- find primary and secondary sources of information appropriate to the task

- use notations and citations accurately

- use a search engine to find information stored on the World Wide Web

- source and reference online information gathered from the World Wide Web

- assess your reading rate

- identify poor reading habits

- use the SQ3R reading method

- create a suitable study environment.

Evaluate your communication skills by completing the self-check in the chapter.

The research process is a matter of finding information and using the appropriate aids and techniques to collect, store and retrieve your material.

Your completed assignment, essay, work project or report is the culmination of the whole research and study process. Before the task begins, identify your subject and main purpose and determine what sources of information you need.

Sources of information

Research both primary and secondary sources.

Researchers refer to primary and secondary sources of information. **Primary sources of information** spring from people or organisations whose activities become part of society's store of information. Those who review and write about these activities and events prepare the **secondary sources of information**. These secondary sources are published and stored after events have taken place.

Finding primary sources

Many primary sources of information are available. Some of these are summarised in Table 14.1.

Finding secondary sources of information

Libraries have special expertise in collecting and storing information on many different subjects, in a form that makes it easy to find. Libraries are an invaluable source of secondary information. Their services are available to the public, though some are limited to library members. Some sources of secondary information are listed in Figure 14.1.

Library catalogues

Library catalogues are databases that list all the information contained in a library's reference sources. These secondary sources include fiction and non-fiction books, reference books, periodicals, journals, newspapers and audiovisual material. Most libraries hold their subject, author and title indexes in online computer information systems and on microfiche. As you search for information, use the catalogues.

Figure 14.1 Examples of secondary sources of information

Handbooks or guides
Australian Business Handbook
Australian Parliamentary Handbook
Australian Postal Commission Postal Guide
Business Who's Who in Australia
Commonwealth and State year books
Telephone directories
Universal Business Directory (UBD)

Dictionaries and encyclopaedias
Australian Commercial Dictionary
Australian Encyclopaedia
Black's Medical Dictionary
Concise Oxford Dictionary
Dictionary of Acronyms and Abbreviations
Macquarie Dictionary
Science Dictionary in Basic English
Webster's Geographical Dictionary

Table 14.1 Primary sources of information

Source	Purpose	Strategy
Observation	To collect information and evaluate it objectively	Observe the event several times. Check that it is a typical event, not an unusual one. Try to interpret your observations objectively.
Experiment	Carry out a trial operation or test to find out how it works.	Explore alternatives. For example, if you want a better office environment, try screens between desks in an open-plan office. Then ask experts such as Occupational Health and Safety Officers to assess the results. Offer these as evidence gained from the experiments.
Interviews	Gather facts and opinions that can be analysed and evaluated	Prepare the questions and their order of presentation first. Then conduct the interview by asking questions and recording the answers. Finally, compile the results.
Questionnaires and surveys	Gather valid facts and information from small groups, larger organisations or the community	Plan the questions so that they focus on your subject and purpose. Make the survey, then extract and compile the information. Finally, analyse the information.
Human resources	Gather information by direct contact with the primary source	First, design the questions. Then interview and/or administer surveys or questionnaires to primary sources such as the Migrant Resources Centre, Working Women's Centre or the Department of Land and Water Conservation. Analyse the information and draw conclusions.
Files and records	Collect information on a particular industry or company	Focus on a particular company. Gather current and background information from office files and records. Follow up any other source of expertise that is relevant to your needs.
Professional associations	Gather professional information	Contact professional associations, their support services, trade associations or trade unions. Interview your own business and professional contacts.

Online computer information systems

You can find information from library online systems and computer database systems. Some libraries use sophisticated technology such as the Clann Database, which is updated quarterly. Searches on the Clann Database can be made by title, author, author/title, subject or key word.

Key words are often called search terms.

Compact disk read-only memory

The compact disk read-only memory (CD-ROM) uses a variety of information-handling software. Use the software to find the library's catalogue disk, the *Grolier's Encyclopaedia* disk and the *McGraw-Hill Encyclopaedia of Science and Technology.*

The CD-ROM also supplies abstract-only services such as the Educational Resources Information Centre (ERIC). A brief summary, two to three paragraphs in length, on each publication is printed as an *abstract.* You can then decide if you want to borrow it. It is worth asking the librarian if other catalogues are available. Library staff also use online searching services to find Australian and international electronic databases such as Aussinet, an Australian database.

Periodicals and journals

To find periodicals and journals relevant to your topic, use the library's periodical index. Another specialised index, created by the National Library of Australia in Canberra, is the Australian Public Affairs Information Service (APAIS). It is a subject index to current literature on the humanities and social sciences. Look up the key words in the index to find all the current literature related to your key word.

If you join a library, ask for a complete tour to help you become familiar with its different sections and the whereabouts of the various indexes. Ask for an interlibrary loan if the library does not have a book you need.

Audiovisual and other services

Some libraries provide audiovisual facilities to view videos and films or to listen to tapes. Most also provide at least one photocopier, at a price per copy.

It is worth considering information stored in teletext and videotext form. Initially, the task may seem difficult, but each time you use these systems your skills improve.

Archives

Archives store historic and public information. For example, each state government keeps records of its past activities. Many large corporations such as Arnotts and the Commonwealth Bank also keep old records and files. It is possible, although sometimes time-consuming, to find this kind of organisation and government department data for your work projects, assignments or reports.

Mass media

The media produce up-to-date information via newspapers, magazines, television, radio and film. Study the media critically. Separate and identify facts from opinions.

When gathering information from the range of sources indicated so far, make sure you record in your notes full details of the source of your information. You will need to present these details with your essay, project or report. You should always supply full source references to acknowledge the author, speaker, film, and so on. This is explained in the next section.

Sources of information

SKILLS
APPLY

Work in groups of three.
1. a. Briefly describe the difference between primary and secondary sources of information.

b. Give an example of each and describe its purpose.

2. a. Name two library catalogues you could use for a library search.

   b. List three resources or services that libraries offer.

3. Assume that the Local Council has commissioned your consultancy firm to compile a report titled 'Beach Front Amenities and Developments: Council's Responsibilities'. The finished report is to be presented to local resident action groups.

   a. Name three organisations that could provide information for your initial researching stage.

   b. Are these primary or secondary sources of information?

   c. List three words you could use in a library search for secondary sources of information.

Notation

When you write reports, assignments and workplace documents with information you have obtained from either primary or secondary sources, you must acknowledge your source by using some form of **notation**. This notation can be inserted in three different places in the document.

Notation acknowledges your information sources.

1. As a citation in the text.
2. As a footnote at the bottom of the page.
3. As an endnote placed at the end of the document and before the list of references or bibliography.

Citation in the text

When you make a factual statement supported by another author's (or group's) work, or when you quote someone else's work, acknowledge (cite) them as shown in Figure 14.2.

Footnotes

Number your **footnotes** by using superscripts. These are small numbers placed in the main body of the text slightly above the line at the end of the sentence.[1] The traditional placement of a footnote is at the bottom of the page. However, it is easier to place the reference at the end of the document, unless you are using a word-processing program that can insert footnotes correctly at the bottom of each page. Otherwise, as you move the text around, you may have difficulty keeping the footnotes in the right place.

Endnotes

Number your **endnotes** in sequence throughout your document and list the matching endnotes in the same numerical order at the end of the document, before the list of references, as shown in Figure 14.3. For more about notation see the *Style Manual for Authors, Printers and Editors* in the Bibliography.

Figure 14.2 The author–date (Harvard) system of reference notation

---

The author–date (or Harvard) system is widely accepted because it is easy to use and economical in terms of time and space. When you refer to someone else's work, identify it there on the page by giving, in brackets, the author's name and year of publication – for example (Cole 2001). Sometimes it is also useful to give the page or volume numbers – (Cole 2001, pp. 83–5).

In the list of references at the end of the document, give full publication details of the works cited: author's surname and initials or given name, year of publication, title, publisher and place of publication.

Timm, Paul, R. 2001, *Customer Service: Career Success through Customer Satisfaction*, 2nd edn, Prentice Hall, Upper Saddle River, New Jersey.

Check the method of notation and documentation preferred by your instructor, employer or organisation. If no particular method is preferred, use your own judgment about how to organise your references.

Figure 14.3 The note (or traditional) system of reference notation

> For a footnote or endnote, the information required for the first reference to a work is the same as that required for the author–date system list of references, but presented in a slightly different order: the note number is followed by the author's initials or given name and surname, title, publisher, place of publication, year of publication and page number/s.
>
> 1. Kris Cole. *Supervision: The Theory and Practice of First-Line Management*, Pearson Education Australia, Sydney, 2001, pp. 83–7.
> 2. Timm, Paul R. *Customer Service: Career Success through Customer Satisfaction*, Prentice Hall, Upper Saddle River, New Jersey, 2001.
>
> Second and subsequent references to a source do not have to be as detailed as the first reference to it. The simplest way is to abbreviate them; for example:
>
> 3. Timm, p. 66.
>
> Because full publication details are given in the notes, a list of references at the end of the document is optional, though advisable.

Bibliography and list of references

A **list of references** gives details only of those works cited in your report or essay. A **bibliography** not only gives these details but also lists other relevant sources you may have consulted for your work. These may include:

- primary sources such as interviews or responses to surveys
- secondary sources such as books, journals, newspapers and government publications.

In some cases you may prefer or be required to present these separately – background reading and other relevant sources are sometimes presented under the heading 'Further reading' or a similar heading.

Arrange your list of references or bibliography in alphabetical order by authors' surnames, not by title. Be sure that all references are accurate and consistent.

There are two main methods of presenting a list of references or a bibliography: one is the **author–date (Harvard) system**, the other is the **note (traditional)** system. The main difference between the two is the order in which they present information. Both methods use the same presentation for a bibliography and for a list of references. Both methods are shown in Figure 14.4.

References

APPLY SKILLS

1. a. What is 'notation'?
   b. Explain the difference between a footnote, a citation and an endnote.
   c. What information is required in an endnote?
2. Differentiate between the note (traditional) reference style and the author–date (Harvard) style.
3. a. Briefly explain the term 'bibliography'.
   b. Organise a bibliography by choosing two books, an article from a journal and a video cassette. Present the author's name, title, publisher, place and date of publication according to each method.

4. a. Compile a list of four key words (search terms).
   b. Use the library's catalogues to find a book, an article in a journal, an entry in an encyclopaedia and an audiovisual item that contain useful information for a particular project or report.
   c. List these four items as a bibliography, using either the author–date method or the note method.
   d. Name five ways to search for information on a database such as the Clann Database.

Figure 14.4 Compiling a list of references or bibliography

---

1. The author–date (Harvard) method
Information is presented in the following order:

Books
1. Author's surname and initials or first name
2. Year of publication
3. Title of book in italics
4. Name of publisher
5. Place of publication

Anderson, Jonathan & Poole, Millicent. 2001, *Assignment and Thesis Writing*, 4th edn, John Wiley & Sons, Brisbane.
Rose, Jean. 2001, *The Mature Student's Guide to Writing*, Palgrave, Basingstoke, UK.

Articles
1. Author's surname followed by initials or first name
2. Year of publication
3. Title of article in single quotation marks
4. Title of journal in italics
5. Volume number and issue number, if applicable
6. Page number/s

Nguyen, Maria. 2002, 'The graduates', *The Sydney Morning Herald*, 26–27 January, pp. 4–5.

2. The note (traditional) method
Information is presented in the following order:

Books
1. Author's surname and initials or first name
2. Title of book in italics
3. Name of publisher
4. Place of publication
5. Year of publication

Anderson, Jonathan & Poole, Millicent. *Assignment and Thesis Writing*, 4th edn, John Wiley & Sons, Brisbane, 2001.
Rose, Jean. *The Mature Student's Guide to Writing*, Palgrave, Basingstoke, UK, 2001.

Articles
1. Author's surname followed by initial or first name
2. Title of article in single quotation marks
3. Title of journal in italics
4. Volume number and issue number, if applicable
5. Date of publication
6. Page number/s

Tovia, Joanna. 'Superior service costs nothing', *The Daily Telegraph*, 29 January 2002, p. 32.

Note that, in both methods, references are listed in alphabetical order. Careful documentation assists your reader and adds to your credibility as a writer. The authority followed here is the *Style Manual for Authors, Editors and Printers* (see Bibliography).

Researching on the web

Research data, text, images and sound to gather information.

Business writers draw on primary and secondary sources of information. Regardless of whether the information is taken from printed or online sources, it must be fully acknowledged and dated. The World Wide Web (WWW) offers business writers a universally accessible network of low cost and speedy communication and publication tools and resources. This network connects individuals, organisations and communities of all kinds and cultures across all time zones and geographical boundaries.

Key words in web page titles make it easier for researchers to find sites of interest because the search engine looks for these key words. Then the main information and comments on these key words are placed in the body of the electronic text. An individual, company or organisation that creates a website should always inform the search engine of its key word/s.

A search engine is a program that receives a research request, compares it to the index created by the 'robot' or 'web crawler' and returns the results of the search to the researcher. A search engine not only finds relevant web pages. It can also find new pages on any server anywhere in the world, and can index those pages. By typing in key words you can locate a list of the page/s that contain the key word/s.

The web pages are linked together via hypertext links – a piece of text on a web page that allows any visitor to that page to click on the hypertext link to visit another address on the Net. The hypertext link is an address to another web page.

Each web page has:

▓ a header that identifies the company or organisation by name and page number
▓ a footer that contains a uniform resource locator (URL) protocol/site/path/file – for example, <http://www.anta.gov.au/>
▓ a title that contains the key word/s
▓ details such as headings, information and hyperlinks

How to do a search on the World Wide Web

A search engine is a coordinated set of programs that uses hypertext links.

Any researcher who wants to find information on the web will need to choose a **search engine**. It is worth trying several because each search engine's coverage, ease of use, currency, authority, loading time and way of finding information varies. Alta Vista, for example, has detailed search information and easily modified search requirements. Some of the parameters on Alta Vista are quick search tabs defining Business, People, Subject and Health categories. Its easily modified search lets you choose from a wide range of relevant topics, with fewer irrelevant topics to sort through.

For example, suppose you made a general search for *coffee*. Alta Vista will ask the researcher to break down the search by giving it other key words such as 'coffee coloured', 'coffee cake', 'coffee beans'. Rather than finding every instance of coffee, the engine uses these more specific terms to refine its search. Unless the specific URL is known, your only way to find the information is to search the World Wide Web.

Most search engines provide advanced features for constructing search parameters. For example, key words can be combined by using boolean operators (such as 'and', 'not', 'or') and wild cards (such as * which matches any number of characters in that position in the key word). Some search engines also have other advanced features – for example, the 'near' operator can locate two key words within a certain distance (number of words) of each other.

Various comprehensive search tools are available. All search engines do the same thing – search according to key words – but the way each one presents information is probably a matter of personal choice. Some search engines are shown in Figure 14.5.

Figure 14.5 Comprehensive search tools

Subject search engines

- *Single engines* (fast access to large database by single search engine):
  Alta Vista, Excite, Google, HotBot, Infoseek, Lycos, Open Text Index.
- *Multiple engines* (slower access to multiple databases by multiple search engines):
  All-in-One Search Page, Dogpile, Internet Sleuth, Meta Crawler, Mother Load, SavvySearch, Search.Com.
- *Engines restricted* to or specialising in certain world regions; for example,
  ANZWERS for Australian and New Zealand content.
- *Hierarchical search engines*: Magellan Internet Guide, Starting Point, World Wide Web Virtual Library, Yahoo.

Miscellaneous databases

- *Telephone directories*
  Switchboard (white-page listings); BigBook (business listings), BigYellow (business listings), Yell (United Kingdom Yellow Pages), Yellow Pages Online (business listings).
- *Email addresses*
  Four11 White Pages Directory, Internet @ddress Finder, PeopleSearch, Usenet-Addresses, WhoWhere.
- *Usenet group messages*
  DejaNews Research Service, Reference COM, Excite News.
- *Mailing lists*
  Liszt (searchable directory of email discussion groups), Mailbase (UK mailing list service for research in higher education), Publicly Accessible Mailing Lists.
- *Shareware and freeware sources*
  Association of Shareware Professionals, Shareware.com (search engine), Shareware Trade Association and Resources.

Bookmarking

Once researchers find their areas of interest, the rule is to **bookmark** the site through a web browser (e.g. Netscape Browser). The bookmark records the URL you have visited. It is easy to go back then to the bookmark menu and click on the URL to go directly to the site. The bookmark file can be ordered into a hierarchy of folders according to your areas of interest. For example, in a folder labelled 'Goats' every site on goats would be bookmarked. This folder could then be subdivided into 'Dairy Goats', 'Meat Goats', 'Fibre Goats', and each of those subdirectories would contain the sites of interest in that category. Microsoft Explorer, for example, refers to bookmarking as favourites. Favourites are organised into a hierarchical order of choice.

> A bookmark, or favourite, is a saved link to a web page that has been added to a list of saved links.

Referencing or sourcing online information

The formats and examples given here offer models for online references that are included in the bibliography of a business writer's research paper, assignment or report. They follow the bibliography formats outlined for print materials in Chapter 15, Organise Workplace Information. The URL provides the specific location of online materials. It is the unique address of a single file on the Web. When the information downloaded is an extract from a paper publication, the publication and URL details should be recorded.

> Each file on the Web has a unique address.

Uniform resource locators

The citation formats for electronic publication are still subject to change and will be revised as they change. Currently, there are four necessary parts to citations of information gathered from a web page:

> A uniform resource locator gives the address of a web page.

1. protocol
2. site
3. path
4. file.

For example, The World Clock can be found at the URL address here. The World Clock shows the current local time in every part of the world.

http://www.timeanddate.com/worldclock
1. protocol   2. site   3. path   4. file

This site is the Flinders University of South Australia Library news page:

http://www.lib.flinders.edu.au/new

For print material downloaded from the Internet and online sources, most Australian students follow the traditional (note) method or Harvard method of referencing and add the URL details. For American students, the MLA Style Guide is one of the most popular methods. It is best to ask your lecturer which style is preferred by your faculty. The style shown in Figure 14.6 follows the note (traditional) reference method.

Figure 14.6 Example of a list of references or bibliography for online materials, using the note (traditional) reference method

---

Books online
1. Author's surname and initials or first name
2. Publication information for printed source (if available):
   - ▨ title of book in italics
   - ▨ name of publisher
   - ▨ place of publication
   - ▨ year of publication
3. Publication medium online
4. Name and repository of the electronic text if applicable
5. Available on URL – that is, protocol/site/path/file
6. Access date

Example
Sarsfield, L. *The Cosmos on a Shoestring: Small Spacecraft for Space and Earth Science*, RAND Publications United States, 1998, Online http://www.rand.org/publications/MR/MR864/24 April 1998

Journal article online
1. Author's surname followed by initials or first name
2. Title of article in single quotation marks
3. Title of journal in italics
4. Volume number and issue number, if applicable
5. Page number/s if applicable
6. Publication medium online
7. Available on URL – that is, protocol/site/path/file
8. Access date

Example
Cooper, C.S. 'Display your Family on the Web with JavaGED', *Journal of Online Genealogy*, Vol. 2, No. 9, March 1998. World Wide Web http://www.onlinegenealogy.com/current/sof006.htm 24 April 1998

Journal article on CD ROM
1. Author's surname followed by initials or first name
2. Title of article in single quotation marks
3. Title of journal in italics
4. Volume number and issue number, if applicable

Cont'd

---

5. Date of publication
6. Page number/s
7. Publication medium CD ROM
8. Database name
9. File identifier or number
10. Accession number

Example

Zorn, Theodore E. and Violanti, Michelle T. 'Communication Abilities and Individual Achievement in Organizations', *Management Communication Quarterly*, Vol. 10, No. 2, November 1996 139–167. CD Rom Business Periodicals on Disc.

World Wide Web home page
1. Author/editor (if known)
2. Title of page in single quotation marks
3. Revision or copyright date (if available)
4. Publication medium online
5. Page publisher
6. Available on URL – that is, protocol/site/path/file
7. Access date

Example

Williams, Peter. 'What's New', 8 May 2002 online. Austraining (NSW) Pty Ltd
http://www.austrainingnsw.com.au/main.htm 8 May 2002

World Wide Web secondary page
1. Author/editor (if known)
2. Title of page
3. Revision or copyright date (if available)
4. Publication medium online
5. Page publisher
6. Available on URl – that is, protocol/site/path/file
7. Access date

Example

Williams, Peter. 'Stop Press', 8 May 2002 online. Austraining (NSW) Pty Ltd
http://www.austrainingnsw.com.au/main.htm 8 May 2002

Newspaper article online
1. Author (if known)
2. Article title
3. Newspaper title
4. Date
5. Edition
6. Section
7. Page (if available)
8. Publication medium online
9. Available on URL – that is, protocol/site/path/file
10. Access date

Example

Wood, Alan. 'Broadband the decade's boomer, says Budde', *The Sydney Morning Herald*, 1 May 2002 online. Available http://www.smh.com.au/articles.html 1 May 2002

Personal electronic communication (email)
1. Sender's email address
2. Subject of message
3. Receiver's email address
4. Message date

Example

bhughes!@bigpond.com.au 'Canadian Holiday'
john.walsh@austrainingnsw.com.au 6 May 2002

Searching on a CD ROM

Say you are looking for information about cars.

Have I	Yes	No	Unsure
▨ typed the word 'car' and pressed <enter>?	☐	☐	☐
▨ renewed the search when too many records came up by entering the word AND, for example, typed 'car' AND 'sports' and pressed <enter>?	☐	☐	☐
▨ widened the search when not enough records came up by entering the word OR, for example, typed 'cars' OR 'sports' and pressed <enter>?	☐	☐	☐
▨ excluded something from the search by entering the words AND NOT; for example, typed 'cars AND NOT family cars' and pressed <enter>?	☐	☐	☐

Placing online information in a bibliography

1. Gather relevant information for an essay or business report by using:
   - ▨ a single engine subject search engine such as Alta Vista, Excite, HotBot; and
   - ▨ a multiple search engine such as All-in-one Search on Meta Crawler
   to find at least two documents to use as source data.
2. Put the two documents in the bibliography by using the note (traditional) reference method.
3. Find a newspaper article online and include it in the bibliography.
4. Use the Business Periodicals Ondisc (BPO) in your library to find a relevant online article and put the details of this article in the bibliography. Use Self-check 14.1 as you search the CD ROM.

The physical process of reading

Once you have found your sources of information, your next challenge is to extract information efficiently by reading and note-taking. Take notes that categorise, order and paraphrase information. An effective set of notes is an aid to memory, provides fresh ideas and material and makes it easy to retrieve the information.

Determine your reading rate.

Reading is a physical and intellectual exercise which requires you to identify and understand what is written. Your eyes and brain work together to decode the message. This section explains how this is achieved.

Efficient reading

Vary your reading method and speed to suit your purpose and the type of material. The speed at which you read can be calculated by using the simple formula shown here:

$$\text{Reading rate} = \frac{\text{number of words read per minute}}{\text{number of minutes}}$$

Three examples of different reading rates for the same article are shown in Table 14.2.

The formula has been created for use with straightforward writing. Technical or other styles of writing may produce a slower reading rate. In contrast, your previous knowledge of the subject of any written material will increase your reading rate. About 400

Table 14.2 Reading rates

Number of words per minute	Reading rate	Applying the formula
100	Slow	A 600-word article divided by 6 minutes of reading time equals 100 words per minute.
200	Slow to average	A 600-word article divided by 3 minutes of reading time equals 200 words per minute.
400	Average	A 600-word article divided by 1.5 minutes of reading time equals 400 words per minute.
600	Fast	A 600-word article divided by 1 minute of reading time equals 600 words per minute.

words per minute is suggested as an average reading speed that will still maintain the reader's level of understanding.

Efficient readers are fast and also fully understand what they are reading. Inefficient readers have developed one or more poor reading habits (see Figure 14.7).

Figure 14.7 Poor reading habits

Habit	Description	Result
Fixation	When the eye stops on words as you read along the line. The number of pauses or fixations depends on your reading ability – a fast reader may fixate on only four words, a slow reader on ten words.	Too many eye fixations on each line. An efficient reader can read a line with only three eye fixations. A slow reader may use up to six fixations on one line because they are unable to group the words as whole phrases or units.
Regression	When the reader does not understand a word or phrase and goes back to read it again; also when a reader stops at the end of each line and returns to check something.	Regressive eye fixations or backtracking slow down the reading speed and interfere with the flow of information.
Interrupted return sweep	When the eye makes a return sweep to the beginning of the line, to read a word or phrase again.	Movement back to a word or phrase that is not understood slows down the reading.
Subvocalisation	When the words are spoken under the reader's breath.	Someone who mouths the words can read no faster than they speak.

The SQ3R reading method

A useful and well known reading technique suited to all types of reading, including studying and reading at work, is the SQ3R reading method. This method breaks the reading process into five stages, as shown in Figure 14.8.

The SQ3R reading method has five stages.

Figure 14.8 The five stages of the SQ3R method

Assume you are reading a long report. Consider each of the five stages of this reading method, as follows.

Survey first

Making a survey means skimming quickly through the report for particular information. Survey its table of contents, the terms of reference and introduction to identify its title, author, outline and purpose. Then survey the conclusions and recommendations.

Question

What is the purpose of your reading? Do you intend just a quick read before filing the information or do you need to read the report carefully, absorb it all and use it for your next meeting?

Read

First, you surveyed the report quickly to see whether the information was useful. If it is, read it carefully so that you can identify the details and evidence on which the author based the conclusions and recommendations. Study the appendices and sources of information. Are they up to date and suited to a report of this nature?

Recall

You may want to memorise the information to recall it later for use elsewhere. Take particular care to recall the report's purpose, conclusions and recommendations.

Review

Review by reading the report again, to make sure that the information you recall is accurate. Take notes to help your memory.

Reading methods

1. Briefly describe the five stages in the SQ3R reading method.
2. a. Briefly explain the difference between skimming and reading.
   b. Briefly describe three poor reading habits. How can reading habits be improved?
   c. Name and explain the main aspects of efficient reading.
   d. Read a journal article of interest to you, using the SQ3R reading method.
3. Select an article from today's newspaper.
   a. Skim the article.
   b. Show, by means of underlining, the important points on which a person skimming the article would concentrate.
   c. What is the article's purpose?

Creating a suitable study environment

If you manage your research skills, study time and resources efficiently, you will achieve more. Organise a comfortable study environment. Lighting should be adequate and your desk must be roomy enough to accommodate paper, pens, equipment and research material. A chair that supports you comfortably is also essential.

Managing your study time

You might set an immediate short-term study goal – revise your notes tonight; an intermediate goal – to complete the assignment that is due in six weeks; or a long-term goal – to pass the examination at the end of the semester. To achieve your goals, spend time preparing your schedule for an assignment, essay or project. Prepare a list of things to do in order of priority. Identify the deadlines for completing each item on this list.

Make the effort to evaluate how you use your study time. Decide whether it is worth changing your routine and, if so, what you would like to change to make the most of your study time. This is how you start a **study time management plan.** Then follow the ten steps listed in Figure 14.9.

Study goals can be short term, intermediate or long term.

Figure 14.9 Ten-step approach to a study time management plan

1. List your goals for this assignment, essay, project or report.
2. List the activities you will need to complete to achieve each of these goals.
3. Classify the activities as *important activities, not so important activities* and *things to do later*.
4. Focus on the important activities and allocate time to each.
5. Prioritise the not so important activities from high to low priority and allocate time to each.
6. Allocate time to the 'things to do later'.
7. Check priorities and time allocations against your deadlines.
8. Place your time-management plan or study guide on a desk or wall planner in a prominent position. This is your time log.
9. Tick or mark off on your time log each completed step. This acknowledges your success in achieving research and time-management goals.
10. Present your completed project on or before time.

CHECK 14.2

Note-taking

Have I	Yes	No	Unsure
Read to			
read the entire article?	☐	☐	☐
identify the article's main purpose?	☐	☐	☐
Created a set of notes with			
an outline?	☐	☐	☐
headings?	☐	☐	☐
subheadings?	☐	☐	☐
Created a set of notes that is easy to understand			
by identifying the source information?	☐	☐	☐
by keeping the writer's original arguments, points of view and meaning?	☐	☐	☐
Created notes that			
are easy to file and retrieve?	☐	☐	☐
are easy to understand?	☐	☐	☐
break information into manageable units?	☐	☐	☐
give a clear summary of the original material?	☐	☐	☐
need to be reviewed?	☐	☐	☐
should be reduced?	☐	☐	☐

Visit the Companion Website at **www.prenhall.com/dwyer_au**. Choose the Good Practice/Bad Practice activity in Chapter 14 and practise researching online by answering question 2.

Chapter summary

Find primary and secondary sources of information appropriate to the task. Primary sources spring from the activities of people or organisations. Publications and stored information are secondary sources of information. By identifying your main topic and writing purpose clearly before you research you can determine your best sources of information. This saves you research time.

Use notations and citations accurately. Always acknowledge the work of another author, either by citation in the text, or by footnotes or endnotes. Use either the Harvard or note (traditional) reference system.

Use a search engine to find information stored on the World Wide Web. Search engines find information on a particular topic. The three main types are subject search engines, hierarchical subject indexes and miscellaneous databases. A search engine is a coordinated set of programs that uses hypertext links to read pages on websites. An engine can search any subject using a key word, by information organised into subject areas in hierarchical subject areas and by directories, for example telephone directories, in the form of an online database.

Source and reference online information gathered from the World Wide Web. Many business writers now research information from online sources. The specific location of online materials is found by using the uniform resource locator (URL). The URL gives the protocol, site, path and file details of the online document.

Assess your reading rate. Use the simple formula: the number of words read per minute divided by the total number of minutes equals a person's reading rate. The average reading speed is about 400 words per minute.

Identify poor reading habits. These include fixation, regression, interrupted return sweep and subvocalisation. Poor reading habits make it hard for the reader to find the main ideas in a piece of writing.

Use the SQ3R reading method. The SQ3R reading method identifies five stages in the reading process: survey, question, read, recall and review.

Create a suitable study environment. Make sure it is quiet and free from interruptions. This helps you to manage your study time, concentrate on the subject, and use your reading skills efficiently.

REVIEW QUESTIONS

1. What is a search engine?
2. Distinguish between subject search engines and miscellaneous databases.
3. What is bookmarking?
4. What is a uniform resource locator (URL)?
5. Describe the characteristics of a multiple search engine.
6. A researcher who wants to use online information in a report must acknowledge that source of information in the bibliography. What details should they put in the bibliography?
7. Distinguish between eye fixation, regression, return sweep and sub-vocalisation.
   a. Give the formula used to determine a person's reading rate.
   b. How many words a minute are read by slow, average and fast readers?
8. a. What is the purpose of surveying first, using the SQ3R reading method?
   b. Briefly explain the difference between the 3 Rs: read, recall and review.
9. a. Why is it important to create a suitable study environment?
   b. List two benefits gained by preparing a study time management plan.
   c. How can you improve your study environment?

Researching and reading

BUILD SKILLS

1. Read the following passage, then check your understanding by answering the questions.

   How to approach an assignment, essay, work project or report
   Break the title and/or topic of the written task into key words. A dictionary or an encyclopaedia will help you to check the meaning of the key words, phrases and concepts. Look in the library catalogue for key words that will lead you to secondary sources of information.

   Once you have found your sources, write down the details of each book, periodical or audiovisual item. Ensure that you are in the right section of the library to find the item you want and check the shelves for its catalogue or index number.
   When you find the book, check that the publication is up to date. Check the scope of the book by reading the contents page. Does it cover your needs? Check the index to see whether it contains information and details suited to your purpose.

You may find more recent or additional information from a periodical index such as APAIS. Your library can organise an inter-library loan to lend you books not held in the library.

Libraries hold many sources that are useful for written work in business and commercial fields.

a. Reread the passage and highlight each key word. Explain briefly why it is useful to do this.

b. List three other strategies for preparing an essay. Briefly explain why each one is useful.

c. What are dictionaries and ency-clopaedias used for?

d. When you use the library catalogue, what does the passage above suggest you:
   ▓ look for?
   ▓ write down?
   ▓ check?

e. Why would you use APAIS?

2. a. What reading purpose is served when you survey first?

b. Read the section in Chapter 20, Writing Long Reports, by surveying first for specific items.

c. Break into groups of three to iden-tify, memorise and recall the report writing sequence presented in Figure 20.2, Sequence of parts when writing a long report. Take five minutes to read it carefully.

d. In your group of three, recall the information by listing the ten steps described in Figure 20.2.

e. Finally, discuss as a group the writer's main purpose in preparing the chapter section titled Planning a Long Report (pages 388–91). Is the presentation objective? Justify your answer.

Key terms

author–date (Harvard) reference system

bibliography

bookmark

endnotes

footnotes

list of references

notation

note (traditional) reference system

primary sources of information

reading

search engine

secondary sources of information

study time management plan

Cowboys & engines

STUDY CASE

by Tasker Ryrie

Estimates of the number of Web pages now run into the billions, and the figure grows daily. No search engine can do anything but trawl a fraction of them. Still, not all search engines are alike, and if one doesn't turn up what you are after, another may. Knowing the strengths and limitations of the various search engines can help you find what you seek.

Bear in mind, though, that the Web is freedom of expression gone mad. In addition to the mind-numbing banality of most per-sonal Web pages and the boring reams of information that some people believe the world wants to know about, never has it been

so easy for nutters of every description to promulgate their particular hobbyhorses. Beware 'Institutes for this' and 'Centres for that' – if the information you seek doesn't come from a reputable source, or it seems a bit dodgy or too good to be true, then it probably is.

Accuracy and truthfulness aside, first you have to find what you are looking for and this is not always easy. A search can some-times yield hundreds or even thousands of results. And yet when it works, searching the Web not only saves time but gives you access to a diversity of resources no library can match.

Athough the term 'search engine' is used almost universally, there are several types of search engine, although sometimes the distinction isn't that clear. Search engines use programs, usually called 'spiders', to seek out new information on the Web. This information is then added to the search engine's database.

Search engines or directories?

Search engines are best used when you want to obtain a wide range of results about a specific topic. Directories, on the other hand, use people to index websites, and the quality and bias of a particular directory depends on the people behind it. Directories categorise Web pages under headings such as Arts & Humanity, News & Media, Recreation & Sports, and then provide subcategories and so on. Directories are more likely to list entire sites, whereas search engines are more likely to list specific pages within a site.

Directories are best used when you are vague about what you are looking for and can't provide a specific search term or phrase, and when you don't want too many results to search through. If your searches don't work, then you can send your search to several other search engines simultaneously (using a meta search engine), which will then catalogue the results to you.

Ixquick and Ask Jeeves allow you to ask questions in plain English, although you'll probably get better results using ordinary search techniques. Note, however, that by using a meta search engine you have much less control over your search parameters, and also that meta search results are only as good as the search engines your request is sent to. Meta search engines are best used when you want a wide-ranging search without too much detail.

So-called 'deep Web' search engines search the billions of pages of information believed to be in databases and other sources which are, according to Bright-Planet, 500 times greater than the known Web and hidden from standard search engines. Deep Web search engines are best used when you want detailed, authoritative information, often from academic and other professional sources.

If none of these options give you what you want, then turn to topic-specific or specialty search engines, which concentrate on particular topics such as domain names, government, law and medicine. These are databases with a search engine on top, and they can cover anything. An example is the growing number of search engines catering to news junkies – hourly updates around the world like Excite NewsTracker (nt.excite.com), News Index (www.newsinde.com) and 1stHeadlines (www.1stheadlines.com).

Where to find search engines

You can find lists of the major search engines in each category at Search Engine Watch (searchenginewatch.com/) and ZDNet's Search IQ (www.zdnet.com/searchiq/), which also provides opinions on the qualities of each search engine. Search Engine Watch is also a wonderful source for tips on how to use search engines.

Using a search engine is simple: enter a word or phrase and press enter. Many search engines require a phrase to be enclosed in quotation marks, whilst others like Anzwers and HotBot allow you to stipulate 'exact phrase' from a menu. More complex search syntax can usually be found on a search engine in the section called 'Advanced', which is nearly always next to the search window.

If you conduct regular and complex Web searches, then you will need to pay close attention to search syntax. Boolean search expressions (AND, OR, NOT) are the mainstay, or you can use + and – symbols in front of keywords to indicate which ones should or should not appear in a search. You can then refine your search by, for example, changing the order in which keywords appear and including more complex conditions.

Some search engines enable you to search within the results you have found rather than initiate a new search. However, more and more search engines are using the menu approach to searches, such as 'Exact phrase', 'Match all Words', or 'Match any Words'.

It's nearly always worth trying your search at more than one type of search engine, but watch out for searches which are at the top of the list, especially if they are marked by the term 'features site' or are in colour, bold type or have a border. Many of these are paid advertisements which is why they appear at the top of the search page.

And so to the million-dollar question: which are the best search engines? I favour Google for its clean, uncluttered interface, its simple syntax (just enter words separated by spaces) and its ranking system which tends, most of the time, to provide interesting sources on the first page of results. I also like HotBot and Anzwers for their search parameter menu system, and Anzwers because it provides Australian content.

For local content, always try the Australian site of the search engine. Yahoo is my directory search engine, and then LookSmart. Again, there are Australian sites. For a meta search engine, I use Ixquick because, as its name implies, it is quick. Happy hunting.

Source: Tasker Ryrie, 'Cowboys & Engines', *Charter,* September 2001, pp. 48–9.

Questions

1. Differentiate between the 'best use' of a search engine and a directory, and give examples of each.
2. What do you see as the key features of an effective Web-based search?
3. What are some of the factors that influence the way you choose to research an essay, assignment or project?

Search engines
All The Web   www.altheweb.com
Northern Light   www.northernlight.com
Alta Vista   www.altavista
HotBot   www.hotbot.com
InfoSeek   www.infoseek.com
Excite   www.excite.com
Lycos   www.lycos.com
Google   www.google.com
Anzwers   www.anzwers.com.au

Directories
Ask Jeeves   www.askjeeves.com
Yahoo   www.yahoo.com
Open Directory   www.opendir.com
MSN Search   www.msnsearch.com
LookSmart   www.looksmart.com

Meta search engines
Ask Jeeves   www.askjeeves.com
Ixquick   www.ixquick.com
MetaCrawler   www.metacrawler.com
Dogpile   www.dogpile.com
Profusion   www.profusion.com
Qbsearch   www.qbsearch.com

Deep Web search engines
CompletePlanet   www.completeplanet.com
Northern Light   www.northernlight.com
Invisible Web   www.invisibleweb.com
WebData   www.webdata.com

Organise workplace information

In this chapter you will learn how to:

- choose from three methods of organising information

- use practical strategies for planning complex work documents

- apply various strategies for sorting information

- organise relevant information to suit audience, purpose and context.

Evaluate your communication skills by completing the self-check in the chapter.

Good written communication plays a crucial role at work. It may well affect an organisation's prosperity; it is certainly important to an individual's success.

Good workplace correspondence gets results. It does this by organising relevant information, identifying the writer's purpose, and presenting it in a way that suits the context.

Planning

Careful planning is the key to clear, concise writing.

There are several ways you can tackle the task of planning a document. The following steps are a useful way of getting started and of ensuring that the result is appropriate, readable and clear.

1. Identify your reason for writing the document.
2. Consider the needs of your receiver.
3. Decide what points and ideas you need to include.
4. Decide the best way to organise these points.

Before you start sorting the information it is worth considering three different ways of organising it.

Methods of organising information

Choose the organising method appropriate to your writing purpose.

The following methods of organising material will help your reader understand it readily.

1. The *direct method* presents the main points and/or conclusions early in the document, either before or after the introduction.
2. The *indirect method* leads the reader from the introduction, through the body of information and on to the conclusion.
3. The *problem-solving method* begins with a description of the problem, then discusses the factors that caused it and finally indicates the solution.

Direct method

The **direct method of organising information** begins with the main points and/or conclusions, and then provides detailed evidence to support it and discussion about it (see Figure 15.1). This method is often useful at work because your receiver usually appreciates being able to grasp the point of your document straight away. The direct method is ideally suited to simple documents. The kite-shaped structure illustrated in Figure 15.1 shows how the main point is presented first.

Indirect method

The **indirect method of organising information** starts with the introduction, then provides the detailed evidence and discussion, and finishes with the conclusion or recommendation. Here the order of information has changed. In Figure 15.2 the top triangle has become the bottom triangle and the bottom triangle is now at the top.

Problem-solving method

The **problem-solving method of organising information** is used when you wish to focus the reader's thoughts on a problem. Start with a detailed discussion of the factors that caused the problem and conclude with the solution (see Figure 15.3).

Figure 15.1 The direct method of organising information

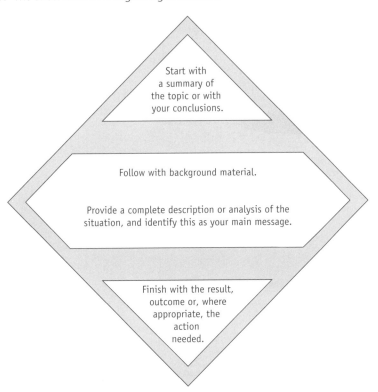

Figure 15.2 The indirect method of organising information

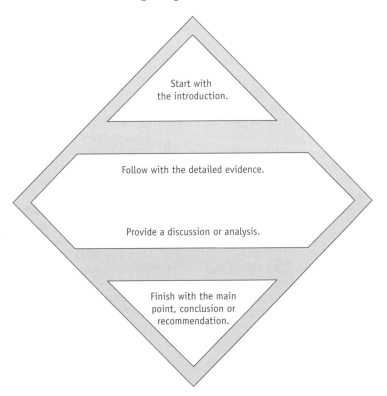

Figure 15.3 The problem-solving method of organising information

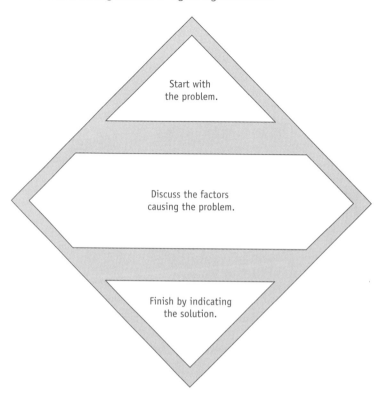

Start with
the problem.

Discuss the factors
causing the problem.

Finish by indicating
the solution.

Planning your writing

APPLY SKILLS

1. You have received a letter from a customer asking why it was necessary to wait 25 minutes to have a credit card authorised on a final lay-by payment.
   a. Write down your purpose in replying to the customer.
   b. List any details about the customer that may affect your reply.
   c. List the points you need to make in your reply.
   d. Choose an appropriate method of organising these points.
2. You have examined the workstation of a staff member and found it unsatis-factory in several ways. Your task is to plan a one-page report requesting improvements to it. Use the direct method presented in Figure 15.1.
   a. What is your purpose? Write a one-sentence summary of your main point.
   b. What aspects of your receiver will you consider when you write the report?
   c. Develop an appropriate description of the background to the issue. What points will you include?
   d. How will you organise these points?
3. Good workplace writing requires planning. Assume you have been asked to provide information about local tourist attractions to a visiting family.
   a. Identify your purpose.
   b. Note any details about the family that may influence your suggestions.
   c. Jot down some details you might include.
   d. Group these under appropriate headings and put them into logical sequence.

4. In pairs, discuss three methods of organising information.
   a. Define the terms 'direct', 'indirect' and 'problem-solving' methods.
   b. List two written tasks suited to each of the above methods.
   c. Which organising method is best suited to each of the tasks presented in Table 15.1?
   d. Explain the benefits of organising your information before you start writing.

Table 15.1

Task	Receiver	Organising method
A request for a new computing system	Unsympathetic to the request	_____
A proposal to move to new premises	Sympathetic	_____
A request for approval to fix the drainage system	Non-technical, neither sympathetic nor unsympathetic	_____
Proposal to offer staff a weekend conference	Informed receiver	_____

Strategies for sorting information

During the planning stage of a complex document you will sort your material before you decide what sequence or order to put it in. Any of the four sorting techniques shown in Table 15.2 may be helpful.

Sorting information assists logical ordering.

Table 15.2 Techniques for sorting information

Technique	Purpose
A traditional written outline or list	To list the most important points. In addition to providing the outline or structure of the document, the list is likely to suggest headings and subheadings.
A tree diagram	To place the most important points as branches on the tree. Specific points are then placed on the branch to which they relate. In this manner, related points are grouped together.
A triangle	To organise your writing one step further than the traditional and tree diagrams by providing a visual limit to the amount of information you can include. It shows you whether you are keeping an appropriate balance between important and less important parts of the document.
A Mind Map®	To represent the thought pattern visually. The map begins with the main idea at the centre. Key concepts project from this. The map prompts you to make associations between them.

Traditional written outline

The **traditional written outline** can be either formal or informal.

Formal outline

A **formal outline** shows the main ideas, the supporting information, their position and the connections between them. It is useful for dealing with many complex ideas or details. A formal outline with headings and subheadings organises information into manageable pieces.

Informal outline

An example of an **informal outline** is shown in Figure 15.4. It lists the main ideas and their supporting information. To create an informal outline, list all the points you wish to make. Then organise them into the sequence in which they will be written. Think about this sequence: will it be easy for the reader to follow? You may decide to remove some irrelevant points or include extra points to expand the content or make the document easier to follow.

Figure 15.4 Example of an informal written outline

Purpose statement: To discuss the consequences of the changes to the Terms of Reference (TOR) for the General Insurance Enquiries and Complaints Scheme (The Scheme) on the community

Outline

    Current Terms of Reference for the Scheme

        Strengths
        Weaknesses

    Changes Proposed by the Insurance Enquiries and Complaints Board

        Review Consultation and Board Obligations
        Deletion of Aggregation of Claims
        Procedural Fairness

    Impact on the Community

        Authorised Insurers
        Self Insurers
        Insurance Brokers and Investigators
        Employers
        Unions
        Employer and Industry Associations
        Workers Compensation Authority
        Others

An informal written outline is one of the easiest ways to organise simple, uncomplicated information. However, for more complicated information this kind of outline may become long and unwieldy because it is so easy to keep adding ideas

Consider the list in terms of your message. How do the ideas link together? Are there any gaps in the information? What issues are the most important? The outline becomes more useful, both as a planning and first draft document, if you create topic headings to indicate the paragraphs you will need to write.

Tree diagram

The tree diagram groups and orders ideas logically.

The **tree diagram** is a planning strategy that groups particular points or ideas together. It is a technique suited to complicated ideas and it is best to use it after you have fully developed them. This is because it shows up any similarities, differences, overlaps or gaps in your ideas, and identifies their order of importance.

The main topic, or theme, becomes the trunk of the tree. Then each idea that stems from this trunk becomes a branch. The tree diagram defines the document's three levels of importance.

1. The **purpose statement** (main topic/theme)
2. The general headings that divide the document into sections
3. The specific ideas grouped under each of the general headings.

You can use the tree diagram to connect your ideas. The branches provide extra information that is related to the main idea or purpose statement (trunk). Check the branches to see which ideas are the most important. Should some of the branches be subdivided into smaller branches? A tree diagram is shown in Figure 15.5.

Figure 15.5 A tree diagram

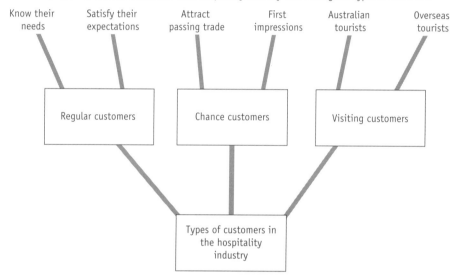

As it is possible to go on adding smaller branches and twigs, too much information may creep into the document and confuse the reader. Is the sequence easy to follow, or is the document becoming dense with too much information and too many words so that the main theme is lost?

Aim to create a tree diagram that keeps the trunk (main topic) clearly defined, and does not have too many general ideas as branches. The diagram is a useful planning strategy; if you are willing to remove excess information, it is also a useful editing strategy.

Planning

Is my	Yes	No	Unsure
purpose statement clear?	☐	☐	☐
organisation method suited to the receiver's needs?	☐	☐	☐
list of points complete, but as concise as possible?	☐	☐	☐
list of points relevant?	☐	☐	☐
Does my information-organising method			
suit the purpose?	☐	☐	☐
suit the audience?	☐	☐	☐
suit the context?	☐	☐	☐

SELF CHECK 15.1

Figure 15.6 A triangle outline

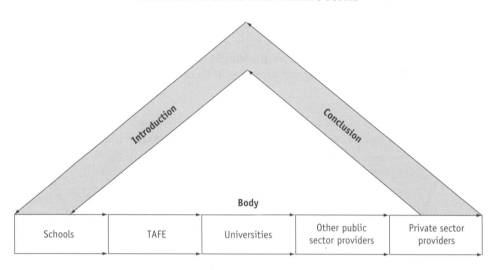

A triangle
outline contains
the main ideas as
a unit.

Triangle

The shape of the **triangle** emphasises the lead-in or introduction to your topic and the conclusion. As a closed shape it contains the main ideas in boxes along the bottom, as a unit. Consequently, it helps you to limit your material to what is necessary. A triangle outline for the topic 'Australian Education and Training Bodies' is shown in Figure 15.6.

Once you have created the triangle, check that:

- each box in the main body relates to the title
- each box is in logical order from left to right across the bottom
- each box is related to your writing purpose
- there is no gap in the information or flow of ideas.

The heading 'Australian Education and Training Bodies' is the theme linking the ideas presented in the boxes. The introduction's purpose is to link the heading and the first idea, which is placed on the left side of the bottom line of the triangle. The conclusion is placed on the right-hand side. Visually, it brings readers back to the starting point, your introduction. As a way of organising information, it emphasises the flow of ideas and is best suited to the first draft of your writing project.

Tony Buzan
created the
technique of
Mind Mapping.

Mind Map®

Some writers organise their information by using a **Mind Map®,** where key concepts project from a central theme. Instead of the linear approach to note-taking, the Mind Map offers key concept overviews to which descriptive details can be added.

A Mind Map helps us to make associations between key concepts and relevant experiences. This way of sorting and selecting information is more efficient than making the traditional kind of structured notes which contain unnecessary words that interrupt the key words.

Figure 15.7 Mind Map® of a company's emergency procedure

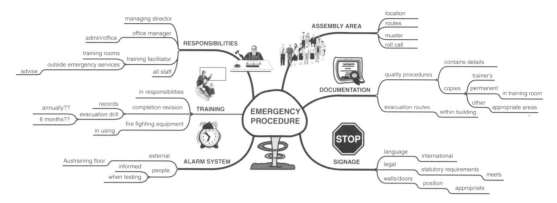

Create the Mind Map by placing the main idea (theme) in the centre, with key concepts branching out from it. In the Mind Map shown in Figure 15.7 the key concepts are linked to each other and to the central theme: emergency procedure. Other concepts flow from each main concept. The Mind Map becomes a visual representation of a thought structure. From this Mind Map a report could be written on emergency procedure.

Some of the advantages offered by Mind Mapping are:

- focus on the main theme
- identification of the key concepts
- links between key concepts and other concepts
- organisation
- structure.

The more important points are closer to the centre, while the less important ones are further out. It is easy to add new ideas to the Mind Map. Table 15.3 shows the relationship between the key and related concepts.

Table 15.3 Concepts for emergency procedure

Key concepts	Related concepts
1. Assembly area	Location, routes, muster and roll call
2. Documentation	Quality procedures and evacuation routes
3. Signage	Language, legal, walls and doors
4. Alarm system	External and people
5. Training	In responsibilities, completion revision and fire fighting equipment
6. Responsibilities	Managing director, office manager, training facilitator and all staff

WISE
WEB

Visit the Companion Website at **www.prenhall.com/dwyer_au**. Choose the Net Search activity in Chapter 15 to conduct a literature search online and use the problem solving method to organise the information.

Chapter summary

Choose from three methods of organising information. Once you have identified your audience and purpose, use the direct, indirect or problem-solving method.

Use practical strategies for planning complex work documents. Plan the order in which you will present the information.

Apply various strategies for sorting information. A traditional written outline, a tree diagram, a triangle or a Mind Map. These help you to sort and group the main topics and headings, and to create the outline or structure of the document before you write it.

Organise relevant information to suit audience, purpose and context. This helps you to analyse and evaluate your key concepts. Consider the needs of your audience, the document's purpose and the context in which it is presented.

QUESTIONS
REVIEW

1. Nominate four steps that help you start your writing.
2. Why is it important to plan a document?
3. List ways of organising information.
4. What is the difference between the direct and indirect methods of organising information?
5. What is the purpose of a traditional written outline?
6. Explain what a tree diagram is.
7. Name the three levels of importance defined by a tree diagram.
8. How can a triangle help to structure a document?
9. What is a Mind Map?

10. List Buzan's seven laws of Mind Mapping.
11. a. Nominate three techniques for sorting information at the planning stage.
   b. Which of these techniques would most suit you? Why?
   c. Briefly explain how a written outline can help to show clear relationships and develop balance in your writing.
12. What benefits do you gain by considering:
   a. the needs of your audience?
   b. the context in which the information is presented?

Key terms

direct method of
   organising information
formal outline
indirect method of
   organising information

informal outline
Mind Map
problem-solving method
   of organising
   information

purpose statement
traditional written outline
tree diagram
triangle

Planning your document

1. Prepare a Mind Map of your favourite sport or hobby, as preparation for an essay. Begin by placing a sketch in the middle of an A4 sheet of paper. For example, if your favourite sport is tennis, draw a tennis ball and then project your ideas from that point. Apply Buzan's seven Mind-Mapping rules.

2. Prepare a traditional written outline for an essay on the topic 'How to eat well'. Clearly distinguish your first-level and second-level headings.

3. Assume you have to write a short report for your supervisor on the benefits of completing your course of study. Include in your report a request for the payment of your course fees.
   a. Prepare a title for the report.
   b. Write a purpose statement.
   c. Prepare a triangle outline for your report.

4. Which method was easiest to prepare – the Mind Map, the traditional outline or the triangle outline? Which method gave you more information to include in a piece of writing?

Get to the power point

Use Word as the basis of a Power-Point presentation

Word, Excel and PowerPoint are designed to share information. For example, you can insert an Excel chart or a PowerPoint slide into a Word document. This project shows you how to create a PowerPoint presentation based on a Word outline. You can complete this project using Word 95 (version 7) and PowerPoint 95 (version 7) or Word 97 and PowerPoint 97.

When you create a PowerPoint presentation, keep your intended audience in mind. That way you'll find it easier to make decisions about content, style and format. In this project, the audience is a workgroup about to get a new computer system. Imagine you're a manager giving the presentation to inform your staff about the new system. We will design the presentation to be shown on an overhead projector, but we'll not actually print the overhead transparencies.

Creating the outline

Start a new document in Word and type the following headings (when you see [Enter], press the Enter key):

Staff Presentation [Enter]
How the New Computer System will Affect

You [Enter]
About the New System [Enter]
What it is [Enter]
Why we need it [Enter]
When it's arriving [Enter]
Where you can get help with the New System [Enter]
The Help Desk [Enter]
The Training Department [Enter]
Your Manager [Enter]

You must format the outline with the built-in Word styles. Click in the first heading and then open the Style drop-down list on the Formatting toolbar and choose the Heading 1 style (Figure 1). Click in the second heading and format it with the Heading 2 style. Click in the third heading and format it with the Heading 1 style. Select the fourth, fifth and sixth headings and format them with the Heading 2 style. Click in the seventh heading and format it with the Heading 1 style. Select the last three headings and format them with the Heading 2 style. Your outline should look similar to the one in Figure 2.

Before you can import the outline into PowerPoint you must save it. Open the File menu and choose the Save As command. In the Save As dialog box, choose the folder in which you want to save the outline, then

Figure 1

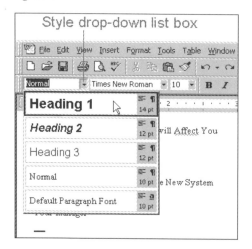

type a name for the outline in the File Name text box. After you have saved the outline, close Word.

Importing the outline

Start PowerPoint and, in the PowerPoint dialog box, select the Blank Presentation radio button and then click on the OK button. In the New Slide dialog box that opens, click on the Blank Slide option (fourth column, third row) and then click on the OK button.

Open the File menu and choose the Open command. In the Open dialog box, click on the Files of Type drop-down list and choose the All Outlines option. Now open the folder in which you saved your

Figure 2

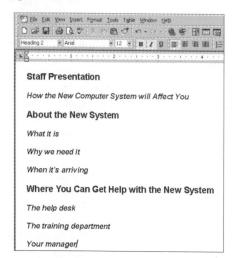

outline, select it and then click on the Open button. PowerPoint opens the outline, converts it into a presentation and displays it in Outline view. Each heading formatted with Word's Heading 1 style becomes a slide. All headings formatted with the Heading 2 through Heading 9 styles become subheadings on the slides.

Specifying page setup

When working with PowerPoint it is important to make sure you specify the size of your slides before you start formatting them. To specify the slide size, open the File menu and choose the Page Setup command (in PowerPoint 95, it is called the Slide Setup command). In the Page Setup dialog box, click on the Slides Sized For drop-down list and choose the Overhead option. The Orientation section of the dialog box lets you specify the orientation of the overheads. Click the Portrait radio button and then click the OK button.

Formatting the presentation

The best view for looking at slide formatting is Slide view. To switch to Slide view, open the View menu and choose the Slide command. In Slide view, PowerPoint displays one slide at a time. To move through the slides, you can use the Next Slide and Previous Slide buttons at the bottom of the vertical scroll bar (Figure 3).

So far, our slides are very plain and boring. Let's jazz them up by applying one of PowerPoint's built-in slide designs. Open the Format menu and choose the Apply Design command (in PowerPoint 95 it is called the

Figure 3

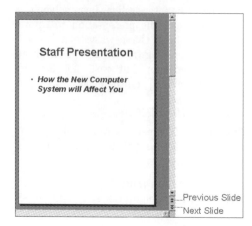

Apply Design Template command). In the Apply Design dialog box, choose a design template and then click on the Apply command. If you don't like the design, re-open the Apply Design dialog box and choose another.

Inserting clip art

Let's insert a piece of clip art on the first slide in the presentation. Make sure the first slide is displayed and then click on the Insert Clip Art button on the Standard toolbar (Figure 4). In the Clip Gallery dialog box, choose the clip art you want to use, then click on the Insert button. You might want to reposition the clip art. To do this, move your mouse pointer over it, then drag it and drop it where you want it to go.

Figure 4

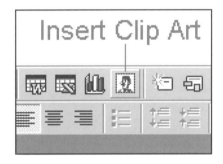

Replacing fonts

Rather than select each piece of text and format it with a new font, you can use the Replace Fonts command to replace every occurrence of a particular font. In Word 95, the Replace Fonts command is on the Tools menu; in Word 97, the Replace Fonts command is on the Format menu. Choose the Replace Fonts command to open the Replace Font dialog box (Figure 5). From the Replace drop-down list, choose the font you want to replace, and from the With drop-down list, choose the new font.

Now click on the Replace button. Power-Point replaces the selected font with the new font. When you've done this, the Replace Font dialog box stays open so you can replace other fonts in the presentation.

When you have finished replacing fonts, click on the Close button.

Inserting the date

To insert the date on the first slide of the presentation, make sure the first slide is displayed, then open the View menu and choose the Header and Footer command. On the Slide tab of the Header and Footer dialog box, make sure the Date and Time check box is selected. Click on the Update Automatically radio button and, from the drop-down list, choose a date format. Make sure none of the other check boxes is selected, then click on the Apply button. PowerPoint adds the date to the bottom-left corner of the first slide.

Saving the presentation

Open the File menu and choose the Save As command, or click on the Save button on the Standard toolbar. In the Save As dialog box, open the folder in which you want to save the presentation, type a name in the File Name text box and then click on the Save button.

Figure 5

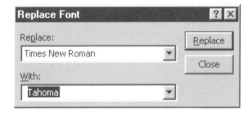

Running the presentation

We can preview our presentation by running it as a slide show. To do this, open the View menu and choose the Slide Show command (after you choose the Slide Show command in PowerPoint 95, it opens the Slide Show dialog box where you should click on the Show button). PowerPoint switches to Slide Show view and displays the first slide in your presentation. To move to the next slide, click on the screen. When you have moved on to the last slide, click on the screen to return to Slide view.

This presentation was designed to be shown on an overhead projector. Make sure your printer is capable of printing transparencies before you try it and buy transparencies that meet the specifications in your printer's manual.

Source: Vanessa Waller, *Sydney Morning Herald*, 12 June 1999. The complete series of Projects 101 is available on CD-ROM from Webster Publishing <http://www.websterpublishing.com>. Reproduced with permission.

Webster Publishing is an Australian company that produces training material to teach people how to use popular commercial software. In addition to publishing books and computer-based tutorials, the company produces an ever-expanding range of multimedia titles on CD-ROM.

Questions

1. How does the Style drop-down list box in Word help you sort and organise information?

2. Why should you keep your intended audience in mind as you prepare a PowerPoint presentation?

3. Use one of the techniques in Table 15.2 to construct an outline of this article.

4. Why did you choose this technique instead of one of the other three?

5. A PowerPoint presentation is a visual aid. Describe the characteristics that make a visual aid effective.

Using plain English in workplace documents

In this chapter you will learn how to:

- define the term 'plain English'

- plan workplace documents in plain English

- write workplace documents in plain English

- edit documents according to the principles of plain English

- discuss three advantages of a plain English writing style

- advocate the use of plain English in the workplace.

Evaluate your communication skills by completing the self-check in the chapter.

A plain English writing style – that is, a reader-friendly writing style – is good clear writing that considers the reader's needs and gets the message across easily and quickly. It reduces the chances of misunderstanding and ambiguity and is particularly suited to workplace documents.

Good workplace writing results from thoughtful planning, writing in plain English and careful editing. Each stage is part of the writing process. At the planning stage, take time to identify your purpose, consider your receiver, decide what you want to say and put this in a logical sequence. Chapter 15, Organise Workplace Information, offers you a range of strategies to use for the planning stage. At the editing stage check your work for accuracy and completeness and make sure that your writing is logical, clear and concise.

At the writing stage, your tools are words, sentences, paragraphs and layout. Make these work for you to convey your meaning concisely and courteously. The receiver of business correspondence wants to understand what should happen, why it should happen and how to go about making it happen. The main purpose when writing in plain English is to get the message across.

The seven components of writing style

Good workplace writing uses the following seven components of writing style appropriately:

1. words (language)
2. sentences
3. paragraphs
4. rhythm or flow
5. tone
6. order of information
7. layout or format.

Words should be familiar, not frightening.

Appropriate words, well structured sentences and paragraphs, a logical progression of ideas and an appropriate tone all ensure a good writing style.

Language

Language is the communication tool that expresses meaning and gives a form to ideas, feelings and events as you transmit them to others. Your vocabulary is your stock of words. These words have been assigned their meaning or range of meanings by use and convention.

When choosing words for workplace writing, remember that it's always good practice to use **plain English** – the language that is familiar and friendly to your receiver. Keep the following guidelines in mind.

Use simple language

Familiar, unambiguous words that move straight to the point make the reader's task simple, and ensure that the message is immediately clear. Choose words that are appropriate to the audience and situation.

Remove unnecessary words

Using more words than are necessary to convey the meaning irritates the reader, who may decide to read no further. Avoid repetition. Some examples of the use of too many words, and suitable alternatives, are given in Table 16.1.

Table 16.1 Unnecessary words

Poor or incorrect use	Better use
precedes before	goes before, or 'precedes' by itself
reverse backward	reverse
possible benefit	benefit
repeat again	repeat
actual fact	fact
the majority of	most
progress forward	progress
on the occasion of	when
a number of different	various
I personally	I
wise words of wisdom	wise words
completely eliminate	eliminate
end results	results

Avoid clichés

Hackneyed expressions, or **clichés**, are overused words and phrases that have lost meaning and impact. Examples of clichés that are often used in official documents and sometimes creep into our own writing are given in Table 16.2. Avoid them.

Use specific language

Specific language describes details precisely. It is easier to understand and makes more impact than general or theoretical language. The receiver may interpret a general term quite differently from the way you intended. Concrete language conveys a specific image that is easy to interpret. The phrase 'a rusted green late seventies Torana' has a much clearer message for the reader than the more general phrase, 'an old vehicle'.

Precise language is easier to understand than general language.

Table 16.2 Clichés

Poor use	Better use
reside	live
terminate	end
utilisation of	use
optimum	best
finalise	finish
at this point in time	now

Use technical terms carefully

Technical terms (**jargon**) have a precise meaning that is specific to a particular subject, procedure or process (e.g. computer terminology: motherboard, port, pixel). They are useful when you write for those who are familiar with them. Avoid them when you write for those who are not familiar with them. Readers may simply 'turn off' or become 'worried' by the difficult terms. Use technical terms only when you know they will help your reader to understand, not to show how knowledgeable you are.

Avoid 'buzz words' – for example, the term 'coal face', meaning the operational end of management. Acronyms are another difficulty (e.g. ASEAN). You may understand its meaning but others will need it spelt out. Use an acronym only if you are sure it is known to your reader, but it is good practice to spell it out in full the first time you use it.

Use the active voice

The active voice
is strong and
direct.

The **active voice** communicates simply and directly, and lets the reader know exactly who does what.

In a sentence using the active voice, the subject comes first – for example, 'Jane hailed the taxi'. Jane is the subject and the action word (the verb) is 'hailed'. This subject-and-verb sequence links the subject directly to the action in the structure of the sentence.

The sentence 'The taxi was hailed by Jane' uses the **passive voice**. In other words, 'taxi' is the passive receiver of the action 'was hailed'. The sentence is longer and less direct than 'Jane hailed the taxi'. By putting 'taxi' first, it emphasises 'taxi', rather than 'Jane', who is responsible for the action. The passive voice is less direct than the active voice. Sometimes it also leaves out important information such as who or what is performing the action – for example: 'The taxi was hailed.'. For examples, see Table 16.3.

Overuse of the
passive voice
slows down your
message.

Using the passive voice too much can slow down your writing, whereas the active voice creates a sense of immediacy and energy. It also reduces formality, as in 'I enclose a cheque' rather than 'A cheque is enclosed'.

Using the passive voice is sometimes appropriate. For example, it conveys a more diplomatic tone to write: 'Your payment has not been received' rather than 'You have not sent payment'.

Choose non-discriminatory, inclusive language

Language often carries hidden meaning. Some words carry sexist or racist messages that are offensive or demeaning to others. Think about your own language use. Do you use racist or sexist terms? Can you identify them?

Sexist language gives one gender more prominence than the other. Three strategies for removing sexism in written language are suggested here.

Table 16.3 Active and passive voice

Active voice	Passive voice
The business reached its highest sales figures for the year this month.	Record sales figures for the year were reached by the business this month.
Ling completed the assignment.	The assignment was completed by Ling.
Third-year management students prepared the project.	The project was prepared by third-year management students.
Barbara finished the work.	The work was finished by Barbara.

1. Avoid using male-dominated terms to describe occupations or roles that are shared by both men and women – for example, instead of 'chairman' use 'chair' or 'chairperson'.
2. Eliminate the unnecessary mention of a person's gender, as in 'lady doctor' or 'female engineer'.
3. When referring to someone whose gender is not specified, avoid using the male pronoun 'he' exclusively. Use 'he or she', or simply use the plural pronoun even when referring to just one person. For example: 'If a student is late, ask them to explain'. The *Macquarie Student Writer's Guide* suggests this approach. You could also rewrite the sentence entirely, in the plural form – for example: 'If students are late, ask them to explain'.

Non-discriminatory, **inclusive language** includes all your readers. Even if your occupation is currently female-dominated, as nursing is, or male-dominated, as engineering is, changing attitudes and education trends mean that both women and men are working in all industries. Resentment and communication barriers can occur when language is addressed exclusively to one sex. It is discriminatory (see Table 16.4).

Inclusive language includes all readers.

As you mix and correspond with business men and women, use language that includes both groups. To write an engineering job description that says 'The best man for the job will have the following characteristics . . .' ignores women engineers. To write a nursing job description that says 'She will have the following characteristics . . .' excludes male nurses. Whether you are writing for local, regional or international business readers, make sure that you use non-discriminatory, inclusive language.

Use parallel language

You can sometimes link related ideas more closely by expressing them in an equivalent grammatical form.

Also, use words that give the same weight or emphasis to two different but equally important things or people. 'The man and the woman' is an example of parallelism, but 'the man and the lady' is not. 'The gentleman and the lady' are parallel terms, though outdated.

Table 16.4 Discriminatory language

Sexist	Non-sexist
Each student must submit his assignment by August.	Each student must submit their assignment by August.
When a person is employed he must contact Personnel.	When people are employed they must contact Personnel.
My girl will answer the telephone.	My assistant will answer the telephone.
You and your wife are invited to the Christmas party.	You and your partner are invited to the Christmas party.
Lady lawyer	Lawyer
Actress	Actor
Manpower	Staff or workforce
Workman	Worker, employee
Foreman	Supervisor

A sports commentator who says, 'The men are really holding their strength', and then describes a female event by saying 'The girls are holding their strength' is not using parallel language. 'Men' describes adult males, but 'girls' does not describe adult females and therefore can be interpreted as patronising or discriminating.

Words are your tools as a writer. Make them work well for you. Use simple, familiar language, free of jargon, repetition and clichés. Be prepared to work at becoming competent with language. A dictionary and a thesaurus are both useful. A quick check in the dictionary will ensure that your spelling is correct, while the thesaurus offers you a range of words suitable for your purpose.

The word processor is another useful aid to writing. Some packages include a thesaurus, spell check and dictionary in their software.

Sentence structure

The sentence is the pattern in which your written ideas are presented. These patterns are then interpreted by your receiver. As a writer, your aim is to convey information in sentences that are easy to understand. Clarity and coherence in writing are achieved by carefully and correctly constructed sentences.

Correctly constructed sentences make writing clear and coherent.

There are three main types of sentences. Each uses a particular structure or pattern of words.

1. A *simple sentence* has one clause – the main clause – which stands alone.
2. A *compound sentence* has two main clauses that could stand alone – that is, two simple sentences usually joined with a connecting word such as 'and' or 'but'.
3. A *complex sentence* has one main clause and one or more subordinate (dependent) clauses.

A **simple sentence** contains only one idea or action, expressed in one clause. It thus has only one finite verb – that is, one verb with a subject. The sentence 'James carried the baby.' is a simple sentence containing one clause, one finite verb ('carried') and its subject, 'James'.

A **compound sentence** contains two or more main ideas or actions, expressed in two main clauses. It has at least two finite verbs – that is, two verbs with subjects. 'James carried the baby and Mary pushed the stroller.' is a compound sentence containing two verbs ('carried' and 'pushed') and their subjects, 'James' and 'Mary'.

A **complex sentence** contains more than one idea. The main idea is contained in the main clause, but a complex sentence has at least one other idea that relates to or depends on the main clause. Thus the sentence 'James carried the baby who was crying.' is a complex sentence containing the main idea – that James carried the baby – plus additional information – that the baby was crying.

The value of understanding these basic facts about sentences is that you can avoid two of the most common errors in writing sentences: writing fragments instead of whole sentences; writing sentences that lack unity.

A sentence fragment does not make complete sense on its own. An example is: 'Writing to the clients'. Clearly, the reader needs more information – for example, 'Writing to the clients was an important task for the manager.'. The incompleteness in the sentence fragment is caused by the absence of a finite verb – that is, a verb with a subject. Beware of treating sentence fragments as whole sentences. They can confuse your reader.

A second very common fault in sentence structure occurs when a sentence lacks unity because it contains two quite separate ideas that need separate sentences.

Advice about ensuring sentence unity is given in the subsection, 'Sentence Sprawl' below.

The correct use of grammar gives order to sentence structure and the flow of ideas, and enables the reader to understand the writer's intention and information. It follows certain conventions to allow the expectations of writer and reader to intersect. Accordingly, the reader relies on the writer to use these conventions and the writer knows that the reader expects them.

The Business Communication Handbook does not aim to explain and develop correct grammatical use and punctuation. However, it is suggested that you practise and check carefully the details of spelling, grammar and punctuation in all your writing.

Sentence length

The general rule when writing plain English is to keep sentences short and compact because they are easier to read. Long, involved sentences can be difficult to follow. On the other hand, too many short sentences can make the connections between each idea hard to follow. As you write, make sure that you connect your points or ideas clearly. Lead the reader through them without causing confusion. Variety in sentence length improves the flow of ideas.

Sentence sprawl

Sprawling sentences with too many words often try to cover too much at once. This can confuse the reader because there are:

Long involved sentences may confuse the reader.

■ too many points or ideas to grasp
■ too many qualifications or modifications to each point.

You can make a document more readable by breaking long sentences into two or three sentences, to form a paragraph. Variety in sentence length also helps to keep the reader's interest.

If a sentence looks awkward, read it aloud. If it sounds too long, or the ideas tangle together, you have a poorly constructed or perhaps over-complex sentence. The following guidelines can help you to shorten long complicated sentences.

■ Sort out your ideas or points.
■ Limit each sentence to one or two ideas.
■ Break up a long sentence into two or three shorter sentences.
■ Put explanations into separate sentences.

If the writing sounds choppy and interrupted, your sentences may be too short. In this case, join two sentences with words like 'or', 'and', 'but', 'so', 'because', 'unless', 'although' and 'otherwise'.

Readability

The general rule in business correspondence is to keep sentences short and compact: 15–20 words each will make them easier to understand, which is what '**readability**' means here.

Table 16.5 measures readability against the average number of words in sentences in a passage. A sentence with eight words or less is very easy to read. An average reader would have no trouble with a sentence of 17 words, so the 17-word sentence is defined as the standard sentence. A sentence of 29 words or more is more difficult to read. However, variety in sentence length can increase the reader's interest.

The Fog Index

The Fog Index is a readability test. It can be used to assess the density of your writing. To use the Fog Index follow these steps.

1. Choose a piece of your writing of, say, half a page in length.
   a. Count the number of words that have three or more syllables.
      (There are exceptions to this rule: do not count:
      - the main topic words and proper nouns (e.g. communication, Conservative, Canberra)
      - verb tense endings (e.g. ing, ly and ed)
      - plural words)
   b. Count the number of sentences.
2. Divide the number of words with three or more syllables by the number of sentences to give you the Fog Score.

Interpretation

A Fog Score of:

2–3: a reasonable average for business writing

4–5: a rather heavy use of long words

6+: typical of much academic and technical writing.

In general, a low Fog Score means that more people will be able to understand the document, although a low Fog Score does not guarantee good writing. A score of 5 or more warns you that your document is difficult to comprehend.

To reduce a high score:

- omit unnecessary words
- replace long words with shorter words
- divide long sentences into shorter ones.

Even if your writing style is so good that you can construct complex sentences of 30 words or more correctly, think of alternatives. The average reader, who makes up the greatest part of your readership, may be able to read and understand only a simpler construction that uses about 17 words. If you always use complex sentences, many readers are likely to have problems understanding your message.

Table 16.5 Sentence readability

Number of words	Readability
8 or less	Very easy
11	Easy
14	Fairly easy
17	Standard
21	Fairly difficult
25	Difficult
29 or more	Very difficult

Punctuation

Punctuation achieves for written communication what pauses and inflection do for spoken communication. Using it correctly will help to keep your points distinct and your message clear. Remember to use a capital letter to begin a sentence and a full stop to complete it. Use a comma to mark a pause, or to give one part of the sentence equal weight with the other.

Correct punctuation keeps meaning clear.

Paragraph structure

The coherence and rhythm of your writing will depend not only on your word choice and sentence structure, but on how well you construct your paragraphs. A paragraph is a cluster of sentences built around one main idea or point. Its most important function is to group together the sentences that are dedicated to one main idea, and to separate them visually from the ideas that precede and follow them.

A paragraph is dedicated to one main idea.

To make your paragraphs work this way you must ensure that the main point of each one stands out sharply. Some strategies that will help you with this are as follows.

Strategies to create different types of paragraphs

For an opening or introductory paragraph, organise the ideas or thoughts around:

■ a statement of the subject
■ a statement of the intention of the piece of writing
■ background information
■ a question
■ an anecdote
■ an opinion.

The first three of these strategies are used most often in workplace documents because of their objective nature.

A **topic sentence** that states the main idea of a paragraph is also useful. It is usually presented at the beginning or end of the paragraph. When it occurs at the beginning, follow it with sentences that explain or discuss the paragraph's main idea.

A topic sentence is usually placed at the beginning of a paragraph.

Alternatively, you may discuss the supporting information first, and then present the main idea in the last sentence of the paragraph. Either way the topic sentence identifies for the reader the main point of that paragraph. In a closing or concluding paragraph you may organise the content around:

■ a course of action
■ a recommendation
■ a summary
■ a quotation
■ a question or challenge
■ a restatement of the introduction.

Grouping sentences

The structure of your paragraph is important. Organise the sentences it contains to provide a logical progression of information. Use linking words such as 'therefore', 'consequently', 'however' to tie the whole together and carry your reader comfortably from point to point. Summary statements are discussed more fully further on. Always aim to put the sentences of each paragraph in an order that will make them easy to understand.

To achieve this sort of coherence, attention to punctuation and grammar is very important. For more information and exercises, see the Bibliography. *The Little Brown Handbook* is particularly useful.

Paragraph length

In business writing, the usual rule is to have at least two sentences in a paragraph. However, a sentence can stand alone as a 'paragraph' to emphasise a particular point. Use this device sparingly.

Consider varying paragraph length to give variety to your writing. Remember that paragraphs provide relief to the eye. White space is important as it breaks up blocks of printed material that could otherwise overwhelm or discourage the reader.

Short paragraphs are usually easier to comprehend.

A good writing style presents correct, concise information. Paragraphs must also be linked together in a logical order to make your piece of writing clear and unified.

Write your paragraphs so that the reader can follow the development of your idea in each one, and then progress from one paragraph to the next. At the concluding paragraph the reader should comprehend the purpose and meaning of your entire piece.

Sentence constructions

APPLY SKILLS

1. Define the terms 'simple sentence', 'compound sentence' and 'complex sentence'. Write an example of each type of sentence.
2. Define 'sentence sprawl' and briefly discuss three ways to avoid it in your writing.
3. Divide the following sentence into at least three shorter sentences. You may need to change a few words to clarify the writing.

    My strong interest in your organisation and in the field of publishing is based on a long-term involvement with data and people and I am writing to offer multi-faceted employable skills to meet your organisation's needs.

4. Combine the following two simple sentences to make one compound sentence.

    Marie and Jarek attended the conference. Charles decided to stay at home.

5. Identify the main clause and the subordinate clause in the following complex sentence.

    The child who is wearing the Collingwood sports jumper is my cousin.

6. Reorganise the following long involved sentence into a paragraph of shorter

sentences, so that it can be read and understood more quickly.

Like many other ways of writing, a piece of persuasive writing uses several different strategies to persuade readers including gaining the readers' attention, interest, desire for the product or service and their willingness to take action, although there are two general strategies underlying any type of writing; a good piece of writing will consider its purpose and the needs of the receiver and persuasive writing also uses these two strategies.

Suggestions for beginning each sentence:
Like many other ways of . . .
Some of these are to . . .
Two general strategies . . .
Of course . . .

7. a. Reorganise the following passage by combining short statements into longer ones wherever you think that you can improve the expression.

    Seating arrangements can affect communication between members at a meeting. Round or oval tables are ideal. People see each other's actions and reactions. Rectangular tables are less ideal. They give power to the people at either end of the table. Tables do not invite informality. Sit above the rest and you have more power. Sit below other people and they have more power.

A suggestion for beginning the first sentence:
    Different seating arrangements . . .
Suggestions for connecting your sentences:
        because . . .

as . . .
while . . .

b. Use 'or when' to connect two short sentences to make one concluding sentence.
Suggestion for beginning the concluding sentence:
    In any one of the arrangements above . . .

Rhythm

As people read, they follow the writer's **rhythm** – the flow of ideas and the pauses that halt the flow to emphasise a point. To vary your writing rhythm this way, practise the following techniques:

- a full stop
- a new paragraph
- a topic sentence
- a simple sentence
- a longer complex or compound sentence
- repetition of key words
- headings and subheadings
- linking words and phrases.

Rhythm is the flow of words.

Read your work aloud and listen for the rhythm. First, does it flow and, second, does it provide variety? A balanced rhythm in writing is important because it helps to make your writing interesting and easy to follow.

Tone

Tone is an important part of your message. The reader, like the listener, interprets meaning not only from the words, but from your choice of words, and even from the way you arrange them. A courteous, confident tone is appropriate for business writing, or for offering an opinion, stating a fact or asking a question. An aggressive or patronising tone is unacceptable.

Tone is the mood or feeling expressed by a piece of writing.

When we give a command or direction we use the imperative tense. For example: 'Pass the ball to the left-winger' or 'Leave the computer turned on'. The imperative changes tone and becomes more courteous if we add: 'Please'.

The question 'How could you have been so stupid as to post the cheque to the wrong address?' has an angry and belittling tone. The words 'How could you' and 'stupid' in the sentence would make the receiver defensive, because the tone is judgmental and unkind.

Tone reflects your attitude towards the receiver and your subject. Take time to place yourself in the receiver's position and write courteously and positively.

The 'you' approach

The **'you' approach** in writing speaks personally to the receiver by addressing them directly as 'you' from time to time in the document. 'Thank you for your inquiry' is an example of this approach. It projects an empathetic, personal tone and includes both

The 'you' approach creates a personal tone.

male and female readers – that is, all readers. Sometimes, you can add the word 'us' to create a rapport between the writer and the receiver. However, for workplace writing it is usually better to focus on the document's purpose and the receiver's needs.

Composing paragraphs

1. a. List six words about a public transport system.
   b. Create a topic sentence around one of these words.
   c. Prepare a draft paragraph by using the other words in clear sentences that discuss, explain or outline the topic. Try to vary the length of your sentences.
   d. Reread the draft paragraph and highlight the topic sentence. If the topic sentence is not the first sentence of the paragraph, reorganise the paragraph so that the topic sentence does come first and put the other three sentences in an appropriate order.
2. Assume you are preparing a pamphlet on the topic 'The Harmful Effects of Excessive Sunlight on your Skin'. Write a paragraph that summarises this topic in general terms.
   a. Start the paragraph with a topic sentence that contains the words 'skin cancer'.
   b. Follow the topic sentence with two or three other sentences.
   c. Conclude with a sentence that repeats at least one of the key words from your topic sentence.
3. In a reply to a request from a new employee for information about the Social Club, write a four-paragraph account of the company's Social Club activities.

Begin each paragraph with a topic sentence, then complete it with sentences that build upon the idea expressed in the topic sentence. In at least one of the paragraphs, use a key word from its topic sentence in the last sentence.

4. Consider the sentence: 'Various strategies can be used to make paragraphs approachable and easy to understand.' Briefly explain two different strategies that make a paragraph easy to understand.

5.
   > No Plant Operators
   > Beyond This Point

   This sign, posted by management at the entrance to the administration block, caused a serious conflict between workers at the manufacturing plant and workers in the administration office. Yet management intended nothing personal. They simply wanted to prevent the new floors of the administration block from being damaged by the heavy boots normally worn by the plant operators.
   a. Discuss why the above sign is an example of bad communication.
   b. Compose a sign that you believe will achieve what management wants without offending the plant operator workers. Briefly explain why you consider your sign would be an improvement.

Order of information

Choose a logical order of information.

The order in which you present your information must suit your communication purpose. You probably do this instinctively. After all, you would adopt one kind of order to inform a client that they had won the store's $100 000 Art Union prize, but a different one to advise a longstanding client that you were cancelling their credit with the store.

Some of your communication purposes at work are:

- to inform
- to persuade
- to instruct.

A discussion of different ways of organising information to achieve your objective is presented in Chapter 15, Organise Workplace Information. It is vital to choose a method that suits your purpose, the content, and the needs of the receiver. To develop the content in business writing, the rule (as for any writing) is to place the important points in positions that will draw the reader's attention to them. When you relate the content clearly to the purpose of your document, you create a balance between your information and the changes or action that should take place as a result of the communication.

Layout

Layout is the arrangement or presentation of information on the page. It gives your reader their first impression of your message. Therefore, to project a professional image, set out any document to:

Layout creates the first impression for your reader.

- make a maximum impact
- achieve your communication purpose
- improve readability.

Set out the material clearly and space it so that it is easy to understand; the reader will welcome the break provided by the white spaces.

A wide variety of layouts is used for business documents. The first step is to decide which one suits your communication purpose and channel. Documents that use formal communication channels have a formal layout – for example, a submission or a short report – whereas a handwritten note will suit communication that goes through an informal channel. As a rule, internal channels of communication require a less formal presentation than external channels.

Organise your information so that the reader can follow its progress through the document. Highlight the main points with:

- headings
- numbered lists or sections
- underlining
- indenting
- shading
- white space.

The appropriate professional layout of your communication is an integral part of it. You will achieve its purpose when you provide specific information that is set out carefully.

Good paragraphs

SELF CHECK 16.1

The following points can be used to evaluate your competence in paragraph construction.

Does each paragraph	Very well	Satisfactorily	Not satisfactorily
present an idea or thought?	☐	☐	☐
discuss, explain or develop?	☐	☐	☐
express ideas, thoughts or facts as clearly as intended?	☐	☐	☐
use a suitable strategy for an introductory, main body or concluding paragraph?	☐	☐	☐
emphasise the main points?	☐	☐	☐
lead the reader easily through the ideas?	☐	☐	☐
connect the sentences well?	☐	☐	☐
relate to and achieve the writer's purpose?	☐	☐	☐

Editing according to principles of plain English

At the final stage of writing your document, have the courage to edit your work and the work of others. Do this critically, and from the receiver's point of view. This is your chance to ensure that what you set out to say is not only clear, but correct and appropriate to the receiver.

As an editor of other people's documents, your aim is to ensure:

- that they have said what they set out to say; and
- that the result is clear, correct and appropriate to the receiver.

As you edit, assess the document according to the seven characteristics of a good writing style, as shown in Table 16.6.

Busy people appreciate specific information that is well organised and expressed simply. A document written in plain English encourages them to respond quickly. Readers who struggle with a poorly constructed message, unfamiliar language or unprofessional layout are much less likely to respond.

Table 16.6 Seven characteristics of good writing style

Characteristic	Features
1. Clear	Readable, coherent and unambiguous
2. Complete	Containing all necessary detail
3. Concise	Having no more detail than is necessary
4. Considerate	Aware of the receiver
5. Courteous	Tactful and sensitive
6. Concrete	Not vague or abstract
7. Correct	In detail, grammar, punctuation and spelling

The advantages of writing in plain English

Plain English contributes to efficiency, equity and effectiveness.

Plain English makes the process of giving information and receiving feedback easier. A document written in plain English has three advantages.

1. Efficiency
2. Equity
3. Effectiveness.

These advantages of a plain English writing style make a significant impact on your organisation and on your receiver.

Efficiency

A document in plain English is easier to read and understand. As a result, more people can understand it, and there will be fewer inquiries from clients who cannot. The use of plain English also reduces the number of incorrectly completed forms or survey responses, and this increases **efficiency** and saves clerical time.

Equity

A document is a major communication channel in the workplace, especially between organisations and their clients. It is important to write in plain English so that all people are able to understand the information, how it applies to them, and whether it is necessary to take any action. **Equity** is the quality of being fair or impartial.

Access to information is a right for people living in a democratic society. A great deal of the information received in written form affects people's lives – for example, a contract for the purchase of a home or information on Social Security benefits.

Language can be used to exercise power over people. Language that is clear and easily understood can empower people, but if it is obscure it can deny them their right to know something, or take action.

It is important for people to understand the meaning of laws, rules and contracts. A lack of information or misunderstanding can put them at a disadvantage, and can cause problems and even hardship. Thus, people must be able to understand written forms and documents. Plain English gives them easy access to information.

Effectiveness

An effective document expresses its purpose clearly, is well organised and meets the needs of the receiver. It uses an appropriate tone and its message is easily understood by the receiver. In addition, an effective document is one written to match the way the receiver thinks rather than the way the writer thinks. Once you put yourself in the place of the receiver and focus on their need to know and understand the information, your documents will be more effective. The **effectiveness** of a document refers to how well it achieves its purpose.

> Express your purpose clearly.

A clear, concise and unified message, written in plain English, helps readers to understand, and thus enables them to make decisions and take actions on the basis of the information and so exercise their democratic rights as citizens.

The principles of plain English apply to any document you create. This does not mean that you must write every document in the same style. You can adapt your style to suit the context. Technology now enables us to communicate quickly with larger audiences through new media.

Correct use of language

In each of the following sentences, identify any faults and correct them.

1. I apologise for the way our product reached you and it seems the panels have broken through insufficient packaging.
2. Mrs Jones, the attractive wife of the manager, opened the new store.
3. We must repeat again and again, Mrs Jackson, how deeply apologetic we are, that our service to you has been so very poor.
4. We beg to acknowledge receipt of your gracious letter of the 16th.
5. You have not paid this month's account.
6. Our tardiness in replying has been due to the fact that we hoped to arrange for an account manager to call upon you.
7. West Carlingford is the only place where the substantial investment necessary for the new freeway network is justified from the financial viewpoint.

APPLY SKILLS

Visit the Companion Website at **www.prenhall.com/dwyer_au**. Choose the Internet exercise in Chapter 16 to analyse the writing style used in an article published on the Web.

WEB WISE

Chapter summary

Define the term 'plain English'. A plain English writing style is reader-friendly writing. It makes the information and ideas easy to understand. It suits the needs of the intended audience and will achieve results.

Plan workplace documents in plain English. Think about the content from the point of view of the receivers, their level of knowledge, familiarity with and approach to the topic.

Write workplace documents in plain English. Base the structure of your sentences and paragraphs on one main point, in language appropriate to your industry. A courteous tone and inclusive, non-sexist and non-racist language are important in written (as well as spoken) communication. Consider rhythm in your written presentation and the order in which you present information and ideas. Appearance makes an impact on the reader straightaway. Set out your information in a clear, professional format.

Edit documents according to the principles of plain English. As you check your work, try to prevent misunderstanding. Remove the communication barriers caused by ambiguity, wordiness, obscure and archaic language, and unnecessary technical jargon and officialese.

Discuss three advantages of a plain English writing style. A plain English writing style has three advantages: increased efficiency, equity and effectiveness in communicating the message.

Advocate the use of plain English in the workplace. In your own writing, set a good example to encourage others to use plain English.

REVIEW QUESTIONS

1. a. Define the terms 'plain English'.
   b. Briefly explain the phrase 'reader-friendly writing style'.
2. List three advantages of writing in plain English.
3. List the seven characteristics of good writing style.
4. Briefly explain the difference between the planning, writing and editing stages.
5. Define the term 'inclusive, non-discriminatory language'.
6. a. What is a sentence?
   b. Give one example of a simple sentence and one of a complex sentence.
7. What is wrong with the following sentence? 'Thank you for your letter regarding delivery of your order and we suspect damage was caused in transit.' Correct and rewrite the sentence.

8. a. How do sentences and paragraphs organise information and help the reader to progress through a piece of writing?
   b. List two techniques that help to organise information efficiently into a paragraph.
   c. List three techniques for emphasising a point.
9. What is an appropriate tone to use in a set of instructions to employees?
10. What is the difference between a negative and a positive tone? Give examples of two negative and two positive phrases.
11. Define the term 'layout'.

Business writing

1. Describe the tone of the following response to a customer, and rewrite the letter to give it a more appropriate tone.

   Dear Sir
   Your allegations of a delay in processing your credit claim have been considered by this section and dismissed.

   Please consider the needs of an overworked staff before you put pen to paper and write to this organisation again.

2. Nominate three ways of removing sexism from language. Should sexism be removed from writing? Justify your answer.

3. A member of your staff has produced the following letter. You are unhappy with its language and sentence structure and would like to talk to her about how she could correct these weaknesses.

   Dear Sir/Madam
   It has come to our attention that your account is currently in arrears, due perhaps to an oversight on your part or to some temporary pecuniary difficulty. It is the long-held policy of this company that clients responsible for bad debts should be denied further access to credit until such time as the overdue amount has been received. In view of this, it would appear imperative that you attend to this matter without further loss of time. Should payment not have been received at the above office, or indeed have been posted to same, within a month of the date hereon, continued credit in this store will be impossible.

   a. Identify three errors in language and one in sentence structure.
   b. Rewrite the document.

4. Define the term 'topic sentence'. The topic sentences of four different paragraphs are given below. Copy each topic sentence and construct a paragraph around it.
   a. Tennis should receive radio and television coverage.
   b. A large V8 car can be an expensive purchase.
   c. The family is looking forward to taking a holiday in New Zealand.
   d. Speaking before a business audience requires special skills.

5. Consider the first draft of the following memo.

   A computing system is a useful tool for the report writer. A powerful word processing package that is easy to use is highly recommended. The features of a word processing package are not always easy but make it easy to format, edit and rewrite the document. The main advantage for staff of these over the typewriter is the freedom to vary the information and format of the report without the need to key in the information again. Once the text is keyed in, it is there to stay until it is moved or deleted. Word processors allow the writer to move the text to different locations in the document and to change the layout. Sometimes the operators make mistakes. Layout is part of the communication and the report writing process.

   After reading this first draft, the writer decided that the wording was vague, tended to be negative, and failed to emphasise the benefits of training all staff in word processing.

   Assume you wrote the first draft. Rewrite it to remove irrelevant details, and list the main points to clarify and emphasise their importance.

6. Choose a piece of your writing of, say, half a page in length and apply the Fog Index.
   a. How did your piece of writing score, according to the Fog Index?
   b. Should all writing have a low Fog Score? Give reasons for your answer.
   c. The Fog Score is a simple formula for working out how well readers can understand your writing. Why should you be interested in this?

Key terms

active voice	equity	readability
cliché	inclusive language	rhythm
complex sentence	jargon	simple sentence
compound sentence	layout	tone
effectiveness	passive voice	topic sentence
efficiency	plain English	'you' approach

Plain English: Choosing the most effective sentence structure

STUDY
CASE
C

by Elizabeth M. Murphy

Sentence length

Sentences can be long or short. The shorter they are, the easier they are to read. In this sentence, two main ideas have been added together, forcing the reader to try to retain too much in one go:

> Courses for next semester will include one-day seminars on stress management, plain English awareness and personal development AND will be held in the small meeting room. (26 words)

It would be better to split this according to its two main ideas. Here's just one solution:

> Courses for next semester will be held in the small meeting room. They will include one-day seminars on stress management, plain English awareness and personal development. (12 + 14 words)

Likewise, sentences containing qualified main ideas, such as this overlong sentence, are hard to read:

> It would be anticipated that, WHEN the company takes over all the complex, ITSELF a significant item of local history, it would be possible to have, PERHAPS in association with a visitors' lounge, a display of significant locally produced artefacts and art of the district OR indeed combine OR co-locate the lounge and something WHICH for want of a better term might loosely be called a museum. (68 words)

Again, it would be better to separate out and rewrite the main ideas. Where feasible, write any qualifications or conditions as separate sentences too:

> The company will soon take over the complex which is of historical interest locally. We would like to have a visitors' lounge and a museum of local art and artefacts. It may be possible to combine these in one room. (14 + 16 + 10 = 40 words)

A lot of wordiness disappeared in that rewrite. A word of warning: sentences that are consistently very short become boring, lack meaning, and seem like a burst of machine gun fire! Variety in sentence length helps to keep up reader interest.

Parallel structure

This is sentence organisation that sticks to the same structure for items in any kind of list or series. In this short example,

> His experience in that dead-end job has made him BITTER, SULLEN and a CYNIC.

the words 'bitter' and 'sullen' are adjectives, while 'a cynic' is a noun phrase. To put in into parallel structure, we need to have all three in the same form, so let's make them all adjectives:

> His experience in that dead-end job has made him bitter, sullen and CYNICAL.

This is much easier to read because the reader doesn't have to think about the structure at all – only the meaning.

In a lot of business and public service writing, long sentences containing series of items under one opening statement are set out as 'dot-point' or 'bullet-point' structures. The parallel structure rule applies to these as well, and the easiest way to apply it is to make sure that each item begins with the same kind of structure. This avoids reader confusion. Here's one that could be improved:

> Recycling cans, bottles and cardboard is worthwhile because:

- DOING SO re-uses valuable resources
- PREVENTS piles of rubbish accumulating and
- IT HAS MADE Australians aware of the ecology of their environment.

Here we have three different beginnings: subject + present tense verb; present tense verb with no subject; subject and present perfect tense verb – confusing! Let's make them all the same, to achieve parallel structure:

Recycling cans, bottles and cardboard is worthwhile because doing so:

- RE-USES valuable resources
- PREVENTS piles of rubbish accumulating and
- MAKES Australians aware of the ecology of their environment.

Notice the punctuation: no line-end commas or semi-colons are necessary because there is no internal punctuation in any of the items.

Sentences in paragraphs

Paragraphs are organised clusters of sentences – a paragraph is a unit of thought, not of length. One main idea should produce one topic sentence and perhaps several supporting sentences, plus a final sentence that leads the reader to the next paragraph. It is all too easy in this computer age to let paragraphs wander on to fill up the screen. Some planning about main and supports ideas, linking devices and transitions from one paragraph to the next is worthwhile.

Source: Elizabeth M. Murphy, 'Plain English – Style of Choice', *Stylewise*, Vol. 7, No. 1, 2001, pp. 1–2. Reproduced by permission of Elizabeth Murphy, from *Stylewise*, published by the Department of Finance and Administration, and *Effective Writing: Plain English at Work*, published by Pitman, Melbourne, 1989, 1994. © Elizabeth Murphy, emmurphy@ozemail.com.au.

Questions

1. How could you solve the problem of too many qualified main ideas in a sentence?
2. Why should you vary the length of your sentences in a business document?
3. Briefly explain 'parallel structure'.
4. The article ends: 'Some planning about main and supporting ideas, linking devices and transitions from one paragraph to the next is worthwhile'. What are the benefits gained by planning and organising the paragraphs in a business document?

Communicating through technology

In this chapter you will learn how to:

- define the terms 'information technology', 'intranet' and 'Internet'

- explain an intranet's purpose

- explain two different uses of the Internet

- apply the principles necessary for planning, writing and editing online documents

- explain the advantages of email

- identify the barriers to using technology.

Evaluate your communication skills by completing the self-checks in the chapter.

In the 21st century organisations must make decisions quickly because of the pace and global nature of modern business. Once a decision is made it may have to be sent anywhere in the world quickly. Many businesses now use numerous forms of information technology to store, send, receive and present information. Information technology allows an organisation to apply its knowledge systematically to practical tasks so that relevant data is on hand for decision making.

These forms of technology include email, mobile phones, facsimile machines, personal organisers, Computer-Aided-Design (CAD), conference calls, intranet, Internet and personal computers (PCs). The choice of technology depends on the needs of the business. One piece of technology can print a document in black and white or colour, send it as a fax, scan and copy it. Various forms of technology convey information between people for various purposes. By itself technology does not cause change, but it enables the people using it to make changes. Those who do it efficiently build a more responsive and competitive organisation.

Good communicators use strategies that suit whatever form of technology they use to send spoken, written, nonverbal and graphic messages. Spoken communication, such as voice messages, voice mail and electronic conferences, can send and receive information via different technologies. Technology also enables us to store, send, receive and present written information via word-processing packages, database spreadsheets, fax and graphic applications.

Intranets

An intranet, a private version of the Internet, is used by individual enterprises to share computer resources and company information.

An **intranet** is an internal or **local area network (LAN)** which individual enterprises use to share computer resources and company information among their employees. It is a kind of **website**. The PCs in the company are networked, and files with **online information** that is shared by staff are placed on the intranet. It is an information system that processes data in a form that is appropriate to that organisation's needs.

Types of information

The main purpose of an intranet is to share company information.

The information in a company's intranet is available to all staff. However, confidential information can be protected by a password so that only a select group has access to it. Some examples of materials published on a company intranet site are:

- internal telephone directory
- latest procedures
- product information
- employee-suggestion form
- customer database
- sales and inventory base
- order form for supplies
- marketing materials
- schedules and calendars
- reference manuals.

An intranet allows staff to share information on word-processing files, database spreadsheets, graphic and other software applications. The people who manage the information system must fully understand the organisation and its business if the system is to work well. They also need policy, organisational and communication skills, and the ability to manage people. At least one member of the senior management team must understand the system's strategic planning requirements and long-term implications. They must also know how to integrate it so that the organisation can benefit fully from the system.

Network components

An organisation's efficiency is increased when an intranet is used to full advantage. The automation of routine administrative tasks saves time. For example, processing and filing student enrolment forms on an intranet is much faster than the old manual systems. An intranet can schedule an appointment, record an event, set up a meeting and print a calendar. Staff can view all this on PC screens.

The components of a network are:

- user workstations
- file servers and print servers
- network hardware
- network operating system
- peripherals – printers, storage devices, plotters, scanners, modems.

A network is supported by an operating system that controls the queues of users waiting for printers and other services. It also requires physical hardware to:

- pass information from one place in the network to another – *hubs*
- connect PCs to the network – *interface cards*
- provide alternative paths through a network – *switches*
- select the optimum path for moving information – *routers*
- allow exchange of information between different networks – *gateways*.

An intranet improves an organisation's efficiency as well as saving time. For example, an educational organisation processing student enrolment forms on an intranet can analyse the information on the forms to help it make better decisions about students' present and future needs, courses, attendance patterns and so on. The organisation can then plan to improve its courses and perhaps extend their range. The organisation is able to do its core business – education and training – better.

A company that wants to share information on the intranet between offices in different cities can use a modem to connect the sites. Most larger enterprises also have connections to the Internet. They screen incoming and outgoing messages to maintain security by using 'firewalls'.

Many companies now use a combination of texts, graphics, sound and images for various purposes, including presentation materials, catalogues and computer-based education.

Suppliers, customers, advertisers and others with common interests can form networks to share information such as training programs and product catalogues. Such networking is a form of 'groupware' – its services let people who are far apart, geographically, share calendars, email handling, collective writing and electronic meetings. Microsoft Exchange is an example of groupware.

Intranets

SKILLS
APPLY

Work in small groups.

1. Brainstorm to find as many meanings as possible for the term 'information technology'. Record your ideas on a flipchart.

2. a. List two activities that require a fast-food outlet (e.g. McDonald's) to use technology.

   b. Boutique fashion outlets need to contact customers and suppliers. What sort of information technology are they likely to require to support their daily business operations?

3. 'Your goal in using information technology for your business is to provide the right information to the right people at the right time and at the right cost.' Discuss this statement.

4. The online help system in your suite of software applications is designed to replace a hard copy manual and to make it more convenient for you to use the PC. An online help system enables you to search for something by using a combination of words, whereas hard copy has only an index and table of contents.

   a. Use the Help command to find out how to get online help with formatting a document and with using the spell check and grammar check.

   b. A dialogue box opens on the screen when the software application needs you to supply certain pieces of information before it can carry out a particular command. For example, Microsoft Word's Open dialogue box asks you for the name and location of a document to open.

   c. List some of the difficulties of using software applications. How can dialogue boxes help to overcome these difficulties?

5. Why do people have to be considered at every step of planning, building and managing information systems?

The Internet

The **World Wide Web (WWW)** consists of those who use Hypertext Transport Protocol (HTTP). The Web is a collection of pages that is uploaded by individuals, companies or organisations onto an Internet service provider's computer. The associations that link together the information units (**web pages**) for a WWW user are called *hypertext*. The **Internet** is a worldwide system of computer networks.

Throughout the 1970s and 1980s organisations used written and graphic communication on the WWW. Now they are using sound and spoken communication more extensively to publish and share information on the Web. Multimedia means several types of media, or channels, such as sound, images, graphs and text, and its use is becoming more common.

Multimedia uses a variety of channels.

Communication purposes

Organisations send and receive messages on the Web for many purposes. Some of these are shown in Table 17.1.

Anyone with a computer that can connect with the public telecommunications network and has installed the two-layer software program Transmission Control Protocol and Internet Protocol (TCP/IP) can gain access to the different routes by which information travels on the Internet. **Protocols** are the special set of rules that begin and end a message sent via a telecommunication connection. As the technology improves, both small and large organisations can connect more easily to the WWW's wide area network (WAN). Communication in the form of data, text, images or sound conveyed by electromagnetic energy is defined as **electronic communication**.

The Internet is a cooperative public tele-communications network accessible to tens of millions of people worldwide.

Table 17.1 Purposes of WWW messages

1. To promote greater awareness of themselves and their products
2. To provide customer support
3. To sell products or services
4. To sell website advertising space to other companies
5. To offer electronic information services
6. To find information
7. To distribute information

The Internet has various uses. Three of these are to:

1. communicate by email
2. trade electronically
3. use search engines to browse the World Wide Web.

Users need to develop skills for each of these activities. The next section discusses the first two. Search engines are described in Chapter 14, Analyse and Present Research Information.

Benefits of an internal information system

Does the intranet	Very well	Satisfactorily	Not satisfactorily
let the organisation respond quickly to customer inquiries?	☐	☐	☐
process orders quickly?	☐	☐	☐
issue invoices and statements on time?	☐	☐	☐
eliminate the need to rekey data?	☐	☐	☐
provide accurate data?	☐	☐	☐
provide timely reports?	☐	☐	☐
improve decision making?	☐	☐	☐

SELF CHECK 17.1

Electronic mail (email)

Electronic mail is sent via intranets (LANs) and via the World Wide Web (WAN). An electronic mail system lets the sender and receiver create, send, receive, file, copy, print and delete electronic messages. Email is the most widely used Internet service.

Email is the electronic transmission of messages from computer to computer through devices such as modems, telephone lines and mail servers.

Netiquette

Netiquette maintains and promotes goodwill between writer and receiver. A professional email message should be courteous and confident. Writers using netiquette not only consider their own needs and writing purpose but also the receiver's need to understand and take action.

'Netiquette' describes the conventions that an online message sender observes.

Net address

Each part of a net address has a specific purpose appropriate to the writer and the reader. The minimum acceptable format is the least a writer can use to make their email message readable. However, the extra or additional parts can be used for specific purposes.

The net postal systems work much the way letter postal services do. For example, the header on the piece of email is the equivalent of a postmark on a letter. The date and time of sending and receiving the message (and the difference from Greenwich Mean Time) are shown on the header.

Net addresses must be accurate. One incorrect digit will send the email to the wrong location. Although net addresses can be put in upper or lower case, the general rule is to use lower case.

A net address contains the user's ID at a site or domain. The domain identifies the organisation running the site and the kind of site. The organisation suffix at the end of the email address identifies the type of organisation. Examples are shown in Table 17.2.

To offer the receiver several ways to make contact is helpful. Telephone and fax numbers can be placed under the complimentary close and signature block. Add the web page address so that the receiver can quickly use their browser to find the web page.

Table 17.2 Suffixes on net addresses

Suffix	Meaning
Com	Commercial business
Org	Non-profit organisation
Gov	Government organisation
Net	Company or organisation that runs large networks
Mil	Military organisation
Edu	Educational institution

Layout

The layout of an email message is the frame for your message. The acceptable minimum number of parts for an email message is as follows:

- receiver's name
- sender's name
- subject
- date
- body
- email address
- at least one other way, apart from the email address, of contacting the sender.

Give the message a structure

When responding to an email message, you can create a structure for your own message by asking the following questions:

- What is the writer's relationship with me?
- Why are they writing to me?
- What do they want?
- How can I help?

Because dense documents are difficult to understand, use a new paragraph for each new point. This will highlight it and leave some welcome white space between points. Check that the tone of your message is courteous and confident, and spell check.

Email conventions and standards are still evolving because online communication is relatively new. Common usage and acceptance of a certain practice eventually establish it as an online communication convention. Email is a fast means of communication and will have greater use in the future. It is important to choose a suitable format and to think through and present ideas clearly and professionally.

Write clear and professional emails.

Advantages and disadvantages

The advantages and disadvantages of email are outlined in Table 17.3. The rapid changes in technology and its increasing accessibility mean that more and more messages will be sent online.

Electronic trading

The Internet offers online shopping services on the WWW. This enables organisations to target markets and sell their products. These services are supported by marketing and advertising strategies. Companies set up electronic kiosks to let their customers gain information and perform transactions on the WWW. **Electronic trading** allows people to order and pay directly online.

The Smart Card (also known as digital cash) is moving us closer to the 'cashless economy'. This small piece of plastic looks like a normal credit card, but contains a tiny computer chip. This enables customers to interact electronically with businesses and financial institutions. The Smart Card gives its owner access to funds and payment facilities on the Web.

Electronic trading, e-business and e-commerce are terms used to describe transactions conducted online.

Table 17.3 Advantages and disadvantages of email

Advantages	Disadvantages
■ Email is a faster and more efficient channel than regular mail (sometimes referred to as snailmail). Most messages reach anywhere in the world within minutes of being sent.	■ It can be difficult to distinguish between casual and formal messages because of their similar layout.
■ It can be sent at any convenient time and avoids telephone tag.	■ There may be a time lag if the receiver does not read their email for a few days.
■ It can be sent to many receivers at the same time.	■ The system is inaccessible to those who are computer illiterate or not online.
■ Email can be stored and sent at off-peak telephone rates.	■ Its content may reappear later in a variety of printed forms.
■ It saves paper.	■ It lacks nonverbal communication cues to add meaning.
■ A message can be written and edited quickly by several people before it is sent.	■ It can be overused.
■ Email can combine text, pictures and diagrams.	■ It can be used to send messages unrelated to company business.
■ Documents or files can be attached to the email.	■ It can have an abrupt and rude tone if the writer does not take the time to read and edit.
■ Copies of emails can be forwarded.	

As soon as privacy and security issues are resolved, the Smart Card is likely to gain wider acceptance. Some of the current concerns about online payments are whether or not third parties can:

- gain information about transactions
- invade the privacy of the Smart Card user
- break password and PIN codes.

Online shopping services must identify and attract customers. They advertise and communicate with customers to promote an awareness of their services and products.

Online persuasion

Electronic advertisements, like all other kinds, use persuasive techniques to influence our behaviour and attitudes towards their products. They use emotional appeals, objective appeals and appeals to authority. The main characteristics of each appear in Table 17.4.

Table 17.4 Online persuasion

Emotional appeal	▓ Indirect rewards often outweigh the direct rewards
	▓ Generalisations are used
	▓ Comparisons are made between unlike events
	▓ Appeal to feelings is emphasised
	▓ Appeal is made to the subconscious mind
Objective appeal	▓ Direct rewards outweigh indirect rewards
	▓ Advantages and disadvantages are presented
	▓ Comparisons are made between two similar events
	▓ Statistics and facts are presented
	▓ Logic is used and appealed to
	▓ Appeal is made to the conscious mind
Appeal to authority	▓ Suggests security and safety
	▓ Invites trust in the authority figure
	▓ Offers prestige
	▓ Invites the customer to enjoy the product too
	▓ Implies that the buyer will become the person they would like to be

AIDA formula

Motivation to act comes from within the person.

Online businesses use chat rooms, newsletters and information sheets to persuade customers to buy. The goal of those writing the newsletters and information sheets is to motivate or persuade the reader to buy the product. Motivation prompts action or behaviour that is directed to a goal – buying the product or taking the action (such as paying a bill) using online services. A motivated person wants to satisfy the need the persuasive writer has created.

The AIDA formula identifies four steps in persuasive writing.

The aim of the AIDA formula is to attract the reader's attention, create interest, arouse desire and provoke willingness to take action (Figure 17.1). It is a four-step process that is suited to persuasive writing.

Figure 17.1 The AIDA formula

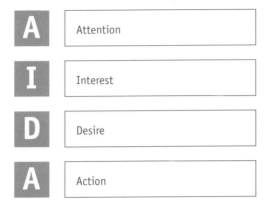

It is not enough to attract the reader's attention, interest and desire. They must also be willing to take action to fulfil their desire for the product or service. Throughout the online newsletter or information sheet, be enthusiastic and interested in the reader. Put the reader in the picture. Use the 'you' approach in writing. Visit the home page of one of the online shopping sites such as www.davidjones.com.au to find examples of the 'you' approach and how to use it in online persuasive writing.

Writing principles still apply

Online documents should be readable. If they are not the reader may lose interest and your message will be unsuccessful. An effective online writing style uses the key elements shown in Table 17.6 on page 325. Improve readability by using correct font sizes and reducing document clutter. Some simple design guidelines that improve readability are shown here.

Online writing should be efficient, effective and equitable.

- Aim for simplicity – keep your layout and structure simple and concise.
- Use appropriate typography – ensure that your font is of appropriate size, style, type and colour.
- Enhance text flow – ensure that line spacing, paragraph alignment and shading is appropriate.
- Plan the page layout – ensure that page borders, shading, margins, indents and tabs are appropriate for the task.
- Position text and objects – ensure that the relative position of text, graphics, tables, textboxes, charts and other objects is not confusing for the reader.
- Avoid clutter – edit to remove extra text, graphics, textboxes and other objects throughout your document.

Prior to designing a business text document, you must establish your organisation's requirements or standards. Check primary sources of information such as the policies and procedures for text document design. Organisational requirements or standards may include:

- company logos
- corporate images
- templates
- content restrictions

- letterheads
- header and footer information.

Consistent structure and layout

Business text documents of the same type should be consistent in both structure and layout. This is especially significant when sending documents to external customers or clients. Consistency of structure and layout mimimises confusion and improves your efficiency and the reader's understanding. Document layout includes the positioning of text, paragraphs and graphics on a page. It also involves the page layout as a whole: margins, borders, shading, tabs, indents and other features.

Pre-designed templates with layout features appropriate for the particular task save time and reduce the likelihood of errors. The template maintains consistency because the same document design and layout is used over and over again. When you use templates, be careful not to modify the template in any way. Simply open the appropriate template and enter the required information.

Apply styles

Styles can be defined as collections of paragraph- and character-formatting attributes that you can apply and create to enhance the structure of your document. As the producer of a document, it is essential that you follow any organisational guidelines with regard to style standards. Styles ensure that everyone within the organisation is using the same set of standards.

Other advantages of styles include:

- creation of a consistent organisation-wide standard
- improved document structure and layout
- capacity to create a table of contents easily
- improved document navigation, especially for long documents, using a tool called the Document Map.

Three general tips for using styles in your word processing package include:

1. Become familiar with the styles already provided by templates before deciding to create your own. This will obviously save you time.
2. Establish organisation-wide style sheets and style-naming conventions. This makes it easier for groups to work together on projects.
3. Establish one or two base styles for complex styles.

Styles can be used to divide your document into sections, thereby maintaining a level of consistency. An example of the various heading styles and the normal paragraph style is shown in Table 17.5.

Table 17.5 Heading and normal paragraph styles

Heading 1 style

Heading 2 style

Heading 3 style

Heading 4 style

Normal paragraph style

Table 17.6 Elements of a good online writing style

Key element	Purpose	Strategies
Clarity	To communicate clearly	Create single-subject messages whenever possible Open the email message with a sentence that either: ■ connects it to previous correspondence, or ■ identifies its purpose, or ■ reflects an awareness of the reader's needs. Focus on the subject and purpose. Show the reader how the content affects them. Present new ideas clearly. Arrange ideas in a logical sequence.
Readability	To make information accessible	Use 15–20 words per sentence. Limit each sentence to one idea. Use complex sentences of 25–35 words sparingly as they require a high level of reading skill. Vary the length of sentences to add rhythm and interest to your writing. Use the active voice. Avoid slang. Remove ambiguous and unnecessary words. Avoid technical terms unfamiliar to the reader.
Positive language	To create a positive first impression	Use direct and courteous language. Choose positive rather than negative words.
Punctuation	To keep the meaning clear	Start a sentence with a capital and end with a full stop. Check that the sentence is not too long. Separate ideas by using paragraphs. In general, use more full stops than commas.
Paragraphs	To organise information around one idea	Use an average paragraph length of three or four sentences. Avoid breaking up a point that should be presented as a complete unit in one paragraph. Create short paragraphs that are easy to read. Occasionally, let a sentence stand alone, for extra emphasis.
Tone	To establish the communication climate	Avoid emotional responses (called 'flaming'). Use a courteous and tactful tone. Use an appropriate level of formality.

The majority of today's advanced word processing software packages include inbuilt default styles that allow you to display various types of headings as well as normal paragraph text. They also provide you with the opportunity to create your own styles depending on your organisation's requirements.

Format text and paragraphs

Formatting of a business text document involves both character formatting and paragraph formatting. Character formatting refers to the specific characteristics of the letters you type into a document, such as changing text to bold or underlined. On the other hand, paragraph formatting refers to the characteristics of an entire paragraph, such as the alignment or indentation.

The purpose of formatting text and paragraphs is to increase the readability of the document. Often text needs to be formatted to add emphasis to a particular word. This is also true for the formatting of paragraphs. The first step to format text or paragraphs is to make sure the particular text or paragraph is selected. This allows your word processing program to know which area of your document it needs to format.

The following four steps are used in Microsoft Word to format text within a document:

1. Select the text that you wish to format.
2. Click on the Format menu.
3. Select Font.
4. Select your font characteristics and click OK.

The options available in formatting text include the following:

1. font type
2. font style
3. font size
4. font colour
5. underline style
6. text effects
7. character spacing.

There are numerous options available as you use software packages to write a text document. Bulleted or numbered lists, tables, borders and shading, page layout, headers and footers, clip art and pictures and other features can be used to create a clear pathway though your document. By using them well you are able to identify your writing purpose clearly, help the reader understand the message and meet your own need to convey information and the intended message clearly.

Regardless of whether you are preparing a short formal report, email or any other document online, the content should be as objective as possible. Assume a piece of written communication is permanent. It may be archived for years on disk to reappear later in either formal or informal print media in a situation unrelated to its original purpose. Some receivers for example may print all the email messages they receive and file and index them for ease of retrieval and reference later. Always read the document and edit carefully.

SELF CHECK 17.2

Editing an online document

Have I considered the receiver's	Yes	No	Unsure
■ viewpoint?	☐	☐	☐
■ experience?	☐	☐	☐
■ knowledge?	☐	☐	☐
■ need?	☐	☐	☐

■ position in the company? ☐ ☐ ☐
■ cultural differences? ☐ ☐ ☐
■ access to technology? ☐ ☐ ☐

Have I presented

■ a clear purpose statement? ☐ ☐ ☐
■ a logical order of information? ☐ ☐ ☐
■ an appropriate, concise and complete message? ☐ ☐ ☐
■ a clear, readable writing style? ☐ ☐ ☐
■ positive language? ☐ ☐ ☐
■ paragraphs focused on one idea? ☐ ☐ ☐
■ a courteous and confident tone? ☐ ☐ ☐
■ carefully edited work, using spell check and grammar check? ☐ ☐ ☐

Have I met

■ the reader's need to understand the information? ☐ ☐ ☐
■ the document's purpose? ☐ ☐ ☐
■ the writer's need to convey particular information? ☐ ☐ ☐

Barriers to using technology

Information technology enables an organisation to store, transmit and present information much more efficiently and quickly than was possible previously. However, barriers exist that can affect the efficient use of this technology.

Staff may feel reluctant to use the available technology because of fear of making mistakes, particularly if they lack training in information technology or typing skills. Many older staff members may feel at a disadvantage. They often do not want to admit their lack of expertise and refuse to ask for assistance, particularly from junior staff members.

Computer terminology can be confusing to inexperienced users. They may be unable to distinguish between an intranet and the Internet, the World Wide Web (WWW) and the Hypertext Transport Protocol (HTTP), the modem and a hub. Computer jargon causes problems.

Frustration can occur when a web address cannot be accessed or when an email address is incorrect and the email does not reach the receiver. Similarly, using a search engine on the Internet can result in hundreds and thousands of websites if the key words are not specific.

Being unable to access the Internet because of power failure, malfunction or network disruptions can cause frustration and incur additional expense. This is often outside the control of the organisation – for example, it may be the fault of the Internet service provider.

Time is wasted when information is lost because of a failure to save or back up when using computer applications.

Although many households now have access to the Internet and email, organisations cannot be certain that their email messages are received. Many households only access their email infrequently because of lack of competence or competing interests. Many are reluctant to transmit credit card details on the Internet, fearing a lack of security.

Mobile phones can cause frustration. Similar to a computer, they require the user to

Avoid barriers to communication.

have some knowledge of cursors and an ability to retrieve stored information. For some business organisations, the mobile phone is their main source of communication and essential to ensure their economic viability. Being out of range or forgetting to recharge a mobile phone can be not only frustrating but also costly. It is not unusual for customers' mobile phones to be switched off for long periods of time.

Electronic communication

APPLY SKILLS

1. 'It has been suggested that email is reviving the art of writing.' Discuss some of the strategies that email writers can use to make their messages more readable.

2. Explain what skills people need to research, send and receive business information through online sources.

3. Prepare an email message to a colleague that outlines the steps required for conducting a search online. Use the following headings in the body of the message:
   ■ Pick the search engine
   ■ Learn how to use the search boxes on the site
   ■ Choose the key words carefully
   ■ Widen and narrow the search
   ■ Use more than one search engine.

4. Edit your email message by using Self-check 17.2.

5. Locate a single page of a website. Apply the criteria in Self-check 17.2 to assess and edit the page. Suggest how the page could have been designed better and how you would improve the written message.

6. Work in small groups to discuss this statement.

   To those online, email offers a general and often substantial improvement in productivity and access to information.

   When the discussion is over, work individually to prepare an email message that outlines the advantages that email offers.

7. What are the advantages and disadvantages of email? How can you avoid the disadvantages?

8. Work in small groups to discuss the following and to prepare an email message presenting your conclusions.
   ■ The importance of electronic communication channels

   ■ The impact that these channels have on commerce
   ■ How electronic communication channels have changed the way people communicate.

9. Work in small groups to discuss this statement.

   Barriers occur with accessing the Internet when, for example, the Internet service provider merges with another organisation. It can cause major inconvenience and become quite expensive when there is very little information from the provider as to what is happening.

10. In small groups, brainstorm how to overcome the barriers to using information technology.

11. Compared with younger persons, becoming a skilled Web surfer is more difficult for older Australians because of lack of familiarity with the technology. Those who missed this basic skills training at school and at work often feel alienated by the technology and the speed with which it changes. The Government plans to spend $24 million over the next four years to fund IT training for Australians aged 45 and over.

    To be a fully functioning member of society, everyone should be able to turn on and use a computer. Many people over the age of 45 in Australia feel too ashamed to speak about their lack of computer or Internet literacy. (Maria Nguyen, 'The Graduates', ICON, *Sydney Morning Herald*, 26–27 January 2002, Review, pp. 4–5).

    a. Why is surfing the Net more difficult for older Australians?
    b. Why do you think older Australians are ashamed to speak about their lack of computer or Internet literacy?
    c. How is the Government planning to overcome this situation?

Visit the Companion Website at **www.prenhall.com/dwyer_au**. Choose the Internet exercise in Chapter 17 to prepare a short instruction email to assist staff in checking their email, filing and managing the volume of email.

WEB WISE

Chapter summary

Define the terms 'information technology', 'intranet' and 'Internet'. Information technology allows us to apply knowledge systematically to practical tasks such as storing, sending, receiving and presenting information. An intranet makes information available when and where it is needed. The Internet makes information available anywhere in the world, 24 hours a day. Users can send or find information at any convenient time instead of only when workplaces or libraries are open. They can use search engines to browse the World Wide Web at any hour of the day or night.

Explain an intranet's purpose. An intranet is an internal network that allows an individual company to share computer resources and company information. It does not change the basic nature of tasks, but it does change how we perform them. Technology makes our communication more productive.

Explain two different uses of the Internet. The two Internet uses discussed in this chapter are communicating by email and electronic trading. An email identifies the receiver, sender, subject and date. In the body of the email use a courteous and confident tone. Structure the context and edit before you send the message. Online trading sites require clear and persuasive messages. Newsletter and information sheets often use the AIDA formula. The Internet's standards, services and conventions are constantly changing in response to users' demands and developing technologies.

Apply the principles necessary for planning, writing and editing online documents. Business writing is successful when it follows the four steps of the systematic approach – step 1: research and investigate; step 2: plan and structure; step 3: write; and step 4: edit.

Explain the advantages of email. Email is faster and more efficient than regular mail. It can reach a person anywhere in the world within a matter of minutes. Email also avoids the frustration caused by attempts to telephone someone who is not available.

Identify the barriers to using technology. Some people are reluctant to use information technology because of lack of skills or confidence, or through frustration.

REVIEW QUESTIONS

1. What is the Internet?
2. Outline three advantages of using the Internet.
3. Why is the Internet constantly changing?
4. What is the acceptable minimum number of parts for an email message? List them.
5. What are the elements of a good email writing style?
6. a. What is the four-step AIDA formula?

b. How can you use the AIDA formula for online writing?
7. Outline some of the current and potential uses of email.
8. What are the advantages and disadvantages of email?
9. What are the errors to avoid when sending a message online?
10. List four barriers to using technology.

Online writing

SKILLS
BUILD

1. Choose a half-page advertisement for a motor vehicle from a newspaper.
   a. List six words used in the advertisement that catch the reader's attention.
   b. What other details are likely to catch the reader's interest?
   c. What sort of people would desire the motor vehicle in the advertisement?
   d. Which statement in the advertisement encourages the reader to take action?
   e. Use the AIDA formula to prepare an Internet advertisement for the motor vehicle, and include its main features.

2. a. Analyse a website that describes goods and services. Present your conclusions about it in a 10–15 minute talk. Evaluate the site by the following criteria:

   ■ purpose
   ■ audience
   ■ structure
   ■ graphic design (colour, balance, consistency, continuity, layout, texts and fonts)
   ■ communication efficiency (suitability for international audience, language)
   ■ ease of access, registration and fee requirements (if any).

   b. In your presentation you will be expected to:
   ■ analyse
   ■ provide specific evidence from the site to support your observations
   ■ organise your presentation well
   ■ use visuals to demonstrate and reinforce your conclusion.

Key terms

electronic communication
electronic mail
electronic trading
Internet

intranet
local area network (LAN)
netiquette
online information

protocol
web page
website
World Wide Web (WWW)

STUDY
CASE

A small fish plans a big splash on the Web

by Patrice Gibbons

Michael Heine is pinning his hopes on the World Wide Web to relaunch his career in funds management. Heine left the funds management industry two years ago, selling Heine Management, the firm he created in 1982. He returned in August last year, starting the online investment site netwealth. His new business faces stiff competition in the crowded financial services market.

Heine has spent $10 million developing netwealth over the past two years. The website offers share trading, managed funds, wrap services and personalised portfolios that allow users to monitor their investments. Users can see their transaction records, the value of their investments, profit-and-loss statements, and data on the performance of stocks and funds. 'It is the merging of finan-

cial services and technology,' Heine says. 'The Internet provides access to a traditional service – the two go hand in hand.' Netwealth offers 400 free entry funds from managers, including AMP and BT Financial Group. It also offers 10 netwealth-branded funds in sectors such as property and Australian shares.

Heine is competing in an industry that will undergo consolidation over the next few years. A report released by the United States research and consulting firm Cerulli Associates in March 2001 stated that Australia's managed-funds industry will be dominated by a handful of companies by 2004. Consolidation, it said, will stem from low margins and no differentiation between the companies selling managed funds.

An associate director of the investment research firm van Eyk Research, Rashmi

Mehrotra, says, the industry is overserviced. In any round of consolidation, small operators such as netwealth would be likely targets for a takeover. Netwealth has about 600 customers, but no other details of its performance are available.

Heine already knows the dangers of being small in a big market: that was the reason he sold Heine Management in October 1999. Heine owned 43% of the company and advised shareholders to accept a $111.6 million takeover offer from Mercantile Mutual (now Axa). Heine Management had $2.7 billion of assets under management at the time. 'We were approached and I went through a huge amount of agonising, for a number of reasons,' he says.

He says that one of his talents is knowing when to leave a business and relaunch his career. His father Walter started a commodities trading company in 1945 after emigrating to Australia from Germany. Heine Brothers focused on international trade in products such as steel, wheat, wool and coal. Heine says: 'A trader played a very big role in facilitating international trade because communication and financial markets were unsophisticated at the time.' He and his brother worked in the company.

As the commodity trading business started to change, because of new communications technology and the opening up of financial markets around the world, the Heine brothers shifted into funds management. 'The commodities trading business had lost its value,' Heine says.

Heine has big plans for netwealth. Superannuation funds will be added to the netwealth site in the next few months. A financial planning service is due to be set up in January, operating as a portal for financial planners to work with their clients. Heine says more than 200 financial planners

will use the service, but he will not release their names.

'The financial planners will do all of the traditional research on the needs of the investors, and a financial plan,' he says. 'But then the financial planners will go online and do a buy or sell, or any other application.' The recommendations will be emailed to clients and will require approval before any transaction can go ahead.

Large companies such as RetireInvest, Westpac and AMP are starting to provide their clients with financial planning services similar to those offered by netwealth. The head of financial planning and advice at Westpac, Brett Himbury, says big financial planners will continue to develop services themselves, rather than outsourcing the development of an online portal to small companies such as netwealth. However, he says: 'There will always be smaller, niche players who will outsource this service.'

<www.netwealth.com.au>

Source: Patrice Gibbons, 'A small fish plans a big splash on the Web,' *BRW*, 10–16 January 2002, p. 39.

Questions

1. Explain how the use of the Internet can impact on business.
2. The article suggests '. . . financial planners will go online and do a buy or sell, or any other application . . . The recommendations will be emailed to clients . . .'. Detail the writing skills that businesses such as netwealth need to communicate effectively with their clients.
3. Should all businesses use technology as a channel of communication? Give reasons for your answer.

Producing workplace documents

Part V

Writing business letters

In this chapter you will learn how to:

- use conventional layout

- follow format conventions

- identify reader and purpose

- include information appropriate to your purpose

- use words, sentence forms, structure and style appropriate to your reader and purpose

- take the demands of context into account

- follow a writing plan that is suited to good news, bad news or persuasive letters

- reply to a letter of complaint.

Evaluate your communication skills by completing the self-check in the chapter.

A successful business letter is one that elicits the expected response. You can achieve this by expressing your ideas in a way that makes your purpose clear to the reader, and by writing in a suitable style. A business letter that is clear, direct, courteous and set out in the correct format will create a good first impression and help to persuade the reader to accept your ideas.

At work we write letters for many different reasons: to initiate a business contact, to reply to someone, to give directions, to make requests. Some are written to persuade a potential customer to buy something, or to encourage a customer to pay an overdue account.

The four main types of business letters are good news letters, bad news letters, neutral letters and persuasive letters. Each has a different purpose. Each requires a structure suitable for that purpose.

Layout of a business letter

A business letter layout has seven essential parts, each with a specific purpose.

The **layout** of the letter provides the frame for the body of your letter. It consists of seven essential parts and sometimes includes other parts. The seven essential parts are listed in Table 18.1, together with some of the optional parts.

Table 18.1 Essential and optional parts of a layout

Essential parts	Optional parts
1. Writer's name and address	Subject line
2. Date	Attention line
3. Inside (intended reader's) address	Reference initials
4. Greeting	Enclosure
5. Body of the letter	File number
6. Complimentary close	Sender's telephone extension
7. Writer's signature and job title or designation	Sender's email or website details

Function of the parts

Each part of a business letter serves a particular purpose. The parts and their purpose are described here by referring to the business letter from Mountain Retreat (Figure 18.1). The purpose of this letter is to acknowledge cancellation of a holiday booking. It is a good news letter and, therefore, follows the good news order of information described later in this chapter.

Letterhead

The **letterhead** identifies the writer, their address and telephone number. Most business organisations use company stationery with a letterhead that includes the company's name, postal and email addresses, and telephone, telex and facsimile numbers. Some companies also include a reference (Our Ref. or Your Ref.) and telephone extension.

Date

The date is placed between the letterhead and the inside address – for example, 4 August 2003. Numerals such as 4/8/03 can be misleading; this format could refer to the eighth or the fourth month. Spell out the month in words.

Figure 18.1 Letter of acknowledgment in full block layout – a good news letter

MOUNTAIN RETREAT

Bluegum Creek
PMB 3
SOMEWHERE NSW 2628
Telephone (02) 7654 3210
Email: mountainretreat@blue.com.au
[enter]
[enter]
4 August 2003
[enter]
[enter]
Mr Howard Johnson
14 Robinson St
PETERSHAM NSW 2049
[enter]
[enter]
Dear Howard   *Order of information*
[enter]
Change to Holiday Booking   Subject line
[enter]
I am confirming the cancellation of your booking of Chalet 10 for the week 25 Septem-   Acknowledgment
ber to 1 October 2003.
[enter]
At your request, I have changed your booking of Chalet 10 to the period 3 September   Clear 'yes'
2004 to 9 September 2004. The remainder of your deposit for this booking has been
carried forward.
[enter]
You will note from our enclosed booking conditions that a cancellation fee of 25% has   Details
been deducted from your original deposit of $465, leaving a balance of $349 to be
carried forward to next year.
[enter]
I do not expect any increase for the 2003 winter tariffs. Therefore your balance for next   Actions to be taken
year will be $581, the payment of which would be appreciated six weeks prior to your
booking date.
[enter]
I trust that the building extensions work out well for you and look forward to seeing   Courteous close
you next year.
[enter]
[enter]
Yours sincerely
[enter]
[enter]
[enter]
Janice Hayden
Manager
[enter]
[enter]
encl Booking Conditions

Inside address

The **inside address** is the intended reader's address. It is placed between the date and the salutation, two lines below the date.

Attention line

Some organisations, such as local government councils, ask that all correspondence be directed to the General Manager. In this case, identify in an **attention line** the specific person who is to attend to your letter. Place it two lines below the inside address.

Greeting

The writer's **greeting** to the reader (sometimes called the 'salutation') is placed two lines below the inside address or the attention line.

If you know the receiver's name, use this instead of 'Dear Sir' or 'Dear Madam'. When you know the person well enough to call them by their first name, use it to make the letter more personal. Use your own first name when you sign the letter only if you are sure that it will not be confused with another's.

On many occasions you will have to use Mr, Ms, Mrs or Miss. Mr and Ms distinguish between people by their gender. Mrs and Miss distinguish a woman's marital status. If you know that a particular woman prefers Mrs or Miss, then use this form of address. Otherwise, use Ms.

Subject line

Identify your
purpose clearly
in the subject
line.

The **subject line** identifies the letter's subject or purpose. It should be no more than ten words. It is placed below the greeting.

Body

The **body** of a letter has three parts, and each part has a particular purpose (Table 18.2). A successful combination of opening and closing paragraphs in the body of the letter catches the reader's attention and helps to prompt the response you want (Figure 18.2).

Figure 18.2 Examples of openings and closings

Openings
- The brochure you requested is enclosed.
- Thank you for your request for information.
- You should receive the goods in your Purchase Order No. 6543 by 28 July.
- I am happy to accept your invitation to address the new committee.

Closings
- I think the brochure will answer your questions but, if you need more information, please let me know.
- If I can help in any way please let me know.
- I am pleased to be able to fill this order for you.
- Please forward me a copy of the agenda and the names of the committee members.

Figure 18.3 Greeting and complimentary close

Dear Sir	Dear Mr Johnson	Dear Irene	Dear Ms Jones	Dear Mrs Bean
Yours faithfully	Yours sincerely	Yours sincerely	Yours sincerely	Yours sincerely

Table 18.2 The body of a letter

Part	Purpose	Strategy
Beginning	The beginning has two purposes: to open courteously and, when appropriate, to link the letter to previous transactions. The first sentence of the letter in Figure 18.1, 'I am confirming the cancellation of . . .', clearly links the letter to previous transactions.	In the opening paragraph, aim to catch the reader's attention, and create a desire to read further. State your intentions. Explain the situation. Present the alternatives and related information. Use plain English for your opening statement and avoid clichéd beginnings such as, 'We are pleased to inform you . . .'.
Middle	The middle part of a letter contains material appropriate to its purpose. It should prompt the reader to take the intended action (response).	The middle of the letter presents details and information. In the letter in Figure 18.1, the middle consists of three paragraphs. Decide on the length of your paragraphs with the aim of creating a concise message that is easy for the reader to understand.
Ending	The ending has two purposes: to indicate future action and to close courteously.	The closing paragraph states what action the reader is to take. The final sentence concludes with the same courteous tone used throughout the letter. 'I trust that the building . . .'. This tone maintains goodwill between writer and reader.

Complimentary close

The **complimentary close** should match the form of address used in the greeting. For a business letter that opens with 'Dear Sir' or 'Dear Madam', close with 'Yours faithfully' followed by your signature, name and job title or designation. When you write to a person you have met, to a specific person in the organisation or to someone who has corresponded with you before, use their name in the opening and 'Yours sincerely' at the close.

The ending should be confident and courteous.

The traditional rule is to use 'Yours faithfully' when you do not know the receiver's name, and 'Yours sincerely' when you know their name and have used it for your opening (see Figure 18.3).

Signature block

The writer's signature and name follow the complimentary close. It may be appropriate to place the position or job title you hold under your signature and typewritten name.

Types of layout

The effect of your letter will be improved by a suitable and correct layout. The parts of a business letter can be arranged in different ways. There are three main types of layout:

1. Full block layout (see Figure 18.1)
2. Full block layout with centred letterhead (see Figure 18.4)
3. Modified block layout.

The parts of all these layouts are arranged to create a good first impression.

Figure 18.4 A 'thank you' letter in full block layout with centred letterhead

MOUNTAIN RETREAT

**Bluegum Creek PMB 3 SOMEWHERE NSW 2628
Telephone (02) 7654 3210 Email: mountainretreat@blue.com.au**

16 May 2003
[enter]
[enter]
Mr Gregory Highton
Development Manager
Kosciusko National Park
Sawpit Creek
PMB via COOMA NSW 2630
[enter]
[enter]

Order of information   Dear Gregory
[enter]
Subject line   **Recent Services Provided to Mountain Retreat**
[enter]
Good news   I would like to thank you and your staff for the provision of the following services.
[enter]
Details   1.   Repainting of the water treatment plant on our leasehold.
                         2.   Processing our Development and Building Application for the relocatable cabins.
                         3.   Attending to correspondence required by the XYZ Bank.
[enter]
                         We very much appreciated the efficiency with which each task was completed. Your
                         prompt attention to the Development and Building Application and the correspon-
                         dence required by XYZ Bank has enabled us to offer new accommodation in the cabins
                         before the mid-year school holidays.
[enter]
Goodwill close   Please convey our sincere thanks to your staff for their excellent service.
[enter]
[enter]
                         Yours sincerely
[enter]
[enter]
[enter]
                         Janice Hayden
                         Manager

Full block layout

Full block layout places each part of the letter – the sender's address, the date, the inside address and the greeting – against the left margin. Each paragraph starts against the left margin, and so do the complimentary close and the signature block. Extra parts such as enclosures, file numbers and copy notations are also set out this way. Full block is an attractive modern layout that is easy to read (see Figure 18.1).

Full block is the most popular form of layout.

Full block layout with centred letterhead

In the full block layout with centred letterhead, the organisation's name, address, telephone and email address is centred across the top of the page (see Figure 18.4). The remainder of the letter follows the full block format. This form of layout is used extensively by organisations.

Modified block layout

Modified block layout centres the sender's address, or aligns it with the right-hand margin. The date is placed straight underneath and in line with the sender's address. The inside address and the greeting are placed against the left-hand margin, and so is each paragraph. The complimentary close and signature block are centred in line with the writer's address and the date. Modified block is a more conservative style of layout and used less often than the previous two layouts.

Punctuation styles

Punctuation styles for business letters include the open style and the mixed style. Open style omits punctuation from all parts of the letter except the body. It does not use punctuation for the greeting or complimentary close. The mixed style places a comma after the greeting and after 'Yours faithfully' or 'Yours sincerely' at the close. The examples in Figures 18.1 and 18.4 use the open style and the example in Figure 18.5 uses the mixed style.

Letter writing

1. In a business letter, what is the function of the following?
   a. letterhead
   b. greeting
   c. subject line
   d. body
   e. complimentary close
   f. signature block.
2. In groups of three, discuss the following.
   a. How does full block layout differ from modified block layout?
   b. Where do you place extra parts such as enclosures, file numbers or notations in a letter that is set out in modified block layout?
   c. Why is it important to format your business letters well?
3. Some examples of poor letter writing style and clichés to avoid are listed below. Correct and rewrite the sentences.
   a. I am pleased to inform you that you are required to attend the next meeting.
   b. For all practical purposes, time could be saved if you used the new terminals.
   c. It is important here to take into account the fact that prices will increase in May.
   d. In most cases, goods are delivered within 14 days of the date on the order form.
   e. I desire to inform you that our representative is unable to call next week.
   f. You are advised for your information that we will not agree to your proposal.
   g. Due to the fact that State Rail will be repairing the lines tomorrow, train travel will be unavailable between 10–12 pm next Friday.
   h. Before examining the reasons for this, I should state that all staff are expected to use electronic mail.
   i. In this, comparatively the most fragmented, most competitive media market in Australia (four commercial television networks, five commercial radio stations, three weekly community newspapers and one daily newspaper), the rates charged

are already the most competitive possible, consistent with the standards demanded by our advertising clients.

4. Assume that you are Clive Ferguson, writing in response to an advertisement offering digital cameras at $100 below normal retail price. You want to know the brand name, the availability of service and repairs, delivery times and method of payment. Write the letter, using full block letter layout and the seven basic parts of a letter. For the opening paragraph, prepare a clear, courteous request.

Figure 18.5 Letter of request in full block layout with mixed punctuation style

	MOUNTAIN RETREAT
	Bluegum Creek **PMB 3** **SOMEWHERE NSW 2628** **Telephone (02) 7654 3210** **Email: mountainretreat@blue.com.au** [enter] [enter] 12 February 2003 [enter] [enter] Carmel Walsh Simkins Publishing Group Pty Ltd GPO Box 706 MELBOURNE VIC 3001 [enter] [enter] Dear Carmel, [enter]
Order of information	**Order for Advertising Brochure** [enter]
Subject line	I would like to place an order for the third print run of the Mountain Retreat's advertising brochure.
Identify the request	[enter] Our advertising is booked on Order No. 2255. I have enclosed a proof for the printer to assess the colours. Please return the films and proofs after the third print run.
Background details	[enter] I would appreciate your prompt handling of this order so that we may have the brochures by 24 March.
Specific response	[enter] Please contact me if you have any questions. I am most happy with the quality of the first two print runs and look forward to the third.
Courteous close	[enter] [enter] Yours sincerely, [enter] [enter] [enter] Janice Hayden Manager

Planning the business letter

It is your responsibility as a business letter writer to know your purpose for writing, and to express this message courteously. The following seven steps will help you achieve this.

1. Decide on the purpose of the letter.
2. Decide what you want to say.
3. Note down all the ideas in point form.
4. Order these ideas into a sequence appropriate to the type of letter.
5. Write the first draft, using plain English (see below).
6. Read the letter to ensure that you have achieved your purpose.
7. Rewrite if necessary.

As your letter writing becomes more skilful, you will complete many of these steps automatically. Be careful to avoid the ten common errors listed in Table 18.3.

Table 18.3 Ten common errors to avoid

1. Obscure, unfamiliar words and highly technical jargon
2. Lengthy sentences and paragraphs
3. A discourteous or too familiar tone
4. Long sections of unbroken text
5. A structure unsuited to the letter's purpose
6. Clichéd routine openings that sound insincere
7. Negative, pessimistic expressions
8. New ideas in the closing paragraph
9. A closing that does not state what is required
10. An untidy format

Using plain English

A **plain English** writing style uses clear expressions and a courteous tone. Combine these features with a logical structure to create a letter that is easy to understand. Plain English is discussed fully in Chapter 16. Some of the key elements of a good letter writing style are shown in Table 18.4.

Clarity of expression aids the reader's understanding and makes your writing more convincing. If you present new ideas clearly the reader is more likely to accept them. Arrange ideas in a logical sequence so that the reader can follow the flow of your thoughts.

Try to avoid technical jargon unless you are certain that the reader will understand it. Also avoid ambiguous and unnecessary words. Limit each sentence to one idea.

Writing good news or neutral letters

In these types of letter, the writer and reader share favourable or neutral information. **Good news letters** and **neutral letters** are common at work. They are written to grant

Good news and neutral letters announce the news first.

Table 18.4 The key elements of a plain English writing style

Key element	Purpose	Strategies
Clarity	Clarity of expression aids the reader's understanding and makes your writing more convincing.	Present new ideas clearly, in a logical sequence. Avoid jargon and technical terms unless you are certain the reader will understand them. Avoid ambiguous and unnecessary words.
Readability	Make your information accessible to an average reader.	Use 15–20 words per sentence. Limit each sentence to one idea. Use complex sentences of 25–35 words sparingly as they are more demanding. Avoid slang.
Courtesy (see Table 18.5)	Polite language creates a good first impression.	Project your desire to communicate with the reader. Use a courteous and tactful tone.
Active voice	The active voice tells the reader who or what is responsible for an action.	Using the active voice conveys information directly and concisely. For example, 'I report to . . .', 'I act as Manager . . .'. The passive voice leaves out details. The active voice creates an energetic image.
The 'you' approach	The 'you' approach addresses readers directly and establishes rapport.	Speak directly to your readers and acknowledge their needs. Open the letter with a sentence that reflects your awareness of readers' needs. Show consideration for the readers and tell them how the content affects them.
Punctuation	Punctuation clarifies meaning.	Start with a capital letter. End a sentence with a full stop. Decide whether you need to use a comma by reading the sentence aloud and noting pauses. Check that the sentences are not too long. Apply the general rule: always use more full stops than commas.
Paragraphs	Paragraphs organise information around one idea.	Use an average paragraph length of about six lines. Avoid spreading a point or idea (a complete unit) into two or more paragraphs. Occasionally, let a sentence stand alone to add emphasis.

a loan or extend credit, make an inquiry, introduce your organisation or service to potential customers, acknowledge receipt, inform members of an organisation about its activities, extend an agreement, make a request or create goodwill.

Direct order of information

As you write a good news letter, arrange your information in the order shown in Figure 18.6. This produces a structure suitable for any good news or neutral letter.

Table 18.5 Positive and negative language

Negative	Positive
'It is not unlikely that . . .'	'This can possibly . . .'
'I see no reason why . . .'	'It seems possible . . .'
'Do not use the telephone for personal calls . . .'	'Please use the telephone for business calls only . . .'
'I am not required to do that'	'I am responsible for . . .'
'Stop doing that'	'Is there a reason for that?'

Figure 18.6 Writing plan for a good news letter

> 1. Identify the letter's purpose in the subject line or opening paragraph.
> 2. Place the good news in the opening paragraph.
> 3. State the details that support the good news in the middle paragraphs.
> 4. Close with a statement of goodwill.

The subject line helps you to focus the reader's attention on the letter's content. It should be 6–10 words in length. If you choose to omit the subject line, identify the letter's purpose and good news in the opening paragraph. This draws the reader's attention to the information or good news immediately, and prompts them to read further.

In the middle paragraphs, give details and information. A good news or neutral letter benefits the writer and reader; there are no existing or expected problems. Provide all necessary information clearly and logically. Use the closing paragraph to state any action you would like the reader to take and close on a positive note. The letter of request in Figure 18.5 is an example of a good news letter.

Four types of good news letters

The writing plan or strategy outlined in Figure 18.6 is suitable for preparing any good news or neutral business letter. The content of good news and neutral letters will, of course, vary. This section offers specific guidelines for planning the following good news letters and neutral letters:

1. an inquiry
2. a request
3. an acknowledgment
4. an introduction to someone.

An inquiry

A **letter of inquiry** asks others to supply information and/or ideas. Most inquiries are routine – for example, about a product or service. This kind of practical information will be used by someone who has to fill an order or provide a service; or they may pass it to someone else. The order for setting out information for a letter of inquiry is shown in Figure 18.7.

When you need specific information, open with a question. When you need to ask more than one question, open with a summary statement. Then, in the body, list and number the questions from most important to least important. Indicate what you would like the reader to do and close courteously.

An inquiry seeks information.

Figure 18.7 Writing plan for an inquiry

> 1. Identify the inquiry in the subject line.
> 2. Open with the inquiry and a short background if necessary.
> 3. Indicate how the receiver is to respond.
> 4. Close in a courteous and friendly manner.

A request

A request asks for specific action.

A **letter of request** is different from an inquiry in that it asks for a specific action. The writing plan for a letter of request is given in Figure 18.8.

A purchase order is an example of a specific request. A purchase order is made usually by ordering from the sales representative in person, by telephoning the company, or by filling out and sending off an order form. When you order by writing a letter, authorise the purchase in the first sentence. The reader then knows that the letter is an order, not simply a request for information. Make sure you include all the relevant details – order number, quantity, price and date of delivery – and describe the item in detail. State how you would like to have the product delivered: by rail, post or private transport carrier. In the conclusion, specify the method of payment.

Figure 18.8 Writing plan for a request

> 1. Identify the request in the subject line.
> 2. If you choose to omit the subject line, identify the request and give a brief reason or background for it in the opening paragraph.
> 3. Ask for a specific response to your request.
> 4. Close courteously to maintain goodwill.

An acknowledgment

An acknowledgment recognises the action or quality of another.

A **letter of acknowledgment** acknowledges requests for information, confirms orders, supplies information and thanks the reader. It also maintains goodwill. The plan for writing a letter of acknowledgment is shown in Figure 18.9, and an example of this kind of letter is shown in Figure 18.11.

Figure 18.9 Writing plan for an acknowledgment

> 1. Start with the acknowledgment.
> 2. Say 'yes' clearly, when relevant.
> 3. Supply any necessary information or details.
> 4. Close courteously to maintain goodwill.

It is courteous and helpful to acknowledge orders immediately. If a delay in delivery is likely, send an interim acknowledgment letter thanking the customer for the order. Explain the reasons for the delay so that the customer knows what is happening and when to expect delivery. Close the letter courteously.

Some letters of acknowledgment are written in response to a request for service or help. The same writing strategy applies.

- Begin with an acknowledgment – for example, 'Thank you for your invitation to address your students'. Say yes clearly: 'I will be delighted to do so'.
- Supply necessary information – for example, 'I have work commitments on the date you nominated, so I would prefer the later time of 8 pm'.

■ Close courteously: 'Please contact my secretary to confirm these details. I look forward to seeing you'.

Figure 18.11 gives an example of a letter acknowledging an inquiry about training facilities.

A letter of introduction

A well timed **letter of introduction** reaches the reader when they need the type of service it offers. By using correct business letter format and all the basic parts of a business letter, your letter will make a good impression.

Letters of introduction aim to establish contact, goodwill, and an opportunity for future sales. Many real estate agents and car salespeople send them. Local council candidates also send letters of introduction.

Personalise the letter with the reader's name. Write in a courteous tone, using the 'you' approach to show interest in the reader. Provide interesting details with believable information. Close by letting readers know what you can do for them. Explain how they can make contact with you. The writing plan for a letter of introduction is shown in Figure 18.10.

A letter of introduction aims to create a link between sender and receiver.

Figure 18.10 Writing plan for a letter of introduction

1. Use the subject line to catch the reader's attention.
2. Open by explaining your reason for the introduction and aim to catch the reader's attention.
3. Supply details and information in the middle paragraphs to create a desire to read further.
4. Close by saying what you can do for the reader and what you want the reader to do.

A successful introduction creates a communication link between you and the potential client. Some letters of introduction combine good news with persuasive elements. Remember that this kind of letter is unrequested, so try to make it short, complete and courteous to avoid irritating the reader.

Each of the four good news letters presented so far has its own writing plan, but for each one you use the same arrangement: the direct method of organising information. The bad news letter uses the indirect method of organising information and is discussed in the next section.

Writing good news letters

1. What is the main purpose of a letter of acknowledgment?
2. Briefly explain the writing plan for a letter of acknowledgment.
3. Assume you are Stathi Korda, a Council Development Officer. You have been asked to draft a letter of acknowledgment on behalf of the Lord Mayor's Appeal. The purpose of the letter is to thank people for their donations or help after the recent floods. Format the letter in block layout and organise it by using the method suited to a good news or neutral letter. (Invent the Council's address or find the address of your local council in your telephone directory.)
4. Write a letter of inquiry to your bank asking for information on its range of accounts and interest rates. You wish to open a new account. Assume you are interested in savings accounts, fixed term accounts, cheque accounts and online banking. You also need to know the minimum amounts that each account requires to receive the best interest rate.

APPLY SKILLS

Figure 18.11 Letter of acknowledgment – good news letter

Longworth Function Centre

15 Douglas Street
MEREWETHER NSW 2290
02-4929 8642
www.longworth.com.au
[enter]
[enter]
30 April 2003
[enter]
[enter]
Mathew Lloyd
New Training Pty Ltd
PO Box 546
BRISBANE QLD 4001
[enter]
[enter]

Order of information   Dear Mathew
[enter]

Acknowledgment   Thank you for the opportunity to submit a proposal for an all-day seminar.
[enter]

Say 'yes' clearly   Naturally we would be delighted to hold your function at the Longworth Function Centre and to help out in any way to make the seminar a great success.
[enter]

Details   Mathew, I would like to offer you the use of the Boardroom and the Saloon Room. For an all-day seminar we can offer you:
[enter]

Morning tea, coffee & biscuits	$6.00 per guest
Substantial morning tea including cakes and biscuits	$8.00 per guest
Light conference luncheon including gourmet sandwiches, fruit platters, tea, coffee and orange juice	$18.50 per guest
Afternoon tea (as above)	

[enter]
Any other beverages can be charged to you on a consumption basis. Alternatively, guests can purchase their own drinks.
[enter]
Any equipment required during the seminar, such as overhead projectors, whiteboards, videos and screens, will be available for hire on the day at a cost of $20.00 per unit. A microphone and lectern will be set up at no additional charge.
[enter]

Courteous close   I look forward to helping you organise the function. If you have any questions, please call me any time.
[enter]
[enter]
Yours sincerely
[enter]
[enter]
[enter]
Francene Lee
Functions Coordinator

Follow the writing plan for a letter of inquiry. Start with the inquiry and explain why you are making it. Close with a courteous paragraph.

5. Assume you are Mark Vestor, the secretary of a local service club. Write a letter of acknowledgment to members thanking them for their participation and support in the club's activities during the past year. You might mention club activities such as fundraising to buy extra sporting equipment for the local Police Citizens Youth Club. Club members have also organised an exchange study scheme between Australian and European 16–18-year-olds. Invent your address. Use Self-check 18.1 to edit your letter.

Edit your business letter writing style

Read your first draft and ask yourself these questions.

Have I	Yes	No	Unsure
deleted unnecessary words and phrases?	☐	☐	☐
used courteous, inclusive language?	☐	☐	☐
used the appropriate order of information?	☐	☐	☐
used correct punctuation?	☐	☐	☐
written paragraphs that:			
■ have a topic sentence	☐	☐	☐
■ develop one idea	☐	☐	☐
■ flow from one idea to the next?	☐	☐	☐
used a courteous tone?	☐	☐	☐
provided a balance of information and action?	☐	☐	☐
stated the action to be taken on the customer's behalf?	☐	☐	☐
closed on a firm positive note?	☐	☐	☐
been concise and to the point?	☐	☐	☐
checked that the information is correct?	☐	☐	☐
checked whether some of the information should be placed as an attachment instead of in the body?	☐	☐	☐

Writing a bad news letter

A **bad news letter** is a refusal. It is, therefore, likely to disappoint the reader. It is a difficult letter to write successfully because you must convey the bad news yet maintain the receiver's goodwill. This means that you must write it so that the reader has every chance of understanding and accepting your explanation.

In business, bad news letters are written for many reasons. They are written to refuse credit, refuse a request, decline to speak at a function, decline to donate time or money, notify an unsuccessful job applicant or explain why you are unable to fulfil an order.

Most people dislike writing bad news letters. They are difficult to write successfully. The message may anger, disappoint, offend or antagonise the reader. It is most important to use the correct writing strategy to keep the customer's goodwill.

A bad news letter gives the reader unwelcome news.

Indirect order of information

Someone who receives bad news may read no further than the bad news unless you guide them gradually through the letter to the bad news. Then any reasons and explanation for the refusal are seen and read before the reader reaches the bad news. The writing strategy or plan in Figure 18.12 leads the reader from a courteous opening to relevant information and explanation, then to the bad news towards the end of the letter.

Figure 18.12 Writing plan for a bad news letter

1. Open with a courteous greeting.
2. Explain the situation fully.
3. State the bad news.
4. Close with a positive paragraph.

The buffer is neutral yet relevant.

Open with a sentence that acknowledges the original request as this restates the information on which both writer and reader agree. It is a courteous, neutral opening that acts as a buffer before the refusal. If the refusal is stated before this opening, the customer may not read the rest of the letter. Examples of neutral openings are:

- 'Thank you for your order No. 18-652.'
- 'Your inquiry for vacation employment is appreciated.'

A courteous explanation is vital.

In the middle paragraphs, explain the situation clearly and courteously. Express bad news tactfully, avoiding anything that sounds sarcastic, patronising or insulting. Write the letter so that the reader fully understands the reasons for the refusal.

The conclusion is courteous and pleasant.

Never place the refusal in the last sentence of the letter. Avoid referring again to the bad news, apologising repeatedly or using clichés. Close with a sentence or paragraph that is courteous and pleasant.

Four types of bad news letters

This section offers specific guidelines for planning four types of bad news letters.

1. Order refusals
2. Saying 'no' to a request for credit
3. Refusing an adjustment
4. Declining invitations and requests for favours.

An order refusal

An order refusal declines an order.

Sometimes orders are refused because buyers have overextended their credit level, or are poor or slow payers. Alternatively, your organisation may not deal with the requested line of stock. The writing plan for an order refusal is given in Figure 18.13.

Figure 18.13 Writing strategy for refusing orders

1. Start by acknowledging the order.
2. Explain the reasons for the refusal.
3. State the refusal.
4. Close with a courteous expression of interest in continuing your relationship with the customer.

A credit refusal

Credit is sometimes refused if the applicant has spent too little time at one address or in current employment, lacks assets, or has too low a level of income. The most usual request for credit and, therefore, the one that incurs the most usual credit refusal, is for a loan or credit card. The writing plan for refusing credit uses the four steps shown in Figure 18.14.

A credit refusal rejects a request for credit.

Figure 18.14 Writing plan for credit refusal

1. Start with a neutral (buffer) opening.
2. Explain the factors considered in the decision.
3. State the refusal clearly and courteously.
4. Close by courteously inviting the receiver to contact your organisation in the future.

An adjustment refusal

A genuine adjustment request is a request to change, replace or adjust a transaction that has already taken place. Examples include requests to replace damaged goods or missing parts, replace an incomplete order, or correct an error on an account. An adjustment refusal is given when the organisation believes that the adjustment request is unjustified, or that it is not responsible for the problem, or that a problem does not exist at all.

An adjustment refusal is given with convincing reasons.

The writing plan for refusing an adjustment follows the four steps shown in Figure 18.15, and an example of this kind of letter is shown in Figure 18.16.

Figure 18.15 Writing plan for an adjustment refusal

1. Start with a buffer paragraph acknowledging the adjustment request.
2. Explain the reasons for the decision.
3. State the refusal courteously.
4. Close with a courteous attempt to maintain the customer's goodwill.

Refusing an invitation or request

Invitations and requests often come from other business people or community groups. To maintain goodwill, it is necessary to write the refusal in a manner that expresses your interest in the reader.

By giving valid reasons for a refusal, you are sometimes also able to soften the bad news. The writing plan for declining invitations and requests follows the four steps listed in Figure 18.17, and an example of a letter declining an invitation is shown in Figure 18.18.

In each of these bad news letters, the writing strategy is the indirect order of information. The most important part of the letter, to the reader, is the decision – in this case, the refusal. All the contents – the reasons as well as the decisions – should be written in an attempt to maintain the reader's goodwill.

Figure 18.16 Effective bad news letter refusing an adjustment

Bayside Realty

12 Bayview Avenue PEARLY HEADS QLD 4033
Tel: 07 6553 3333 Email: bayside@blue.com.au

[enter]
[enter]
12 July 2003
[enter]
[enter]
Mr S Lee
1 Scenic Drive
PEARLY HEADS QLD 4033

Order of information [enter]
[enter]
Subject line Dear Mr Lee
[enter]
Neutral buffer **Rental Property – 1 Scenic Drive**
[enter]
The property you are renting is located in one of the most scenic areas in Pearly Heads.
As the property has extensive views, is close to both the bay and the surfing beach,
Positive explanation many people are keen to rent in this area.
[enter]
During the initial inspection of the property and interview, the rental price and terms
and conditions of the lease were identified by our Rental Property Manager and dis-
cussed with you. When the lease was signed, both you and the owner of the property
Refusal agreed to the rental value.
[enter]
The weekly rent is $300.00 which is the current market rent for a property in this area.
We are therefore unable to meet your request to have the rent reduced by $25.00 per
Positive close week.
[enter]
A list of services we offer to people renting properties through our agency is enclosed.
Please contact me if you would like to use any of these services.
[enter]
[enter]
Yours sincerely
[enter]
[enter]
[enter]
Jennifer Dewar
Managing Director
[enter]
[enter]
encl List of Services

Figure 18.17 Writing plan for declining an invitation or request

1. Start with a neutral buffer, preferably by expressing your appreciation of the invitation or request.
2. Give a full explanation.
3. State the refusal clearly, courteously and tactfully.
4. Close by expressing interest in the other person or organisation.

Figure 18.18 Effective letter declining an invitation

GRAPHIC ART DESIGNS

17 Floraville Avenue FAIRWEATHER NSW 2256
Tel: 02 8996 6666 Email: graphicart@blue.com.au

[enter]
[enter]
18 July 2003
[enter]
[enter]
Mr J Marconi
Marketing Enterprises
30 Park Street
ULTIMO NSW 2206
[enter]
[enter]
Dear Mr Marconi   *Order of information*
[enter]
Thank you for your invitation to deliver a presentation at your seminar on Wednesday,   Neutral buffer
1 September 2003.
[enter]
Although I would be pleased to be involved in this seminar, I already have a commit-   Explanation
ment on this date.
[enter]
Regrettably, I am unable to accept your invitation.   Refusal
[enter]
I wish you every success with this seminar. I would be very pleased to present my ideas   Positive conclusion
to your group at another time.
[enter]
[enter]
Yours sincerely
[enter]
[enter]
[enter]
Jack Fenwick
Design Consultant
Graphic Art Design

Writing persuasive letters

A **persuasive letter** is written to influence the reader in some way. In business, this may mean persuading the reader to buy a product, to pay an overdue account or to consider an application for work.

Clearly, the motivation to respond comes from the reader; the suggestion that prompts their response comes from the letter writer. Some examples of persuasive letters are collection letters, sales letters and job applications.

Persuasive letters aim to change attitudes or produce action.

Writing plan

To motivate your readers to take action, aim to gain their attention, interest, desire and willingness to respond.

Persuasive letters are written when you expect resistance, want to change an attitude or persuade the reader to take some action. The writing plan for a persuasive letter is shown in Figure 19.19. Notice that it follows the **AIDA formula**: Attention, Interest, Desire and Action shown in Figure 18.20.

Figure 18.19 Writing plan for a persuasive letter (the AIDA formula)

> 1. Open with a sentence or paragraph that catches the reader's attention.
> 2. In the next paragraph, develop an idea that might interest the reader, or show how the product could benefit them.
> 3. Use the middle paragraphs to build the reader's desire for the product or service, or to encourage them to respond to your letter.
> 4. State in the concluding paragraph what action is to be taken.

Catch the reader's attention immediately, follow with the details that explain and create interest and desire, then provide any additional information in a logical way. This provides the foundation for the action you want the reader to take.

At the beginning of the letter, capture attention by focusing on the reader in a positive way. Then, in the second paragraph, make your appeal in the form of direct or indirect benefits – for example, comfort, popularity, economic benefit, distinctiveness, prestige, quality of life or convenience.

Next, state the main reason for your letter, explaining it fully. Restate the benefits that the reader will receive.

In the concluding section, identify the action you would like the reader to take. Close positively, indicating your wish for future contact. Figure 18.22 shows how the writing plan follows the AIDA formula.

Figure 18.20 Persuasive letter writing plan, following the AIDA formula

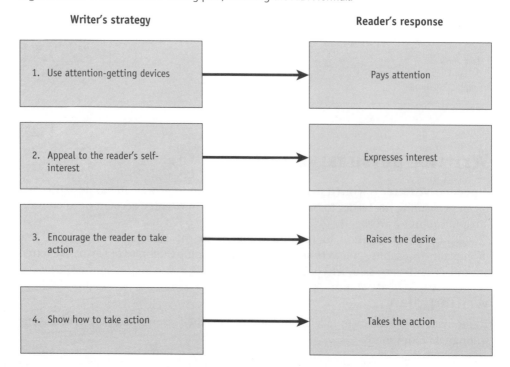

Writer's strategy	Reader's response
1. Use attention-getting devices	Pays attention
2. Appeal to the reader's self-interest	Expresses interest
3. Encourage the reader to take action	Raises the desire
4. Show how to take action	Takes the action

The next section discusses the first two types of persuasive letters: collection and sales letters. Chapter 23 discusses a third type of persuasive letter: the job application.

Collection letters

Collection letters usually appeal to fair play, cooperation, reputation, self-respect or self-interest. Each letter of this kind sets out to demonstrate that the desired action is reasonable and in the receiver's best interest.

Positive appeals focus on cooperation, fair play and self-respect, whereas negative appeals tend to focus on self-interest – for example, losing a credit rating. In all such communication, the writer's aim is to develop positive relationships with others and to maintain goodwill. The positive appeal is the one that is most likely to get the desired response and establish good relationships between the organisation and the reader.

When writing to collect money from those who are slow to pay, some organisations break the collection letter process into four stages:

1. Reminder stage
2. Strong reminder stage
3. Inquiry stage
4. Urgency stage.

Others break the collection process into three stages by writing a single (strong) reminder.

The time taken for the process to develop from a reminder to the urgency stage depends on the type of credit account, your knowledge of the debtor and the organisation's collection policy. All collection letters, at each stage, should specify the amount owing and the account number.

The writing plan for collection letters is shown in Figure 18.21.

Figure 18.21 Writing plan for a collection letter

```
1. Identify the letter's purpose in the subject line or introductory paragraph.
2. In the introductory paragraph, focus the reader's attention on the issue.
3. In the middle paragraphs, give all relevant details and state what action the reader should take.
4. Close with a neutral statement.
```

The reminder

At the first stage, the organisation gives the customer a **reminder**. It assumes that the customer has forgotten to pay, so the letter is a courteous reminder to pay. This stage usually takes place 30 days after the purchase.

The strong reminder

At this stage, the writer still assumes that the customer has forgotten to pay. This second reminder is offered only to an established customer or someone who might have a valid reason for not paying. For other customers, move straight to the inquiry stage, which usually occurs when the account is 60 days overdue.

Inquiry

By this stage, the situation is serious. The writer suspects that something is wrong. The persuasive letter becomes a direct request to the customer to explain their problem to the organisation, or to take immediate action to correct it. The letter also appeals to the

Collection letters use persuasion.

customer's self-interest, reputation or sense of fair play. By this stage, the account is usually 90 days overdue.

The reason for this inquiry is to ask the reader to explain why the overdue account has not been paid and to pay it if possible. If you can persuade the customer to respond with a reason for their non-payment, there is a reasonable chance of working out a payment plan.

Urgency

By this stage, the account is at least 120 days overdue. The need to collect the money is urgent and you assume there is a reason for not paying. At this stage, the writer clearly states what action the customer should take. The tone of the letter suggests that the payment must be made; it is more demanding but still courteous. See Figure 18.22 for an example of a collection letter, urgency stage.

Figure 18.22 Effective letter of collection: urgency stage

Orange Marketing Solutions

342 Bourke Street
MELBOURNE VIC 3000

Phone: 03 9909 0011
Fax: 03 9909 0126
Email:orama.blue.com.au

[enter]

[enter]
21 September 2003
[enter]
[enter]
Ms Kim Daley
Kim's Fashions
200 Browning Street
MELBOURNE VIC 3000
[enter]
[enter]
Dear Ms Daley
[enter]

Gain attention   **Overdue Account**
[enter]

Appeal to reader's self-interest   Over the last three years you have had a monthly charge account with our company. By paying this account every month you have built a strong credit history with us.
[enter]

Encourage reader to take action   It is therefore difficult to understand why your account is 120 days overdue. The account is a net 30 day account. The amount outstanding is $480.00.
[enter]
As we have sent you an account and a reminder letter, we are now requesting your urgent attention to this account to prevent cancellation of your credit facilities.
[enter]

Action   To enable us to maintain your credit facilities, please forward the outstanding $480.00 by cheque today.
[enter]
[enter]
Yours sincerely
[enter]
[enter]
[enter]
Liz Smithson
Credit Officer

If your organisation is going to take some other action over the non-payment, let the customer know what will happen if they ignore the urgent request. The account may, for example, be placed in the hands of a collection agency, or legal action may be initiated.

In the first stages of the collection process, it is best to assume that the customer has simply forgotten to pay. In the third and fourth stages, it is easier to write courteously if you still assume that the customer wants to pay but cannot do this for some reason.

Sales letters

Sales letters follow the same writing plan as other persuasive letters. They aim to motivate readers to act by gaining their attention and interest and prompting their desire and action. When you write a sales letter you need to know what you want to sell, what kind of people will buy the service or product (that is, the market) and who your competitors are. Then decide what type of appeal will persuade the reader to buy.

Sales letters aim to persuade the reader.

The AIDA formula is again useful for planning a sales letter, as shown in Figure 18.23.

Figure 18.23 Writing plan for a sales letter

1. Catch the reader's attention in the subject line or introductory paragraph.
2. Use the introductory paragraph to focus on readers' self-interest and the benefit to them.
3. In the middle paragraphs, emphasise the central selling point, create a desire and give the price.
4. Close by stating the action you want the reader to take.

An unusual opening statement, a sample, photographs or sketches, a solution to a problem or even gimmicks may attract attention. You can develop readers' interest further with a description that highlights the features and benefits of your product or service. Offers of proof to support your claims include samples, trial offers, statistics and guarantees.

The persuasive sales letter shows readers what is in it for them. Although a product may have many features, highlight just one or two of the best. Listing too many features may confuse the reader. Instead, place all the features in an attachment such as a brochure.

Appeal to the reader with one or two selling points.

To motivate the reader to take action, you need to relate the benefits of the product directly to the reader: for example, an advertisement for a hotel chain might say '. . . and kids stay free'. What you want the reader to do is then stated clearly – for example, 'Come in and test drive today' or 'Telephone your order today'.

Create desire by emphasising the benefits.

Specific, objective language gives the reader a clearer image of the product than abstract language and overstatement. Show you are confident that the customer will be satisfied by offering a money-back guarantee or free samples. Keep your sales letters short (no more than one page) and include any extra information as enclosures or attachments. Figure 18.24 is an example of a sales letter that uses the AIDA formula.

Replying to a letter of complaint

Organisations often receive telephone calls or letters of complaint from customers. The complaint can refer to, for example, the quality of service received, the condition of goods or the amount of the charges.

Many organisations regard this as essential feedback and a necessary component of ensuring quality customer service. When the complaint is justified and you acknowledge

Figure 18.24 A persuasive letter

74 Lambton Quay
WELLINGTON 1 NZ
Phone: (04) 472 6111
Fax (04) 472 6104

	[enter]
	[enter]
	17 October 2002
	[enter]
	[enter]
	Ms Maureen Talbot
	93 Port Street
	LOWER HUTT 6009
	[enter]
	[enter]
Order of information	Dear Ms Talbot
	[enter]
`*`Attention	Congratulations! You have been chosen to receive the XYZ Credit Card which establishes your ability to pay and your reliability as a desirable customer in selected stores throughout the world.
	[enter]
Focus on interests	The use of your credit card means you will no longer be worried about carrying extra cash around with you when travelling. As well, if you should become stranded overseas or run out of money, our nearest office will provide you with cash immediately, up to $1000.
	[enter]
Desire	There are no hidden costs for users of this prestigious credit card and only a small interest charge for extended repayments.
	[enter]
Action	Fill in the enclosed application form and slip it into the supplied postage paid envelope today. You will soon be enjoying the freedom, prestige and courteous attention this card will give you.
	[enter]
	[enter]
	Yours sincerely
	[enter]
	[enter]
	[enter]
	James Mason
	Marketing Director

this, you are writing a good news letter. When you believe the complaint is unjustified, you are writing a bad news letter. The important factor in both situations is to retain the customer's goodwill.

The writing plan for replying to a complaint follows the four steps listed in Figure 18.25. An example of an effective reply to a complaint is shown in Figure 18.26.

Figure 18.25 Writing plan for a reply to a letter of complaint

1. Start with the action you have taken as a result of the complaint.
2. Acknowledge the complaint clearly.
3. Give an apology and acknowledge any inconvenience caused.
4. Close with a goodwill statement.

Figure 18.26 Effective reply to a complaint

Austral Travel Agency

16 Sydney Street
ADELAIDE SA 5000

Phone: 08 2232 5555
Fax: 08 2232 5588
Email: austravel.blue.com.au

[enter]
[enter]
30 July 2003
[enter]
[enter]
Ms Janet Williams
15 Jacaranda Avenue
GLENELG SA 5045
[enter]
[enter]
Dear Ms Williams
[enter]

Overbooked Flight
[enter]
We have investigated your complaint regarding overbooking on your flight to Sydney (Headway Flight No. 68) on Saturday 10 July.
[enter]
We understand this overbooking resulted in you being delayed for several hours at Adelaide airport.
[enter]
Headway Airlines state that computer overbooking of seat allocations at Perth had resulted in seats on this flight being unavailable at Adelaide. They apologise for the error and regret the inconvenience caused.
[enter]
We appreciate you informing us of the situation. We value your custom and will make every effort to ensure this does not occur again.
[enter]
[enter]
Yours sincerely
[enter]
[enter]
[enter]
Sam Macklin
Manager

Order of information

Action taken

Acknowledge complaint

Apology

Goodwill close

Writing business letters

1. Working in pairs, assume you have received a request from the local high school Careers Adviser to accept a Year 10 student for work experience.
   a. Discuss two differences between the writing plans for a good news letter and a bad news letter.
   b. Decide who will write a letter accepting the student for work experience, and who will write a letter refusing the request.
   c. Discuss and evaluate each letter by using Self-check 18.2.

2. Consider this faulty opening for a letter of request.

   I received a brochure outlining the details of the Great New Zealand Ski Holiday for 17 days at $2995. Since I want to travel with my family some time within the next 12 months, I would like to know the dates of departure and any other details. Could you please send me specific details?

   Rewrite the request with a clear direct opening.

APPLY SKILLS

3. Work in pairs to complete the following tasks. A client asks you to replace a faulty appliance outside warranty conditions. Since the fault is clearly the result of misuse, you decide that the request is unjustified.
   a. Outline the writing plan for this letter.
   b. Discuss and prepare an opening statement to provide a neutral, relevant buffer.
   c. Prepare a concluding statement which avoids reference to the bad news, apology and clichés.
   d. Write your letter of refusal.
4. Select a sales letter that your household has received.
   a. In groups of three, evaluate the letter by referring to the AIDA formula. Decide whether the letter succeeds or fails to use the persuasive writing plan effectively.
   b. Discuss any devices it uses to highlight special features.
5. a. What is the main difference between the first and fourth stages of a collection campaign?
   b. Assume you have to write to a customer whose account is outstanding for an amount of $2400. Write the first reminder letter. The customer does not pay during the next three months. Write a letter suited to the fourth collection stage.

SELF CHECK 18.2

Good news, bad news and persuasive letters

In a good news letter, have I	Very successfully	Successfully	Unsuccessfully
used the direct method of organising information?	☐	☐	☐
clearly identified the letter's purpose in the introduction?	☐	☐	☐
closed with a statement of goodwill?	☐	☐	☐
In a bad news letter, have I			
opened with a neutral buffer?	☐	☐	☐
explained the news tactfully and fully?	☐	☐	☐
concluded with a positive statement?	☐	☐	☐
In a persuasive letter, have I			
gained the reader's attention?	☐	☐	☐
aroused the reader's interest and desire?	☐	☐	☐
concluded with an action statement?	☐	☐	☐

WEB WISE

Visit the Companion Website at **www.prenhall.com/dwyer_au**. Choose the Net Search activity in Chapter 18 to prepare a critique in business letter format of a document published online.

Chapter summary

Use conventional layout. There are several layout options for workplace correspondence. A uniform, professional layout makes it easier for both reader and writer. The writer can organise the information readily and the reader can quickly grasp the purpose of the letter.

Follow format conventions. Each part has a purpose specific to the reader's needs and the writer's needs. The acceptable format has a minimum of seven parts, and sometimes additional parts.

Identify reader and purpose. Remember to organise your information to suit the letter's purpose, the receiver's needs and the type of news you convey. If you take the time to do this before you write the letter, it is more likely to achieve its intended result.

Include information appropriate to your purpose. Some letters convey good news or bad news, some are neutral, and some aim to persuade the reader to take some action. In each type of letter, treat the reader with courtesy and write in a concise, confident manner that is easy to understand.

Use words, sentence forms, structure and style appropriate to your reader and purpose. Plain English is the most appropriate style for workplace correspondence. Readability, courtesy, the active voice and the 'you' approach help you to maintain readers' goodwill, encourages them to read the entire letter and identifies what action, if any, they should take.

Take the demands of context into account. When writing any letter, it is important to consider its purpose and effect on the receiver. Keep in mind your main objectives, and remember to retain the goodwill of the reader. Present your information in a way that is most likely to produce the result you want.

Follow a writing plan that is suited to good news, bad news or persuasive letters. Each type of letter has three sections: an introduction, a body and a conclusion. The purpose of each section is always the same: to open the letter, to give information and details, and to close the letter. However, the writing plan will vary the order of information. In a good news letter, the writing strategy is direct order of information. In a bad news letter, the writing strategy is an indirect order of information. A persuasive letter follows the order of information determined by the AIDA formula.

Reply to a letter of complaint. A reply to a letter of complaint aims to retain the customer's goodwill. Its order of information follows four steps. Start with the action you have taken as a result of the complaint. Then acknowledge the complaint clearly. Follow with an apology and acknowledge the inconvenience caused. End the letter with a goodwill closing.

1. List the seven basic parts of a business letter.

2. When is an attention line useful in a business letter?

3. What is the advantage of a subject line in a letter?

4. How is the choice of complimentary close determined by your greeting?

5. List the features of full block layout.

6. What are the advantages of full block layout?

7. A good business letter follows seven steps. Describe them, and explain how they could help you to prepare a difficult letter.

8. Briefly explain the 'you' approach in writing and justify its use.

9. List three different types of persuasive letters.

10. a. What do persuasive letters aim to do?
   b. Why is the AIDA formula used?

11. Why does a positive appeal achieve more than a negative appeal?

12. What are the four stages of the collection process?

13. a. List four different ways to gain attention in the first sentence or paragraph of a sales letter.

REVIEW QUESTIONS

b. Name one way of creating a reader's desire for a product or service.

14. a. Explain how a writing plan is helpful.

b. What is the writing plan for a letter of acknowledgment?

15. Define the terms 'good news letter' and 'bad news letter'. Give an example of a business situation that requires each type of letter.

16. What writing plan is used for:

a. a good news letter?

b. a bad news letter?

17. a. Define a request, an inquiry and an acknowledgment.

b. What does a letter of introduction do?

18. a. Give two reasons for refusing an order.

b. Give two reasons for refusing credit.

c. Give two reasons for refusing an adjustment.

19. How can you soften bad news when refusing an invitation or request?

20. What writing plan (or order of information) is used in a letter of complaint?

Write a good news, a bad news and a persuasive letter

SKILLS
BUILD

1. You are James Woods, Manager of North-West Copiers, a firm that supplies office equipment. On 19 May you receive a letter from Bryan Randall of 1001 Newmarket Street, NEWINGTON 3201. Bryan Randall, who runs a small advertising agency, complains that the digital photocopier installed by North-West Copiers is continually presenting problems to staff trying to send print jobs from their personal computer (PCs) to the digital copier. In his letter he says that, even though North-West's sales representative has been back three times to inspect the copier, it is still receiving only about half the print jobs from staff's PCs. He claims that the product is faulty and wants it replaced with another copier.

You discuss the content of the letter with the sales representative who visited Bryan Randall on 15 April, 26 April and 14 May. He says that he cannot find a fault although he has tested the copier on six occasions and, on two of these, the print jobs did not reach Bryan Randall's copier. The sales representative believes that a different model of digital copier is more suited to Bryan Randall's needs.

After this discussion you decide to replace the copier at no charge to Bryan Randall. In your letter you want to emphasise Bryan's value as a customer, the quality service North-West Copiers always gives, the offer of a free service call one month after the new digital copier is installed, and your interest in a business relationship with Bryan to meet his future needs for office supplies.

a. What is the good news and where should it be placed in the letter?

b. What details will you give in the body of the letter?

c. Write the letter to Bryan Randall using the writing plan for a letter of acknowledgment.

2. Rewrite the following tactless letter of refusal.

> Dear Mr Johns
> Further to your letter dated 28 January 2000, we regret to inform you that your request for a refund on your washing machine has been denied. The appliance has been badly treated since you bought it. Please feel free to contact me if you would like to discuss this matter further.

3. As a group, think of a new product or service you would like to buy. Write a sales letter to yourself and include the following features:

a. Block letter format

b. The seven basic parts of a business letter, plus two additional parts

c. The AIDA formula

d. An appropriate opening

e. One or two central selling points.

Key terms

adjustment refusal
AIDA formula
attention line
bad news letter
body
collection letter
complimentary close
credit refusal
full block

good news letter
greeting (salutation)
inside address
layout
letter of acknowledgment
letter of inquiry
letter of introduction
letter of request
letterhead

modified block
neutral letter
order refusal
persuasive letter
plain English
reminder
sales letter
signature block
subject line

Plain English: choosing your words

CASE STUDY

by Elizabeth M. Murphy

Taking care of sentence length and carefully choosing active or passive sentence constructions are essential to plain English. However, all the structural care in the world falls apart if we don't take care of the words.

Can we ever forget the words – the very many words – used by Sir Humphrey Appleby in *Yes Minister* when asked for a straight yes or no to a simple question: 'Minister, if I am pressed for a straight answer I shall say that, as far as we can see, looking at it by and large, taking one thing with another, in terms of the average of departments, then in the last analysis it is probably true to say that, at the end of the day, you would find, in general terms that, not to put too fine a point on it, there really was not very much in it one way or the other – as far as one can see, at this stage'?

Sheer wordiness

We may smile, but why is this quote so woolly? There are long phrases, redundancies and fillers. If we attend to these, the rest is clearer. Some people use *extra words as written 'throat-clearing'* while they decide what to say. Plan what you want to write and get to the point quickly.

Have you received a letter that begins something like 'I am writing to inform you that it would seem that there is a possibility that roadworks will cause noise outside the building tomorrow'? Get rid of the 'throat-clearing' to reveal the real message: 'Roadworks may cause noise outside the building tomorrow.'

Other examples include such phrases as 'due to the fact that', 'in light of the fact that' and 'for the reason that' when the one word 'because' would do. What one-word replacements can you suggest for 'in the event that', 'in anticipation of', 'concerning the matter of' and 'at this point in time'?

Redundancy occurs when the same idea is repeated in a phrase, for example:

> First and foremost, I want to stress forcefully that we must cooperate together in our initial preparation in order to achieve a fair, just and equitable end result that will have meaningful relevance to each and every researcher in the field of psychology.

Cut out the redundancies for a more readable sentence:

> First, I want to stress that we must cooperate in our preparation in order to achieve a just result that will have relevance to every researcher in psychology.

Fillers are words that creep into sentences while the writer is still thinking – omit them. Some can be misinterpreted because they are vague (e.g. 'it would seem that') and some can be actually insulting to the reader (e.g. 'as we can plainly see' or 'obviously'). Here is an example:

> At our last meeting, it was generally agreed that no decision could be made. Obviously there has been a misunderstanding.

Better: 'At our last meeting, everyone agreed that no decision could be made. There has been a misunderstanding.'

Pomposity

Don't drive the reader to a dictionary. Use words that are sure to be familiar to your target audience. Most people are not 'cognisant of' – they 'know'. We do something 'now' rather than 'instantaneously' and we 'end' a task rather than 'terminate' it. Pompous words can also be vague, and plain English is precise; rather than 'educational institution' it is often better to specify school, college or university; rather than 'yours' or 'your esteemed communication' write 'your letter', 'your memo' or 'your phone call'.

Pompous words need deflating. They get in the way of the message.

Verbs or verbal nouns?

Verbal nouns are nouns made from verbs – for example, 'management' from 'manage' or 'discussion' from 'discuss'. The very nature of verbs is to indicate action, so a lively sentence will contain more verbs than verbal nouns. Look at this lifeless sentence:

> The workers will hold discussions about the project with whoever has the responsibility for its coordination.

Compare it with this which says the same thing but uses dynamic verbs instead of verbal nouns. It is shorter and you can visualise action:

> The workers will discuss the project with whoever is responsible for coordinating it.

Positive, idiomatic, non-technical English

We think positively, so we respond better to *positive writing* than to negative writing. 'When your cheque reaches us, we will be able to fill your order' is more acceptable than 'It is not possible for us to fill your order as you neglected to enclose a cheque'.

English is a living language, so some constructions change in acceptability over time – this is particularly so with *prepositional idiom*. Some years ago, 'different from' was a strick rule; now 'different to' is also acceptable. 'Different than' may be acceptable in speech, but has not yet made it into acceptability in workplace writing. Use the acceptable preposition to make your meaning clear – for example, you can agree with, to, on, between, among and in, depending on the meaning you want to convey.

Jargon is the technical language of a particular industry or job. A doctor might talk about 'prognosis', but most people would use 'outlook'. Remember to whom you are writing, and choose words that will be understood at first reading.

English is a rich language – we rarely need to resort to *foreign* or *dead languages* in writing. We can have a 'conversation' rather than a 'tête-à-tête', we can ask people to 'reply' rather than 'rsvp', we can spell out 'for example' rather than using 'e.g.', and so on.

There are many more aspects of word choice to be considered when writing, but they all boil down to one piece of advice: consider your reader. In most writing, we are trying to inform, not to teach English vocabulary. Relax – use words you would use in ordinary conversation, and your message will be clear.

Source: Elizabeth M. Murphy, 'Plain English – style of choice', *Stylewise*, Vol. 7, No. 3, 2001, p. 2. Reproduced by permission of Elizabeth Murphy, from *Stylewise*, published by the Department of Finance and Administration, and *Effective Writing: Plain English at Work*, published by Pitman, Melbourne, 1989, 1994. © Elizabeth Murphy, emmurphy@ozemail.com.au.

Questions

1. The article states: 'There are many more aspects of word choice to be considered when writing, but they all boil down to one piece of advice: consider your reader'. Why should business letter writers consider the needs of their readers as well as their own needs?
2. Why is it important to use plain English rather than repetition, fillers and pomposity in a business letter?
3. What do you see as the key characteristics of a plain English writing style?

Writing memos and short reports

In this chapter you will learn how to:

- organise memos and reports

- plan and write effective memos

- apply a five-step plan for a short report

- follow the format conventions for the short formal report, letter report and memo report

- write justification, progress and periodic reports.

Evaluate your communication skills by completing the self-checks in the chapter.

The term **memo** (short for **memorandum**) is used to describe the standard format of internal communication that an organisation uses for its own staff. A memo may communicate information, explain new procedures, announce changes, make requests, confirm results or offer advice. Memos are rarely sent to other organisations, although government departments may use them to communicate with other government departments or authorities.

Short reports collect and communicate different types of information to a variety of people within and outside an organisation. Their main purpose is to provide objective information to support ideas or proposals, to inform people about the progress of a project or to present information periodically (bulletins).

The systematic approach

As a writer of memos and short reports, your purpose may be to inform people or to encourage some action. Your readers may or may not be aware of the issue already. The contents may vary from simple to complex. You should organise the memo and short report in a way that helps the reader to grasp the main points quickly.

This is best achieved by a systematic process:

■ researching
■ planning and structuring
■ writing
■ editing.

Throughout this process you will need to apply your thinking and analytical skills.

The memo format

The memo is an internal organisation communication.

The parts of a memo parallel those of a business letter. However, they are fewer and simpler, and dispense with some of the courtesies of the letter.

Parts of a memo format

The memo format is less formal than the business letter format.

As the memo is an internal means of communication and less formal than a letter, there is no need to include an inside address, greeting, complimentary close or full signature. The four headings that a memo usually includes are: 'To, From, Date, Subject' as set out in Figures 19.1. to 19.5. The headings 'To' and 'From' clearly identify the receiver and sender of the memo. 'To' usually precedes 'From' as a courtesy to the receiver. The subject line indicates the topic of the memo; for example, 'Delivery Schedules for March'. Make the title informative but brief.

The body of the memo carries a clearly structured message, often written in short numbered paragraphs. The body, including the subject sentence, should be blocked to the left margin. Write in plain English to present readers with an objective, factual description of the topic.

Advantages of a memo

As a memo is a written form of communication, it has four advantages over the spoken word.

1. It reaches a large number of people at the same time.
2. It provides a written record for filing and reference.

3. It allows the writer to convey detailed or difficult information logically and accurately.
4. It can indicate, by a company letterhead, that its information is part of the organisation's procedures.

Writing a memo

Memos vary enormously in length and complexity. Some make brief, routine announcements; others present complicated or sensitive information. Any memo, however, warrants the following four steps:

Consider the context and required level of persuasion.

1. Identify the subject.
2. Select and organise your information.
3. Write simply.
4. Use a suitable tone.

Five types of memos

Memos are used often, for many purposes – for example, to request, instruct, authorise, acknowledge. In each instance, the nature of the message and the writer's purpose determine the structure of the memo. This section describes five examples of routine memos and sets out some guidelines for producing them.

Clarity is the key to a useful memo.

1. Instruction memo
2. Request memo
3. Announcement memo
4. Transmittal memo
5. Authorisation memo.

Instruction memo

The objective of the **instruction memo** is to give your receivers all the information they need to carry out the instructions confidently. The example shown in Figure 19.1 will probably achieve this aim; it works well, for several reasons. Its style is simple and direct. The instructions are logically arranged so that they stand out clearly: introduction, main point, secondary information and action. The tone is pleasant and it includes all the necessary details.

Request memo

The aim of the **request memo** is to ask the receiver for certain information or action. The request memo in Figure 19.2 tells the receiver clearly and precisely what is required. It is arranged in the following way: first, the main point, then the secondary idea or details, then the action required.

The request memo asks for action or information.

Announcement memo

The **announcement memo** provides information. It follows the organisation method suggested for writing good news letters. The announcement comes first, followed by the secondary details or information, and then the required action. An example of an announcement memo is given in Figure 19.3.

The announcement memo informs.

Figure 19.1 Instruction memo

	MEMORANDUM
	To: All Staff
	From: Elaine Thomas, Administrative Officer
	Date: 12 May 2003
Introduction	Subject: Operating instructions for new copying machines
Main point	A new photocopier has been installed in the general office. All staff are welcome to use it.
	To ensure the copier's survival, it is important to keep the following procedures in mind:
Secondary information	■ Use the machine for no longer than 30 minutes at a time. ■ After use, allow the machine to cool for at least 5 minutes. ■ Make sure the switch is turned off after use.
	Please speak to me if you have any questions about the machine.

Figure 19.2 Request memo

	MEMORANDUM
	To: Section Heads
	From: Phillippa Allertz, Operations Manager
	Date: 10 April 2003
Main point	Subject: Planning of work schedules July–December
Secondary idea	Work schedules for July to December are now being prepared.
Action	To help us plan these in a way that will suit all sections, please let me have holiday schedules for the employees in your section by 24/5/03.

Figure 19.3 Announcement memo

	MEMORANDUM
	To: All Staff
	From: Sonia Browne, Personnel Manager
	Date: 21 April 2003
	Subject: Staff discounts
Announcement	Employees are entitled to a 12% discount on books at any of our branches.
Secondary details	To obtain a discount, simply present your discount card so that your staff number is keyed in with each purchase.
Action	You may collect your employee discount card at my office.

Transmittal memo

The **transmittal memo** is the cover note that accompanies a more formal or lengthy message. In the example in Figure 19.4, the memo accompanies the statistics on staff absenteeism requested by the receiver. It introduces the reader to what follows: the full details and the action required.

The transmittal memo accompanies the main message.

Figure 19.4 Transmittal memo

	MEMORANDUM
	To: Mr Byrnes
	From: J. Pike, Human Resources Manager
	Date: 21 April 2003
Main point	Subject: Statistics on Staff Absenteeism
	The statistics on staff absenteeism that you asked for are attached.
Secondary details	These figures are for the last five years. A table projecting absenteeism for the next quarter is also attached. If you would like to discuss the statistics, my extension is 7304.
Action	Please forward me a copy of the report you prepare from these statistics.

Authorisation memo

The **authorisation memo** gives someone permission or authority to do something. It presents the background information first, then the main point and, finally, the secondary details and action (Figure 19.5).

The authorisation memo gives authority to take action.

In all memo examples presented so far, the information is direct, simple and concise. Each one is brief: it clearly outlines all that is necessary, but no more. This approach encourages prompt action.

Sometimes, however, your memos will be more complex and much longer. Whatever the length or complexity, it is always important to set out your information clearly and logically and to convey it in simple, suitable language. Do this and your memo writing will be successful.

Figure 19.5 Authorisation memo

	MEMORANDUM
	To: M. Leung
	From: K. Doherty, Manager
	Date: 21 April 2003
Background information	Subject: Purchase of Accounting Computing Packages
Main point	Your findings identified inadequacies in our computing packages. Your proposal indicated two new packages suited to our current and projected needs.
Action	Action 1. Please order these packages from the supplier nominated in the proposal and arrange for their installation on our terminals as soon as possible. 2. Could you organise and be involved in training for each of our computer operators? 3. Please see me some time on Wednesday to arrange a reduction of your regular responsibilities to give you time to complete the project.

Memo writing

SKILLS
APPLY

1. The memo below is disorganised and discourteous. Rewrite the memo by:
   a. grouping similar ideas so that the structure is logical
   b. setting a courteous, positive tone.
2. Assume you are the manager of a chain of natural health food stores. As you check the stock of breakfast cereals, you notice that the seal is broken on more than half the packages. You decide to return all the new delivery of breakfast cereal to the manufacturer.

   Write a request memo to the Stores Officer, asking him to prepare the stock for return to the supplier. Use Self-check 19.1 to evaluate your memo.

EXAMPLE OF A DISCOURTEOUS MEMORANDUM

To: H. Lin

From: J. Morriss

Date: 29 September 2003

The Conference Plans you submitted last week were considered at the Committee Meeting. Make reservations for three more people. You have made some errors in the planning.
It was foolish to consider that all participants would be willing to share accommodation. Two more workshop leaders have to be chosen. Have you written the invitation to the keynote speaker or has that already been completed? The conclusions of the committee are as follows: A mistake was also made in the order of the conference proceedings. See me as soon as possible so that I can tell you what things need to be done.

SELF CHECK 19.1

Writing a memo

Read the first draft of your memo and ask yourself these questions:

Have I	Yes	No	Unsure
used correct memo layout?	☐	☐	☐
decided the memo's purpose?	☐	☐	☐
included a subject line?	☐	☐	☐
written a clear message?	☐	☐	☐
organised the information logically?	☐	☐	☐
closed by stating the required action to be taken, or by making a positive statement?	☐	☐	☐

Writing short reports

Good planning ensures effectiveness.

A report, whether long or short, presents comprehensive information on a specific subject. Its main function is to inform. Sometimes, it also offers expert opinion or advice to managers, to help them check on progress, plan for the future and make decisions.

The key to success in developing an effective report that is also easy to read lies in planning carefully. The following guidelines will help you achieve this.

■ Indicate your purpose clearly.
■ Give accurate and objective information.
■ Apply suitable headings.
■ Organise it so that it highlights the main points and leads logically to your conclusions.

When faced with the task of producing a short report, the following five-step approach will help you plan and write it.

Five-step plan for a short report

At the investigation and planning stage of your short report, consider the following five steps.

1. Take time to identify your task precisely.
2. Consider your readers' needs, knowledge level and familiarity with technical terms. Do this at the beginning as these will affect both the content and language of your report.
3. Identify and list your information and sourcing requirements. Create ideas by brainstorming, consulting co-workers or considering previously successful examples.
4. Gather your information purposefully, and avoid being side-tracked. Sometimes you may need to research both primary and secondary sources.
5. Sort your information and discard anything irrelevant. Organise your material into sections under suitable headings, in a logical sequence.

By this stage, you have a logical outline that should allow you to work swiftly to produce a complete yet concise report.

Order of information

In deciding how to arrange your information for a short report, it is useful to consider the following three methods:

Choose the order of information appropriate to your purpose.

1. indirect order
2. direct order
3. routine order.

The purpose of each method is given in Table 19.1.

Some of the characteristics of poor short reports are listed in Table 19.2. A systematic approach to memo and report writing – researching, planning and structuring, writing and editing – will help you to avoid these mistakes.

Table 19.1 Purpose of each order of information

Indirect order	Direct order	Routine order
A problem-solving method for a reader unfamiliar with the content	A problem-solving method for a reader familiar with the content	A decision-making or routine order for readers who need to base their decisions on the information
The indirect order moves the reader through the short facts and options The criteria and alternatives are then fully explained.	The direct order leads the reader from the solutions to the problem, then to the reasons for suggesting the solutions, and finally to the facts supporting these reasons.	The routine order of information is used within the context of an overview – each main idea is presented with its related secondary ideas to give accurate information on which to base decisions, or to communicate information to others in the organisation.

Table 19.2 Characteristics of poor short reports

No clear purpose statement

No significant information

Irrelevant detail

Illogical order of information

Overuse of technical terms

Poor use of white space

Inappropriate format

Irrelevant attachments

Short report formats

A short report format places information on the page in a way that is easy to understand. Writers have developed various types of format to convey certain types of information, but discussion here is limited to three typical short report formats:

- **formal format**
- **letter format**
- **memo format.**

Table 19.3 summarises the details required for each type of report format.

Table 19.3 Three types of report formats

Formal format	Letter format	Memo format
1. A title page	**1.** The writer's address	**1.** Reader's name
2. An introduction	**2.** The date	**2.** Writer's name
3. Sections with headings in the body	**3.** Inside or reader's address	**3.** Date
4. Conclusions	**4.** Greeting (salutation)	**4.** Subject line or title
5. Recommendations (when required)	**5.** Subject	**5.** Body
	6. Body	
	7. Complimentary close	
	8. Signature block	
Attachments are included if their information is useful.		

Plan the short report

1. Assume you are to prepare a short report stating some proposed changes and asking for new computer technology. The following instructions will guide you.
   a. Plan your report by placing the information into the correct order.
   b. Prepare an outline that clearly identifies each heading.
   c. Create a title for the short report.
   d. Open by stating the changes. Then explain the current problems of using computing software that is inadequate for the size of your company. This is your introduction.
   e. Open the body of the report with some examples and a brief explanation of the advantages of the new software. Remember to be clear and not to overload your short report with technical information that would be more easily understood by word-processor operators than by management. Then present the problems of your current system. Next, state advantages and any disadvantages of the new proposal.
   f. Place the conclusions and recommendations at the end of the report.

2. Distinguish between the problem-solving method of organising information for a reader unfamiliar with the content, and the method suitable for a reader familiar with the content.

Four types of short reports

There are four widely used short reports that usually follow the memo format, but may sometimes follow the format for a letter or formal report.

- Justification report
- Progress report (and completion report)
- Periodic report
- Form report (and incident report).

These short reports have different purposes and suit different situations. They are discussed next.

Format the short report to suit your writing purpose.

Justification report

The **justification report** presents an idea or proposal and follows this with evidence to support it. As this kind of report usually seeks approval for some action and the resources involved, it is usually sent upwards in the organisation.

A justification report must explain clearly why the proposal is made. The details of any proposed changes are placed in the body of the report.

A report that balances the advantages and disadvantages of the current situation with the changes outlined in the proposal allows for clear conclusions and recommendations. If it is necessary to follow up, review or check on progress, remember to recommend this.

Always present facts to support your request for approval or change in a justification report. Achieve the correct emphasis by organising your information as shown in Table 19.4.

The justification report presents an idea or proposal.

Table 19.4 A justification report: indirect order of information

1. Purpose statement
- Identify the report's purpose with a subject line or purpose statement.

2. Body of information
- Describe the current situation.
- Describe the change.
- Detail the cost factors.
- Discuss the advantages or disadvantages.

3. Conclusion
- Make a conclusion.
- Close with the recommendation/s.

A short report suggesting or asking for a change to normal procedures may meet with some resistance. In this case, use the indirect order of information shown in Table 19.6 for a progress report. Start with a purpose statement, and keep the writing neutral to lead the reader through the problem and the details supporting the change. It is essential to remind or persuade the reader that there is a problem, not to assume that they are familiar with it (see Figure 19.6). Close by pointing the way ahead, or by using a neutral statement or a goodwill statement.

One of the advantages of a short report is that the information and written approval are eventually put on file for future reference. Justification reports may apply to the situations listed in Table 19.5.

Table 19.5 Justification report: possible situations

A short justification report may deal with:

- a change of procedure

- a change of funding source

- a change of accommodation

- a change of operating times

- a drop in sales

- a need to replace current computer software with a more powerful package

- a change to a department budget

- a change of switchboard

- a discount pricing policy.

Figure 19.6 Justification report in memo format

To:	Jennifer Adams, Managing Director
From:	Jim Dyer, Customer Service Manager
Date:	13 March 2003
Subject:	Proposed changes to lunch breaks

Numerous complaints have been received over the past six months over delays in service during the lunch period. Feedback from a client survey indicates that approximately 56% of our clients are dissatisfied with our customer service during the hours of 12.30 pm to 1.30 pm. Over the past half-year we have experienced a 10% decline in sales.

The current practice is for half the staff to take a lunch break from 12.15 pm to 1.00 pm and the remainder from 1.00 pm to 1.45 pm.

Staff consultations have resulted in the proposal that the staff lunch breaks be changed to improve customer service. The suggestion is that the two lunch breaks be 11.30 am to 12.15 pm and 1.30 pm to 2.15 pm. Staff would nominate which time period they prefer. This would mean that all staff would be available over the busy period of 12.30 pm to 1.30 pm.

It is recommended:
1. that the changed lunch times be introduced for a trial period of three months;
2. that, after this trial period, staff are consulted and customers surveyed for their comments.

Marginal notes: Purpose statement in subject line / Body of information / Recommendation

Progress report

The **progress report** is an essential part of the organisation's management information system. It sends objective factual information, usually to management, on the progress of a task and on timetables for future work and completion.

Progress reports usually move upwards through the organisation to inform management of the rate of progress according to schedule, to identify goals for subsequent periods or to provide a forecast. They are written as required rather than at regular intervals. For a progress overview, organisations often compare the latest report with previous reports on file.

Present your progress report in positive language and emphasise achievements and progress. Aim to maintain a balance between successes and any problems encountered or anticipated.

Table 19.6 sets out the main parts of a progress report, in their appropriate sequence. Progress reports often compare the results achieved so far against the anticipated or intended results. Table 19.7 lists some typical situations requiring progress reports. A typical progress report is given in Figure 19.7.

The progress report provides objective factual information on specific progress.

Completion report

A **completion report** is the last report to prepare. It complements the progress reports generated during the life of a project, and is written to state that the project has been completed. It is also a courteous way of thanking management for the opportunity to work on the project.

Table 19.6 Progress report: indirect order of information

1. Purpose statement
- ■ Identify the report's purpose with a subject line or purpose statement.

2. Body of information
- ■ Open the body of the report with the current status, work or goals completed so far.
- ■ Follow with details of the operation's achievements.
- ■ Present any problems and state how they were resolved or will be resolved.

3. Conclusion
- ■ Indicate future actions.

Table 19.7 Situations requiring progress reports

Short progress reports are required for:

- ■ checking the rate of work on a new building

- ■ updating progress on office renovations

- ■ reporting progress on a rezoning application lodged with Council

- ■ informing union members about wage negotiations

- ■ providing daily medical details on a patient's progress.

Figure 19.7 A progress report in memo format

To:	John Wilson, Project Manager
From:	Les Smith, Building Supervisor
Date:	30 June 2003
Subject line Subject:	Progress Report on 26 Elkhorn Street, Sommerville
	Unfortunately, rain over the past two weeks has hindered progress.
Body of information	The timber framework of the building has been completed, underground pipes have been laid and electricity connected. It is anticipated that the brick veneer exterior will be completed this week.
Conclusion	The revised completion date for this building is 10 August 2003.

Periodic report

The periodic report supplies objective information regularly.

A **periodic report** is the most common report prepared in business. Its purpose is to inform management, at regular intervals, about some aspect of the organisation's operation over a specified period.

A periodic report may be prepared and circulated daily, weekly, fortnightly or monthly. An accounts receivable clerk may, for example, prepare a monthly report on debtors, showing accounts overdue, with an explanation of the steps taken to recover the debts. Management then considers this report and decides whether to pursue the debt with a collection letter, telephone call or legal action. Or a real estate agent may prepare a monthly report for management on the percentage of listed houses sold during that time.

Many periodic reports are prepared on standard printed forms that are easy to complete, read and file. They follow the same format each time so that it is easy to compare information from one period with that of another.

Writing plan

In the body of the report, emphasise the most important points. Group related details under headings. Use tabulation, indents, lists or numbers to make it easier for your reader to find and understand information. To plan a periodic report, use the routine order of information shown in Table 19.8 and refer to Figure 19.8 for an example. Table 19.9 lists some situations that require periodic reports.

Table 19.8 Routine order of information for a periodic report

1. Purpose statement
- Identify the report's purpose with a subject line or purpose statement.

2. Body
- Open the body of the report with facts and figures.
- Present objective information on achievements and problems.

3. Conclusion
- Summarise the findings.
- Close with the recommendation/s.*

* The recommendation can also be placed at the beginning of the report, if this position is more appropriate.

Table 19.9 Situations requiring periodic reports

Short periodic reports may deal with:

- monthly staff absenteeism

- annual figures on unauthorised leave from each section

- monthly revenue reports

- audit reports

- weekly sales figures

- outstanding accounts.

Figure 19.8 A periodic report in letter format

<table>
<tr><td colspan="2">

Walkom Linehan

—————————————————

FIRST NATIONAL REAL ESTATE

</td><td>

Walkom Linehan Real Estate
Pty Ltd
447 Hunter Street Newcastle 2300
Facsimile: (02) 4926 2077
Telephone: (02) 4929 4053

</td></tr>
</table>

Order of information	
	2 April 2003
	Broadfield Pty Ltd 54 Rachel Street Drayton NSW 2323
Subject line	**Rental figures for Suites 1–4 Raymond Street, Newcastle**
Purpose	The rental statement for the first quarter of 2003 shows the total rental figures for the quarter as $33 600.00.
Facts and figures	**Rental summary**

Month	Suite 1	Suite 2	Suite 3	Suite 4
January	$3200.00	$3200.00	$4000.00	$3200.00
February	$3200.00	$3200.00	$4000.00	$3200.00
March	$3200.00	$3200.00	Outstanding	Vacant
Total	$9600.00	$9600.00	$8000.00	$6400.00

All tenants are paid up to date with the exception of Suite 3. Suite 4 is vacant.

Marketing

Objective information	We have sent letter/s to accountants, solicitors and doctors and have erected signs in the foyer to encourage offers. We will keep you informed of progress.
Recommendation	It may be worthwhile placing an advertisement for Suite 4 in the *Newcastle Herald* Saturday Classifieds for the next two weeks.

Yours faithfully
WALKOM LINEHAN FIRST NATIONAL

SCOTT WALKOM

Form report

A **form report** is a cost-effective way to collect information. Its standard layout enables information from various sources to be gathered and arranged consistently. Headings and subheadings enable the writer to quickly place related information into the same section so that there is no need to spend time on planning the order of information. Forms make it easy to keep accurate and up-to-date records. They also help the receiver to interpret, analyse and compile the information quickly (see Figure 19.9).

Figure 19.9 A form report

WEEKLY CUSTOMER SERVICE REPORT

Date	Time	Customer	Service delivered	Service charge	Mileage
	Arr. Dept.				
	Arr. Dept.				
	Arr. Dept.				
	Arr. Dept.				

Incident report

An **incident report** gives management a clear, factual account of an incident that is non-routine. It is primarily an information report, offering the receiver objective, factual details rather than a full analysis or justification of the incident. The writing plan for an incident report is shown in Table 19.10 and an example in Figure 19.10.

Incident reports may be written on:

■ incidents involving client/staff interaction
■ unusual delays in normal procedures
■ accidents
■ special events.

Table 19.10 Writing plan for an incident report

■ A short general statement about the incident.

■ A description of the circumstances that led up to the incident.

■ An outline of what happened, in appropriate detail.

■ An indication of the outcome: the effect the incident had or is having.

Figure 19.10 An incident report

Name of injured person _____

Department _____

Name of Supervising Officer _____

Where the incident occurred _____

When the incident occurred _____day _____date _____time

Duties being undertaken by the injured person at time of incident _____

_____

How the incident occurred _____

_____

_____

_____

_____

_____

_____

What injuries were sustained _____

_____

Witnesses of the incident _____

_____

_____

Action taken (identify doctor or hospital if injured person taken to a surgery or hospital) _____

_____

_____

Any other details observed (such as bleeding, vomiting, limping) and whether the injured person was able

to continue working _____

_____

Supervisor/Manager's comments _____

_____

Date _____

Signature _____

Name (in block letters) _____

Department _____

Designation _____

Applying the 4-step systematic approach to memo and short reports

1. Assume you are a holiday employee with a large engineering firm. Your next holiday employment depends on the successful completion of your current course work. The engineering firm has asked you to write a short report on your progress with your studies and to include your subject choice for the next year of study.

   Write this report with details on the number of subjects, your performance in these subjects, and any further subjects you need to complete your course.

2. Assume you are the manager of the plant nursery of a large mining company. This nursery regenerates areas affected by the mining operations, and you have to prepare a monthly report for the General Manager.
   a. Write the report, following the memo report layout. Include the following statistics:
      ■ number of plants in the nursery: 6000
      ■ number of plants planted on the site: 4500
      ■ number of work hours on the job: 120
      ■ number of hectares cleared: 10 000
   b. What type of short report is prepared at regular intervals?

3. Prepare a letter report on one of the following topics.
   a. Three pieces of technology used by accountants
   b. Five job functions performed by the Human Resources Officer
   c. Why marketing is so important to an organisation
   d. Three different services usually provided by a welfare agency.

4. Write a letter report to business students, explaining how to use the AIDA formula for a piece of persuasive advertising. A new brand of joggers has just been released in Australia. Your potential customers are 20- to 35-year-old men and women who play sport. Refer to Self-check 19.2.

Writing short reports

Read the first draft of the letter report produced in question 4 of Apply Skills and ask yourself these questions:

Have I	Very well	Moderately	Unsatisfactorily
prepared a purpose statement?	☐	☐	☐
followed the five-step approach to planning a report?	☐	☐	☐
organised information in an order suitable for a letter report?	☐	☐	☐
used a suitable format?	☐	☐	☐

Visit the Companion Website at **www.prenhall.com/dwyer_au**. Choose the Good Practice/Bad Practice activity in Chapter 19 to prepare a request, announcement and instruction memo.

Chapter summary

Organise memos and reports. Your task is to write effective memos and short reports that produce the response you want. If you select and arrange your information carefully, your material will be easy to read and more likely to produce action.

Plan and write effective memos. The internal memo form uses a consistent, standard format to convey information, requests and instructions quickly and simply. It requires a concise statement of fact and matter-of-fact tone. It speeds up the flow of communication that is essential to an organisation's efficiency.

Apply a five-step plan for a short report. This will help you to produce a logical outline and a readable report that is accurate and complete. The purpose of a report is to provide concise information that will enable the reader to make a decision, check progress or plan for the future.

Follow the format conventions of the formal, letter and memo report formats. Format your document correctly using one of three formats regarded by convention as acceptable: short formal report, letter or memo.

Write justification, progress and periodic reports. Each of these short reports has a specific purpose – to inform, advise or persuade. Your task is to help the reader to consider, analyse or evaluate new information quickly. Aim for a balanced view. Base your interpretations, conclusions and recommendations on the facts, and arrange these in an order that is suitable for your purpose and distribution.

REVIEW QUESTIONS

1. Define the term 'memo'.
2. Name three objectives that a memo sets out to achieve.
3. What is the typical format for a memo?
4. What is the purpose of the subject line?
5. List four steps for preparing memos.
6. What is the objective of a request memo?
7. Briefly describe a transmittal memo.
8. Name four functions that memos can perform.
9. Why is it important to identify the memo's purpose?
10. a. List four different types of memos.
    b. What is the purpose of each?
11. Define the term 'short report'.
12. List the five steps for planning a short report.
13. Name the five essential parts of a memo report format.
14. Name the eight essential parts of a letter report format.
15. Name the five essential parts of a formal short report format.

16. a. Define the terms 'direct', 'indirect' and 'routine' order of information.
    b. What is the purpose of each?
17. Define the terms 'justification report', 'progress report' and 'periodic report'.
18. Define 'form report' and give an example of a situation that would require one.
19. What is a completion report?
20. List six characteristics of a poor short report.
21. Explain the difference between the introduction, body and conclusion of a short report.
22. Show how to plan a justification report by using the kite shape.
23. Briefly explain the main difference between a memo report and a letter report.
24. Briefly discuss three differences between a progress and a periodic report.

Writing memos and short reports

1. Assume you are Head of a large government Administrative Division, and that you supervise 25 staff. Your staff are to take part in a new training program, 'An Introduction to Management', on separate dates.
   a. List three advantages of using a memo for this situation instead of a spoken message.
   b. Write the announcement memo to staff.
   c. Write an authorisation memo to the Training Manager. State that the funds are available for the program. Make up the details of times, dates, venue and content.

2. Assume you are employed by the Local Council as Manager of the local ocean baths. The annual Christmas and New Year high tides are a hazard to swimmers. Heavy seas break into the pool and cause a rip that can drag swimmers from the pool and into the ocean. As Baths Manager, you have taken the following precautions:
   ■ placed warning signs in prominent positions
   ■ installed a safety chain across the ocean end of the baths
   ■ installed a loudspeaker system
   ■ stored safety and rescue equipment in an accessible position.

This year, on the last Saturday in December, the swell and winds have created a particularly heavy surf. You have clearly announced over the loudspeaker system that the situation is very dangerous. Everyone is to leave the pool.

Three people have refused to leave the pool. As you walk towards them, a very large wave drags them back into the dangerous surf.

You radio the Surf and Rescue helicopter, then use the rescue equipment to try to save the three swimmers. Two people are rescued unharmed. The third person is seriously injured.

   a. Write an incident report to the Council. Include all the information provided.
   b. Ensure that you use each section of the short report correctly.
   c. Give each section a heading. You may place the conclusions and recommendations at either the beginning or end of your report. Use Self-check 19.2 to ensure that you have completed each step of the task to a suitable standard.

Key terms

announcement memo
authorisation memo
completion report
form report
formal format
incident report

instruction memo
justification report
letter format
memo
memo format
memorandum

periodic report
progress report
request memo
transmittal memo

STUDY
CASE

February a cracker, says NAB survey

by Matt Wade and Laura Tingle

Business conditions were the best for two years last month, according to a major survey, while home lending figures pointed to a backlog of building work that should boost economic activity for some time.

The National Australia Bank's February business poll, released yesterday, showed an economy graining momentum with trading conditions, profitability and employment all rising.

The survey's measure of business confidence was marginally off its recent seven-year highs, but was still strong.

NAB's chief economist, Alan Oster, said the results were consistent with non-farm growth of about 4.5 per cent. 'Putting it all together, it seems Australian growth in 2002 and 2003 will be higher than previously forecast,' he said.

The survey showed retailing, wholesaling and construction were among the best performing industries.

Housing finance grew by 1.5 per cent, seasonally adjusted, in January, the Bureau of Statistics reported yesterday. This defied expectations of a cooling in the demand for housing finance as the First Home Owners Scheme was wound back from January 1.

The demand for finance for construction of new dwellings – the indicator of continuing building activity – rose a strong 2.8 per cent to be 105 per cent higher than in January last year.

HSBC economist Anthony Thompson said yesterday that strong gains in finance for new construction over the last two months meant the trend line for new construction financing was rising, with no signs yet of a peak.

Trend construction finance was now above the pre-GST peak in November 1999 by 6.7 per cent.

'The continued uptrend in finance suggests that the backlog of dwelling construction work to be done in the pipeline is still rising,' he said.

'This creates a growing chance that positive GDP growth contributions from dwelling investment could spill over into the third quarter of 2002, creating a further positive impetus for domestic demand, and adding to the case for tighter monetary policy.'

Westpac estimates that the number of first home buyers in the loan market fell by just 4.1 per cent, despite the winding back of the FHOS scheme.

Despite this, Westpac economist Harley Dale warned the housing market could turn very quickly and there was still a risk that the bullish outlook for housing suggested by yesterday's figures would not transpire.

The Housing Industry Association said the strong housing finance numbers were consistent with reports from some of the nation's largest builders, who experienced significant increases in New Year display home traffic.

The ACCI/Westpac Survey of Industrial Trends for the March quarter added further economic gloss yesterday.

It showed that all activity measures continued to rise, and business confidence rebounded strongly.

More than a third of the manufacturers surveyed predicted an improvement in the general business situation in the next six months.

The net outcome for new orders more than doubled while output also firmed, with more firms nominating insufficient capacity as their main constraint.

There was also a pause in reported job shedding, which the authors of the survey said reinforced predictions of strong employment growth in the next quarter.

Source: Matt Wade and Laura Tingle, 'February a cracker, says NAB survey', *Sydney Morning Herald*, 13 March 2002, p. 21.

Task

Assume you have been asked by Adbrill Advertising Agency to use the information in the NAB survey to write a short report. The purpose of the report is to recommend at least two growth industries that Adbrill Advertising can target to find new clients.

1. Write the short report and include recommendations.
2. Use the short formal report format.

3. Use the order of information for a justification report (purpose statement, body of information, conclusions and recommendation(s)) to plan and structure your report.

4. Use a business writing style.
5. Use the checklist on page 381 to assess your short report.

Writing long reports

In this chapter you will learn how to:

- identify the purpose of a report

- determine the main issues of the report

- organise material according to purpose, audience and context

- use technology for faster distribution and better visual presentation

- format a long report

- use language suitable for the task and audience

- develop an argument logically

- present solutions that are based on evidence

- evauate your solutions objectively

- write the conclusions

- offer recommendations appropriate to the purpose of the document

- edit a report.

Evaluate your communication skills by completing the self-checks in the chapter.

Formal reports are major documents written to provide comprehensive information and expert opinion. They are written for specific purposes – for example, to investigate the suitability of a particular site or to analyse achievements over a set period. They are therefore usually long, and require careful organising.

Your task in preparing a long formal report is to produce a document that is accurate, objective and complete. It must give your readers a reliable basis for checking progress, planning or making a specific decision.

Planning a long report

The planning stage of a **long report** is the most time-consuming and, in one sense, the most important part of the task. Good planning allows you to write and edit more easily. There are six steps to planning a report.

1. Define its purpose.
2. Consider the reader.
3. Determine what issues are involved.
4. Collect information.
5. Sort and evaluate your information.
6. Prepare the outline.

Complete each step before you start writing the long formal report.

Step 1 Define the purpose

First, decide what the **purpose** of your report is. If, for example, you have been asked to develop a local traffic management plan, you need to determine at the beginning whether your report must identify a problem, or present a plan to prevent problems arising.

Or suppose you are examining the feasibility of opening a new office in the city: your purpose will be to evaluate the site according to what you believe essential and acceptable – for example, access to public transport or parking. In this case, your report will investigate the options.

Once you have defined your purpose clearly, develop your report to help your reader solve the problem or make a decision.

Step 2 Consider the reader

Consider the needs of the reader.

Think about who will read the long report: for example, a supervisor, fellow worker, client or government department. Your reader will determine your definition of the problem and how you develop your arguments, analyse problems and present solutions. As you plan and write, consider the readers' point of view, their need for detail, their preference for a particular order of information, and their experience and understanding of technical terms. All this will affect the content, structure and language of a long report. At the same time you must consider your own needs as a writer. Table 20.1 distinguishes the needs of the writer and reader.

In many cases a report is written in response to someone's request. That person will have certain expectations about your report, and if you consider these early in the planning stage you will write it more efficiently.

Table 20.1 Writer and reader needs

The writer needs	The reader needs
■ to define the purpose of the long report	■ information and evidence
■ to define its scope and limitations	■ an analysis of the information
■ to know all the facts	■ conclusions
■ to know how the long report will be used	■ recommendations

Step 3 Determine the issues involved

What issues or topics do you need to deal with? For example, if you are proposing a local traffic management plan you will need to explore its effect on the environment, the availability of parking and its effect on residents. List these issues, then create a preliminary outline of headings – that is, your plan for writing. As you formulate assumptions or propositions, check their accuracy and relevance to the report's purpose.

Identify the issues involved.

Step 4 Collect the information

After identifying the relevant issues, find sources of information on each. Gather information from primary and secondary sources, checking that they are credible and reliable. Review Chapter 14 for further details on researching primary and secondary sources of information.

Step 5 Sort and evaluate the information

During this stage you will sort the material you have gathered before placing it in sequence, or order. Four kinds of outlines are discussed in Chapter 15, Organise Workplace Information – the traditional, tree, triangle and Mind Map® outlines. Any one of these may be used in the planning stage of a long report.

Put aside irrelevant information.

Once information has been sorted, review your material. Highlight key words and your most important material, and place it in a working file. Put irrelevant information into another file to be checked later. It is unwise to throw out any details until the report is finished. Check your information is sufficient to achieve the report's purpose.

As you evaluate the information try to answer the following questions.

1. Does the evidence relate to the report's purpose and provide objective information?
2. Does the evidence I have gathered answer the right questions?
3. Does the information provide a clear, concise, consistent and complete picture?
4. Are my sources of information credible?

Step 6 Prepare the outline

The sequence of information varies according to what the report presents. However, in each case your outline must present your data in a logical sequence. Organise all your information into sections, under the headings you have chosen. Then see whether any section could be subdivided, under subheadings. In the report on local traffic management, for example, there may be a major section on 'Current Traffic Problems'. As you plan this section you may decide to have a subsection, 'Peak Hour Congestion'.

Decide on a logical sequence of headings.

Organise information under appropriate headings.

Organising information

Information can be arranged logically as follows:

■ chronological sequence (a time progression)

- order of importance (from most important to least important, or from least to most important)
- geographical identity (e.g. by states)
- inductive order (from the general to the specific)
- deductive order (from the specific to the general)
- from cause to effect
- a problem-solving method.

In the planning stage an outline guides your investigation.

If you were preparing an **outline** for the local traffic management plan, for example, you may choose the chronological sequence, identifying problems as they occurred over the last five years, starting from the first year. Alternatively, you may choose the problem-solving order: identifying the nature of the problem, its causes and possible solutions.

Organise your material according to the preliminary outline of headings you created earlier. Your task now is to be sure that you are ready to prepare the writing outline for your report. Determine this by considering the whole picture. How do ideas link together? Are there any gaps in the information? What headings are the most important? If you are dissatisfied with your preliminary outline, revise it and include new topics to replace those that are no longer relevant.

The outline you prepare at this stage is crucial. It provides you with the structure of the main body or text of the report, and enables you to present your information logically and clearly.

Order of presentation

Sequence the information to suit your writing purpose.

Your decision about the sequence of the introductory, central and final sections of the main text is largely determined by the purpose and nature of your report. It is a decision you may take after you have written it, but remember – how you organise the report affects how it is received and whether action is taken. If you are trying to persuade a reluctant reader that restructuring in the workplace is essential, you will choose a different sequence from the one you would use if you are endorsing a proposal to which the reader is already committed.

Indirect order of information

Use the indirect order of information when the report gives bad news or news different from the receiver's opinion.

The indirect order of information in the main body or text of a long report is suited to a reader who may resist the conclusions, or will not understand the conclusions and recommendations until the whole text or main body has been read. The indirect order of information usually starts the main body with an introductory section followed by the centre section and then the final section. The indirect order of information used in the body of the Fairways Golf Club report (see Figure 20.11) is the most common indirect order. It follows this order:

- introductory section
- central section
- final section with the conclusions followed by the recommendations.

This indirect order introduces your readers to what you are about to do and why, and to the limits of the report. Readers are then led through the central section and on to the conclusions and recommendations. By reading the findings in the central section of the report first they are able to understand the reasons for the conclusions and recommendations.

Direct order of information

The direct order is more appropriate when the receiver is knowledgeable about the subject and likely to understand the conclusions without having to read the whole text of the report. Two direct orders of information are shown in Table 20.2.

Use the direct order of information for an expert reader.

Table 20.2 Two direct orders of information for the main text

Choice 1	Choice 2
Introductory section	Final section with conclusion(s) first, followed by the recommendation(s)
Final section with conclusion(s) first, followed by recommendation(s)	Introductory section
Central section	Central section

Choice 1 starts the main text or body with the introductory section, followed immediately by the final section (conclusions and recommendations) and then the central section with the full details of your findings.

Choice 2 is the order to use when writing to an expert. It allows you to present an overview and your conclusions first. You follow with the recommendations, then the introductory section to the central section that contains the body of information supporting the conclusions (findings) and recommendations. This direct order focuses the reader's attention on the conclusions and recommendations first.

Once you have chosen a sequence and outline that suits your purpose and your reader's needs, the planning of your report is complete. Your task now is to write the main text or body of the long report and prepare its additional components.

Writing the long report

At the writing stage of a long report, your first task is to produce the body or main text. It contains the introduction to the findings, the body of your findings, your conclusions and recommendations.

Writing style

The principles of an appropriate report-writing style apply to all sections of the report. **'Writing style'** means how the report writer uses words, sentences and paragraphs to present ideas to the reader. A person's report-writing style may be described as crisp and clear, verbose, academic, theoretical, factual or businesslike.

Report-writing style avoids emotional language.

Although plain English is suitable for most business writing, overuse of the 'you' approach is unsuitable for long reports. The language in a long report is more formal and should present facts and information as objectively as possible (see Table 20.3). The impersonal objective approach is more suited to a long report than the personal 'you' approach. The impersonal approach removes all reference to 'I', 'we', 'us', 'our' and 'you'. Take care, however, to limit your use of the passive voice as it can make a document dull and wordy.

Table 20.3 Personal/impersonal language in a long report

The personal 'you' approach	The impersonal approach
I undertook research	Research was undertaken
My results were	The research results demonstrated
I found that	The findings are
My recommendations are	It is recommended that

CHECK 20.1
SELF

Appropriate use of language in report writing

How does your writing rate? Is it	Yes	No	Unsure
appropriate to the report's purpose?	☐	☐	☐
courteous?	☐	☐	☐
easily understood?	☐	☐	☐
concise?	☐	☐	☐
non-sexist, non-racist and inclusive?	☐	☐	☐
suited to the reader's needs?	☐	☐	☐

Using technology

Technology has revolutionised the way in which writers research, plan, write and edit their work. It has also revolutionised the way organisations present their information. Word processing, facsimile machines, email and the Internet have changed the nature of communication.

Software packages such as Word, Excel and PowerPoint are designed to share information. In the report-writing stage you can insert an Excel chart or a PowerPoint slide into a Word document. The ability to move information between packages makes the report-writing task easier.

Formatting and outlining

Use the features in software packages effectively.

You can format and create the outline for the body of a report with the built-in Word styles. The Format menu in word-processing packages provides options for formatting paragraphs, bullets and numbering, borders and shading, columns and changing case. Other standard menus such as Edit and Insert let you cut, copy and paste material as you write. By using the software packages to their full capacity, you can structure, format, write and edit your long report more effectively.

Additionally, PowerPoint slides can be inserted into a long report to provide graphic presentation. Use PowerPoint to format original ideas and information in the graphic or insert a piece of clip art.

Efficiency

Organisations need to access data and make decisions quickly. Technology allows relevant information such as long reports to be forwarded immediately within and outside the organisation. Reports can be forwarded internally through the intranet or to institutions outside the organisation via the Internet or fax machine. (See Chapter 17, Communicating through Technology, for the uses of information technology and the principles involved in writing online documents.) Competent use of the technology and its packages improves your efficiency and effectiveness as a report writer.

Readability and credibility

You need your readers to respond to the message in your report so you want them to understand its contents and be able to implement the recommended action. As well as being sufficient to document and explain the problem, the evidence and facts in the report must come from reliable and credible sources. As your readers expect a report to have information presented objectively and organised under headings follow these **conventions**. Information should be presented in the most useful way for your readers.

Headings

Headings highlight the main ideas and give them an order that suits the purpose of the report and helps the reader. Bovée and Thill state, 'When wording outlines you must choose between descriptive (topical) and informative (talking) headings . . . descriptive headings label the subject . . . informative headings (in either question or summary form) suggest more about the meaning of the issues.' (p. 370). In Figure 20.1, the heading *Cost Comparison of Existing and Proposed Watering Systems* is a descriptive heading.

Well chosen headings lead readers through the report's structure so that they can identify its content and order easily. For example, Section 2 of the Fairways Golf Club report shown in Figure 20.1 is divided into four levels of heading. The first and largest heading, 2.0, is bold and upper case. The second heading, 2.1, is bold with upper case initials. The third heading, 2.1.1, is lower case. The fourth heading, 2.1.1.1, is lower case. The intention is to show the reader that a completely new section is beginning, with subsections within it.

Headings should be used for each new aspect of the content, to break the text into manageable sections. Pages without headings make it hard to find information quickly.

Numbering systems

Choose a numbering system that suits your document. Numbers and headings give the reader an outline that makes reading and reference easy. Figure 20.1 is an example of a decimal numbering system. An example of an alphanumeric system is shown in Figure 22.1 in Chapter 22, Writing Technical Documents. By using multi-level numbering or outlining in your word-processing package, you can renumber and make changes easily.

Statistics

Check statistics for relevance and reliability. Statistics collected by the Australian Bureau of Statistics (ABS) carry more authority than those collected personally. ABS statistics provide objective, accurate information. For example, the ABS Consumer Price Index figures are compiled from a survey of thousands of items and placed into a simple format. Conclusions (e.g. on the rate of inflation) can then be drawn from these figures.

Graphics

Graphics in the central section can add meaning and emphasis to your report. However, if they could distract readers from the argument or interrupt the progression of ideas, place them in an appendix. Once you decide to use a graphic in the main text, draw the reader's attention to it by following this three-step method:

Graphics create interest.

1. Refer to the graphic in the text.
2. Explain how the graphic relates to the information.
3. Place the graphic or diagram immediately after this reference and explanation.

Figure 20.1 Numbering system for Section 2 of the Fairways Golf Club report

---

2.0 COST COMPARISON OF EXISTING AND PROPOSED WATERING SYSTEMS

2.1 Costs of Existing System
    2.1.1 Current operating costs
        2.1.1.1 Greenkeeping
        2.1.1.2 Water Board usage charges
        2.1.1.3 Electricity
        2.1.1.4 Maintenance
        2.1.1.5 Staffing

2.2 Costs of Proposed System
    2.2.1 Installation costs
        2.2.1.1 Installing pump machinery, cables and machinery housing
        2.2.1.2 Landscaping
    2.2.2 Anticipated operating costs
        2.2.2.1 Greenkeeping
        2.2.2.2 Water Board charges
        2.2.2.3 Electricity
        2.2.2.4 Maintenance
        2.2.2.5 Staffing

Use only graphics or diagrams that add meaning and interest to your report. When and how to use business graphics is discussed further in Chapter 21, Graphic Communication.

Notations

If you use author–date references, endnotes or footnotes to direct the reader to extra sources of information or views on the topic, make sure that all these are accurate and complete. All sources should be fully acknowledged in the list of references or bibliography. If your information cannot be traced and checked, it loses credibility. Refer to Chapter 14, Analyse and Present Research Information, for more about notation.

Additional parts

After the text is written you will prepare a range of additional parts that appear either before or after the main text. Details about these additional parts and a suggested sequence to follow as you write them are given in Figure 20.2.

Figure 20.2 Sequence of parts when writing a long report

You complete a sequence of steps when writing a long report:
1. Create an outline. Include the major headings and subheadings.
2. Write the purpose statement.
3. Write the introductory section of the main text.
4. Write the central section of the main text or body.
5. Draw and write the conclusions from the information you have gathered. As you write, relate these to the purpose you defined for the report.
6. Write the recommendations.
7. Prepare an executive summary, abstract or synopsis *after* presenting facts and findings.
8. Construct a list of references or bibliography as you research, plan and write the report. Each time you use a source of information, add it to the references or bibliography.
9. Construct the table of contents and the table of illustrations. Place items in the order they appear in the report.
10. Write the letter of transmittal.
11. Prepare the title page to complete your report.

Formatting the long report

While the format should suit the purpose and nature of the report you must also follow the in-house style of your organisation and its formal report-writing conventions. Organisations and individuals have tried out and adjusted report formats for years. An effective format achieves a professional appearance and smooth transfer of information.

Parts of a long report

The parts of a long report can be grouped into three sections: **front matter**, **body** and **end matter**. Plan and write the long report around these and your task will be completed more efficiently. Many writers find there is less need to write and rewrite if they place their information in the correct sections as they go (Table 20.4). All the possible parts of a long report are presented in Figure 20.3.

Table 20.4 The three main sections of a long report

Section	Essential parts	Optional parts
Front matter	■ title page ■ letter of transmittal ■ table of contents	■ list of tables ■ list of figures ■ abstract or synopsis or executive summary ■ authorisation document
Body (text)	■ introduction ■ discussion and analysis of the report's findings ■ development of ideas ■ conclusions ■ recommendations	■ tables ■ graphics
End matter	■ bibliography	■ appendix ■ glossary ■ index

Front matter

In the format used in the Fairways Golf Club report, the parts placed before the main text are the title page, letter of transmittal, authorisation document (letter or memo), table of contents, list of illustrations and executive summary. These make up the front matter.

The front matter consists of the preliminary parts that appear before the body.

Title page

On the **title page** include the long report's title, the name of the person who authorised the report and their organisation. Usually, the report is submitted to this person. Also include the name and designation of the report writer and the date of submission. Create a title that indicates the purpose and nature of the report. For a report that is to be distributed to other departments, sections or staff members, indicate these on the title page. Figure 20.4 shows a sample title page.

Figure 20.3 Parts of a long formal report

Part	Purpose
Title page	Identifies the report's title, the receiver's name and title, the writer's name and title and the date.
Letter of transmittal	Indicates in the form of a formal covering letter the person who authorised or requested the report, the terms of reference, the scope of the report and problems addressed. It serves as a record of transmittal, identifies the writer and acknowledges others who contributed.
Terms of reference	State clearly and concisely the scope of the report.
Acknowledgments	List the names of persons and institutions who assisted in preparing the report.
Table of contents	Records the name of each part of the report and the name of each first and second order heading within the body and the page on which each occurs.
List of figures/tables	Records page numbers of tables, illustrations and diagrams.
Executive summary	Provides the reader with a brief summary of the material in the main text of the report. It includes the report's purpose, scope, methods, findings and conclusions.
Synopsis or abstract	Provides a brief description or informative overview of the report's most important points.
Glossary	Defines and explains technical words.
Body: introductory section	Defines the research task and problem and includes: ■ the purpose statement ■ background information ■ scope, aims, limits of the report, size and complexity ■ authorisation – when, how and by whom.
Body: central section	Presents factual, objective information. Analyses and discusses findings and evidence presented. Uses headings and a numbering system to signal to the reader when new ideas are to be introduced and developed. Includes enough detail to support conclusions and recommendations.
Body: final section Conclusion	Provides an analysis of the report's findings and evaluates the main facts.
Recommendations	Offers reasoned and logical solutions or courses of action.
Signature block	Contains the signature, name and job title of the writer; usually placed after the recommendations and before the appendices and bibliography.
Appendices and attachments	Present additional details and material such as charts and tables that are relevant to the report.
References and bibliography	References list the sources of the information quoted in the text. The bibliography contains recommended reading material on the subjects covered in the report, or other relevant subjects. The list of references and further reading are often presented together and called either 'References' or 'Bibliography'.

Figure 20.4 Title page for the Fairways Golf Club report

Proposed New Watering

System for

Fairways Golf Club

Prepared for
Mr John Cunningham
Hon. President
Fairways Golf Club

Prepared by
Alan Westbury
Secretary/Manager
Fairways Golf Club
28 October 2003

Letter of transmittal

The **letter of transmittal** is the covering letter for the report. It is set out in block business letter format and addressed to the person who authorised or requested the report. The date is important, as it is the formal way of stating that the report has been completed as requested, within the terms of reference and by a certain date. Figure 20.5 shows an example.

In the letter of transmittal, state who wrote the report and thank any others who worked on it. Indicate the purpose and scope of the report. Remember that the letter of transmittal may be the first part of the report to be read, so use it to impress.

Authorisation document

The memo of authorisation in Figure 20.6 identifies the scope of the report and the terms of reference. It also identifies who is authorising the report, the date the report is requested and the date the report is due.

Table of contents

Include the main sections and subsections of the report in the **table of contents**. Check that the numbering system for the main section headings and subheadings of the body is easy to use. Indicate the page number on which each main heading appears. In a

Figure 20.5 Letter of transmittal for the Fairways Golf Club report

FAIRWAYS GOLF CLUB

Driveway Avenue, Merrylands Vic 3055
Tel/Fax: 03 6653 2948 Email: fairgolf@blue.com.au

28 October 2003

Mr John Cunningham
Hon. President
Fairways Golf Club
Driveway Avenue
MERRYLANDS VIC 3055

Dear John

Here is the report you requested on 3 July on the proposed new watering system for the golf club.

I have detailed in this report an examination of the differences between the existing watering system and the proposed system. I have included a cost effectiveness analysis as well as a detailed comparison of the physical and engineering differences of the two systems.

Additionally, I have included an analysis of the possible effect on golfers and the results of a survey of golf club staff, golfers and nearby residents. The County Council's requirements and the results of an inspection of the new watering system in operation at the Riverview Golf Club are also detailed.

My recommendation is that the Golf Club should postpone implementation of this system until other options are considered.

Please contact me if you have any questions regarding this report.

Yours sincerely

Alan Westbury
Secretary/Manager

---

formal report, the page numbers for the front matter are written in lower case roman numerals (i, ii, iii, iv, etc.). The page numbers for the remainder of the report are written as arabic numerals (1, 2, 3, etc.). An example of a table of contents for the Fairways Golf Club report is shown in Figure 20.7.

List of illustrations

Use visuals to improve understanding.

Visual aids such as tables, figures, maps and diagrams are used in reports because they are easy to understand. Business reports may refer to all visual aids as illustrations or exhibits in the table of contents. When only a few illustrations are used, place the list of illustrations straight after the table of contents. If you include a large number, start a new page for the list.

The list of illustrations in Figure 20.7 gives their titles and page numbers. It is included in the table of contents because there are only four illustrations. Use a new

Figure 20.6 Example of authorisation document or terms of reference

To:	Alan Westbury, Secretary/Manager
From:	John Cunningham Hon. President
Date:	3 July 2003
Subject:	Proposed new watering system for Fairways Golf Club

The Board authorises you to submit a report on the proposed new watering system for the Golf Club discussed at our last meeting.

We require you to compare the existing system and the proposed new system in terms of cost effectiveness as well as any physical or engineering differences. Additionally, an analysis of the possible effects on golfers and nearby residents is required.

The County Council should be contacted for their comments regarding any environmental requirements.

Also include your findings resulting from an inspection of the proposed new system already in operation at another golf course.

The Board would like this report submitted by 30 October 2003.

Figure 20.7 Table of contents for the Fairways Golf Club report

Table of Contents

An executive summary is an essential part.

page if there is not enough room under the table of contents. If you decide to number tables and figures separately, create two separate lists – a list of tables and a list of figures.

Executive summary

Business reports usually have an **executive summary** rather than a synopsis or abstract. Putnis and Petelin state, 'A summary should be an acceptable substitute for the whole report.' (p. 410). It states your reasons for writing the report and gives a brief outline (half to one page) of the report's purpose, scope, methods, findings and conclusions. This helps non-expert readers to grasp the topic. When you are writing a very long report, the executive summary may be longer than this, but no more than two pages.

An executive summary is one of the essential components of a long business report. It may be the only part of a long report read by people who are too busy to read the whole report. Bovée and Thill state, 'So an executive summary is more comprehensive than a synopsis, often as much as 10% as long as the report itself.' (p. 517).

Figure 20.8 is the executive summary for the Fairways Gold Club report.

Figure. 20.8 Executive summary for the Fairways Gold Club report

Executive Summary

This report was commissioned by the Fairways Golf Club to study the effects of the introduction of a new watering system at the golf club. This new system is based on recycling effluent to irrigate the greens.

A detailed examination was made of the differences between the existing watering system and the proposed system. This entailed a cost effectiveness analysis as well as a comparison of the physical and engineering differences of the two systems. Advantages and disadvantages for golfers were analysed. The study also examined the proposed new system in operation at another golf course.

A survey was conducted to ascertain the views of golf club staff, golfers and nearby residents. An informal meeting with nearby residents to discuss the survey was also held. The County Council was contacted for comment.

The study concluded that the new system was beneficial in terms of cost and effectiveness. However, there were negative effects that outweighed the positive benefits. The staff, golfers and nearby residents were opposed to the introduction of the new system on the basis of possible health issues, odour, machinery noise, visual pollution, lowered house values and possible drainage problems. The City Council was of the opinion that the system could impact detrimentally on the environment and an Environmental Impact Statement would be required.

The recommendation is that the Golf Club postpone the implementation of this system until other options are considered.

Synopsis (abstract)

Bovée and Thill say, 'A **synopsis** is a brief overview (one page or less) of a report's most important points . . . Because it's a concise representation of the whole report, it may be distributed separately to a wide audience.' (p. 516). Depending on the report's intended audience, a synopsis can be either descriptive or informative.

An *informative synopsis* is suited to a report using the direct order of information. As the informative synopsis focuses on the key points and conclusions the receivers know these directly before they read the long report.

A *descriptive synopsis* describes what the report is about in slightly more detail than the table of contents. It is suited to a report using the indirect order of information because it does not give the report's findings and conclusions before the readers have read the report's main text. The indirect order of information in the main text of a long report leads the reader through the introductory section and central section to the final section with the conclusions and recommendations.

A synopsis can also be called an **abstract**. The term 'abstract' is more commonly used in articles in academic journals than business reports.

The synopsis or abstract is well suited to a long information report. It improves a long technical, professional or academic report by providing a concise overview of the whole report.

The decision to include an executive summary, synopsis or abstract is determined by your organisation's in-house style. If there is no in-house style, make the choice on the basis of your report's purpose and intended audience.

Body or text

The largest part of a long report is the body or **text**. Plan and write this in three sections:

1. introductory section
2. central section
3. final section.

Organise the body or text into three sections.

Your task is to present your ideas clearly for the reader. For this reason, use headings and subheadings to divide your material into manageable sections. Use plenty of spacing; otherwise, material becomes too dense on the page and therefore more difficult to read.

Introductory section of the main text

The **introduction** defines the report's main task or topic, so it makes sense to begin it with the purpose statement. It is helpful to think clearly about the goals of the report and to state these next. Then present the terms of reference. As they are the instructions for writing the report, they should be available to both writer and reader.

Finally, state the report's **scope** (limits). For example, you may decide that a report on 'Information Technology in Australia' is too broad for your purpose. You may prefer to limit your report to 'Information Technology in the Commercial Sector in New South Wales'. Let the reader know by stating this in the introductory section.

Figure 20.9 lists the parts of the introductory section. Figure 20.10 is the introductory section of the main text of the Fairways Golf Club report.

Central section of the main text

When you are producing the central section of the body (or text) of the long report, focus on the report's purpose by continually asking yourself: 'What am I reporting on?' Then write according to your outline and the order of information you have decided on. If the outline is causing difficulties – for example, by giving undue weight to a particular issue, or introducing issues that are not vital to the report – revise it. Do this by reconsidering the report's purpose, scope and findings.

As you are creating a report, not an essay or narrative, take care to keep it factual, relevant, objective and up to date. This will help you argue your case convincingly. Subsections with headings order the information in the central section of a long report.

The central section of the report body usually investigates and analyses the **findings**, and proposes solutions for any problem involved. Aim to present a balanced, comprehensive view and to support your findings with documented evidence. Figure

Figure 20.9 Parts in the introductory section of the body of a long report

Part	When is it used?
Authorisation	In every case, except when the decision to prepare the report is the writer's own.
Problem	In every case where the report addresses a problem.
Purpose	In every case.
Scope	In every case.
Methodology	In every case.
Sources	In every case, except when you are writing the report on the basis of your own experience.
Background	Only when it is necessary for the reader to have the background information to understand the findings presented in the report.
Definition of terms	Only when technical or unfamiliar terms are used in the report. Even then, it may be better to place the definitions in a glossary at the end of the report.
Limitations	In every case where constraints such as available information, research assistance, time or money have limited the extent of research.
Brief statement of results	Only when the conclusions and recommendations are placed at the end of the body of the report.

Figure 20.10 Introductory section of the main text of the Fairways Golf Club report

1.0 INTRODUCTION

Fairways Golf Club has endeavoured to ensure that the most efficient and cost-effective watering system has been used to keep the golf course in the best condition for golfers.

Recent drought conditions have resulted in the greens requiring more water to maintain their current condition. However, increased Water Board charges have necessitated the club limiting the amount of water required for the greens. This has led to detrimental conditions for the golfers and golfer dissatisfaction. The club's aim is to make certain that the greens are maintained to golfer satisfaction. To ensure this under present conditions would incur additional Water Board costs. This would result in an increase in fees.

In the light of these anticipated increased costs, the Board of the Golf Club has requested an investigation into the effects of the introduction of a proposed new watering system at the golf club. This proposed system would reduce the amount of water necessary to irrigate the greens by incorporating recycled treated effluent.

This reports details the results of these investigations. The results show that, although the new system would be beneficial in terms of cost and effectiveness, there are negative effects that outweigh the positive benefits.

1.1 Purpose, Scope and Limitations
The purpose of this report is to analyse the differences between the existing system and the proposed system, the effects on golf club staff, golfers and nearby residents, and to determine whether the proposed new system should be introduced.

1.2 Sources and Methods
In preparing this report a cost effectiveness analysis as well as a detailed comparison of the physical and engineering differences of the two systems was made.

A survey was conducted to ascertain the views of golf club staff, golfers and nearby residents. An informal meeting was also held with the nearby residents to discuss the survey.

An analysis was made of the advantages and disadvantages to golfers. The City Council was contacted for comment and possible objections.

Inspection was made of the proposed new system in operation at Riverview Golf Club for comparison purposes.

20.11 (see page 404) is the central section of the main text of the Fairways Golf Club report.

As you research sources of information, distinguish between facts, opinions, beliefs and prejudice. Keep in mind that any source of information presents a case or a point of view. Analyse this point of view to determine whether it is based on fact or opinion. A **fact** can be determined to be true.

An **opinion** is a judgment, viewpoint or belief. As you develop your argument, present as much accurate, relevant information as you can. Consider how reliable your argument and conclusions are. Remember that opinions may be challenged. **Prejudice** is another term for bias, and sometimes indicates a person's refusal to examine or even acknowledge facts and evidence. Keep your report free of prejudice.

The statement 'Your new venture will be successful' expresses an *opinion* that may depend on one or more factors. One year later, an analysis of the new venture might reveal that it is *in fact* successful. Base business decisions on factual evidence, not on unsupported beliefs.

Present advantages and disadvantages in the body of your report to give balance to your work and point of view. Include all relevant information even if it is unpleasant or against your point of view. The findings may lead you to a new conclusion. To present only the information that suits your point of view is misleading. A situation considered from all angles allows greater understanding and can give new insights.

Develop a convincing **argument** by thinking clearly and then writing clearly. As you present the argument in writing, break it into three parts:

1. the givens
2. the operations
3. the goals.

The *givens* are what you know. The *operations* are the actions required to reach the goals, and the *goals* are what you hope to achieve. A convincing argument emphasises each part in a way that encourages the reader to agree with it. It must persuade readers to take a different course of action or change their attitude.

A convincing argument is sound, thoughtful and coherent. It expresses the writer's knowledge of the subject well, so that the reader can follow the ideas. Start by clearly identifying your purpose, then focus on the main points.

Be objective – that is, base your argument on accurate, relevant evidence. Facts that can be supported with statistics or other verifiable evidence are the most credible. Avoid making statements that depend on opinion or your own experience, values and beliefs.

> Present clear, well supported arguments.

If you support your opinions with facts collected in research, your argument will be more credible. When making assumptions, ensure that they are reasonable. Try to develop your own reasoning abilities, and base your conclusions on the evidence. Then, in the main part of the document, show how you have analysed the material. When several complex issues are involved, your task is more difficult. You need to show that you have thought about them all from various perspectives. Then your argument is thoughtful and balanced.

> Investigate all the issues involved.

As you present a particular issue and reason it through, keep all your arguments about it in one place. If you find that you come back to it after two or three paragraphs' discussion of another issue, reorganise your arguments so that they are all together.

> Highlight the relationships between ideas.

It is not enough simply to present information. An argument does more. Writers gather information, think about it, and then produce an argument that shows the relationships between their ideas, in order to make a proposition to the reader. The reader is asked to accept the writer's reasoning.

Clear logical
thinking
improves the
quality of your
writing.

Indicate criteria
clearly and
concisely.

List any alternative solutions and show clearly and concisely why you have chosen one in particular. Then make the propositions or recommendations that you hope will lead to action. As you write, look for central themes and connecting ideas that relate to your argument and to the recommendations you suggest.

Define and explain your criteria for evaluation clearly and concisely so that your readers can weigh up the evidence for themselves. Your argument can be presented by analysing, comparing, criticising, evaluating and summarising. Table 20.5 presents strategies you can use to develop a strong argument.

Avoid exaggeration and take care to present a balanced, non-biased view. Exaggeration is quickly recognised by the perceptive receiver. It can only diminish the credibility of your argument.

Table 20.5 Developing an argument in writing

Purpose	Strategy
Analyse	Identify and explain each element.
Compare	Show similarity or differences.
Distinguish	Point out the differences between two or more factors.
Illustrate	Make clear by written examples, diagrams, pictures or other devices.
Contrast	Show differences between two or more factors.
Criticise	Make judgments or show the relative merits of something.
Interpret	Explain or bring out the meaning.
Evaluate	Give a reasoned appraisal or assessment of something.
Summarise	Provide a brief account.
Justify	Demonstrate a satisfactory reason.

Figure 20.11 Central section of the body of the Fairways Golf Club report

---

2.0 COST COMPARISON OF EXISTING AND PROPOSED WATERING SYSTEMS

Costs of both the existing and proposed new watering systems were investigated. Initially, there would be the cost of installing the new system and additional landscaping. However, results showed that over subsequent years there would be considerable cost benefits in installing the new system that would compensate for the cost of installation.

The important difference is that the recycled treated effluent would considerably reduce Water Board charges, resulting in a large cost saving.

Since the commissioning of this report, advice has been received that a large engineering works is being closed. As the Water Board will not be supplying water on a large scale to this site, it is possible that the Water Board may consider supplying additional water to the golf course at a reduced rate.

2.1 Costs of Existing System

The existing system has been in operation for over thirty years. Currently, the overall costs of the existing system amount to $86 690 annually. This includes depreciation of equipment ($15 500) as well as the day-to-day operating costs listed below.

    2.1.1 Current operating costs
        2.1.1.1 Greenkeeping

Includes replacement of turf and fertilising, also petrol for mowers	2 505.00

        2.1.1.2 Water Board usage charges

Includes increased charges this year	11 685.00

        2.1.1.3 Electricity   5 000.00
        2.1.1.4 Maintenance

Includes lawnmower repairs and pumping equipment service calls	1 300.00

        2.1.1.5 Staffing

Includes salary of one greenkeeper and one apprentice	50 200.00

$70 690.00
Cont'd

2.2 Costs of Proposed System

The proposed system would incur initial costs of installing the pump machinery, cables, pipes, and housing for the machinery, as well as landscaping. The existing sprinkler system would be incorporated into the new watering system. The club presently has this amount available so it will not be necessary to obtain a loan. However, loss of interest on this amount should be taken into account.

Depreciation of equipment would be marginally higher. The anticipated operating costs are based on quoted figures from the Water Board and the installing company.

2.2.1	Installation costs	
	2.2.1.1 Installing pump machinery, cables and housing	200 000.00
	2.2.1.2 Landscaping	3 000.00
		$203 000.00
2.2.2	Anticipated operating costs	
	2.2.2.1 Greenkeeping	1 000.00
	2.2.2.2 Water Board charges	
	(costs reduced using the recycling process)	2 000.00
	2.2.2.3 Electricity	5 500.00
	2.2.2.4 Maintenance	
	(costs reduced owing to new equipment installed)	800.00
	2.2.2.5 Staffing	50 900.00
		$60 200.00

3.0 COMPARISON OF PHYSICAL AND ENGINEERING DIFFERENCES

There are considerable physical and engineering differences between the two systems. These are detailed below.

3.1 Physical Differences

The major physical differences would be in the installation of the plant to treat the effluent and the construction of plant housing. This would be situated near the tenth dam behind the sixth tee.

The housing for the new machinery would differ markedly from the present plant housing, which is small and unobtrusive. The new housing, a recycled shed, would be covered with treated pine lattice cladding to blend into the landscape. The housing roof cover would be Caulfield Green Colorbond zincalume custom orb roof cladding. (A sketch of the housing is shown below.)

Landscaping would be required to ensure minimal visual effect from the housing. A 'buffer' of native plantings would need to be created.

Figure 1 Sketch of machinery housing

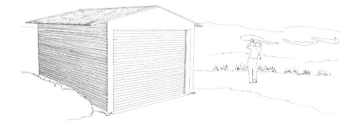

3.2 Engineering Differences

The main engineering difference between the two systems is in the transfer system to recycle the sewerage water. Cables would be laid underground from an access shaft in Salisbury Street and the effluent pumped to a plant on the golf course. The effluent would be treated by ozone to separate the contaminants. The contaminants would be discharged back into the sewer. The clean, treated water would then be pumped to the main storage dam before being distributed to other dams on the course. The treated effluent would be of a high quality, but marginally lower than the World Health Authority standard for drinking water.

The new system differs from the existing system in that the pumps would be in operation during night hours. Watering of the greens, however, would occur on the same cycle as presently exists.

4.0 ADVANTAGES AND DISADVANTAGES FOR GOLFERS

There are considerable advantages for golfers with the introduction of the proposed system. However, there are also some disadvantages that could affect golfers. Perceived advantages and disadvantages are listed below.

4.1 Advantages

The main benefit for golfers would be the improved condition of the greens, both in summer and winter. Additionally, the saving on Water Board charges would mean that fees could remain at their present level.

The savings made by the golf club would also result in the club being able to improve the clubhouse and its facilities. This would give golfers better amenities without the need to increase fees.

4.2 Disadvantages

There would be some disruption during the installation of the cables and machinery and the creation of new ponds. Attempts would be made to keep this at a minimum.

There may be some opposition from golfers to increased operating noise but, as most of the operations will be confined to evening hours, this should be minimal. The company supplying the new system has given assurance that the noise level will be within acceptable decibel levels.

The golfers may be opposed to treated effluent being used to water the greens. Signs will be erected advising golfers of this fact.

5.0 THE PROPOSED NEW SYSTEM IN OPERATION AT RIVERVIEW GOLF CLUB

The Secretary/Manager and head greenkeeper inspected the proposed system in operation at the Riverview Golf Club during August and September.

They also consulted the greenkeeper and manager of Riverview Golf Club regarding financial advantages for the club. They asked for comments or objections the club may have received from golfers and nearby residents relating to the new system.

5.1 Inspection Results

The irrigation of the golf course worked well. The greens were regularly watered and were of a high quality and a lush green.

There appeared to be no discernible noise effects from machinery operation.

5.2 Manager's and Greenkeeper's Comments

5.2.1 Financial savings

The manager reported that there had been considerable saving on water costs since the installation of the new system.

The recycling had greatly increased the club's ability to maintain the greens in an acceptable condition at much lower cost.

5.2.2 Golfers' and nearby residents' comments and/or objections

5.2.2.1 Golfers

According to the manager, there had been some adverse comments from golfers during the installation period. Golfers were at first reluctant to have treated effluent used as irrigation. However, golfers now appreciate the improved condition of the greens. They also appreciate the removal of the water levy imposed during the earlier drought period.

5.2.2.2 Nearby residents

Riverview Golf Club differs from Fairview Golf Club in that a large proportion of the green is adjacent to a river. As a result of this only a very small number of residents adjoin the golf course.

The machinery and housing is located near the riverbank away from any residential property.

The only objections from residents were in relation to run-off from the dams during a recent heavy rainfall and the fear of possible health problems from the treated effluent. Over four years of operation, there have been no health issues.

6.0 SURVEY RESULTS

Surveys were made of golf club staff, golfers and nearby residents. Additionally, an informal evening meeting was held to inform nearby residents of the reasons for the survey.

There was a 100% return from golf club staff. Of the golfers, the return was 20%. A very high percentage (89%) of the residents of the four streets adjoining the golf club returned completed surveys.

Overall, results showed that golf club staff and golfers were in favour of a new watering system. They appeared to have few objections to the proposed system. The main objection was in respect of the machinery housing.

Nearby residents, however, raised very strong objections to the introduction of this proposed watering system. They were concerned about possible odour and drainage problems. A particular concern was the likelihood of health risks if there was run-off from the golf course into their properties. Noise levels were also a problem, particularly as the machinery would operate mainly during evening hours. Visual pollution from the proposed machinery housing construction was an added concern. At the informal evening meeting they also expressed concerns about possible devaluation of their properties. Many had already lodged objections to the construction of the proposed new watering system directly to the City Council.

Cont'd

Survey results from the different groups are listed below and shown in the graphs.

6.1 Golf Club Staff (*n* = 14)

6.1.1 A majority of the staff (78.6%) were in favour of the introduction of a new watering system.

6.1.2 A small number (21.4%) were in favour of increasing fees and retaining the existing system.

6.1.3 Numbers were equally divided on the possibility of increased noise from the machinery of the proposed watering system.

6.1.4 A small majority (56.4%) were concerned with possible health problems.

6.1.5 A majority (85.7%) felt that the introduction of new clubhouse facilities and the improved condition of the greens would attract new members.

6.1.6 A large percentage (92.85%) considered that the machinery housing located near the ninth tee would be visual pollution.

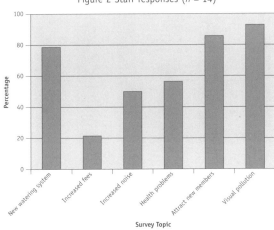

Figure 2 Staff responses (*n* = 14)

6.2 Golfers (*n* = 223)

6.2.1 A majority of the golfers (89.2%) were in favour of the introduction of a new watering system.

6.2.2 A very low percentage (10.3%) was in favour of increasing fees and retaining the existing system.

6.2.3 A slight majority (53.36%) felt that there could be noise pollution.

6.2.4 A significant number (78.4%) felt that there was a heath risk.

6.2.5 Similar to golf club staff, the golfers (89.6%) felt that the introduction of new clubhouse facilities and the improved condition of the greens would attract new members.

6.2.6 Similar to golf club staff, 99% of the golfers felt that the machinery housing would be visual pollution.

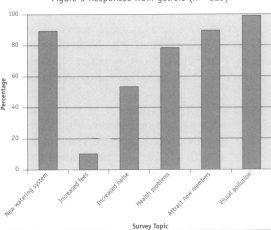

Figure 3 Responses from golfers (*n* = 223)

6.3 Nearby Residents (*n* = 98)

6.3.1 96% of residents were opposed to the introduction of the new system.

6.3.2 100% were in favour of increasing the fees.

6.3.3 Numbers were equally divided on the possibility of increased noise from the machinery of the proposed watering system.

6.3.4 A large majority (96%) felt there was a health risk.

6.3.5 75% felt that the introduction of new clubhouse facilities and greens would attract new members.

6.3.6 90% felt that the machinery housing would be visual pollution.

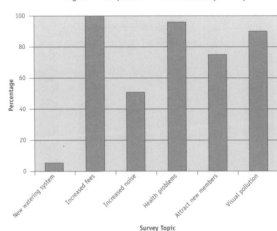

Figure 4 Responses from residents (*n* = 98)

7.0 CITY COUNCIL REQUIREMENTS

The City Council was contacted to ascertain if there were any objections to the implementation of the proposed new watering system based on recycling treated effluent. Detailed plans of the proposed system were submitted.

The City Council's engineers inspected the golf course and consulted golf club management.

After the inspection, a letter was received from the City Council stating that there were concerns about the introduction of this system. They were of the opinion that there could be detrimental effects. They have requested an Environmental Impact Statement before any consideration of the implementation of the proposed watering system.

Final section of the main text

The final section of the body of the long report contains the conclusions and recommendations. Set these out as separate subsections. However, placing your conclusions in the final section is a matter of choice. You may prefer to place them before the body of the report or, in some cases, even before the introduction. The sequence of introduction, body and conclusion is discussed earlier in this chapter in the section 'Planning a Long Report'.

The **conclusion** analyses and evaluates the report's main facts. It is usually short – half a page or so. Do not present new material in the conclusion. Figure 20.12 gives the conclusion to the Fairview Golf Club report. The findings in the report demonstrated that it would be cost-effective to install a new watering system at Fairways Golf Club. However, there would be considerable opposition from staff members, golfers and nearby residents. The local County Council also had objections. Your conclusion should reflect the report's findings.

Recommendations are the writer's attempt to provide at least some answers to questions and issues raised by the report. See the recommendations in Figure 20.12. They are based on the report's findings and are both reasoned and logical.

Recommendations flow logically from the conclusions.

Always relate the recommendations clearly to your analysis and the discussion set out in the body or text of the report. Then the reader can evaluate them against the report's purpose – that is, what it aims to do and why it was put together.

Present each recommendation as a separate point or paragraph, numbered and in descending order of importance. Clearly state what action is required. For example, if you recommend the Fairways Golf Club should postpone the implementation of the new watering system until other options are explored, you need to justify this with supporting evidence in the central section of the long report. Supporting tables are placed either in the body of the report or in an appendix, not in the final section. Also include in the body figures on items such as total outlay, borrowings and period of repayment, and relate these to figures for projected earnings and cash flow.

A useful strategy is to recommend a specific, achievable action plan. Then, if the reader agrees, your recommendations can be carried out more easily and quickly.

Recommendations are not needed if the long report is intended as a source of data for others who will be responsible for planning and recommendations.

Signature block

Report writers usually place their signature, name and job title in a signature block at the end of the final section of the main text, after the recommendations and before the appendices and bibliography. Sometimes the date is placed after the signature block. See Figure 20.12.

Figure 20.12 Conclusions, recommendations and signature block for the Fairways Golf Club Report

---

8.0 CONCLUSION

Although the new system is beneficial in terms of cost and effectiveness, the negative effects outweigh the positive benefits.

8.1 There is strong opposition from golf club staff, golfers and nearby residents that could lead to a loss of goodwill and long-term revenue on the basis of:
possible odour
health risk
machinery noise
possible drainage problems
lowering of land values.

8.2 The City Council requires an Environmental Impact Statement and this would have an impact on costing. Additionally, the City Council might impose conditions that would make the introduction of this system cost-prohibitive.

9.0 RECOMMENDATIONS

9.1 That installation of the proposed new system be postponed.
9.2 That other options be explored:
  9.2.1 Approaching the Water Board for a reduction in rates (closure of the large engineering works may make this a feasible option)
  9.2.2 Reviewing other watering systems currently available.

Alan Westbury

Alan Westbury
Secretary/Manager
Fairways Golf Club
28 October 2003

End matter

The end matter includes the appendix, glossary of terms and bibliography. These are placed after the final section of the body or main text of the long report.

Appendix

An **appendix** contains facts and findings that are useful but not vital to the main text. It may also contain information that is too long for a report section or highly technical. Examples of what can be placed in appendices include statistics, copies of surveys or questionnaires, graphs, charts and maps, and extracts from journals, newspapers or other reports.

Two or more appendices should be identified by numbers or letters (A, B, etc.). If you include an appendix, refer to it in the table of contents and at an appropriate place in the main body of the report.

Glossary

The **glossary** lists alphabetically special terms or phrases used in the report, and briefly explains each one. Refer to the Glossary in this book for an example.

Bibliography

As explained in Chapter 14, a **bibliography** sometimes lists all the references and sources of information along with background or recommended reading. However, some organisations and writers prefer to present a separate list of references for the information sources cited in the report, and a bibliography for background reading and information sources not cited in the report.

Editing the long report

Once the long report is written and presented, you want the reader to act on its findings, conclusions and recommendations. Any blocks in the communication flow between the writer and reader can prevent this from happening. The editing process will help you to check the report for accuracy, consistency and clarity.

The six-step approach

These six steps provide a systematic approach to editing. See also Self-check 20.2.

Step 1

Edit the long report to eliminate obscure or sexist language, unnecessary jargon and abbreviations. Delete any irrelevant information or repetition to make your report more concise. Rewrite any sentences that are too long, and avoid exaggeration as this irritates the reader and distorts the message. Also remove any imprecise expressions such as 'a terrific result' – this statement conveys very little. It is much better to say 'the percentage changes are high' or 'the figures and results are significant', and make sure that you have provided these figures in a graph or table near your statement or as an appendix.

Step 2

Revise and correct your report in the editing stage.

Correct any spelling, punctuation or grammatical errors to ensure that what you have written is clear at the first reading. Rewrite sentences that are poorly structured and check that they are concise.

Check that each paragraph has a concise topic sentence, and that each following point relates to it. Restructure paragraphs that lack unity and make sure that each one follows on logically from the previous one.

Step 3

Check that you have clearly identified in the introduction the scope of your report and your reasons for preparing for it. Edit so that the reader can find these in the first paragraph, and ensure that the report does in fact deliver what it sets out to do.

Step 4

Check for any unsupported opinions as these will cast doubt on your credibility as a report writer. Presenting factual, objective information with accurate references is an essential part of report writing. As you edit, make sure the arguments are logical and check the information for accuracy.

Step 5

Remove any extra information that is not vital to the main argument, findings or discussion. If it is still useful, put it in an appendix or endnote. Extra information in the body of the report can distract the reader and interrupt the progression of ideas.

Step 6

Edit the layout or format of the report. Check the sequence of information and ideas, and the numbering of sections. In addition, check that each essential component of a long report is included and achieves its purpose.

Long reports

1. a. In groups of three, discuss the following statement.

   If you can answer questions such as what the report will do, how it is to be prepared, why it has been requested and when it will be completed, you will have defined the purpose and scope of your report.

   As you discuss the statement, take note of the terms 'purpose' and 'scope'.

   b. In your group of three, discuss the following statement.

   The purpose statement is the most important component of the introductory section of the report. It conveys the report's purpose to the reader. Other words that can be substituted for the term 'purpose statement' are 'goal', 'aim' or 'objective'.

   c. On your own, write a purpose statement for a long report that aims to investigate student amenities provided at your college. Compare your purpose statements.

2. Discuss three ways in which an outline and headings can improve a report's capacity to communicate.

3. Find a long report in the library or at work. Evaluate the report by answering these questions.
   a. What improvements could you make to the title page?
   b. Does the report use an executive summary? Is it a suitable length?
   c. Is the table of contents well constructed?
   d. What headings does the report have? Are they suitable?
   e. What is its order of presentation?
   f. Is the conclusion well written and convincing?
   g. Use Self-check 20.2 to analyse the report you used.
   h. Can you suggest any changes or improvements?

APPLY SKILLS

CHECK 20.2
SELF

Editing a long formal report

Have I	Yes	No	Unsure
identified the report's purpose clearly?	☐	☐	☐
fulfilled the purpose statement?	☐	☐	☐
used the correct long-report format?	☐	☐	☐
written an introduction that:			
a. explains the report's purpose?	☐	☐	☐
b. defines the main issues?	☐	☐	☐
c. guides the reader to the main section (body) of the report?	☐	☐	☐
presented a main section that:			
a. has headings and perhaps subheadings?	☐	☐	☐
b. uses language appropriate to the report's purpose, content and readers?	☐	☐	☐
c. progresses in well connected paragraphs?	☐	☐	☐
d. presents factual and objective information?	☐	☐	☐
e. analyses the findings?	☐	☐	☐
written a conclusion that:			
a. draws the main points together?	☐	☐	☐
b. summarises all the material?	☐	☐	☐
recommended solutions to any problems in the body?	☐	☐	☐

WISE
WEB

Visit the Companion Website at **www.prenhall.com/dwyer_au**. Choose the Good Practice/Bad Practice activity in Chapter 20 to develop a best practice checklist to assist a long-report writer to evaluate their report.

Chapter summary

Identify the purpose of a report. This must be clear in the writer's mind before work is started, and presented in the introduction.

Determine the main issues of the report. These should be set out clearly for the reader. At the planning stage of writing the report, base your preliminary outline of headings on these issues.

Organise material according to purpose, audience and context. Before you write the report, decide on the order of information. The indirect order is used when the reader may disagree with your conclusions or not understand them until the main text of the report is read. The direct order is suited to a report prepared for a receiver who has the background to understand it, or is too busy to read the whole report. When the conclusions contain good news the direct order is appropriate.

Use technology. Many word-processing features such as built-in Word styles and menus will help you structure, format and write your reports. The intranet can be used for faster internal distribution of the report and the fax and Internet for distribution to outside organisations. Use PowerPoint for better visual presentation.

Format a long report. The standard long-report format consists of three sections: front matter, body and end matter. The reader of a long report expects it to follow this format.

Use language suitable for the task and audience. Your report is often the only communication you have with those who read it. Therefore, use a report-writing style that is clear, readable, factual and relevant. The writing style should also be impersonal and avoid repetition and redundancy. A report that is too wordy is often obscure and difficult for the reader to understand.

Develop an argument logically. Break a problem into givens, operations and goals. Present objective supporting evidence. Write the body of your report in a way that is thoughtful and coherent, to demonstrate all the work you have put into gathering material and thinking about it. In this way, you may persuade your readers to change their mind, or take the action you recommend. Show clearly how your argument or analysis develops by using headings and a numbering system to connect ideas and to give structure to your argument. Remember always to acknowledge your sources of information fully.

Present solutions that are based on the evidence. A report gathers factual information and makes findings on the basis of the information. In the discussion of the findings in the body of the report, you investigate and analyse the findings. The solutions should follow from the analysis of the evidence and ideas.

Evaluate your solutions objectively. By keeping the purpose in mind and gathering appropriate information, you will be equipped to write a report that is easy for readers to understand. You will also be better placed to check the likely outcome of the solutions and their relevance to the report and its purpose.

Write the conclusions. This should round up the main information and arguments of the report. It helps the reader to grasp the report's main points.

Offer appropriate recommendations. These are your suggestions or solutions. They should be specific and realistic. Others should be able to base their decisions and/or actions on them.

Edit a report. Aim for accuracy, objectivity and completeness. Check the structure and writing style for logic, clarity and conciseness. As a long report is a formal document, it requires a professional and appropriate form of presentation.

QUESTIONS
REVIEW

1. What is the purpose of planning a long report?
2. What are the seven steps of this planning process?
3. Identify four ways of organising information for a long report.
4. List two different sequences for presenting the introduction, body, conclusions and recommendations in a long report. Briefly explain the reasons for using different sequences.
5. Define the following terms and explain one purpose for each:
   a. table of contents
   b. bibliography
   c. title page
   d. appendix
   e. letter of transmittal
   f. summary
   g. conclusions
   h. recommendations.
6. Identify how technology assists in the distribution and presentation of a report.
7. Explain the difference between the front matter and the introductory section of the body of a long report.
8. Name the parts of the report that belong to the:
   a. front matter
   b. body, or main section
   c. end matter.
9. Define the term 'purpose statement'.

10. Choose one of the following statements:
    a. The sport of rugby league is now a carefully marketed commodity.
    b. Essays are not a good way of communicating.
    c. Communication is the key to business success.
    d. A leader must understand how a team works.

    Write (in about one page) a convincing argument that supports or refutes the statement. Present arguments for and against the statement, and illustrate with factual examples.

11. Briefly explain the three-step method of drawing the reader's attention to a graphic.

12. Explain the difference between a long report's conclusions and its recommendations.

13. What is the difference between a long report's synopsis and its conclusion?

14. List the six steps of the editing process.

15. Define the terms 'facts', 'opinion' and 'prejudice'.

16. What is the difference between an analysis and an evaluation?

Writing a long report

Prepare and plan a long report for the graduates of your study course. The topic is 'Job Availability for Graduates of this Course'. Provide information on all the job skills and qualifications required, positions available, practical experience, career paths, salaries, other conditions of work and categories of employment.

Complete the following steps.
a. Identify your most likely sources of information and research the topic.
b. Prepare a purpose statement.
c. Prepare an outline of the report's structure.
d. Write the first draft.
e. Submit a short progress report to your teacher halfway through the report-writing project.
f. Write the long report.
g. Use each essential part of a long formal report as you set it out.
h. Edit the report by using Self-check 20.2.

Key terms

abstract	findings	prejudice
appendix	front matter	purpose
argument	glossary	recommendations
bibliography	graphics	scope
body	headings	synopsis
conclusion	introduction	table of contents
conventions	letter of transmittal	technology
end matter	long report	text
executive summary	opinion	title page
fact	outline	writing style

Tips for electronic documents

While a recent survey of electronic versions of Commonwealth agencies' annual reports found that standards of online reporting are rising, it also revealed that some conventions are not being followed, thereby reducing the effectiveness of Internet publications. There are several conventions applicable to electronic publications, designed to benefit the reader. As with any conventions, as users become familiar with them they develop expectations of what information they will get and how it will be presented.

Electronic documents or publications should conform to the following conventions:

■ Clearly identify the author and publisher. The logo of the publisher – be it a government department or agency, or commercial entity – should be placed in a prominent position on the opening page.
■ Structure the document as a book formatted with each chapter on a separate 'Internet page'. Smaller pages are more user-friendly and also help to reduce the time taken to open each part of the document.
■ Give the publication its own International Standard Book Number (ISBN) different from that of any printed version. If, in addition, a portable document format (PDF) version of the publication is available, it too should have its own ISBN.
■ Display a copyright notice so that anyone wishing to use the information knows who owns the work and can readily contact the copyright owner.
■ Provide an index. Each document should have its own search facility, rather than relying on that of the website as a whole.
■ Create links to the front page from the top and bottom of every page; and a link between the bottom and top of each page.
■ Create links between every page and the contents list.

■ Indicate a feedback and contact mechanism in the document.
■ Insert a consistent masthead on every page. Keep this simple – the document name and essential links – to help minimise the time taken to open each part of the document.
■ Use links to other documents to provide access to further information. It is polite to seek permission before linking to another site.
■ Include metadata, the equivalent of Cataloguing in Publication (CiP) data in a book. Metadata will increase the probability of Internet browsers finding the document.
■ Say when the site was last updated.
■ Carefully read, edit and check the document before publishing it on the Internet. While it is true that Internet publications can be corrected easily, and that, unlike a traditional book, thousands of copies are not produced, mistakes can nevertheless be embarrassing.

Source: 'Tips for Electronic Documents', *Stylewise*, Vol. 7, No. 2, 2001, pp. 1, 4, Department of Finance and Administration. Copyright Commonwealth of Australia. Reproduced by permission.

Questions

The article says that, although '. . . a recent survey of electronic versions of Commonwealth agencies' annual reports found that standards of online reporting are rising . . . some conventions are not being followed'.

1. Why is it important to follow online standards for Internet publishing before submitting an annual report for publication on the Internet?
2. Why should an annual report use long-report writing conventions?
3. Explain the similarities and differences between a long report published on the Internet and a long report published as a paper-based bound copy.

Graphic communication

In this chapter you will learn how to:

- identify the purpose of the main types of graphics

- select an appropriate form of graphic

- describe what message each graphic conveys

- construct and place graphic material with appropriate lettering, numbering, text references and sources

- present graphic material to convey a specific message for a specific purpose.

Evaluate your communication skills by completing the self-check in the chapter.

The task of a writer is to collect, analyse and present information in a way that is intelligible and interesting to the reader. Frequently, this task involves discussing data that are crucial to the document, but difficult to explain clearly and concisely. Graphics enable the writer to incorporate these data so that they demonstrate the meaning simply and clearly.

Your own experience will tell you that 'graphics' means more than just graphs. Graphics include photographs, diagrams of assembly, graphs of escalating profits or foreign debt, pictures of people and places and cartoons.

Graphics use visual techniques to focus the reader's attention on the main points and to clarify discussion and findings. They reinforce written or spoken words and help the reader to connect the relationships between things and ideas. A designer of a graphic must determine what the most important concept is and how to illustrate it.

What do graphics do?

Graphics simplify complex information.

Graphics help to sort, classify and group data such as percentages, numbers and rates of change. They highlight trends and relationships, clarify technical ideas and emphasise important points. They are valuable for catching the reader's attention and for conveying complex information.

Graphics convey information visually, for a variety of purposes:

- to reinforce and complement written material
- to clarify complex material, particularly figures and statistics
- to show the total picture
- to clarify and link ideas expressed in text
- to catch the reader's attention
- to help the reader remember information.

Graphics should convey accurate, specific and up-to-date material.

Major types of graphics

A range of graphics is available to the report writer. Concepts, related data, trends, movement and changes in time, comparisons and spatial distributions can all be shown graphically. Some of the major types of graphics used in report writing are tables, line graphs, column graphs, bar graphs, dot graphs, pie charts, diagrams and drawings, photographs, illustrations and maps.

Each has particular strengths and weaknesses. The advantages and disadvantages of each are shown in Table 21.1. When you use graphics well, your ideas and information are complemented and are more easily understood by the reader.

Tables

Tables present precise data.

Tables present data, facts and figures. They can compare a large amount of data in a way that is easy to understand and emphasises similarities or differences.

Tables present related information in parallel lists or columns (see Table 21.2). In this form, relationships are shown more clearly and a table takes up much less space than a long description interspersed with figures. It is also easier to find specific figures in a table than from a string of sentences. The data in tables should be right-hand justified in each column as this makes it easy to read down the column. When tabled data are also graphed, the data and their relationships are further simplified.

Table 21.1 A comparison of different kinds of graphics

Graphic	Advantage	Disadvantage
Table	Allows comparisons between large amounts of data	Difficult to read and connect data quickly
Diagram	Emphasises details with a simple representation; can show a cross-section	Easy to miss the main point if the diagram becomes too cluttered with detail
Line graph	Indicates movement and trends in data clearly	Inappropriate labels and scales can make it difficult to interpret
Column or vertical bar graph	Simplifies comparisons between items, or periods	Size and proportions can be hard to interpret
Horizontal bar graph	Allows direct comparisons of size	Difficult to read if too many bars are grouped or stacked in one graph
Dot graph	Illustrates values quickly and easily	Awkward to read unless it progresses from the largest down to the smallest figure
Pie chart	Shows relative proportions and importance of each part to the whole unit	Difficult to judge differences between area and size
Photograph and illustration	Shows immediate impact of subject	Difficult to see the point if too much detail appears
Map	Shows a large amount of detail in one representation	Difficult to read if highly detailed or if the scales, legends and labels are not clear

Table 21.2 Population size and rate of growth for selected countries

	Population as at June		
Country	1999 million	2000 million	Increase %
Australia	18.9	19.2	1.2
China	1250.5	1261.8	0.9
Canada	31.0	31.3	1.0
Germany	82.6	82.8	0.3
Hong Kong (SAR of China)	7.0	7.1	1.8
India	997.9	1014.0	1.6
Indonesia	221.1	224.8	1.7
Japan	126.3	126.6	0.2
Korea, Republic of	47.0	47.5	0.9
New Zealand	3.8	3.8	0.5
Papua New Guinea	4.8	4.9	2.5
Singapore	4.0	4.2	3.6
Taiwan	22.0	22.2	0.8
United Kingdom	59.4	59.5	0.3
United States of America	273.1	275.6	0.9
World	**6002.5**	**6080.1**	**1.3**

Source: Australian Demographic Statistics (3101.0); Statistics New Zealand, National Population Estimates; US Bureau of the Census, International Data Base.

Tables make comparisons possible but graphs and charts explain, simplify and emphasise data and their key relationships even further.

Line graphs

Line graphs indicate trends.

Line graphs (charts) show movement through time. Their main purpose is to indicate trends. They do this by showing the rate at which specific items or values change over time (see Figure 21.1). When a line graph presents quantities, it marks the beginning point, called the *point of origin*. A vertical line and a horizontal line (the *axes*) are drawn at right angles to one another from this point of origin. Each point on the graph shows a relationship between the variables. These points occur in the space created by the axes, and are plotted wherever the two **variables** meet. The horizontal axis is usually referred to as the *x* axis and the vertical axis as the *y* axis.

Figure 21.1 A line graph showing population of Australia from 1788 to 2000

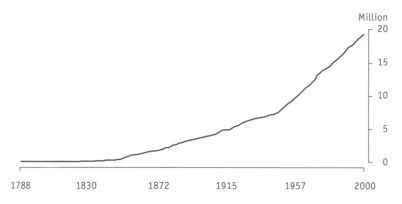

Source: *Official Year Book of the Commonwealth of Australia 1901–1910*; Australian Demographic Trends (3102.0); Australian Demographic Statistics (3101.0).

A line graph with only one line is known as a simple line chart (see Figure 21.1). If it has several lines it is called a multi-line chart, and should be limited to three or four lines. On all line graphs the data are plotted as points connected by segments of a line.

Column (vertical bar) graphs

Bar graphs compare one item with another.

Column (vertical bar) graphs are used to show changes from one time period to the next, or to compare one item with another. Their columns can be single, grouped or stacked. A 100% column chart shows the relative size of sections if a whole unit is broken up this way. This kind of information is best shown in grouped columns as it is more difficult for the eye to interpret size and proportions on a stacked bar graph.

Vertical bar graphs usually show a maximum of five or six items. The vertical bar graph shown in Figure 21.2 is a grouped column graph showing household computer and Internet access in the years 1998 to 2001. The legend indicates what each column represents.

Dot graphs

The Australian Bureau of Statistics now tends to use dot graphs instead of bar charts because a reader's eye picks up and interprets the value more quickly this way.

Figure 21.2 A column (vertical bar) graph showing household computer and Internet access 1998–2000 and projected to 2001

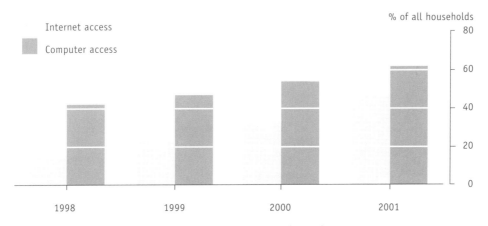

Source: Household Use of Information Technology, Australia, 2000 (8146.0).

The **dot graph** is used to present six or more variables. This kind of graph makes it easy, visually, to connect the graphed point to its label on the vertical axis. The information is easier to read. The dot graph presented in Figure 21.3 shows the proportion of crimes recorded by police where a weapon was used.

Figure 21.3 A dot graph showing the proportion of crimes recorded by police where a weapon was used in 1999 and 2000

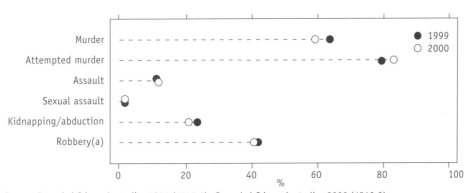

Source: Recorded Crime, Australia, 1999 (4510.0); Recorded Crime, Australia, 2000 (4510.0).

Pie charts

A **pie chart** shows the parts or divisions of a whole unit in a circle. Its main use is to compare or emphasise the proportions of each part and it works best when only a few parts need to be shown – say no more than five or six. For a circle, these are called 'sectors' or 'segments'.

Pie charts compare parts of a whole unit.

A pie chart presents a simple illustration that is easy to understand. It is not so clear if too many segments are presented. If a whole unit is broken into more than six parts, the 100% column chart is more suitable. The first sector of the pie chart is the largest and starts at the 12 o'clock point. The remaining sectors are arranged in decreasing order of size (see Figure 21.4).

Figure 21.4 A pie chart showing distribution of annual income from XYZ Credit Union to members

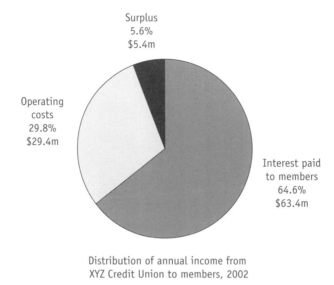

Distribution of annual income from
XYZ Credit Union to members, 2002

The Australian Bureau of Statistics prefers not to use pie charts as they do not convey the area and size differences accurately and cannot show negative values.

Diagrams and drawings

Diagrams
illustrate
structures.

A **diagram** is useful for showing the structure of something – its parts and their relationship to each other (see Figure 21.5). The organisation chart and flow chart are often used as report graphics, although any kind of structure can be shown in a diagram (see Figure 21.5). Diagrams are particularly helpful for demonstrating technical procedures and details – for example, how to assemble a model aeroplane.

Drawings and diagrams can simplify and highlight special features and details that may not stand out in a photo. They can also show the interior or inner workings of something by presenting it in cross-section.

Figure 21.5 A diagram showing the storage tank of a petrol station

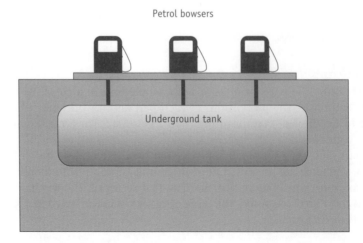

Photographs and illustrations

A **photograph** is easily understood, makes an immediate impact and shows the physical appearance of a subject. It can often enhance or even replace a lengthy description. For example, the site descriptions of a valuation report are more easily understood if photographs of the site are included. A description of Sydney's Centrepoint Tower is easier to visualise if it is accompanied by a photograph of the building.

Photographs have three main disadvantages. They are expensive, sometimes present too much detail and cannot show a cross-section.

Maps

A **map** is a specific type of diagram that uses scale, grids, symbols, lines, colours, legends, labels, figures and text to locate landforms, cities, towns, rivers, roads and so on. Maps use a wide range of graphics to transfer a large amount of detail onto the page. If you decide to use a map, ensure that it is easy to reproduce, either as an enlargement or reduction. Maps are used to convey information in a small space. **Symbols** can be described as a shorthand form of writing – for example, a street directory may use a red cross to represent a hospital and a solid red dot for traffic lights. Symbols should be clear, simple, instantly recognisable and easy to reproduce. Figure 21.6 shows Australia's land mass elevation on a map.

Maps show a large amount of detail about location.

Figure 21.6 Australia: land mass evaluation

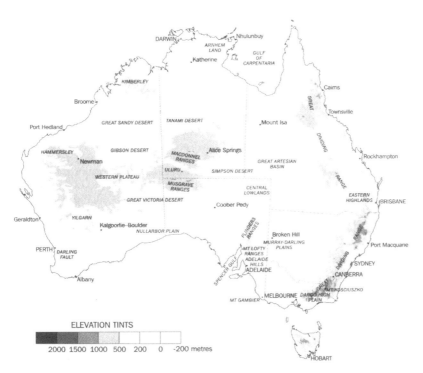

Source: ABS *1999 Year Book Australia*, Catalogue No. 1301.0, p. 5. © Commonwealth of Australia. Reproduced with permission.

Computer-generated graphics

Focus attention
on the main
points.

Presentation graphics packages are designed to paint pictures, create drawings manipulate or enhance scanned pictures. They are used to illustrate business presentations, lectures, oral presentations and documents such as reports. MS PowerPoint is a popular presentation package.

Graphics packages such as Adobe Photoshop or Microsoft Photo Editor enhance photos by adjusting the shading, contrast and context. It is even possible to crop the photo to highlight a particular aspect. Adobe Illustrator can create or change logos. The photo packages let you touch up the graphics before you transport them into a publication package such as Adobe Pagemaker, Microsoft Publisher or Quark Express. Newsletters, flyers, business cards and calendars are produced on the publication packages because the page layout and size can be varied. Publication packages are more flexible. The publication packages allow you to manipulate a document into various types of layout. Figure 21.7 is a computer-generated graphic, showing how files are uploaded to and downloaded from an Internet service provider.

Presentation and graphics packages are available for use in the home, school or office. Many of these packages now have multimedia capabilities such as sound and movement.

Figure 21.7 Computer-generated graphic showing how files are uploaded to and downloaded from an Internet service provider

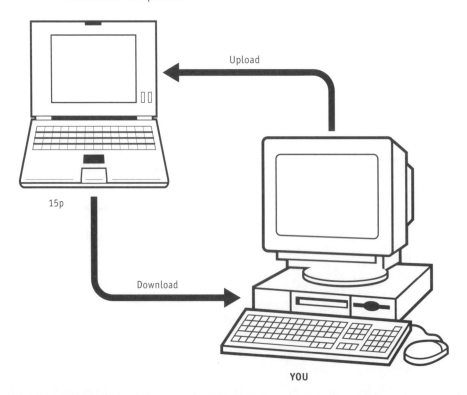

Source: Peter J Williams for Computer Services, 27 July 1999. Reproduced with permission.

Analysing graphics

1. a. Collect six different types of graphics from the print media and analyse them using Self-check 21.1 to prepare for the next task.
   b. In groups of three compare your individual analyses.
2. Still in your group of three, prepare a set of instructions on how to construct a useful graphic.
3. In your same group, discuss the following statement. 'It is possible to prove anything with statistics, so for our next report we should apply our data to suit our own findings.' Do you agree or disagree with the statement? Comment on this report writer's credibility and the likely result if someone relies on such misinformation.
4. Report back to your large group.

Constructing graphics

Some graphics are obtained from external sources – for example, photographs, maps and diagrams by planners. Others may be constructed from information you have gathered in your research – for example, tables, graphs and pie charts.

Designing the graphic

A graphic can be enlarged or reduced to give particular emphasis to one element. Or you may prefer to interrelate various parts of it, to compare their similarities, differences or dependencies. Simplicity in design is better than too much detail, so keep the graphic simple and easy to follow. Include plenty of space and avoid cluttering your diagram or map. Ensure that each part of the graphic is labelled clearly (see the next subsection).

Keep graphics simple.

It is essential to use a **scale** that covers the range of data. As a general rule, the width of a graph should be twice its height. If you use a key, place it inside the frame of the graph. Written text on either side of a graphic is distracting so avoid placing written comments on either side of the graph. Comments relating to the graph are usually placed before the graph.

When you use several graphics in a report, aim for a consistent presentation. Keep them to a similar size and use the same style for headings and labels. Always give the source of your information and state clearly whether you have reproduced or adapted someone else's work.

Graphics

Before you decide to put a graphic in your report, ask the following.

Does the graphic	Yes	No	Unsure
have a title?	☐	☐	☐
label everything clearly?	☐	☐	☐
represent the subject accurately?	☐	☐	☐
have a definite purpose?	☐	☐	☐
illustrate only one subject?	☐	☐	☐
add interest to the report?	☐	☐	☐
support the text?	☐	☐	☐

Labelling the information

Give each graphic an explanatory title or heading, and label all units of measurement clearly. Help the reader to identify and think about the aid's purpose and ideas. Clear labels should be placed on each line or piece of information to identify the graphic's purpose and its main features or concepts. To avoid cluttering a graph too much, use a key as in Figure 21.2.

Graphics and text should be integrated.

When you use more than one graphic for a report, number each one. Place a graphic as close as possible to the text it is illustrating. For example, if you present text about unemployment in the 1990s, place the graph or diagram illustrating this immediately after the text. In the report, refer to and explain the graphics. Your text should lead up to and away from each graphic to integrate them with the discussion. They should not look like optional pieces of artwork.

Selecting the graphic

Graphics should project an accurate image.

Select graphics that present a true and accurate picture of your written information. Otherwise, your credibility and the value of your writing is likely to be questioned. Be careful not to exaggerate similarities or differences. Graphics can demonstrate complex ideas simply and concisely and emphasise their relationships. Select your graphics with these criteria in mind.

Visit the Companion Website at **www.prenhall.com/dwyer_au**. Choose the Internet exercise in Chapter 21 to find and analyse the graphics on the home page of three Free Clip Art sites. How would you describe each site?

Chapter summary

Identify the purpose of the main types of graphics. Graphics should catch readers' interest and encourage them to think about the report writer's main ideas or data. Tables simplify and compare, line graphs indicate trends or movement over time. Column or vertical bar graphs compare one amount or time period with another. Dot graphs are used by the ABS to compare six or more variables. Pie charts compare the parts or relative proportions of a whole unit. Diagrams illustrate structures and the relationships between their parts. Photographs show the physical appearance of a subject or place. Maps convey a large amount of detail about areas, sites, cities, states or countries.

Select an appropriate form of graphic. This helps to focus the reader's attention. The right graphic makes the information more intelligible and interesting.

Describe what message each graphic conveys. Read the titles, units of measurement, labels, keys, symbols, lettering and numbering to determine the subject and focus presented in the graphic.

Construct and place graphic material with appropriate text references and sources. When large amounts of data are presented in tables and charts rather than in paragraphs of writing, the visual impact of a document is improved. Appropriate references and sources allow the receiver to gather further information.

Present graphic material to convey a specific message for a specific purpose. Always present accurate information in graphs or charts and avoid misrepresenting or distorting it. Make sure that the graphic emphasises or relates important points and adds meaning to the written text.

1. What are three advantages of using a graphic in a report?
2. What are three features of a useful graphic?
3. List five major types of graphics.
4. Name three elements that a table should include.
5. Which graph or chart is used to represent and compare the parts of a whole unit?
6. Name three disadvantages of using a photograph.
7. Identify the strengths and weaknesses of a diagram.
8. Define the term 'symbol' and give an example of one.
9. a. Refer to Table 21.2. By what percentage (%) did Australia's population increase from June 1999 to June 2000?
   b. Which is the fastest growing and which is the slowest growing country?
   c. Why is it important to collect population size and rate-of-growth figures?
10. a. What sort of graph appears in Figure 21.2 and Figure 21.3?
    b. Briefly explain the difference between these two types of graphs.
    c. Why is a legend used for each graph?
11. a. How many different measurements are shown on the dot graph in Figure 21.3?
    b. Briefly describe two features that make a dot graph easy to follow.
12. Briefly explain the following statement: 'Simplicity helps; too much detail is confusing.'

Construct a graphic

1. a. Construct one line graph and one column graph from the information in Table 21.3, Flower Corporation Profit and Share Prices (below). The figures represent Flower Corporation's annual profit and share prices over six years. As you plot the line and column graphs, show the profit against time as a line graph, and the share price for each year as a series of columns. Use years as the scale on the horizontal axis, $A million on the left-hand vertical axis and $ share price on the right-hand axis.
   b. i. What advantages does the column graph representation have over the table?
      ii. Briefly discuss two relationships shown on the line graph.

Table 21.3 Flower Corporation profit and share prices

Year	Profit ($A million)	Share price ($)
1996	185	1.80
1997	220	3.40
1998	315	5.00
1999	375	6.00
2000	410	7.80
2001	580	9.50

2. a. Summarise the following data by placing them in a table.
The Mercury Superannuation Fund's portfolio covers a wide range of assets. The largest proportion, 30%, is in *Australian shares*, followed by 20% in *international shares*.
Liquidity has to be part of the fund, so 5% of the portfolio is held in *liquid assets* to ensure profitability. *Property shares* make up another 15%. Safety is provided by placing another 15% of Mercury's assets in *Australian fixed interest deposits* and 15% in *international fixed interest holdings*.

b. To present a visual comparison after you have compiled this table, draw a pie chart showing Mercury Superannuation Fund's division of assets.

3. Consider the line graph, column graph and pie chart you have plotted.

a. Identify which of the graphs shows the following:
i.   changes over time
ii. relative size
iii. comparison between items.

b. Decide which graph is the most or least successful and justify your answer by briefly outlining what it communicates.

Key terms

column (vertical bar) graph	line graph	symbol
diagram	map	table
dot graph	photograph	variable
graphics	pie chart	
	scale	

Data collection on schools

Schools

In August 2001, there were 9596 schools in Australia, of which 6942 (72.3%) were government schools and 2654 (27.7%) were non-government schools.

During the decade from 1991 to 2001 the total number of schools fell by 3.8%. Government school numbers declined by 7.1% whereas the number of non-government schools rose by 5.7%. In the year to August 2001, the number of government schools fell by 19 and the number of non-government schools increased by 20.

The number of combined primary/secondary schools has grown from 841 in 1991 to 1051 in 2001 (an increase of 25.0%), with combined schools now representing 11.0% of all schools.

Students

In 2001 there were 3 268 141 full-time school students, 68.8% of whom attended government schools.

Over the period 1991 to 2001, the number of full-time students attending government schools grew by 1.4%, while the number attending non-government schools increased by 18.9%. Compared to 2000, the number of full-time students attending government schools in 2001 was virtually static (a marginal decrease of 68), while non-government school student numbers increased by 20 784 or 2.1%.

There were 28 429 part-time school students in 2001, an increase of 6.9% since 2000, and 23.4% higher than in 1996. Tasmania had the highest proportion of part-time students (3.6%), followed by South Australia (2.9%) and the Northern Territory with 2.8%.

In 2001 there were 115 465 full-time Indigenous school students, a 3.5% increase over the number in 2000. Approximately 57% of Indigenous students attended schools in New South Wales or Queensland.

Age participation rates

At the Australian level, the age participation rates for full-time school students in 2001 were 93.0% for 15-year-olds, 82.4% for 16-year-olds and 62.2% for 17-year-olds. Over the last decade, the age participation rate for 17-year-olds has risen from 56.9% (1991) to 62.2% (2001).

non-government schools in 2001, representing 221 927 full-time equivalent (FTE) teachers, an increase of 1.8% from the previous year.

The number of FTE teaching staff in government schools increased by 5.7% since 1996 compared to a 16.3% growth in the non-government sector. In the year to 2001,

Participation rates of full-time students aged 17 – 1991 and 2001

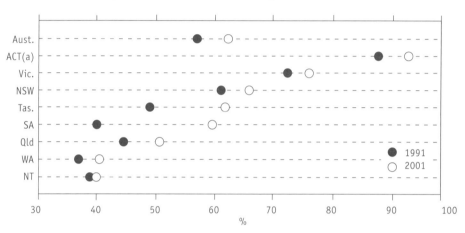

(a) The ACT figure includes some students who are not ACT residents.

Apparent retention rates

In 2001 the apparent retention rate of full-time school students from Year 7/8 to Year 12 was 73.4% compared to 72.3% in 2000 and 71.3% in 1991. As in previous years, the apparent retention rate for females (79.1%) was significantly higher than the rate for males (68.1%).

Over the last decade the apparent retention rate from Year 10 to Year 12 increased slightly from 73.4% in 1991 to 75.4% in 2001, with the rate for females in 2001 again being considerably higher than that for males (80.1% and 70.8% respectively).

Apparent retention rates for full-time Indigenous school students, from Year 7/8 to both Year 10 and Year 12, have continued to rise over the last five years – the rate to Year 10 increased from 74.8% in 1996 to 86.0% in 2001, and the rate to Year 12 increased from 29.2% to 36.3%.

Staff

There were 249 629 teaching staff (both full-time and part-time) at government and

government school teacher numbers increased by 1.0% and non-government school teacher numbers grew by 3.5%.

The proportion of teaching staff who are female continues to rise slowly – in 2001 just over three-quarters (78.7%) of FTE teaching staff in primary schools were female, with the secondary school figure being 54.9%; the comparable figures in 1996 were 76.2% and 52.6% respectively.

Over the last five years the largest percentage increases in FTE primary school teaching staff occurred in Queensland (17.6%) followed by Victoria (13.2%). Queensland and Western Australia reported the largest percentage increase in the number of secondary school teaching staff (FTE) over the same period (15.4% and 10.7% respectively).

Overall, the average number of full-time primary school students per FTE teacher was 17.0. In the government sector the average was 16.8 and in non-government schools it was 17.6. In secondary schools the equivalent figure was 12.4, with no difference between government schools and non-government schools.

Source: Australian Bureau of Statistics, *Schools,* Cat. No. 4221.0, 2001, pp. 3–4.

Questions

1. Suggest reasons why data is collected on schools.
2. Are there some issues within schools for which data should not be collected? Give reasons for your answer.
3. Use the data in the report to construct column graphs that show the
   a. number of full-time school students in 2001
   b. number of part-time school students in 2001
   c. number of full-time indigenous school students in 2001.
4. The number of full-time students attending government schools appears to be declining while the number attending non-government schools is increasing. Detail how the statistics in the report explain this.
5. What reasons would you suggest for the changing age participation rates for 17-year-olds from 1991 to 2001?

Writing technical documents

22

In this chapter you will learn how to:

- identify a technical document's intended audience, purpose and scope

- choose material appropriate to your purpose and the audience

- use a direct, concise technical writing style

- organise a technical document

- present headings, lists and instructional steps consistently

- write different types of technical documents

- present the technical document in an appropriate format

- edit a technical document to industry standards.

Evaluate your communication skills by completing the self-checks in the chapter.

Technical writing communicates highly specific information. Most of it is prepared by professionals such as engineers, scientists, computer specialists and other technicians. Even though it presents technical, industrial or specialist material, a technical document should be easy to understand.

As a technical writer you will be communicating with people from widely different backgrounds. Some of your readers will be technical experts and managers, others will be non-expert general readers. For a technical writing task at work, consider your range of readers and your writing purpose. These elements affect the document's content, organisation and format.

The purpose of technical writing

Technical writers use factual information for a specific purpose.

Technical writing deals with facts that can be measured, categorised, analysed, proved or disproved. It is objective and practical. Technical writers have to do all the following:

- convey technical information for managerial and other specific purposes
- instruct
- describe
- explain technical and/or industrial processes.

Technical writing tasks

At work a great deal of information is conveyed in technical documents. Some of the tasks tackled by their writers are:

- proposals
- reports
- definitions
- instructions
- explanations of processes and procedures.

Identify the intended audience

Select and organise the information.

Technical writers must identify the intended audience first and then sort, organise and shape the content of their document so that their audience grasps the main points easily. The readers of technical documents need to:

- understand and interpret the information
- recognise the purpose of the writer's work
- follow instructions.

The audience may have varying technical or non-technical backgrounds, knowledge and experience. Before you plan a piece of technical writing, use Self-check 22.1.

Identify the purpose, audience and scope

Have I	Yes	No	Unsure
defined the writing purpose?	☐	☐	☐
considered the reader's technical background?	☐	☐	☐
determined the scope of the document?	☐	☐	☐
identified the components needed in the document?	☐	☐	☐
identified what I want the reader to do after reading the document?	☐	☐	☐
organised the information to make it accessible?	☐	☐	☐

A technical writing style

In choosing words for your technical writing tasks, aim for a style that is concise and straightforward. The technical writer must be especially careful to use technical terms precisely and consistently.

Convey your exact meaning to the reader.

Repetition

In a technical document, such as a word-processing guide, you may have to repeat instructions (e.g. 'click the right mouse button to use shortcuts') several times. Select a simple phrase to describe the action and use the same phrase each time. The precise and consistent repetition of key words and phrases helps to link sentences and paragraphs throughout the document. This strategy is known as **keynoting**: restating key words and phrases.

Technical terms

Technical terms have a precise meaning specific to a particular subject or organisation. When you write to someone who understands this precise meaning, the proper technical term is the most appropriate one to use. Define its meaning if you are writing for a non-technical reader.

The active voice

The active voice shows who or what is doing something, identifying and emphasising the subject of the sentence. The sentence 'The operator loaded the software' demonstrates the active voice. It tells us that the operator loaded the software. If you used the passive voice and wrote: 'The software was loaded', the reader does not know who or what did the loading. Information is omitted this way.

Technical instructions are often written in the form of a specific command (e.g. fasten, lift, put, close). Technical descriptions explain the steps of a process (e.g. the driver lifts, the kitchen hand spreads, the electrician removes). The active voice is always more useful in technical writing than the passive voice, because the passive voice often leaves out important information. Parallel language should also be used in technical writing, particularly in tables and lists (see Chapter 16, Using Plain English in Workplace Documents).

Sentences and paragraphs

The general rule in technical writing is to keep sentences short (15–20 words). Technical material is easier to follow this way. Try breaking long sentences into two or three sentences per paragraph. Every word and sentence in a technical document should help the reader understand each detail.

Topic sentence

The **topic sentence** announces the main point of each paragraph. It is usually the first sentence of the paragraph, followed by two or three more sentences containing the supporting details (*comment sentences* – see Table 22.1). Table 22.2 shows how different types of topic sentences organise a paragraph.

Topic sentences identify the main point.

Paragraph structure

A paragraph expands or clarifies the main point expressed in the topic sentence. In technical writing, each sentence in the paragraph adds and explains further relevant details. It is sometimes helpful to repeat the main point in the final sentence.

A paragraph connects or relates details.

Table 22.1 The purpose of topic and comment sentences

Topic sentence	Comment sentence
1. Announces the main topic	1. Adds supporting details
2. Indicates the purpose of the document	2. Explains who or what does what
3. Sets the scene (context)	3. Gives proof
4. Gives a framework	4. Gives examples
	5. Shows reasoning

Table 22.2 How different types of topic sentences organise a paragraph

Type	Example
Specific to general	The unemployment rate is decreasing because the economy is moving out of a recession.
General to specific	The economy is moving out of a recession and as a result the unemployment rate is decreasing.
Spatial order	To transfer a call to another line, lift the handset. Press the hash button on the bottom left-hand side. Push button 2, then button 4. Press the circular button on the top right-hand side.
Chronological order	Today at 10.30 am I attended a Beginners' Class in aerobics. The instructor started with warm-up exercises and then moved on to a group of power exercises for about an hour. Then, finally, the instructor led us through the wind-down exercises.

Linking and summary statements

Linking and summary statements enable the reader to make logical connections between the main points. This gives continuity to the writing. Table 22.3 gives some examples.

Table 22.3 Linking and summary statements

Linking statements	Summary statements
On the other hand . . .	In other words . . .
In contrast to this view . . .	To return to the previous example . . .
Following on from . . .	Some of the approaches discussed so far . . .
Associated with . . .	The ideas presented here include . . .
A different point of view . . .	A final point before we move on . . .
Alternatively . . .	As shown earlier . . .
In the case of . . .	Finally . . .

Format

Choose a **format** or layout that makes the technical information as accessible as possible. Signalling devices such as headings and numbers help to highlight each part of the document and move the reader through it. Signals should be used to:

■ identify the main point
■ indicate connections between the main point and supporting points
■ indicate the connections between all the main points
■ highlight any warnings or cautions.

Use signalling devices to highlight the main points.

Headings

Headings help the readers to find specific information by dividing it into sections and paragraphs. The first-level heading indicates each main section, while the second-level heading indicates a subdivision, and so on for third-level and fourth-level headings. Headings help the reader in five ways.

1. To locate specific material
2. To show the relationships between different sections of material
3. To give the reader a place to stop and think
4. To reduce the reading time by indicating the main points
5. To give a brief survey of the information that follows.

Numbering systems

A numbering system can be used with headings. Numbered headings help writers and readers to sort out highly detailed material. Each main section requires a main heading. Adding numbers to headings gives an outline that is easy to follow and revise.

Number headings to give a clear outline.

The example in Figure 22.1 presents the alphanumeric system for numbering the main section and subsection headings, if you decide to subdivide your main sections. The decimal system is shown in Figure 20.1 in Chapter 20.

The numbering of subdivided sections is not always necessary, but is useful for technical or very long documents. Check to see if an in-house style is used at your workplace. If not, create your own numbering system.

Figure 22.1 Alphanumeric system of outlining

I. **Heading for first main section**
    a. Heading for first subsection of first main section
    b. Heading for second subsection
    c. Heading for third subsection

II. **Heading for second main section**
    a. Heading for first subsection of second main section
    b. Heading for second subsection
    c. Heading for third subsection

The subsections may require further subdivision:

III. **Heading for first main section**
    a. Heading for first subsection
        1. Heading for subdivision of first subsection
        2. Heading for the next subdivision of first subsection
    b. Heading for second subsection

Lists

Lists are useful if your readers need to gather items such as materials, parts or tools. If special operating conditions apply, list these in sequential order (e.g. safety procedure).

Instructional steps are easier to understand when they are placed in a list. Start each step with the essential action word (verb) – for example, 'release', 'unscrew', 'turn off'.

Warnings

Cautions and warnings should be highlighted in bold or italic capital letters. Box frames and symbols are also useful. A technical writer should place a warning before the steps or procedures it applies to.

Notes

Notes (i.e. NB, followed by a short statement) highlight important aspects of text or diagrams. Avoid using too many notes as this defeats their purpose: to attract attention.

Tables

Tables present data in a concise form that separates yet relates them. The information is usually presented in lists or columns so that the reader can recognise key relationships or make comparisons easily.

Illustrations

Illustrations (graphics) make an immediate impact.

Illustrations are particularly helpful for explaining technical details concisely, and simplifying or emphasising the main points of interest. Whenever you need to describe what, where and how things happen, diagrams and photographs are particularly useful.

However, if you decide that your graphics are not essential to the text, or interrupt its progression, place them in an appendix. Once you decide to use a graphic in the main text, focus the reader's attention by using the following three-step method.

1. Explain the point in writing.
2. Relate the illustration to the text.
3. Place the illustration straight after the text explanation.

Use only graphics that add meaning and interest to the text. When and how to use graphics is discussed in Chapter 21.

Different types of technical documents

Technical writing provides factual information for a specific purpose. There are various ways of presenting this information. Five are discussed here.

1. technical definitions
2. technical descriptions
3. technical instructions.
4. technical proposals
5. tenders.

Technical definitions

Define technical terms clearly.

A **technical definition** sets out to explain a special technical term. Many technical terms have no familar, equivalent term, so they must be clearly defined by the writer for readers who are not expert in that field.

Situations calling for definitions

Technical writers should make it a rule to use a definition in the following four situations.

1. A technical writer must include definitions for all highly specialised terms when technical information originally written for expert readers is revised for non-expert readers.
2. A technical document intended for a range of expert and non-expert readers must include definitions for the non-expert.
3. A technical writer must define any term that is new or rarely used – for all readers, expert or otherwise.
4. A term that changes its meaning according to context must be defined so that both writer and reader are clear about its meaning in the document.

Table 22.4 lists three kinds of definitions and their purpose.

Table 22.4 Definitions and their purpose

Type of definition	Purpose
Informal	To give a brief explanation of a term, in the first sentence that uses it – most helpful for non-experts
Formal	To define a term or concept, using a three-part formula: 1. the term 2. all objects or actions to which the term applies 3. any features that distinguish this term from other similar terms
Extended	To define the term and to emphasise and discuss other related qualities and aspects – usually in a full paragraph

Technical descriptions

A **technical description** is a factual account of a technical subject. There are two main types of technical descriptions.

Describe a technical subject factually.

1. Descriptions of a mechanism or piece of equipment
2. Descriptions of a process.

Description of a mechanism

A technical description of a mechanism requires at least four parts: a definition, a list and description of the parts, an explanation of how these work, and a logical explanation of its general operation (see Table 22.5).

A description of a mechanism should include:

- its purpose or function
- model numbers and names
- weight, shape, measurements, materials
- major and minor parts, their location and how they are connected
- features such as texture, sound, colour and size

Table 22.5 Description of a mechanism

Part	Purpose
1. A summary statement, often in the form of a definition	■ state main use ■ show how it works ■ explain when it is used
2. A logical explanation of the general operation	■ break into main sections or steps ■ explain human and mechanical controls ■ describe any pre-operational conditions and controls
3. A list and description of each part of the mechanism	■ describe general size and dimensions ■ compare and/or contrast with other related mechanisms
4. A logical explanation of the operation of each part	■ explain *how* each part functions ■ explain *when* each part functions

- operating cycle
- special conditions for appropriate use such as time, temperature, safety features.

The amount and kind of detail depends on your readers' needs and their level of knowledge about the subject.

Description of a process

A **process description** describes how something works, why it works that way, and each step of the process. How to write a description of a process is shown in Table 22.6.

Technical instructions

Technical instructions must be clear and factual.

Technical instructions must guide the reader to a full understanding and efficient, safe performance of a procedure. Failure to convey instructions properly can have serious consequences for those who rely on them.

Table 22.6 Technical description of a process

Step	Purpose
1. Definition of process	■ why process happens ■ when process happens ■ where process happens ■ who performs process
2. Overall description of process	■ main steps of the process ■ essential materials for the process ■ special skills required for the process ■ any actions or conditions to complete before the process begins ■ special time requirements for the process
3. Description of each step of the process	■ how each step is carried out ■ why each step occurs ■ when it occurs ■ time needed for each step to occur

Technical instructions may be suitable for general (non-expert) readers – to explain the operation and functions of a DVD (Digital Versatile Disc) player, for example; or for more expert readers – explaining how to set up the sound specifications for a DTS surround sound system, for example. Technical instructions usually consist of three main steps, shown in Table 22.7.

Table 22.7 Technical instructions

Step	Purpose
1. State the purpose of the instructions	■ what the instructions are for ■ when to perform them ■ where to perform them
2. List conditions that must be met before performance	■ safety considerations and consequences ■ environmental factors ■ essential material and equipment ■ special skills required ■ time constraints
3. Provide the order of steps to follow	■ list instructions in order of performance ■ provide brief description ■ use the direct 'you' approach ■ use visuals where necessary ■ add brief notes if necessary

Most readers are interested in how to use something or, if it malfunctions, how to fix it. For experts, only a brief description of how it works may be necessary, but you need to know what your readers' requirements are. Whether they are highly trained or beginners, all readers require a well organised set of instructions. These can be presented in the form of an introduction, body and conclusion.

Introduction

Use a summary statement or definition to explain what the instructions are for, and when and where to perform them.

Body

Next, explain each step in a logical numbered list. Notes and warnings should be inserted where appropriate. As you proceed through the instructions, begin each step with its definition. The reader must understand each step and the reason for it. Numbering the steps and/or placing them in lists helps to avoid confusion and separates the steps from one another.

Conclusion

The conclusion should summarise the major steps, and repeat safety warnings. It helps readers to revise the instructions.

Offer follow-up advice and any additional instructions for what can be done next – for example, how to adjust the levels of individuals speakers of a surround sound system to ensure maximum effect. It is also useful to tell the reader what to do if something goes wrong.

Different types of documents

1. Write three different definitions for a car wheel:
   a. an informal definition
   b. a formal definition
   c. an extended definition.
2. a. Write the procedure for archiving or storing documents on a CD ROM for an audience of computer specialists.
   b. Rewrite the procedure for readers who have never copied documents onto a CD ROM.
3. Write a technical description of a mechanism such as a juice blender or a supermarket shopping trolley. Follow the four steps shown in Table 22.5.

SELF CHECK 22.2

Procedures and processes

Have I provided	Effectively	Satisfactorily	Unsatisfactorily
a clear, specific title?	☐	☐	☐
concise information?	☐	☐	☐
background information?	☐	☐	☐
each step of the process?	☐	☐	☐
a logical order for the steps?	☐	☐	☐
appropriate graphics?	☐	☐	☐
an appropriate level of technical language?	☐	☐	☐

Technical proposals

Technical proposals put forward a plan of action.

The **proposal** is a plan or scheme sent to a decision maker, either a specific person or an organisation. It should be a well organised and persuasive document.

A proposal that clearly identifies its objectives and the organisation's need, presents strategies for meeting that need, outlines the direct benefits of these strategies, and offers a way of evaluating the results has a high chance of success.

Written proposals are submitted for a variety of reasons:

- to obtain funds for research
- to present a feasibility study
- to solve a problem
- to express interest in a project
- to ask for approval for a change or a new course of action.

Formal proposal

Make sure your proposal gains maximum benefit from the time, energy and costs involved in preparing it. Your proposal should include:

- a cover page
- an executive summary
- an introduction, briefly describing its purpose
- details of the management of the project
- the qualifications and experience of all those involved in proposing the project
- a detailed budget
- a proposed schedule
- terms or conditions
- attachments (if any).

Present factual information and lead the reader from the proposal's purpose, through the facts and supporting details to the conclusion.

- Clearly identify the subject, purpose and scope of the proposal.
- Briefly analyse the situation or project.
- Detail the steps of the project in a logical order, usually chronological.
- Provide a timetable and date of completion.
- Identify the resources, time and money needed.
- Present a conclusion that summarises the findings and show how the results of the proposal will be evaluated.

When the reader is already informed about the project, you may decide to move the conclusion forward. The risk of doing this is that the reader may disagree with your conclusion and read no further, so the order of information suggested here is usually preferred.

Proposals can vary in length from a one-page memo or letter report to a short or long formal report. A major project may require a long report before it begins, and progress reports once it starts. (See Chapter 20, Writing Long Reports, for the long report format.)

The body of the proposal should outline the plan of action for the project, and the procedures involved. Include details of the research and resources required, and the organisations and other people involved. Include the experience, qualifications and any special skills or facilities offered by the proposing organisation. Show how the intended results will be achieved and how they will be evaluated and reported.

One section of the body will detail the budget, another will present a schedule. These will need headings, and perhaps subheadings, lists or numbers to emphasise important points. A widely accepted rule is to keep the body of a long formal proposal to four parts:

The body of a technical proposal has four main points.

1. two detailed pages on how the project will be managed
2. two pages for the costs
3. two pages for the schedule
4. two pages for selling the idea and the special qualities of the proposing organisation.

Detailed technical information is presented as attachments. This helps to keep the proposal as short as possible. Most people are overwhelmed by a 50-page document: a maximum of eight pages for a proposal is recommended.

Base your conclusions on the information presented in the proposal. Emphasise its benefits and results, the advantages offered by the proposing organisation, and explain how these can be taken up during and after the project.

Work request

This type of proposal is usually submitted as a request to carry out a work project. It should include:

- details of work to be carried out
- descriptions of facilities and capabilities of proposer
- complete technical information
- a detailed budget for the project
- a schedule.

A **work request** proposal often uses graphics to clarify details.

Funding request

A **funding request** is a proposal for funds. As well as giving details about a project, it should emphasise the proposer's credibility and ability to complete the project.

A funding request usually includes:

- an introduction to arouse interest and gain approval
- reasons supporting the request, such as the proposer's special facilities or expertise
- an explanation of any benefits to be derived from the project, supported by specific data
- a specific request for funds
- a brief summary
- appropriate graphics.

If the organisation asking for funds has previously received funds, and used them for a successful project, this should be mentioned along with any benefits gained by the community or others. This emphasises the proposer's ability to manage a project.

Tenders

A tender is a bid to provide something in exchange for a fee.

A tender document is a bid or offer to provide a product or service in exchange for a fee. It should do more than make a statement about money: you want to persuade the receiver to accept it and offer you the contract. As a plan of action, it must set out clearly how the service or product will be provided, and how this will satisfy their needs.

The tendering process

Tendering, particularly government tendering, is usually competitive. The contract is awarded to the company who can supply quality goods and services in the time specified and at a reasonable cost. Quality and value for money are important considerations.

The invitation-to-tender document lists the organisation's requirements. These documents are designed to ensure that all who tender receive the same information and specifications.

In some cases, such as in public works tendering, there is an accredited list of companies to whom the invitation to tender is sent. In others, advertisements may call for statements of intent or registrations of interest before the tenders are sought. Negotiation with a preferred company may occur after a registration of interest or statement of intent is received. For routine purchases, many government agencies have a list of preferred companies who are invited to tender.

Tendering costs can be prohibitive. You should only tender if you have a reasonable chance of securing the contract. You may be required to pay a specified amount to purchase the tender documents. This amount may be refunded once you have submitted a tender.

Successful tendering

To be successful in tendering, you need to:

- find the opportunities – for example, through national and state advertisements, trade journals, Internet sites
- know the customers' needs, wants and expectations
- know the right person/s in the organisation to approach
- know the strengths and weaknesses of your potential competitors
- realistically assess your ability to provide quality goods and services within the specified time and give good customer service.

Additionally, it is important that your tender:

- follows the organisation's tender guidelines

- includes background material on your organisation, such as previous successful tenders, staff qualifications, your mission statement
- includes details of Quality Assurance accreditation and Occupational Health and Safety accreditation as well as level of public liability insurance
- is submitted by the specified closing date.

Before tendering

Before preparing and submitting a tender, ask yourself what will be the costs involved, and whether they are within your working budget. Do you have adequately trained staff available to deliver the required goods and services? Are you able to complete the project by the specified time?

After purchasing the tender documents, it may be necessary to check out any details that are not readily understandable. You might need to read and reread the documents to ensure that important criteria are addressed. If the document is very large, you may need to divide it into sections for easy handling. You may need to make a site inspection or attend a pre-bid conference or briefing.

Parts of a tender document

As you plan and draft the tender document, focus on the project description – its purpose, and any other relevant details of the project. The tender document should contain the following:

1. the project's purpose
2. your willingness to achieve the project's objectives
3. the costs
4. the anticipated completion schedule
5. your capacity to deliver.

The organisation inviting the tender identifies its main objectives and expectations in the specification document. Preview these, and rank them from most to least important. Then prepare a tender document based on sound reasoning and reliable data.

Preparing the tender document

Address the objectives in the specification document. Show how your tender fulfils their expectations and emphasise the special benefits you offer. Remember, how you address the specific criteria and plan to meet the organisation's objectives are used to compare the tender documents.

Sometimes, it may be necessary for you to divide the tender into several sections to address the specifications. Alternatively, the tender may have to be submitted on a printed form supplied by the organisation.

You should have your tender checked by someone else to make certain that all aspects have been covered. Remember also to check and recheck your maths. It is quite easy to write $5000 instead of $50 000. Table 22.8 lists the various sections that may be required in a tender document.

Editing

The editing stage is your chance to ensure that you have said all that you intended to say. When you edit your writing, consider each sentence from the reader's position. Will it be easier to understand if the sentence is:

Editing is crucial to successful writing.

Table 22.8 Suggested sections in a tender document

Section	Content
Method/Timing	The order and timing of the completion of the tasks. You could include a timetable.
Technical	How you will carry out the work, and the technology and methodology you will use. Any problems anticipated, and contingency plans to counter them, should be included.
Management	Describe your organisation's structure, special expertise and projects already completed or under way. Include your organisation's mission statement and proposed administration of the project. Collaborative ventures and use of local resources should be mentioned.
Financial	Include a breakdown of the tender price. Itemise the costs involved. The quoted price should be firm; include a statement that any other options requested later will be charged at a negotiated price. Say whether you will offer a discount for early payment.
Benefits	List the key benefits to the organisation as well as the special features you can offer.
Value	The lowest bid is usually accepted. Calculate your tender to ensure quality and price. Quote only on what is requested by the organisation. Increase your chance of winning by including extras such as staff training or service at no extra cost.
Executive summary	Include a summary of the whole proposal. As this is often the first part of the proposal read, be clear, concise and convincing.

- broken into two or more sentences?
- written in a different order?
- rewritten to replace jargon or difficult words with simpler, clearer words?

Common writing errors

Four common writing errors that make a document difficult to follow are:

1. confusing language
2. discriminatory language
3. verbose language
4. information overload.

Confusing language

Words that can mislead the reader include the following:

- ambiguous words (those that have more than one meaning)
- vague, imprecise words that do not clearly convey or define anything (e.g. 'implement')
- sexist words that seem to direct the message to only one gender
- trendy words (buzzwords) that are imprecise, or hackneyed terms that have lost their impact (e.g. 'a level playing ground')
- pompous words ('undertake' instead of 'do')
- archaic words that are no longer part of everyday vocabulary (e.g. 'herewith').

Discriminatory language

In any document, avoid sexist, racist or other words that discriminate against a group of people. Avoid sexist words by checking that the document:

- does not use male-dominated terms to describe occupations or roles that are shared by both men and women – for example, 'chairman'
- does not mention gender unnecessarily, as in 'male nurse' or 'female barrister'
- does not use only the male pronoun; replace with 'a person' or 'people', or 'they' or he/she'.

Non-discriminatory, inclusive language includes all readers.

Verbose language

Verbose means 'too many words', which can interfere with comprehension. For example: 'Your attention is drawn to the fact that the stock order is fulfilled and on the way to reach you by Tuesday' uses too many words. Simply say, 'The stock you ordered will be delivered on Tuesday'.

Too many words and unnecessary expressions interrupt the reader's understanding of the message. Present the facts and content as concisely as possible. Verbosity can confuse or bore the reader.

Information overload

Information overload means that too much information is provided so that the reader becomes overwhelmed and confused. Too much detail at once may frustrate readers, and may create the impression that the writer is over-anxious to impress. The receiver does not need to consider all your knowledge or background reading. Decide how much of your information is absolutely relevant.

Technical writing

1. Prepare a set of technical instructions, following the three steps outlined in the chapter. Present an introduction, body and conclusion. The instructions are for a worker who must either:
   - change the linen on a hospital bed occupied by a patient; or
   - replace the spark plugs in a car.
2. What is the difference between active and passive voice? Write a sentence in the active voice, then one sentence in the passive voice, on each of the following topics.
   - The winner of the men's singles at Wimbledon
   - The current rate of interest on Bankcard
   - Motivation and its impact on a person's work performance
   - Alcohol.
3. Rewrite the following sentences by placing the action word (verb) at the beginning.
   a. A safety hat must be worn at all times.
   b. The equipment must be placed in the tool box.
   c. Heavy planking is to be used to support digging equipment on soft ground.
   d. The printer paper is inserted from the front.
   e. The jack is placed under the marked support.
   f. The knives need to be sharpened at the end of each day.
4. Complete Table 22.9. List four common writing errors and how to avoid them.

Table 22.9

Four common writing errors	How to avoid each error
1.	■ ■ ■
2.	■ ■ ■
3.	■ ■ ■
4.	■ ■ ■

5. a. In a small group, discuss the differences between a work request proposal and a funding request proposal.

b. In this same group, prepare a work request to refurbish the student amenities at your college. Invent the technical information your request will need.

Visit the Companion Website at **www.prenhall.com/dwyer_au**. Choose the Net Search activity in Chapter 22 to find examples of business writing and technical writing. What are the distinguishing features of each type of writing?

Chapter summary

Identify a technical document's purpose and scope. Technical writing informs, instructs, describes, explains and documents technical material. It is important to identify the audience, and determine the scope of the document and the level of technical information to include in it.

Choose material appropriate to your purpose and the audience. Consider your need as a writer to communicate the information in the technical document. As well as achieving your purpose as a writer, the document should also meet the audience's need for specific technical information. Consider carefully the audience's background, range (or lack) of technical knowledge and detail.

Use a direct, concise technical writing style. An expert reader may not require a definition of a particular system, but they may still require a detailed description of it. Apprentices and/or students may require full definitions, descriptions and installation instructions. In each case, the writing style should be clear and precise.

Organise a technical document. A technical document is organised to give concise, accurate information that the reader can follow easily.

Present headings, lists and instructional steps consistently. This helps the reader to identify the main points and connect them with each other and with other relevant supporting points. Special points, such as warnings and safety issues, as well as procedural steps, must be easy to find and understand.

Write different types of technical documents. Technical definitions briefly explain specific subjects. Technical descriptions explain the subject more fully. Technical instructions explain how to perform precise procedural steps. A proposal is a plan or scheme sent to a decision maker or a funding body. A tender is an offer to supply a particular product or service for a fee.

Present the technical document in an appropriate format. Use headings, a numbering system, warnings, notes, tables and illustrations consistently.

Edit a technical document to industry standards. As a writer your aim is to convey accurate, appropriate information. The final stage in writing is editing or checking your own work. Keep in mind the reader's point of view and the standard expected by your workplace and industry.

REVIEW QUESTIONS

1. a. List three purposes of technical writing.
   b. List three technical writing tasks.
   c. Give three reasons for identifying your intended audience before you begin writing a technical document.
   d. Why should you determine the document's scope before you begin writing?

2. List three ways in which you can make your technical writing easier for the reader to understand.

3. a. Define the terms 'topic sentence' and 'comment sentence'.
   b. List the main purposes of a topic sentence and a comment sentence.
   c. Why do writers use linking and summary statements?

4. a. Name three different strategies for improving the layout of a technical document.
   b. List six ways in which headings can help a reader understand the information in a technical document.
   c. Why should lists and instructional steps be used consistently throughout the document?

5. a. Define the terms 'technical definition', 'technical description' and 'technical instruction'.
   b. List four situations calling for definitions.

6. a. Describe the four parts of a description of a mechanism and briefly explain the purpose of each.
   b. Describe the three steps of a process description and briefly explain the purpose of each.
   c. Describe the three steps for writing technical instructions and briefly explain the purpose of each.

7. Name three features of an efficient technical writing style.

8. a. Define the terms 'proposal' and 'tender'.
   b. List the main differences between a proposal and a tender.
   c. Name three different purposes for writing a proposal.
   d. List five essential elements to include in a tender document.
   e. Name the six sections into which a tender document can be divided.
   f. Define the terms 'work request' and 'funding request'.

Writing a technical document

1. Work in small groups. Collect two or three operation manuals for equipment such as a camera, dishwasher, fishing gear or laser printer. Analyse the manuals as follows:
   a. label each section of the manual as definition, description or instruction
   b. identify their major strength as a piece of technical writing
   c. identify any weaknesses
   d. comment on layout.

2. Write a technical description of a process – for example, how to install door frames, operate a facsimile machine, scan supermarket items or enrol as a student in a course of your choice. Follow the three steps required for a process description. Use Self-check 22.2 to assess your work.

Key terms

format
funding request
information overload
keynoting

process description
proposal
technical definition
technical description

technical instructions
topic sentence
work request

The technical writing FAQ

by John Hewitt

What are the primary skills of a technical writer?

The first skill a technical writer should have, of course, is writing. You should be able to write in a clear, concise manner. Technical writing is not poetry or prose. Depending on where you work, you may or may not be able to add some stylistic flair. Either way, your job is to clearly tell your audience exactly what they need to know, and everything they need to know.

The second skill you should have is knowledge of a technical subject. My emphasis has always been in the field of computers, which is probably the largest segment of the technical writing market. Your knowledge can be in many other areas, however, such as science, medicine, engineering, mechanics or law.

No matter what your area of knowledge, you will need computer skills, especially desktop publishing skills. At minimum, you should know the Microsoft Office suite of applications, especially Microsoft Word. Beyond Office, there is Adobe FrameMaker, which is used in many technical-writing environments. Other publishing packages such as PageMaker, Quark Express and Interleaf can also be useful. In addition, online documentation tools such as RoboHelp, Doc-to-Help and Lotus Notes are great applications to have on your résumé, as are HTML and other Internet skills.

In addition, you should try to develop interviewing skills, because you will probably find yourself interviewing technical people to get the information you need for your documents. Often, they will have no idea how to tell you what you need to know, so it is up to you to figure out how to draw the information out of them.

Why don't companies value technical writing?

Technical writers are a luxury, pure and simple. As valuable as I feel my skills are, and can be to a company, the company can still function without me. If the programs or systems are undocumented, or if they are poorly documented by programmers or analysts, it will not damage the company as obviously as if the program fails to get developed. I happen to feel that a company that spends money on good technical writers can get a very high return for their investment, in more satisfied customers, smoother processes and greater institutional memory. I believe that dollar-wise this can make money for the company, but those are categories that are difficult to measure and often hard for management to comprehend.

Also, some companies do not understand what a technical writer does. Some consider writers to be glorified secretaries, and do such things as give them notes to type up or even have them take minutes at meetings. Part of the problem is that secretaries and administrative assistants have also become a thinning breed, and companies (not the upper management, who have secretaries, but the lower management and team members) are desperate for anyone who can make a document look good. I have occasionally been forced to type up notes, and I have comforted myself with the fact that I was paid US$36 an hour to do it.

What types of documents do technical writers create?

The range of writing a technical writer performs varies widely. Much is dependent on the technical specialty of the writer and of the needs of the company. You may find yourself a part of one large project, or overseeing dozens of smaller projects. You might write manuals, articles, proposals, white papers, product descriptions or any of a hundred other types of documents.

My specialty is writing manuals, especially user manuals and programmer manuals for specific software applications. This is the technical writing I enjoy most, because for me it involves solving problems and figuring out puzzles. To write a user manual, I need to think like the people using the program and try to tell them what they need to know, rather than what I would need to know or what the programmer would need to know. For me, this is a lot of fun and very fulfilling.

There are dozens of different types of writing that come under the banner of techical writing, however. Many people document processes. Processes can be just about any system by which something gets done. For example, in order for a company to generate a payroll, certain actions must be taken, such as logging hours and generating checks. All of those steps are part of a process, and intelligent companies document those processes so that, if an employee leaves or a system goes down, they have something to consult in order to get themselves on track. One name for this type of documentation is SOP (Standard Operating Procedure).

Another type of documentation is SLA (Service Level Agreement). The SLA describes exactly what a provider (company or department) will do for a customer (another company, another department, or an individual). These can be highly technical documents or busywork, depending on the service and the company.

RFP (Request for Proposal) responses are much like SLAs. They describe what work will be done, but they often require a little more finesse because they are also pitching the service. The company is proposing to sell a service. I have written several proposals and, depending on the request and the company, they can be quite interesting or more busywork.

Source: John Hewitt, 'The Technical Writing FAQ', <www.poewar.com/articles/twfaq.htm>, accessed 30 August 2002. Writers Resource Center Copyright © 1993–2002.

Questions

1. What primary skills should a technical writer have?
2. What are the benefits to a company of using technical writers?
3. What are some of the different types of documents created by technical writers?
4. In what ways does the writing of manuals differ from the documenting of processes?

Job search skills

VI

Part

Applying for a job

In this chapter you will learn how to:

- collect information on employment opportunities from a variety of sources

- evaluate your preferences, skills, aptitude, qualifications and experience

- make inquiries about a position

- prepare a résumé that shows how your qualifications match the job requirements

- write a covering letter for the job application

- use a search engine to find an online recruitment website

- identify the main components of an online recruitment site.

Evaluate your communication skills by completing the self-check in the chapter.

Careful preparation is vital to the success of your job-seeking campaign. Whether you are looking for a first job, a change in career or a promotion, you are making a job search. A successful approach involves knowing yourself and knowing how to find available positions.

Prepare for the job-seeking process by assessing your strengths and weaknesses, studying the newspapers and contacting employment agencies.

A successful job search depends on your ability to market yourself, and this requires a well written application. It is essential to the initial stage of the job search. The job application has two parts: a résumé and a letter of application.

Searching for a position

Try several different ways to find a job.

When searching for a position, you have the option of consulting various established services, or using contacts and your own initiative.

Newspapers

Check the 'Positions Vacant' section in the newspapers.

The most common way of finding a position is to check the 'Positions Vacant' section in newspapers. National, metropolitan and local newspapers advertise jobs, particularly on Mondays, Wednesdays and Saturdays. The national papers advertise professional positions all through their pages and in their 'Positions Vacant' sections, so if you are in the market for a higher-level position it is necessary to scan the whole paper. The 'Positions Vacant' or 'Professional' sections of metropolitan and national papers have many headings. Suburban newspapers have a smaller general 'Positions Vacant' section.

Government organisations advertise as early as August or September for the general intake of employees for the next year. Some private employers advertise around October or November. School leavers and TAFE and university graduates apply for many of these positions.

Employment agencies

Many employers use employment agencies to select their staff.

Many employers avoid advertising in the press because such large numbers of people apply for each position. It is too time-consuming to sort through all the applications and choose the best applicants to interview. Instead of advertising, these employers use the services of a private **employment agency** to match the skills and qualifications of people on its register with the requirements of the position. If your qualifications are suitable, the agency will also arrange an interview. In this way, countless jobs are filled without being advertised in the newspapers.

Networking

Networking assists in gaining a position.

Many vacant positions are never advertised. Employers fill the position through their own networks of professional and business contacts, social or family contacts. Thus, it is important to create your own **network** of friends, neighbours, sport and social clubs and contacts at work. Your network includes people you knew in previous employment and socially. Local community services can also become part of your network if you join them, participate in their activities, and exchange ideas and information with their members.

Let people in your network know that you are in the market for a job or change of employment. One way to do this is to ask someone to be your personal or professional referee. If they agree, tell them about your needs and aspirations. This way, people in your network can pass on the information to co-workers and associates. They may even recommend you for a position. So let them know what kind of work and position you are looking for, and ask them to tell you about any prospective leads or positions in their organisation.

Publications

Most professional associations publish journals, and many of these carry advertisements for positions. Use the computer facilities at the library to find journals published by companies and potential employers. The library also files government gazettes such as the 'Public Service Notices'.

Information about an organisation can be found in the business news section of local and national newspapers. The Yellow Pages telephone directory gives up-to-date listings of businesses. Industry publications indicate current developments and trends in industry – for example, the *International Journal of Contemporary Hospitality Management*. Company brochures and annual reports outline the company's history, size and activities. Employer directories such as *The Business Who's Who* and *Kompass* list the names and locations of business people who may be potential contacts for employment.

Journals of professional associations can carry advertisements for positions.

Online job search

The Internet allows you to search quickly for vacant positions. Using a website such as <www.employment.com.au> will give you access to suitable vacancies, nationally or by state or capital city. You key in the position you are looking for – for example, accounts clerk. You can also select key words to identify the type of position – for example, full-time/permanent or casual/temporary and also the industry area you would prefer, such as Sales & Marketing or Telecommunications.

The Internet allows you to search for vacant positions.

Using a search engine and the words 'employment agencies' will give you both national and international agencies (e.g. Drake International). You can register and store your profile and résumé with an employment agency. As well as listing job opportunities, recruitment agencies will scan résumés and place them on the Web. Recruitment agencies that use the Internet will allow you to display relevant work experiences via a questionnaire and, on occasions, on the Web. The questionnaire asks for details about qualifications, experience, professional memberships, software skills and specific industry experience. Many of these websites will also give you help with preparing a résumé and advise on how to prepare for an interview.

The Internet also allows employers to find suitable people quickly. Employers can advertise through employment agencies' websites. They can do this either permanently or on a casual basis. Alternatively, employers can request an agency to forward the details of suitable applicants on their database.

You can also use the Internet to search the 'Positions Vacant' in state and national newspapers. Newspapers such as *The Sydney Morning Herald* at its website <www.smh.com.au> list all government, educational, health industry and generalist positions advertised in their daily paper.

Direct mail campaign (cold canvassing)

When looking for a job, you may decide to go one step further and seek opportunities by writing directly to companies. This is known as **cold canvassing**, or a **direct mail campaign**. Applying for unadvertised positions widens your opportunities.

Widen your job search by using a direct mail campaign.

The first step of your campaign is to determine the skills you have and the type of position suited to them. Then decide which companies might offer employment suited to your qualifications and aspirations.

Search for your targets in the index of the Yellow Pages telephone book to choose the areas of work that may interest you, and note what employment agencies are listed there.

If your résumé is ready, the next step is to prepare the unsolicited letter of application. Résumés are discussed later in this chapter.

Unsolicited letter of application

An unsolicited
letter inquires
about a position
not advertised.

An **unsolicited letter of application** is the most important part of your direct mail campaign. It is difficult to write. Its purpose is to find a position that has not been advertised, and you do not know whether a position is available.

The unsolicited letter of application is your initial contact with a potential employer. It is the covering letter and has four main parts.

1. A paragraph introducing yourself.
2. An explanation of the type of position you are looking for and are qualified for – say what you have to offer the employer.
3. A paragraph saying why you have asked this particular organisation for work.
4. A statement of where and how you can be contacted.

In this covering letter, emphasise your main strengths and write no more than one page. If you write too much or too little you defeat your purpose.

Evaluating yourself

Assess your qualifications, skills, interests, values and attitudes towards different sorts of work. Before you can develop this comprehensive list, you need to know what you do well and what you like doing.

Interests and experience

Determine your
skills, interests,
values and
attitudes.

Evaluate all your experiences and interests to reveal your major strengths and weaknesses and any talents or skills you may have overlooked or considered unimportant.

People who feel they have little or no work experience relevant to an advertised position, or those who have been out of the workforce for some time, may underrate their skills and abilities. For example, women returning to the paid workforce after being full-time homemakers have developed skills in stock control, budget management, organisation, planning and getting along with others. Many school leavers have developed their planning skills by organising school functions or by leadership and teamwork in sporting activities. School leavers also know how to manage time, set goals and work under pressure.

In voluntary social and welfare work you meet a wide range of people and become part of an organisation. Even though the work is unpaid, you gain valuable contacts, experience and skills that can be useful in other positions.

Identify your strengths and weaknesses by researching yourself. Then you can let potential employers know why you might suit a postion with them. You are the only person, apart from your referees, who can present a case on your behalf to a potential employer. Further education at Technical and Further Education (TAFE), agencies or private business colleges can upgrade your skills and qualifications to the level required by your preferred type of work.

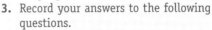

Finding a suitable position

1. a. List two people in your personal network who may be able to give you ideas or leads to potential jobs.
   b. Prepare three questions you could ask to find out about potential jobs that might match your particular strengths and aspirations. These three questions are to be asked during informal conversation with your network contacts.
2. a. What is the first section or heading in the 'Positions Vacant' section of one of your city's large newspapers? List at least two other headings or sections that might contain positions that are suited to your interests and qualifications.
   b. Make a note of two jobs listed in this week's 'Government Positions' section of the newspaper.
   c. List three publications (newspaper, trade journal or government publication) which advertise 'Positions Vacant' or courses of study that lead to employment opportunities.
   d. Use the Yellow Pages telephone directory to find the names and addresses of two private employment agencies or consultancies that advertise positions and recruit people.
3. Record your answers to the following questions.
   a. What work environments encourage success?
   b. What have I done successfully?
   c. What are my attitudes to work?
   d. What gives me greatest satisfaction in a position?
   e. What are my likes and dislikes?
   f. What have others acknowledged as my particular strengths?
   g. What types of positions do my qualifications suit?
   h. What training and development activities have extended my skills?
   i. Which of my skills can be applied to more than one position?
   From these answers develop a comprehensive list of your skills and abilities.
4. a. In Table 23.1 tick the factors that are important to you in a job.
   b. List six other factors that are important to you in a job.

Table 23.1 Important factors in a job

creativity		supervision		individualism	
routine		comfort		guidelines	
security		challenge		leadership	
initiative		risk taking		promotion	
decision making		teamwork		membership	
support		variety		fringe benefits	
groupwork		communication		tangible outcomes	

Writing a good job application

The written application is the only source of information a potential employer can assess when it comes to deciding whether you should be invited to an interview. Therefore it is important to make it as interesting, informative and persuasive as possible. A job application has two parts:

A job application consists of a covering letter and a résumé.

457

1. the résumé
2. the covering letter, or letter of application.

The **covering letter** is another term for the letter of transmittal for your résumé. It introduces your qualifications for the job and sets out to persuade the employer to invite you to an interview.

A résumé is the summary of your personal data: education, skills, qualifications, work experience, references, hobbies and interests. It is also referred to as a curriculum vitae or CV.

Résumés

Plan the résumé to suit your needs.

The **résumé** is the document that contains all your qualifications, experience and achievements. A well designed résumé presents the information in sections with headings. Choose a structure that suits your particular qualifications and experience and makes the résumé informative and interesting. The two most common types of résumé are:

■ basic (general)
■ functional.

Types of résumé

Résumés can be either basic or functional.

Once you have completed your research, choose the type of résumé and résumé format that makes the most of your suitability for the job. Table 23.2 describes these two types of résumé. Remember to use white space to emphasise particular parts of the résumé and to make it easier for the potential employer to read.

Table 23.2 Types of résumé

Type	Description
Basic résumé	Includes all the usuall parts of a résumé with appropriate headings, but is simpler and shorter than the functional résumé. The basic résumé suits those who have just left school or have little work experience. The headings shown in Figure 23.1 will help you to organise it.
Functional résumé	Uses a different order of presentation from the basic résumé to make the most of a wide range of skills and work experience (see Figure 23.2). As most employers are interested in seeing how your most recent experience matches their needs, present your work experience first, starting with the most recent, and put the rest in reverse chronological order. Develop subheadings that highlight the job functions in which you have demonstrated expertise – for example, supervisory, marketing, or training skills and responsibility. Use the advertisement as a guide for highlighting specific functions.

Headings

The résumé is organised into sections, each with a heading. The main sections could be headed as follows:

■ personal details – name at the top (easy to find), rest at the end
■ employment objective
■ education
■ work experience

Figure 23.1 Layout and function of each part of a basic résumé

Brad Anniston

1012 South Sydney Road
BONDI NSW 2026

02 9204 0011

banniston@excelmail.com.au

Employment objective

Open with a sentence or paragraph stating your reasons for wanting this position. Write the objective with a clear and confident style that shows you have something to offer the potential employer.

Educational qualifications	List all your certificates, the subjects they cover, the year each was completed, and the name of the institution that awarded each one. Never assume that the interviewer is familiar with your courses. Attach copies of these to support your application, with the most recent one on top and the rest in reverse chronological order.
Work experience	Mention all work experience, including voluntary, part-time and student vacation work. Highlight your particular strengths.
Achievements	Identify any special achievements from school or other organisations – for example, school captain, prefect or local club leader. Highlight special communication skills (e.g. public speaking, debating), as these are essential to most positions.
Activities and interests	Present your most recent activities first, with the rest following in reverse order. The employer is interested in your interests and special skills.
Referees	Nominate people who have agreed to recommend your skills and recent work.

- achievements
- interests
- referees.

You may want to vary the order of these headings, or change them to suit a particular application or to highlight your particular strengths. However, always remember to include the names of referees or people prepared to recommend your professional competence and experience.

Order the headings.

It is no longer necessary to mention your marital status or age in a résumé. If either of these personal details is necessary for the position, the interviewer will ask for them. If age and marital status have nothing to do with your ability to do the job, the question should not be asked. In Australia it is illegal for an employer to discriminate on the basis of marital status.

Research the position

When a job advertisement provides a contact telephone number, use it to find out more about the position before you prepare the résumé. Even if a contact number is not provided, you could telephone the organisation and ask for more details, research online or in business magazines in the library.

Figure 23.2 Layout of a functional résumé

Brad Anniston

1012 South Sydney Road
BONDI NSW 2026

02 9204 0011

banniston@excelmail.com.au

Employment objective

State your reason for wanting the position.

Employment experience	Present your employment history, starting with the most recent position, then proceeding in reverse order to your first position. Your most recent job functions and achievements are of greatest interest to the employer or selection panel. Give the title of each position, then briefly describe each job function, particularly those relevant to the position you are applying for. Indicate any specific achievements or initiatives you accomplished in any of your previous positions.
Educational qualifications	Fully identify your qualifications, the institutions where they were gained, and the details of course subjects. Again, present these in reverse chronological order, starting with the most recent. Emphasise any that are particularly important to your potential employer.
Activities and interests	Offer potential employers evidence of your ability to mix with others and mention any special skills that may be relevant – for example, community involvement or sporting interests.
Professional memberships	List any memberships of professional associations as these indicate that you are keeping up with the latest developments in your industry or occupation.
Referees	Present at least one who is professional and work-related, and one who will provide a character reference. An academic reference could also be useful.

It is also worth considering the length of your résumé, because this will affect the amount of time the potential employer spends reading it. If it is too long, it may be scanned rather than read carefully. If it is too short, check to see whether you have left out any important information. Bullet points and short phrases may suit some parts of the résumé better than sentences.

Whenever you use either of the two types of résumé, make it easy for the selection panel or the person responsible for the **cull** to identify your strengths. Interviewers eliminate on the basis of the job application those people considered unsuitable because of lack of qualifications, experience, ability or motivation for the position. In the résumé concentrate on the attributes that are essential and desirable for the job. Irrelevant details make it very difficult for the panel or interviewer to find what they are looking for.

Show how your qualifications match the job requirements.

After preparing your résumé, you must write a covering letter that will persuade the reader to attend carefully to your application.

Letter of application

The **letter of application** is the covering letter for your application. It should make a good first impression and should be brief (about one page). Its main purpose is to draw attention to the particular qualifications and experiences, listed in the résumé, that equip you for the job. The aim is to achieve a balance between your belief that you are suitable for the job and the potential employer's needs. It should persuade the reader to consider your application carefully, as someone potentially well suited to the advertised position. An example of a letter of application is given in Figure 23.3. Table 23.3 lists the characteristics of a poor covering letter.

Plan your covering letter carefully.

Figure 23.3 Example of letter of application or covering letter

Jennifer Omega
11 Excelsior Parade
NORTH SYDNEY NSW 2060

7 July 2003

Mr Dennis Rikkimatto
Wentworth Technology
12 Everton Avenue
NORTH RYDE NSW   2113

Dear Mr Rikkimatto

Position: Retail Sales Trainee

I am applying for the position of Retail Sales Trainee advertised in the Ryde Gazette on 5 July 2003.

I have a Certificate 111 in Information Technology (General) and I am currently studying for my Certificate 111 in Information Technology (Software Applications). I have had considerable experience in IBM-compatible hardware and software and also in server/client network hardware and software in my courses. My present position as sales assistant in a city computer store also requires me to be familiar with computer hardware and software.

I am very keen to secure the advertised position with your company. The rest of my qualifications and experience are outlined in the accompanying résumé.

The duties of my present position require me to have a high level of written and verbal communication skills as well as interpersonal skills. Essential components of the position are liaising with customers and other staff and maintaining good customer relations.

Over the past five years I have developed similar skills in previous positions as a sales assistant. These are supported by the enclosed references.

I look forward to discussing my application at an interview. I can be contacted at the above address or by telephone at 02 8867 7444.

Yours sincerely

Jennifer Omega

Table 23.3 Characteristics of a poor covering letter

- Messy appearance
- Poor layout
- Incorrect spelling
- Ambiguous words or 'buzzwords'
- Unclear, rambling sentences
- Incorrect punctuation

- Exaggeration of the applicant's abilities
- Superior, discourteous or pushy tone
- Apologetic tone
- More than one page in length
- Not enough details
- Photocopy rather than a signed original letter

The covering letter, or letter of application, has three main parts.

1. The *introduction* expresses your interest in the job.
2. The *body* points out specific qualities, qualifications and experience mentioned in your résumé, and states your interest in this organisation.
3. The *conclusion* indicates where and how you can be reached for interview.

Write the letter using the AIDA formula.

The **AIDA formula** is a helpful strategy to use for writing the application (see Table 23.4). A well planned letter is more likely to arouse a potential employer's interest in your application – enough to call you for an interview.

Table 23.4 Applying the AIDA formula to a covering letter

AIDA formula	Purpose
Attention	A covering letter should make an impact on potential employers. It states your interest in the position, and aims to catch the reader's attention. See Table 23.5 for examples of openings.
Interest	In the body of the letter, your aim is to arouse the interest of potential employers. Show how your qualifications and experience equip you for the position. One of the easiest ways to do this is to start one or two of your paragraphs with a topic sentence that includes some of the words used by the advertisement to describe the job essentials.
Desire	Refer the reader to the particular part of the résumé that supports your special strengths for the position (see the list of action words on page 469). At this point you want them to recognise your value, and to want to call you for an interview.
Action	The conclusion invites the reader to take action. As you want an interview, close by stating again that you are interested in the position and are available for interview. See Table 23.6 for examples of closings.

The advertisement in Figure 23.4 is for the position of Retail Sales Trainee to join the retail sales team of a computer store. The person must have experience in IBM-compatible computer hardware and software. A basic knowledge of server/client network hardware and software is desired and previous sales experience in the computer industry is preferred. Essential qualifications are good written and verbal communication skills.

If you applied for this job, you could include some of the words in the advertisement in your covering letter, then refer the reader to your résumé for more information.

Figure 23.3 is an example of the covering letter that could accompany an application for the position of Sales Trainee shown in Figure 23.4. In the covering letter, take care to present information that is relevant to the position you want. The potential employer is trying to achieve two things:

1. To identify the person with the required personal attributes
2. To choose someone who has the appropriate qualifications, experience and motivation to do the job, or to be trained for it.

About two weeks after you have sent off a job application, it is appropriate to make an inquiry about it, by letter or telephone. State again, courteously and clearly, your interest in the organisation and the fact that you are available and would like an interview.

Figure 23.4 'Position Vacant' advertisement

RETAIL SALES TRAINEE

FULL TIME

We require an enthusiastic, well presented and self-motivated person to join our Retail Sales team in our busy North Ryde store. You will be required to assist our existing retail customers in both computer hardware and software in a timely and accurate manner. You should have a good working knowledge of IBM-compatible computer hardware and software. A basic knowledge of server/client network hardware and software would also be desirable. Previous sales experience within the computer industry is preferred, but not essential. Good written and verbal communication skills are also essential for the role.

Please send résumé to Dennis Rikkimatto by fax 02 8945 6789 or email Dennis.rikkimatto@blue.com.au

Wentworth Technology
12 Everton Avenue
North Ryde NSW 2113

References

Work-related **references** are documents that highlight and recommend your skills and experience. They are usually written by your immediate supervisor, manager or employer. A potential employer will check these references to establish your stability, loyalty, capabilities, personality and ability to accept and carry out instructions.

Before you offer someone's name as referee, or present a written reference, it is business courtesy to warn them in advance. This can also produce a more positive report from them when they receive a telephone call about you. Prospective employers rarely accept a written reference at face value. They prefer to check by telephone with the named referees to establish the character and work history of a potential employee.

In the job application, it is wiser to include photocopies of references, not your originals. However, be prepared to present the originals at the interview. A reference is a form of report from a previous employer or co-worker that verifies your suitability for the position. Some positions may require at least one personal and one workplace or academic reference. Each reference should come from a credible source, and be professional in appearance.

Before you leave a position, think about whom you will ask to be a referee. They should be willing to recommend you and able to assess your abilities competently.

A well presented résumé is the first step towards reaching the interview. Good verbal references are invaluable when it comes to applying for a position. References from previous employers can confirm the claims you make in your résumé, particularly references that highlight your most relevant experience or skills.

Work-related references are usually written by your immediate supervisor, manager or employer.

Table 23.5 Openings for letters of application

Solicited letter

■ Identifying a common interest between you and the potential employer

'I am a trained microcomputer operator with two years' experience. I was, therefore, most interested to see your advertisement for a trained Microcomputer Operator.'

■ Focusing on the position

'I am applying for the position of Accounts Clerk.'

■ Naming the particular advertisement

'I am interested in the position of Marketing Manager – Head Office that you advertised in the *Melbourne Age* on 4 October 2000.'

■ Stating your employment interest and job objective

'I am most interested in applying for the position of Merchandise Representative. I have a thorough knowledge of your range of products, and would like to apply this knowledge to selling.'

Unsolicited letter

■ Itentifying qualifications

'As a qualified Accounts Clerk with five years' experience and an Associate Diploma in Accounting, I am seeking a position in a large organisation where I can apply my knowledge and skills.'

■ Explaining how you heard about the position

'I am inquiring about the prospects of employment in the Marketing Division of your company. An article in the *Shire News* stated that this division is rapidly expanding now that XYZ has extended its operation to include distribution.'

■ Expressing interest in work

'I wish to apply for a position with your company.'

CHECK 23.1
SELF

Covering letter

Have I	Very successfully	Successfully	Unsuccessfully
used each part of a business letter?	☐	☐	☐
named the position in the first paragraph?	☐	☐	☐
used words from the advertisement in the main body?	☐	☐	☐
mentioned attributes and qualifications suited to the position?	☐	☐	☐
expressed in the concluding paragraph my wish for an interview?	☐	☐	☐
limited the letter to one page?	☐	☐	☐
prepared an original letter suited to the position?	☐	☐	☐

Table 23.6 Closings for letters of application

Solicited letter

■ Asking for more information	'Could I call at a time convenient to you to find out more about the position? My telephone number is (04) 6562 2244.'
■ Offering to present more information at an interview	'I look forward to discussing my application at an interview.'
■ Indicating how you can be contacted	'I can be contacted on (02) 9818 5468 or at the address above.'
■ Expressing interest in an interview	'Could you advise me of the time and place of the interview? My telephone number and address are shown above.'
■ Indicating when you are available	'I am available for interview between 8.30 am and 5.30 pm Monday to Friday.'

Unsolicited letter

■ Expressing an interest in employment	'I would welcome the opportunity to discuss employment prospects with you.'
■ Indicating a desire to make further contact to arrange an interview	'I will contact your office by telephone next Tuesday to see if I can meet you to discuss my qualifications and what I can offer your organisation.'
■ Inviting a reply	'I look forward to an early reply.'

Application forms

Some employers prefer applicants to fill out a job **application form**, for at least four reasons.

1. The form uses standard questions, which makes it easier to compare the applicants.
2. The applicants' answers provide the same sort of information about them all.
3. The potential employer can see whether an applicant can interpret and answer written questions.
4. The company places the questions in such a way that the answers can be used in the order required for processing.

Read the whole form carefully, take time to think about your answers and answer every question. Then read it through and check for any spelling mistakes or incomplete answers. Mention your résumé on the form.

Complete forms carefully and accurately.

When a potential employer sends you an application form before an interview, decide whether it has sufficient space for all your relevant details. If not, your résumé and a covering letter may be attached to the form.

If the form is given to you to fill out just before your interview, attaching the résumé is not necessary as you will have the opportunity to present it and speak about it there. However, as you answer the questions, refer the reader to particular parts of your résumé that support your answers.

Temping

Temping is a growing part of the job market. Many job hunters and recruitment agencies are now using the Internet to find and place specialist temporary staff. The Internet does not replace traditional methods of selecting the right person for the role, but recruitment agencies find it useful for this purpose. Interviews, assessment of applicants, reference checks and other methods of matching people and roles are a long way from being replaced by the Internet.

Recruitment agencies

Recruitment agencies maintain a database of positions and candidates online.

Agencies build up a database of positions and candidates in an address book online. This way they can email details of permanent and temporary positions to suitable people. A job search can be emailed within an hour of a request from a company. Candidates can respond by email and attachment as soon as they receive the email. The turnaround is much faster than ordinary post ('snail mail'). Up to 30% of positions are filled by the email network.

You can also contact agencies direct to register your availability as a temporary worker. Most agencies will interview, test for competency in word-processing and communication skills and cross-check with the details on your résumé before placing you on their register. After a period of time, particularly if you have not secured any work with them, agencies will make contact to update their register. They will make certain that you are still available as a temporary and that your employment details have not altered.

Freelancing

Freelancing using the Internet is a saving for the employer.

Freelance telecommuting from home is another growing sector of the job placement market. People working from home save the employer a lot of floor space, equipment and overhead costs. Most of their communication is done by telephone, fax and email. Up to 50% of temporary placements are telecommuting positions.

Online opportunities

More and more positions are being posted on the Web. The real difficulty is for potential candidates to find job listings appropriate to their skills. Because there is so much information on the Web, useful indexes or directories are hard to find. Searches are still very broad. As the Web develops, it will become easier for potential employers, candidates and recruitment agencies to match person with position.

When surfing the Web for job opportunities, try starting at one of the generalist sites that list vacancies published in leading newspapers. For example, try <www.f2.com.au> or <www.monsterboard.com> for global vacancies. For jobs in Australia or New Zealand, try <www.monsterboard.com.au>.

People working or seeking work in the information technology and associated industries find the Internet easy to use in a job search. People working in manual industries, manufacturing, processing, building and construction are less likely to use it.

If you want to freelance, as well as searching on the Internet you can apply directly to an organisation either by email or by letter, offering your services and requesting an interview. In your covering letter you can emphasise the benefits that freelancing has for an employer – for example, flexibility, contract rates and reduced overheads. If the organisation does not reply within a reasonable period, say fourteen days, follow up with a telephone call.

Applying for a position

1. Why is it important to make a job application interesting, informative and persuasive?

2. a. List the two parts of a job application.
   b. List two types of résumé. Briefly explain the similarities and differences between them.

3. Why is it important to present your special knowledge, qualifications, skills and personal qualities in the résumé?

4. Why should you communicate with the advertisement's contact person?

5. Outline why a reference from a previous employer is invaluable to your application for a position.

6. a. Choose from a newspaper a position suited to your qualifications and interests.
   b. Prepare a résumé for this position in the format most suited to your qualifications, abilities and experience.
   c. What qualities is the employer likely to require from the applicant?

7. The Web can help employers search for and recruit temporary, contract, part-time and full-time staff. Job candidates can search for jobs and give employers direct access to their résumés and references.

a. Use a search engine to find either
   ■ an online national recruitment website or
   ■ an online global recruitment website.

b. What benefits does this site offer to candidates?

c. What services does the site offer to employers?

d. How do employers and candidates register on the site?

e. How can an employer
   ■ add a job registration to the site?
   ■ search a current candidate list according to specific job criteria?

f. What key words would you use to search the Web for a job position as a
   ■ management accountant?
   ■ website designer?
   ■ temporary professional desktop publisher?

g. What are three items you could discuss on a recruitment agency's chat page?

h. Visit a generalist site such as a newspaper website and key in the words 'temporary + jobs'. Prepare a résumé suited to one of the positions you find in this search.

Visit the Companion Website at **www.prenhall.com/dwyer_au**. Choose the Net Search activity in Chapter 23 to describe the job search tools, strategies and techniques you would use in a job search.

Chapter summary

Collect information on employment opportunities from a variety of sources. Sources include newspapers, employment agencies, professional publications and your personal networks.

Evaluate your preferences, skills, aptitude, qualifications and experience. This helps you to identify the type of work and career objectives that suit your abilities.

Make inquiries about a position. Focus your job search so you can match your strengths and abilities to the job requirements.

Prepare a résumé that shows how your qualifications match the job requirements. Once you choose an appropriate type of résumé, present your educational qualifications, your range of experience, your achievements and attributes and any special interests in the most appropriate way. The two main types of résumé are the basic résumé and the functional résumé.

Write a covering letter for the job application. This is a persuasive letter that aims to attract a potential employer's attention and enough interest to call you for an interview. It has three main parts: introduction, body and conclusion, and should be short, no more than one page in length.

Use a search engine to find an online recruitment website. The Web can help employers search for and recruit temporary, contract, part-time and permanent staff. A key-word search is the easiest way to narrow down the search for the position that best matches your qualifications and experience.

Identify the main components of an online recruitment site. These sites offer job advertisements and other services free to job seekers. Candidates register their details online, to form a database for search criteria. Employers register their positions online. Contact details are not released to anyone until a candidate's suitability is assessed and the employer and candidate give permission to release the details.

REVIEW QUESTIONS

1. Why should you try several different ways to find a position?
2. List two reasons for analysing your experience and interests.
3. Identify two organisations that can help you collect information on employment opportunities.
4. a. Define the term 'direct mail campaign'.
   b. Briefly explain its purpose.
   c. What is an unsolicited letter of application?
   d. List the four parts of an unsolicited letter of application (covering letter).
5. Give three reasons for investigating a position.
6. What is the main purpose of the letter of application?
7. What kind of result does a covering letter or letter of application attempt to achieve? Why must the covering letter be a persuasive letter? Explain how the AIDA formula is used in a covering letter.
8. The résumé demonstrates your skills, experience and qualifications. What does the covering letter do?
9. List the three important parts of a letter of application.
10. Name four characteristics of a poor covering letter. How could you avoid each of these?
11. a. List two different types of résumé.
    b. Name and describe the parts of a basic résumé.
    c. What is the difference between a basic and a functional résumé?
12. How do references support your application?
13. List two reasons why employers use application forms.
14. What is the purpose of an online recruitment website?
15. What are the advantages and disadvantages of conducting a job search online?

Prepare a résumé

SKILLS
BUILD

From one of last Saturday's national or metropolitan newspapers, choose a position that interests you.

1. Analyse this advertisement by listing
   a. the educational qualifications it requires
   b. any additional qualifications required
   c. any special skills needed
   d. any conditions that apply
   e. the extent of experience required
   f. the contact person to ring, or to whom the application should be sent
   g. your particular interest in this position.
2. Analyse your qualifications for this position.
3. Write a career objective suited to this position.

4. What sections or headings would you use when preparing a résumé for this position?
5. Draft the Work Experience section of a résumé, using at least six of the action words listed below.
6. Complete your résumé in the basic or functional résumé format.
7. If you were placing your résumé with an online recruitment agency, list at least six key words that would make it easy for an online employer to determine whether you suit the position they want to fill.
8. Would you change the résumé before you asked the recruitment agency to scan and place it on the Web? How?

■ expand	■ obtain	■ communicate
■ initiate	■ evaluate	■ interpret
■ report	■ operate	■ supervise
■ maintain	■ program	■ analyse
■ install	■ print	■ negotiate
■ solve	■ create	■ analyse
■ design	■ liaise	■ delegate

Key terms

AIDA formula
application form
basic résumé
cold canvassing
covering letter

cull
direct mail campaign
employment agency
functional résumé
letter of application

network
reference
résumé
unsolicited letter of
   application

People power

CASE STUDY

by Matt Buchanan

For many people, 'networking' is a dirty word and a vile concept. Why? Because its smacks of ulterior motive, premeditation and insincerity. Is there anything more distasteful than the habit of buttering up strangers – *using* them – for personal gain?

But, here's a surprise. Networking does not have to be double-dealing, bogus or crafty. Most of us, including a good per-centage of those who sniff disdainfully at the idea of creating and maintaining a network of professional relationships, have at some stage arrived at a job, courtesy of a contact. We might even have employed people based on a colleague's recommendation. (As everybody knows, a snappy CV and a reference that sings doesn't stand much of a chance against a colleague's recommendation.)

That is not to say that networking 'snobs' are hypocrites, even if they have been prospering from vigorously practising what they purport to loathe. They – all right, let's be honest, we – just don't recognise when we're doing it.

'At any gathering of people in a function, whether it's a funeral, wedding or professional association, networking takes place,' says Paul Stevens, the founder and director of the Centre for Worklife Counselling and author of *How to Network and Select a Mentor, Sponsor or Coach*.

'It's not a discrete career management technique. It's a natural human condition. It's well-nigh impossible for people to enrich their careers without alliances and partnerships with others. And to get alliances and partnerships with others you need to network. QED.'

Stevens agrees that if we can accept we're always inadvertently networking, then the logical next step is to impose, well, a little logic concerning how we go about it.

'You could enhance the manner of how you network,' he suggests. 'A thank-you letter or thank-you email as a follow-up after a person has facilitated your information gathering. Think back to what grandma said: fundamental politeness is the real issue. But no one minds sharing information if the motive is an ethical one and, secondly, the approach is civil.'

Stevens crisply defines networking as 'information gathering, or introducing to another person'.

'You're after data, or people, or both,' he says. 'The most critical thing is to define for yourself what it is that you are seeking. You can't just go into a meeting of people and bail someone up, glass in hand, and say, "I'm seeking career happiness, can you help me?".

'You've got to get your information need quite specific before you open your mouth. Otherwise,' Stevens says, 'people think, "Who's this weird person. Bugger it. I won't help them".'

The trick to networking, then, appears to be twofold. First of all, admit the necessity of nurturing alliances and partnerships. And then, rather than feeling slippery and counterfeit in your dealings, cast aside your copy of *Brown-nosing for Beginners* and

instead be unambiguously – and unapologetically – open.

It makes sense. After all, how else could you respect yourself in the morning?

'State the reason for your request,' suggests Stevens. 'You don't have to be secretive about it. The person you ask either says, "I know the person who could facilitate this", or they don't.'

The next step in your new networking life is to start casting about for someone willing to take a lasting interest in your career.

In short, you need to go shopping for a mentor. And don't be intimidated. The big bosses want to help you. Really.

'Think of fundamental human nature,' says Stevens. 'People like being asked for their opinions. It's a fundamental vanity of humankind. That is why senior people, subject to the nature of the approach and the stated reason, are only too willing to help.'

All of this assumes, of course, that you have a job. But don't assume that if you're unemployed you're living in a network-free zone. Stevens says he has just seen a poll of career counsellors from 33 countries that surveyed job success rates.

Networking accounted for 65 per cent of job placements, and for executives it was 75 per cent. Responses to print media advertisements accounted for 9 per cent. He adds that this does not mean the unemployed are simply cold-calling companies and hoping for the best. Rather, they are simply following the basic principles of networking.

'Work out what it is you want to find out,' says Stevens, 'get in contact with whoever you think has the information you require and state the reasons why you're asking in essentially a civil and polite fashion.'

<wetfeet.com> <monster.com>

Ten tips for killer networking

1. You scratch my back, I'll scratch yours.

Trust the principle that if you ask for ideas or referrals people will respond because in the future they may come to you. What goes around...

2. Don't be intimidated.

Most people in business understand networking and will welcome your inquiry. Also, even if you think you're inexperienced, consider what you have to offer.

3. Be polite and clear.

A civil, polite inquiry that doesn't beat around the bush is more likely to be welcomed.

4. Plan your networking.

Create a list of people you know and ask them for ideas, referrals and contacts. Every contact you make while working is a potential jewel in your networking crown.

5. Maintain your contacts.

Once you have your job, don't forget who helped get you there. Maybe there's something they need that you can help them with.

6. Don't wait until you're desperate.

Keep your network healthy so that if the work climate changes you're ready for it. In other words, don't rest on your oars.

7. Look close to home.

Sometimes the most valuable networking you can do is within your company. They know you and you know them.

8. Always ask permission to use a name.

By mentioning names, you are able to capitalise on your contact's reputation and implicit approval. So it pays not to offend by assuming their concurrence beforehand.

9. Report back.

Show you understand and appreciate others' effort and contribution. It paves the way for future contact.

10. Find a mentor.

Senior executives are not as remote or hostile to your inquiries as you may think and are often only too happy to be asked their opinion.

Source: Matt Buchanan, 'People Power', *Sydney Morning Herald*, 9–10 February 2002, My Career, p. 1. Reproduced with the consent of the author.

Questions

1. The article suggests '… a snappy CV and a reference that sings doesn't stand much chance against a colleague's recommendation'. Discuss the importance of networking when seeking or apply for a job.

2. Briefly describe three strategies used by successful networkers.

3. Self-promotion is a key component of networking when seeking a position. Comment.

The job interview

In this chapter you will learn how an interviewer:

- plans an interview

- prepares suitable questions

- gives clear information

- uses appropriate questioning techniques

- conducts an interview

- proposes appropriate follow-up activites.

Evaluate your communication skills by completing the self-check in the chapter.

Before you attend an interview, it is important that you understand why and how interviews are organised and conducted. An organisation uses a job interview to select the best applicant for a position. The interview is structured to ensure that the questions asked will differentiate between candidates.

To perform successfully in an interview, you should know the various stages in an interview, the interviewer's goals and the types of questions an interviewer will ask. Chapter 25, Being Interviewed for a Job, will help you to prepare for an interview and present yourself competently.

Characteristics of an interview

An interview is a means of gathering or exchanging information.

An **interview** may be planned and highly formal, or it may be the informal information-gathering interview that is part of daily problem solving in the workplace. Whatever its purpose, it is important that an interview is conducted well.

An interview involves the **interviewer** (the person conducting it) and the **interviewee** (the person being interviewed). In a successful interview, information flows between them. Both interviewer and interviewee can express views and use the interview process in a purposeful manner.

An interview is essentially an exchange of information. What distinguishes it from a casual conversation, which is also an exchange of information, is that it:

■ is planned
■ is prearranged
■ is structured
■ is controlled by the interviewer
■ has a predetermined purpose
■ takes place between two or more people of different status.

A crucial factor is that the interview is controlled by the interviewer. This means that the interviewer encourages the interviewee to answer questions fully, stops the interviewee who talks too much, handles upset or hostile interviewees, paces the interview so that adequate time is available, and guides and directs it to a successful conclusion. The interview loses focus if there is a lack of control.

Stages of an interview

The interview has five stages.

The interview structure generally includes the five stages shown in Table 24.1.

Types of job interviews

Interviews can be either a single interview, panel interview or series interview.

The three main types of job interview are shown in Table 24.2.

Goals of a job interview

Select the candidate with the best credentials for the position.

When conducting a **job interview**, the interviewer wants to attract and choose the best applicant for the position. The interviewer's goals are to:

■ gather information from interviewees to assess their future performance
■ inform applicants about the job and the organisation
■ determine applicants' ability to work with others and fit into the organisation's culture.

Table 24.1 Summary of tasks completed by the interviewer at each stage

Stage of the interview	Tasks	Specific examples
Pre-interview stage	■ Identifies essentials and desirables ■ Prepares questions: open, closed, probing ■ Short-lists candidates	■ Uses position description ■ Asks manager for any particular skills and attributes ■ Finds application, telephones the referees, checks qualifications
Opening	■ Opens the interview ■ Puts the interviewee at ease ■ Answers questions	■ Greets the interviewee ■ States the interview's purpose ■ Builds the interviewee's confidence
Body	■ Obtains specific information ■ Asks open, closed and problem-solving questions	■ Listens carefully and with empathy ■ Uses positive nonverbal behaviour ■ Paraphrases
Closing	■ Summarises what has taken place ■ Indicates clearly that the interview is over ■ Closes the interview	■ Asks interviewees if they would like to ask any questions ■ Encourages further questions ■ Thanks interviewee for attending
Post-interview stage	■ Evaluates each interviewee objectively ■ Makes selection ■ Completes records ■ Informs successful candidates ■ Informs unsuccessful candidates	■ Uses rating scales ■ Discusses respondent's document ■ Completes notes ■ Maintains confidentiality ■ Records result

Potential problems

Interviews do not always succeed in choosing the best person for the job. Problems include:

■ poor planning
■ lack of objectives
■ lack of structure
■ little knowledge of the job under discussion
■ judging the applicant on inappropriate or irrelevant criteria
■ poor listening, so that the interviewer hears only part of the interviewee's answer
■ the influence of personal bias.

These problems are avoided if the interviewer has planned the interview carefully and conducts it skilfully. Ways of achieving an interviewer's goals are discussed in the next section.

Table 24.2 Types of job interviews

Type of interview	Description
1. The single interview	Is conducted by a single interviewer responsible for interviewing all applicants and selecting the new staff member. It can be affected by the interviewer's bias because he or she is the sole person involved in assessing the applicant's abilities.
2. The series interview	Is conducted by several interviewers in turn, in separate interviews. Each one evaluates each applicant on a specific area of expertise. After the series of interviews the interviewers consult each other to make a group selection. The process of a series interview and its result are not very different from the panel interview. In each case, a group of interviewers assesses the quality of the applicants.
3. The panel interview	Is conducted by a group of interviewers all together. Each member of the panel asks specific questions relevant to their special experience and expertise. This range of experience allows for a wider selection of questions and answers and helps to minimise personal bias. The panel works together to assess the applicant.
	The interview panel should include at least one woman and one man, to support the principles of Equal Employment Opportunity. Members of an interview panel should know how to conduct and participate in an interview. They should try not to allow bias to affect the quality of their decision.

Planning an interview

Much of the work done by the interviewer must be completed before the interview, in the pre-interview stage. The following steps are usually planned before the interview takes place.

Pre-interview stage

Identify the essential and desirable job qualifications.

The interviewer analyses the job by identifying all the tasks, activities, skills and personal attributes it requires. A job specification or description is created if one does not exist already. The **job specification** is the basis for the essential and desirable qualities listed in the advertisement and is also the basis for the questions in the interview. The job specification is made available to interviewees to enable them to become familiar with any relevant information that may be needed.

Before the interview, the interviewer finds out as much as possible about the interviewees by checking their application forms and references.

The interviewer determines the style and structure of the interview. Is it to be a directive or non-directive style of interview? **Directive interviews** are controlled and organised by the interviewer. A **non-directive interview** involves a cooperative effort by the participants and the organisation in setting its goals and process. Employment interviews are usually directive.

Equal Employment Opportunity

The merit principle selects the best person for the position.

Equal Employment Opportunity (EEO) and Affirmative Action policies and programs have been created in response to legislation, and aim for the fairer representation in employment of all groups in the community. EEO applies the **merit principle**: the best and most efficient person must be selected. As a result, no person should be discriminated against on the basis of:

- gender
- marital status
- ethnic or racial grounds
- physical handicap
- intellectual impairment
- sexual preference
- age.

Equal opportunity occurs when people's chances of employment, promotion, training or obtaining any other employment benefit or opportunity are neither reduced nor increased on the basis of the characteristics listed above.

Equal employment opportunity has become a part of management practice in the public and private sectors. It aims to avoid discrimination. **Discrimination** in the workplace means denying people equal treatment for reasons other than those relating directly to the job. One of the purposes of this legislation is to ensure that an organisation's recruitment is based on merit. The person with the skills, experience and qualifications best suited to the job should get the job.

Question preparation

A set of questions about the interviewee's qualifications, previous job experience, career ambitions, goals, and attitudes towards the organisation's products or policies are prepared. The interviewer's aim is to create clear, specific questions that will adequately establish the applicant's capacity to meet the demands of the job. Questions should also be relevant, unambiguous and free from bias, so that no particular community group is favoured or disadvantaged. The interviewer should take into consideration federal and state anti-discrimination legislation.

Clear, specific questions are prepared.

The interviewer should ask a range of questions to evaluate the extent of the interviewee's knowledge. The four types of questions in Table 24.3 are particularly important. They should all be asked in a well structured interview. If questions are prepared carefully, the interview should be conducted effectively.

The interview process should be fair and open to scrutiny. Below each question, in the interviewer's notes, the type of response expected should be identified to enable the interviewer to check as each applicant answers the questions.

Questions may cover topics such as communication skills, energy and motivation levels, creativity, ability to handle stress, career ambitions, persuasiveness, initiative, planning, controlling and analytical skills.

Short-listing candidates

Sometimes more applications for a position are received than the number of applicants the interviewer is willing to interview. In this case, a **short list** of those who best suit the position is prepared. First, the information in their applications is compared against what the job requires – the essential and desirable qualifications and skills. This tells the interviewer which applicants are suitable. The interview short list is then compiled. Next, the interviewer should, as a courtesy, inform all applicants whether or not their application is successful. Those who are successful are invited to an interview, and those who are not should be thanked.

Candidates are short listed according to the essential and desirable requirements.

An appropriate room and seating should be organised for the interview. The interview should be held in a comfortable, private place free from all distractions. The interviewees should be advised of details such as time, room and what documents they should bring to the interview.

Table 24.3 Types of interview questions

Type	Purpose	Examples
Open questions	Open questions encourage interviewees to speak freely and talk about themselves, while the interviewer listens, observes and makes notes. Interviewees' trust and confidence determine how much information and opinion they offer. The open question helps to overcome some of the apprehension and defensiveness an interviewee often feels. Open questions should be used carefully and sparingly as they can elicit time-consuming answers and irrelevant information. Their success depends on the interviewee's communication skills and on the interviewer's skill at analysing the response.	As interviewers listen, they may decide to probe for further information or clarification of a point: ■ 'Could you tell me a little about how you got your promotion?' ■ 'What did you do then?' ■ 'How do you induct a new person into your team?'
Closed questions	Closed questions are designed to limit interviewees' responses and to establish familiar facts, such as address, previous employment and qualifications. The main disadvantage of closed questions is that they elicit very little information, and discourage further explanation by the applicant.	Closed questions can clarify or fill any gaps in the answers to open questions: ■ 'Have you used Dataflex?' ■ 'Have you got a First Aid Certificate?'
Mirror questions	Mirror questions restate the interviewees' previous answer and invite them to add further information. They give the interviewee accurate feedback and allow the interviewer to check their understanding of the applicant's reply.	■ *Interviewee's answer:* 'I thought the team I worked with on the project was great.' ■ *Mirror question:* 'The team was great?' ■ *Interviewee:* 'Yes. We shared ideas and I liked the support of working in a team.'
Probing questions	Probing questions follow on from the interviewee's last response. This type of question is spontaneous rather than planned. It aims to probe the basis for the interviewee's response and gather more information.	■ *Interviewee's response:* 'My present job requires me to manage my time.' ■ *Interviewer's probing question:* 'How do you manage your time?'

An interview

1. Work in groups of four to complete the following tasks.
   a. Discuss and list five tasks you would complete as interviewer in the pre-interview stage of a job interview.
   b. Consider an interview you have attended and discuss what you liked and disliked about the way it was opened.
   c. As a group, list three ways of opening an interview that help the interviewee to relax and feel comfortable.
   d. Identify and discuss three responsibilities an interviewer has in the closing stages of an interview.

2. a. In groups of four, describe your best and worst interview experience. If you have not been for an interview, imagine the best and worst experience.
   b. Create a list of the group's worst experiences and brainstorm to suggest ways of improving the situation for an interviewee.

Conducting an interview

Once the content of the interview has been prepared, the interview is ready to be conducted. By distinguishing between directive and non-directive techniques, the interviewer will be able to use each to keep the interview open and to encourage interviewees to express themselves clearly.

Non-directive techniques use minimal questions, maintain a conversational rather than an interrogatory tone, and adopt positive nonverbal cues such as pauses and nods to encourage the applicant. **Directive techniques** include open-ended questions and specific probing questions to focus on a particular topic and gain further information or clarification.

Non-directive techniques depend largely on nonverbal communication.

Opening the interview

The interviewer should create a friendly environment to put the interviewee at ease. People who feel at ease are better able to answer questions.

Interviewers should greet applicants by name and introduce themselves and the panel by name and job designation. Simple courtesies make a person feel welcome. The interviewee is shown to a chair and perhaps offered refreshment. Some interviewers like to talk about general topics such as local events or sport to make the applicant feel at ease; however, care is taken not to stray too far from the interview's purpose.

The interviewer starts the interview by stating its purpose and intended result. Interviewers should be specific and avoid generalities. They tell the interviewee whether they intend to take notes and explain the length of time allotted to the interview.

There is no single correct interviewing style or method of establishing and maintaining rapport. Interviewers should be aware of their own communication style, particularly the use of nonverbal cues such as eye contact, facial expressions, body posture, gestures and voice level – the interviewee reads these as well as hearing the spoken words. Interviewers should be aware of different personalities and cultural backgrounds, project an encouraging, positive attitude and maintain a professional and courteous manner.

The interviewer's nonverbal cues are important to the interviewee.

Body of the interview

In the body of the interview, the interviewer should begin with simple questions to help the applicant build confidence. The interview should then progress with questions on

The interviewer's questions should be clear and purposeful.

work experience, education and personal details. Questions should be kept clear and purposeful. **Open questions** are used to encourage the interviewee to speak freely; closed questions limit the response. Some examples of open questions are:

- 'I see from your résumé that you are currently working in retail management. Please summarise your major responsibilities.'
- 'I see you are currently employed as an accounts clerk. What does that job involve?'
- 'Would you please summarise your main responsibilities as an accounts clerk?'

For applicants with little or no work experience, begin with their interests or training and education. Ask such questions as:

- 'I notice that your course included a major project. What skills did you require to complete it?'
- 'You've had experience as a volunteer in a welfare agency. In what ways did you find that work satisfying?'

Throughout the interview, the purpose is twofold: to obtain specific information from the applicant and to make the interview comfortable for the applicant. Interviewers generally take notes to jog their memory at the post-interview stage when they must choose one of the applicants. However, the interviewer should take care to maintain eye contact with, and interest in, the interviewee.

At this stage of the interview, the interviewer is forming an impression of how well the applicant can speak and relate to others. Sometimes, however, the interview situation does not allow interviewees to demonstrate all their skills and ability to perform the job.

Some interviewee responses may be inadequate, irrelevant, poorly organised or inaccurate. The interviewer should listen carefully and with empathy. On occasion, the interviewer will vary the type of question, to clarify information or to allow the applicant to elaborate.

The interviewer questions, listens and gives answers.

Interviewers should check their understanding and give interviewees accurate feedback by summarising what they have said. For example:

- *Interviewee:* 'As well as liaising with wholesalers and suppliers regarding stock control, I was also responsible for controlling finances.'
- *Interviewer:* 'So your major responsibilities were to keep stock inventory, deal with day-to-day problems with suppliers and check their deliveries? You also controlled all finances for the company?'

A **panel interview** can be stressful for an inexperienced interviewee because several people have to be addressed. Panel members can help the applicant to remain calm by asking one question each, in turn, and by maintaining interest and supportive eye contact.

The applicant also has questions that should be answered. The interviewer should encourage the applicant to ask questions by such statements as:

- 'Are there any points you would like clarified?'
- 'Do you have any questions for the panel?'
- 'Can we give you more information about . . .?'

The interviewer should anticipate the questions the applicant may ask and have relevant information ready – for example, written summaries of policies, or guidelines. Some organisations always give these to applicants. However, it is the interviewer's responsibility to give applicants accurate job information, to answer their questions, and to allow them scope to discuss their abilities.

Types of questions asked at interviews

1. What is the purpose of
   a. an open question?
   b. a closed question?
   c. a probing question?
   d. a mirror question?
2. Prepare a final question that invites the interviewee to ask the panel any questions.
3. In groups of three:
   a. Discuss which characteristics of the interviewer and the interviewee can affect the result of an interview.
   b. Consider the interviewer's messages in Table 24.4. Decide on appropriate nonverbal behaviour for each spoken message and write it in the second column. The interviewer is trying to create an open, supportive environment to encourage interviewees to talk about their skills and abilities.

   c. When you have completed Table 24.4, two people in your group will role-play the situation while the third person watches and records the interviewer's nonverbal communication. Then compare the nonverbal messages used in the role play with the appropriate nonverbal messages that you noted in Table 24.4.

   If you have trouble listing suitable nonverbal messages, try the role play first and then list the appropriate behaviours.
   d. Which nonverbal factors expressed by interviewees are likely to make the most impact on the interviewers?

Table 24.4 Consistent verbal/nonverbal communication

Verbal message	Appropriate nonverbal behaviour
■ 'Good morning. How are you?'	Smiles, leans forward, shakes hands.
■ 'Did you have any trouble finding us?'	
■ 'The interview is for the position of Purchasing Officer. Why are you interested in this position?'	
■ 'In your application you state that you check all invoices. Could you tell me how you do this?'	
■ 'Where do you expect to be one year from now?'	
■ 'Which software package do you use?'	
■ 'Are you satisfied with that package?'	
■ 'Do you have any questions about the job?'	
■ 'Thank you for your application and for coming to the interview.'	

Closing the interview

The main points and facts presented during the interview should be summarised and highlighted to avoid any misunderstandings. The interviewer should indicate any further action that must be completed. The interviewer then indicates clearly that the interview is over and thanks applicants for their application and for attending the interview.

Post-interview stage

Immediately after the interview, the interviewers record or complete notes on all the important points. They must now try to form an objective opinion of each applicant from the information provided by applicants and from any other information available. At this stage, interview evaluation sheets or rating scales are often used. Some organisations require interviewers to complete a report on the interview. Apart from that, all notes, documents and results are kept confidential.

The interviewers need to inform everyone of the decision within a reasonable amount of time, usually ten working days. Follow up in writing to the successful person. Unsuccessful applicants should also receive a courteous letter.

Common mistakes made by interviewers

There are several common mistakes that interviewers make. Each mistake places someone in the interview process at a disadvantage or at an advantage. The aim of a selection interview is to choose the best person for the job. By avoiding these mistakes an interviewer is able to choose the best person more effeciently.

Some of the mistakes made by interviewers are:

- relying on first impressions
- rating towards the average
- relying on overall impression: the 'halo' effect
- placing too much emphasis on negative information
- making a rushed decision.

By relying on first impressions, interviewers often miss important information or the opportunity to judge it fairly. The first impression could come from the application file, the way interviewees dress or how they perform in the opening stages of the interview. If favourable information is presented first, less favourable answers given later in the interview may slip past unnoticed.

When interviewers rate towards the average, it is harder to distinguish between applicants. If 15 people are interviewed and they are all clustered around the average rating, it is much harder to make the final decision.

At the interview, applicants should be evaluated according to specific criteria required by the position. The 'halo' effect describes a decision based on an overall impression gained from general characteristics rather than from these criteria.

A rushed decision based on first impressions can miss important information given by applicants. It is better for interviewers to take time to discuss and evaluate each interviewer's impressions of each applicant. A considered decision is more likely to produce the best choice of applicant.

After the interview, as an interviewee you can follow up the interview with a 'thank you' letter or a phone call. If you are notified that you were unsuccessful, you can contact the convenor of the interview panel and request information on how you performed. This may provide an opportunity for you to point out information that you feel could have been overlooked by the interview panel.

Visit the Companion Website at **www.prenhall.com/dwyer_au**. Choose the Multiple Choice activity in Chapter 24 and answer the questions. How would you describe your knowledge of the interviewer's role in a job interview?

Chapter summary

Plan the interview procedure as an interviewer. An interviewer and an applicant for a position have different goals and different roles. Both should prepare for the interview. A job interviewer should plan an interview opening that establishes the relationship, a body that seeks and gives information, and a closing stage that summarises what has taken place.

Prepare suitable questions. Questions should be asked that are relevant to the job requirements and possible answers anticipated. The applicant's abilities should be discussed. Interviewers should choose the most appropriate style of question to obtain the information they need. The four types of questions an interviewer can use are open, closed, mirror and probing questions, and each has a particular purpose. Open questions encourage others to speak freely. Closed questions limit the response to facts. Mirror questions restate the interviewee's response in different words. Probing questions follow up the last response to gather more information or clarify a point.

Give the interviewee clear information. Interviewing is based on sending and receiving messages. Interviewers should listen carefully, give feedback and provide whatever information the interviewee needs. They should speak clearly, show empathy for the interviewee and behave courteously.

Use appropriate questioning techniques. To encourage interviewees to express themselves clearly, the interviewer uses either non-directive or directive techniques.

Conduct an interview. To conduct a structured interview, the interviewer moves through the opening stage, the body and the concluding stage.

Propose appropriate follow-up activities. In the post-interview stage of a job interview, interviewers evaluate the applicant and the results of the interview. They complete the necessary records and maintain confidentiality. The interviewee follows up the interview with a 'thank you' letter or telephone call if they have not been contacted. Interviewees can contact the panel convenor to ask why they were unsuccessful. The interviewer notifies the successful and unsuccessful applicants in writing.

1. How does an interview differ from a conversation?

2. List the five stages of an interview.

3. a. What is the difference between a single interview, a series interview and a panel interview?
   b. Compare the merits of the panel interview with those of the single interview.

4. What responsibilities does the

interviewer have in preparing for a job interview?

5. Briefly explain three problems that may arise for the job applicant in an interview.

6. Why is it important for the interviewer to let job applicants demonstrate their abilities and skills at an interview?

7. a. List four types of questions you could use as an interviewer.
   b. Describe the advantages of each.
8. List three tasks to be completed at the pre-interview stage.
9. What is the difference between a directive and non-directive interview?
10. a. What is the interviewer's role in the opening stage of the interview?
    b. What is their role in the body of the interview?
    c. What is their role in the closing stage?
11. a. What is the purpose of a closed question?
    b. What is the purpose of an open question?

The job interview

BUILD SKILLS

Working in groups of three or four, prepare the interviewer's questions to those applying for this advertised position of Sales Representative. Read the questions that follow first.

SALES REPRESENTATIVE
NEW AND USED VEHICLES

Essential

We require a salesperson with proven selling skills. You will be a skilled communicator and happy to deal with the public. You will also need skill in maintaining records. We are looking for someone who is highly motivated to succeed.

Desirable

Ideally, you will have experience with both new and used vehicle sales and be able to prospect for new clients. We offer a generous retainer, a commission scheme and a company demonstrator vehicle.

For confidential interview, please forward your application to:
N. Gibson, General Sales Manager, 651 Princes Road, Adelaide 5000.

---

1. Create two questions to open the interview and two questions to close it.
2. Create five questions that will help you evaluate each applicant's ability to carry out the essential and desirable tasks outlined in the advertisement.
3. Be sure to include at least one open, one closed, one probing and one mirror question.
4. Create an evaluation sheet to help you evaluate and compare the answers given by each interviewee.
5. Conduct a panel interview. Two people interview another for the Sales Representative position. A fourth person observes and uses Self-check 24.1 to evaluate the performance of the two interviewers.

SELF CHECK 24.1

Behaviour as an interviewer

As an interviewer, did you	Very successfully	Successfully	Unsuccessfully
define the interview's purpose?	☐	☐	☐
show interest and involvement?	☐	☐	☐
prevent interruptions?	☐	☐	☐
prepare questions?	☐	☐	☐
prepare answers?	☐	☐	☐
prepare an evaluation sheet?	☐	☐	☐

	Very successfully	Successfully	Unsuccessfully
listen carefully?	☐	☐	☐
show empathy for the interviewee?	☐	☐	☐
show courtesy?	☐	☐	☐
assess your own behaviour?	☐	☐	☐
dress appropriately?	☐	☐	☐
respect the interviewee's personal space?	☐	☐	☐
complete each stage of the interview?	☐	☐	☐
the interview's purpose?	☐	☐	☐

Key terms

closed question
directive interview
directive techniques
discrimination
Equal Employment
   Opportunity (EEO)
interview

interviewee
interviewer
job interview
job specification
merit principle
mirror question
non-directive interview

non-directive techniques
open question
panel interview
probing question
series interview
short list
single interview

Choose or lose

by Simon Lane

The recruitment process is often a time-consuming exercise. First you have to ensure that the job is designed properly, that you can afford to hire, that the recruitment ad is in the right place and looks good, and that internal employees have been advised about the opportunity. Then there's whether or not to engage the services of a recruitment agency, that the screening is appropriate, that the interviews are conducted using appropriate techniques and interviewers, that references are checked . . . *gasp, choke, puff* . . . and only then do you find someone you want to hire!

Yet it constantly amazes me that people think that when you arrive at *this* point, recruitment and selection is almost at an end. WRONG!

There is a strong expectation – not unfounded – that someone interested in joining your business who has got to the point of selection by you has demonstrated interest in winning the job. However, there are many mental checks that an applicant goes through before they agree to a job offer. These include whether:

- the job is advertised in a way they find attractive
- the job represents some of their desires in terms of location, career opportunity, salary package, and duties and responsibilities
- the company presents itself well through its interviewer
- the company itself presents well
- the job is represented similarly to or better than the advertisement that initially attracted them
- it's an improvement on their current position.

It should be no surprise that many of these issues can be addressed by the way a company puts together its recruitment advertisement, and the way the interviewer supports and supplements it.

By doing this well, no candidate should arrive at the job-offer stage and be completely surprised by things such as salary, benefits, hours of work, duties and responsibilities, location, or even starting date. They all should have been discussed at some point, even in general terms.

For example, if you wish to consider the

salary you want to pay *after* you have made your selection, then you could set expectations in the ad or at the interview in general terms. Statements such as 'a package of around $60,000' or 'salary between $45,000 and $55,000, plus benefits depending on experience' are ways in which you can frame the candidates' expectations.

There are two issues that research has shown to affect attraction to advertised jobs. The first is that jobs that advertise with some salary or package information will attract more applicants than those ads without such information.

The second is that most applicants will need assistance from the recruiter to understand what a job is actually paying. As such, a company that advertises a position as 'a package of around $60,000' may only be paying $45,000 base salary, but may attach to this superannuation above the legislated requirements, car allowances, free mobile phone and laptop (that may also be for personal use), educational support, parking, discounted product, etc.

The worth of this needs to be spelt out as some components will be included in the final contract signed. My point here is that by taking the time to add up what goes with the job, you can make the conditions just that bit more attractive without being misleading.

So with all of the excitement you can muster, you ring the selected applicant and break the good news! If your explanations and conditioning have been strong, the reac-tion should be a mixture of happiness and excitement. If it's not, it might be because:

- you haven't given them enough information for them to know whether your offer of a job is a good thing yet, or
- the offer isn't as good as they thought it would be.

Source: Simon Lane, 'Choose or Lose', *Charter*, October 2001, p. 40.

Questions

1. An effective interviewer (or interview panel) completes a number of activities before the interview takes place. Discuss these.
2. The article suggests '. . . no candidate should arrive at the job-offer stage and be completely surprised by things such as salary, benefits, hours of work and responsibilities, location or even starting date'.
   a. Discuss the advantages of ensuring the candidate has clear and complete information about the position.
   b. Discuss any barriers that can impede interviewer(s) in an interview.
3. a. What are the mental checks you would go through before you would agree to a job offer?
   b. Why should the interviewer(s) and company present themselves well in an interview?

Being interviewed for a job

In this chapter you will learn how to:

○ make inquiries about a position

○ prepare for a job interview

○ work out probable questions and suitable answers

○ present yourself competently at a job interview

○ evaluate your own performance

○ follow up after the job interview.

Evaluate your communication skills by completing the self-check in the chapter.

A job interview is your chance to speak in support of your application for the position. You are able to demonstrate, by your responses to questions and by your general behaviour, your interest in the position.

As an applicant for a job, it is important that you present yourself well. You need to impress the interviewer. The interview itself has a structure and a purpose. At the interview your role is to demonstrate your interest in, and suitability for, the job. How well you do that influences your immediate career opportunities. Chapter 24 outlines the types of job interviews and how an interview is planned, structured and conducted. As an interviewee, it is important to be aware of the different stages of an interview, and the types of questions that you will be asked. Your responses will allow you to demonstrate your capabilities, interests and expertise.

Before the interview

The letter inviting you to an interview arrives. Immediately, write the place, date and time of interview in your diary. Check that you will have enough time to prepare yourself for it. As the applicant, you have several different tasks ahead of you.

Finding out about the position

Research the company and its values.

Try to find out as much as possible about the position and the company before the interview. Do this by telephoning your contacts or the company. Usually, the job advertisement provides the name of a contact person, and a job description outlining the duties and responsibilities of the position. You may even see whether it is possible to visit the company to find out more. An online search lets you find out about the company quickly. Using a search engine and the company's name will take you to the home page. As you research, find out what you can about the company's values and the kind of people it employs. This will help you to decide whether you will be able to fit in.

Identifying your strengths

Research, prepare and identify your strengths.

Make a self-evaluation. Know your own aims and the requirements for the job. Analyse the advertisement to assess what essential and desirable skills and qualities the job requires. Check these against your résumé and the cover letter for your application. Let your referees know that they might be contacted to speak on your behalf. See Chapter 23, Applying for a Job, for discussion of the résumé and covering letter.

Summarise all your work experiences that are relevant to the job, along with any other skills, qualities, responsibilities, initiatives and achievements you think are relevant.

Consider your competence across a range of areas: for example, the personal skills necessary to work as part of a team. You will need to demonstrate these skills to the interviewer or the interview panel. In addition, consider your skill at dealing with information and handling activities such as driving a car or performing as a first aid officer.

Refer to the job description

As a potential employee you are interested in the type of tasks the job involves. Ask for the **job description** and look at the main tasks and other duties it sets out, to determine what you will be asked to do. Sometimes it also lists the company's objectives.

General information about the company – such as how many people it employs, how many divisions it has, what the main products are and what the company's main market is – can be obtained by telephoning its department of Human Resources, Public Relations or Customer Services.

Job search control sheet

The **job search control sheet** is a systematic way to organise a job search. Record the details on a sheet similar to that shown in Figure 25.1. The job search control sheet records your ideas and impressions in one place as a useful time-management tool.

Manage your time well during your job search.

Practising your presentation

In the interview you are judged on how you act and what you say. Take time beforehand to think about the questions you may be asked and what you will say in answer to each. Even consider the sort of question that may be awkward to answer. It is easier to appear relaxed and confident during the interview when you have practised your presentation.

Practice helps you to be relaxed and confident.

Figure 25.1 Job search control sheet

Name of position:	....
How I made contact, and date:	....
How I found out about the position:	....
Date job application forwarded:	....
Date and time of interview:	....
Place of interview:	....
Name of potential employer:	....
Address:	....
	....
Telephone, fax and email numbers:	....
	....
Research on the position:	....
Comments on the interview:	....
	....
My particular strengths in the interview:	....
What would I do differently next time?	....
Material left with the employer:	....
Follow-up action:	....
Dates:	....
To whom:	....

Consider your personal presentation

The way you dress makes an impression at the interview. Choose business-like clothes and take care over your personal grooming.

Pack your things carefully. Include copies of your résumé on good quality paper. Also include the originals and copies of your references. Include any relevant samples of work, and originals of course qualifications such as degrees, diplomas, certificates and work qualifications. Also pack your pen, paper and **interview memory jogger** (see Figure 25.2).

Place only the most important points that warrant special mention on the interview memory jogger. This aid is most useful if it is placed on your lap or on the table in front of you. At the end of the interview, when the interviewer asks if you have anything to ask or add, quickly scan it to check you have covered the main points.

Remember to record important points on your interview memory jogger.

Figure 25.2 Interview memory jogger

Summarise your strengths:	1. _____ 2. _____ 3. _____ 4. _____
Determine the personal and physical factors required for the job:	_____ _____ _____ _____ _____
Date and time of interview:	_____
Things to take to the interview:	1. _____ 2. _____ 3. _____
Accomplishments relevant to this position:	1. _____ 2. _____ 3. _____
Key points to bring out in the interview:	1. _____ 2. _____ 3. _____ 4. _____ 5. _____
Emphasise why I am interested in this position:	_____ _____ _____

At the interview

A job interview is your opportunity to convince a potential employer that you are the best person for the job. It is an opportunity that your résumé and covering letter have gained for you, and it is often your first face-to-face contact with the employer. Be ready to speak clearly and to ask appropriate questions. Table 25.1 provides some hints to help you perform well at an interview.

Table 25.1 Hints for an impressive performance

1. Interviewers are influenced by personalities. Be pleasant, listen carefully and respond to questions with interest. Make a good first impression by greeting the interviewer in a friendly manner.

2. Reply to questions with full sentences, rather than 'yes' or 'no', to show the interviewer you have prepared for the interview and are interested.

3. Nonverbal behaviour indicates your feelings. Practise, or be videotaped, to check movements of your head, arms, feet, legs and shoulders and your facial expression.

4. Focus on your most relevant skills. Give examples of how you have solved problems in previous positions.

5. Show interest in specific aspects of the position. Describe what you have learnt from previous positions, and how these will help you in future positions.

6. Be positive and confident when you communicate. Practise suitable responses to questions. Prepare questions to ask about career paths, staff development and future changes to the company, to indicate that you have thought about your goals.

Beginning the interview

Create a good first impression by entering the interview room confidently with body upright, shoulders relaxed. Make direct eye contact, and greet the interviewer or panel with a firm handshake. Take time to organise your thoughts and your papers and seat yourself comfortably. Make sure that you can sit comfortably without fidgeting but are still able to use your hands for emphasis. If you need to change the position of your seat, state politely why you are doing so. For example, if you cannot see all the members of the interview panel, say 'I'm sure you won't mind if I move the chair so that I can see everybody'. As the interviewee, you are also assessing the company or organisation, so behave politely but assertively.

Begin the interview confidently and courteously.

Firm eye contact shows confidence. Keep your head upright and encourage the interviewers by smiling and nodding when appropriate. Voice volume and clarity and knowing what you want to say are important for creating a good impression. Vocal inflection adds variety and interest to your presentation. Nonverbal communication is discussed more fully in Chapter 2.

Body of the interview

This is the working stage of the interview where you must present yourself confidently and persuasively. Listen carefully to questions and try to answer them thoughtfully and confidently. Maintain eye contact with the person who is questioning you, but avoid making them uncomfortable. Keep your posture upright, but be relaxed and natural. It almost goes without saying: never chew gum or smoke at an interview.

Listen carefully.

Be confident and persuasive.

Answer questions

A variety of questions are asked at interviews. An expert interviewer should make you feel comfortable and encourage you to tell them about yourself. Experienced interviewers design the questions to focus on the job and keep them free of bias and discrimination. The examples of questions in Table 25.2 will allow you to prepare and rehearse possible answers.

Table 25.2 Commonly asked questions

By the interviewer

■ How do you organise your day?

■ What have you done to make your job more satisfying?

■ What are your hobbies and interests?

■ Have you conducted a meeting or done any group speaking? What kind of feedback did you receive?

■ What reports or proposals do you write? Tell me about one of your documents and how it was received.

■ Tell me about the positions you have held.

■ In your last job, what accomplishments gave you the most satisfaction?

■ Why did you leave your last job?

■ Do you feel pressure in your job? How do you deal with it?

■ What do you see as your strengths and weaknesses?

■ Are you able to travel?

■ What are your career goals for the next five years?

■ Tell me about a problem you've solved in the last six months.

■ Can you give an example of a good decision you made in the last six months?

■ What were the alternatives to that decision?

■ What do you understand about Equal Employment Opportunity?

■ What do you consider your best abilities?

■ Why did you apply for this position?

■ What can you bring to this position that others can't?

By the interviewee

■ How many people are employed in the organisation?

■ Where would I be working?

■ What projects would I be working on?

■ Will training be available?

■ Does the company intend to expand into other areas?

■ How many have applied for this position?

■ When will I hear the results of my interview?

■ When would you like the successful applicant to start work?

Ask questions

Prepare your
questions.

Be prepared to ask questions when the opportunity arises. They should indicate your genuine interest in the possibility of a career with the organisation. Ask the interviewer questions about the:

■ opportunities for promotion or training
■ channels for communicating with others at work
■ long-term and short-term goals of the organisation
■ nature of the work.

Then, if you are offered the position, you will be able to decide whether you want the job or not.

If the interviewer does not ask certain questions that would let you identify all your relevant skills or qualities, take the initiative to mention them towards the close of the interview. This is when your interview memory jogger is so important. It is also your opportunity to clear up any doubts you may have about the position.

Close of interview

The interviewer will indicate that the interview is over. Be ready for this, and express thanks for their time and consideration. If you are still interested in the position, let them know at this point and ask when they will make their decision. Try to leave the interview with a sense of control as well as a sense of relief!

Thank the interviewer.

After the interview

It is worth reviewing your performance. After the interview, identify everything you did well and not so well. Learn from them all, and decide how to improve any parts of your performance that were weak.

Learn from your performance at the interview.

Evaluating your performance

If you were unhappy about any part of your interview performance, decide how you can do better on another occasion. What experiences were pleasant, unpleasant, challenging, awkward or uncomfortable?

Evaluate the way you:

■ answered questions
■ presented yourself.

Reflect on aspects of the interview that you handled well and those that you might have handled better.

Reflect on the positive and any negative aspects of your performance.

Follow-up

Once you have attended an interview, it is appropriate to follow up with:

■ a letter of inquiry, if you have not heard from the company within two weeks, or
■ a letter of acceptance if you are offered the position.

Send either a letter of acceptance or a letter of inquiry.

Follow-up letter

The **follow-up letter** may be posted the next day or up to two weeks after the interview if you have not received a reply by then. How soon you send it depends on you and on your impression of the company. Sometimes, one or two days later may seem too 'pushy'; or it may simply refresh the interviewer's memory of your particular skills and interview performance.

The goal of a follow-up letter is to reconfirm your interest.

The follow-up letter format follows the seven basic parts of a business letter, as presented in Chapter 18, plus a subject line. Follow these steps when you write it.

1. Start with a 'thank you' for the opportunity to present yourself at interview.
2. Identify the job sought and the date of interview.
3. Mention the responses you made to the points covered in the interview.
4. State how you feel about the company and explain why you want to work for it.
5. Present a short summary of your particular strengths, qualifications and value to the organisation.
6. Thank the interviewers for their time and confirm your interest in the position.
7. Close with a statement of goodwill.

A follow-up letter should be courteous and concise – no more than a page long. It confirms again your interest in the job.

Telephone call

A follow-up telephone call also confirms your interest in the position. If you have not heard from the organisation within seven days, call the interviewer, express your interest again and ask when you are likely to hear. The interviewer will explain the delay or let you know if you were successful or unsuccessful.

Letter of acceptance

Accept or decline a job courteously.

Sometimes the job is offered by telephone, other times it is offered in writing. An offer in writing is preferable, and it should set out the conditions of employment, such as hours of work and salary.

Once you decide to accept the job, telephone the contact person and let them know. Then write a courteous **letter of acceptance**. This letter should:

- thank the employer for the job offer
- state your pleasure in accepting the position
- identify the position fully
- clarify the duties it requires and name the person who will be your supervisor
- acknowledge the salary and conditions
- state how much you are looking forward to the new challenge and opportunity to contribute to the organisation.

Your tone should be courteous, expressing how much you are looking forward to working with the company.

Being interviewed

SKILLS
APPLY

Work in pairs.
1. Prepare a set of guidelines for school leavers to follow before they attend their first job interview. Explain the purpose of each part of a job interview.
2. Discuss three differences between the opening and closing stages of an interview. Why is it important to make a good first impression?
3. a. Why should an applicant ask questions at an interview?
   b. Prepare three questions you could

ask at an interview to find out more about the position.
c. Each person thinks of an interview question that could be awkward to answer. Discuss these and prepare appropriate answers.
4. As the interview closes, you leave the room. The post-interview stage is still ahead of you. What steps should you follow at the post-interview stage? Why are they important?

SELF CHECK 25.1

Behaviour at an interview

Use this checklist to assess your performance at an interview.

Did I	Yes	Successfully	Unsuccessfully
find out as much as possible about the position before the interview?	☐	☐	☐
consider and prepare answers to possible questions?	☐	☐	☐

	Yes	Successfully	Unsuccessfully
dress appropriately?	☐	☐	☐
arrive on time?	☐	☐	☐
present a confident and courteous attitude?	☐	☐	☐
control my nervousness?	☐	☐	☐
speak clearly?	☐	☐	☐
answer questions thoughtfully and fully?	☐	☐	☐
answer each question in terms of my qualifications and the job requirements?	☐	☐	☐
prepare beforehand a short list of my main strengths?	☐	☐	☐
present all necessary documents and information?	☐	☐	☐
ask appropriate questions?	☐	☐	☐
learn all that I needed to know?	☐	☐	☐
use the interview memory jogger?	☐	☐	☐
create a good first impression?	☐	☐	☐
maintain the interviewer's attention and interest?	☐	☐	☐

Visit the Companion Website at **www.prenhall.com/dwyer_au**. Choose the Internet exercise in Chapter 25 to research the oral, written and interpersonal communication strategies used in job applications and job interviews.

Chapter summary

Make inquiries about a position. By doing this you can prepare yourself fully for the interview and feel confident that your skills and qualifications suit the position.

Prepare for a job interview. The job search control sheet enables you to plan each step of the job search. Remember to give yourself enough time to complete each step.

Work out probable questions and suitable answers. Certain questions are common to most job interviews. If you have thought about the most likely questions and how you will answer them, you are more likely to answer confidently at the interview and make a good first impression.

Present yourself competently at a job interview. This is your opportunity to convince the potential employer that you are the best person for the job. Present yourself confidently and honestly. At the interview, use your effective speaking, listening and nonverbal skills when responding to questions. Speak clearly and ask appropriate questions.

Evaluate your own performance. Review your performance and learn from each experience. Familiarise yourself with strategies to improve your performance and increase your chances of success at the next interview.

Follow up after the job interview. Two letters may be written after the interview. One is a brief letter reminding the employer that you are still interested in the job. The other is the letter accepting a job offer – the last step of a successful job search.

QUESTIONS
REVIEW

1. List four tasks you should complete before the interview.
2. What are the advantages of being prepared?
3. What is the purpose of:
   a. the job search control sheet?
   b. the interview memory jogger?
4. List three kinds of nonverbal behaviour that help to create a good first impression.
5. a. What are the three stages of an interview?
   b. Why should you ask questions at an interview?
6. What are three follow-up activities you should complete after the interview?
7. What is the format of a follow-up letter?
8. A letter of acceptance aims to do six things. List these.

The job interview

SKILLS
BUILD

In groups of three, role-play job interviews for three different positions. Read through the whole exercise before beginning.
1. Choose three 'Positions Vacant' advertisements from a national or metropolitan newspaper.
2. Each person selects one position and prepares a set of questions for the interviewer to ask. Follow the order of questions shown in Table 25.3, as these will structure the interview in a way that enables interviewees to talk about their skills and abilities.
3. Each person in the group is to be interviewed by the other two for one of the positions. Each group member prepares a set of answers for one of the positions, using some of the action words in Table 25.4. Also prepare at least one question to ask the interviewer (see Table 25.2 for some suggestions). In your answers include positive phrases such as:
'I like my work . . .'
'My relevant experience in . . .'
'I can communicate . . .'
'I have extensive experience in . . .'
4. Take turns to role-play the three interviews so that each person is interviewed by the other two, and so that each person is interviewed for a different position.
5. Discuss the results of the role play and use Self-check 25.1 to evaluate your performance as interviewee.

Table 25.3 Interviewer's questions

Interviewer's question	Purpose
How do your qualifications . . .?	To ensure that the interviewee's qualifications are suitable for the position
In what ways will . . .?	To consider the interviewee's experience
What do you . . .?	To identify strengths
What could you . . .?	To identify weaknesses
Why did you . . .?	To consider the interviewee's reason for applying
What do you hope to . . .?	To identify career goals
What would you do if . . .?	To consider the interviewee's problem-solving abilities
Any other questions . . .?	To clarify issues for the interviewee

Table 25.4 Action words for interview responses

Communicating	Managing	Creating	Administering
persuade	solve	plan	arrange
mediate	produce	shape	achieve
write	review	design	organise
develop	analyse	prepare	prepare
cooperate	initiate	invent	accomplish

Key terms

follow-up letter
interview memory jogger

job description
job search control sheet

letter of acceptance

At the interview: tips and techniques

CASE STUDY 1

by Ambrose McKinnery

Interviews can be stressful for many people, as being judged and assessed tends to provoke the stress response. Unfortunately, when we become anxious, one of the first things to fail is our memory, with our thought processes not as sharp as they would be otherwise.

Trained interviewers are aware you may be a little nervous, and will attempt to settle you with humour and rapport-building questions; other interviewers may launch into the process without preamble. Preparation will engender confidence, which will manifest both verbally and nonverbally. Preparation will also reduce the chances of you fumbling on a question.

Achievements

The workplace is full of demands, issues to address and problems to solve. All questions are directly or in some way connected to these workplace aspects. Positions become available because of current or perceived future deficits in company operations. These deficits are basically problems that need to be solved. In a way, the interviewer is looking for someone who is a problem solver; this is why your preparation in self-assessment and identifying your past achievements is so vitally important and cannot be overemphasised.

Many interviews will use targeted sel-ection techniques, otherwise known as *behaviour interviewing*. You will be asked for evidence where you have shown certain actions in the past. This is your opportunity to record achievements relevant to the question. Be sure to mention what the problem was, what you did, and what was the outcome or result. Try to avoid verbosity, keeping your answer concise and to the point. Other interviews will not be behaviourally based. However, whether you are asked a behavioural question or not, you should try to answer as if you had been.

For example:

Behavioural question
'Can you tell me a time when you had to meet a deadline? What did you do?'

Behavioural/achievement answer
'Yes, last term my course structure required the submission of four pieces of work simultaneously. From the outset I developed a schedule which enabled me to portion and better manage my time. I was able to avoid a last minute panic, and was very happy with the standard and result I achieved.'

Non-behavioural question
'What are you like with deadlines?'

Non-behavioural answer
'I always meet deadlines. I've never had a

problem' (This tells the interviewer very little.)

Behavioural/achievement answer
'I'm quite used to deadlines. In fact, last term . . .' (and you recite as above)

This will impress the interviewer a great deal, as you continue to build value as a problem solver.

Asking questions

It is essential that you find out what needs to be done or solved, what are the responsibilities and major tasks. What is critical to the role, its essence, and what would you be primarily involved in? The onus is on you to find out and convey interest by asking questions. Many people think they can be a passive responder, which gives all the control to the interviewer. Some interviewers even believe this is how they should proceed, and may even say, 'I'll give you a broad overview of the position, then ask you some questions, and then I'll give you the opportunity to ask me some questions. How's that with you?'

While you would answer in the affirmative, you should try and come in with questions as soon as you can. Asking a question at the end of your answer is one technique – e.g. following from above answer:

'. . . very happy with the standard I submitted. Are deadlines common with this role?'

In reality, everyone in an interview is both interviewer and interviewee at the same time. You can help turn it more into a conversation and communicate your interest by asking questions. This leaves the interviewer with the impression that you really want to find out about this job – i.e. you are enthusiastic. When you leave, the interviewer will think that you have got a pretty good handle on the position's requirements. Contrast this to the passive responder, who finds out very little about the position and company. The interviewer is unsure that you know what you could be getting yourself into, and will be less impressed with you.

In closing the interview it is common to be asked if you have any (more) questions. It is quite acceptable to overtly refer to your question list at this time, or during the session. This will show some preparation,

some systematic thinking, preparedness and orderliness, all of which imply enthusiasm and career motivation.

Be an active listener

Active listening refers to communication techniques that help us to follow and understand each other. Foremost is that you must listen attentively, and confirm that you are listening by using clarification. Always seek clarification on questions you don't understand. For example:

Your question
'Are you saying that I would be able to plan for all deadlines?'

Answer
'Well, not really. What I mean is things get sprung on you . . .'

This is a clarification attempt from the interviewee, which turned out to be not quite right. However, the attempt to clarify, even if incorrect, conveys a powerful message in that you are trying to understand the role and expectations.

The better your understanding of the position, through questioning and clarification, the better your capacity to selectively recall and respond with relevant material, including achievements, in relation to the position's requirements.

One more thing to note is whether you are the 'interrupting type' or not. Interrupting gives the message that what you have to say is more important than what the interviewer is currently saying, and will cause this person to become irritated, and develop a less favourable perception of you.

How to present yourself

We've all heard of first impressions. The reality is that first impressions are crucial in determining how well you come across throughout the interview. First impressions tend to last so that, once you have been 'boxed', subsequent information is assimilated into how you have been first perceived, with impressions being quite resilient to reality checks. Therefore, aspects of presentation are critical.

Presentation means dress and grooming, and how you carry yourself. Walk with confidence, shake hands firmly with eye contact and a smile. Ladies, offer your hand first. Show courtesy by sitting simultaneously, not before the interviewer. Vitality, enthusiasm, manners and style will foster the development of a positive impression. You should be well groomed and wear the kind of clothes most commonly worn in the job environment you wish to enter. If you are uncertain, err on the side of caution. Better to be slightly overdressed than vice versa.

Follow-up

Make sure you know what the next step is, so that you can act at that time, or follow up if they have not responded as agreed. Why not continue to market yourself by sending a brief thank you letter confirming this. You will also show some style, and differentiate yourself with your courtesy.

Source: Ambrose McKinnery, 'At the interview: tips and techniques', Employment.com.au <www.employ-ment.com.au/news/dsp_news_item.cfm?NEWS_ID=26>, accessed 24 January 2002. By Ambrose McKinnery, psychologist at Chandler Macleod, supplied by employment.com.au.

Questions

1. The article claims: 'The reality is, first impressions are crucial in determining how well you come across throughout the interview.' Discuss the importance of presenting yourself competently at a job interview.

2. 'In reality, everyone is both interviewer and interviewee at the same time.' Analyse this statement and explain what the writer means.

3. Discuss the job interview follow-up strategies that you have used, or will use, following a job interview.

How to succeed at interviews

by David Hughes

In most cases, where an organisation has more than one candidate to choose from for a given position, with the same basic skills set, the key differentiator is how they come across at interview. Here are some thoughts on how you can improve your interviewing, starting with the important issue of preparation.

Interview preparation

Good preparation is crucial – the best prepared candidate invariably gets the job. This is why.

Preparation is evidence of professionalism and interest in the company but, above all, it is indicative of the way a candidate is likely to work. If someone doesn't prepare properly for an interview which may have an impact on their entire career, what kind of an employee are they likely to be? Preparation is vital.

So what do we mean by preparation?

First, we mean research, gathering as much information as possible. You need to:

- visit the company's website;
- read their corporate brochure, annual report and accounts;
- ask for divisional brochures and further literature if available;
- review the job spec and seek as much information about the role as is available;
- regularly monitor the financial press.

Good ways to get this information include asking your recruitment consultancy for as much help as possible, making use of contacts and searching press coverage at websites such as <www.ft.com>.

Having done your research, use it to develop questions and points of view, which will help you gather key information at the interview as well as impressing. Also, plan answers to questions they are likely to ask.

The final stage of preparation is rehearsal. Practise at presenting yourself. The best way to do this is to arrange a mock interview with your recruitment consultancy or another trained interviewer.

Preparation done, it's now time for the real thing.

The interview

Here are some important points to bear in mind:

CASE STUDY 2

1. Interviews are unlike the CV filtering stage, in that people will be looking for your positive points rather than reasons to reject you. Most interviewers want to be impressed with the people they are interviewing. Be confident. Believe in yourself.

2. First impressions are crucial. Most interviewers make a decision within minutes of meeting someone. Here's a checklist to help those opening minutes go well:
   - Be on time.
   - Be polite to the receptionists and support staff – they can be very influential.
   - Dress smartly and professionally.
   - Smile and give a confident handshake.
   - Politely thank the interviewer for taking the time to meet with you.
   - Have an easy topic of non-work conversation ready as an ice breaker.
   - If they don't take the initiative immediately, open the conversation.
   - Listen as well as talk.
   - Be friendly and appear enthusiastic.

3. When the interview gets under way, let the interviewer lead. They may well have a series of topics they need to cover and a set time limit, so let them control the conversation.

4. Be mindful of the questions the interviewer is trying to ask and help give them the answers. Remember, the most important question is always, 'Would I like to work with this person?'

5. Ask good questions which demonstrate you have done your research and thought about it.

6. When answering questions, don't be afraid of taking a moment to think before plunging in.

7. If asked for your strengths and weaknesses, start with your strengths, and offer only one weakness.

Following these guidelines should increase your chances of winning at interview.

Source: David Hughes, 'How to succeed at interviews', *Insider CIMA*, September 2000. Reprinted with the kind permission of *Insider CIMA Magazine*.

Questions

1. 'Good preparation is crucial – the best candidate invariably gets the job.' The planning stage is complex. Briefly describe what should be done before you attend a job interview.

2. a. Asking good questions at the interview demonstrates that you have done your research. What sort of questions should you ask at an interview?

   b. Discuss the value of having prepared relevant questions for the interview.

3. 'Preparation is evidence of professionalism and interest in the company but, above all, it is indicative of the way a candidate is likely to work.' What do you see as the key factors to presenting professionally at an interview?

Bibliography

Part I Interactive communication

Chapter 1 How communication works

BLACK, OCTAVIUS. 'Analysing the process gets the point across', *People Management*, 2 May 1996.

COUTTS, LOUIS. 'None the wiser', *Management Today,* January–February 2002, p. 37.

GUFFEY, MARY ELLEN. *Essentials of Business Communication*, PWS Publishing, Boston, 1991.

HELLRIEGEL, D. & SLOCUM, J.W. *Organizational Behavior*, 4th edn, West Woodman, St Paul, USA, 1988.

LEWIS, GLEN & SLADE, CHRISTINA. *Critical Communication*, 2nd edn, Prentice Hall, Sydney, 2000.

MCGUIGAN, J. *Cultural Populism*, Routledge, London, 1992.

MURRAY-SMITH, S. *Right Words: A Guide to English Usage in Australia*, 2nd edn, Penguin, Ringwood, Victoria, 1989.

MYERS, GAIL E. & MYERS, MICHELE TOLELA. *The Dynamics of Human Communication: A Laboratory Approach*, 5th edn, McGraw-Hill, USA, 1988.

PETERS, P. (ed.) *Macquarie Student Writer's Guide*, Jacaranda Press, Sydney, 1989.

ROGERS, C.R. & ROETHLISBERGER, F.J. 'Barriers and gateways to communication', *Harvard Business Review*, 30, 1952, pp. 46–52.

SAMOVAR, L.A. & PORTER, R.E. *Intercultural Communication: A Reader*, 5th edn, Wadsworth Publishing, Belmont, California, 1988.

TAYLOR, A., ROSEGRANT, T. & MEYER. A. *Communicating*, 4th edn, Prentice Hall, Englewood Cliffs, New Jersey, 1986.

'Teaching the bear how to dance', *Manufacturers' Bulletin*, June 1996, pp. 12–14.

WILLING, K. *Talking it Through: Clarification & Problem Solving in Professional Work*, National Centre for English Language Teaching & Research, Sydney, 1992.

Chapter 2 Interactive skills: nonverbal communication and listening skills

ABRAMS, K.S. *Communication at Work: Listening, Speaking, Writing and Reading*, Prentice Hall, Englewood Cliffs, New Jersey, 1986.

ADAMSON, G. & PRENTICE, J. *Communication Skills in Practice: Workbook 1 Speaking and Listening*, Nelson Wadsworth, Melbourne, 1987.

BOLTON, R. *People Skills*, Simon & Schuster, Sydney, 1987.

BOLTON, R. & GROVER, D. *People Styles at Work: Making Bad Relationships Good and Good Relationships Better*, AMACOM, New York, 1996.

COLE, K. *Crystal Clear Communication Skills for Understanding and Being Understood*, Prentice Hall, Sydney, 1993.

DEVITO, J.A. *The Interpersonal Communication Book*, 9th edn, Longman, New York, 2000.

EKMAN, P. *Telling Lies: Clues to Deceit in the Marketplace, Politics and Marriage*, Norton, New York, 1985.

EKMAN, P. & FRIESEN, W.V. 'The repertoire of non-verbal behaviour: categories, origins, usage, and coding'. *Semiotica I*, 1969, pp. 49–98.

JOHNSON, D.W. *Reaching Out: Interpersonal Effectiveness and Self-Actualization*, 3rd edn, Prentice Hall, Englewood Cliffs, New Jersey, 1993.

KAYE, MICHAEL. *Communication Management*, Prentice Hall, Sydney, 1994.

KNAPP, M.L. *Essentials of Nonverbal Communication*, Holt, Rinehart & Winston, USA, 1978.

KNAPP, M.L. & MILLER, G.B. *Handbook of Interpersonal Communication*, Sage Publications, California, 1985.

KNAPP, M.L. & VANGELISTA, ANITA L. *Interpersonal Communication and Human Relationships*, Allyn & Bacon, Boston, 1996.

LEWIS, G. & SLADE, C. *Critical Communication*, 2nd edn, Prentice Hall, Sydney, 2000.

MACKAY, HARVEY. 'Listening is the hardest of the easy tasks', *Minneapolis Star Tribune*, 24 May 2001, on the International Listening Association web page <www.listen.org/pages/mackay.html>, accessed 4 January 2002. Reprinted with permission.

MICHULKA, J.H. *Let's Talk Business*, 3rd edn, South-Western Publishing Co., Cincinatti, 1988.

SAUNDERS, S., KAYE, M., GILPIN, A. & COLLINGWOOD, V. *Managing Adult Communication: Experiential Activities Workbook*, University of Technology, Sydney, 1990.

SCHERER, K.R. & EKMAN, P.K. *Handbook of Methods in Nonverbal Behavior Research*, Cambridge University Press, New York, 1985.

VALLENCE, K.E. & MCWILLIAM, T. *Communication that Works*, Thomas Nelson, Melbourne, 1987.

Chapter 3 Interactive skills: interpersonal communication

ABRAMS, K. *Communication at Work*: *Listening, Speaking, Writing and Reading*, Prentice Hall, Sydney, 1986.

ADAMSON, G. & PRENTICE, J. *Communication Skills in Practice: Workbook 1 Speaking and Listening*, Nelson Wadsworth, Melbourne, 1987.

ANEMA, D. & LEFKOWITZ, W. *Don't Get Fired! How to Keep a Job*, Simon & Schuster, California, 1990.

BOLTON, R. *People Skills*, Simon & Schuster, Sydney, 1987.

BOLTON, R. & GROVER, D. *People Styles at Work: Making Bad Relationships Good and Good Relationships Better*, AMACOM, New York, 1996.

DEVITO, J.A. *The Interpersonal Communication Book*, 9th edn, Longman, New York, 2000.

FORGAS, JOSEPH P. *Interpersonal Communication*, Pergamon Press, Sydney, 1985.

FORGAS, JOSEPH P. *Interpersonal Behaviour: The Psychology of Social Interaction*, Maxwell Macmillan, 1992.

NEASEY, MICHELLE, CLARE, FLORENCE & FORAN, MATTHEW. 'Think tank', *Management Today*, January–February 2002, p. 13.

NELSON-JONES, R. *Human Relationship Skills: A Practical Guide to Effective Personal Relationships*, 3rd edn, Harcourt Brace, Sydney, 1996.

SCHUTZ, W. *The Interpersonal Underworld*, Science and Behaviour Books, Palo Alto, California, 1966.

SCHUTZ, W. *The Human Element: Productivity, Self-esteem and the Bottom Line*, Jossey-Bass Publishers, San Francisco, 1994.

VALLENCE, K.E. & MCWILLIAM, T. *Communication that Works*, Thomas Nelson, Melbourne, 1987.

WOLF, P.M. & KUIPER, S. *Effective Communication in Business*, South-Western Publishing Co., Cincinatti, 1989.

Part II Communicating in the workplace

Chapter 4 Effective workplace communication

COLE, KRIS. *Office Administration and Supervision*, Prentice Hall, Sydney, 1992.

COLLIS, JACK. 'Developing the human resource', *Australian Business News*, Vol. 32, March 2002, p. 27.

GEORGE, CLAUDE S. JR & COLE, KRIS. *Supervision in Action*, 3rd edn, Prentice Hall, Sydney, 1992.

JACOBS, RONALD L. & JONES, MICHAEL L. *Structured On-the-Job Training*, Berrett-Koehler Publishers, Inc., San Francisco, 1995.

LOCKER, KITTY O. *Business and Administrative Communication*, 5th edn, Irwin/McGraw-Hill, Boston, Mass., 2000.

RENTON, N.E. *Guide for Meetings and Organisations*, 6th edn, The Law Book Co., Melbourne, 1994.

TOVEY, D. *Training in Australia*, Prentice Hall, Sydney, 1996.

Chapter 5 Effective meetings

BLICQ, R.S. *Communicating at Work: Creating Messages that get Results*, Prentice Hall, Scarborough, Canada, 1991.

DEJEAN, D. 'Selling your ideas', *Australian PC User*, October 1989.

DEWEY, J. *How We Think*, Heath, Boston, 1933.

HODGETTS, R.M. *Management: Theory, Process and Practice*, Holt Saunders, New York, 1986.

HODGETTS, R.M. *Organizational Behavior: Theory and Practice*, Merrill, New York, 1991.

LEWIS, G. & SLADE, C. *Critical Communication*, 2nd edn, Prentice Hall, Sydney, 2000.

PENDERGAST, ANNETTE. 'Meetings and conferences are big business', *National Business Bulletin*, February 2002, pp. 36–7.

Queensland Tourist and Travel Corporation, *Understanding Asia*, <www.qttc.com.au/international/asia/busprotocol.htm>, accessed 13 March 2002.

RENTON, N.E. *Guide to Meetings and Organisations*, 6th edn, The Law Book Co., Melbourne, 1994.

STRANO, Z., McGREGOR, H. & MOHAN, T. *Communicating! Theory and Practice*, 4th edn, Harcourt Brace, Sydney, 1997.

WAINWRIGHT, G.R. *Meetings and Committee Procedure*, Hodder & Stoughton, UK, 1987.

Chapter 6 Speaking in public

ADAMSON, G. & PRENTICE, J. *Communication Skills in Practice: Workbook 1 Speaking and Listening*, Nelson Wadsworth, Melbourne, 1987.

BATEMAN, D.N. & SIGBAND, N.B. *Communicating in Business*, 3rd edn, Scott Foresman & Co., Boston, 1989.

BLICQ, R.S. *Communicating at Work: Creating Messages that get Results*, Prentice Hall, Scarborough, Canada, 1991.

DONALDSON, L. & SCANNELL, E.E. *Human Resource Development: The New Trainer's Guide*, 2nd edn, Addison-Wesley, Massachusetts, 1986.

GRAY, M. *Public Speaking*, Schwartz & Wilkinson, Melbourne, 1991.

MICHULKA, J.H. *Let's Talk Business*, 3rd edn, South-Western Publishing Co., Cincinatti, 1988.

SLAN, JOANNA. *Using Stories and Humor to Grab your Audience*, Allyn & Bacon, Needham Heights, MA, 1998.

TUPMAN, SIMON, 'Avoid presentation panic', *Charter*, September 2000, pp. 56–7.

VALLENCE, K.E. & McWILLIAM, T. *Communication that Works*, Thomas Nelson, Melbourne, 1987.

Part III Workplace relationships

Chapter 7 Organise personal work priorities and development

BASS, JEREMY. 'Wake up to yourself', *My Career*, *Sydney Morning Herald*, 2–3 February 2002, p. 1.

Blanchard, K., Oncken, W. & Burrows, H. *The One-minute Manager meets the Monkey,* Collins, London, 1990.

Business Services Australia Ltd. *BSB01 Business Services Training Package Vol. 1,* Australian National Training Authority (ANTA), Brisbane, 2001.

Cole, Kris. *Supervision: The Theory and Practice of First-line Management,* Pearson Education Australia, 2001.

Ellyard, Peter. 'Challenges in the years ahead' *National Business Bulletin,* November 2001, p. 24.

Neasey, Michelle, Florence, Clare & Foran, Matthew. 'Think tank', *Management Today,* January–February 2002, p. 13.

Chapter 8 Develop teams and individuals

Borkowski, Mark & Alaily, S. 'Finding a fresh perspective. Do you need a consultant, coach or mentor?' *CMA Management,* December/January 2002, pp. 12–13.

Dewey, J. *How We Think,* Heath, Boston, 1993.

Handy, C.B. *Understanding Organisations,* 3rd edn, Penguin Books, Harmondsworth, England, 1985.

Hellreigel, D., Slocum, J.W. & Woodman, R.W. *Organizational Behavior,* 4th edn, West Publishing Company, St Paul, USA, 1986.

Janis, I.L. *Victims of Groupthink,* Houghton Mifflin, Boston, 1972.

Luthans, Fred. *Organizational Behavior,* 5th edn, Prentice Hall, Englewood Cliffs, New Jersey, 1989.

Taylor, A., Meyer, A., Samples, B.T. & Rosegrant, T. *Communicating,* 4th edn, Prentice Hall, Englewood Cliffs, New Jersey, 1986.

Tuckman, B.W. 'Developmental sequence in small groups', *Psychological Bulletin,* May 1965.

Welbourne, Michael. *Understanding Teams,* Prentice Hall, Sydney, 2001.

Chapter 9 Lead work teams

Fieldler, F.E., Chemers, M.M. & Mahar, L. *Improving Leadership Effectiveness: The Leader Match Concept,* John Wiley, New York, 1977.

Hellriegel, D., Slocum, J.W. & Woodman, R.S. *Organizational Behavior,* 4th edn, West Publishing Company, St Paul, USA, 1988.

Hersey, Paul & Blanchard, Kenneth H. *Management of Organizational Behavior: Utilising Human Resources,* 8th edn, Prentice Hall, Englewood Cliffs, New Jersey, 2001.

Hodgetts, R.M. *Modern Human Relations at Work,* 3rd edn, The Dryden Press, New York, 1987.

House, R.J. 'Path-goal theory of leadership', *Journal of Contemporary Business,* Autumn 1974.

Kaye, Michael. *Teaming with Success: Building and Maintaining Best Performing Teams,* Prentice Hall, Sydney, 1997.

Luthans, Fred. *Organizational Behavior,* 5th edn, Prentice Hall, Englewood Cliffs, New Jersey, 1989.

McGregor, Douglas. *The Human Side of Enterprise,* Penguin, Harmondsworth, 1987.

McWalters, M. (ed.) *Understanding Psychology,* McGraw-Hill, Sydney, 1990.

Pirie, James, Haddy, Michael & Woodard, Peta. 'Think tank', *Management Today,* November/December 2001, p. 13.

Robbins, S.P. *Organizational Behavior: Concepts, Controversies and Applications,* 4th edn, Prentice Hall, Englewood Cliffs, New Jersey, 1986.

Robbins, S.P. *Human Resource Management,* Prentice Hall, Sydney, 1997.

Welbourne, Michael. *Understanding Teams,* Prentice Hall, Sydney, 2001.

Chapter 10 Deliver and monitor a service to customers

BOVÉE, COURTLAND L. & THILL, JOHN V. *Business Communication Today*, 6th edn, Pearson Education, USA, 2000.

CRAIG-LEES, M., JOY, S. & BROWNE, B. *Consumer Behaviour*, Wiley, Brisbane, 1995.

DWYER, JUDITH. *Communication in Business: Strategies and Skills*, 2nd edn, Prentice Hall, Sydney, 2002.

FINE, S. & DREYFAK, K. *Customers: How to Get Them, How to Serve Them and How to Keep Them*, Dartnell Corp., New York, 1983.

GAMBLE, TERI KWAL & GAMBLE, MICHAEL. *Communication Works*, 5th edn, The McGraw-Hill Companies, USA, 1996.

GERSON, RICHARD F. *Beyond Customer Service: Keeping Customers for Life*, Crisp Publications, California, 1992.

LEGGE, W.L. *Successful Marketing Strategies in the 1990s*, Michael Wilkinson Publisher Information, Melbourne, 1989.

MORGAN, REBECCA L. *Calming Upset Customers and Staying Effective during Unpleasant Situations*, Crisp Publications, California, 1989.

SCHIFFMAN, L., BEDNALL, D., COWLEY, E., O'CASS, A., WATSON, J. & KANUK, L. *Consumer Behaviour*, 2nd edn, Prentice Hall, Sydney, 2001.

SCOTT, DRU. *Customer Satisfaction: The other Half of your Job,* Crisp Publications, California, 1991.

TOVIA, JOANNA. 'Superior service costs nothing', *Daily Telegraph,* 29 January 2002, p. 32.

WARNER, JON. *Improving Customer Service,* Training Solutions Group Pty Ltd, Queensland, 2000.

WHITELEY, P. *The Customer-driven Company*, The Forum Co., Massachusetts, 1990.

WILKE, W.L. *Consumer Behavior*, John Wiley & Sons, New York, 1986.

Chapter 11 Coordinate and implement customer service strategies

ALBRECHT, K. *Customer Service: The Only Thing that Matters*, Harper & Row, New York, 1992.

ALBRECHT, K. *Delivering Customer Values: It's Everyone's Job,* Productivity Press, Portland, Oregon, 1995.

COLE, K. *Supervision: The Theory and Practice of First-time Management*, Prentice Hall, Sydney, 2001.

Editorial: 'Customer service: the seven deadly sins', *Australian Small Business Portfolio,* December, 1995.

FRAENKEL, JACK. 'Great service is a learned skill', *Australian Business News,* Vol. 31, February 2002.

GERSON, R.F. *Keeping Customers for Life*, Crisp Publications, California, 1992.

GERSON, R.F. *Measuring Customer Satisfaction*, Kogan Page, London, 1994.

HOROVITZ, J. & Jurgens, M. *Total Customer Satisfaction*, Pitman Publishing, London, 1992.

LEGGE, J.M. *Successful Marketing Strategies in the 1990s*, Michael Wilkinson Publisher Information, Melbourne, 1989.

TIMM, PAUL R. *Customer Service Career Success through Customer Satisfaction*, 2nd edn, Prentice Hall, New Jersey, 2001.

WARNER, JON. *Improving Customer Service,* Training Solutions Group Pty Ltd, Queensland, 2000.

Chapter 12 Negotiation skills

ACLAND, A.F. *A Sudden Outbreak of Common Sense*, Hutchinson, London, 1990.

ALBRECHT, K. & ALBRECHT, S. *Added Value Negotiation*, Illinois Business, Irwin, 1993.

CARKHUFF, R.R. *Helping and Human Relations: A Primer for Lay and Professional Helpers*, Vols I & II, Holt, Rinehart & Winston, New York, 1969.

CARKHUFF, R.R. *The Art of Helping*, Human Resource Development Press, Amherst, Mass., 1993.

FISHER, R. & BROWN, S. *Getting Together*, Houghton Mifflin Company, 1988.

FISHER, R. & URY, W. *Getting to Yes*, Business Books, London, 1991.

FISHER, R. & URY, W. *Getting to Yes: Negotiating an Agreement without Giving In*, Random House Business Books, London, 1999.

HAYES, CHRISTINE & HARDIE, LILLIAN. *Negotiation Skills*, 2nd edn, Eastern House, Victoria, 1997.

HELLREIGEL, D., SLOCUM, J.W. & WOODMAN, R.W. *Organizational Behavior*, 4th edn, West Publishing, St Paul, USA, 1988.

JENKINS, LINDA. 'Everything is negotiable', *Salarycom's negotiation clinic*, <www.salary.com/SalaryAdvice/LayoutScripts>, accessed 31 December 2001.

URY, W. *Getting Past No*, Business Books, London, 1991.

WATSON, DESLEY. *Communication in the Workplace*, Prentice Hall, Sydney, 2000.

Chapter 13 Conflict management

ACLAND, A.F. *A Sudden Outbreak of Common Sense*, Hutchinson, UK, 1990.

ACLAND, A.F. *Perfect People Skills: All you Need to get it Right First Time*, Random House, London, 1999.

ALLENBY, GUY. 'A nasty piece of work', *My Career, Sydney Morning Herald*, 13 March 2002, p. 4.

CORNELIUS, H. & FAIRE, S. *Everyone Can Win*, Simon & Schuster, Sydney, 1989.

GAMBLE, TERI KWAL & GAMBLE, MICHAEL. *Communication Works*, 5th edn, The McGraw-Hill Companies, USA, 1996.

HAYES, CHRISTINE & HARDIE, LILLIAN. *Negotiation Skills*, 2nd edn, Eastern House, Victoria, 1997.

HELLREIGEL, D., SLOCUM, J.W. & WOODMAN, R.W. *Organizational Behavior*, 4th edn, West Publishing Company, St Paul, USA, 1988.

SAUNDERS, S., KAYE, M., GILPIN, A. & COLLINGWOOD, V. *Managing Adult Communication: Experiential Activities Workbook*, ITATE, Sydney College of Advanced Education, Sydney, 1989.

STEINER, C.M. *Scripts People Live*, Grove Press, New York, 1974.

TILLETT, GREGORY. *Resolving Conflict: A Practical Approach*, Sydney University Press, Sydney, 1992.

VALLENCE, K.E. & McWILLIAM, T. *Communication that Works*, Thomas Nelson, Melbourne, 1987.

Part IV Workplace writing and research skills

Chapter 14 Analyse and present research information

ANDERSON, JONATHAN & POOLE, MILLICENT. *Assignment and Thesis Writing*, 4th edn, John Wiley & Sons, Brisbane, 2001.

BERNARD, J.R.L. (ed.) *The Macquarie Thesaurus: The Book of Words*, Macquarie Library, Macquarie University, Sydney, 1986.

BERNARD, J.R.L. (ed.) *Macquarie Writer's Friend*, Macquarie Library, Macquarie University, Sydney, 1999.

BUZAN, TONY. *Speed Reading*, E.P. Dutton, New York, 1984.

COLE, K. *Crystal Clear Communication Skills for Understanding and Being Understood*, Prentice Hall, Sydney, 1993.

DELBRIDGE, A. (ed.) *The Macquarie Dictionary,* Federation edn, Macquarie Library, Macquarie University, Sydney, 2001.

Education Network Online *Home Page* <www.edna.edu.au>, accessed 13 March 2002.

Flinders University of South Australia, *Library News Page,* <www.lib.flinders.edu.au/new>, accessed 8 May 2002.

Google *Home Page,* <www.google.com>, accessed 13 March 2002.

GUFFEY, MARY ELLEN. 'Formats for the citation of electronic sources in business writing', *Business Communication Quarterly,* Vol. 60, No. 1, March 1997, pp. 59–76.

HOGER, ELIZABETH A., CAPPEL, JAMES J. & MYERSCOUGH, MARK A. 'Navigating the Web with a typology of corporate uses', *Business Communication Quarterly,* Vol. 61, No. 2, June 1998, pp. 39–48. Reproduced by scanning into CD Rom BPO98_07_10, 21 September 1998.

LACHMAN, BETH E. *Linking Sustainable Community Activities to Pollution Prevention: A Sourcebook,* RAND Publications, USA, 1997; <www.rand.org/publications/electronic>, accessed 25 April 1998.

McGARVEY, PAT 'Search Engines and Searching' 1997; online *What is . . . A Tour of the Internet: Where to Go,* <www.whatis.com/tourwhse.htm>, accessed 26 April 1998 (assistance given).

RYRIE, TASKER. 'Cowboys and engines', *Charter,* September 2001, pp. 48–9.

Style Manual for Authors, Editors and Printers, 6th edn, Australian Government Publishing Service, Canberra, 2002.

The World Clock – Time Zones, <www.timeanddate.com/worldclock>, accessed 8 May 2002.

Whereis Online *Home Page,* <www.whereis.com.au>, accessed 13 March 2002.

Yahoo *Home Page,* <www.yahoo.com.au>, accessed 13 March 2002.

Chapter 15 Organise workplace information

BUZAN, T. *Make the Most of your Mind*, Pan Books, London, 1988.

BUZAN, T. *Use both Sides of your Brain*, 3rd edn, Plume, New York, 1991.

EAGLESON, R.D. *Writing in Plain English*, Australian Government Publishing Service, Canberra, 1990.

WALLER, VANESSA. 'Get to the Power Point', *Sydney Morning Herald*, 12 June 1999.

Chapter 16 Using plain English in workplace documents

ADAMSON, G. & PRENTICE, J. *Communication Skills in Practice: Workbook 2 Reading and Writing*, Nelson Wadsworth, Melbourne, 1987.

BARNETT, M.T. *Writing for Technicians*, 3rd edn, Delmar Publishers, Canada, 1987.

Capital Community College, *Guide to Grammar and Writing*, <http://ccc.commnet.edu/grammar>, accessed 13 March 2002.

EAGLESON, R.D. *Writing in Plain English*, Australian Government Publishing Service, Canberra, 1990.

FLESCH, R. *How to Write, Speak and Think More Effectively*, Signet Books, New York, 1990.

FOWLER, H.R. & AARON, J.E. *The Little Brown Handbook*, 4th edn, Scott Foresman, Boston, 1989.

MERRIAM-WEBSTER. *Online Language Centre*, <www.m-w.com>, accessed 13 March 2002.

MURPHY, ELIZABETH M. 'Plain English – Style of Choice', *Stylewise*, Vol. 7, No. 1, 2001, pp. 1–2.

MURPHY, H.A. & HILDEBRANDT, H.W. *Effective Business Communication*, 6th edn, McGraw-Hill, New York, 1991.

PETERS, PAM. *The Cambridge Australian English Style Guide*, Cambridge University Press, Melbourne, 1994.

Rose, Jean. *The Mature Student's Guide to Writing*, Palgrave, New York, 2001.

Style Manual for Authors, Editors and Printers, 6th edn, Australian Government Publishing Service, Canberra, 2002.

Vallence, K.E. & McWilliam, T. *Communication that Works*, Thomas Nelson, Melbourne, 1987.

Walsh, B. *Communicating in Writing*, 2nd edn, Australian Government Publishing Service, Canberra, 1989.

Wolf, M.W. & Kuiper, S. *Effective Business Communication*, South-Western Publishing Co., Cincinatti, 1989.

Chapter 17 Communicating through technology

Angell, David & Heslop, Bret. *The Elements of E-Mail Style,* Addison Wesley, Reading, MA., 1994.

Australian eBusiness Guide, CCH Australia Limited, Sydney, 2001.

Baskin, Colin & Adam, Stewart. *Managing on the Internet*, Pearson Education Australia, Sydney, 1999.

Blogger *Home Page,* <www.blogger.com>, accesssed 13 March 2002.

David Jones *Home Page,* <www.davidjones.com.au/home>, accessed 8 May 2002.

Gibbons, Patrice. 'A small fish plans a big splash on the Web', *Business Review Weekly*, 10–16 January 2002, p. 39.

Globalise Interactive Solutions. Press release: *Corporations' search for alternative means of communication, boosts videoconference and online technology,* <www.globalise.com.au/article1.shtml>, accessed 13 March 2002.

Google *Home Page,* <www.google.com>, accessed 14 March 2002.

Louhiala-Salminen, Leena. 'Investigating the genre of a business fax: a Finnish case study', *Journal of Business Communication*, Vol. 34, No. 3, July 1997, pp. 316–33.

McCabe, Kathleen. 'On-line documentation: its place in a two year college's technical writing curriculum', *Journal of Business and Technical Communication*, Vol. II, No. 1, January 1997, pp. 74–82.

Merrier, Patricia A. & Dirks, Ruthann. 'Student attitudes toward written, oral, and e-mail communication', *Business Communication Quarterly*, Vol. 60, No. 3, June 1997, pp. 89–99.

Nguyen, Maria. 'The graduates', *Sydney Morning Herald*, Review, 26–27 January 2002, pp. 4–5.

Online Information Service Obligations, <www.dcita.gov.au/infoaccess>, accessed 4 April 2002.

Price, Rodney P. 'An analysis of stylistic variables in electronic mail', *Journal of Business and Technical Communication*, Vol. II, No. 1, January 1997, pp. 5–23.

Schramm, R.M. & James, M.L. 'The impact of e-mail in today's organizations', *Office Systems Research Journal*, Vol. II, No. 1, 1992, pp. 3–13.

White Pages *Home Page,* <www.whitepages.com.au>.

Part V Producing workplace documents

Chapter 18 Writing business letters

Bailey, B. *Effective Language*, Campus Publishing, Sydney, 1986.

Barnett, M.T. *Writing for Technicians*, 3rd edn, Delmar Publishers, Canada, 1987.

Bateman, D.N. & Sigband, N.B. *Communicating in Business*, 3rd edn, Scott Foresman & Co., Boston, 1989.

GARTON, KAREN & GARRETT, JENNY. *Word Processing Simple Business Documents*, Pearson Education Australia, Sydney, 2002.

MURPHY, ELIZABETH M. 'Plain English – Style of Choice', *Stylewise*, Vol. 7, No. 3, 2001, p. 2.

Style Manual for Authors, Editors and Printers, 6th edn, Australian Government Publishing Service, Canberra, 2002.

TREECE, M. *Communication for Business and the Professions*, 4th edn, Allyn & Bacon, Massachusetts, 1989.

VALLENCE, K.E. & McWILLIAM, T. *Communication that Works*, Thomas Nelson, Melbourne, 1987.

WALSH, B. *Communicating in Writing*, 2nd edn, Australian Government Publishing Service, Canberra, 1989.

WATSON, DESLEY. *Communication in the Workplace*, Pearson Education Australia, Sydney, 2000.

Chapter 19 Writing memos and short reports

BATEMAN, D.N. & SIGBAND, N.B. *Communicating in Business*, 3rd edn, Scott Foresman & Co., Boston, 1989.

GALVIN, M., HUSEMAN, R. & PRESCOTT, D. *Business Communication: Strategies and Skills*, 4th edn, Holt Rinehart & Winston, Sydney, 1992.

TOLMIE, L.W. & TOLMIE M.J. *Handbook of Communication Skills*, Prentice Hall, Melbourne, 1980.

TREECE, M. *Communication for Business and the Professions*, 4th edn, Allyn & Bacon, Massachusetts, 1989.

VALLENCE, K.E. & McWILLIAM, T. *Communication that Works*, Thomas Nelson, Melbourne, 1987.

VAN ALSTYNE, J.S. *Professional and Technical Writing Strategies*, 2nd edn, Prentice Hall, New Jersey, 1990.

WADE, MATT AND TINGLE, LAURA. 'February a cracker, says NAB survey', *Sydney Morning Herald*, 13 March 2002.

WALSH, B. *Communicating in Writing*, Australian Government Publishing Service, Canberra, 1989.

WOLF, M.W. & KUIPER, S. *Effective Communication in Business*, South-Western Publishing Co., Cincinatti, 1989.

Chapter 20 Writing long reports

ABRAMS, K.S. *Communication at Work: Listening, Speaking, Writing and Reading*, Prentice Hall, New Jersey, 1986.

BARNETT, M.T. *Writing for Technicians*, 3rd edn, Delmar Publishers, Canada, 1987.

BATEMAN, D.N. & SIGBAND, N.B. *Communicating in Business*, 3rd edn, Scott Foresman & Co., Boston, 1985.

BLICQ, RON. *Writing Reports to get Results: Guidelines for the Computer Age*, IEEE Press, New York, 1987.

BLICQ, RON & MORETTO, LISA, A. *Writing Reports to get Results: Quick, Effective Results using the Pyramid Method*, 2nd edn, Institute of Electronic and Electrical Engineers, New York, 1995.

BOVÉE, COURTLAND & THILL, JOHN V. *Business Communication Today*, 6th edn, Pearson Education, New Jersey, 2000.

GUFFEY, MARY ELLEN. *Essentials of Business Communication*, 2nd edn, PWS-Kent Publishing Company, Boston, 1991.

MURPHY, R. & PECK, M. *Effective Business Communications*, 5th edn, McGraw-Hill, New York, 1988.

PRENTICE, J. & ADAMSON, G. *Communication Skills in Practice: Workbook 2 Reading and Writing*, Nelson Wadsworth, Melbourne, 1987.

PUTNIS, PETER & PETELIN, ROSLYN. *Professional Communication: Principles and Applications*, 2nd edn, Prentice Hall, Sydney, 1999.

'Tips for Electronic Documents', *Stylewise*, Vol. 7, No. 2, 2001, pp. 1, 4.

WATSON, DESLEY. *Communication in the Workplace*, Prentice Hall, Sydney, 2000.

Chapter 21 Graphic communication

Australian Bureau of Statistics, *Schools Australia*, No. 4221.0, Australian Bureau of Statistics, Canberra, 2001.

Australian Bureau of Statistics, *2002 Year Book*, Australian Bureau of Statistics, Canberra, 2002.

BARNETT, M.T. *Writing for Technicians*, 3rd edn, Delmar Publishers, Canada, 1987.

STRANO, Z., McGREGOR, H. & MOHAN, T. *Communicating! Theory and Practice*, 4th edn, Harcourt Brace Jovanovich, Sydney, 1997.

TUFTE, E.R. *Visual Display of Quantitative Information*, Graphics Press, Cheshire, Connecticut, 1983.

TUFTE, E.R. *Visual Explanations: Images and Quantities, Evidence and Narrative,* Graphics Press, Cheshire, Connecticut, 1997.

WAXMAN, P. & MAUTHNER, P. *Business Mathematics and Statistics*, 2nd edn, Prentice Hall, Australia, 1990.

Chapter 22 Writing technical documents

BARNETT, M.T. *Writing for Technicians*, 3rd edn, Delmar Publishers, Canada, 1987.

'Chemical alert – TCE reclassification', *WORKCOVER NEWS* 46, September–November 2001.

EAGLESON, R.D. *Writing in Plain English*, Australian Government Publishing Service, Canberra, 1990.

EISENBERG, A. *Writing Well for the Technical Professions*, Harper & Row, New York, 1989.

FOWLER, H.R. & AARON, J.E. *The Little Brown Handbook*, 4th edn, Scott Foresman & Co., Boston, 1989.

HARAMUNDANIS, K. *The Art of Technical Documentation*, Digital Equipment Corporation, USA, 1992.

Queensland & New South Wales Tender Magazines, *How to Prepare Winning Tenders*, Mudgerraba, Qld, 2001.

REEP, D.C. *Technical Writing: Principles, Strategies and Readings*, Allyn & Bacon, Massachusetts, 1991.

RINEY, L.A. *Technical Writing for Industry – An Operations Manual for the Technical Writer*, Prentice Hall, New Jersey, 1989.

Style Manual for Authors, Editors and Printers, 6th edn, Australian Government Publishing Service, Canberra, 2002.

TARUTZ, J.A. *Technical Editing: The Practical Guide for Writers and Editors*, Hewlett Packard Press, USA, 1992.

Part VI Job search skills

Chapter 23 Applying for a job

BLICQ, R.S. *Communicating at Work*, Prentice Hall, Canada, 1991.

BUCHANAN, MATT. 'My Career', *Sydney Morning Herald,* 9–10 February 2002, p. 1.

GROSE, R.W. *Your First Job: How to Get It, Keep It and Do Well in It*, Polondo Pty Ltd, Sydney, 1992.

mycareer.com.au, *Advertise a Job*, <www.f2.com.au>, accessed 8 May 2002.

STEVENS, P. *Win that Job!* 6th edn, Centre for Worklife Counselling, Sydney, 1994.

STEVENS, P. *The Australian Résumé Guide: Making your Job Application Work*, 2nd edn, Centre for Worklife Counselling, Sydney, 1998.

Chapter 24 The job interview

ADAMSON, G. & PRENTICE, J. *Communication Skills in Practice: Workbook 1 Speaking and Listening*, Nelson Wadsworth, Melbourne, 1987.

BATEMAN, D.N. & SIGBAND, N.B. *Communicating in Business*, Scott Foresman & Co., Boston, 1989.

CLEMIE, S. & NICHOLSON, J.R. *The Good Interview Guide*, Wrightbooks, North Brighton, Victoria, 1990.

GOODALE, J.G. *The Fine Art of Interviewing*, Prentice Hall, Englewood Cliffs, New Jersey, 1982.

LANE, SIMON. 'Choose or lose', *Charter,* October 2001, p. 40.

MURPHY, H.A. & HILDEBRANDT, H.W. *Effective Business Communication*, 5th edn, McGraw-Hill, New York, 1988.

SAUNDERS, S., KAYE, M., GILPIN, A. & COLLINGWOOD, V. *Managing Adult Communication: Experiential Activities Workbook*, ITATE, Sydney College of Advanced Education, 1989.

Chapter 25 Being interviewed for a job

DEET *Jobsearch for Adults*, Australian Government Publishing Service, Canberra, 1991.

FLETCHER, C. *Get that Job! Your Guide to a Successful Interview*, Unwin Paperbacks, London, 1992.

GROSE, R.W. *Your First Job: How to Get It, Keep It and Do Well in It*, Polondo Pty Ltd, Sydney, 1992.

HUGHES, DAVID. 'How to succeed at interviews', *Insider CIMA*, September 2000, p. 42.

LUDDEN, L. *Job Savvy: How to be a Success at Work*, J. Michael Farr, CES Job Search Kit, Indianapolis, 1992.

MCKINNERY, AMBROSE. *At the Interview: Tips and Techniques*, <www.employment.com.au/news/dsp_news_item.cfm?NEWS_ID=26>, accessed 24 January 2002.

STEVENS, P. *Your Career Planner*, Centre for Worklife Counselling, Sydney, 1991.

STEVENS, P. *Win that Job!* 6th edn, Centre for Worklife Counselling, Sydney, 1994.

Glossary

abstract   Provides a brief description or informative overview of the report's most important points.

accommodation   A negotiation style in which one party is willing to oblige or adapt to meet the needs of the other party.

action plan   The working document for the implementation of chosen options.

active listening   A listening technique in which the listener works at paying attention to the whole message – that is, the content and the feeling.

active voice   A writing style in which the subject is placed before the action to give a stronger link between them and to show who or what is doing the action.

adaptors   Nonverbal acts performed unconsciously in response to an inner desire.

adjustment refusal   A refusal given when an organisation believes that a request for an adjustment is unjustified.

advertise   To offer a particular product or service for sale.

affective displays   Changes in facial expressions that display emotion.

agenda   A list of a meeting's business prepared by the secretary in consultation with the chairperson and distributed before a meeting.

aggressive behaviour   When one person seeks to dominate others.

agreement chart   Differentiates between three different outcomes: the negotiated agreement, the BATNA and the WATNA.

AIDA formula   This formula describes the process suited to persuasive writing. It aims to catch the attention, interest, desire and willingness of the customer or potential customer to take action.

amendment   A proposal to alter a motion in a formal meeting.

anecdote   Examples from your own experience, someone else's experience or a past experience common to the group.

announcement memo   A memo that provides information.

apologies   The names of people who have apologised for not being present at a meeting.

appeal   Emotional appeals, informative appeals and appeals to authority often used in persuasive messages.

appendix   Information relevant to a report but which would interfere with the flow of ideas if included in the body text.

application form   A form with standard questions asking for the same sort of information from each applicant for a job.

argument   A process of reasoning that shows the interrelationship between ideas and aims to convince others of the truth of something.

artefacts   Objects used to convey nonverbal messages about self-concept, image, mood, feelings or style.

assertion   Behaviour that acknowledges your rights as an individual and the rights of other people.

assertive behaviour   A constructive style of behaviour that acknowledges the needs of the sender and the receiver of a message.

assertive statement   A statement used to make people aware of your rights while respecting theirs.

attending listening   Focusing on the speaker by giving physical attention.

attention line   Names the person who is to attend to a letter's contents.

audiovisual aids   Aural and visual devices used by a speaker to improve the audience's understanding.

author–date (or Harvard) system of referencing   Acknowledging work written by someone else by identifying, in the following order, the author's surname and initials or given name, year of publication, title, publisher and place of publication.

authorisation memo   A written statement giving the reader authority to take some action.

authoritarian leader   A leader who determines the policies and work of the team with little discussion or input from other members.

authority   The characteristic given to a person with the accepted source of information or the right to determine actions or the respect or acceptance that commands influence.

autonomous or semi-autonomous work groups   Sections or groups in an organisation that are provided with general objectives and targets by senior managers and then left to decide the work process.

bad news letter   A letter of refusal.

barrier   See communication barrier.

basic résumé   The informative part of a job application summing up the experience of those who have just left school or have little work experience.

BATNA   The best alternative to a negotiated agreement.

belief   A personal conviction.

bibliography   A list of all the references and sources of information used in a report as well as further recommended reading.

body   The main part of a spoken or written presentation.

body movement   A form of nonverbal communication conveyed by the hands, head, feet, legs or posture.

bookmark   A saved link to a web page, added to a list of saved links.

brainstorming   A group process for generating ideas and creative solutions.

briefing   A short, accurate summary of the details of a plan or operation.

casting vote   A vote by the chairperson that decides an issue in a meeting in the case of a tied vote.

chairperson   Is either elected or appointed to conduct the meeting according to the standing orders or rules of the organisation, committee or meeting.

clarifying   A communication technique that aims to bring accuracy to an area of confusion. The listener explains how they have interpreted the message.

cliché   Expressions that have been so over-used that they have lost meaning and impact.

client records   Information about the type and level of service expected and received by a customer.

climate   The atmosphere created by the team reflects the quality of the team's communication.

closed question   A question that is designed to limit the response.

coaching   Is about being aware of what people need to be able to do, guiding them in how to do it and encouraging them to do it well.

coercive power   Power based on coercion or punishment.

cohesion   A sense of belonging and inclusion that allows team members to satisfy their needs and objectives.

cohesiveness   Refers to the level of common purpose and commitment to the team among members.

cold canvassing   Seeking job opportunities by mailing applications directly to companies. Also known as 'direct mail campaigning'.

collaboration   People cooperating to produce a solution satisfactory to everyone.

collection letter   Uses persuasion to collect money from those who are slow to pay.

column (vertical bar) graph   A graphic that shows changes from one time period to the next or compares one item with another.

committee   A meeting in which a group of people have the delegated authority to consider, investigate and report or act on some matter.

communication   Any behaviour, verbal or nonverbal, that is perceived by another.

communication barrier   Anything that distorts or interrupts the message and its meaning.

communication channel   The means or techniques that are used to send a message.

communication climate   Refers to the tone of the relationship as expressed by the verbal and nonverbal messages between people.

communication process   The seven main elements of the communication process are sender, message, receiver, feedback, channel, context and interference.

competence   The ability to complete a task to the standard required.

competition   A situation in which one party negotiates to maximise its results at the expense of the other party's needs.

completion report   A report that states the project is finished.

complex sentence   A sentence that contains more than one idea.

complimentary close   The use of 'Yours sincerely' or 'Yours faithfully' placed before the signature in a letter.

compound sentence   A sentence that contains two or more main ideas expressed in two principal clauses.

compromise   The settlement of differences by mutual concessions.

concerns   Issues that engage a person's attention or interest. See also needs.

conclusion   A closing overview of the main points of a presentation.

conclusions   The findings from your investigations.

conditional instructions   These explain the objectives, provide background information and describe the intended outcome.

conducting or content phase   The part of the interview during which the content is covered.

confidence   The ability to feel comfortable with the other person and the situation.

conflict   A clash of opinions, values, contexts and so on.

conflict map   A tool used to find the cause of a conflict.

confrontation   A situation where people are in opposition or antagonistic toward one another.

connotation   The association that is placed on a word by past experience, attitudes, values, context and so on.

consensus   An agreed position.

constitution   A document that contains an organisation's name, aims and objectives, rules of administration, membership, office bearers and committee.

consult   A process to gather information from customers about their needs and expectations.

consultative power   Power that is based on a capacity to seek information, consider advice from others and make plans with others.

consulting   The action of gathering information from customers about their needs and expectations.

content phase   See conducting phase.

context   The situation or setting within which communication takes place or the circumstances that surround a particular piece of communication. In business, the context is that organisation setting within which people work and communicate to achieve a common goal.

convention   An accepted standard or practice.

correspondence   A meeting's incoming and outgoing mail.

counselling interview   An interview that aims to provide support for employees dealing with problems.

cover page   Part of a proposal that includes the name of the proposing organisation or person, their contact address and telephone number, title of the project, the name of the person to whom the project is submitted and the date.

covering letter   The persuasive part of a job application that aims to make a positive first impression and to focus attention on the relevance of the qualifications to the position.

credit refusal   A rejection of a request for credit.

crisis level   A level of conflict where behaviour and normal functioning is affected.

cross-cultural communication   Communication between people living in different countries.

cull   Elimination, on the basis of the job application, of those people considered unsuitable because of lack of qualifications, experience, ability or motivation for the position.

cultural differences   These arise from the various rules, backgrounds and interpretations that affect our perception – for example, values, attitudes and life concerns.

cultural diversity   The differing characteristics resulting from belonging to a cultural group.

cultural nonverbal communication   Nonverbal behaviour learnt unconsciously by observing others in the society or group – the behaviour becomes characteristic of, or common to, a group of people.

cultural sensitivity   Awareness of the common rules and patterns of behaviour in other countries.

customer   A person who purchases and/or seeks goods or services from another person or organisation.

customer complaint   A customer's expression of dissatisfaction with a good or service supplied by another.

customer inquiry   A customer's seeking of information, usually by questioning about a good or service provided by another.

customer records   Up-to-date records of a customer's requirements, personal details and/or history.

customer value package   The range of strategies designed to give customer service based on the things that customers value.

customer values   The four types of customer values are basic, expected, desired and unanticipated value.

data or information collection interviews   Interviews that are designed specifically to collect information.

decision block   The space provided for the receiver of a submission to give written approval.

decision by authority   A situation in which the group discusses the issue and then either the leader or an outside supervisor makes the decision.

decision by compromise   A decision that appeals to all members of a group without fully satisfying everyone.

decision by consensus   A decision that is made by mutual agreement among group members.

decision by majority   An agreement that is reached among the majority of group members.

decision-making agenda   A nine-stage process that encourages all members of a team to participate in planning the actions to be taken to complete a task.

decode   To interpret a message to achieve understanding.

deductive reasoning   Argues from the general to the particular.

defensive roles   Behaviours that are intended to protect the group from anxiety when it is unable to function effectively.

delegate   To give someone else the authority and responsibility for carrying out a task while retaining accountability.

denotation   The literal meaning of a word.

diagram   A graphic that is used to compare structures.

direct instructions   These are to the point and indicate who, what, when, where and how a task will be completed.

direct mail campaign   See cold canvassing.

direct method of organising information   Presents the main points and/or conclusions early in the document, either before or after the introduction.

direct order of information   This leads the reader from the solutions to the problem, then to the reasons for suggesting the solutions, and finally to the facts on which these conclusions are based. It begins with the main point, then provides detailed evidence and discussion about this.

directive interview   An interview that is controlled and organised by the interviewer.

directive techniques   Used in interviews to focus on a particular topic and gain further information.

discipline or reprimand interview   An interview that aims to discuss unacceptable or inappropriate behaviour and to create and discuss the plans to take action to change the situation.

discretionary time   The time available to think, plan and create ideas. Discretionary time is under your control.

discomfort level   A level of conflict where things do not feel right or you feel uncomfortable in a situation.

discrimination   In the workplace, discrimination means denying people equal treatment for reasons other than those relating directly to the job.

dot graph   A graph that is used to present six or more variables.

drama triangle   An illustration of non-assertive behaviour in which people play the role of victim and behave in a helpless manner.

dysfunctional roles   Behaviours that are intended to distract the group from its purpose or to inhibit the group's progress towards its objectives.

edit   To revise and correct your writing.

effectiveness   Refers to how well an activity achieves its intended purpose.

efficiency   Refers to how well and how quickly a task (for example, writing a letter) is achieved.

electronic communication   Data, text, images or sound conveyed by electromagnetic energy.

electronic mail (email)   A form of communication in which the writer keys the message directly into the computer and the receiver either reads it on a screen or as a printout.

electronic trading   This allows people to order and pay for products and services directly online.

emblems   Nonverbal acts that are learnt through imitation.

empathy   The ability to understand and feel as the other person feels.

empathy blocker   These have a negative impact on communication and may cause barriers between the sender and receiver of a message.

employment agency   A broker of jobs – a middle person between employers and job applicants.

employment interview   An interview that aims to attract and choose the best applicant for a position.

encode   To send a message to achieve understanding.

encouraging listening   Inviting the speaker to disclose their thoughts and feelings.

end matter   The final part of a report that contains the appendix, bibliography, index and glossary of terms.

endnotes   Supplementary material placed at the end of a chapter or article.

environment   Surrounding circumstances, conditions or influences.

Equal Employment Opportunity (EEO)   A policy that aims to achieve fairer representation in employment for all groups in the community.

equality   An interaction that recognises each person in the interaction as worthwhile and with something to contribute.

equity   The quality of being fair or impartial.

ethics   A set of moral principles by which we judge human actions and proposals as good or bad or right or wrong.

executive summary   Provides the reader with a brief summary of the material in the main text – includes the report's purpose, scope, methods, findings and conclusions.

expectations   The type or level of service the customer anticipates.

expertise power   Power that is held because of a person's knowledge, aptitude and ability.

expressiveness   Involvement, both as a sender and receiver, in interpersonal interaction.

external channels of communication   Means of communicating to people outside the organisation.

external conflict   Conflict between people caused by an unsatisfied need or an unresolved experience or emotion.

external customers   Customers from outside the organisation, i.e. the general public.

fact   A fact can be determined to be true.

feedback   The receiver's response to a sender's message which tells the sender how their message is being received and helps the receiver confirm whether their perception of the message is correct.

fight response   Used in a conflict situation to control or defend a position.

findings   Facts and other verifiable information.

flight response   Used in a conflict situation to escape the situation and avoid the results.

flow response   Used in a conflict situation to acknowledge the situation and respond appropriately.

follow up   A telephone call or letter to the company or organisation after a job interview that inquires about the result of the interview.

follow-up letter   A concise, tactful, one-page letter that again shows your interest in the position and your ability to perform the job.

footnotes Comments at the foot of the page giving extra information about points in a text.

form of communication The three forms of communication are verbal (either spoken or written), nonverbal and graphic.

form report Provides a standard layout which enables information to be gathered in a consistent manner from a number of different sources.

formal format A defined form or structure used in formal documents such as reports.

formal group A group established by management that is usually regulated through formal or contractual processes.

formal meetings Meetings that are structured, unchanging proceedings.

formal outline Contains headings and subheadings that identify the main ideas and support the information.

formal short report format The minimum acceptable format for a short report includes a title page, introduction, sections with headings in the main body, conclusions and recommendations (when required).

format Layout and appearance of a document.

front matter The first part of a report that contains the title page, letter of transmittal, table of contents, abstract or synopsis and authorisation document.

full block Alignment of a business letter on the left of the page.

functional résumé A résumé that focuses on skills demonstrated in previous employment. See also résumé.

funding request A formal request for money.

general business The heading on the agenda of a meeting under which 'new' business may be introduced.

given Something that is stated, fixed or already determined.

glossary A list of terms and definitions.

goal An aim or end towards which effort is directed.

good news letter or neutral letter Presents positive, favourable or neutral information, using the direct order of information.

goodwill The reputation of a business and its relations with its customers.

graphic communication Ideas, relationships or connections represented visually using shapes, diagrams and lines.

graphics Visual representations that organise information, show relationships, highlight trends and help to sort, classify and group data.

greeting (salutation) The writer's greeting to the receiver.

group cohesion The level of common purpose and commitment to the group among members.

groupthink A situation in which group cohesiveness prevents disagreement, constructive criticism and full assessment of alternatives.

headings Highlight the main ideas and give them an order that suits the document's purpose.

high-quality service The act of providing a good or service to the expected, desired or unanticipated level of service.

horizontal bar chart A diagram that emphasises the differences or similarities between two or more items at a certain point in time.

horizontal channel A communication channel that operates between colleagues at the same level of an organisation's structure.

'I' messages   These messages are assertive statements that help to send a clear message.

Illustrators   Nonverbal acts that relate to, and illustrate, the spoken word.

immediacy   The sense of contact the other person receives from the person communicating.

impromptu speech   An unexpected speech which is delivered without preparation.

incident level   A level of conflict where some short, sharp exchange has occurred and caused a slight irritation.

incident report   Offers a clear factual account of something that happens which is non-routine, for example an accident or any other unusual occurrence.

inclusion   Includes all groups in a society – gender, race or other factors.

inclusive language   Language that does not exclude any group on the basis of their gender, race or some other factor.

indirect method of organising information   Emphasises the problem at the beginning and end of the document, starting with the result or action needed, then providing the detailed evidence and discussion, and concluding with the main point.

inductive reasoning   Argues from the particular to the general.

informal meetings   Unstructured meetings.

informal organisational structure   The links between individuals, groups and whole sections of the company that are not legitimised by management.

informal outline   The creation of all the points which it is desired to make before any sequencing or editing.

information overload   Excessive amounts of information.

in-house   Work done within the organisation without seeking outside help.

inquiry   A letter that asks others to share information and ideas.

inside address   The receiver's address in a business letter.

instruction memo   A memo that gives directions.

intentional message   The message that the sender means to send.

interaction management   The balance between the sender and listener as they interact with one another.

interactive skills   The nonverbal, listening and interpersonal skills that enable people to interact effectively.

intercultural communication   Takes place between people living in the same country but from different cultural backgrounds.

internal channels of communication   Means of communicating to people within the organisation.

internal conflict   Conflict within a person caused by an unsatisfied need or an unresolved experience or emotion.

internal customers   Customers from within an organisation.

Internet   Worldwide cooperative public telecommunications network accessible to anyone with suitable technology.

interpersonal communication   Interaction either between two people on a one-to-one basis, or in small groups.

interpersonal concerns   The three interpersonal concerns within teams are the need for inclusion, the need to know who has control and the need to be accepted.

interview   An exchange of information that has a purpose and is planned, structured and controlled by the interviewer.

interview memory jogger   A summary of the main points you want to put forward in your answers at the job interview.

interviewee   The person being interviewed.

interviewer   The person conducting the interview.

interviewer skills   The ability to plan, structure and control an interview using effective interactive skills.

intranet   A private version of the Internet used by individual enterprises to share computer resources and company information.

introduction   The first part of a spoken presentation or written document that prepares your audience for what you are going to say and identifies the aim or main theme.

jargon   The language peculiar to a trade or profession.

job description   A list of the objectives of the position and the duties completed by a person in the position.

job interview   An interview conducted to choose the best applicant for a position.

job search control sheet   A systematic way to organise a job search.

job specification   An outline of duties and responsibilities.

Johari Window   This theory explains the parts that make up each person's self-concept in two broad divisions: the areas of yourself known to you and the areas of yourself known to others.

justification report   A report that presents an idea or proposal and then uses evidence to justify the proposal or request.

justified complaint   A valid and reasonable complaint from a customer.

key competency   A generic competency required in all workplaces – communicating, organising, collecting, analysing, planning, problem solving, using mathematical ideas and working with others and in teams.

keynoting   Restatement and repetition of the key words.

kinesic behaviour   Body movement that includes movement of the torso, limbs, hands, head, feet or legs; posture; eye movement such as blinking; and facial expressions such as smiles.

laissez-faire leader   A leader who has a policy on non-interference and lets the group run itself.

lateral thinking   A creative thinking technique in which the thinker explores a situation or idea from many different points of view.

layout   The arrangement of information on a page.

leader   A person who achieves the organisation's goals through the work of others without relying on his or her position of power – the ability to influence others.

leadership style   The consistent pattern of behaviour adopted by a leader.

leading question   A question that directs the interviewee to clarify answers.

learning   The hierarchy of learning follows this sequence: recall, comprehension, application, analysis, synthesis and evaluation.

legitimate power   Power held because the organisation has given authority to that position.

letter format   Format includes the seven basic parts of a business letter plus a subject line.

letter of acceptance   A courteous letter stating your acceptance of a job offer.

letter of acknowledgment   A letter that acknowledges requests for information, confirms orders, supplies information and thanks the receiver.

letter of application   The persuasive part of a job application. It is a covering letter and should be brief (about one page) and specific.

letter of inquiry A letter requesting information regarding a product or service.

letter of introduction A letter that aims to maintain contact and to create goodwill and the opportunity for future sales.

letter of request A letter that asks for information.

letter of transmittal The covering letter for a report.

letterhead Identifies the writer, their address and other contact details.

liaison-related role The behaviours that are needed to communicate and collaborate with members of other teams or groups.

line graph A diagram that shows movement. Its main purpose is to show trends over time in a situation in which there is a continuous relationship.

linking phrases Phrases that let the writer make logical connections between ideas and give continuity to the writing.

list of references Gives details only of those works cited in your report or essay.

listening Involves both hearing and striving to understand the other person's message.

local area network (LAN) The network or interconnection of computers, hubs and other network devices in a limited area like a building.

long report A formal document written to provide comprehensive information and expert opinion.

lose–lose situation A situation in which both parties are dissatisfied with the negotiated result.

lose–lose strategy A strategy which results from a situation in which the objectives of the two parties are too rigid or when both parties are unable to collaborate.

lose–win strategy A strategy which focuses on one party's problem to the exclusion of the other and results in one party feeling dissatisfied and the other satisfied with the negotiated result.

maintenance-related functions Behaviours that focus on what is happening in the group, the way members listen and relate to each other within the group.

maintenance-related role The roles that are done in groups or meetings to focus on people and their relationships with one another – for example, to support and encourage the contributions of members or to reconcile disagreements.

manager A person who achieves the organisation's goals through the work of others.

manuscript speech A written style of speech suited to technical and complicated information which is often read.

map A type of graphic that uses scale, grids, symbols, lines, colours, legends, titles, figures and text to show the location of landforms, cities, towns, roads and other features.

Maslow's Hierarchy of Needs The hierarchy identifies five needs: physiological, safety and security, belonging, esteem and status, and self-actualisation.

media Means of communication that reach large numbers of people – for example, television, radio, newspapers and magazines.

media release Announcements made in the media.

meeting A forum or group of people that can provide and clarify information, give and receive feedback, encourage problem solving and allow discussion.

memo (memorandum) The standard form of internal written business communication.

memo format A report in memorandum format for circulation within an organisation.

memo proposal A proposal that uses a standard memorandum layout.

memorised speech A speech that is learned and recalled.

memory   The capacity to recall or recognise something that has been previously experienced.

mentoring   A relationship in which those with experience and knowledge facilitate and support those with less experience and knowledge.

merit principle   A principle which states that the person with the best qualifications, experience and capabilities should have the position.

message   The idea or feeling transmitted from the sender to the receiver to achieve understanding.

Mind Map®   A problem-solving technique that begins with the main idea as the focus. Key concepts then project out from the main idea.

minutes   The written record of what happened during a meeting.

mirror question   A question that restates the interviewee's previous answer and invites them to add further information.

misunderstanding level   A level of conflict where motives and facts are often confused or misperceived.

modified block layout   A business letter format that centres the sender's address or blocks it to the right margin.

motion   A proposal for action put by a member to the rest of the meeting.

motivation   A process that directs action or behaviour towards a goal.

multicultural society   A society which consists of people of diverse cultural, racial, religious and ethnic backgrounds.

needs   The major requirements of each negotiating party. See also concerns.

negotiation   Negotiation is a process in which two or more parties try to resolve differences, solve problems and reach agreement. Effective negotiation meets as many interests as possible in an agreement that is durable.

netiquette   The conventions and accepted standards used by a sender of messages online (made up of Internet and etiquette).

network   A group of people who exchange ideas and information with one another.

neutral letter   A letter sending information on which the sender and receiver agree.

noise or interference   An interruption to the message or communication flow between the sender and receiver which can lead to misunderstanding.

nominal group technique   A technique that enables the members of a group to work as individuals to think about and present new ideas.

non-assertive behaviour   Behaviour described as aggressive or submissive that ignores our own rights by failing to express honest thoughts and beliefs.

non-directive interview   An interview technique that involves the participants and the organisation in setting the goals and process of the interview.

non-directive techniques   Using minimal questions, creating a conversational tone and adopting positive nonverbal cues in an interview to encourage the applicant to speak.

non-discriminatory behaviour   Attitudes and actions that support the principle of equality.

nonverbal behaviour   Behaviour that includes body movement of the hands, head, feet, legs, posture; eye movements; facial expressions; vocalisations and voice qualities.

nonverbal communication   Communication that is sent by any means other than words or graphics. It modifies, changes or complements the verbal communication.

notations   Acknowledge the sources of information.

note (or traditional) system of referencing   When someone else's work is presented in an essay or project, identify the work in the following order – author's surname, given name or initials, title, publisher, place of publication and year of publication.

notice of meeting   A document convening a meeting that is sent to all members at a time specified by the organisation's rules.

obscure writing   Imprecise language that obscures meaning, such as clichés, lead-ins, topic announcements and qualifiers.

online communication   Communication on the Web that includes bulk email, advertisements, electronic mail, bulletin boards, newsletters and web page promotions and designs.

online information   Information held on company intranets or the World Wide Web.

open question   A question that is designed to encourage the interviewee to speak freely and to provide a range of information.

openness   The inclination of a person to respond frankly and spontaneously to people and situations, and the ability to acknowledge personal feelings and thoughts as their own.

operation   Action taken to reach goals.

opinion   A personal judgment; belief or viewpoint.

options   The range of alternatives from which the appropriate choice can be made.

oral report   Describes what, where, when, who and why something happened in spoken words.

order of information   The sequence in which information is organised.

order of presentation   The sequence in which information is presented.

order refusal   Declines a request.

organisational time   Time that is organised on the basis of the boss' imposed time, the system-imposed time and self-organised time.

organisational writing   Writing developed for and within the organisation.

other-orientation   The ability to attend to and focus on the other person in an interpersonal interaction.

outline   Provides a structure or writing plan for a document.

overhead transparency   A prepared visual aid projected onto a screen using an overhead projector to illustrate or reinforce points in a presentation.

palm card   Cards with the main points and supporting information on them which you hold in the palm of your hand as you give a speech.

panel interview   An interview that is conducted by a group of interviewers.

paragraph   A clustering of sentences that is built around one main idea.

paralanguage   How something is said.

paraphrasing   Expressing the meaning of what was said using different words from those originally used.

paraphasing question   Asks the receiver to restate the content in the message.

participative leader   A leader who encourages the members of the group to have an active role in decision making.

passive voice   A sentence with a verb describing action done to the subject.

perception   How people understand or give meaning to their environment.

performance appraisal   Evaluates an employee's performance and provides feedback to the employee.

performance interview   An interview that seeks to evaluate the employee's performance and provide feedback on the organisation's perception of the employee's performance.

periodic report   A report that keeps management informed by providing, at regular intervals, information on some aspect of the organisation's operation.

permissive leader   See laissez-faire leader.

persecutor   A role from the drama triangle played by those who put the other person down or bully them into action.

personal nonverbal communication   The use of nonverbal actions in a way that is personal or unique to that person.

persuasive interview   An interview that aims to influence the interviewee to think or act in a particular way.

persuasive letter   A letter that is written to influence the reader to take some action.

persuasive writing   Writing that aims to influence the reader to change an attitude or take some action to satisfy a need.

photograph   A graphic used to show the physical appearance of the subject.

pie chart   A graphic that represents the parts or divisions of a unit to give a comparison between each of the parts.

plain English   A writing style that is easy to understand. This style uses positive language, clear expression and a courteous tone.

point of order   The interpretation of the rules or standing orders that govern the way in which a meeting is to be conducted.

positiveness   The ability to communicate in a confident way while acknowledging the other person.

power   The capacity to influence, the possession of delegated authority or an ability to act.

pre-interview stage   Preparation for an interview when the purpose of the interview is defined, details of time and location are decided, and research is undertaken to establish the responses required and the questions to be asked.

prejudice   Any preconceived opinion or feeling, favourable or unfavourable.

prepared speech   A speech that is planned and organised before the time of presentation.

primary activities   Activities that produce the most important results.

primary sources of information   The people or organisations who take the action or cause the events that become part of society's store of information.

principled bargaining   A negotiation method made up of four elements: people, interests, options and criteria. The negotiating purpose is to satisfy the underlying interests of the parties.

priorities   The most important things.

probing question   A question that follows on from the last response of the interviewee.

problem-solving method of organising information   Used when you wish to focus the reader's thoughts on the problem. Start with the problem. Provide a detailed discussion of the factors that caused the problem and conclude with the solution.

process description   Describes how something works, why it works that way and each step in the process.

professional development   Activities undertaken to improve our knowledge, skills and abilities – for example, training, mentoring, coaching and attendance at professional associations.

professionalism   Behaviour that reflects the standing, practice or methods in an organisation offering service to the expected, desired or unanticipated level of service.

progress report   A report that keeps management informed about progress on a project or activities.

proposal   See motion.

proposal   A plan or scheme sent to a decision maker in the form of a well organised and persuasive document.

protocol   The special set of rules of communication used by the terminals/nodes (and related software) in a telecommunication network as they send and receive messages.

proximity   Nearness in place or position.

public relations   Activities that are concerned with the presence or image of an organisation and the positive public acceptance of this image.

purpose   Your objective in writing a document.

purpose statement   A sentence identifying a document's theme or subject.

quorum   The minimum number of people that must be at a meeting in order for business to be conducted.

RADAR approach   A five-step communication approach discussing practical problems and turning ideas into actions.

readability   How easy or interesting a document is to read. To improve the readability of business writing, keep sentences short and logical.

reading   A physical and intellectual exercise that involves identifying and understanding what is written.

realistic conflict   Conflict that can be resolved if people are willing to use effective strategies and negotiation skills.

receiver   The receiver decodes or interprets the sender's message to achieve understanding.

recommendations   Proposed as a result of the findings of a report or proposal.

reference   A document written by other people that highlights and supports certain skills and experiences you have gained.

reflecting listening   Restating to the speaker the feeling and content of their message.

reflective statement   Restates to the speaker the listener's understanding of the feeling and content in the speaker's message.

regulators   Nonverbal acts, such as head nods and movements, that regulate communication between people by maintaining and controlling the flow of speaking and listening.

reminder   A courteous letter reminding a customer of an overdue account.

request memo   A memo that asks for information.

rescuer   A role played from the drama triangle by those people who offer help and support while denying their own needs.

response time   The time a person makes available to respond to other people's problems, inquiries or complaints.

resolution   A motion put to the meeting and carried.

results   Outcomes that support and contribute to an organisation's business plans.

résumé   An informative and comprehensive document about your qualifications, experience and achievements.

reward   Something given or received in return for taking some action.

reward power   Power held by a person in authority who has control over resources desired by others.

rhythm   A measured flow of words that is used to emphasise the flow of ideas or to provide pauses that halt the flow in order to emphasise a point.

role   A way of behaving in a particular situation; a set of expected behaviours associated with a position.

routine instructions   Regular instructions that only require questions that check if the person can remember, restate and apply the information to a new situation.

routine order of information   Factual information that is presented in logical order, as an overview of the complete picture.

routing information   The list of signatures or initials on a circulating memo that is usually prepared in alphabetical order or in order of seniority of position.

sales letter   A persuasive letter that follows the order of information in the AIDA formula.

scale   A series of marks covering the range of data on a graph set out in succession at determinate distances to indicate times, lengths or amounts.

scope   Extent, or set of limitations.

search engine   Computer program that receives requests from Internet researchers, compares them with the index created by the 'robot' or 'web crawler' and returns the results of the search to the researcher.

secondary activities   Activities with a lower priority than primary activities.

secondary sources of information   Material published and stored after an event has taken place.

secretary   Conducts correspondence, prepares the minutes, keeps records and completes other duties for a meeting.

self-actualising person   Someone who realises their own potential.

self-bargaining person   Someone who will show you their feelings and ideas if you show yours first.

self-denying person   Someone who is introverted and reticent in providing information, especially feedback.

self-disclosure   Involves showing how you react and feel about a situation.

self-exposing person   Someone who wants to be the centre of attention.

self-image   A person's view of themselves.

self-protecting person   Someone who uses diversionary tactics such as discussing other people or sidetracking to other issues.

sender   The sender encodes an idea or feeling in words or signs that the receiver will recognise and transmits this message to the receiver.

sequence   A required order of tasks.

series interview   Several interviews conducted in turn by a number of interviewers.

service conditions   Statements about any limits or restrictions on service that help to avoid false expectations by the customer.

service culture   The way in which service is offered across an organisation.

service strategy   The techniques used to offer service.

short list   A list of the most suitable candidates who have been selected for interview from a larger group of applicants.

signalling devices   Subject headings, introductory paragraphs, prefaces or summaries all signal either that the flow of ideas, the importance of ideas or the emphasis in the document is about to change.

signature block   The letter writer's signature, name and job title.

simple sentence   A sentence that contains only one idea expressed in one clause.

single interview   A job interview that is conducted by a single interviewer responsible for interviewing all applicants and selecting a new staff member.

skills audit   A process to identify skills and competencies.

SMART formula   A goal-setting technique in which goals are specific, measurable, achievable, relevant and time-referenced.

solicited job application   A job application responding to an advertisement or a known vacancy.

specification document   A document that lists the selection criteria and the selection mechanism to be used to differentiate between tenders.

SQ3R reading method   Breaks the reading process into five stages: survey first, question your reading purpose, read, recall and review.

stage fright   Anxiety or fear about making a presentation before an audience.

standing orders   The rules that govern the manner in which a meeting's business is to be conducted.

stress   Any pressure or demand, physical or psychological, that creates a state of tension.

study time management plan   A plan of action to make the best of study time.

subject line   Identifies a letter's subject or purpose.

submission   A request for funds or approval for a different course of action.

submissive behaviour   When a person accepts opinions of others without asserting their own point of view.

success triangle   An illustration of the flow response or assertive behaviour in a conflict situation.

summarising   Restating in a condensed way the most important points.

summary   A brief overview that captures the essence of the ideas discussed and findings presented.

supportive communication   Genuine, spontaneous and non-evaluative communication.

supportiveness   The ability to supply descriptive and spontaneous feedback to another person in a provisional manner.

symbol   A shorthand form of writing – for example, a red cross indicating a hospital on a map.

synopsis   Provides a brief description or informative overview of the report's most important points.

table   A graphic in which related information is presented in parallel columns.

table of contents   A list of what a document contains.

task-related functions   Actions and behaviours that focus on achieving the group or meeting's objectives and goals.

task-related role   The behaviours needed to focus on the specified goals to be completed as a group or meeting achieves its purpose – for example, goal setting, decision making and problem solving.

tautology   Unnecessary repetition of an idea.

team   A group with a charter or reason for being.

team briefing   A presentation designed and delivered by team members.

team structure   The elements that make up the whole team as it moves through the stages in the development of a team.

teamwork   When trust, cooperation and compatibility exist between the leader and team members.

technical competencies   The knowledge, skills and attitudes required to perform the duties, tasks and activities in the job.

technical definition   A clear statement of the meaning of a specialised word.

technical description   Factual descriptions that give the reader a clear image of the object.

technical instructions   The steps to follow in order to understand and complete a process.

technical writer   Writer of documents containing specialised facts and information belonging to a particular trade, occupation or profession.

technology   The knowledge, equipment and application of scientific and engineering practices used to store, send and receive information. Forms of technology include email, mobile phones, facsimile machines, personal organisers, Computer-Aided-Design (CAD), conference calls, intranet, Internet and personal computers (PCs).

tender document   A bid or offer to provide a product or service in exchange for a fee.

tension   A level of conflict where relationships are weighed down by negative attitudes and fixed opinions.

text   The main body of matter in a document.

Theory X   A leadership approach based on the assumptions that people do not like to work and will avoid it; people lack ambition; people prefer to be told what to do.

Theory Y   A leadership approach based on the assumptions that people like to work; will work together to achieve a goal; prefer to set their own goals; use their imagination and creativity to solve problems; not only accept responsibility but seek it.

thinking   The process by which new concepts or representations of information are created in the mind. It is the action of knowing or perceiving the facts or conceiving or creating new concepts and logical ideas.

time-management plan   A personal management tool to identify and organise different types of time, to prioritise and set goals.

time wasters   Distractions caused by human nature, environmental factors and poor management skills.

title page   The first page of a report that includes the report's title, the name of the person who authorised the report and the name and designation of the report writer.

tone   The mood or feeling expressed.

topic sentence   Signals the point in a paragraph.

total message   The words, the nonverbal behaviour and their meaning.

total quality management (TQM)   The process by which everyone in the organisation focuses on providing quality customer service.

traditional written outline   A way to prepare for writing a report in which the main ideas and their supporting information are listed.

transitional expressions   Words or phrases that make connections between two ideas or subjects.

transmittal memo   The cover note for a more formal lengthy message.

tree diagram   A way to prepare for writing a report in which the general points are organised as branches on a tree.

triangle   A way to prepare for writing a report that provides a visual limit to the amount of information you can include and lets you see if an appropriate balance is maintained between those parts of the document that are important and unimportant.

undercurrent message   The hidden part of the message that may contain feelings or content, or a combination of both.

unintentional message   The meaning placed on the message by the receiver is different from the sender's intended message.

universal nonverbal communication   Body movements common to humankind such as a smile or tears.

Universal Resource Locator (URL)   The unique address of a web page.

unjustified complaint   An unreasonable complaint from a customer.

unrealistic conflict   Conflict that cannot be resolved because the people involved are unwilling to change their attitudes.

unrelated nonverbal communication   Random nonverbal behaviour, such as a sneeze, which is unrelated to the verbal message.

unsolicited letter of application   A job application that seeks a position or expresses an interest in working for an organisation when a vacancy has not been advertised.

urgent activities   Actions necessary to deal with interruptions that must be done.

urgent matters   Interruptions that must be dealt with.

validity   The soundness or authority of research.

variable   An element in a graph that is analysed and compared with one or more other elements.

verbal communication   Communication between two or more people in the form of spoken words.

verbosity   The unnecessary use of too many words.

vertical channel   The channels of communication that move communication up and down between different levels in the organisation.

victim   A role played in the drama triangle in which a person who is not a real victim plays the role of a victim in order to have someone else rescue or persecute them.

vision   A clear view of what the work team is doing and will do in the future.

visual aids   Graphics and visual devices used by a speaker to improve the audience's understanding.

visual materials   See graphics.

visuals   See graphics.

vocal characterisers   Nonverbal vocal behaviour which includes laughing, crying, sighing, yawning, clearing the throat, yelling, whispering.

vocal qualifiers   How something is said – for example, its intensity and pitch.

vocal segregates   Nonverbal sounds such as 'uh-huh', 'um', 'uh', 'ah'; silent pauses and intruding sounds.

vocalisations   Vocal characterisers, qualifiers and segregates such as sighing, pitch height and 'uh-huh' or 'um' sounds that give clues to the meaning of the spoken message.

vote   At formal meetings members vote to make decisions. This vote is usually by a verbal 'aye' or 'nay' or by a show of hands.

WATNA   The worst alternative to a negotiated agreement.

web page   A page on a website made up of a related collection of web files.

website   A collection of web pages.

win–lose situation   A situation in which one party is satisfied and one is dissatisfied with the settlement negotiated.

win–lose strategy   A strategy which focuses on the initiator's problem to the exclusion of the other's. The initiator wins.

win–win approach   Aims to satisfy the needs and interests of both parties in the situation.

win–win situation   A situation in which both parties are satisfied with the settlement negotiated.

win–win strategy   Negotiates the situation on its merits.

withdrawal   A negotiation style in which one party retracts their point of view or backs away from the situation.

work request   A proposal that is submitted as a request to complete a work project.

work team enablers   The team's capability, power transparency, direction and account-ability; they enable communication and collaboration to take place within the team.

workplace instructions   Explain the objectives, provide background information and describe the intended outcome.

workplace language   Language actually used on the job.

World Wide Web (WWW)   All the resources and uses on the Internet that are using Hypertext Transport Protocol (HTTP).

writing style   The way a writer uses words, sentences, paragraphs and layout to present ideas.

'you' approach   A writing style that speaks personally to the reader by addressing them directly as 'you' throughout the document

Index